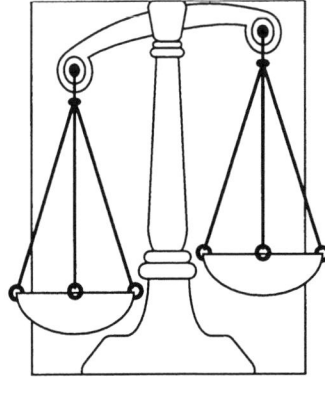

West's Advanced Topics and Contemporary Issues
Second Edition

Expanded Coverage for:

West's Business Law
West's Legal Environment of Business

FRANK B. CROSS
Associate Director, Center for Legal and Regulatory Studies
Univesrsity of Texas at Austin

WEST
WEST EDUCATIONAL PUBLISHING COMPANY
An International Thomson Publishing Company

Publisher/Team Director: Jack Calhoun
Acquisitions Editor: Rob Dewey
Developmental Editor: Jan Lamar
Production Editor: Bill Stryker
Marketing Manager: Scott D. Person

Copyright © 1998
by West Educational Publishing Company
An International Thomson Publishing Company

All Rights Reserved
The text of this publication, or any part thereof, may not be reproduced or transmitted in any form or by any means, electronic or mechanical, including photocopying, recording, storage in an information retrieval system, or otherwise, without prior written permission from the publisher.

ISBN: 0–538–87987–4

2 3 4 5 6 7   C6   3 2 1 0 9 8

Printed in the United States of America

I(T)P®
International Thomson Publishing
West Educational Publishing is an ITP Company.
The ITP trademark is used under license.

Contents in Brief

Cross-Reference Chart   viii

Preface   ix

1 Business Ethics   1
2 International Business Law   21
3 Individual Employee Rights   37
4 Employment Discrimination Law   55
5 Occupational Safety and Workers' Compensation   73
6 Accounting and the Law   89
7 Securities Law and Regulation   105
8 Mergers and Acquisitions   127
9 Insurance Law   145
10 Real Estate Finance and Liability   161
11 Bank Regulation and Liability   177
12 Unfair Competition   193
13 Advertising Law   209
14 Environmental Liability   227
15 Health Care Law   243
16 Sports and Entertainment Law   259
17 Hospitality Management Law   281
18 Communications Law   297
19 Government Contracts   319
20 Legal Representation of Business   337

Glossary   355

Table of Cases   363

Index   369

Contents

Cross-Reference Chart   viii

Preface   ix

1 Business Ethics   1
Key Background,   1
Profit Maximization as Ethical Duty?   1
Obeying the Law as Business Ethics?   2
Sources of Business Ethics,   5
The Requirements of Business Ethics,   6
Does Ethics Pay?   11
Business Beneficence,   12
Putting Business Ethics into Effect,   15
Questions and Case Problems,   19

2 International Business Law   21
Key Background,   21
Performance and Remedies in International Contracts,   21
Regulation of Exports,   22
International Intellectual Property Protection,   26
Customs and Regulation of Imports,   26
Foreign Capital Markets,   31
Foreign Direct Investment,   33
Questions and Case Problems,   35

3 Individual Employee Rights   37
Key Background,   37
Employment at Will,   37
Implied Contract of Employment,   38
Public Policy Exception,   41
Whistle-Blowing,   44
Good Cause,   44
Tortious Discharges,   45
Employee Privacy,   48
Family and Medical Leave Act,   50
Additional Employee Rights,   51
Ethical Perspectives: Whistle-Blowing,   51
International Perspectives: Wrongful Discharge in Japan,   52
Questions and Case Problems,   53

4 Employment Discrimination Law   55
Key Background,   55
Title VII,   55
Sexual Harassment,   59
Affirmative Action,   61
Section 1981,   62
Age Discrimination,   62
Americans with Disabilities Act,   65
Arbitration of Antidiscrimination Claims,   68
Ethical Perspectives: Ethics and Comparable Worth,   69
International Perspectives: International Prohibitions on Employment Discrimination,   70
Questions and Case Problems,   71

5 Occupational Safety and Workers' Compensation   73
Key Background,   73
Occupational Safety Standards,   73
Employer Responsibility,   78
Inspections and Citations,   79
Penalties,   79
Workers' Compensation,   80
Benefits,   83
Exclusivity,   84
Ethical Perspectives: The Cost of Occupational Safety,   85
International Perspectives: International Occupational Safety Protection,   86
Questions and Case Problems,   87

6 Accounting and the Law   89
Key Background,   89
Malpractice Liability to Clients,   89
Liability to Non-Clients,   94
Accountants and Confidentiality,   97
SEC Rules,   98
Management Consulting,   99
Ethical Perspectives: Accounting Conflicts of Interest,   100

International Perspectives: International Accounting Standards, 101
Questions and Case Problems, 102

7 Securities Law and Regulation 105
Key Background, 105
The Securities Act of 1933, 105
Registration and SEC Review, 106
Section 11 Private Actions, 108
Section 12 Private Actions, 108
The Securities Exchange Act of 1934, 110
Insider Trading, 110
Fraudulent Corporate Disclosure, 113
Proxy Regulations, 115
The Williams Act, 116
Regulation of Broker-Dealers, 117
RICO, 120
Ethical Perspectives: Ethics and Insider Trading, 123
International Perspectives: The International Law of Insider Trading, 125
Questions and Case Problems, 126

8 Mergers and Acquisitions 127
Key Background, 127
A Factual Scenario for a Takeover, 127
Directors' Duties, 128
Directors' Duties in Mergers and Acquisitions, 131
State Anti-Takeover Statutes, 138
LBOs, MBOs, and Second-Step Mergers, 139
Federal Regulation of Takeovers, 141
Ethical Perspectives: Stakeholder Rights, 141
International Perspectives: Foreign Takeover Laws, 142
Questions and Case Problems, 144

9 Insurance Law 145
Key Background, 145
Insurance Coverage Issues, 145
Policy Exclusions, 148
Insurer's Duty to Defend, 149
Wrongful Treatment of Claimants, 150
Wrongful Nonrenewal of Policy, 152
Insurance Company Defenses, 152
Wrongful Issuance of Life Insurance, 156
Ethical Perspectives: Insurance and the AIDS Crisis, 157
International Perspectives: Insurance and Europe, 158
Questions and Case Problems, 159

10 Real Estate Finance and Liability 161
Key Background, 161
Real Estate Finance, 161
Commercial Leasing, 166
Real Estate Fraud, 170
Ethical Perspectives: AIDS Disclosure and Residential Real Estate, 174
International Perspectives: Foreign Investment in U.S. Real Estate, 175
Questions and Case Problems, 176

11 Bank Regulation and Liability 177
Key Background, 177
Bank Regulation, 177
Lender Liability, 184
Mortgage Lender Liability, 187
Ethical Perspectives: An Ethical Duty to Loan? 188
International Perspectives: U.S. Banks in Europe, 189
Questions and Case Problems, 191

12 Unfair Competition 193
Key Background, 193
Wrongful Interference with Business, 193
Trademark Infringement, 197
Disparagement, 202
Robinson-Patman Act, 203
Sections 2(d) and 2(e), 205
State Laws, 205
Ethical Perspectives: Opportunistic Behavior and Business Transactions, 206
International Perspectives: Trademark Protection and Grey Market Goods, 207
Questions and Case Problems, 208

13 Advertising Law 209
Key Background, 209
First Amendment Rights of Advertisers, 209

Federal Trade Commission Regulation, 212
Comparative Advertising, 215
Private Regulation of Advertising, 219
Advertising Misappropriation, 219
Advertising Negligence, 222
Ethical Perspectives: Social Responsibility in Advertising, 223
International Perspectives: International Advertising, 224
Questions and Case Problems, 225

14 Environmental Liability 227
Key Background, 227
CERCLA/Superfund, 227
Environmental Liability in Business Transactions, 231
Individual Liability for Environmental Violations, 234
Compliance and Criminal Liability, 235
Ethical Perspectives: Export of Hazardous Wastes, 239
International Perspectives: Foreign Environmental Regulations, 241
Questions and Case Problems, 241

15 Health Care Law 243
Key Background, 243
Government Regultion of Health Care, 243
Malpractice, 246
Hospital Direct Liability, 249
Patient "Dumping," 250
Antitrust Liability, 253
Ethical Perspectives: The Value of Human Life, 256
International Perspectives: AIDS and International Health Care, 257
Questions and Case Problems, 258

16 Sports and Entertainment Law 259
Key Background, 259
Sports Law, 259
Entertainment Law, 266
Ethical Perspectives: Sports Agents and Ethics, 276
International Perspectives: International Marketing of Motion Pictures, 278
Questions and Case Problems, 279

17 Hospitality Management Law 281
Key Background, 281
Guest-Innkeeper Relationship, 281
Responsibility for the Safety of Guests, 282
Responsibility for Guest's Property, 286
Liability for Refusing or Evicting Guests, 289
Reservations, 290
Rights of Guests, 292
Rights of Innkeepers, 292
Licensing and Regulation of Hotels, 293
Licensing and Regulation of Restaurants, 293
Ethical Perspectives: Ethics and Overbooking, 294
International Perspectives: International Hospitality Management Law, 295
Questions and Case Problems, 296

18 Communications Law 297
Key Background, 297
Federal Communications Commission Regulation, 297
New Communications Technologies, 305
Telecommunications Act of 1996, 306
Communications Law and the First Amendment, 307
Mass Media Liability, 309
Ethical Perspectives: Free Press vs. Fair Trial, 315
International Perspectives: Cross-Border Broadcasting, 316
Questions and Case Problems, 318

19 Government Contracts 319
Key Background, 319
Types of Contracts, 319
Contract Formation, 320
Contract Requirements, 321
Collateral Policies, 324
Contract Challenges, 324
Contract Administration, 326
Contractor Fraud, 328
Suspension and Debarment, 330
Ethical Perspectives: Government Contracts and Corporate Codes of Ethics, 332
International Perspectives: International Government Contracting, 334

Questions and Case Problems, 335

20 Legal Representation of Business 337
Key Background, 337
Attorney-Client Relationship, 337
Attorney-Client Privilege, 339
Work Product Privilege, 342
Legal Representation of the Corporation, 342
Documentation Retention and Destruction, 346
Management of Legal Affairs, 347
Ethical Perspectives: Whistle-Blowing and the Corporate Counsel, 350
International Perspectives: International Practice for U.S. Attorneys, 351
Questions and Case Problems, 352

Glossary   355

Table of Cases   363

Index   369

Cross-referencing to
West's Business Law, Seventh Edition
by Clarkson, Miller, Jentz, and Cross
and
West's Legal Environment of Business, Third Edition
by Cross and Miller

Chapter in	Compares with chapter in	
West's Advanced Topics and Contemporary Issues, Third Edition	*West's Business Law, Seventh Edition*	*West's Legal Environment of Business, Third Edition*
1 Business Ethics	2	2
2 International Business Law	11, 55	1, 7, 8
3 Individual Employee Rights	35, 36	20, 21, 22
4 Employment Discrimination Law	36	21
5 Occupational Safety and Workers' Compensation	35	20
6 Accounting and the Law	54	-
7 Securities Law and Regulation	43	28
8 Mergers and Acquisitions	42	18
9 Insurance Law	52	-
10 Real Estate Finance and Liability	50, 51	25
11 Bank Regulation and Liability	28	23
12 Unfair Competition	7, 47	13, 26
13 Advertising Law	45	23
14 Environmental Liability	46	24
15 Health Care Law	-	-
16 Sports and Entertainment Law	-	-
17 Hospitality Management Law	-	-
18 Communications Law	-	-
19 Government Contracts	-	-
20 Legal Representation of Business	55	-

Preface

Even a casual reader of the *Wall Street Journal*, or other business periodicals, quickly becomes aware of the importance of legal requirements in modern business. Detailed government regulations and multimillion-dollar liability actions have become an integral part of conducting businesses of all types. Consequently, a solid understanding of the law and the legal environment is critical in today's business world.

West's Advanced Topics and Contemporary Issues goes into greater detail than the typical business law or legal environment text on some of the most pressing issues confronting business today. It also addresses special legal topics that are not covered in these introductory texts.

The chapters can be used in any order. Students will gain much greater value from the book, however, by using it to build upon knowledge gained from their business law or legal environment of business text. The book can be used in tandem with an introductory text or in a follow-up course.

West's Advanced Topics and Contemporary Issues is keyed to two texts—*West's Business Law, Seventh Edition,* and *West's Legal Environment of Business, Third Edition.* There are numerous specific references to these texts. Consequently, this text will be of particular value to students who use or have used *West's Business Law, Seventh Edition,* or *West's Legal Environment of Business, Third Edition.*

Coverage

West's Advanced Topics and Contemporary Issues begins by introducing two topics of critical concern today: business ethics and international business law. These first two chapters provide a detailed analysis of these topics, building upon the discussion of business ethics and international business law found in business law and legal environment texts. Ethical concerns are also addressed in each succeeding chapter.

The next twelve chapters offer expanded and more detailed coverage of selected topics covered in business law and legal environment texts. The topics selected involved legal issues which are of particular importance in management, finance, accounting, and marketing. Some of the issues covered in this section are employee rights, mergers and acquisitions, accountant liability, and advertising law.

The remaining six chapters of the text address legal topics of special concern in business. This last section deals with issues that are generally not covered in business law and legal environment texts. Some of the topics involve the unique legal problems faced by particular industries, such as the health care industry and the hospitality management industry. Other topics are of general interest, such as the legal representation of business.

Special Features

In addition to the expanded coverage and special topics described above, this text also contains special features to enhance student understanding.

Ethical Perspectives After Chapter 2, each chapter concludes with an "Ethical Perspective" that relates to the subject matter of the chapter. Ethics has become a critical concern of businesspersons and is an integral part of business law and legal environment courses.

The "Ethical Perspective" for each chapter analyzes an ethical concern that is both current and controversial. Different perspectives of the ethical controversy are presented. The text then attempts to offer some resolution to these ethical dilemmas that confront business.

International Perspectives In light of the increased importance of international business and applicable legal standards, Chapters 3 through 20 conclude with an "International Perspective." As business becomes more global in scope, managers have a greater need to understand the international legal environment.

The "International Perspective" for each chapter discusses issues that are relevant to that chapter. While it is obviously impossible to detail every international legal requirement for a given issue, the text selects highly relevant and representative international requirements. For example, the text discusses the environmental law controlling hazardous waste in Europe and the law of employer–employee relations in Japan.

Cases In order to illustrate and amplify important legal principles discussed in the text, excerpted cases are interspersed throughout each chapter. Most of the cases have been decided recently, but some classic cases are included when they stand as landmarks in the law.

Each case presented in *West's Advanced Topics and Contemporary Issues* follows a special format: case title and full case citation, background and facts, case excerpt, and discussion and remedy.

Exhibits When appropriate, the text contains exhibits to illustrate important legal principles or rules. These exhibits are designed to enhance the material and aid the reader's understanding of the legal concepts discussed.

Questions and Case Problems Each chapter ends with questions and case problems. Some questions are hypothetical and are intended to help review the understanding of key legal issues in the chapter. Others are actually cases that exemplify the issues discussed in the chapter. The answers to the questions and case problems are available free to professors and can be placed on reserve in the library for students.

Acknowledgments

Many individuals have contributed to the second edition. I wish to thank my editor, Clyde Perlee, Jr., who provided the basic ideas for this text and provided considerable assistance in designing its framework. Jan Lamar, Barri Breeden, and Bridget Neumayr of West also provided substantial assistance. Roger LeRoy Miller performed helpful service in reviewing the chapters for this text and in providing many useful suggestions and comments. Morli Fidler and Bill Stapleton assisted me greatly in researching the issues addressed in this text.

Of course, any errors that may remain are my own responsibility. Please write to me with any ideas about how to improve the usefulness of this work. I welcome your ideas so that I can incorporate them in subsequent editions.

This is dedicated to Linda Fay.

CHAPTER ONE

Business Ethics

KEY BACKGROUND

Business ethics seems to some a contradiction in terms. The concept of ethical business took a black eye in the 1980s, with misconduct in the savings and loan industry, insider trading, "junk bonds," Department of Defense supplier overcharges and other scandals. Yet most Americans believe that business should behave ethically. The exact nature of the ethical obligations of business is not so clear. This chapter will set forth the sources of business ethics, the scope of ethical duties, and the interface of ethics and the law.

The nature of ethical behavior has long been debated by philosophers, some of whom argue for universal rules of behavior, while others argue for a utilitarian maximization of human welfare, and still others employ other approaches. The scope of this debate is well beyond our chapter. Rather, the chapter will focus on how the business context influences ethical duties of individuals.

The specific focus of this chapter will be on the ethical duties of the officer or employee of the corporation. The corporate context is not the only scenario for business ethics. For example, the sole proprietor of a business has ethical duties. The problem of business ethics for the corporate officer, though, is the most common situation and also the most difficult to resolve.

Profit Maximization as Ethical Duty?

Cynics about business ethics argue that business is only interested in making a profit. Some authors on business ethics contend, however, that making a profit is *the* ethical requirement for business managers. It is a useful starting point to consider this position, which contends that the only ethical duty of corporate employees is to maximize corporate profits. This position seems contrary to what most persons consider business ethics. A duty to maximize profits could possibly necessitate breaking the law, polluting water supplies, cheating on contracts, and other acts that seem questionable.

Yet a case can be made for profit maximization as an ethical duty. Milton Friedman, the conservative economist and Nobel prize winner, has declared: "Few trends could so thoroughly undermine the very foundations of our free society as the acceptance by corporate officials of a social responsibility other than to make as much money for their stockholders as possible."[1]

The corporate employee, even a chief executive officer is, after all, managing someone else's money—that of the shareholders. This surely gives the employee some duty to the shareholders. By what authority do such employees have a right to spend their shareholders' money for whatever purpose the employee deems "ethical"? What makes such employees ethical experts, anyway?

Suppose that Barbara Bookman is a majority shareholder in Tiller, Inc. William Puckett is

---
[1] "The Social Responsibility of Business Is To Increase Its Profits," printed in *Ethical Issues in Business* (T. Donaldson and P. Werhane, eds. 1983), p. 239.

Tiller's president and chief executive officer. Puckett decides that it would be ethical to make a large contribution to Planned Parenthood for use in promoting birth control. Barbara, however, for religious reasons believes that use of birth control is immoral. Regardless of whether birth control is ethical or not, why should William decide how to spend Barbara's money for what he personally considers ethical?

It seems clear that corporate officers such as William have some ethical duty to shareholders such as Barbara. It is troublesome to have such officers using "others' money" to advance their own ethical agenda. It does not follow, however, that William's only ethical duty is to maximize Barbara's profits.

Consider the implications of an ethical duty only to maximize profits. Under the most extreme form of this theory, the officer should violate the law, even market illegal drugs, at least if the corporation would not be caught and punished. Indeed, the most extreme form of this theory dictates that the employee should lie, cheat and steal whenever such actions would actually increase corporate profits. Something is wrong with such a theory of business ethics. Even Milton Friedman does not adopt this extreme view of profit maximization. He says that corporations have an ethical duty to obey the law as well as to maximize profits. This leads to a second theory of business ethics.

▬ Obeying the Law as Business Ethics?

A more widely held vision of business ethics contends that business should maximize profits within the bounds of legal behavior. The corporate officer acting within the context of this theory would rely on the government to set the bounds of ethical behavior. If an action is illegal, businesspersons should avoid it. If, however, the law permits a certain business action, and if that action is profitable, a company has an ethical right to take the action.

This theory has appeal, for it reflects some duty to shareholders and recognizes the limitations of corporate employees. After all, what qualifies officers to determine ethical behavior? Corporate managers are hired for their ability to make business decisions, not ethical ones. The laws reflect the ethical decisions of society as a whole and perhaps offer a better ethical guide than the instincts of corporate officers.

This theory is frequently invoked by business. For example, the government recently brought an action against Neil Bush, the son of former President Bush, and a savings and loan official regarding allegedly unethical loans that he made. The government argued that Bush had a conflict of interest when he made loans in order to advance his own businesses. An expert witness law professor contended at a hearing that Mr. Bush had not behaved unethically. The witness emphasized that ethical standards varied from state to state and that Mr. Bush should be judged by the laws of Colorado, where the savings and loan institution was located. Because Bush apparently violated no Colorado statute, the expert argued that his behavior was ethical.[2]

This reliance on the law as the only ethical standard, however, is misused and a misunderstanding of both the law and ethics. The law was never meant to define the full scope of ethical duties. Earl Warren, former Chief Justice of the Supreme Court, wrote that "Society would come to grief without Ethics, which is unenforceable in the Courts and cannot be made part of Law."[3]

There are two reasons why the law cannot define all ethical duties. First, our lawmakers have limited time and cannot write laws to cover every possible ethical problem. Congress is busy with foreign policy, the national budget, and innumerable other issues. Lawmakers cannot consider all of their own ethical problems, let alone every ethical issue in business. Second, Congress cannot deal well with all types of ethical problems. For example, no law could prevent a person from lying to friends or parents. Yet such action would often be unethical. Ethics must go beyond the law.

Indeed, it could be harmful for the law to attempt to enforce business ethics fully. The following opinion emphasizes the difference between law and ethics and contends that the law already has gone too far in attempting to enforce business ethics.

---

[2] *New York Times*, September 27, 1990, p.C2 (National edition).

[3] Speech quoted in *Trends in Business Ethics* (C. van Dam and L. Stallaert, eds. 1978), p.9.

Case 1.1
Oki America, Inc. v. Microtech International, Inc.
United States Court of Appeals
Ninth Circuit, 1989
872 F.2d 312

Background and Facts *Oki America, Inc., and Microtech International, Inc. were involved in a contract dispute. In connection with this dispute, Oki argued that the parties had no contract. Microtech then brought suit for the tort of "malicious denial of the existence of a contract." The district court granted summary judgment for Oki and Microtech appealed. The appellate court affirmed on the grounds that Microtech had failed to meet its burden of proof. Judge Kozinski wrote an interesting concurring opinion, in which he challenged the basis for such a tort as malicious denial of a contract.*

KOZINSKI, Circuit Judge, concurring:

* * * *

Nowhere but in the Cloud Cuckooland of modern tort theory could a case like this have been concocted. One large corporation is complaining that another obstinately refused to acknowledge they had a contract. For this shocking misconduct it is demanding millions of dollars in punitive damages. I suppose we will next be seeing lawsuits seeking punitive damages for maliciously refusing to return telephone calls or adopting a condescending tone in interoffice memos. Not every slight, nor even every wrong, ought to have a tort remedy. The intrusion of courts into every aspect of life, and particularly into every type of business relationship, generates serious costs and uncertainties, trivializes the law, and denies individuals and businesses the autonomy of adjusting mutual rights and responsibilities through voluntary contractual agreement.

* * * *

It is impossible to draw a principled distinction between a tortious denial of a contract's existence and a permissible denial of liability under the terms of the contract. The test—if one can call it such—seems to be whether the conduct "offends accepted notions of business ethics." *Seaman's*, 36 Cal.3d at 770, 206 Cal.Rptr. 3554, 686 P.2d 1158. This gives judges license to rely on their gut feelings in distinguishing between a squabble and a tort. As a result, both the commercial world and the courts are needlessly burdened: The parties are hamstrung in developing binding agreements by the absence of clear legal principles; overburdened courts must adjudicate disputes that are incapable of settlement because no one can predict how—or even by what standard—they will be decided.

* * * *

The eagerness of judges to expand the horizons of tort liability is symptomatic of a more insidious disease: the novel belief that any problem can be ameliorated if only a court gets involved. Not so. Courts are slow, clumsy, heavy-handed institutions, ill-suited to oversee the negotiations between corporations, to determine what compromises a manufacturer and a retailer should make in closing a mutual profitable deal, or to evaluate whether an export-import consortium is developing new markets in accordance with the standards of the business community.

* * * *

Perhaps most troubling, the willingness of courts to subordinate voluntary contractual arrangements to their own sense of public policy and proper business decorum deprives individuals of an important measure of freedom. The right to enter into contracts—to adjust one's legal relationships by mutual agreement with other free individuals—was unknown through much of history and is unknown even today in many parts of the world. Like other aspects of personal autonomy, it is too easily smothered by government officials eager to tell us what's best for us. The recent tendency of judges to insinuate tort causes of action into relationships traditionally governed by contract is just such over-reaching. It must be viewed with no less suspicion because the government officials in question happen to wear robes.

Decision and Remedy *The court affirmed the dismissal of plaintiff's claim.*

Notwithstanding Judge Kozinski's commentary, the state of California continues to recognize a tort action for wrongful denial of a contract. The California courts have restricted the tort, however, to cases when there was a special relationship between the parties, when one party to the contract had inferior bargaining power and was particularly vulnerable. There is no tort if the contract is an arm's length bargain.[4] Does this limitation cure Judge Kozinski's problem with the doctrine?

As Judge Kozinski indicated, it can be inefficient to "judicialize" all ethical precepts. This fact makes voluntary private recognition of business ethics all the more important. Indeed, failures of business ethics explain a great deal of government and judicial regulation of business practices.

The law is an important part of ethics, however. The law does reflect societal standards of ethics and provides the context in which business operates. There is considerable overlap between legal and ethical requirements. Legal principle will be used to illustrate ethical duties throughout the remainder of this chapter. Prevailing approaches to business ethics inevitably influence the law as well. The following case indicates how business ethics helps the law of fraud.

[4] *Freeman & Mills, Incorporated v. Belcher Oil Co.*, No. B069559 (Cal. App. 1994).

■ Case 1.2
First Federal Savings and Loan Association v. Twin City Savings Bank, FSB
United States Court of Appeals,
Fifth Circuit, 1989
868 F.2d 725

Background and Facts *Twin City Savings Bank sold to the First Federal Savings and Loan Association participation in a multi-million dollar loan to Sea Oats of Juno Beach, Inc., a condominium developer. In negotiating the sale of loan participation, Twin City concealed facts regarding Sea Oats' credit worthiness. Sea Oats ultimately was unable to pay off the loan. First Federal sued Twin City for fraudulent concealment. The district court found that Twin City had indeed fraudulently concealed facts but held for Twin City because First Federal was negligent in investigating the facts and in failing to detect Twin City's concealment. For example, First Federal had access to Twin City's files on the loan, which revealed that Sea Oats was behind in construction. First Federal appealed the judgment.*

RUBIN, Circuit Judge.

* * * *

To permit the perpetrator of a fraud to escape liability because of the failure of his victim to take precautions to prevent deception imposes on an innocent party a duty of care to avoid the culpable conduct of a miscreant.

* * * *

Prosser and Keeton state in their standard work on Torts:

> The last half-century has seen a marked change in the attitude of the courts toward the question of justifiable reliance. Earlier decisions, under the influence of the prevalent doctrine of "caveat emptor," laid great stress upon the plaintiff's "duty" to protect himself and distrust his antagonist, and held that he was not entitled to rely even upon positive assertions of fact made by one with whom he was dealing at arm's length. It was assumed that any one may be expected to overreach another in a bargain if he can, and that only a fool will expect common honesty. Therefore the plaintiff must make a reasonable investigation, and form his own judgment. The recognition of a new standard of business ethics, demanding that statements of fact be at least honestly and carefully made, and in many cases that they be warranted to be true, has led to an almost complete shift in this point of view.
>
> It is now held that assertions of fact as to the quantity or quality of land or goods sold, the financial status of corporations, and similar matters inducing commercial transactions, may justifiably be relied on without investigation, not only where such investigation would be burdensome or difficult, as where land which is sold lies at a distance, but likewise where the falsity of the representation might be discovered with little effort by means easily at hand. The plaintiff is not required, for example, to examine public records to ascertain the true state of the title claimed by the defendant. It is only where, under the circumstances, the facts should be apparent to one of his knowledge and intelligence from a cursory glance, or he has discovered something which should serve as a warning that he is being deceived, that he is required to make an investigation of his own.

Decision and Remedy *The court reversed the district court's judgment for Twin City and remanded the case for trial.*

■ Sources of Business Ethics

Assuming that business ethics must be more than maximizing profits and obeying the law, ethical behavior is still difficult to define. While the two preceding theories are incomplete, they make important points. Certainly, corporate officers have some ethical duties to their shareholders. Also, those officers are not necessarily the best judges of ethical behavior. Why and when should these employees go beyond the law and act ethically?

One potential flaw in the first two theories is the assumption that shareholders are only interested in maximizing their profits from a corporation. Ultimately, shareholders are people with their own personal ethics. Shareholders may not want their money used in unethical ways.

In addition, a corporation and its officers may have some duty to society over and above their duties to shareholders. The ability to form a corporation is granted by government. When the government permits a business to incorporate, it grants important benefits to shareholders. For example, the government limits the potential liability of shareholders in corporations. (This benefit is discussed in Chapter 37 of *West's Business Law, Seventh Edition*, and in Chapter 17 of *West's Legal Environment of Business, Third Edition*.) Many philosophers believe that corporations owe a duty to society in exchange for the benefits provided from incorporation. They argue that corporations have a duty not to act in a way that injures the society at large.

Finally, maximizing profits (even within the law) does not usually conform to our sense of ethical behavior. If a sole proprietor (individual owner) took advantage of every legal loophole to trick customers, suppliers, etc., we would probably not think that he or she was acting ethically. Why should a corporation be judged by a lesser standard?

The Requirements of Business Ethics

The above section explained only the reasons why business may have some ethical duties beyond profit maximization and obeying the law; it did not state what these duties are. Defining ethical obligations is difficult. This is an issue that philosophers have struggled with. The businessperson, who is likely not a philosopher, might simply try to live by several general rules. The following rules are widely accepted by our society. Some refer to these rules as "moral minima" or *prima facie* ethical duties that should always be followed. The requirements of business ethics include: (1) honesty, (2) promise keeping, (3) loyalty, (4) the avoidance of causing harm to others, and (5) fairness.

Honesty

There is widespread agreement that people ordinarily should be honest. Honesty generally means that a person should not intentionally lie to, or deceive, another person. Most people expect some level of honesty from others and should abide by this rule themselves. Telling the truth is expected, unless a person has a good excusing condition. Philosophers dispute the conditions that may excuse dishonesty. St. Augustine considered every lie to be a mortal sin, but Plato supported the "noble lie" as necessary to preserve social harmony.

Many philosophers agree that honesty is not an absolute rule of ethical behavior. It is easy to imagine times when honesty may be inappropriate. One common example suggests that a murderous maniac bursts into your house and confronts you on the first floor. The murderer asks you if anyone else is home. No one would argue that honesty requires you to say that your infant sister is asleep upstairs. These examples are unusual, however. As a general rule, honesty is an appropriate guide to behavior.

Honesty is particularly significant in many business transactions. Suppose that Tom Olsen is the chief financial officer of a large company. The firm needs a major loan from a bank for expansion of the company's operations. The company will be more likely to receive the loan if Tom exaggerates the value of its assets on the loan disclosure form. Honesty dictates that Tom report the true value of the corporate assets, even if that may risk losing the loan.

Honesty is a more difficult rule for other types of business transactions. Suppose that Tom is in charge of marketing his company's products. A rigid standard of honesty could require that Tom objectively describe all of the advantages and disadvantages of the product in its advertising. Such a standard might even say that Tom should tell consumers that his company's product is inferior to that of it competitors. While businesses have some duty of honesty in advertising, they need not necessarily adopt such an extreme position.

Like all ethical duties for business, honesty should be considered in the context of business. Tom is a representative of his company, not of *Consumer Reports*. He has some duty to the company and its shareholders. Moreover, Tom is trying to get customers to engage in an arms-length business transaction. These customers are not wholly dependent on Tom for information, and the customers probably do not expect him to be rigidly honest in his advertising. As customers, we realize that advertisers will promote the benefits of their products. Customers are unlikely to trust advertising completely, and they assume some responsibility to protect their own interests. Nevertheless, Tom still has a duty of honesty and should not claim that his product has certain attributes that it clearly does not possess. If he is selling computers, he should not lie about the objective processing speed of his products.

The American Association of Advertising Agencies has its own ethical code. This code declares that its members "will not knowingly produce advertising which contains:

a. False or misleading statements or exaggerations, visual or verbal.

b. Testimonials which do not reflect the real choice of a competent witness.

c. Price claims which are misleading.

d. Comparisons which unfairly disparage a competitive product or service."[5]

The code sets additional standards and provides for disciplinary action by the Association if an advertising agency violates the code.

---

[5] American Association of Advertising Agencies, "Standards of Practice," reprinted in *Ethical Issues in the Professions* (1989), p. 540.

Promise Keeping

An ethical duty related to honesty is that of promise keeping. If a person makes a promise to another, he or she generally should keep that promise. Some promises are explicitly made, but others are implied. An agent makes an implied promise not to engage in conflicts of interest, for example.

Promise keeping is also very important in a business context. Our free enterprise system depends on promise keeping among businesses. Contracts are a form of promise, and businesses depend on contracts being made and kept. If companies could not rely on contracts, the system could degenerate into commercial anarchy.

Like honesty, promise keeping is not a rigid or absolute rule. Sometimes a business cannot keep a contract for reasons beyond its control. The law recognizes this in the doctrine of impossibility of performance (discussed in Chapter 19 of *West's Business Law, Seventh Edition*). Other times, it would be inefficient to keep a contract. Society justifies this situation by permitting a company to breach a contract and pay damages to the injured contractual party. Still other promises may themselves be illegal or unethical to carry out. There is generally no ethical obligation to carry out these contracts.

Nor can businesses expect every promise to be kept. Sometimes, a person or business may make a promise out of excessive generosity and think better of it later. If someone saves your life, you may promise them anything, out of gratitude. While you should always consider your promise and your gratitude, you need not necessarily keep this promise to the letter.

A similar situation arises in the business context. Principles of contract require that you keep promises made in exchange for consideration but need not keep all other promises. (This principle is described in Chapter 14 of *West's Business Law, Seventh Edition*.) If I promise to sell my car to someone for $10,000, I must keep that promise, which would be a contract. Promises to make a gift, however, need not always be carried out. If I promise simply to give my car to a student, I may not be required to carry out the gift. The ethics of breaking such a promise may depend on specific circumstances.

Even a gratuitous promise to make a gift should be kept if the promise has caused the promisee to rely to her detriment. Suppose Red Owl Stores promises Hoffman a franchise. In reliance on this promise, Hoffman sold his previous business, obtained a loan, and purchased fixtures and inventory necessary to running a Red Owl store. Red Owl then reneged on the promise. Both law and ethics would require Red Owl to go through with its promise to grant Hoffman a franchise.[6]

Loyalty

Another ethical issue is that of loyalty, sometimes called the **duty of fidelity**. This ethical duty is highly dependent on the facts of a situation. The loyalty duty is not the same for all persons. A person has a greater duty of loyalty to his family than to strangers. Usually, certain facts must arise before a strong duty of loyalty is triggered.

The business context creates several circumstances in which loyalty is important. Business creates situations in which one person is given a special position of trust and confidence. If Carol Velarde hires Jesse Mack to manage her investment portfolio, Jesse has some duty of loyalty to Carol's best interests. He should manager her investments in her own interests, not his own. He should not invest Carol's savings into his own business enterprises in order to make more profits for himself. If Jesse thinks that it is in Carol's best interest to invest in his businesses, he should disclose his potential conflict of interest to Carol, so that she is aware of the potential problem.

The loyalty duty is a source of the duty that corporate officers owe to their shareholders. As discussed above, the loyalty duty is not absolute. While loyalty to shareholders is important to corporate officers, this principle does not give officers the moral right to disregard all other ethical duties, such as honesty and promise keeping.

Many difficult loyalty problems arise in business. One area of considerable dispute is loyalty in the employment context. In Japan, employees are extremely loyal to their employer and highly dedicated to the company's success. Many of these employees would not even consider leaving their employer for a higher-paying job with a competitor. Of course, Japanese employers also show a high degree of loyalty to their employees. Japanese companies will go to great lengths to avoid laying off workers, even in an economic downturn.

---

[6] *See Hoffman v. Red Owl Stores, Inc.*, 133 N.W. 2d 267 (Wis. 1965).

The situation in the United States is somewhat different. Workers show less loyalty to employers, but this may be because they expect less loyalty in return. This argument has been made by basketball coaches at major universities. Many basketball coaches, such as Rick Pitino of the University of Kentucky, have quit their former jobs in mid-contract in order to take a more prestigious or better-paying job with another team. These coaches often justify their actions by noting that the university would be quick to fire them after a losing season. If the coach receives little loyalty from the school, they ask, why should the coach be loyal to the school? The loyalty duty is highly dependent on context and understandings among the parties.

Employees clearly have some loyalty duties to their employer. For example, if an employer informs an employee of an important trade secret of the company, that employee has a loyalty duty not to disclose the trade secret to competitors. Such a disclosure of trade secrets could also be a violation of the ethical duties of honesty and promise keeping.

Avoid Causing Harm to Others

It seems obvious that persons have some ethical responsibility not to harm others physically. At a most basic level, it is unethical to murder someone. One should also avoid doing emotional or financial harm to others. While this duty seems simple, it is actually quite complex in practice. Often it is impossible to do good without running some risk of causing harm.

Consider the environmental pollution situation. Pollution, almost by definition, causes harm. This harm may be to the natural environment, but often the harm will create some health risk to persons. Under this standard, causing pollution would be unethical. Yet an absolute rule against polluting would be disastrous. The production of electrical power unavoidably causes some pollution. Emission control devices and other measures can reduce the amount of pollution, but they cannot eliminate it. Eliminating all pollution would require abolishing electrical power production. Surely ethics does not require us to forego electricity, which has offered enormous health benefits to Americans.

As another example, the free enterprise system necessarily involves doing at least some financial harm to others. When one company provides a better service at a better price, that company inevitably does financial harm to its competitors and their employees. Yet providing a better service at a better price is at the heart of our economic system and is something to be encouraged. In our current business context, an ethical duty of never doing any harm would be impossible and unwise.

A better conception of ethical duty would be to avoid doing any unnecessary or unjustified harm to others. This ethical rule could prohibit pollution that could be easily prevented. It would also prohibit unfair competition aimed only at destroying competitors. This rule would also make it unethical to cause harm recklessly or negligently. The ethical duty could be not to cause harm without sufficient justification. Of course, this raises other difficult ethical questions. What justifications should be considered adequate for causing physical or financial harm in the course of doing business?

Fairness

Another widely accepted ethical responsibility is that of fairness. Fairness, though, is even more vague than the other ethical duties described above. While everyone would agree that fairness is good, individuals might disagree about what is fair.

Fairness arises in a number of business contexts. One component of fairness is acting in good faith and not arbitrarily. If the automobile manufacturing company of Sportsco, Inc., is suffering business setbacks, it may have to lay off workers. Suppose the company decides, for simplicity's sake, to lay off all its workers who are of the Jewish faith. Even if this were legal, which if is not, such an action would be unfair and unethical.

Fairness also means the use of fair procedures. Sportsco is a company that has suffered many employee thefts and is concerned with the drug problem in society. Suppose that Steve, a Sportsco employee, tells the company president about a rumor that another employee, Janice, is stealing from Sportsco in order to support her drug habit. If Sportsco fires Janice purely because of this rumor, is that fair? Such an action seems unfair to most observers. Janice should have an opportunity to answer the accusation and convince the president that it is false. If Janice agrees to take a drug test and a lie detector test, the employer should giver her a chance to prove her innocence.

The Bill of Rights of the United States Constitution requires certain procedures for criminal trials. For example, the Sixth Amendment gives each criminal defendant a right to confront his or her accuser. The Fifth Amendment contains a general requirement of due process, which broadly compels fair procedures. These procedural protections legally apply only to the government's actions and not to those of most private employers. Yet the Constitution's requirements provide some guidance about what procedures are considered fair by our society. These procedures offer help to businesses seeking fair procedures. Because the constitutional rules apply to government prosecution of crimes, they need not always be strictly applied to duties of business ethics. Nevertheless, employers should consider these principles when defining their own rules of fairness. Like other rules, the requirements of fairness depend on circumstances and the understandings of the parties involved.

The above five rules for business ethics—honesty, promise keeping, loyalty, avoiding doing harm to others, and fairness—are not a complete list of ethical concerns for business. Some ethics experts have suggested other duties, including confidentiality, due care, respect for liberty and other responsibilities.[7] The five rules discussed in this chapter provide a good foundation for considering the ethical requirements of business.

Applying Business Ethics to Decision Making

It is easy to acknowledge the importance of ethical duties, such as fairness or honesty. It is much more difficult to apply these rules in business decision making. Often these basic ethical duties may appear to be in conflict. At the beginning of this chapter we discussed how the directions of a duty of loyalty to shareholders could conflict with other duties, such as honesty and promise keeping. This creates a moral dilemma that must be resolved. How should a corporate officer resolve these moral dilemmas?

Most people have some experience in resolving moral dilemmas that arise in everyday living. Often, people make moral decisions based on their "gut instinct" about the right thing to do. This approach may yield the proper result; an ethical person usually has ethical "gut instincts." Reliance on this immediate intuition, however, is inadequate to resolve complex ethical problems. Also, one's "gut instinct" may be subconsciously influenced by selfish interests. In many cases, a decision maker should use a more thoughtful and rigorous methodology for making ethical decisions. Pure logic usually cannot answer ethical questions, but logical thought can help reach a better ethical solution. The following analysis can help make ethical choices when a person is confronted with a moral dilemma. A business manager should: (1) identify the ethical issues, (2) evaluate the ethical issues, and (3) apply the issues to the business context. The manager can then better resolve the ethical problem.

Identify the Ethical Issues

The first step in ethical analysis is to identify or find the ethical issues in question. It is difficult for a person to make a reasonable ethical decision until all the concerns are recognized. Return to the example in which Sportsco fired Janice because of a rumor of drug use and theft. The president of Sportsco may have acted rashly due to the company's great concern over drugs and theft. If the president stopped and considered the fairness of his decision toward Janice, he or she would be better prepared to do the right thing.

The very nature of an ethical dilemma suggests that two or more values are in conflict. Consideration of these values is necessary to define the existence of such a dilemma. Nor can the dilemma be reasonably settled until all relevant values have been acknowledged.

Evaluate the Ethical Issues

Once the possible ethical issues have been identified, the corporate decision maker should evaluate the significance of all relevant values. Sometimes, value conflicts are more apparent than real. An action that seems to violate an ethical duty may not actually do so.

Consider a corporate president whose company, Multinat, Inc., has substantial investments in the country of South Africa. These investments have been quite lucrative for the company and have yielded great profit for the Multinat shareholders. Individuals outside the corporation have protested these investments, because the government of South Africa denies fundamental rights to native Africans, who form a majority of that country's

---

[7] Dunfee, "The Case for Professional Norms of Business Ethics," 25 *American Business Law Journal* 385 (1987).

populace. These individuals argue that the company's investments help prop up a repressive government. The president is concerned about whether the Multinat investments cause harm to South Africans, yet she is also concerned about her duty of loyalty to shareholders. This appears to be a dilemma. It is possible, though, that her shareholders do not want to profit from investments in South Africa. If so, this step in the analysis can provide an easy answer to the apparent ethical dilemma.

Apply the Issues to the Business Context

The next critical step of the analysis is to apply the identified and evaluated ethical concerns to the specific business decision at issue. Philosophers debate ethical issues in the abstract, but the businessperson must make a decision in a specific set of circumstances. This chapter already has described how context and expectations can properly influence ethical choices. The correct decision depends on consideration of all the facts relevant to the perceived dilemma. These relevant facts must be found, and the decision maker should ensure that the perceived facts are accurate.

Applying relevant facts can shed considerable light on the ethics of a business decision. Return to the case of Multinat's investment in South Africa. Perhaps the Multinat shareholders do wish to maximize profits, even through South African investments. A full review of the facts may show that the South African investments are not as profitable as they seem at first glance. These investments may be quite risky, given the unstable situation in South Africa. Such investment may also give the company a bad name in the marketplace. Multinat may be shunned by potential customers and employees. Such facts should be considered in ethical decision making. Of course, the president of Multinat should also consider the possibility that the South African investments could be used to promote reform of that nation's government.

Full consideration of all relevant facts can improve ethical decision making, but it does not necessarily make decisions easier. Say that Diopaper, Inc., runs an old pulp and paper mill in a small town on a river in the state of Washington. Environmentalists complain that the mill is polluting the river, killing fish, and endangering humans who live near the river. Diopaper's executives determine that the old mill is not very profitable and that closing the mill would appear environmentally responsible and enhance the corporation's goodwill towards the public. Here, the company's responsibility to society seems consistent with its own self-interest. A full consideration of the facts, however, might reveal that the old Washington mill employs hundreds of local workers. Some of these workers may not have alternative job opportunities. The Diopaper mill may even be essential to the entire economy of the small town where it is located. How should the company consider the economic effects of closing the mill on its employees and on the small town? What ethical issues are implicated in this decision?

This step in ethical analysis, full factual investigation and the application of ethical values in the business context, may simplify business decisions. In other cases, such an analysis may make the decisions more complicated. In any event, understanding the facts is essential to ethical judgment.

Problem Resolution

The final step in ethical analysis is problem resolution. The above three steps may filter out some ethical problems and show that apparent dilemmas are actually easy to resolve. Unfortunately, some ethical dilemmas truly are dilemmas in which fundamental values conflict. In these cases, the businessperson faces a more difficult problem in decision making.

When fundamental ethical duties conflict, the businessperson is required to sacrifice some ethical objectives in order to satisfy other duties. Resolving this problem should include two important considerations. First, the businessperson can still attempt to escape from the dilemma through "alternatives analysis" (considering more than one alternative plan). Perhaps some alternative policy can achieve both ethical goals. Second, if the alternatives analysis fails to produce an ideal compromise, the businessperson must make a choice between the conflicting ethical objectives and decide which is the more important.

The first step of alternatives analysis if often critical. Ethical dilemmas are too often perceived as binary or "yes/no" decisions. Few real-world problems actually require a "yes or no" answer. Often, some unconsidered third approach is available to help escape an ethical dilemma. Consider the Diopaper dilemma discussed above. Perhaps the company could upgrade or convert the old mill into a more modern, less polluting facility, while saving the jobs of many (though not all) of their workers.

Each new alternative may raise new ethical issues, however. If Diopaper is to upgrade or convert its old facility, this action will cost money. If the improvement is not the best use of corporate resources, this third alternative could violate some duty of loyalty to shareholders interested in maximizing their profits.

Even after searching for all alternative approaches, the moral dilemma may remain. This is a true dilemma, and the decision maker must choose among imperfect options. The conflicting ethical duties and goals must be compared and weighed. The decision maker must choose which ethical requirement is paramount under the circumstances.

Comparing and balancing conflicting ethical duties is not a simple matter. One cannot simply say, for example, that promise keeping is always more important than fairness. The decision maker also must consider the probability that a course of action will violate an ethical objective and must consider the seriousness of the violation. The seriousness of failure to keep a promise, for example, depends on the significance of the promise to the other party. The seriousness of the duty to avoid doing harm will depend centrally on the type and extent of harm that could be caused.

The resolution of an ethical problem is not a mathematical calculation, but requires thoughtful judgment. Ethical values such as honesty cannot be reduced to equal units that can be traded off. A pure utilitarian (one concerned only with maximizing human happiness) may attempt to reduce ethical decision making to a calculation. Since happiness cannot be readily measured, however, even such a utilitarian must employ judgment. There are no easy, all-purpose answers to ethical dilemmas in business. Motivation is important. If the decision maker is sincerely determined to make the ethical choice, ethical results are likely.

Another way to improve ethical decision making is to emphasize the importance of ethics to corporate employees. Employees will find it easier to be ethical in a corporate culture that rewards ethical behavior. Many corporations have developed codes of ethical conduct to guide their actions, as described later in the chapter.

Does Ethics Pay?

Corporate officers often seek to justify ethical behavior on the grounds that "ethics pays." Under this theory, good ethics is good business. If the ethical company succeeds in the marketplace, there is no reason not to act ethically. If ethics pays, there is no dilemma between loyalty to shareholders and other responsibilities to society. Unfortunately, the case that ethics pays is not so clear.

There are logical reasons why ethics pays in some circumstances. For a company that depends on repeat customers, behaving responsibly toward these customers should promote future business opportunities. Behaving ethically toward employees can induce better work habits and can help attract better employees. Ethical companies are less likely to suffer the penalties resulting from violating the law.

There are real-world examples of bad ethics having hurt a company. The leader of the investment firm of E.F. Hutton openly "regarded Hutton's retail customers as sheep waiting to be sheared, and he often said so."[8] Perhaps because of this attitude, Hutton engaged in a series of questionable financial practices. For example, it would write checks simultaneously against accounts in Chemical Bank and Manufacturers Hanover Bank and deposit the checks in the other bank. By so doing, it had a period when the checks were credited to its account (with interest) before their other account was charged for the money. For this and other check-kiting schemes, Hutton pleaded guilty to two thousand counts of fraud. In addition to the legal sanctions, the episode destroyed Hutton's reputation in the business community. E.F. Hutton was once the nation's second largest broker; the ethical scandal all but destroyed the company, and it was eventually taken over by another company.

An example of good and profitable business ethics was the response of Johnson & Johnson after persons were found to be poisoned by contaminated Tylenol, a Johnson & Johnson product. Although the company apparently was not at fault for this tragedy, Johnson & Johnson immediately pulled its product off the market in order to protect its consumers, and then promptly reintroduced the product, this time with tamper-resistant packaging. The after-tax cost of the recall alone was $50 million,

---

[8] *New York Times Book Review,* October 21, 1990, p.13.

but Johnson & Johnson almost immediately recaptured its market share in painkillers and established ample goodwill with consumers.

The E.F. Hutton and Johnson & Johnson examples illustrate that bad ethics can be bad business and good ethics can be good business. Unfortunately, ethical decision making does not always pay. A recent article by two Harvard Business School professors found that "[c]ompared with the few ambiguous tales of treachery punished, we can find numerous stories in which deceit was unquestionably rewarded."[9] Ethical behavior can be expensive, giving less ethical competitors a price advantage. Good ethics and profit maximization are not always correlated.

In addition, the economic benefits of ethical action tend to show up only in the long run. Cultivating an ethical reputation in business dealings may take years. While good ethics may avoid government regulation and legal penalties, these effects also take years. Today's business climate, however, often demands short-run results, creating pressures to cut corners on ethical duties and show more profit in the next fiscal year.

Sometimes ethical behavior will pay off, and at other times such behavior will require some financial sacrifice. It is easy to be ethical when ethics is profitable. Truly ethical behavior requires sacrifices, however. Ethics is tested when self-interest conflicts with ethical responsibilities.

▬ Business Beneficence

The above discussion focused on the ethical responsibilities of business in making everyday business decisions. Another central ethical issue is that of business beneficence, which means doing acts of kindness and charity. Business beneficence may involve contributing to housing for the homeless or to a local symphony orchestra. How appropriate and necessary is it for business to act with beneficence toward its external society?

Many businesses would argue that they owe no ethical duty of beneficence or philanthropy. Rather, they consider beneficence as going "above and beyond the call of ethics" in order to help the needy and improve the community. This action is usually considered praiseworthy. Beneficence raises significant issues, however. First, it is difficult to decide how much beneficence is appropriate. After a corporation has given a contribution to the symphony orchestra, why shouldn't they also give to the opera, ballet, public television, local educational institutions, poverty aid groups, etc.? It is difficult to decide which organizations merit contributions and how much they should receive.

Second, beneficence seems a direct taking of the shareholders' money. When a business gives money to a charity, it is donating its shareholders' profits. Perhaps the corporation should distribute the profits to the shareholders and let them decide whether to give to charities. Corporate contributions are particularly problematic when the shareholder may not agree that the recipient of charity is a worthy cause. This risk was illustrated in the Tiller, Inc., example near the beginning of this chapter.

Of course, much corporate beneficence returns to help the corporation. A company with a reputation for charitable giving to worthwhile causes may be especially attractive to potential customers. An opera fan may be more likely to purchase gasoline at a Texaco station because of that company's long-standing sponsorship of Metropolitan Opera broadcasts.

Most corporations see some benefit to philanthropic contributions. The Caterpillar Tractor Company's code of international business conduct has a section called "public responsibility" in which the code provides:

> [Another] category relates to initiatives beyond our operations, such as helping solve community problems. To the extent our resources permit—and if a host country or community wishes—we will participate selectively in such matters, especially where our facilities are located. Each corporate facility is an integral part of the community in which it operates. Like individuals, it benefits from character building, health, welfare, educational, and cultural activities. And like individuals, it

---

[9] Bhide & Stevenson, "Why Be Honest if Honesty Doesn't Pay," *Harvard Business Review* (September/October 1990), p. 122.

also has citizen responsibilities to support such activities.[10]

While there may be some business benefit from corporate contributions, this code seems to treat beneficence as almost a duty to the local community.

---

[10] "A Code of Worldwide Business Conduct," reprinted in Frederick Sturdivant, *The Corporate Social Challenge* (1985), p. 167.

Corporate law has itself struggled with the legitimacy of corporate beneficence. Under traditional principles, the directors and officers of a corporation were required to manage the company in the interests of shareholders. Some argued that corporate contributions to charity were contrary to this legal duty. The following case is a landmark in the law of corporate charitable contributions.

Case 1.3
A. P. Smith Manufacturing Company v. Barlow
Supreme Court of New Jersey, 1953
98 A.2d 581

Background and Facts The A.P. Smith Manufacturing Company, located in New Jersey, was incorporated in 1896. A.P. Smith manufactured valves and other special equipment for water and gas companies. Over the years, the company had made small contributions to local schools. In 1951, the corporate board of directors resolved to make a $1500 contribution to Princeton University. Some stockholders questioned this action. The company then brought this case to court, seeking a declaratory judgment on the lawfulness of its contribution. The New Jersey Chancery Court found the contribution to be a legal exercise of corporate power, and the stockholders appealed.

JACOBS, Justice.

* * * *

Mr. Hubert F. O'Brien, the president of the company, testified that he considered the contribution to be a sound investment, that the public expects corporations to aid philanthropic and benevolent institutions, that they obtain good will in the community by so doing, and that their charitable donations create favorable environment for their business operations. In addition, he expressed the thought that in contributing to liberal arts institutions, corporations were furthering their self-interest in assuring the free flow of properly trained personnel for administrative and other corporate employment. Mr. Frank W. Abrams, chairman of the board of the Standard Oil Company of New Jersey, testified that corporations are expected to acknowledge their public responsibilities in support of the essential elements of our free enterprise system. He indicated that it was not "good business" to disappoint "this reasonable and justified public expectation," nor was it good business for corporations "to take substantial benefits from their membership in the economic community while avoiding the normally accepted obligations of citizenship in the social community."

* * * *

When the wealth of the nation was primarily in the hands of individuals they discharged their responsibilities as citizens by donating freely for charitable purposes. With the transfer of most of the wealth to corporate hands and the imposition of heavy burdens of individual taxation, they have been unable to keep pace with increased philanthropic needs. They have therefore, with justification, turned to corporations to assume the modern obligations of good citizenship in the same manner as humans do. Congress and state legislatures have enacted laws which encourage corporate contributions, and much has recently been written to indicate the crying need and adequate legal basis therefor[e]...

During the First World War corporations loaned their personnel and contributed substantial corporate funds in order to insure survival; during the depression of the 1930s they made contributions to alleviate the desperate hardships of the millions of unemployed; and during the Second World War they contributed to insure survival. They now recognize that we are faced with other, though nonetheless vicious, threats from abroad which must be withstood without impairing the vigor of our democratic institutions at home and that otherwise victory will be pyrrhic indeed. More and more they have come to recognize that their salvation rests upon sound economic and social environment which in turn rests in no insignificant part upon free and vigorous nongovernmental institutions of learning. It seems to us that just as the conditions prevailing when corporations were originally created required that they serve public as well as private interests, modern conditions require that corporations acknowledge and discharge social as well as private responsibilities as members of the communities within which they operate.

* * * *

In the light of all the foregoing we have no hesitancy in sustaining the validity of the donation by the plaintiff. There is no suggestion that it was made indiscriminately or to a pet charity of the corporation directors in furtherance of personal rather than corporate ends. On the contrary, it was made to a preeminent institution of higher learning, was modest in amount and well within the limitations imposed by the statutory enactments, and was voluntarily made in the reasonable belief that it would aid the public welfare and advance the interests of the plaintiff as a private corporation and as part of the community in which it operates.

Decision and Remedy *The New Jersey Supreme Court affirmed the lower court holding that the contribution was legal.*

A corporate governance project of the American Law Institute has grappled with the law's response to corporate philanthropy. The ALI's corporate governance project has long recognized that the fundamental duty of corporate directors and officers is to enhance corporate profit and shareholder gain. The Institute's influential Principles of Corporate Governance, however, provide that a corporation "may devote a reasonable amount of resources to public welfare, humanitarian, educational and philanthropic purposes."[11]

Some corporate beneficence is regarded as legally and ethically appropriate. It remains difficult to decide how much beneficence is right and where to distribute this beneficence. The following principles can provide some guidance for corporate contributions:

---

[11] *Principles of Corporate Governance and Structure: Restatement and Recommendations,* section 2.01(c) (Tent. Draft No. 2, 1984).

1. The amount of any contributions should be "reasonable" and not threaten the value of the corporation as an ongoing enterprise.

2. The contributions should focus on benefitting the corporation's "community." For some multinational corporations, of course, the relevant community may be the entire world.

3. The contributions should consider need. Rather than giving to the most popular local charity, the corporation should find where its contributions would do the most good.

4. The contributions should consider shareholder opinions. Corporations should avoid contributions that offend the values of a significant proportion of their shareholders.

5. A portion of the contributions should involve areas of interest to the corporation. If a corporation's business activities unavoidably injure the local environment, that corporation should consider making contributions to environmental improvements.

These principles are not meant to be exhaustive, and corporations may reasonably consider other factors. Corporate contributions should not be determined by the "pet charity" of the company's president, however. The beneficence comes from the corporation and should reflect the corporation's position, not that of individual officers.

Putting Business Ethics into Effect

After a corporation affirms the fundamental principles of business ethics, there remains the need to implement these principles in corporate decision making. The company must convince its employees to act responsibly. Three tools for putting business ethics into effect are corporate codes of conduct, social audits, and creation of positive corporate culture.

Codes of Ethical Conduct

In recent years, many corporations have adopted ethical codes of conduct for their employees. Establishing such a code of conduct can provide guidelines for the actions of employees at all levels in the company. Codes may assure executive officers and managers that a single-minded pursuit of profit should not be their sole objective.

Corporate codes of conduct are especially effective in setting specific rules for situations that can commonly arise. For example, some codes of conduct flatly prohibit payments to government officials, to avoid even the perception of bribery. Another provision might prohibit employees from taking any gifts from suppliers or might limit the value of gifts that could be received. A code can also establish fair procedures for disciplining employees. These specific prohibitions can be enforceable rules for the corporation.

Codes of conduct are less effective for larger and more ambiguous ethical controversies. It is difficult to set clear rules for issue such as product quality or environmental protection. Many corporate codes of ethical conduct contain no provisions for these large issues. One study found that only 20 percent of corporate ethical codes mentioned environmental affairs, and only 35 percent of the codes mentioned civic and community affairs.[12] When codes do address large issues, there provisions are typically quite vague.

Notwithstanding these limitations, writing a code of ethical conduct can be valuable. The simple act of writing such a code "is in itself worthwhile, especially if it forces a large number of people in the firm to think through, in a fresh way, their mission and the important obligations they as a group and as individuals have to the firm, each other, their clients or customers, and society as a whole."[13] The mere presence of such a code can encourage employees to act ethically and reassure customers and the public of the corporation's good intentions. Standing alone, an ethical code has only limited benefit. The principles of the code must be reinforced by supervisors and other corporate officers. The code also should be transmitted directly from the corporate president to employees throughout the company.

A 1986 study by the Center for Ethics at Bentley College found that nearly 80 percent of the companies surveyed were taking steps to implement ethical concerns in daily operations.[14] Of the

---

[12] Donald Cressey & Charles Moore, "Manager Values and Codes of Ethics," 25 *California Management Review* (Summer 1983), p. 56.

[13] Richard T. DeGeorge, *Business Ethics* (1986), pp. 345-346.

[14] Center for Business at Bentley College, "Are Corporations Institutionalizing Ethics?," 5 *Journal of Business Ethics* (1986), p. 85.

> **Exhibit 1-1**
>
> **TOPICS COVERED IN CORPORATE ETHICS CODES**
>
> | Issue | % of companies dealing with this issue in their codes of ethics |
> |---|---|
> | Relations with U.S. Government | 76.7% |
> | Employee Duties to Corporation | 69.0% |
> | Responsibility to Customers and Suppliers | 75.0% |
> | Relations with Foreign Governments | 42.2% |
> | Community Affairs | 34.5% |
> | Environmental Affairs | 19.8% |
> | Personal Character Issues | 9.5% |
>
> Source: Donald Cressey & Charles Moore, "Manager Values and Codes of Ethics," 25 *California Management Review* (Summer 1983), p. 56.

companies that were implementing ethics policies, 93 percent were using some corporate code of ethics. Nearly every major American corporation has some form of ethical code in effect.

These corporate codes vary considerably and address a range of topics. The issues covered in corporate codes of ethics, as found in one study, are displayed in Exhibit 1-1.

Adoption and enforcement of a corporate code of ethics can have legal benefits for a company. The following decision used a code of ethics as an important factor in ruling for a defendant.

■ Case 1.4
O'Connor v. CertainTeed Corporation
United States District Court for the Eastern District of Pennsylvania, 1990
Civil Action No. 87-3866

Background and Facts *Glidden O'Connor, employed by CertainTeed Corporation, was promoted to Vice-President. He thus became a participant in CertainTeed's Executive Retirement Plan, which provided deferred compensation. Payments would not be made under the plan if a participant voluntarily resigned or was fired for cause. In 1985, CertainTeed became aware that O'Connor had given corporate contracts to his personally owned company without disclosing that fact, in violation of the CertainTeed code of ethics. CertainTeed resolved to fire O'Connor but, in recognition of his service, the company offered to allow him to resign. O'Connor agreed to resign.*

CertainTeed refused to pay O'Connor benefits under the retirement plan. O'Connor claimed that his resignation was not voluntary and that he was due pension benefits. O'Connor sued to recover these benefits.

SHAPIRO, United States District Judge.

* * * *

Since March, 1974, CertainTeed has had a written Business Code of Ethics and Conduct Policy ("Code of Ethics"). The Code of Ethics lists certain prohibited activities and provides that situations possibly creating conflicts must be disclosed. In the case of a group president, such disclosure must be made to the Chief Executive Officer, who reports to the Board of Directors on the possible conflict. For certain activities, such as an outside directorship, the Code of Ethics requires that employees obtain prior approval of the Board of Directors.

The Code of Ethics also requires annual completion of a "business Code of Ethics and Conduct Statement and Questionnaire" ("Code of Ethics Statement" or the "Statement") by certain employees including Vice-Presidents. The Code of Ethics Statement requires that the employee set forth activities resulting in possible conflicts of interest, such as CertainTeed employment of any immediate family member or ownership interest in an entity doing business with or competing with CertainTeed or its subsidiaries.

Besson became President and Chief Executive Officer of CertainTeed in July, 1980. As Chief Executive Officer of CertainTeed Besson placed great emphasis on the importance of complying with the Code of Ethics. Besson stressed the importance of the Code of Ethics by sending cover letters in 1982, 1983, and 1984 to employees required to complete the Code of Ethics Statement.

* * * *

If O'Connor's resignation had not been voluntary, the court would find that he had been dismissed for cause. Besson decided to ask for O'Connor's resignation because of his failure to abide by the Code of Ethics. O'Connor was given the option of resigning only because he had worked for the Company for so many years and the issue of his entitlement to Plan benefits was specifically and explicitly reserved. On the facts surrounding his departure as established by the credible testimony, particularly the events of the day his letter of resignation was signed, O'Connor could not have reasonably believed he was resigning voluntarily with Company approval and consequent entitlement to the additional benefits he now seeks. His failure to abide by the Code of Ethics in more than one way on more than one occasion was flagrant and clear cause for dismissal.

Decision and Remedy *The court granted summary judgment for CertainTeed.*

A code of ethics may create litigation. As business codes become more common, terminated employees are increasingly likely to sue their former employers for a breach of the code. Such codes typically contain statements about dealing fairly with employees. These cases have failed when the ethical code's promises were general and when the code contained a disclaimer indicating that it was not meant to create a contract.[15]

Social Audits

Some corporations have begun conducting "social audits" that review corporate policies and actions and inform the public of where they stand on key social issues. There is no defined structure for social audits, which often address and omit a variety of issues.

Social audits are regularly used by European corporations. One very large Swiss corporation, Migros-Genossenschafts-Bund, issued a social audit report conceding that the company underpaid women, provided needlessly boring jobs, and had increased its air pollution emissions over a recent period. Such unusual candor is praise-worthy if the corporation takes steps to correct the problems.

United States companies have not fully employed social audits, but some corporations (e.g., Bank of America, Norton Co. and others) have issued audit reports. It is understandable if American corporations have not been quick to confess wrongdoing. Under U.S. law, such admissions could be used against the company in expensive litigation. Moreover, confessing blame is not as important as correcting ethical shortcomings. Of the companies that conduct social audits, only about half report the results to the public or to their shareholders.

Social audits can be quite beneficial. To be effective, though, audits require a thorough and rigorous consideration of all significant ethical issues. Audits also should be conducted by some independent auditor who has no self-interest in the outcome of the audit. Some corporations have established an office of ombudsman with the charge of conducting ongoing investigations of the ethics of the corporation's activities.

Social audits are not as common as business codes of ethics. The Bentley College survey found that nearly 44 percent of companies had some form of social auditing and reporting. Many of the social auditors, however, came from within the corporation, rather than an independent outsider. Approximately 7 percent of these companies had an ethics ombudsman.

Corporate Ethical Culture

Perhaps the most important method for promoting business ethics is the creation of a corporate culture that rewards ethical behavior. Employees are usually sensitive to the standards and objectives of higher officers. Whether these officers reward or discourage ethical action can have a great effect on ethics throughout the corporation.

In some companies, the prevailing corporate culture can actively discourage ethical action by middle managers. Some corporations have led employees to believe that illegal behavior is practically a job requirement. Many corporations have fired or otherwise punished employees that have "blown the whistle" on illegal corporate actions. Employees caught up in this type of atmosphere will make unethical corporate decisions that they would not consider when acting independently.

Creating an ethical corporate culture should start at the top. Edwin Epstein, a professor of Business Administration at the University of California, stressed that the "ethical sensitivities and proclivities of top management, and, more specifically, the CEO, can and do have a profound impact on the moral ethos of a corporation." The use of codes of ethical conduct and social audits can contribute to a positive ethical culture.

Another measure used to create an ethical corporate culture is ethics training for managers and other employees. In the Bentley College study, 44 percent of responding firms had initiated some program of training in ethics. Most of these programs were addressed to middle managers, but some included everyone from executive officers to administrative staff. While no rigorous studies prove the effectiveness of such training, common sense suggests that the program should have some benefit.

A positive ethical culture has direct benefits for the corporation itself. If employees recognize that the company values ethical behavior, they are more likely to act ethically in many respects. Such

---

[15] *Kapossy v. McGraw-Hill, Inc.,* 921 F.Supp.234 (D.N.J. 1996).

employees will be less likely to take corporate supplies for personal use. If employees act ethically toward one another, morale is sure to improve. Companies benefit when employees care about their workplace and their employer.

Of course, even a bad corporate culture cannot excuse unethical actions by employees. Middle managers and other corporate employees can improve the corporate culture from the bottom up. Some such employees have blown the whistle on illegal actions, even at the cost of their jobs. While it is obviously difficult to endanger your own employment, ethics can dictate running such a risk.

Evidence suggests that most companies have a neutral corporate culture with respect to ethics. Business professors have studied advertising and marketing executives to determine whether high ethical standards help or hinder an individual's success in a company. A review of this evidence concluded that executives "appear neither to be penalized nor rewarded based on social responsibility."[16]

[16] Hunt, Kiecker & Chonko, "Social Responsibility and Personal Success: A Research Note," *18 J. of Acad. of Marketing Science* (1990), p. 243.

Questions and Case Problems

1. While still working for Duane Jones Co., an advertising agency, the employees of Jones conspired to start a new firm. After leaving Jones, these employees took along many of their former agency's principal clients as well as many files. Jones Co. filed suit against their former employees. Have the employees who formed the new firm acted unethically? Have they acted illegally? [*Duane Jones Co. v. Burke*, 117 N.E.2d 237 (N.Y.)].

2. Brooks Lee works as a sales assistant at XYZ Co.—a large, publicly held New York corporation. Brooks grew up in a poor family and felt fortunate to get the job. She would rather be an actress but has immediate financial needs that could not be met in an acting career. She has many friends in the theater. At XYZ, Brooks overheard a conversation about a likely merger of the company that would increase its stock price dramatically. Knowing that she could not take advantage of this information as an employee, Brooks tells her acting friends so that they can make enough money to survive in the theater. She saw this as a small correction for society's undervaluation of the arts. The actors buy XYZ shares and profit substantially. Has brooks behaved unethically?

3. Dale Thomas has worked as an engineer for Perfect Swing Golf Products (PSGP) for many years. The latest product out of PSGP is an attachment for the driver that creates the right "feel" for a perfect stroke. The company developed an expensive marketing campaign for the product and sales have been good. Dale inadvertently discovered that the new product is apt to fly off the driver and injure other golfers. Dale developed a simple safety mechanism to correct the problem. The mechanism will cost little in production but could be quite costly if all the previously sold products had to be recalled. Dale informed his supervisor who told him to "keep quite" about the problem. How should Dale act?

4. Eddie and Kris received civil engineering degrees from the same university twenty years ago and have maintained their friendship ever since. They still visit at football games and occasionally go on fishing trips together. Eddie is now the president of a large construction company that performs many projects for the state. Kris was recently promoted to the position of construction contract officer at the state highway department and is in charge of reviewing and approving highway contract bids. At a football game, Eddie told Kris that he had the company plane for the weekend and invited Kris on a trip to the Gulf of Mexico for some deep-sea fishing. How should Kris respond to this offer?

5. Bob Maxon works as an account executive at ABC advertising and has made his living in the beauty products area. Bob is currently working on campaigns for a whitening toothpaste and a hardening agent for a nail polish. The toothpaste company is trying to dispel a rumor that their product ruins the finish on nail polish. Bob is wondering whether to provide the toothpaste company with the details of the hardening agent so that they might be able to improve their product. Bob did not sign a nondisclosure agreement with the nail polish client, but they did inform him that the product details were a trade secret that should not be disclosed. What action should Bob take?

6. The Boy Scouts of America have a policy of refusing to admit gays as members or troop leaders. A large California corporation, U.S. West, has traditionally made contributions to the Boy Scouts but has a policy of encouraging pluralism and diversity. The donations to the Boy Scouts were challenged by gay and lesbian U.S. West employees as contrary to this policy. After consideration, the company decided to continue its contributions. Levi Strauss & Company, however, eliminated its support for the Boy Scouts because it chose not to fund an organization that discriminates. Whose decision do you agree with and why?

CHAPTER TWO

International Business Law

KEY BACKGROUND

The essential background for this chapter on international business law is found in Chapters 11 and 55 of *West's Business Law, Seventh Edition,* and in Chapter 8 of *West's Legal Environment of Business, Third Edition.* These chapters cover international business transactions and the international legal environment. Among the important points to remember from these chapters are:

- the application and provisions of the Convention on Contracts for the International Sale of Goods
- the provisions for making payments on international transactions
- the United States laws applicable to international transactions
- the laws governing imports and exports.

* * *

Globalization is the watchword for business in the 1990s. International transactions in goods and services threaten to make the concept of a national economic market obsolete. Hundreds of billions of dollars of imports and exports pass through United States ports every year. A new and important development is the globalization of securities markets.

As business becomes increasingly international in scope, legal rules applicable to international business must follow. This chapter addresses the key legal issues of international contracting, U.S. regulation of exports and imports, and investments in overseas securities markets and in foreign production facilities.

Performance and Remedies in International Contracts

Chapter 56 of *West's Business Law, Sixth Edition,* provides considerable detail on the formation of transnational contracts governed by the United Nations Convention for the International Sale of Goods. This section focuses on requirements imposed after the contract is made. It covers the presence of warranties, performance, discharge, breach of contract and remedies.

The U.N. Convention does not expressly speak of any implied warranties in the goods sold, but certain provisions are similar to warranties. Article 35(2) of the Convention requires that the goods be fit for ordinary use, be properly packaged, and conform to any samples or models provided the purchaser. This Article also requires that goods be fit for any particular use that the purchaser made known to the seller prior to the conclusion of the contract. As under U.S. law, this obligation only arises when the buyer has relied reasonably on the seller's skill in selecting the goods. All these warranties may be disclaimed by agreement of the parties.

Article 41 of the Convention obliges sellers to deliver title to the goods free from any encumbrances and free from any claims by third parties. This goes beyond the Uniform Commercial Code, Section 2-312, which does not require warranty of freedom from third-party claims.

In the event of defective goods, the Convention provides that a seller is not liable for defects of which the buyer was aware or "could not have been unaware" at the time the contract was concluded. For subsequently arising defects, the buyer must inspect the goods "within as short a time as is practicable" and notify the seller of any defects "within a reasonable time" in order to recover damages. The precise meaning of these terms depends on the circumstances of individual cases.

If the seller breaches the contract by providing defective goods, the Convention provides remedies different from those of the U.S. law. The purchaser may demand specific performance (the shipment of conforming goods), but only if the defect is so significant as to be a "fundamental breach." A "fundamental breach" is defined as one that "substantially deprive[s] [the buyer] of what he is entitled to expect under the contract." This appears to be a stricter test than under American law. The purchaser may require repair of the defective goods if that is reasonable under "all the circumstances."

The Convention also permits a buyer to avoid payment on the contract if there has been any "fundamental breach" by the seller. The Convention, however, permits a seller the opportunity to cure the defect and hold the buyer to the contract, even in the event of a fundamental breach. This remedy is unavailable, though, when a cure would cause "unreasonable delay" or "inconvenience."

The Convention also enables buyers to sue for damages, both direct and consequential. As under U.S. law, the buyer has a duty to mitigate its damages. Article 50 of the Convention contains an interesting provision permitting buyers who receive defective goods to "reduce the price" paid to the seller. The rules for determining the amount of price reduction are unclear, however, and the buyer must allow the seller to attempt to cure the nonconforming goods before reducing the price paid. Foreseeability of damage is also a condition on recovery.

The Convention's rules for risk of loss are similar to those of U.S. law. Article 67 provides that the buyer bears the risk of loss to the goods once the goods are handed over by the seller to the first carrier, even if that carrier is a local trucker. The parties may change this rule by contract, however, and provide that the seller would bear the risk of loss until the goods reach the buyer's place of business.

If a buyer breaches a contract and refuses to pay for the goods, the Convention provides that the seller may bring a damages action for the price of the goods. The seller may win such damages only if the seller has performed to the extent required by the contract. If the seller is unable to obtain the price, he or she may be able to reclaim the goods that were delivered to the defaulting buyer. Such reclamation is rather difficult under American law but easier under the U.N. Convention.

Regulation of Exports

Although the United States generally encourages the export of products, federal law places controls on certain categories of exports. The United States government restricts exports under the Export Administration Act of 1979, as amended in 1981 and 1985. This law is administered by the Department of Commerce's Office of Export Administration. The Act's coverage is quite broad and prohibits the export of commodities or technical data, unless the exporter obtains a license.

U.S. law is not limited to controlling direct exports from the United States. The law also applies to re-exports of United States-origin commodities and technical data among foreign countries and export from foreign countries of products with United States-origin parts or technical data.

Suppose that CompuTech exports oil production software containing advanced technical data to Taiwan. A Taiwanese corporation then incorporates this software into computers, to sell to corporations in Indonesia. A United States export license is required in order to ship the U.S.-origin goods from Taiwan to Indonesia.

Some exporters are also subject to the Arms Export Control Act, which applies to exports of defense-related products, services and technical data. Exporters subject to this act must obtain an export license from the State Department, which can deny a license on the grounds that the export is inconsistent with U.S. foreign policy interests.

The Export Administration Act and Arms Export Control Act enable the President to restrict exports as necessary for national interest. The greatest use of the Act has been to restrict exports of military-significant commodities and technology to communists countries. The Act also authorizes restrictions as necessary to "protect the domestic economy from the excessive drain of scarce materials" and "to further significantly the foreign policy of the United States and to fulfill its international responsibilities."[1] When a grain shortage occurred in the 1970s, export controls were placed on soybean and grains.

The Department of Commerce maintains a Commodity Control List (CCL) that contains all the commodities subject to export regulation. The list is based on factors such as the potential military uses of the goods, how advanced the technology involved is, and the availability of comparable goods from other nations. The CCL is an almost two-hundred-page listing of products and components. Computer equipment has been especially sensitive.

In addition to the commodities list, the Department's Office of Export Administration also regulates export of technical data, which is defined as "information of any kind that can be used, or adopted for use, in the design, production, manufacture, utilization or reconstruction of articles or materials."[2]

Exporting Licensing

Every export of goods and technology is subject to some measure of export control. Exports are broadly defined to include exports of goods, exports of technical data from the United States, re-exports of goods from one foreign purchaser to another in the same country. Restrictions on exports of technical data may be overlooked. Such a regulated data export can occur when operating manuals or other technical manuals are sent to a foreign purchaser of a U.S. product or when a sales representative delivers written product specifications on a sales trip abroad.

The Commerce Department enforces its export regulations through a process of licensing. Federal regulations prevent the export of any commodities or technical data until a license is obtained. The Export Administration Act provides for two different types of licenses: the **General License** and the **Validated License**. The Validated License is the more restrictive of the two.

A Validated License is required for the export of certain products listed on the Commodity Control List, for certain technical data, and for exports to certain destination countries. When the Validated License is required, the government scrutinizes specific shipments to consider whether to grant a license.

To obtain a Validated License, a company first needs a customer. The Commerce Department generally requires an "order" from a foreign person or firm for a particular commodity or technical data. The next step is to determine whether a Validated License is required by the export regulations, which can be a complicated determination. The company then applies for a license to fill the order, with full documentation regarding (i) the materials to be exported, (ii) the destination country, (iii) the names and addresses of all parties, and (iv) the proposed utilization of the exported commodity.

The Commerce Department generally approves such license requests within three weeks, when the shipper may go forward with the export. The license typically requires shipment only to the approved destination country and may contain other restrictions, such as the use of the exports by the foreign nation. When shipment is made, the company posts this fact on the reverse of the Validated License forms and returns it to the Commerce Department.

In addition to applying for a Validated License, the exporter also generally must submit a Form DIB-629P, a consignee and purchaser statement. This form must be completed by the importer in the foreign country and restates the essential facts of the export transaction as set forth in the application. This is to prevent the unauthorized diversion of exported commodities.

A company may avoid some of the complexity of the Validated License by obtaining a **Distribution License**. This Distribution License permits an exporter to ship even commodities requiring a Validated License to certain destination countries (e.g., any nation in the Western Hemisphere except Cuba). In order to obtain a Distribution License, the exporter must gain advance approval of the Office of Export Administration and must have a written agreement in which the importer agrees to comply with U.S. export control restrictions.

For many commodities, a company can use the more flexible General License, which requires no government documentation for specific exports. There are different types of General Licenses. One

---

[1] 50 U.S.C. Sec. 2402(2).
[2] 15 C.F.R. Sec. 379.1(a).

type authorizes the export of commodities to certain specified countries in a single shipment, up to a certain total value specified in the license. Another type of General License authorizes the export of technical data that is "generally available" or of scientific or educational data to all destinations. Obtaining a General License simplifies the export process.

An exporter must do some research to determine if it qualifies for a general license. At minimum, the exporter must employ the following procedure:

1. Check to see if the commodity is on the CCl. If so, make a note of the Export Commodity Control Number ("ECCN").

2. Check to see if the destination country is on the embargo list, which requires a Validated License for any exports. Embargoed countries include Libya, North Korea and Cuba.

3. If the country is not embargoed, check to see of the destination country requires a validated license for the quantity of the ECCN commodity to be exported.

4. Check to see that the exported commodity does not contain technical data requiring a Validated License (e.g., electronic equipment containing computer software).[3]

The Export Act also places record-keeping requirements on exporters. These records must include all correspondence, contracts, financial records and "other written matter" relating to an export transaction. These records must be retained for two years.

Enforcement and Penalties

The Export Administration Act makes licensees strictly liable for compliance with the terms of their license, and penalties under the Act can be severe. Whoever knowingly violates the act is punishable by a fine of up to five times the value of the exports involved and imprisonment for up to five years. Willful exports to a prohibited destination country are subject to potentially greater sanctions. Even inadvertent violations can yield fines of up to $100,000. In one case, a company exported $3 million in equipment to the Soviet Union for an air traffic control system. Before obtaining the required Validated License, the company went forward with the exports. Although the license was eventually granted (with many conditions), the company was found criminally liable for violation of the Export Administration Act and fined $3 million.

In the 1980s, a California company purchased airplanes, which it routed through West Germany, France, and Benin, before delivering the planes to Libya. At least one of the planes became part of the Libyan air force. This was in violation of the company's license with the Commerce Department. The company's owner was given a fifteen-year jail sentence and a fine in excess of $6 million.[4]

The penalties under the Export Administration Act and Arms Control Act are criminal, so the government must prove the willfulness of the violation. In the following recent case, the government failed to meet this burden.

---

[3] J. Land & D. Hall, "Overview of the U.S. Export Administration Regulations," *10 Whittier L. Rev. 305* (1988).

[4] *United States v. Elkins*, 885 F.2d 775 (11th Cir. 1989).

■ Case 2.1
United States v. Adames
United States Court of Appeals
Eleventh Circuit, 1989
878 F.2d 1374

Background and Facts *Ivonne Adames was a vice-consul at the Panamanian consulate in Miami, Florida. Her brother, Ivan Blasser, owned a security firm in Panama. Blasser began traveling to Miami to purchase supplies, including firearms, from a police surplus store in Miami. Adames obtained letters from the Panamanian consulate authorizing her brother's purchases and delivered the goods to Air Panama for shipment to his Panamanian address. She also cosigned the shipment forms. One of these forms included an "Export Notice," which stated that certain products could not be exported without a license.*

After relations between the U.S. and Panama had deteriorated, Adames refused to sign the export forms. An inexperienced sales clerk released the firearms, however, without her or her brother's signature. Blasser then delivered the guns to Air Panama for shipment, but they were seized by the Customs Department. Adames then issued a backdated consular letter authorizing the purchase of the firearms. The exports were unlicensed, and the Customs Department prosecuted Adames under the Arms Export Control Act. A jury found her guilty, but the district judge overturned the verdict and entered a judgement of acquittal. The government appealed this decision.

PER CURIAM.

* * * *

The commercial export of arms and ammunition from the United States is governed by the Arms Export Control Act (AECA), 22 U.S.C.A. § 2778, and the International Traffic in Arms Regulations, 22 C.F.R. §§ 121-30. Persons desiring to export certain listed munitions must register with the State Department's Office of Munitions Control and obtain an export license for each shipment of arms abroad. 22 C.F.R. §§ 122-23. It is undisputed that Adames twice assisted her brother in exporting controlled firearms without having obtained a license, as alleged in the indictment.

Section 2778(c), however, imposes criminal sanctions only on those persons who "willfully" violate the AECA and the regulations promulgated thereunder. 22 U.S.C.A. § 2778(c) (West Supp.1989). In *United States v. Davis*, 583 F.2d 190 (5th Cir.1978), the court held that this requirement of willfulness connotes a voluntary, intentional violation of a known legal duty. *Id.* at 193 (adopting the Ninth Circuit's analysis in *U.S. v. Lizarraga-Lizarraga*, 541 F.2d 826 (9th Cir.1976). "Because the items covered by the statute are spelled out in administrative regulations and include items not known generally to be controlled by the government, [we infer] that Congress did not intend to impose criminal penalties on innocent or negligent errors." Davis, 583 F.2d at 193.

The government acknowledges its burden of proving specific intent under each count of the indictment; it concedes that it must prove that Adames knew that it was unlawful to export the unregistered firearms. *See id.* On appeal, the United States asserts, as it did in the court below, that Adames' execution of the Export Notice and her conduct throughout this period of time amply supports the inference that she acted willfully.

Having studied the transcription of the testimony elicited at trial, especially those portions to which the government eludes, we conclude that the government failed to prove that Adames acted willfully. The evidence demonstrates, at most, that Adames was negligent in not investigating the legal prerequisites to the exportation of firearms. It does not prove that she intentionally violated a known legal duty not to export the firearms or purposefully perpetuated her ignorance of the AECA to avoid criminal liability. Though it reasonably could be inferred from Adames' suspicious conduct that she was aware of the generally unlawful nature of her actions, that state of mind is insufficient to sustain a finding of guilt under a statute requiring specific intent. See *United States v. Frade*, 709 F.2d 1387, 1392-93 (11th Cir.1983); *United States v. Hernandez*, 662 F.2d 289, 292 (5th Cir.1981).

Decision and Remedy *The court affirmed the judgment of acquittal.*

In addition to fines and imprisonment, the State Department may invoke or suspend the export privileges of a company. The law creates a presumption of denial of export licenses to those who have been convicted of violations of the Arms Export Control Act.

Whatever the type of license, an exporter generally must file a Shipper's Export Declaration. This Declaration must be presented to customs officials at the point where the exports leave the U.S. The Shipper's Export Declaration must contain the name and address of the parties to the transaction, a description of the exported commodities, and the license number for the exports. For many commodities, the Export Administration Regulations require a "destination control statement" on the invoice or bill of lading. This specifies the intended destination of the exports, in order to prevent their diversion.

In 1988, Congress liberalized somewhat the export controls on computers. While exporters once needed a license merely to export floppy disks, they now can sell computers with an 80286 processor to the Soviet Union. In addition, a new general license permits shipment of many computers to a specified group of about 20 countries (most of the world's industrialized nations). A special license is no longer required to export even mid-range computers to a country such as Germany. This new liberalization does not apply to advanced generation supercomputers, however.

▬ International Intellectual Property Protection

The most significant recent developments in international law regard the protection of intellectual property. Some of America's largest imports are movies, music, software, and other products of intellectual property. Unfortunately, companies in some foreign nations have made numerous unapproved copies of these items and sold them for profit. U.S. companies have lost billions of dollars as a result.

Problems of international intellectual property protection have been both legal and practical. Legally, each country had its own regime for protecting such property. Thus, for a patent to be protected in a foreign country, a company had to comply with the substance and procedures of patent law in every country. Practically, the laws that existed were not always enforced, and pirating of intellectual property was widespread, regardless of law. The practical problems are steadily being overcome, as the U.S. government has pressured countries such as China to enforce their laws.

Steps are also being taken to simplify the legal protection of intellectual property overseas. For example, the International Trademark Association (INTA) has developed Model Law Guidelines to harmonize and simplify the protection of trademarks throughout the world. An interesting example of this protection arose in South Africa. McDonald's ceased doing business in South Africa in protest over apartheid. When apartheid ended, McDonald's sought to return to the country but discovered that the McDonald's trademark had in the interim been taken by a local company. McDonald's sued to recover its mark and won.

In 1995, the world's nations agreed to the Trade-Related Aspects of Intellectual Property Agreement, or TRIPS. While not all countries have ratified the Agreement, it is steadily expanding intellectual property protection. The TRIPS agreement provided for clearer protection of computer software.

▬ Customs and Regulation of Imports

The law of importing products into the United States is elaborated and potentially confusing. The relevant laws are generally under the auspices of the Customs Service, an agency of the Department of the Treasury.

Most importing is done by licensed customs brokers, who act as agents for importers. Entry documents for imports must be filed within five days and must include the **bill of lading**, the commercial invoice, and certain forms required by the Customs Service. An entry summary must be filed within ten days, including the estimated customs user fees and duties owed on the imported goods.

Duties

Merchandise that is imported into the United States is either duty-free or dutiable. All goods are presumed subject to duty (a tariff charge) unless specifically exempted. When goods are subject to duty, the rates are usually set on an *ad valorem* basis (based on the value of the goods). Such an *ad valorem* rate might be five percent of the estimated value of the imported goods, plus 50 cents per pound of goods brought into the country. These rates are found on tariff schedules published by the government. Value is usually based on the amount actually paid for the imported goods by the importer.

Rates vary depending on the classification of goods as a particular type. Some categories of merchandise must pay a much higher duty than other categories. The tariff schedules contain over 6700 distinct product categories with associated duty rates. When classifying goods, Customs and the courts look to the "common and commercial" meaning of the description of a product category.

In a recent illustrative case, an importer of camping tents alleged that its product was "sporting equipment" (with a 10 percent import duty), and the Customs Service claimed that the tents should be classified as "textile articles not specially provided for (with a duty of 15 percent plus 25 cents per pound). The Court of International Trade held that camping was not a sport, so the higher duty claimed by the Customs Service had to be paid by the importer.[5]

The proper classification of goods under the tariff schedules is a common source of international trade litigation. The following decision represents an example of how these disputes are resolved.

---

[5] *Camel Manufacturing Co. v. United States*, 686 F.Supp. 912 (1988).

Case 2.2
Richards Medical Company v. United States
United States Court of Appeals, Federal Circuit, 1990
910 F.2d 828

Background and Facts *Richards Medical Company imports into the United States three different kinds of hip prosthesis systems (for replacement of hip joints) and medical instruments that are specifically designed to implant the prostheses. A 1982 law provides for duty-free entry of articles that are for the benefit of handicapped persons. Congress specifically excluded, however, devices that are considered "therapeutic." Customs initially classified the prostheses as duty-free under the law but assessed a duty on the medical instruments, ruling that they were therapeutic in nature.*

Richards appealed to the U.S. Court of International Trade ("CIT"), which held that the medical instruments were not therapeutic in nature and should be admitted to the country duty-free. Customs appealed the ruling to this court. Customs now argues that the prostheses themselves are therapeutic and therefore should not be entitled to duty-free status.

RICH, Circuit Judge.

* * * *

The first issue, that the meaning of "therapeutic," is essentially an issue of statutory construction. As with all questions of statutory construction, we start first with the plain meaning of the statute, and then go to the other extrinsic aids such as legislative history if necessary. *Johns-Manville Corp. v. United States*, 855 F.2d 1556, 1559 (Fed.Cir.1988).

Customs' primary argument with respect to the plain or common meaning of the word "therapeutic" is that it is not limited to treatments which are intended to be curative, but also encompasses treatments which are *alleviative* or *palliative*. In support of this agreement, Customs relies not only on numerous dictionary and encyclopedia definitions, but also on prior case law involving the meaning of "therapeutic" in other statutes. For example, *J.E. Bernard & Co. v. United States*, 262 F.Supp.434, 58 Cust.Ct 23, 28, C.D. 2872 (1967) indicates that "therapeutic qualities embrace the alleviative or palliative, as well as the curative or healing qualities."

However the only conclusion we can reach after reviewing the various definitions from different sources which the parties have provided for us is that the word "therapeutic" has many different meanings and is subject to both broad and narrow interpretations. The question is, which definition best invokes the intent of Congress?

The legislative history is not very helpful on this point. However, one example of an item which is not "therapeutic" is given, and this example definitely cuts against construing this term broadly to include alleviative or palliative treatments, i.e., treatments which help the handicapped person live with his or her handicapped condition.

In particular, the Senate Report accompanying the Act indicates that an automobile fitted with special seats for use by the handicapped or with special attachments to permit a handicapped person to operate the automobile are indicated as being within the scope of the Act.S.Rep. No. 564, 97th Cong., 2d Sess. 20, *reprinted in* 1982 U.S. Code Cong. & Admin. News 4077, 4097. However, such a specially equipped automobile is certainly "alleviative" in the sense that it helps the handicapped person to live with the handicap by helping him or her to ride in or drive a car. Thus, to interpret the word "therapeutic" broadly to include "alleviative" would be inconsistent with the one specific example in the legislative history.

In fact, our impression after reading the legislative history is that the CIT drew a very proper distinction in this case. Congress intended to encourage the importation of that merchandise which is designed to compensate for, or help adapt to, the handicapped condition. At the same time, Congress did not want to allow duty-free importation of merchandise which is used to heal or cure the condition causing the handicap.

Which brings us the second, factual issue: does a hip prosthesis (and consequently the instruments used to implant it) heal or cure a person with a handicap or does it merely allow the handicapped person to better compensate for the handicap? The answer to this question lies heavily in how one defines the underlying condition. Customs argues that a person in need of a hip replacement suffers from an inoperative hip. Thus, they conclude, it is "difficult to imagine a better 'cure' for a diseased hip than the insertion of brand new components to replace the area affected by disease." Appellant's Brief at 15. Richards, on the other hand, points out that a person who needs a hip prosthesis because he or she suffers from, for example, severe arthritis still has arthritis after the operation. The prosthesis merely allows the person to better compensate for the arthritis.

In concluding that hip prostheses merely help handicapped persons adapt to their condition, the CIT relied heavily on the parties' stipulation before trial that:

The Prosthetic Systems are implanted in physically handicapped persons in order to improve their ability to walk or even to allow them to walk when they were severely crippled prior to implantation....

The CIT noted that the implantation of prosthetic hips is performed *because of* the incurable nature of the underlying disease, and that the replacement of the hip joint is a "compensatory remedy of a disability and not a therapy." *Richards Medical*, 720 F.Supp. at 1001.

Decision and Remedy *The court affirmed the CIT ruling that the medical instruments were not therapeutic and were entitled to duty-free status.*

Rates also vary based upon the country of origin. Most countries are granted most-favored-nation status by the U.S. and their duties are lower than those from less favored nations. The country-of-origin determination can be a difficult one, especially when goods have undergone manufacture, processing or assembly in more than one nation.

Other nations receive duty concessions in a special category for the least-developed developing countries. This is know as the Generalized System of Preferences (GSP). Developing countries are excluded from GSP if they are certified as failing to cooperate in the enforcement of narcotics laws, or aiding international terrorism, or having unlawfully expropriated the property of U.S. citizens, among other categories.

Imports of certain goods from these GSP countries are granted duty-free treatment. Approximately 3000 merchandise categories are eligible for GSP duty-free status, including most agricultural products. Countries lose GSP status when their per capita GNP exceeds $8500. Taiwan, South Korea and other countries have succeeded well enough to lose their GSP protection. Other goods also get duty-free status. Intangibles (such as securities or electricity) are not considered goods and are not subject to import duties.

Partial duty-free status is accorded to firms that ship U.S. component parts to a foreign nation, assemble a final product overseas, and then return this product as a U.S. import. Duties are imposed on the value of the final product minus the value of the U.S. component parts. These imports, including automobile and electronic products, amounted to over $67 billion in a recent year.

In addition, there are "foreign trade zones" in the United States that are statutorily declared to be outside the U.S. and therefore free of import duties. While duties must still be paid when the goods are taken from the foreign trade zone into the U.S., the zones provide savings from repacking or assembly of the goods and from direct sales within the foreign trade zone. Merchandise may be held in a foreign trade zone for any amount of time, perhaps awaiting a reduction in rates of duty for the product.

When duties are owed, the Customs Service may accept the importer's estimate and issue a liquidation, which is a final determination of duties. If Customs believes that additional duties are owed, it will send a notice to the importer, who may seek a review of this determination by filing a protest. The protest is heard by the Commissioner of Customs, and the Commissioner's decision may be appealed to the Court of International Trade.

Section 592 of the Tariff Act of 1930 provides strict penalties for violations of importing rules. Violation permits Customs seizure and forfeiture of the imported goods, fines of up to $5000 per violation, and imprisonment for up to two years. In 1989, a South Korean corporation was fined $34 million for false disclosures to Customs officials regarding steel imports.

Import Relief

United States law provides a number of legal protections for domestic businesses against foreign imports. These provisions are designed to insulate the nation's manufacturers from excessive foreign competition. These include the antidumping laws, countervailing duty provisions, unfair import trade practice actions, and what is known as the "escape clause."

Dumping is the name employed when foreign merchandise is sold in the U.S. at less than its fair market value in the exporting country or less than its production costs. An importer might choose to dump goods i the U.S. at such a low price in order to develop its market share. The Antidumping Act of 1921 proscribes dumping that causes material injury to domestic industry.

Proving dumping may be difficult, because defining fair market value is difficult. Some manufacturers do not sell in their own home market. Others may operate in nonmarket economies without established free market prices. Still others may operate in nonmarket economies without established free market prices. Still others may sell directly to retailers in a home market but to wholesalers in the United States. In these instances, the government may consider sales prices in third party nations or production costs as part of a determination of fair market value.

The Secretary of Commerce or any "interested party" initiates a Customs Service investigation into alleged dumping activity. If dumping is found by the Secretary of the Treasury, the Customs Service assesses **antidumping duties** in an amount equal to the extent to which the foreign market value exceeds the price in the United States. An importer may appeal this assessment in the U.S. Customs Court. A Japanese producer of microwave ovens was found to have violated antidumping rules and directed to pay an additional duty of 13.1 percent.

Countervailing duties apply to offset any competitive advantage held by foreign businesspersons due to export subsidies paid by their home governments. As with dumping laws, material domestic injury is required to invoke countervailing duties. Defining subsidies is also difficult. A U.S. Supreme Court decision held that a Japanese law exempting exports from certain taxes was not a subsidy that warranted countervailing duties.[6]

An interested party may initiate a countervailing duty investigation. In addition to demonstrating the presence of foreign subsidies, there must also be a material adverse effect on the domestic industry in order to invoke countervailing duties to offset the subsidies. Determining a material adverse impact may be complicated for various reasons, one of which is illustrated in the following action.

---

[6] *Zenith Radio Corporation v. United States*, 98 S.Ct. 2441 (1978).

Case 2.3
United States Steel Group v. United States
United States Court of Appeals
Federal Circuit, 1996
96 F.3d 1352

Background and Facts *A group of United States steel companies led by Bethlehem Steel Corporation filed a petition with the International Trade Commission alleging that their industry had been harmed by subsidized imports of certain flat-rolled carbon steel products from numerous different countries. The Commerce Department found that such subsidization had in fact occurred. The ITC investigated extensively and concluded that most of the subject imports had not cause and did not threaten to cause material injury to the domestic industry. The steel group appealed this determination, arguing that the cumulation of all the subsidized imports from all the countries had a material adverse effect.*

CLEVENGER, Circuit Judge.

* * * *

In its second assertion of error, Bethlehem asserts that the Commission misapplied the negligibility exception and consequently improperly failed to cumulate the imports of certain countries. Focusing on only one portion of the statute, Bethlehem argues that the Commission may only exclude a country from cumulation if its imports have no "discernible adverse impact." Here, Bethlehem contends, imports from several excluded countries did have a discernible adverse impact since the Commission was able to confirm, in several specific instances, that as a result of these imports various domestic steel producers suffered confirmed lost sales. * * *

Bethlehem, however, misinterprets the statute. The statute requires the cumulation of imports which have a "discernible adverse impact on the domestic industry," . . . not of imports which may adversely affect individual domestic producers. Thus, evidence of specific lost sales or declines in revenue, although important considerations to be taken into account by the Commission in making its negligibility determinations, do not dispositively trigger the cumulation requirement.

* * * the statute contemplates that a country may import small amounts of a product to the United States and still be deemed negligible, although those imports will presumably have some adverse impact on the particular domestic producers who would otherwise supply the demand they fill. Therefore, we disagree with Bethlehem that the Commission improperly excluded several countries from its cumulation and decline to reverse the Commission on this ground.

Decision and Remedy The court affirmed the ITC ruling on these steel imports.

Section 337 of the Tariff Act of 1930 prohibits certain unfair trade practices in international commerce. The law does not list the practices to be deemed unfair, but section 337 can be severe, including daily civil penalties of up to the total value of the imported goods and exclusion of articles from entry into the country.

The escape clause provides domestic companies some relief from imports even without unfair trade practices. Section 201 of the Trade Act of 1974 provides that a domestic industry may obtain relief when an article is being imported in quantities that will be the substantial cause of at least the threat of serious injury to a domestic industry that produces a competitive product.

Under the escape clause, the affected industry first files a petition with the International Trade Commission ("ITC"). The ITC considers factors such as unemployment in the domestic industry, lost market share, and shutdown of producing capacity, among others. The ITC reports its findings to the president, who may increase duties, establish import quotas, or negotiate agreements with foreign nations to reduce the harm to the domestic industry. The president may also expedite readjustment assistance to workers in the affected domestic industry.

For example, a U.S. manufacturer of motorcycles, the Harley-Davidson Motor Co., petitioned for import relief. The ITC found that imports were up and domestic employment was down 12 percent, production was down 36 percent, and profits were down by 20 percent. Importers claimed that these reductions were actually due to a national economic recession. The ITC disagreed and recommended additional duties on motorcycle imports for the next five years at a declining rate (45 percent in the first year, 10 percent in the fifth year). The president accepted the recommendation and imposed these additional duties over and above the prevailing 4.4 percent ad valorem duty that already existed. (A 1980 ruling, however, found that harm to the domestic automobile industry was due primarily to economic conditions rather than due to increased imports.)

Foreign Capital Markets

The financial services industry (including securities, banking, and insurance) is increasingly international in scope. Advanced telecommunications and data processing technologies have made international financial transactions far easier. Companies based in the United States can use foreign markets to raise capital through securities issuances.

The legal and regulatory system has not kept pace with the burgeoning international financial business. There is no global international standard for securities transactions. These transactions are governed by the distinct laws of individual nations. Moreover, any given transaction may be subject to the laws of several different nations.

Japanese Securities Regulation

In spring 1987, the Tokyo Stock Exchange surpassed the New York Stock Exchange as the world's largest. Japanese securities regulation is therefore very important. Trading is governed by the *Shokentorihikiho,* or Securities and Exchange Law. The law is administered by the Securities Bureau, under the national Finance Minister.

The Japanese Securities and Exchange Law was modeled on the United States Securities Act of 1933 and Securities Exchange Act of 1934. In order to issue securities, the issuer must register with the Finance Minister. The law makes exemptions, just as U.S. law does, for private placements and small issuances. As in the United States, the issuer must make full and accurate disclosures.

Japanese securities law also has antifraud provisions. Article 58 of the law prohibits persons from employing "any fraudulent device, scheme or artifice with respect to buying, selling or other transaction of securities," from using documents that contain false statements or omissions of material facts or from using a false quotation of prices.

Foreign companies, including those from the United States, may issue securities in Japan, and foreign stocks are listed on the Tokyo Stock Exchange. Offerings of foreign securities must be registered under Japanese law. Additional information is required of foreign issuers, including a statement on the effect of fluctuations in the exchange rates.

Japan regulates broker-dealers involved in the "securities business." To operate securities companies must obtain a license from the Finance Minister. In 1986, Japan opened Tokyo Stock Exchange membership to foreign brokerage firms. The law imposes minimum capital requirements, and the Minister may revoke licenses as necessary for the protection of investors. A foreign securities firm must deposit in escrow at least 5 percent of its capital (at least 10 million yen) for each of its branch offices in Japan.

Japanese law also restricts practices of securities companies. Article 50, for example, prohibits specific practices, such as "offering a statement of opinion definitively predicting a rise or a drop in the price of certain shares of other securities whose prices fluctuate."

Extraterritorial Application of U.S. Law

United States securities laws will apply to a variety of overseas securities transactions. The details of U.S. laws are set forth in the chapter on Securities Law and Regulation, in Chapter 43 of *West's Business Law, Seventh Edition*, and in Chapter 28 of *West's Legal Environment of Business, Third Edition*. Suppose that PacCorp intends to raise capital by offering their securities on the Japanese market. PacCorp may still be required to comply with the registration provisions of U.S. securities law. If the securities of a foreign corporation are traded in U.S. markets, that company is also subject to United States law and regulations.

In 1985, the Securities and Exchange Commission announced that it would not apply U.S. law to certain foreign offerings of equity securities. The SEC required:

1. An agreement not to offer the shares to North Americans for twelve months following completion of the offering.

2. A conspicuous statement on the cover of the prospectus that the securities were not registered under U.S. law.

3. A restriction on transfer of the securities for twelve months to North Americans.

4. A legend on the stock certificates reflecting the above conditions.

5. Purchaser certification that he agreed to the conditions and was not a North American.

The SEC has also announced that a prospectus meeting the requirements of Japanese law will be generally deemed sufficient for compliance with U.S. law, so long as the offer is not made directly to United States residents.

The antifraud provisions of United States securities law also have extraterritorial application. In the first key case, a Canadian corporation conducting all of its operations in Canada issued shares to its controlling shareholders for "wholly inadequate consideration," thereby diluting the value of the ownership of other shareholders. The court held that U.S. law applied, because the stock was traded in the U.S. and U.S. citizens were among those allegedly defrauded.[7]

■ Foreign Direct Investment

Rather than exporting goods produced in the United States, domestic companies may choose to invest in foreign operations that produce overseas. The primary different approaches to such foreign investment are a joint venture, a branch office, a wholly owned subsidiary, or acquisition of an existing foreign corporation. Multinational enterprises, with investments in numerous countries, are responsible for about 15 percent of the gross world product. The rules for foreign investments vary by nation. This section will consider national rules in three different categories of nations: a large, industrialized country (Japan); a country emerging from communist rule (Hungary); and a group of lesser-developed South and Latin American nations (the Andean nations and Mexico).

Japan

Japanese law is best understood by an illustration of foreign investment rules. Hypothesize that Wessex Chemical, a United States company, wants to produce and market a herbicide for rice crops in Japan.

The joint venture approach is the most common one taken for U.S. companies investing in Japan. This approach takes advantage of Japanese corporations' familiarity with that country's laws and business practices, as well as the existence of a preexisting distribution system for products. Wessex thus could seek out a Japanese chemical company to produce and market its product. As with any joint venture, however, the participant loses autonomy in making business decisions, which must be shared with its venture partner. Wessex would also have to share the profits from its operation.

If Wessex decides to go it alone, they might create a branch office in Japan or establish a new Japanese subsidiary company. Creation of Japanese branch offices or wholly owned subsidiaries is much easier now than prior to 1980. In that year,

Japan amended its Foreign Exchange and Foreign Trade Control Law, to facilitate foreign investment somewhat. The law still restricts investment in some businesses, including agriculture, forestry, mining, petroleum, leather products, and industries pertaining to the national security of Japan. The law places other, general restrictions on foreign investment in Japan. The foreign investor must give advance notice to the Ministry of Finance and wait at least thirty days before proceeding.

An American company such as Wessex, seeking to create a branch office in Japan, must file a "Report on Establishment of Branch Office, Etc." with the relevant government ministries. If approval is granted, the company then must register and appoint an official branch manager. The branch manager becomes the corporation's official representative in Japan and has broad authority to bind the company under Japanese law. Once established, branch offices are subject to little specific regulation, though of course they must comply with the general laws of Japan.

For Wessex to create a new Japanese subsidiary would also require the filing of a report, called the "Report on Acquisition of Stocks." Once approved, the company must comply with the Japanese Commercial Code in the general legal requirements of incorporation. Most Japanese companies incorporate as a *kabushiki kaisha*, or a stock company. The law requires such stock companies to have seven promoters, or incorporators, which prepare Articles of Incorporation. Then the company must select at least three directors. The company must be officially registered with a local office and provide information on the name, purpose, capitalization, directors and shares of the corporation. Once this is complete, and if they comply with the Foreign Exchange and Foreign Trade Control Law, Wessex may begin business in Japan.

Doing business in Japan also requires familiarity with its system of administrative guidance. The Bank of Japan receives the documentation required by the foreign investments law and provides the administrative guidance valuable to gaining approval of investment. The Bank can also inform investors of potential pitfalls to their plans. Under Japanese law, ministries may block transactions under any of the following five criteria:

1. Investments must not harm national security, disturb public order, or hamper public safety.

---

[7] *Schoenbaum v. Firstbrook*, 405 F.2d 200 (2d Cir. 1968).

2. Investments cannot have serious adverse effects on Japanese companies in the same line of business.

3. Investments cannot adversely affect the overall national economy.

4. Reciprocity of investment rights.

5. Investments cannot attempt to evade other restrictions contained in the act.

These criteria are rather vague, and administrative guidance permits U.S. companies to structure their proposals in a way best designed to obtain approval. The Japanese have been particularly protective of their agricultural industry, and a plan such as Wessex's might face obstacles. Administrative guidance can smooth the company's path to entering the Japanese market.

Hungary

Hungary adopted a new business code in the Act on Economic Associations and the Act on Investment of Foreigners in Hungary, effective in 1989. These laws enable domestic or foreign investors to create different forms of enterprises including corporations and partnerships. The most common form is the **limited liability company** (LLC).

To establish an LLC, the company must adopt a "deed of association." This should provide for capital contributions, the number and voting rights of shares, directors and their powers, and other administrative provisions. The LLC has great flexibility under Hungarian law, however, in defining these terms. Hungarian law creates minimum capitalization requirements (one million forints) and requires registration of the LLC.

Government approval is no longer required to establish an LLC. If there will be a foreign majority interest, however, the corporate founders must obtain the permission of the Finance and Trade Ministers. If they do not disapprove the application within ninety days, the law permits the LLC to go forward.

LLC management is not unlike that of a United States corporation. The shareholders' meetings elect directors and can amend the corporate charter, but also arrange for approving any distribution of profits. A simple majority is generally required, though the LLC charter may specify otherwise.

Hungary's Foreign Investment Act guarantees certain protection for foreign investors. Hungary also permits foreign investors to repatriate their dividends and profits and can be exchanged for foreign currency through the Hungarian National Bank. Repatriation of profits is limited by the requirement that the company be able to discharge its obligations to creditors.

Andean Nations and Mexico

Different investment rules govern each country of the world. Investment in poorer, developing countries presents different legal issues. Many of these nations have foreign investment codes in an attempt to capture the benefits of foreign investment. For example, consider the rules of the Andean Common Market, known as ANCOM, which is composed of Bolivia, Venezuela, Columbia, Ecuador and Peru. ANCOM was created by The Cartagena Agreement, which established common rules for foreign investment in member countries, among other joint economic activities.

ANCOM first adopted rules for foreign investment in 1970 in Decision No. 24, which created a Foreign Investment Code. Decision No. 24 created a new set of regulations in addition to the national rules of each member nation. These rules resulted from concern over dependency on foreign investment and technology. The ANCOM rules became a model for nearly every major Latin American country.

Decision No. 24 first prohibited any investment in certain economic sectors. The decision banned investment in sectors including domestic transportation, commercial banking and other financial institutions, the press, and insurance. In addition, members were to exclude direct foreign investment from sectors that they deemed to be "adequately covered by existing enterprises." The Decision also required the "fade-out" of foreign control, such that foreign investment had to be limited to minority ownership in corporations by a certain date and limited the repatriation of money.

The ANCOM rules, along with most other Latin and South American investment codes, had the following characteristics:

1. Screening and approval procedures to be passed by direct foreign investment before the investment is permitted.

2. Performance requirements and maximum ownership percentages for foreign investors.

3. Limitations on the repatriation of capital and profits.

4. Prohibitions or restrictions on direct foreign investment in certain sensitive economic sectors.

5. Restrictions on technology transfer.

The ANCOM nations found that these rules were too restrictive and prevented necessary foreign investment, so they were repealed by Decision 220 of the Quito Protocol of 1987. Individual member states, however, have maintained many of these restrictions. Thus, foreign ownership in all ANCOM countries must still scale back to minority ownership within a certain period (such as thirty years), depending upon the country. Many member states also restrict investment in banking and finance or limit the ability of foreign companies to draw upon local sources of long-term financing.

Other nations also restrict foreign investment based on rules similar to those of ANCOM. For example, Mexico restricts foreign computer manufacturers and investors to 49 percent ownership of most manufacturing facilities and only 40 percent of certain facilities, such as petrochemicals and automobiles. Mexico applies this same 49 percent ceiling to other industries such as mineral extraction. Even those developing countries that do not require a majority of domestic ownership may insist that foreign investment take the form of a joint venture with some domestic participation.

Mexico is currently easing its investment regulations to comply with the terms of the recently adopted North American Free Trade Agreement (NAFTA). The new law will simplify or entirely eliminate official approvals required for U.S. investments, plant expansions, and relocations in Mexico. U.S. Investors will receive "national treatment," that is the same rules that govern domestic Mexican investors.

Questions and Case Problems

1. European unification is designed to eliminate trade barriers among the continent's nations. Germany has a law requiring alcoholic beverages to contain at least 32 percent alcohol to be labeled as spirits. Rewe, an importer, applied to the Federal Monopoly of Spirits for permission to import Cassis de Dijon from France. The Cassis was only 15 to 20 percent alcohol, so Rewe was unable to import the product. Rewe brought an action against the Federal Monopoly, arguing that the restriction conflicted with the EC treaty. Should Rewe prevail in this action? [*Rewe-Zentral*, AG Bundesmomopol ver Waltung fur Branntwein, Case No. 120/78 (Court of Justice of the European Communities)].

2. Teca-Print A.G. is a small company that manufactures machinery in Switzerland. Teca is a small company that bills foreign sales in Swiss francs and does not want to engage in foreign currency speculation. By November 30, 1983, Amacoil Machinery owed Teca 71,224 Swiss francs. On this date the francs were worth $0.45 U.S. dollars. Amacoil breached the contract, and Teca sued in U.S. court, which can grant awards only in dollars. On December 2, 1986, when Teca won its breach of contract suit, the francs were worth $0.61 U.S. dollars. Teca wants payment based on the higher value of the franc on the date of the court judgement, but Amacoil wants to pay the judgement based on the lower value of the franc at the time of the breach of contract. How should a court resolve this dispute? [*Teca-Print A.G. v. Amacoil Machinery, Inc.*, 525 N.Y.S.2d 535 (1988)].

3. Samuels bought a BMW in Alaska. While he was driving, a transmission problem caused him to lose control of the car and wreck it, injuring himself. He sued Bayerische Motoren Werke, AG and BMW of North America, a wholly owned subsidiary, in Alaska, alleging strict liability. Bayerische disputed the jurisdiction of the Alaska court over the German company. Does Alaska have jurisdiction over Bayerische?

4. Japanese cargo containers were temporarily located in California ports for loading and unloading of goods. The average container spent about three weeks out of year in the California ports. Los

Angeles, California, imposed a personal property tax on the containers, which were also registered and subjected to property tax in Japan. Japan Line, Ltd. sued and claimed that the Los Angeles tax was invalid because it subjected the containers to multiple taxation and thereby discouraged international trade. Should the California law be stuck down as unconstitutional? [*Japan Line, Ltd. v. County of Los Angeles*, 441 U.S. 434 (1979)].

5. Smith-Corona is the last remaining manufacturer of portable electric typewriters in the United States. Japanese typewriter companies, Brother and Silver Seiko, export portable electric typewriters to the U.S. Smith-Corona brought an antidumping action, claiming that Brother and Silver Seiko were selling typewriters in the U.S. at a lower price than in Japan. The Japanese companies claimed that the U.S. price only appeared lower, because it had additional advertising and other expenses in Japan. They argued that these factors should be considered in the antidumping action. Do the Japanese companies have a good defense to the antidumping action? [*Smith-Corona Group v. United States*, 713 F.2d 1568 (Fed. Cir. 1983)].

CHAPTER THREE

Individual Employee Rights

KEY BACKGROUND

The essential background for this chapter on individual employee rights is found in Chapters 35 and 36 of *West's Business Law, Seventh Edition,* and in Chapters 20, 21, and 22 of *West's Legal Environment of Business, Third Edition.* This chapter covers employment and labor relations law. Among the important points to remember from this chapter are:

- individual employment rights under contract

- individual protection from wrongful discharge under public policy

- tort liability for wrongful discharge.

The law of the workplace has undergone enormous changes in the past decades. Individual employees once had very few rights in their jobs and had to unionize to obtain protection. Now business faces thousands of individual employee rights cases every year, challenging an improper firing of a worker, claiming invasion of privacy, or other issues. Courts have given employees more bases to sue employers, especially over discharge from employment, and the federal and state governments also have passed statutes to protect workers. This chapter discusses the most prominent issues in the area.

Employment at Will

The traditional employment contract would be either for a defined term (e.g., one year) or for an indefinite term. Most employment contracts were for an indefinite term and these were described as **at-will contracts**. This meant that the employer could at any time fire the employee, and the employee could at any time quit the employer. Neither act would represent a breach of contract. Roughly two-thirds of all employment contracts are at-will.

Under the traditional rule of at-will employment, no reason was required for the discharge of an employee. An employer could fire a worker for a purely arbitrary reason or even for a bad reason.

Thus, suppose Hank Kimble worked for Used Motors Cars, and Hank's employer told him to turn back the odometers of their inventory of automobiles. Hank refuses because the act is both illegal and unethical. If Used Motors were to fire Hank, traditional common law would offer him no remedy.

The once-broad scope of at-will employment has been narrowed considerably. Federal statutes provide protection against specific illegal bases for discharge. For example, an employee may not be fired for participating in a union or on the basis of the employee's race, sex, or religion. These laws are discussed in Chapter 38 of *West's Business Law, Seventh Edition,* and in Chapter 20 of *West's Legal Environment of Business, Third Edition.*

The common law has also created exceptions to the pure employment-at-will contract, as discussed below. While employers still may fire workers for a plethora of reasons, the courts now provide greater job security for workers. The leading doctrines in this regard are the **implied contract of employment**, the prohibition on discharges that are contrary to **public policy**, and the development of a **wrongful discharge tort** cause of action.

Wrongful discharge actions are an important concern of management. A recent survey of these cases found that the employee won in approximately 70 percent of wrongful discharge actions and the average award was over $175,000. In a recent unreported jury verdict, Mobile Chemical Company was ordered to pay $1.375 million to an employee whom it fired in an alleged attempt to cover up environmental violations.

Implied Contract of Employment

Some workers have claimed that their discharge violated an implied contract that they had with their employer. Although the actual employment contract may clearly provide for an indefinite term, employer actions or statements may have modified the contract and promised the employee a long-term job.

For there to be an implied contract of employment, the alleged agreement must contain all the elements of a binding contract. Thus, there must be an offer and acceptance, consideration, capacity, legality, and proper form for an agreement (as discussed below, some agreements must be in writing) in order to be enforceable.

Consider the following circumstance. Denise Booth works as an executive for Bell Diamond & Co. Denise receives a job offer from a competitor at a higher salary. Denise goes to her boss at Bell Diamond and discusses her plans to resign. The boss begs her to stay and promises her that she can keep her job at Bell diamond "for a lifetime" and that she will get a promotion and raise in six months. Denise stays at Bell Diamond. Six months later, with the economy in recession, the company fires Denise. She can sue the company for violation of an implied modification to her at-will employment contract.

Employment Manuals

Many employers publish and distribute an employment manual or handbook that contains a list of their policies. These manuals help establish clear rules for the workplace and help ensure equitable and uniform administration of rules. They also may enhance employee morale by giving security or demonstrating the employer's sense of fairness.

Many courts have held that statements in these employment manuals create binding policies that the employer must follow in dealings with employees. The theory is that employees read the manual and continue working for the employer (do not exercise their legal right to quit) in reliance upon the manual's terms.

Several key provisions in employment manuals have been found to be enforceable implied contracts. These include a guarantee of a certain level of severance pay, a promise that discharge will only be for "good cause," and assurance that certain procedures will be used before an employee is fired.

Not all employment manuals are binding contracts, however. Suppose that the employee did not read the manual or that the manual was not made available to certain employees. Communication of an offer is an essential component of agreement. Nor could the employee have relied on a manual of which he or she was unaware. Most courts hold that an unread manual is not a binding contract.

This principle is illustrated in a Minnesota decision. A discharged employee sued and claimed that his discharge was contrary to an employees' manual that guaranteed certain procedures before he received disciplinary firing and a supervisors' manual that permitted termination for only good cause. The court held that the first claim was good but that the employee could not sue under the supervisors' manual because it was not given to him.[1]

The effect of any employment manual depends on the standard contractual investigation into the intention of the parties. If the language of the handbook appears binding, it will be held binding. Thus, if a manual speaks of the employees' "rights," the manual is likely to be found binding.

Employers may be bound by even policies that are not stated in a manual. The following decision involves a famous instance of wrongful discharge.

---

[1] *Pine River State Bank v. Mettille,* 333 N.W.2d 622 (Minn. 1983).

Case 3.1
Rulon-Miller v. International Business Machines, Corp.
California Court of Appeals
Ninth Circuit, 1984
208 Cal.Rptr. 524

Background and Facts *Virginia Rulon-Miller began work with IBM as a sales person and data processor. She was given the highest employee ratings and steadily promoted within the company. She eventually became a marketing manager, working under Phillip Callahan, her supervisor. Ms. Rulon-Miller had begun dating Matt Blum when he was an account manager for IBM. He eventually left the company and joined QYX, a competitor of IBM's. She dated Mr. Blum while she was working at IBM. IBM was aware of this but gave her a promotion and substantial raise nevertheless.*

Not long thereafter, Mr. Callahan summoned Ms. Rulon-Miller and inquired about her relationship with Mr. Blum. He expressed concern about a conflict of interest and asked her to halt the relationship. After she refused, Callahan first dismissed her and then merely transferred her to another division, removing her from management.

She sued over her demotion, which the court considered a discharge. Among her claims was IBM's breach of an implied contract of employment, based on the company's frequently stated policy of respect for employee privacy. She also sued for intentional infliction of emotional distress. A jury ruled on her behalf and awarded her $100,000 in compensatory damages and $200,000 in punitive damages. IBM appealed the decision.

RUSHING, Associate Justice.

* * * *

When Callahan questioned her relationship with Blum, respondent invoked her right to privacy in her personal life, relying on existing IBM policies. A threshold inquiry is thus presented whether respondent could reasonably rely on those policies for job protection. Any conflicting action by the company would be wrongful in that it would constitute a violation of her contract rights.

* * * *

In this case, there is a close question of whether those rules or regulations permit IBM to inquire into the purely personal life of the employee. If so, an attendant question is whether such a policy was applied consistently, particularly as between men and women. The distinction is important because the right of privacy, a constitutional right in California (*City and County of San Francisco v. Superior Court* (1981) 125 Cal.App.3d 879, 883, 178 Cal.Rptr. 435), could be implicated by the IBM inquiry. Much of the testimony below concerned what those policies were. The evidence was conflicting on the meaning of certain IBM policies. We observe ambiguity in the application but not in the intent. The "Watson Memo" (so called because it was signed by a former chairman of IBM) provided as follows:

"TO ALL IBM MANAGERS:

"The line that separates an individual's on-the-job business life from his other life as a private citizen is at times well-defined and at other times indistinct. But the line does exist, and you and I, as managers in IBM, must be able to recognize that line.

"I have seen instances where managers took disciplinary measures against employees for actions or conduct that are not rightfully the company's concern. These managers usually justified their decisions by citing their personal code of ethics and morals or by quoting some fragment of company policy that seemed to support their position. Both arguments proved unjust on close examination. What we need, in every case, is balanced judgment which weights the needs of the business and the rights of the individual.

"Our primary objective as IBM managers is to further the business of this company by leading our people properly and measuring quantity and quality of work and effectiveness on the job against clearly set standards of responsibility and compensation. This is performance—and performance is, in the final analysis, the one thing that the company can insist on from everyone.

"We have concern with an employee's off-the-job behavior only when it reduces his ability to perform regular job assignments, interferes with the job performance of other employees, or if his outside behavior affects the reputation of the company in a major way. When on-the-job performance is acceptable, I can think of few situations in which outside activities could result in disciplinary action or dismissal."

* * * *

Callahan based his action against respondent on a "conflict of interest." But the record shows that IBM did not interpret this policy to prohibit a romantic relationship. Callahan admitted that there was no company rule or policy requiring an employee to terminate friendships with fellow employees who leave and join competitors. Gary Nelson, Callahan's superior, also confirmed that IBM had no policy against employees socializing with competitors.

This issue was hotly contested with respondent claiming that the "conflict of interest" claim was a pretext for her unjust termination. Whether it was presented as a fact question for the jury. Do the policies reflected in this record give IBM a right to terminate an employee for a conflict of interest? The answer must be yes, but whether respondent's conduct constituted such was for the jury. We observe that while respondent was successful, her primary job did not give her access to sensitive information which could have been useful to competitors. She was, after all, a seller of typewriters and office equipment. Respondent's brief makes much of the concession by IBM that there was no evidence whatever that respondent had given any information or help to IBM's competitor QYX. It really is no concession at all she did not have the information or help to give. Even so, the question is one of substantial evidence. The evidence is abundant that there was no conflict of interest by respondent.

Decision and Remedy *The court affirmed the judgment and award of damages.*

Courts will also look to other factors to determine the intent of the parties. Extensive litigation in California has produced a list of relevant factors. These factors include the length of the employee's service with the country, oral statements supplementing the manual, industry practice, and whether the employee gave any extra consideration for a manual's benefit.

Employers may protect themselves from the binding effects of an employment handbook or manual by including a disclaimer. In one case, a manual's preface stated that the manual was "informational only" and that its terms "are not conditions of employment and may be modified, revoked or changed at any time with or without notice."[2] The court therefore ruled for the employer on a wrongful discharge claim. Companies such as Montgomery Ward and Sears have effectively used disclaimers.

Even a disclaimer will not always insulate an employer from being bound by its employment manual. Courts have emphasized that any disclaimer must be clear and unambiguous. The disclaimer also must be communicated to the employee. Finally, the disclaimer may be undermined by subsequent oral statements that the employer will abide by the terms of the manual.

If a binding manual exists, can an employer modify its policies through issuance of a new manual? Courts are still divided on the issue. Some hold that a new manual creates a new contract which the employee accepts through continued work. Others hold that an employer cannot offer a new manual with reduced protection unless the employer offers the employee some additional consideration for the changes.

Oral Assurances

An implied contract of job security may exist even in the absence of a binding employment manual. If a prospective employee is told in a job interview that she can only be fired for good cause, she may have a binding implied contract. To be enforceable, such assurances must be express and specific.

Oral assurances may even override disclaimers or modifications of employment manuals. In one case, an employment manual provided for severance pay in the event of termination, but the employer retained the right to modify this policy. The employer then modified the handbook to eliminate the assurance of severance pay. A supervisor orally assured employees that the original severance pay policy would remain in effect for them. The court upheld a verdict for the employees based on the oral promises.[3]

As with employment manuals, oral promises must meet the requirements of contract law to be enforceable. One common problem for employees is the Statute of Frauds, which is discussed in Chapter 17 of *West's Business Law, Seventh Edition*. A key Statute of Frauds provision states that contracts which require more than a year to perform must be in writing.

Suppose that a Bell Diamond executive orally promises Henry Washington that he will be retained for at least three years and provided with three years of training. This contract is not enforceable because it cannot be performed within one year and must therefore be in writing to be binding.

The Statute of Frauds provision is narrow, however, and many oral promises will remain binding. Suppose that an employer promises Henry Washington he will be guaranteed a job for the rest of his life. Because Henry could possibly die within one year, this promise is not within the Statute of Frauds and would be binding. Courts do not consider the probability of Henry's dying.

Public Policy Exception

Most states that recognize employment-at-will contracts make an exception for discharges that violate public policy. If the employer's reason for discharge is so objectionable that it violates a fundamental public policy, the employee will have a good case for wrongful discharge.

The public policy exception is a vague one. Governments have innumerable public policies as reflected in thousands of statutes. Most courts have interpreted the public policy exception rather narrowly and limited it to clear violations of fundamental public policies.

The classic case for the exception of public policy occurs when the employer fires a worker for a refusal to violate a law. Examples of discharges under this principle were cases when an employer fired a worker for refusing to participate in a gasoline

---

[2] *Crain v. Burroughs Corp.*, 560 F. Supp. 849 (C.D. Cal. 1983).

[3] *Helle v. Landmark, Inc.*, 472 N.E.2d 765 (Ohio App. 1984).

price-fixing scheme, refusing to perform an illegal medical operation, refusing to fraudulently modify reports on pollutant emissions, and refusing to employ accounting practices that violated state law. The employees prevailed in all these cases.

Another circumstance for the public policy exception occurs when an employer fires an employee for exercising his or her legal rights. One common situation involves a discharge in retaliation for an employee's filing of a legitimate workers' compensation claim. In many states (including Illinois, Florida, Michigan and Oregon), courts prohibit employers from firing workers for filing justifiable workers' compensation claims. Some states, such as North Carolina, have adopted statutes codifying this principle.

Courts are more divided on whether employees are protected for filing other legal claims. New York has held that an employee cannot be fired in order to deprive him of pension benefits, but other courts have disagreed. Courts have recognized a good wrongful discharge claim when workers were discharged for serving on a jury. California has held that an employer cannot fire a worker for suing the employer, as long as the employee had a good claim.

Constitutional principles also may be the basis for the public policy exception. In a Pennsylvania case, an employee was fired for refusing to lobby the state legislature on an issue to which he was opposed. The court held that the discharge violated the employee's political rights of free speech.[4] Other decisions have permitted employers to fire workers over free speech that injured the employer's interests and conflicted with the employee's duty of loyalty.

An employee public policy claim must be closely hinged to a specific law. The following decision explains the limits of the public policy exception.

---

[4] *Novosel v. Nationwide Insurance Co.*, 721 F.2d 894 (3rd Cir. 1983).

Case 3.2
Pierce v. Ortho Pharmaceutical Corp.
Supreme Court of New Jersey, 1980
Ninth Circuit, 1989
417 A.2d 505

Background and Facts *Dr. Grace Pierce was a physician engaged in research by the Ortho Pharmaceutical Corporation. Dr. Pierce was an at-will employee of Ortho. In spring 1975, Dr. Pierce was the only medical doctor on a research team developing loperamide, a drug for treatment of infant diarrhea. The formulation of the drug contained saccharin. Ortho was planning to develop an investigational new drug application ("IND") for filing with the Food and Drug Administration ("FDA") to permit clinical testing of the drug on humans.*

Dr. Pierce objected to the research because of a controversy over the safety of saccharin. She opposed the decision to seek an IND on the grounds that saccharin might be harmful and the formulation would violate her Hippocratic oath as a doctor to do no harm. The company announced that she would not be promoted and would be demoted, so she resigned her position. She then sued for wrongful discharge on public policy grounds. Ortho moved for summary judgment, which the trial court denied. The appellate court affirmed this decision. Ortho then appealed to the New Jersey Supreme Court.

POLLOCK, Justice.

* * * *

In recognizing a cause of action to provide a remedy for employees who are wrongfully discharged, we must balance the interests of the employee, the employer, and the public. Employees have an interest in knowing they will not be discharged for exercising their legal rights. Employers have an interest in knowing they can run their businesses as they see fit as long as their conduct is consistent with public policy. The public has an interest in employment stability and in discouraging frivolous lawsuits by dissatisfied employees. Although the contours of an exception are important to all employees-at-will, this case focuses on the special considerations arising out of the right to fire an employee-at-will who is a member of a recognized profession. One writer has described the predicament that may confront a professional employed by a large corporation:

Consider, for example, the plight of an engineer who is told that he will lose his job unless he falsifies his data or conclusions, or unless he approves a product which does not conform to specifications or meet minimum standards. Consider also the dilemma of a corporate attorney who is told, say in the context of an impending tax audit or antitrust investigation, to draft backdated corporate records concerning events which never took place or to falsify other documents so that adverse legal consequences may be avoided by the corporation; and the predicament of an accountant who is told to falsify his employer's profit and loss statement in order to enable the employer to obtain credit.

* * * *

(2) Employees who are professionals owe a special duty to abide not only by federal and state law, but also by the recognized codes of ethics of their professions. That duty may oblige them to decline to perform acts required by their employers. However, an employee should not have the right to prevent his or her employer from pursuing its business because the employee perceives that a particular business decision violates the employee's personal morals, as distinguished from the recognized code of ethics of the employee's profession. See Comment, 28 Vand. L. Rev. 805, 832 (1975).

(3) We hold that an employee has a cause of action for wrongful discharge when the discharge is contrary to a clear mandate of public policy. The sources of public policy include legislation; administrative rules, regulations or decisions; and judicial decisions. In certain instances, a professional code of ethics may contain an expression of public policy. However, not all such sources express a clear mandate of public policy. For example, a code of ethics designed to serve only the interests of a profession or an administrative regulation concerned with technical matters probably would not be sufficient.

Absent legislation, the judiciary must define the cause of action in case-by-case determinations. An employer's right to discharge an employee at will carries a correlative duty not to discharge an employee who declines to perform an act that would require a violation of a clear mandate of public policy. However, unless an employee-at-will identifies a specific expression of public policy, he may be discharged with or without cause.

* * * *

Viewing the matter most favorably to Dr. Pierce, the controversy at Ortho involved a difference in medical opinions. Dr. Pierce acknowledged that Dr. Pasquale was entitled to his opinion that the oath did not forbid work on loperamide. Nonetheless, implicit in Dr. Pierce's position is the contention that Dr. Pasquale and Ortho were obliged to accept her opinion. Dr. Pierce contends, in effect, that Ortho should have stopped research on loperamide because of her opinion about the controversial nature of the drug.

Dr. Pierce espouses a doctrine that would lead to disorder in drug research. Under her theory, a professional employee could redetermine the propriety of a research project even if the research did not involve a violation of a clear mandate of public policy. Chaos would result if a single doctor engaged in research were allowed to determine, according to his or her individual conscience, whether a project should continue. Cf. Report of the Ad Hoc Committee on the Principles of Medical Ethics, American Medical Association (1979). An employee does not have a right to continued employment when he or she refuses to conduct research simply because it would contravene his or her personal morals. An employee-at-will who refuses to work for an employer in answer to a call of conscience should recognize that other employees and their employer might heed a different call. However, nothing in this opinion should be construed to restrict the right of an employee-at-will to refuse to work on a project that he or she believes is unethical. In sum, an employer may discharge an employee who refuses to work unless the refusal is based on a clear mandate of public policy.

Decision and Remedy *The court reversed the denial of summary judgment and remanded the case for entry of judgment for Ortho.*

Whistle-Blowing

"Whistle-blowing" is the term for an employee who protests, publicly or privately, against the company's participating in criminal or unethical behavior. This is a variant of the public policy exception. Some statutes provide direct protection to whistle-blowers. These include civil rights acts and Department of Defense procurement laws.

Even in the absence of specific statutory protection, some courts have protected whistle-blowing employees from termination. A Connecticut decision protected an employee who objected to his employer over mislabeling of foods. A West Virginia case protected an employee who alerted state authorities over the employer's violation of banking laws.

Other state courts have refused to extend protection to whistle-blowers. In a recent California case, an employee claimed that he was discharged because he notified management that his supervisor was being investigated by the FBI over past embezzlements. The court held that the discharge was legal, and the employee had no right to spread rumors (even true ones) about fellow employees.[5]

Courts also have required the employee to have solid evidence of a violation before protecting whistle-blowers. A mere suspicion of illegal activity is not sufficient justification.

One important issue in both the public policy and the whistle-blowing cases is whether the employee's case is in contract or tort. This is important because damages can be larger in tort claims. For example, punitive damages are available in tort but generally unavailable in contract claims. Most, but not all, states have held that these wrongful discharge cases are torts. Some states have specifically approved the application of punitive damages on wrongful discharge cases.

Good Cause

For any of the above wrongful discharge claims, in contract or tort, the employer has a **good cause defense**. If the employee were fired for good cause, the courts will rule in favor of the employer.

A large number of cases have helped define what constitutes good cause for discharge of an employee. Violation of the employer's rules generally satisfies the good cause requirement. The following is a partial list of conditions that represent good cause for discharge:

- illegal actions
- absenteeism or tardiness

---
[5] *Foley v. Interactive Data Corp.*, 254 Cal.Rptr. 211 (1988).

- alcoholism or drug addiction
- incompetence or poor performance
- refusal of work assignment or overtime
- disruption of work
- dishonesty in job applications
- fighting and threats
- profanity or harassment of coworkers
- moonlighting
- appearance or violation of dress code
- reduction in force due to financial problems

Most courts also defer to employers' decisions regarding good cause. The employer need not prove conclusively that the employee engaged in one of the proscribed behaviors. Rather, courts require only that the employer had a good faith belief in the good cause for terminating the employee.

Tortious Discharges

On some occasions, the act of terminating an employee may constitute a separate tort by the employer. The most common torts alleged in discharge cases are fraud, intentional infliction of emotional distress, negligence, and defamation.

For an employee to succeed on a *fraud* claim, he or she must show a representation of a false fact, made with knowledge of its falsity, which produces reasonable reliance by the employee. Suppose that Anna Juarez is offered a job with Artmark, Inc., but is soon fired. She might be able to allege that she was promised three years employment by Artmark and turned down other opportunities to accept the job. But she would have to prove that Artmark knew that her position would be eliminated before the promised three years.

A fraud claim is difficult to win, because the employee must show that a false statement was knowingly made. In a famous case, Christine Kraft sued a Kansas City television station that had fired her, on grounds of appearance. She brought a fraud claim, based on the statement that she was hired on the understanding that no change was required in her appearance. She lost the case because she could not prove that the hiring assurances were falsely made. The station successfully maintained that it simply changed its mind after she was hired.[6]

Some employees have succeeded in fraud claims. In one case, a company's management hired replacement workers while their regular workers were out on strike. The replacements were hired with a promise that they would be retained after the strike was settled. The strike was settled only one week later, and the replacement workers were fired. The employees sued in fraud and won both compensatory and punitive damages.[7]

Another common tort claim in discharge cases is **intentional infliction of emotional distress**. This claim requires proof of an outrageous act, with reckless disregard of its consequences, which actually causes severe emotional distress.

The mere termination of employment will not constitute intentional infliction of emotional distress. The procedures used in termination can constitute the tort, however. Certain facts can give rise to intentional infliction of emotional distress. If the discharge is accompanied by inaccurate assertions of dishonesty or other unethical practice, a court may permit an employee's recovery. Sexual or racial slurs also constitute the tort.

The following case provides some examples of facts that do or do not constitute intentional infliction of mental distress in connection with an employment termination.

---

[6] *Kraft v. Metromedia, Inc.*, 766 F.2d 1205 (8th Cir. 1985).
[7] *Verway v. Blincoe Packing Co.*, 698 P.2d 377 (Idaho App. 1985).

Case 3.3
Mansfield v. American Telephone & Telegraph Corporation
United States District Court, Western District of Arkansas, 1990
5 IER Cases (BNA) 1383

Background and Facts Martha Mansfield was a national accounts manager for AT&T. Ms. Mansfield was an at-will employee. AT&T officers wanted to hire Beverly Burns as a political favor to an Arkansas state legislator, B.G. Hendrix. Ms. Mansfield refused to go along with this hire, believing it to be illegal. After her repeatedly stated opposition to the hiring of Ms. Burns, Ms. Mansfield was fired.

Before firing her, AT&T officials engaged Ms. Mansfield in six hours of intense questioning, some of which involved personal issues. Ms. Mansfield sued AT&T and among her allegations was a claim for intentional infliction of emotional distress. AT&T moved the court for summary judgment, claiming that the alleged facts did not sufficiently make out a claim for this tort.

ARNOLD, District Judge.

* * * *

Finally, the defendants argue that Ms. Mansfield has failed to produce sufficient evidence to create a genuine issue of material fact as to her claim for outrage. The court disagrees.

To establish such a claim, Ms. Mansfield must present evidence of "conduct that is so outrageous in character, and so extreme in degree, as to go beyond all possible bounds of decency, and to be regarded as atrocious and utterly intolerable in a civilized society." See AMI Civil 3d, 404. The emotional distress suffered as a result "must be reasonable and justified under the circumstances and must be so severe that no reasonable person could be expected to endure it." Id.

Judgments for outrage have been upheld, grants of summary judgment to a defendant reversed, and dismissals for failure to state a claim reversed in Arkansas cases where an employee alleged that she was fired because she would not agree to her supervisor's demands for sexual favors and that her employer then represented in relation to her unemployment compensation claim that she had been fired for misconduct, see *Lucas v. Brown and Root, Inc.*, 736 F.2d 1202, 1206-07 (8th Cir. 1984); where allegations were made that an employee with an outstanding record was intentionally dismissed on account of her age, see *Smith v. Southern Starr of Arkansas, Inc.*, 700 F.Supp. 1026, 1027-28 (E.D. Ark. 1988); where, over a period of two years, the plaintiff was followed by the defendant and people hired by him, the defendant made repeated unwarranted complaints about how the plaintiff was doing his job, and the defendant made numerous threats to get the plaintiff fired, see *Hess v. Treece,* 286 Ark. 434, 440 (1985), cert. denied, 475 Ark. 1036 (1986); where an employee being questioned about alleged thefts from his employer was repeatedly denied the opportunity to take tranquilizing medication during the questioning even though he was highly agitated at the time, see *Tandy Corp. v. Bone,* 283 Ark. 399, 407-08 (1984); where a construction crew unnecessarily drove heavy equipment over family graves, exposed the burial vaults within, and then told distressed family members not to visit the sites if these events were so upsetting, see *Growth Properties I v. Cannon,* 282 Ark. 472, 475-76 (1984); and where evidence was presented that a fired employee was given reasons for her termination inconsistent with the circumstances and, even after passing a polygraph test, was denied her back pay until the state labor department intervened, see *MBM Company, Inc. v. Counce,* 268 Ark. 269, 271-72, 281 (1980).

Judgments for outrage have been reversed, directed verdicts or summary judgment granted to a defendant, and complaints dismissed on outrage claims in Arkansas cases where evidence was presented that an employee was refused a promotion, denied raises, and given poor performance evaluations in an effort to pressure him to resign after he confronted his employer about alleged kickback schemes, see *Puckett v. Cook,* 864 F.2d 619, 620, 622 (8th Cir. 1989); where a religious sect persuaded one of its members to repudiate his family, see *Orlando v. Alamo,* 646 F.2d 1288, 1289-90 (8th Cir. 1981); where an insurance company disputed the plaintiff's interpretation of policy language and refused to pay a claim, see *Glenn v. Farmers and Merchants Insurance Company,* 649 F.Supp. 1447, 1448-50 (W.D. Ark. 1986); where the plaintiff stopped making payments on a camper trailer that had developed multiple problems, the seller secured a warrant for the plaintiff's arrest after having been unable to locate him, and the plaintiff was subsequently arrested and held for two hours until he posted bond, see *Cordes v. Outdoor Living Center, Inc.,* 301 Ark. 26, 29-30, 34 (1989); where an employer was verbally abusive to the plaintiff and had made derogatory comments about a review process of the employer's work in which the plaintiff was involved.

* * * *

Ms. Mansfield alleges that during six hours of questioning, without notice, by AT&T representatives about an alleged conflict of interest, unauthorized use of company property, and submission of false expense vouchers, she was not given a chance to defend herself, she was repeatedly laughed at and accused of lying whenever she tried to speak, was not permitted to smoke even though she told the AT&T representative that she was a heavy smoker, was not permitted to eat, was implicitly accused of having used sexual favors to get customers' accounts, was implicitly accused of having a lesbian relationship with a coworker, was subjected to questioning while one of the AT&T officials had unzipped pants, and was not permitted to leave until she signed a statement; that the reasons given for the interrogation were pretextual; that after she was fired, AT&T refused to pay various benefits due her; and that AT&T representatives suggested to others that she might be having affairs with customers or a lesbian relationship with a coworker.

Decision and Remedy *The court denied defendant's summary judgment motion on plaintiff's claim for intentional infliction of emotional distress.*

Some employees have brought a *negligence* claim in connection with their discharge. Ordinarily, negligent discharge is not a tort, because employers' only duties to employees are those set forth in their contract. An employee may succeed in a case based on negligent evaluation, however, if the employment contract provides that the employee can be discharged only for good cause.

Virtually all employers conduct some form of periodic job evaluation for their workers. Some courts have recognized a cause of action for negligent evaluations. This tort must generally be accompanied by some contract right to be discharged only for good cause.

Michigan courts have recognized a claim for negligent evaluation. If the employee can show a legal right to performance evaluations (such as in contract), the employer has a duty to conduct such evaluations fairly and objectively. If a negligently conducted evaluation causes a worker's discharge, the employee can recover damages.

Another common discharge claim is **defamation**. Defamation requires a false statement about a person, communicated to others, that causes harm to the person's reputation. In one case, a newspaper fired a sportswriter and published an article explaining its decision. The explanation suggested that the writer was insufficiently energetic and was "on the downswing." A court found that this explanation could constitute defamation.[8]

The largest barrier to defamation actions is the requirement of communication to third parties. If a GovCorp Co. manager calls in Jim Jones, privately accuses him of embezzlement, and fires him, there is no defamation. Only Jim Jones heard the accusation.

---

[8] *Falls v. Sporting News Publishing Co.,* 834 F.2d 611 (6th Cir. 1987).

Some courts are creating an important exception to the communication requirement, which is called the **doctrine of compelled self-publication**. When Jim Jones interviews for a new job, the interviewers ask why he left GovCorp. Jim honestly states that he was fired because he was an accused embezzler. Courts have held that this repetition by Jim was foreseeable by the employer, and GovCorp may be liable for defamation if the accusation was false.

Employer comments on employees have a qualified privilege under defamation law. If one employer gives another job reference to another, the qualified privilege protects the first employer from defamation claims. To be protected, however, the employer's reference must meet several requirements. The reference must be communicated in good faith, in a proper manner, to the proper parties (not to the general public), related to job requirements and limited to disclosures that are necessary to performance evaluation.

▄ Employee Privacy

Privacy rights of employees are a major new area of the law. The United States Constitution protects citizens' privacy against the intrusions of the government but generally does not apply to employer "invasions of privacy." Employees generally lack a strong common law basis for privacy protection.

There is a tort of invasion of privacy, but this tort is restricted in the employment context. A leading court case explained that an employer "may seek certain personal information concerning an employee when the importance of the information in assessing the employee's efficacy in his work outweighs the employee's right to keep this information private."[9]

An employer may be liable for invasion of privacy if there is no legitimate or significant employer interest in the matter. In one case, a flight attendant provided her employer with medical information, including the details of planned gynecological surgery. The employer's medical examiner disclosed this information to her supervisor and to her husband. The flight attendant won damages for invasion of privacy, because the employer had no legitimate interest in disclosing this information.[10]

This case was relatively unusual, though, and employers typically will have a legitimate basis for their actions.

While common law will often fail to provide privacy protection to employees, the federal and state governments have passed a series of laws that protect certain privacy rights of workers. The primary areas of concern are in polygraph testing, drug testing, AIDS testing, and monitoring of performance.

Lie Detector Tests

Employers have used polygraphs and other lie detectors to screen job applicants and to investigate for employee theft. After thousands of companies began using these tests, states and the federal government adopted legal restrictions on lie detectors in the workplace.

Employer use of lie detector tests is restricted by the Employee Polygraph Protection Act of 1988. This law makes it illegal for employers to "directly or indirectly, require, request, suggest, or cause, any employee or prospective employee to take or submit to any lie detector test." The law also restricts inquiries about the results of lie detector tests and any discharge of discipline based upon the results of a test or refusal to take a test.

The Act created significant exceptions when lie detector use is allowed. An exemption exists for government employers in national security, private employers of security personnel, and employers authorized to produce or distribute controlled substances.

A more general statutory exemption applies to "ongoing investigations." This exemption allows an employer to request that an employee submit to a polygraph test if the employer can meet the following requirements:

1. The test is used in an ongoing investigation involving losses that result from intentional wrongdoing.

2. The subject employee had access to the property loss in question.

3. The employer has a reasonable suspicion that the employee was involved in the investigated loss.

4. The employer provides a statement to the employee setting forth the legal rights under the act.

---

[9] *Bratt v. International Business Machines Corp.,* 467 N.E.2d 126, 135 (Mass. 1984).

[10] *Lewis v. United Airlines,* 500 N.E. 2d 370 (Ohio App. 1985).

This statement also must specify with particularity the incident under investigation.

This exemption permits tests for employee theft but does not allow random employee testing.

The law provides additional protections even when testing is allowed. The employee cannot be required to take the test. The Act prohibits degrading or needlessly intrusive questions. Thus, questions about religious or political beliefs or sexual behavior are expressly prohibited.

The law provides that employees must be informed of the nature and characteristics of the test. Standards for polygrapher qualifications are established. Disclosure of test results is restricted.

Violation of the law is punishable by a civil penalty of up to $10,000. Employees can sue in a private right of action and obtain reinstatement with the company or the payment of lost wages and benefits.

While the federal legislation applies to many types of lie detector tests, it does not apply to "pencil-and-paper" questionnaires of employees or prospective employees. These tests are used to check for dishonesty and may involve highly personal questions. Note, though, that states have passed laws restricting employee testing, and some state laws may ban these written tests as well. The Massachusetts law expressly bans such pencil-and-paper tests for detecting potential employee dishonesty.

Drug Testing

Recent years have seen an enormous increase in employer testing for drugs or alcohol abuse by employees. Over 80 percent of the Fortune 200 companies and over 30 percent of the total workforce are now subject to such testing.

Many employees have challenged drug and alcohol testing in the workplace. For private employers, drug testing has generally been upheld as an exercise of management discretion.

The U.S. Constitution constrains drug testing of government workers and testing that is required by government action. The Department of Transportation, for example, adopted regulations for drug testing that apply to approximately 4 million private sector employees. These regulations require random testing, periodic testing of some employees, and post-accident testing for transportation workers. Those who test positive must be removed from their duties.

The Supreme Court recently ruled on the constitutionality of these Department of Transportation regulations. The court upheld the rules due to the significant safety concerns in transportation and the protections provided against inaccurate test results.

A federal statute, the Drug-Free Workplace Act of 1988, requires private employers who contract with the federal government to certify their good-faith effort to maintain a drug-free workforce. While this law does not expressly require drug testing, it effectively encourages such testing.

Private employees have little legal protection from employment drug testing campaigns. In California, state law extends state constitutional privacy protections to the private sector, and state courts have restricted drug testing. Other state laws require the use of licensed testing facilities, employee notification, opportunity for employee response, and an opportunity for participation in rehabilitation programs. In a federal case decided under Louisiana law, an individual who was fired after testing positive for marijuana sued and recovered $125,000 in damages for emotional distress and $1 in damages for invasion of privacy.[11]

AIDS Testing

An increasing number of employers are testing their workers for the Acquired Immune Deficiency Syndrome (AIDS). Few public issue are more controversial than this practice.

The primary legal question in AIDS testing was the Rehabilitation Act of 1973. This law applied to companies that received federal grants or contracts. Congress recently passed the Americans with Disabilities Act of 1990 that covers most purely private workforces.

These laws prohibit discrimination against individuals who are handicapped or considered to be handicapped. The term handicapped has been broadly defined to include those who suffer from diseases such as AIDS.

To be protected under the Rehabilitation Act or Americans With Disabilities Act, a handicapped person must demonstrate that he or she is "otherwise qualified." Victims of some communicable diseases will not be otherwise qualified, because they threaten other employees with contagion.

---

[11] *Kelley v. Schlumberger Technology Corp.*, 849 F.2d 41 (1st Cir. 1988).

Courts have generally held, however, that AIDS is not so contagious as to disqualify employees in most jobs. An exception would exist for certain jobs in which infection (such as blood-to-blood transfer) is more likely.

These laws also require that an employer make reasonable accommodation for its handicapped employees and cannot discriminate against them based on their handicap. Thus, the law may not prohibit AIDS testing but may be interpreted to prohibit the discharge of employees based on AIDS tests or even the disclosure of AIDS test results.

Some state laws more directly restrict AIDS testing. In 1985, Florida adopted a law making it illegal for employers to use AIDS tests in making employment decisions. Wisconsin prohibits employers from requesting or requiring employees or job applicants to take an AIDS test. California prohibits involuntary testing and proscribes negligent or willful disclosure of test results. New York encourages testing that is both voluntary and confidential. Some cities, including Los Angeles, San Francisco, Boston and Philadelphia, prohibit AIDS discrimination. State and local handicapped protection laws also limit testing for AIDS and other diseases.

Enhanced Monitoring

As technology advances, so does the employer's ability to closely monitor its employees' work. Companies have increasingly employed monitoring of telephone calls, close-circuit television monitoring, and monitoring of computer work stations. Over 15 million employees are now subject to phone monitoring.

The legality of such enhanced monitoring is an important future issue. To date, most courts have permitted electronic monitoring of employees under the common law. Courts have suggested, however, that employees must be notified of the possibility of such monitoring.

The only directly applicable federal legislation on employee monitoring is the Electronic Communications Privacy Act of 1986, which regulates wiretapping. An employer's telephone monitoring might be an illegal interception of oral communication under this act. The act contains significant exemptions, however, including one for monitoring on an extension of the phone line for business purposes. The act also creates an exception where consent is given to monitoring.

Several states have proposed laws to regulate employee monitoring. Relatively few laws have been adopted, but Connecticut, for example, has legislation that would prohibit electronic surveillance of lounges, locker rooms and other nonwork areas. Some additional restrictive legislation can be anticipated in future years.

Anti-Fraternization Policies

A sensitive area of employment law involves policies on intraoffice dating or the hiring of spouses and relatives. Companies often adopt such policies for morale or to avoid sexual harassment claims. While many employees have found the policies objectionable, courts have generally upheld policies against romantic relationships among workers.[12] If such rules are inconsistently applied, however, they may become unenforceable. In one case, granting exceptions was considered a waiver of the rule, preventing the company from firing a worker for violating an antinepotism policy.[13]

Family and Medical Leave Act

On February 3, 1993, President Clinton signed into law the Family and Medical Leave Act (FMLA). This law provides protection to workers who take time off without pay in order to care for a family member, such as a new child or ill relative. An employer must provide twelve weeks of leave in a twelve month period, though this period may be calculated in several different ways. The FMLA guarantees this leave, reinstatement at its end, and the continuation of health insurance benefits.

Employees have some responsibilities under the FMLA. A worker must provide the employer with thirty days advance notice of the leave, if possible. If the need for leave is unforeseeable, employees must provide notice as soon as practicable. In addition, the employee must make a reasonable effort to schedule the planned leave so as not to unduly disrupt the employer's operations, insofar as possible. A doubting employer may require that the leave request be documented by certification by a health care provider.

---

[12] *See, e.g., Wright v. Metrohealth Medical Center* 58 F.3d 1130 (6th Cir. 1995).
[13] *Goodyear Tire and Rubber Co. v. Potilla*, 897 S.W.2d 47 (Tex. 1994).

Additional Employee Rights

Various laws provide additional rights to individual employees. The right to unionize is protected by federal law and discussed in Chapter 35 of *West's Business Law, Seventh Edition*. Rights against certain forms of discrimination are guaranteed by civil rights laws and discussed in Chapter 36 and in this book's Chapter 4 "Employment Discrimination Law." Rights of workplace safety are discussed in Chapter 35 and in this book's Chapter 5, "Occupational Safety and Workers' Compensation." These topics are also covered in Chapters 20, 21, and 22 of *West's Legal Environment of Business, Second Edition*.

Ethical Perspectives

Whistle-Blowing

Whistle-blowing has been the source of considerable ethical debate. The concept of whistle-blowing sets two moral goals in conflict. First, the employee has a duty of loyalty to the employer. Second, the employee has a duty to external society (such as honesty, doing no harm, etc.)

A large number of employees believe that whistle-blowing should be morally prohibited. There is a strong strain of American opinion against "ratting" to the boss. Blowing the whistle directly confronts and accuses the moral behavior of another. In addition, whistle-blowing may give the entire company a black eye and can produce considerable disruption within the company. Whistle-blowing is a bit like calling a foul on one's own basketball teammate.

Others argue that whistle-blowing is morally required. They contend that whistle-blowing is an altruistic action that places the good of others above selfish personal interests. These advocates would always place societal interest above that of the firm. They would indict an employee who does nothing and fails to blow the whistle on unethical corporate acts. They also have argued that employees have no duty of loyalty to their employing corporation.

A middle ground has been put forth, suggesting that whistle-blowing is morally permitted in some instances, but seldom should be prohibited or required. One leading business ethicist has put forth a three-part test for permitted whistle-blowing:

1. The firm, through its product or policy, will do serious and considerably harm to the public, whether in the person of the user of its product, an innocent bystander, or the general public.

2. Once an employee identifies a serious threat to the user of a product or to the general public, he or she should report it to an immediate superior and make his or her moral concern known.

3. If one's immediate superior does nothing effective about the concern or complaint, the employee should exhaust the internal procedures and possibilities within the firm.[14]

In addition to the above three tests, one might add the existence of strong evidence of the risk of the product. Employees should not be too quick to assume the worst and challenge decisions without good proof. It might also be fair to expect that the whistle-blower seek to correct the problem with the minimum possible damage to the employer.

---

[14] R.T. DeGeorge, *Business Ethics* 230-232 (1986).

International Perspectives

Wrongful Discharge in Japan

The United States has a long tradition of at-will employment that provided employers great freedom and flexibility in discharging workers. Many other nations, including much of Europe, provide much less employer flexibility and, therefore, greater job security. Japan, specifically, has relatively elaborate restrictions on discharging employees.

Interestingly, Japanese statutory law is quite close to U.S. law. The relevant statutes state that an employer may discharge an employee at any time and for any reason. The law simply requires two weeks' notice. The reality is far different, however, as the statutory law is influenced by national culture and by other legal requirements.

Japan draws a distinction between regular (permanent) employees and temporary hires. Regular employees are typically recruited directly from universities and secondary schools. While these workers receive indefinite, at-will employment contracts, they are expected to work for the employer until their retirement. Temporary employees are hired from a pool of experienced workers and are the first (and often only) workers to lose their jobs in the event of an economic downturn.

The Japanese Constitution, adopted in 1946, makes it relatively difficult to fire workers. The Constitution declares that work is a fundamental human right and declares that "the promotion of job security [is] a matter of public order." The constitutional provision has been implemented in part by the nation's Labor Standards Law. The law establishes prohibitions on discriminatory treatment, establishes minimum working conditions, and limits the discharge of employees. Violation of the law can produce criminal penalties.

Japanese courts have placed several restrictions on at-will discharges of regular employees. The Labor Standards Law specifically requires thirty days' advance notice of any discharge. Courts require that an employer provide good reasons for dismissing any worker.

A key protection for workers is found in "employment rules" that each employer (of more than ten employees) must establish and file with the government. These rules provide for the terms and conditions of employment. The rules virtually always contain a dismissal clause. The dismissal clause specifies conditions for which workers may be terminated. The conditions are specific, and Japanese courts have held that a discharge for reasons other than the conditions of the employment rules is invalid. The rules of employment are similar to a detailed employment manual in the U.S.

Even discharges within the employment rules have been overturned by the courts of Japan. The nation's Supreme Court has declared that any discharge is wrongful if it is considered unreasonable on the facts of the case. Any discharge contrary to public policy will be unlawful. The courts of Japan review discharges closely and reject those that are deemed an abuse of employer discretion. If a discharge is invalid, the employee is generally reinstated.

Wrongful discharge law illustrates substantial cultural differences between Japan and the United States. Japan's system typically guarantees lifetime employment to regular employees. This cultural feature is reflected in the application of Japan's laws.

Questions and Case Problems

1. Lincoln Life merged its Wisconsin agency into its Chicago agency. The merger was ordered by Steinhaus, who became manager of the expanded agency. Kumpf, the former manager of the Wisconsin agency, was an at-will employee and lost his job. Kumpf argued that he had been wrongfully terminated, and that Steinhaus had engineered the merger simply to increase his authority and his percentage of revenues from Lincoln Life's business. Does Kumpf have a good claim for wrongful termination? [*Kumpf v. Steinhaus,* 779 F.2d 1323 (7th Cir. 1985)].

2. Charles Toussaint was employed in a middle management position at Blue Cross. After being employed for five years, Toussaint was fired without any reason being given. Blue Cross personnel policies stated that it was the "policy" of the company that employees would be fired for "just cause only." In addition, he was told that he would not be fired so long as he was "doing the job." Toussaint sued Blue Cross, arguing that he had an implied contract of employment that the company violated. A jury ruled for Toussaint and awarded him damages in excess of $72,000. Blue Cross appealed this judgment. Should the court of appeals overturn the jury verdict? [*Toussaint v. Blue Cross & Blue Shield of Michigan,* 292 N.W.2d 880 (Mich. 1980)].

3. Flanigan had worked for Prudential Federal for many years and was promoted to branch office bookkeeper and then assistant loan counselor. She performed satisfactorily in all her positions with the bank. The bank suffered an economic downturn and adopted a new policy that eliminated her position but enabled her to take a new job as a teller. One month later, she was fired from her new position. She argued that the bank had dealt unfairly with her and fired her due to the vindictiveness of her supervisor. She sued for wrongful discharge. A jury awarded her nearly $1.5 million in actual and punitive damages, and the bank appealed. Should the court overturn the jury verdict? [*Flanigan v. Prudential Federal Savings & Loan Ass'n.* 720 P.2d 257 (Mon. 1986)].

4. The manager of a brake shop was directed by its owner not to purchase a new lathe and to reduce inventory. He went ahead with the purchase and did not reduce inventory, because of his sincere belief that this was in the company's best interest. The manager then was fired for insubordination. He claimed that he was given the right to manage the shop and make purchasing decisions and sued for wrongful discharge. Should the manager succeed on his claim? [*Thomas v. Bourdette,* 608 P.2d 178 (Ore App. 1980)].

5. Kelley was a barge engineer on an oil platform in the Gulf of Mexico. His employer had a drug testing policy that involved the taking of a urine sample under the observation of a company agent. Kelley's sample tested positive for marijuana. Subsequently, Kelley was discharged from his job. He sued for negligent infliction of emotional distress, and a jury awarded him $125,000 in damages. The employer appealed this verdict. Should an appellate court overturn the jury award? [*Kelley v. Schlumberger Technology Corp.,* 849 F.2d 41 (1st Cir. 1988)].

CHAPTER FOUR

Employment Discrimination Law

Key Background

The essential background for this chapter on employment discrimination law is found in Chapter 36 of *West's Business Law, Seventh Edition*, and in Chapter 21 of *West's Legal Environment of Business, Third Edition*, which cover employment and labor relations law. Among the important points to remember from these chapters are:

- the coverage and application of Title VII

- the procedures and proof requirements for enforcement of Title VII actions

- the defenses available for Title VII actions

- other antidiscrimination laws providing protection based on age and handicapped status.

* * *

Employment discrimination law is one of the most important issues confronting business today. An informal survey of the daily "law" section of the Wall Street Journal found that it reported more discrimination cases than any other category of law.

Employment discrimination law is also becoming increasingly complex. The categories of individuals protected from discrimination continue to be expanded. The requirements of discrimination law are also expanded as laws are amended and court cases are decided. Even a "pure heart" cannot avoid discrimination liability for an employer who is un-familiar with the details of discrimination law.

Title VII

Title VII litigation continues to grow, as courts extend the section to new forms of discrimination. Different protected classes continue to face different forms of discrimination.

Racial Discrimination

The central protected classes of Title VII are race and color. The primary purpose of the Civil Rights Act was to prevent racial discrimination. Recently, there have been several disputes over what constitutes discrimination based upon race or color.

For example, an Arab university professor alleged that he suffered discrimination based on race. The university defended on the grounds that being Arab is not a distinct race that is protected under Title VII. The United States Supreme Court disagreed and held that race should be interpreted broadly to prohibit discrimination against any subgroup, including "Finns, gypsies, Basques, Hebrews, Swedes," etc.[1]

In a more recent decision, a light-skinned black woman claimed that she had suffered discrimination from darker-skinned black supervisors

---

[1] *Francis College v. Al-Khazraji*, 481 U.S. 604, 611 (1987).

based on her skin color. A court agreed that this type of discrimination was also prohibited by Title VII.[2]

A central form of unlawful discrimination is **disparate treatment**, in which a member of a group is intentionally treated differently. The prima facie case of disparate treatment discrimination is relatively simple, as a plaintiff must first show:

1. The person was a member of a specific protected class under Title VII.

2. The person was qualified for the job in question and undertook other necessary requirements (e.g., applying for the job).

3. The person suffered some loss of employment opportunity (e.g., was fired, not hired, offered lower pay).

4. The employer left the job open or gave the employment opportunity to someone outside the plaintiff's protected class.

Once the plaintiff makes out the prima facie case, the defendant employer need only state a lawful reason why the plaintiff suffered a loss of job opportunity (e.g., was not hired). For example, an employer might state that the plaintiff was not hired because he or she was less qualified than other applicants or was fired due to frequent absences.

---

[2] *Walker v. IRS*, 713 F. Supp. 403 (N.D. Ga. 1989).

While the employer has no burden of proof regarding the stated reason, the employer must state that the legitimate reason was the basis for its action at the time. The employer cannot produce legitimate reasons after the fact.

For example, suppose that a black employee applied for a promotion and was denied as unqualified. Later, a white employee applied and was hired. The black employee sues for unlawful discrimination. The company now concedes that the black employee was qualified but states that the white was more qualified. This is an insufficient reason—the white employee had not applied at the time of the black employee's rejection, so comparative qualifications cannot explain the employer's decision.

Once the employer articulates this reason, the plaintiff has an opportunity to demonstrate that the stated reason is a pretext (a cover-up for discrimination). There are several ways for a plaintiff to show pretext. A plaintiff might show that standards were applied inconsistently. For example, an employer fired a black woman for excessive absences, but white men with an equal number of absences were not fired. Racist or sexist statements by responsible persons also provide some evidence of pretext. If the plaintiff can show pretext, he or she wins the case.

Disparate treatment discrimination involves intentional discrimination but does not require proof of blatant racism or sexism. Any purposeful different treatment, even well-intended, could be a basis for unlawful disparate treatment discrimination. This principle is illustrated by the following decision.

Case 4.1
Vaughn v. Edel
United States Court of Appeals,
Fifth Circuit, 1990
918 F.2d 517

Background and Facts *Emma Vaughn was a black female attorney who worked for Texaco's Land Department. Her supervisors were Robert Edel and Alvin Hatton. In her early years with the company, she received promotions and was the "highest ranked contract analyst" in the department. In 1985, after she returned from a maternity leave, Edel complained to her about her low productivity and excessive visits by other black employees. He was concerned that she was becoming a "black matriarch" for the company and that this hurt her work. Vaughn was offended by these remarks and discussed the matter with another attorney. Concerned about charges of race discrimination, officials told Edel not to criticize Vaughn.*

From 1985 to 1987, neither Edel nor Hatton expressed any criticism of Vaughn's work to her, and her annual evaluations rated her as "satisfactory." There was testimony that the company's satisfaction was overstated. In 1987, to meet cost-reduction goals, Texaco fired its two "poorest performers" in the division, one of whom was Vaughn. Vaughn filed a discrimination claim with the EEOC, which decided that there was no violation of Title VII. She then sued in court, and a magistrate also found that there was no illegal discrimination. Vaughn appealed.

WIENER, Circuit Judge.

* * * *

Vaughn presented direct evidence of discrimination. Keller testified that to avoid provoking a discrimination suit he had told Vaughn's supervisors not to confront her about her work. His "black matriarch" memorandum details the events that led Keller to initiate this policy. Keller also testified that he had deliberately overstated Vaughn's evaluations in order not to start the process that might eventually lead to termination. This direct evidence clearly shows that Keller acted as he did solely because Vaughn is black. Texaco has never offered any evidence to show that in neither confronting Vaughn about her poor performance nor counseling her it would have acted as it did without regard to her race. Vaughn has, consequently, established that Texaco discriminated against her.

* * * *

Although Vaughn's race may not have directly motivated the 1987 decision to fire her, race did play a part, as the magistrate found, in Vaughn's employment relationship with Texaco from 1985 to 1987. Texaco's treatment of Vaughn was not color-blind during that period. In neither criticizing Vaughn when her work was unsatisfactory nor counseling her how to improve, Texaco treated Vaughn differently than it did its other contract analysts because, as the magistrate found, she was black. As a result, Texaco did not afford Vaughn the same opportunity to improve her performance, and perhaps her relative ranking, as it did its white employees. One of those employees was placed on an improvement program. As for the others, Texaco does not deny that they received, at least, informal counseling. The evidence indicates that Vaughn had the ability to improve. As Texaco acknowledges, she was once its "highest ranked contract analyst."

Had her dissatisfied supervisors simply counseled Vaughn informally, such counseling would inevitably have indicated to Vaughn that her work was deficient. Had Keller given Vaughn the evaluation that he believed she deserved, Texaco's regulations would have required his placing her on a ninety-day work improvement program, just as at least one other employee—a white male—had been placed. A Texaco employee who has not improved by the end of that period is fired. Consequently an employee on an improvement program certainly knows what Texaco thinks of his performance, knows that he is in imminent danger of being fired and at least has an option to improve, thereby reducing or removing the risk of being fired.

* * * *

Initially, Texaco's decisions not to criticize Vaughn and not to state her correct evaluations may have appeared beneficial, even—had she been aware of them—to Vaughn. She did, for example, receive a merit pay increase in 1986 that she would not have received had Keller given her the evaluation that he believed she deserved. Ultimately, however, whether Texaco's decisions may have damaged Vaughn's employment status at

Texaco will never be known. Furthermore, whether Texaco's decisions ultimately benefited or harmed Vaughn is irrelevant. The decisions not to apply the usual procedures in Vaughn's case were racial decisions. Texaco has never stated any reason other than that she was black for treating Vaughn as it did. Had Texaco treated Vaughn in a color-blind manner from 1985 to 1987, Vaughn might have been fired by April 1987 for unsatisfactory work; on the other hand, she might have sufficiently improved her performance so as not to be one of the two "lowest ranked" employees, thereby avoiding termination in April 1987. Consequently, Texaco must bear the cost of its lost opportunity to determine whether Vaughn might have remained one of the two "lowest ranked" contract analysts had it not made decisions based on race. This circuit will not sterilize a seemingly objective decision to fire an employee when earlier discriminatory decisions have infected it.

Decision and Remedy   *The court reversed the magistrate's ruling, held that Title VII was violated, and remanded the case for calculation of damages.*

Disparate treatment involves intentional discrimination against a single individual and the employer's overall fair practices are no defense. Some employers sought to use a "bottom-line" defense, by arguing that their work force had proportional representation. After a black worker claimed that a test for promotion was discriminatory, the company defended by showing that it had employed a large number of black employees. The Supreme Court held that this was no defense to a claim of discrimination by an individual employee.[3]

Some of the most difficult discrimination cases involve allegations of sex discrimination, of a type known as **sex plus discrimination**. This arises when an employer has different rules for men and women and, for example, disciplines a woman worker for violating the dress code that is specific to women.

Courts have accepted the legality of applying somewhat different standards to men and women. Different rules were upheld in the following circumstances: a rule requiring that male employees wear ties, a rule prohibiting female employees from wearing pants, a ban on male employees wearing beards or long hair. All these practices were found legal.

Under "sex plus" discrimination, the rules cannot be much stricter for one sex than another and must enable most workers to comply. Courts have struck down rules that placed maximum weight requirements on female flight attendants only and that prohibited female flight attendants from wearing glasses.

A second type of unlawful discrimination is **disparate impact** discrimination. This is unintentional discrimination that results when a seemingly neutral hiring practice has discriminatory consequences. A minimum height requirement for a police department, for example, does not directly discriminate but has the effect of ruling out a higher percentage of women and certain nationalities.

Suppose that Golden Co. used a written test before hiring construction employees, and a member of a minority group contends that this screening test has a discriminatory effect. The plaintiff must show that a higher proportion of qualified minority applicants failed the test. The Equal Employment Opportunity Commission suggests that, if the passing or selection rate of one group is 80 percent or less than that for another group, there is evidence of disparate impact.

Once the plaintiff demonstrates that a specific practice or practices, such as the test, has a disparate impact, the company must then show that the challenged practice is job-related for the position in question and consistent with business necessity. Golden Co. could try to show that their written test

---

[3] *Connecticut v. Teal*, 457 U.S. 440 (1982).

was necessary to ensure that workers could communicate effectively.

The precise standards for showing that a practice is job-related and consistent with business necessity are still unclear. The courts will consider alternatives that might accomplish the employer's objective, without the discriminatory impact upon a protected class. One controversial issue is whether employers can screen workers based upon their arrest records.

The use of arrest records has a statistically disparate impact for blacks, Hispanics, and other groups. The EEOC has found that members of these groups are arrested at a higher rate than are whites.

There may seldom be a good business justification for refusing to hire anyone with an arrest rate. First, an arrest is not a conviction, so there is a poor correlation between arrests and the sort of actions that Golden Co. wants to avoid. Second, one may be arrested for many different crimes. There may be a business justification for not hiring those arrested for larceny, but there is less justification for rejecting those arrested in, for example, a political protest.

Some employers may consider certain arrest records for certain jobs. For example, a trucking company had a policy of refusing to hire anyone as a driver who had been arrested for theft. A court found that this rule had a business justification, because the drivers would be transporting valuable property.[4]

On other occasions, employers may not use arrest records to screen job applicants. The EEOC provided the following example:

> Lola, a black female, applies to Bus Inc. for a position as a bus driver. In response to an inquiry whether she had ever been arrested, Lola states that she was arrested five years earlier for fraud in unemployment benefits. Lola admits that she committed the crime alleged. She explains that she received unemployment benefits shortly after her husband died and her expenses increased. During this period, she worked part-time for minimum wage because her unemployment check amounted to slightly less than the monthly rent for her meager apartment. She did not report the income to the State Unemployment Board for fear that her payments would be reduced and that she would not be able to feed her three young children. After her arrest, she agreed to, and did, repay the state. Bus Inc. rejected Lola. Lola's rejection violated Title VII. The commission of fraud in the unemployment system does not constitute a justification for the rejection of an applicant for the position of bus driver. The type of crime which Lola committed is totally unrelated to her ability to safely, efficiently and/or courteously drive a bus. Furthermore, the arrest is not recent.[5]

Sexual Harassment

Many recent employment discrimination cases have involved sexual harassment. Such harassment is considered a form of discrimination because it is a burden suffered by only one sex. Two types of sexual harassment concern Title VII—**quid pro quo harassment** and **hostile environment harassment**.

Whatever the form of the action, there are five parts to a prima facie case of sexual harassment:

1. Plaintiff belongs to a protected class.

2. Plaintiff was subject to unwelcome sexual harassment.

3. The harassment was based on sex.

4. The harassment affected a term, condition or privilege of employment.

5. The employer is subject to respondent superior liability (responsible for the acts of employees).

Quid pro quo sexual harassment is the stereotypical form of harassment. For example, suppose that a supervisor tells an office worker that she must be physically intimate with him or be fired (or lose a promotion, etc.). If she refuses to comply with the supervisor's demands and loses an employment opportunity, she has a good case for quid pro quo harassment.

Hostile environment harassment is more common. In this form of harassment the employee may suffer no direct adverse financial consequences. The employee must continue to work, however, in an environment made uncomfortable by harassment. This is considered discrimination in the terms and conditions of employment.

---

[4] *EEOC v. Carolina Freight*, 723 F. Supp. 734 (S.D. Fla. 1989).

[5] *EEOC Compliance Manual*, No. 915-061 (September 7, 1990).

Courts have struggled with the definition of what constitutes an unlawful, harassing hostile environment. An occasional sexist comment may be inappropriate but is not illegal. To constitute a harassing environment, the harassment must be both significant and pervasive.

The following Supreme Court decision addressed the standards of proof for a sexual harassment claim.

Case 4.2
Harris v. Forklift Systems, Inc.
Supreme Court of the United States, 1993
114 S. Ct. 367

Background and Facts Teresa Harris worked as a manager at Forklift Systems, Inc. Charles Hardy, the president of Forklift Systems made a number of comments to Harris, such as: "You're a woman what do you know." He suggested that the two of them "go to the Holiday Inn" to "negotiate" her raise. He asked Harris and other female employees to get coins from his front pants pocket and made sexual innuendoes about their clothing. In August 1987, Harris complained to Hardy about his conduct, and he apologized and promised to stop. In September, though, he began again. After she negotiated a deal with a customer, he asked her in front of other employees: "What did you do, promise the guy some sex?" Soon thereafter, Harris quit the job.

Harris brought suit against Forklift under Title VII, claiming an abusive work environment. The district court found it a "close case" and observed that the comments would "offend the reasonable woman." However, the comments were not so severe as to affect Harris' "psychological well-being," and ruled for the defendant. The court of appeals affirmed.

O'CONNOR, Justice.

* * * *

But Title VII comes into play before the harassing conduct leads to a nervous breakdown. A discriminatorily abusive work environment, even one that does not seriously affect employees' psychological well-being, can and often will detract from employees' job performance, discourage employees from remaining on the job, or keep them from advancing in their careers. Moreover, even without regard to these tangible effects, the very fact that the discriminatory conduct was so severe or pervasive that it created a work environment abusive to employees because of their race, gender, religion, or national origin offends Title VII's broad rule of workplace equality.

* * * *

... we can say that whether an environment is "hostile" or "abusive" can be determined only by looking at all the circumstances. These may include the frequency of the discriminatory conduct; its severity; whether it is physically threatening or humiliating, or a mere offensive utterance; and whether it unreasonably interferes with an employee's work performance. The effect on the employee's psychological well-being is, of course, relevant to determining whether the plaintiff actually found the environment abusive. But while psychological harm, like any other relevant factor, may be taken into account, no single factor is required.

Decision and Remedy   *The court reversed the judgment of the lower court and remanded the case for further proceedings consistent with the opinion.*

A defense in sexual harassment cases is that the alleged harassment was welcomed by the plaintiff. There are romantic relationships that occur between employees that are mutually welcome. Indeed, one study found that 55 percent of executive women were romantically involved with men they met professionally.[6] When such a relationship falls apart, a sexual harassment claim may occur.

Whether given actions were welcome is a factual matter to be judged on the available evidence. Evidence suggests that the majority of sexual harassment claims do not involve welcome advances, but rather involve some sort of pressure to comply.

It is important to recognize that "welcome" is not the same as "voluntary." Courts have recognized that a woman may "voluntarily" agree to sex even when it is unwelcome. A woman may agree out of fear of losing her job, even when this threat is unstated. Men also may be victims of sexual harassment and have equal rights to sue if they are so victimized.

Employer Liability

Title VII makes only employers liable. In sexual harassment cases this seems awkward, because a company does not harass a person; individuals do. The employer can be liable under *respondeat superior*, which makes it responsible for the unlawful acts of its employees.

Employers are not strictly liable for the actions of their employees. When sexual harassment was by a supervisory or high-level official, however, the employer is likely to be found responsible. The knowledge of such upper-level employees is generally imputed to the employer under agency law. This is especially likely if the company lacked an effective sexual harassment policy.

When harassment is by coworkers or clients, the plaintiff must show more evidence to find the employer responsible. The plaintiff first must show that the employer was aware or should have been aware, of the existence of the sexual harassment. The employer may be aware because the employee filed a grievance. Alternatively, the employer may be liable for failure to provide an effective, protected grievance policy.

Once the employer is made aware of the harassment, it must respond effectively. Firm actions must be taken to prevent recurrence of harassment, and this action must be taken promptly.

Many companies have adopted policies against sexual harassment. These help avoid liability but are insufficient by themselves. Firms must vigorously apply these policies in seeking out sexual harassment problems and correcting them.

Affirmative Action

Title VII protects all races, colors, sexes, religions and national origins, including white Anglo-Saxon Protestants. Discrimination against white males, for example, is ordinarily illegal under Title VII.

An exception has been created, however, to permit employers to grant certain preferences for certain minority groups and women. This is known as **affirmative action**. Some, but not all, affirmative action plans are legal. Courts strictly enforce the following standards.

First, there must be some demonstrated need for a voluntary affirmative action program. This may be found when a work force has statistical disparities in representation that may be the product of past discrimination. For example, suppose that a private bus company in Detroit had only 10 percent black drivers, though the city has a majority black population. This would probably be grounds for an affirmative action program.

The employer who wants to adopt a voluntary affirmative action program need not concede that it has discriminated in the past. Such a concession would open the employer to innumerable lawsuits. The employer need only demonstrate that some

---

[6]*Success*, April 1986, pp. 34-35.

group in the work force, such as women, are underrepresented in certain jobs.

Courts have also suggested that a second requirement of an affirmative action program is that it only benefit qualified individuals. Affirmative action cannot be used to grant token opportunities to unqualified individuals. Affirmative action can be used to choose among qualified applicants and not necessarily take the most qualified applicant.

Third, affirmative action cannot unduly "trammel" the rights of whites, or males, or whichever protected class does not benefit from the program. Suppose that an employer adopted a plan that said that only Hispanic women could be promoted in a given year. This would be unlawful because it denied all opportunity to other protected classes.

To be legal, an affirmative action plan must leave some opportunity for all. A program that established a training system and reserved 40 percent of the slots in the training system for Hispanics might be legal. This would leave a large number of positions for other protected classes.

Courts have been especially concerned about affirmative action plans that force layoffs of a protected class. Courts have tended to strike down plans that caused white males to lose their existing jobs. Indeed, Title VII contains a specific provision that authorizes seniority systems for layoff protection even if they have a disparate impact on minorities.

Fourth, the affirmative action program must be tailored to, and limited to, correcting the evidence of past discrimination. A plan cannot do more than correct the past statistical underrepresentation of women or a minority group. The plan also must be temporary and must cease once the underrepresentation is corrected.

The above discussion has addressed affirmative action programs adopted voluntarily by private employers. In some circumstances, a court may compel an employer to adopt an affirmative action program as part of a remedy for past discrimination.

Section 1981

While Title VII remains the primary tool to prevent discrimination in employment, other laws also protect victims of discrimination. Laws passed shortly after the Civil War prohibited some forms of racial discrimination. The key provision in these laws is known as Section 1981,[7] which prohibits discrimination in private contracts.

In some respects Section 1981 offers greater benefits to plaintiffs alleging discrimination. Damages under Title VII are quite limited to direct pecuniary losses resulting from unlawful discrimination (such as back pay awards). Section 1981 also permits a court to order damages for pain and suffering and punitive damages. Section 1981 also provides for jury trials, unlike Title VII.

Section 1981's coverage is more limited than that of Title VII. First, this section only prohibits race discrimination. Second, Section 1981 only applies to discrimination in the making of contracts and their enforcement. An important Supreme Court decision held that this section did not apply to discrimination in the terms and conditions of employment.[8] Consequently, a worker who suffers racial or sexual harassment on the job has no claim under Section 1981. Nor is it clear whether this section applies to discriminatory firing of employees.

Age Discrimination

The Age Discrimination in Employment Act ("ADEA"), closely parallels Title VII in its protections. The prima facie case for plaintiffs is similar to Title VII as are the employer's defenses. The ADEA prohibits employment discrimination based on age for anyone who is older than forty. Age discrimination against individuals less than forty years old remains lawful. Mandatory retirement is outlawed, with a few exceptions.

The ADEA applies to all employers with twenty or more employees. An exception permits mandatory retirement for employees who are in a "high policy-making position," such as a chief executive officer. The law is enforced by the EEOC, but unlike Title VII, jury trials are available in ADEA actions.

ADEA cases closely parallel Title VII in terms of types of discrimination and burdens of proof. The following decision reflects unlawful behavior by an employer.

---

[7] 42 U.S.C. section 1981.

[8] *Patterson v. McLean Credit Union*, 491 U.S. 164 (1989).

Case 4.3
Taggart v. Time Incorporated
United States Court of Appeals for the Second Circuit, 1991
Docket No. 90-7318

Background and Facts *In October 1982, Preview Subscription Television, Inc., a subsidiary of Time, Inc., hired Thomas Taggart as a print production manager. At the time, Taggart was fifty-eight years old. After Preview was dissolved, employees were notified that they would receive special consideration for other positions at Time. Taggart applied for thirty-two positions in various divisions of Time and its subsidiaries. He was turned down for all of these.*

Time said that Taggart was not hired because he was underqualified for some positions, was overqualified for other positions, he was argumentative, and received several unfavorable references. No one ever specifically mentioned his age. Taggart stated that the younger and less qualified persons were hired by Time for positions for which he interviewed. He claimed discrimination based upon his age and especially objects to his rejection for being overqualified.

Taggart filed a charge with the EEOC. After they declined to pursue the case, Taggart sued in federal district court under the ADEA. The district court granted Time's motion for summary judgment, and Taggart appealed.

CARDAMONE, Circuit Judge.

* * * *

Research has unearthed no cases when an overqualified applicant was ruled "unqualified" in the context of age discrimination litigation. Since overqualified is defined as having more education, training or experience than a job calls for, Webster's New Collegiate Dictionary 841 (9th ed. 1983), a ruling that overqualified means unqualified is a non sequitur. Thus, it is not surprising that what case law there is comes to the opposite conclusion.

The record reveals that Michele Rios-Nicosia, the hiring manager at HBO, stated that because Taggart was overqualified, she did not think the position would interest or challenge him. Ms. Rios-Nicolsia gave no other reason for not hiring Taggart. Taggart stated he was willing to take any job available simply to continue to earn a decent living, and as a Time employee with preferred status in obtaining the position, alleges he would have been hired had he not been sixty years old. Time admits that its sole reason for refusing to hire Taggart for this position was because he was overqualified. It did not cite any of Taggart's obviously pestering job search techniques as a basis for not hiring him; nor could it since Taggart's interview with Rios-Nicosia took place before all but one of these incidents occurred. If other nondiscriminatory reasons existed for refusing to hire appellant they should have been stated in Rios-Nicosia's affidavit.

Moreover, characterizing an applicant in an age discrimination case as overqualified has a connotation that defies common sense: How can a person overqualified by experience and training be turned down for a position given to a younger person deemed better qualified? Denying employment to an older job applicant because he or she has too much experience, training or education is simply to employ a euphemism to mask the real reason for refusal, namely, in the eyes of the employer the applicant is too old. See EEOC v. District of Columbia, Dept. of Human Services, 729 F. Supp. 907, 915 (D.D.C. 1990) overqualified and overspecialized are buzzwords for too old); Vaughn v. Mobil Oil Corp., 708 F. Supp. 595, 601 (S.D.N.Y. 1989) (overqualified supported employee's contention that she was capable of assuming another position).

An employer might reasonably believe that an overqualified candidate—where that term is applied to a younger person—will continue to seek employment more in keeping with his or her background and training. Yet, that rationale does not comfortably fit those in the age group the statute protects; for them loss of employment late in life ordinarily is devastating economically as well as emotionally. Instead, an older applicant that is hired is quite unlikely to continue to seek other mostly nonexistent employment opportunities.

Consequently, refusing to hire Taggart for the sole reason that he was overqualifed refutes Time's assertion that it was not discriminating on the basis of age. Taggart met the four prongs for presenting a prima facie case of age discrimination for the HBO position. This constitutes circumstances from which a reasonable juror could infer discriminatory animus on the part of Time based upon a finding that the reason proffered was pretextual and unworthy of credence.

Decision and Remedy *The court reversed the district court's grant of summary judgment and remanded the case for a trial on the merits.*

Discharging Older Workers

The most common ADEA problem involves a company that fires a group of older workers in a general reduction in force or replaces them with younger workers who may command a lower salary. This action may or may not be unlawful age discrimination. An employer cannot fire older workers simply because they have high salaries. An employer can fire older workers, however, as long as the decision is based on reasonable factors other than age.

A common ADEA problem involves corporate reductions in the labor force. Corporations may lay off a large number of workers due to an economic downturn or in order to make the company more efficient. If many of the laid-off workers are over forty, they may claim age discrimination.

These workers cannot meet the fourth requirement of the prima facie case, however, because their jobs were abolished and not left open or filled by younger workers. Some courts have therefore modified the prima facie test to require that the laid-off workers produce some evidence showing that the employer intended to discriminate based on age. This might be true if an unusually high proportion of laid-off workers were older.

The business could still state a legitimate reason for the lay-off pattern. For example, it could say that it laid off the least efficient workers. The workers would then be required to prove that this reason was a pretext.

Courts have reached different results in reduction in labor force cases. Some of the factors that courts have considered are:

- Whether the employer had and followed a specific plan for its reduction in force.

- Whether the employer followed seniority policies and considered the plan's impact on older workers.

- Whether the employer gave the fired employees' work to younger employees.

- Whether the employer used objective criteria in determining which jobs were cut.

Voluntary Retirement

Most voluntary retirement programs reflect some age discrimination. Many voluntary retirement programs commence at age sixty-five, thereby discriminating based on age. In addition, many plans provide the greatest incentive for retirement at sixty-five, with declining retirement incentives thereafter for older workers. Nevertheless, the ADEA explicitly permits certain voluntary retirement programs.

The first requirement for a voluntary retirement program is that the employer provide a legitimate business reason for structuring the plan with specific age limitations. Courts have permitted many justifications as legitimate business reasons. For example, if an employer provides a retirement incentive so as to permit replacement by younger workers with lower salaries, courts have found this to be a legitimate business reason for a voluntary retirement program.

The second requirement is that the retirement plan be truly voluntary. Employers cannot compel, or even coerce, employees to accept the retirement offer. In one important case, an employer announced a voluntary retirement program for workers who were sixty and older. The company gave these workers only five days to accept the program, though, and hinted that future layoffs were planned. After accepting the retirement program, the workers sued for age discrimination. A court held that the program was not truly voluntary, because the workers had insufficient time and information to make a free choice.[9]

▬ Americans with Disabilities Act

Restrictions on discrimination against the handicapped traditionally fell under the Rehabilitation Act of 1973, which applied to companies that contracted with or received grants from the government. In 1990, Congress passed the Americans with Disabilities Act ("ADA"), which expanded the coverage of handicapped protection to parallel that of other discrimination laws. In July 1992, the ADA takes effect for employers with twenty-five or more employees, and in July 1994, the Act applies to employers with fifteen or more employees.

The prohibitions of ADA are also similar to that of other discrimination laws. Employers are precluded from discrimination in hiring, promotions, firing and benefits. There are some differences in the ADA, however. The law prohibits employers from asking about the existence or nature of a prospective employee's disability. Under other laws, an employer may ask about a job applicant's race, sex, etc., but cannot use this information to discriminate.

The ADA presents unique problems, however. Unlike race, some handicaps will make it more difficult or impossible for workers to do the job. There is also confusion about exactly what constitutes a protected "handicap."

Definition of Handicapped

In many cases, the existence of a handicap or disability will be obvious. The ADA obviously was intended to protect individuals who are blind, deaf, or reliant on wheelchairs. What about individuals who have a disease, however, or an eating disorder?

The ADA defines the term disability as follows:

- A physical or mental impairment that substantially limits one or more of the major life activities of such an individual.

- A record of such an impairment.

- Being regarded as having such an impairment.

There is some precedent for defining protected handicapped individuals under the Rehabilitation Act. "Major life activities" include walking, seeing, performing manual tasks, and working.

One key controversy was whether an individual with a disease, such as cancer or AIDS, is protected as handicapped. Courts have held that these individuals are regarded as having an impairment and are therefore protected. An exception would exist when the disease was sufficiently contagious to threaten coworkers. Under the Rehabilitation Act, courts were divided on whether hypertension could be considered a protected disability.

Qualified Individuals

The ADA protects those disabled persons who are deemed "otherwise qualified," but for the disability. A qualified handicapped person is one who can perform the essential functions of the job with only reasonable accommodation by the employer.

This provision deals with the following situation. Suppose that Janet Lutz, confined to a wheelchair, applies for a secretarial job at Friendly Cards,

---

[9] *Paolillo v. Dresser Industries, Inc.*, 821 F.2d 81 (2d Cir. 1987).

Inc. Janet is qualified as a secretary but cannot even enter Friendly Cards' building, which has steps up to the door. Janet is not unqualified simply because she cannot enter the building. The employer could make a reasonable accommodation by providing a ramp, after which she would be qualified for the job.

To determine whether an individual is otherwise qualified, the court must determine the essential functions of the job. An accountant may occasionally need to lift heavy boxes, but this is hardly an essential function of accountancy.

A controversial case was decided under a California statute similar to the ADA. A telecommunications equipment installer suffered from asthma that was complicated by certain aspects of her job. A court found that only 12 percent of the work time was spent on the problematic activities and ruled that they were therefore not an essential function of the job.[10]

The following case illustrates a circumstance when a disabled person was deemed unable to perform the essential functions of a job. Although this was decided under the old Rehabilitation Act, the language of the ADA is the same and the result would probably be similar.

---

[10]*Ackerman v. Western Electric Company,* 643 F. Supp. 836 (N.D. Cal. 1986), aff'd, 860 F.2d 1514 (9th Cir. 1988).

Case 4.4
Chiari v. City of League City
United States Court of Appeals, Fifth Circuit, 1991
920 F.2d 311

Background and Facts *Antonio Chiari was a sixty-six-year-old professional engineer who was hired by League City as a construction inspector, which involved the approval of construction plans presented by private contractors and the inspection of their work. About 50 percent of the job involved on-site inspection, which included "climbing into ditches to inspect pipes and climbing up the structure of uncompleted buildings."*

Chiari was diagnosed with Parkinson's disease. He began having trouble walking and on one occasion fell at a construction site. He visited neurologists at the request of his supervisors. After reviewing the physician's reports, the supervisors concluded that Chiari could no longer safely be a construction inspector and sought an alternative position. They could find no such position, and Chiari was fired.

Chiari filed suit against the city, claiming discrimination. The district court dismissed Chiari's claims, and he appealed.

THORNBERRY, Circuit Judge.

* * * *

1. *Could Chiari still perform the essential functions of his job?*

The unchallenged affidavits from Murphy and Nutting demonstrate that Chiari must be able to visually inspect construction sites to perform the "essential functions" of a construction inspector's job. Chiari presented some evidence that he was still competent to make these inspections. For instance, his intellect was unaffected by the disease. Moreover, his immediate supervisor, David Hegemier, testified that Chiari's job performance was satisfactory at the time he was fired. The City's sole justification for maintaining that Chiari was not capable of doing the job was its concern that his loss of balance would endanger him and others working with him.

The regulation that defines a "qualified handicapped person" under section 504 does not explain whether a court may consider the risk which an individual's handicap may pose to himself or others; it requires only that the person be able to perform "the essential functions of the job in question." See 45 C.F.R. § 84.3(k)(1)(1989). But courts which have applied section 504 unanimously have held that a handicapped individual cannot perform the essential functions of a job if his handicap poses a significant safety risk to those around him. *See*, e.g., *School Bd. of Nassau County v. Arline,* 480 U.S. 273, 287 n. 16, 107 S.Ct. 1123, 1131 n. 16, 94 L.Ed.2d 307 (1987) (noting that "[a] person who poses a significant risk of communicating an infectious disease to others in the workplace will not be otherwise qualified for his or her job if reasonable accommodation will not eliminate the risk"); *Bentivegna v. United States Dep't of Labor*, 694 F.2d 619, 622 (9th Cir. 1982) (holding that a job qualification can exclude handicapped individuals if the qualification substantially promotes safe performance). To support its assertion that Chiari's presence would endanger others, the City presented affidavits from two neuro-surgeons, Dr. Sinha and Dr. Borne, who stated that Chiari's unsteady "shuffling gait" and muscle rigidity, which caused him to lose his balance, prevented him from performing the job of construction inspector safely.

Chiari maintains that, despite the testimony of the three physicians, a jury still could find that he is capable of performing his job without endangering others. He contends, and the City concedes, that he has never fallen on anyone or injured anyone in the past. The risk, he stated, is not that he will hurt others but that he will hurt himself, and he argues that this court cannot consider the risk of personal injury to the handicapped individual as one of the factors in determining whether that individual is qualified to do a job. We disagree.

* * * *

Similarly, a significant risk of personal injury can disqualify a handicapped individual from a job if the employer cannot eliminate the risk. In regulations supplementing section 501 of the Rehabilitation Act, 29 U.S.C.A § 791 (West Supp. 1990), the Equal Employment Opportunity Commission defines a "qualified handicapped person" as one who "can perform the essential functions of the position in question without endangering the health and safety *of the individual or others*..." See 29 C.F.R. § 1613.702(f) (1990) (emphasis added). Section 501 refers to the duty of federal, rather than federally funded, employers to accommodate the handicapped, but it imposes a greater burden on the employer than section 504 does: federal employers must take affirmative action toward applicants and employees with handicaps. *See* 29 U.S.C.A. § 791(b). In *Mantolete v. Bolger*, 767 F.2d 1416, 1422 (9th Cir.1985), the court applied section 501 and held that the Postal Service could prohibit an applicant with epilepsy from operating a letter sorting machine if the Postal Service could show a reasonable probability that the applicant could suffer substantial injury.

Decision and Remedy *The court affirmed the district court's dismissal of Chiari's action.*

Reasonable Accommodation

The most significant and controversial provision of the ADA is the obligation on employers to make reasonable accommodations for otherwise handicapped individuals. Testimony before Congress indicated that most accommodations would be inexpensive (about $50), but the law may require employers to undertake more expensive accommodations.

The law itself suggests some examples of accommodations that would be considered reasonable and therefore required. These include making facilities physically accessible, job restructuring through modified-time work schedules, acquisition of equipment or devices, and the provision of readers and interpreters.

The reasonability of accommodations also will vary with the type of business. The law states that courts should consider the overall size of the business and its type of operation in deciding reasonableness.

Perhaps the most difficult issue in reasonable accommodation is the need to hire assistants for some individuals with disabilities. For example, a visually impaired person may be able to perform most office work but may require a person to read memoranda and other papers.

The employer need not hire an assistant who will essentially perform the job of the handicapped individual. For example, a supermarket need not hire someone to operate a cash register so that a visually impaired person could work a check-out stand.

In the case of the office worker, however, the reader would not do the job of the worker and would be much less expensive to hire. The reasonability of this accommodation may depend centrally upon the size of the employer's business and the ability to afford such an accommodation.

Operation and Enforcement

Once the above coverage issues are addressed, the ADA will function much like Title VII or the ADEA. The theories of discrimination developed under Title VII, including disparate treatment and disparate impact discrimination, will apply under the ADA.

The enforcement of the ADA also mirrors Title VII, in the procedures of filing a charge with the EEOC, investigation, and either EEOC or private action against the employer. Remedies of the ADA also parallel those of other antidiscrimination laws.

Arbitration of Antidiscrimination Claims

As antidiscrimination claims have grown in frequency and available damages have grown, employers have sought to avoid the risks of litigation. In consequence, some companies have placed compulsory arbitration clauses in employment contracts. Employees thereby gave up their right to sue for illegal discrimination and are required to take disputes to arbitration. Some clauses apply to all discrimination issues, and arbitration requirements are particularly common for sexual harassment claims.

The EEOC has opposed the requirement to arbitrate antidiscrimination claims, but courts generally have upheld the clauses, at least in theory. In practice, a court may refuse to give effect to an arbitration clause if the worker was not fully informed of its implications. The employee must have made a "knowing waiver" of the right to sue. Courts will also refuse to enforce clauses that take away substantive rights from workers, such as the right to recover punitive damages in appropriate cases.

In an example of an effective arbitration clause, Michele Peacock agreed to work for Great Western Mortgage Corporation, and the company required her to certify on her job application that she understood the company's arbitration requirement. After she accepted a job, the company had her sign another arbitration agreement. Peacock subsequently filed a sexual harassment complaint, which the company believed to be unfounded. After she filed suit, the company successfully had the case dismissed, because she was contractually required to arbitrate the dispute.[11]

---

[11] *Great Western Mortgage Corporation v. Peacock,* Civil Action No. 96-0628 (D.N.J. 1996).

Ethical Perspectives

Ethics and Comparable Worth

Ethics is central to employment discrimination law. Title VII exists because our society considers discrimination to be unethical. When, if ever, should employers go beyond Title VII to fight discrimination?

One controversial example is the "comparable worth" controversy. Some jobs in our society have traditionally been held by women (nurse, secretary, elementary school teacher, etc.), while other jobs have traditionally been held by men (mechanic, construction worker, etc.). The traditionally male jobs historically have paid higher wages than the traditionally female occupations.

One frequently hears the statistic that the average working woman makes only 65 cents for every dollar made by the average working man. This is not primarily because woman mechanics, say, are paid less than male mechanics. It is primarily because mechanics (most of whom are male) make more than secretaries (most of whom are female).

Some argue that these disparities among jobs are unethical because they resulted from and continue to perpetuate stereotypes about males being "breadwinners" and needing higher pay to support a family. They argue that wage rates in these jobs should be modified to reflect the relative value of these jobs to society. This is called **comparable worth compensation**.

While it may seem ethical to pay individuals based on their "worth" or value to society, this approach raises serious problems. What kind of worth should we compensate? Moral worth? How does one compare the moral worth of a mechanic and a secretary? Perhaps most important, who should be given the authority to decide questions of moral worth?

A free enterprise society does not even try to base wage compensation on the relative moral worth of occupations. Under the market a job is worth whatever someone will pay to have it done. This is said to allocate labor efficiently, because the jobs that are in most demand by prospective employers will offer the highest wages and will thereby draw the necessary employees.

This does not mean that the free market is necessarily immoral. By promoting economic efficiency, it can maximize the wealth of the entire society and indirectly benefit everyone. Also, many individuals who take especially "moral" occupations (e.g., charitable work) do so for compensation other than monetary.

To the extent that the free market allocates wages based on sexism, however, it increases inefficiency as well as being ethically dubious. The main problem with comparable worth is designing a solution to this problem. Most people do not want government assigning wage rates for occupations. One must always make sure that the cure is not worse than the disease.

International Perspectives

International Prohibitions on Employment Discrimination

Many millions of individuals work in countries other than their nation of citizenship. It is estimated that over one million Americans work in foreign countries. Many of these U.S. citizens work for branches of U.S. companies operating abroad. To what extent are these individuals protected from discrimination by Title VII or other international prohibitions on employment discrimination?

In one leading case, the Fifth Circuit Court of Appeals held that Title VII did not protect a U.S. citizen who was working for a foreign subsidiary of an oil company incorporated in the United States. Other cases, however, have held that Title VII does have some extraterritorial application, and the EEOC guidelines call for use of Title VII in cases of U.S. employees working for U.S. firms in foreign countries. The Supreme Court recently held that Title VII does not necessarily apply to protect U.S. employees working overseas for U.S. companies.[12]

Even this Supreme Court decision does not answer all questions about overseas discrimination, however. Such discrimination is clearly legal if the laws of a foreign nation compel such discrimination (e.g., a law stating that only members of certain religions may work in certain holy sites). Such discrimination is likely to be illegal if the discriminatory actions were taken in the United States.

Even if Title VII does not apply, foreign workers may receive some protection from discrimination. The International Labour Organization Employment Policy Convention prohibits discrimination based on "race, color, sex, religion, political opinion, national extraction or social origin." This convention lacks enforcement authority, however, unless it is implemented by the laws of member states.

The European Community (EC), an enormous market, has taken steps to implement prohibitions on employment discrimination. In some respects, the EC provisions go beyond Title VII. The EC Treaty prohibits discrimination based on worker nationality or sex but does not prohibit religious discrimination. These provisions are not merely declaratory but impose a duty on the courts of individual nations to prevent discrimination. Individuals suffering prohibited discrimination may sue for compensation.

---

[12] *EEOC v. Arabian American Oil Co.*, 111 S.Ct. 1227 (1991).

Questions and Case Problems

1. Marietta Conner was a bus driver for Fort Gordon Bus Company. She made an illegal left turn when the owner of the bus company happened to be behind her bus. The company had recently paid a $35,000 damage judgment after another driver made an illegal left turn. The owner rushed into the bus terminal and asked who was driving the bus. After discovering it was Conner, he fired her. Conner claimed employment discrimination, because male drivers had not been fired for traffic violations, because the company policy did not clearly state that this was a reason for discharge, and because the owner did not discharge the driver until after he discovered her name and sex. Was Conner's firing unlawfully discriminatory? [*Conner v. Fort Gordon Bus Co.*, 761 F.2d 1495 (11th Cir. 1985)].

2. Cash & Thomas was a pipe-laying firm owned by Jack Thomas. His son, Steve, was employed as a supervisor and was married to Savonda. Jeri Platner was a secretary with the firm. After a time, Savonda began to suspect that Steve was having an affair with Platner and became extremely jealous. Platner dressed and behaved appropriately, but Steve may have fueled Savonda's jealousy by flirting with Platner. Savonda became increasingly upset and her marriage to Steve became jeopardized. Out of concern for his son's marriage, Jack Thomas fired Platner and replaced her with a male employee. She sued the company for employment discrimination. Should Ms. Platner succeed in this action? [*Platner v. Cash & Thomas Contractors, Inc.*, 908 F.2d 902 (11th Cir. 1990)].

3. The owners of a small, closely held corporation made a covenant with God that their business would be a "Christian, faith-oriented business." The company held a devotional service once a week during work hours and required all employees to attend. An employee who was an atheist sought to be excused from the service. The company refused to excuse the employee but told him that he could wear earplugs and read a book or sleep during the service. He still objected and sued for religious discrimination under Title VII. The employer argued that it was simply exercising its own freedom of religion. Should the worker succeed with his discrimination claim? [*Equal Employment Opportunity Commission v. Townley Engineering & Manufacturing Co.*, No. 89-2272 (9th Cir. 1988)].

4. A job applicant placed high enough on a civil service test to be chosen as a clerk but was rejected because of his "heavy Filipino accent." The job involved dealing with 200 to 300 disgruntled people per day regarding their problems with various city services. The job description required that the applicant be able to "deal tactfully and effectively with the public." The city claimed that the accent precluded the applicant, but he claimed that he was subjected to unlawful national origin discrimination. Should the job applicant succeed in a job discrimination claim? (*Fragrante v. City and County of Honolulu*, No. 87-2921 (9th Cir. 1989)].

5. RIA sells publications for tax specialists. Simms Normand, who was hired at age fifty, worked nine years for RIA but then was forced to resign. His sales performance had been excellent for the first seven to eight years but began to decline significantly, and he also missed sales meetings. A supervisor told Normand that he was suffering from the "old salesman burnout syndrome" and suggested that he resign to avoid being fired. On other occasions, RIA workers were referred to as "old geezers" or "old buzzards." Normand resigned, and RIA soon hired a thirty-one-year-old worker for his position. Normand sued and claimed illegal age discrimination by RIA. A jury ruled for Normand and found RIA's action to be willful, enabling him to receive extra damages. The trial court reversed the jury verdict. Normand appealed this reversal. Should an appellate court uphold the trial court decision or reverse and provide Normand with his damages in the jury verdict? [*Normand v. Research Institute of America, Inc.*, 927 F.2d 857 (5th Cir. 1991)].

CHAPTER FIVE

Occupational Safety and Workers' Compensation

KEY BACKGROUND

The essential background for this chapter on occupational safety and worker's compensation is found in Chapter 35 of *West's Business Law, Seventh Edition,* and in Chapter 20 of *West's Legal Environment of Business, Third Edition.* These chapters cover employment and labor relations law. Among the important points to remember from this chapter are:

- the powers of the Occupational Safety and Health Administration
- the requirements for compliance and enforcement of occupational safety regulation.
- the basic rules for coverage and recovery under state workers' compensation statutes.

* * *

Each year, thousands of Americans die because of risks found in their workplace. Every eighteen seconds, an employee is injured on the job. A recent study estimated that, in addition to this human tragedy, occupational injury and death costs the nation over $50 billion per year.

The law has responded to this risk in two different manners. First, the law creates occupational safety and health standards to prevent the risks whenever feasible. Second, the law provides a special compensation system for workers who are harmed on the job. This chapter addresses the two approaches in sequence.

Occupational Safety Standards

The most prominent occupational safety standards are set by the Occupational Safety and Health Administration, known as OSHA, and administratively located within the Department of Labor. OSHA was created and empowered by the Occupational Safety and Health Act of 1970 (the "OSH Act"). The OSH Act has very broad coverage, applying to all companies with employees. A few job categories are exempted from the Act (e.g., agricultural workers, professionals, household domestics).

OSHA has adopted many detailed standards that can be quite expensive to obey. In addition, OSHA has created more generalized, nonspecific standards and duties for employers.

General Duty Clause

The Occupational Safety and Health Act requires that each employer furnish a workplace free from recognized hazards that are likely to cause death or serious physical harm to employees. This duty is above and beyond any specific OSHA standards. The **general duty clause** is violated when (1) a recognized hazard is present, that (2) is likely to cause death or serious physical harm, and that (3) could feasibly be remedied.

The key provision in the general duty clause is that the hazard must be a "recognized" one. Recognized means that the hazard is known or foreseeable by the employer. An employer will be liable under this clause if the industry in general recognized a hazard, but the particular employer was unaware of it. Conversely, the employer also will be liable if the employer was aware of the hazard, even if the industry in general was unaware of it.

Nevertheless, some hazards are not recognized and do not subject an employer to liability under the general duty clause. For example, one court held that an employer could not anticipate that an employee would use a cigarette lighter in examining a propane tank for leaks.[1]

If a recognized workplace hazard exists, the employer must take the maximum feasible protective measures for employees. The employer is not expected to eliminate all risk and guarantee safety, however. One court noted that "demented, suicidal, or willfully reckless employee may on occasion circumvent the best conceived and most vigorously enforced safety regime."[2] this is known as the **unpreventable employee misconduct defense**.

The mere existence of employee negligence, however, is not a defense to violations of the general duty clause. The employer has some responsibility to prevent employee risk-taking, as illustrated in the following case.

---

[1] *William R. Davis & Son, Co.,* 6 O.S.H.C. (ALJ 1978).

[2] *National Reality and Construction Co., Inc. v. OSHRC,* 489 F.2d 1257, 1266 (D.C. Cir. 1973).

Case 5.1
CMI South, Inc. v. Occupational Safety and Health Review Commission
Administrative Law Judge, 1990
OSHRC Docket No. 89-1600

Background and Facts *CMI South, Inc., operates a foundry in Alabama. Early one morning, the foundry began to experience a problem with its sand system, which feeds sand from a 200-ton capacity tank onto a conveyer/feeder and on into the plant. Workers speculated that the sand had become wet, which prevented it from flowing as it should. Employees and supervisors gathered and sought to loosen the sand by beating on the outside of the tank, a method that had worked before. After this failed, two employees opened an inspection plate located over the conveyor and crawled inside. Two workers began to loosen the sand with a shovel, and the sand fell fast, burying and killing one employee.*

CMI was cited for a violation of the general duty clause. CMI contested the citation, the secretary of labor prepared a complaint, and the case was tried before an OSHRC administrative law judge.

BRADY, Administrative Law Judge.

* * * *

CMI contends that the record establishes that, since the plant opened in 1977, no one knew of any person who had entered the tank from the bottom (Tr. 25, 63). There was no known reason for anyone to enter the tank, because there was no machinery or other mechanical devices that required maintenance inside the tank.

CMI's argument does not refute the evidence that entry into the tank was a recognized hazard. CMI argues that it is not a hazard to enter the tank, because everyone knows how dangerous it is. This is circuitous. "Recognition of the hazard can be inferred from the obvious nature of the hazard." Litton Systems, Inc., Ingalls Shipbuilding Division, 81 OSHRC 101/C12, 10 BNA OSHC 1179, 1182, 1981 CCH OSHD P25, 817 (No. 76-900, 1981). In the present case, entry into the bottom of a 200-ton capacity tank to unclog sand in a system that depends on gravity to move the sand is such an obvious hazard that recognition of the hazard is implied.

CMI's second point, that the hazard was not likely to cause death or serious physical harm, is actually an unpreventable employee misconduct defense. CMI states, "The incident that resulted in the death of Leonard Royster was a freak accident. Mr. Royster as the Acting Plant Manager, did something which no reasonably sane person would do—he entered the bottom of a tank containing at least 150 tons of sand over his head and began to dig into the sand, hoping to cause it to fall onto him" (CMI brief, p. 8). CMI is correct in asserting that Royster's behavior is inexplicable.

Hazardous conduct is not preventable if it is so idiosyncratic and implausible in motive or means that conscientious experts, familiar with the industry, would not take it into account in prescribing a safety program. Nor is misconduct preventable if its elimination would require methods of hiring, training, monitoring, or sanctioning workers which are either so untested or so expensive that safety experts would substantially concur in thinking the means infeasible. National Realty and Construction Co., 489 F.2d 1257 (D.C. Cir. 1973).

CMI would perhaps prevail on this argument if the record established that one or two defiant employees had entered the tank without supervision, or even if Royster, as plant manager, had entered the tank unseen, or over the protestations of the other supervisory personnel present. That, however, is not the case. Three supervisors were present at the tank. The supervisor in charge of the entire plant at the time, Royster, was the person who ordered entry into the tank. Another supervisor, Phillips, immediately went into the tank. A third supervisor, Tate, stood by without protest while this occurred. Such conduct by the supervising personnel cannot be excused as idiosyncratic and implausible.

This conduct can also not be explained as a coincidental lapse in the minds of all present as to the danger involved. One man, Earl Hughes (a maintenance employee who should not be expected to be more concerned with safety than his supervisors), did speak up and warn the others not to enter the tank. He was told to shut up by the ranking supervisor. As soon as Phillips and Royster entered the tank, Hughes left to get some rope and two shovels. When asked why, Hughes replied that, in the likely event that the sand would fall, "we would have something to dig them out with and the rope, I was going to tie around his feet" (Tr. 55).

CMI argues that Royster did something "which no reasonably same person would do," but he was joined in this action by Phillips, and the action was condoned by Tate, both of whom are presumably sane. Under these circumstances, unpreventable employee misconduct cannot be established.

Decision and Remedy *The administrative law judge affirmed the citation and imposed a $1000 penalty on CMI.*

OSHA has begun to make greater use of the general duty clause, especially when employers of all types have exposed their workers to toxic substances. For example, OSHA has cited several hospitals and clinics for overexposure of female workers to nitrous oxide, based on citations in scientific literature linking such overexposure to miscarriages and birth defects.

Special Duty Clause

OSHA has adopted many precise standards to protect against specific hazards in certain types of workplaces. These regulations typically involve detailed specifications for employers. Compliance with these standards is under the **special duty clause**.

For example, one traditional source of injury was the mechanical power press, a large machine that produced molded plastic products, among other things. Workers would inadvertently get a hand or a limb inside the press, which would then crush the appendage if the machine was turned on. OSHA adopted safety regulations for mechanical power presses that fill many pages of small print.

If the press is operated by foot pedals, OSHA has a number of requirements, including the type of spring on the pedal and a proper nonslip surface. Some machines require that two hands must be on external levers to activate operations, thereby assuring that one of the operator's hands is not caught in the machine. Another provision states in part:

> (c) Safeguarding the point of operation—(i) it shall be the responsibility of the employer to provide and insure the usage of "point of operation guards" or properly applied and adjusted point of operation devices on every operation performed on a mechanical power press ...
>
> (3) Point of operation devices. (i) Point of operation devices shall protect the operator by:
>
> (a) Preventing and/or stopping normal stroking of the press if the operator's hands are inadvertently placed in the point of operation; or
>
> (b) Preventing the operator from inadvertently reaching into the point of operation, or withdrawing his hands if they are inadvertently located in the point of operation, as the dies close ...[3]

This rule goes on with many more details. The guards required to comply with all provisions of the above rule had a cost of thousands of dollars per machine.

OSHA rules historically focused on industrial workplaces and violent physical accidents. Recent OSHA regulations have shifted to the white collar workplace. Major new proposed rules include standards for indoor air quality in office buildings, cumulative trauma disorders from repetitive motions including computer use, and workplace smoking restrictions. In the future, OSHA compliance issues will not be limited to manufacturing but will increasingly concern lawyers, accountants and other white collar workers.

An employer may apply to the Secretary of Labor to grant a *variance* from a specific OSHA standard. An employer can get a permanent variance if it can show that its practices are "as safe and healthful" as those prescribed in the standard. For example, OSHA has a standard requiring that fire extinguishers be mounted at a specified height above the floor. OSHA provided a variance for an employer whose fire extinguishers were mounted on retractable boards hung from the ceiling and which were just as accessible as under the agency standard. If OSHA grants such a variance, it will usually attach numerous terms and conditions.

OSHA will also grant a temporary variance when an employer can show an inability to comply by the regulation's deadline. This requires a strong showing that material, equipment, or technical personnel are unavailable or a showing that necessary construction or modification of facilities cannot be completed in time.

Employers are expected to be aware of and comply with all OSHA regulations that are relevant to their workplace unless they have obtained a variance. The company must comply with the regulation precisely; the employer's absence of workplace injuries is no defense.

Unfortunately, many OSHA standards are less than specific. This makes the assurance of compliance more difficult and also may provide employers with a defense, as demonstrated in the following decision.

---

[3] 29 C.F.R. Sec. 1910.217 (1990).

Case 5.2
Spancrete Northeast, Inc. v. Occupational Safety and Health Review Commission
United States Court of Appeals
Second Circuit, 1990
905 F.2d 589

Background and Facts *Spancrete Northeast, Inc. was installing precast concrete slabs and grouting the keyways between the slabs in the second floor of a building under construction. Leonard Drew, an OSHA inspector, visited the site and issued a citation to Spancrete. The citation was for violation of a section requiring a "standard railing or the equivalent" on all platforms that are six feet or more above ground level. The proposed penalty was $200. Spancrete contested the citation.*

At a hearing before an administrative law judge ("ALJ"), Spancrete convinced the judge that a railing was unnecessary and would have been difficult to construct. The ALJ did, however, accept Drew's contention that Spancrete should have provided safety belts for workers, with lanyards connecting the belts to wires from the perimeter steel posts. Safety belts could be required under a different OSHA rule that requires the use of "appropriate" personal protective equipment when hazards exist. The ALJ apparently accepted this contention and imposed liability on Spancrete. Spancrete then petitioned for review in federal court.

VAN GRAAFEILAND, Circuit Judge.

* * * *

During the hearing that followed service of Spancrete's answer, the Secretary produced only one witness, Inspector Drew. Drew proved to have a very limited knowledge of general grouting procedures. he had no prior experience with precast concrete and had only inspected one precast construction job prior to Spancrete's. He did not observe Spancrete's employees while they were grouting, and his testimony concerning the grouting and the construction environment in which it was performed was sparse and in some respects erroneous. The exhibits and testimony introduced by Spancrete, none of which is contradicted, illustrate this very well.

* * * *

Spancrete's other witness, Morgan Wildey, was Spancrete's erection foreman. Wildey testified that he had been employed by Spancrete for twenty-two years, that he had not erected a perimeter guard in all that time, and that no one ever had fallen off a building. In his opinion, there was no danger of this occurring.

* * * *

Mr. Drew, the Secretary's sole witness, lacked the experience to testify as an expert on the grouting of precast concrete and could not speak to the customary practices in the industry. He had inspected only one other precast concrete job, and he had never seen any precast erectors wearing safety belts while grouting. He at no time observed Spancrete's employees in the process of grouting. Under 29 C.F.R. § 1926.104(b) provides that lifelines for safety belts "shall be secured above the point of operation to an anchorage or structural member capable of supporting a minimum dead weight of 5,400 pounds." The ALJ made no finding as to how or where the lifelines could be attached in the instant case, and it may be assumed that he adopted Drew's suggestion that the lifelines could be cables strung between the posts that Drew mistakenly believed were near the floor's perimeter. Not only were the posts in question not near the floor's perimeter and thus "above the point of operation," wires connecting them would not be universally parallel to the perimeter of the octagon-shaped core building. In some cases, the outer edge of the floor would run at an angle of 40-45 degrees to the proposed safety cable. Assuming that the existing posts would not be suitable as anchorages, there was no evidence whatever concerning whether other structural members capable of supporting a dead weight of 5,400 pounds could be attached to the precast concrete slabs for the short period of time that perimeter grouting was going on without causing permanent damage to the slabs. This was a matter of particular significance with suspect to the use of safety belts in Wing C where there were no upright posts.

Mr. Wildey, Spancrete's foreman, testified that the use of safety belts would create a hazard of tripping or falling. The ALJ dismissed this testimony as speculation, since Mr. Wildey never had used safety belts while grouting. Having rejected Wildey's testimony as speculative, the ALJ proceeded to speculate on his own to the effect that the use of safety belts would not rise to the level of a greater hazard, an opinion that is not shared universally. See *Ray Evers Welding Co. v. OSHRC, supra,* 625 F.2d at 732-33; *Eagle Sheet Metal, Inc.,* 1979 O.S.H.D. 23,598 (May 1, 1979); *Crouch-Walker Corp.,* 1979 O.S.H.D. 23,227 (November 9, 1978). "Reasonableness is an objective test with must be determined on the basis of evidence in the record." *Ray Evers Welding Co. v. OSHRC, supra,* 625 F.2d at 732. The ALJ's findings should be based on testimony from knowledgeable witnesses experienced in the technical area involved, not upon the ALJ's subjective feelings unsupported by the record.

Decision and Remedy   *The court vacated the citation and penalty against Spancrete.*

Employer Responsibility

Employers cannot satisfy their OSHA obligations simply by making structural changes and installing equipment demanded by the agency. Rather, the employer has the duty of oversight in the workplace.

Employers generally must provide safety training to their workers under the general duty clause, and some specific standards require that employees demonstrate a level of competence before they are permitted to use certain equipment.

An employer sometimes will be liable for unsafe conditions or accidents that resulted from the carelessness of their employees. This is especially true when the risk was foreseeable and preventable or when the risk could have been avoided with better training programs. For example, in one case, an employer instructed employees to keep certain safety doors closed. The employer generally ignored this requirement, and the employer was aware of this fact. The employer was penalized because nothing was done to enforce the safety rules.[4]

Employers are not guarantors of safety. They do have a duty to supervise reasonably but are not expected to anticipate and prevent all accidents. OSHA sought enforcement against one employer after a worker was crushed to death between a logging truck and a crane loading logs onto the bed of the truck. The employer was not liable because it could not be expected to provide constant one-on-one supervision.[5] Less supervision is required if workers are experienced and have good safety records.

---

[4] *Whaley Engineering Corp.,* 8 O.S.H.C. 1644 (1980).

[5] *Hansen Brothers Logging,* 1 O.S.H.C. 1060 (1972).

Inspections and Citations

To ensure compliance with the above clauses, OSHA conducts periodic, unannounced inspections of worksites. OSHA can only inspect about two percent of covered worksites in any given year. Consequently, inspection resources are prioritized to focus on industries and plants with a poor safety record. OSHA also focuses on sites where there have been employee complaints of hazards.

The OSHA inspector is usually prohibited by law from giving any advance warning of the inspection to the employer. Strictly speaking, OSHA requires a search warrant for nonemergency inspections of a plant. These warrants are very easy for OSHA to obtain, and most employers do not insist upon a warrant but consent to an inspection without a warrant.

OSHA inspections follow a fairly standard procedure. The inspector begins by presenting his or her credentials. The OSHA representative has the right to inspect throughout the worksite and to interview workers about potential hazardous conditions.

The law provides "walkaround" rights both to the employer and to employees. This means that each may provide a representative to accompany the inspector on the tour throughout the plant. The employer representative may help the inspector interpret plant conditions and explain why they are legal. The employee representative may help ensure that the inspector does not overlook safety violations.

If the inspection reveals a violation of the law, the Act requires that the inspector issue a written citation to the employer that describes the violation with particularity. This must be done within six months and is generally done while the inspector is still at the worksite.

An OSHA citation will be accompanied with a notice of the proposed penalty. The citation will also contain an abatement period, a time during which the employer must correct the hazard or risk further penalties. An employer may accept the proposed penalty or contest it. In order to challenge the citation and penalty, the employer must file a notice of contest within fifteen working days of receipt of the citation.

After a notice of contest is filed, the government has twenty working days in which to file a complaint against the employer. The complaint sets forth the alleged violations and the standards violated (e.g., general duty or specific duty under standards).

The dispute is tried before an administrative law judge of the Occupational Safety and Health Review Commission ("OSHRC"). OSHA has the burden of proof in this hearing but may rely on circumstantial evidence. The judge's decision may be appealed to the full OSHRC and then to federal court.

Penalties

Penalties under the OSH Act can be quite strict but vary considerably. The amount of penalty depends on the gravity of the violation. OSHA may assess a penalty of up to $1000 for a nonserious violation and must assess a penalty of $1000 for each serious violation.

A serious occupational safety and health violation is one that creates a risk of death or serious physical harm. Nonserious violations vary and some are so trivial as to receive no penalty. An employer violated a standard requiring the availability of a waste receptacle for paper cups at a water cooler but received no penalty.[6] The average penalty for nonserious violations in 1988 was less than $2 per violation.

Penalties are especially strict for willful or repeated violations of the Act. Under recent amendments, employers can be fined up to $70,000 for each willful or repeated violation. This amount is per violation, and USX Corporation was recently fined $7.3 million for violating the OSH Act.

The law also provides for criminal penalties in certain circumstances. A crime is committed if a willful violation causes the death of an employee or if false statements are knowingly made in a required report. Penalties for these crimes include up to six months in prison. Criminal prosecutions have been few, however, and only one person has been convicted and incarcerated for a violation of the Occupational Safety and Health Act.

Employers have long complained of the stringency of OSHA enforcement. A 1996 opinion offered some relief. OSHA cited and fined a company whose worker was once seen using a jackhammer without safety glasses or steel-toed shoes. The employer won on appeal, as the court said that

---

[6] *R.H. Bishop Co.*, 1 O.S.H.C. 1767 (1974).

OSHA was placing an unreasonable burden on companies and that the Act did not require safety measures beyond those just and reasonable.[7]

Workers' Compensation

Under traditional common law principles, an employee injured on the job could sue the employer under a theory such as negligence. Negligence was difficult to prove, however, and the worker lawsuits took considerable court time and expense. By the early twentieth century, virtually all states had adopted a workers' compensation system to supplant the traditional common law approach.

The workers' compensation system was adopted by state legislatures but was presented as a bargain between employer and employee. The employer gave up common law defenses and virtually guaranteed compensation for work-related injuries of the employee. In return, the employee accepted a lower compensation level and gave up the right to sue in court for additional damages.

The workers' compensation system has generally worked well but is beginning to show serious deficiencies. For many workers the recoveries for certain injuries seem insufficient. For employers, the costs of the system doubled between 1985 and 1990 and reached $60 billion per year.

Covered Employees

The workers' compensation systems of the various states are limited to employees and do not attempt to cover independent contractors. The key defining differences between employees and independent contractors are described in Chapter 35 of *West's Business Law, Seventh Edition.*

Nor do the workers' compensation laws cover all employees. Very small businesses are not covered, though the typical state law will cover employers that have three or more employees. In most states, agricultural and farm workers are excluded from coverage. Domestic employees are also excluded. Coverage of professionals varies. Nurses, for example, are generally covered by workers' compensation acts.

Administration

A common feature of state workers' compensation systems is the establishment of a nonjudicial system to administer the statute. A government commission establishes the rules and compensates workers.

The workers' compensation system is invoked when an employee informs the employer that an injury has been suffered. This notice must be given promptly to facilitate effective medical treatment and help in the determination of the injury's cause. States have varying statutes of limitations for the filing of workers' compensation claims.

After notice is filed, many statutes have waiting periods applicable to disability claims. This is to permit the full extent of the injury to be discovered and to encourage the employee's prompt return to the work force.

If the employer disputes liability under workers' compensation, the states provide for an administrative hearing. These hearings are somewhat like a court trial but generally are less formal. For example, hearsay evidence is readily admitted in workers' compensation administrative hearings.

Covered Injuries

The determination of the injuries to be covered by workers' compensation is one of the most controversial issues in this area of law. The standard legal test in most state laws is that of a "personal injury by accident arising out of and in the course of employment."

Many cases have disputed the "arising out of" requirement of workers' compensation coverage. Workers' compensation was originally designed to address the more traditional sources of workplace accidents. Suppose that Joseph Abboud is working on a mechanical power press. He attempts to clear some loose plastic out of the press when it engages and crushes his hand. Workers' compensation will clearly cover this accident.

Modern circumstances have presented nontraditional sources of workplace injuries, however. Suppose that Mr. Abboud is working late one night. While leaving the plant after hours he is mugged and seriously injured. Should this be considered an accident "arising our of" his employment?

Under traditional law, Joseph Abboud's mugging would not be covered, because it would be considered a "common risk." Nonworkers face the risk of mugging just as do workers, so this risk was not peculiar to his employment.

---

[7] *New York State Electric & Gas Corporation v. Sec'y of Labor,* 88 F.3d 98 (2d Cir. 1996).

Modern doctrines are broader, however, and might permit Abboud to recover medical expenses related to his injuries under workers' compensation. Some courts use a **doctrine of increased risk**. If the employment subjects the worker to an increased risk of a certain type of harm, the employee is covered. Abboud could contend that the necessity of his working late in a certain part of town subjected him to such an increased risk of mugging.

Other state courts have adopted an even broader view, known as the **doctrine of positional risk**. This doctrine permits recovery if the injury resulted because the employment placed the worker in the particular position resulting in injury. In a well-known early case, an employee recovered under workers' compensation when he was struck by an arrow fired by a youth outside the work site.[8]

A worker will not be covered if the source of the injury is personal and not work related. In one unusual case, a school janitor noticed a child near his automobile and, fearing vandalism, spanked the child and sent him home. The child's grandmother then approached the janitor on the school premises and shot and killed him. A court said the death was not covered under workers' compensation because it arose out of the janitor's non-work actions.[9]

Courts have construed this personal animosity exception narrowly, however. If an injury is connected to the job duties of the worker, coverage will be applied, as demonstrated in the following decision.

---

[8] *Gargiulo v. Gargiulo*, 95 A.2d 646 (N.J. 1953).

[9] *Porter v. Dallas Independent School District*, 759 S.W. 2d 454 (Tex. App. 1988).

Case 5.3
Security Insurance Co. v. Nasser
Court of Appeals of Texas
Fourteenth District, 1988
755 S.W.2d 186

Background and Facts Izzat Nasser was the manager of a Hamburgers by Gourmet outlet. He became acquainted with Marianne Dawes, who worked nearby and visited the restaurant two or three times a day. Nasser and Dawes would sit and talk at the restaurant. "Although [Nassar] and Dawes did go out on one date, they both claimed that there was no romantic involvement between them." Dawes explained that she had a boyfriend, Victor Daryoush, who had suffered a head injury and had been diagnosed as psychotic and schizophrenic.

Daryoush came to Nasser's restaurant and asked to see him. Nasser suspected trouble and told Daryoush he was busy talking to his girlfriend. Some time later, Nassar was leaving his office, and Daryoush attacked him with a knife. Nasser sought coverage of his injuries under workers' compensation.

At the initial trial, the court granted summary judgment for the workers' compensation insurance agency and against Nasser under the **personal animosity exception**. This ruling was reversed by the state supreme court and the case was remanded. On remand a jury rendered a verdict for Nasser. The insurance company appealed this verdict.

DRAUGHN, Judge.

* * * *

The Supreme Court's holding that the injury in this case was incidental to some duty of Nasser's employment and, thereby, precluded the personal animosity exception, merits further explanation. The court, in reaching its conclusion, reasoned that it was part of Nasser's job to talk with and be nice to customers; as a result of performing this aspect of his job, he was stabbed. The court also held that whenever conditions attached to the place of employment are factors in the catastrophic combination, the consequent injury arises out of the employment. 724 S.W.2d at 19. The Court cited as primary support for this holding *Garcia v. Texas Indem.,* 146 Tex. 413, 209 S.W.2d 333, 336 (1948).

Garcia involved a worker, who because of a pre-existing physical condition, epilepsy, fell against a sharp-edged physical object that was a fixed part of his workplace. (For an analogous comparison of such so-called "idiopathic-fall" cases, see A. Larson, The Law of Workman's Compensation, @12.14(b) (1982).) The Supreme Court similarly concluded that the dispute, if any, between Nasser and Daryoush "arouse in the workplace, or was exacerbated by, or in the very least, was incidental to a duty" of Nasser's employment. Id.

This conclusion is apparently based to a large degree on the Court's earlier finding that had it not been for Dawes' visits to the restaurant as a customer, Daryoush would never have seen Nasser talking to her. However, we find no evidence in the record that Daryoush ever saw Dawes talking to Nasser at the restaurant. There is testimony that Nasser and Dawes dated on one occasion away from the restaurant. We assume the Court's conclusion was grounded on the rationale that the jury must have inferred from the evidence that Daryoush saw Nasser and Dawes together at the restaurant. The jury is entitled to make such an inference if it is reasonable and based on the facts provided. *Walters v. American States Ins. Co.,* 654 S.W.2d 423 (Tex. 1983).

We find the jury could, from the evidence, rationally infer that Daryoush must have seen Dawes talking with Nasser at the restaurant. The evidence shows that for some period of time, between six months and a year and a half, Dawes worked next door to the restaurant and went there as a customer at least twice each day, during which time she would sit and converse with Nasser. The evidence also shows that Dawes never told Daryoush about such meetings or about her one social date with Nasser. This date occurred during the time when Daryoush was in the mental ward of a local hospital. Nasser testified that he did not know Daryoush prior to the assault. Based on this evidence, the jury could reasonably infer that Daryoush must have learned of Nasser's contacts with Dawes by observing them together at the restaurant. This reasonable inference enables the jury to conclude that Nasser's contacts with Dawes at the restaurant were a causal factor in the assault. The Supreme Court has now clearly said that if such causal factors are part of the catastrophic combination of elements which results in injury, it is compensable. The rationale is that Nasser was carrying out a duty of his employment—being friendly with a customer—and this was an important factor in the chair of events that led to the assault and injury.

Decision and Remedy *The court affirmed the trial court decision that Nasser's injuries were covered*

Workers also are not covered for what the law considers to be "Acts of God." If a worker is struck by lightning, the workers' compensation system will not cover the injury. If, however, the worker's job itself made him or her more likely to be struck by lightning (e.g., television antenna repairer), the injury will be covered.

Another common controversy involves the **"in the course of"** employment requirement of workers' compensation coverage. Injuries are only covered by workers' compensation if they arise during the time of employment.

A typical "in the course of" employment controversy would be an employee who was injured while commuting to work. The general rule, sometimes called the "going and coming" rule, holds that the employee is *not* in the course of employment when commuting.

Special circumstances may bring a commuting employee within the scope of workers' compensation. If the employer provides a truck for commuting and places the employee "on call" while commuting, the employee will be in the course of employment even while driving home from work.

Another set of cases involves recreational injuries. Suppose an employer has a company picnic and a worker is injured while playing softball. This injury may be covered by workers' compensation if participation at the company picnic was expected and considered a part of employment at the company.

To be covered, the injury need not occur at work, so long as the injury's cause resulted from the course of employment. For example, an employee inhaled chemical fumes at work shortly before his shift ended. His residual intoxication from these fumes caused him to have an automobile accident on his trip home. A court held that this injury was covered by workers' compensation.[10]

Another "in the course of" employment problem involves preexisting worker conditions. Suppose that an employee with epilepsy has a seizure on the job. This probably would not be covered by workers' compensation. But if the epileptic were a construction worker on a new office building, and if the seizure caused the employee to fall several stories to the ground, the injuries suffered would be considered in the course of employment and covered by workers' compensation.

Just because an injury occurs on the worksite does not automatically render it "in the course of" employment. Injuries from fights among employees are generally not covered. If a worker is intoxicated and is injured, statutes often exclude coverage. Coverage is frequently denied if the worker's injury was caused by the express disobedience of an employer's safety rules.

Christmas parties and other corporate social events have become a controversial new source of liability. Under "business host" liability, a company may be liable for its drunken employees. In one case, an employer was liable for injuries caused by an employee that became drunk after playing "quarters" at a company Christmas party on the company premises.[11] Jury verdicts and settlements have produced liability of more than $10 million for drunkenness resulting from employer parties.

Yet another requirement of workers' compensation coverage is a **personal injury by accident**. For a time, courts distinguished injury from disease and denied coverage to workplace diseases. Now, all courts recognize that at least some diseases will be covered under the workers' compensation statutes.

Some states distinguish occupational diseases from common diseases. An *occupational* disease would be one such as mesothelioma, caused by high exposures to asbestos that are found primarily at work. A *common* disease would be one like pneumonia, which is typically caused by factors other than occupational exposures.

Some courts will allow workers' compensation recovery for even common diseases, if the worker can provide that this disease was caused by the job. For example, a deliveryperson may be required to work outdoors in cold, rain, and snow. If there is proof that this exposure caused the deliveryperson to contract pneumonia, the disease could be covered.

The employer may have a defense to a workers' compensation claim if the employee lied about his condition in a job application. Most states bar benefits if the worker made a knowing false representation about his or her physical condition, the employer relied on this false representation, and there was a causal connection between the false representation and the injury. Some states (such as Arizona) require workers' compensation payments even if the employer has relied on the worker's application misrepresentations.

Benefits

Workers' compensation provides specified recoveries in the event of a covered accident. Death benefits are made available to dependents of the deceased worker. The amount of death benefits is

---

[10] *Technical Tape Corp. v. Industrial Commission*, 317 N.E.2d 515 (Ill. 1974).

[11] *Gariup Construction Co. v. Foster,* 519 N.E.2d 1224 (Ind. 1988).

generally computed on the basis of a percentage of the worker's average wage. Burial expenses are also commonly included.

For workplace injuries, the workers' compensation system provides reimbursement of medical expenses and rehabilitation costs. Recovery of medical expenses is generally unlimited, though some states permit the employer to select the doctor to be used. Some states limit benefits to workers who are incapacitated for at least one week.

Workers can also recover for disability. Statutes generally classify disabilities in one of four categories: temporary partial, temporary total, permanent partial, or permanent total. Temporary partial disabilities are compensated for any wages lost as a result of the disability. Temporary total disability is compensated for economic losses during the worker's recovery period.

Permanent partial disability results from an injury such as the loss of a finger. If the employee is able to return to work, compensation for these injuries is generally based upon a recovery schedule established by the state. Permanent total disability is compensated by such a schedule or by a wage loss calculation. California provides disability payments based on medical and rehabilitation costs plus two-thirds of any income loss resulting from the accident.

▄ Exclusivity

As described above, workers' compensation is an *exclusive* system. This means that an employee has a right to recover in workers' compensation but may not recover in any other forum, such as a negligence claim in court. There are exceptions to exclusivity, which have become more important as court recoveries have become much greater than workers' compensation recoveries in many instances.

The first issue in workers' compensation exclusivity is whether the accident is even within the coverage of a workers' compensation statute. It is not uncommon to find a worker arguing to a court that his or her injury is *not* covered by workers' compensation, so that the worker can bring a lawsuit for damages.

Even covered injuries may permit a lawsuit under certain exceptions to exclusivity. One of these is the **intentional tort exception**. The employee can choose to use either workers' compensation or common law recovery when the workplace injury or death results from the employer's intentional act.

The most common use of the intentional tort exception is when the employer physically assaults an employee. The exception may not apply when coworkers conduct the assault, however. In one case, a waitress was preparing to close a restaurant when she was attacked and raped by her supervisor, an assistant manager. A court held that her exclusive remedy was in workers' compensation.[12]

A number of workers have sought to sue for intentional infliction of emotional stress damages outside of workers' compensation. If the employee claims physical injuries, such as hypertension or a heart attack, courts have generally held that workers' compensation is the exclusive remedy. For purely mental injuries, however, many courts have permitted workers to sue under common law.

Another typical exception to exclusivity is for **fraudulent concealment**. The worker may bring a lawsuit if he or she has suffered a work-related injury and if the employer either aggravates the injury or conceals the presence of the injury from the employee.

In one case, a worker was employed by a company that manufactured and packaged asbestos products. After working for the company for decades, the worker contracted asbestos-related illnesses, including lung cancer. The worker claimed that the company was aware of these risks and fraudulently concealed from him that he suffered the early stages of these diseases. The court agreed and permitted the worker to sue in court.[13]

Another important exception to exclusivity is product liability. Workers' compensation and exclusivity only apply between the employee and the employer. If a workplace injury is caused by a third party, such as a manufacturer of a defective product found in the workplace, the injured worker can go to court and sue that manufacturer. The worker may be limited to workers' compensation, though, if the manufacturer of the product is also the employer.

In most states, the worker also may sue in court if the employer has failed to maintain workers' compensation insurance coverage.

---

[12] *Schatz v. York Steak House*, 444 A.2d 1045 (Md. App.

[13] *Johns Manville Products v. Contra County Superior Court*, 612 P.2d 948 (Cal. 1980).

Ethical Perspectives

The Cost of Occupational Safety

Employers have a variety of financial incentives to improve the safety of their workplaces. Workers' compensation insurance will be less expensive if they suffer fewer claims. Economic studies have shown that workers demand higher wages for jobs that have higher risks. The threat of fines for noncompliance with OSHA standards is always present.

Improving the safety of a workplace is not inexpensive, however. The costs of enhancing safety at times may far exceed the financial benefits to employers. If an OSHA standard requires such enhanced safety devices, the employer must implement the devices, regardless of cost. OSHA cannot regulate every workplace risk, though. The ethical question is how far above and beyond OSHA standards an employer should go.

Some might argue that mere compliance with OSHA standards discharges the employer's safety duties to its employees. The law does not define the limits of ethics, however. Moreover, OSHA has found standard-setting to be a slow, costly and difficult task, subject to challenge by both employers and unions. Everyone agrees that OSHA standards are an incomplete guide to occupational safety. This fact is recognized in the act itself, through the general duty clause.

Suggesting that an employer should go beyond minimum OSHA standards does not answer the question of how far beyond the standards the employer should go. To what extent should the employer consider the costs of workplace safety in deciding whether to adopt additional safety protections for employees.

Some argue that costs should not be considered. The idea of balancing costs against human lives seems repugnant. Who can say how many dollars a life or limb is worth? This ethical vision is too simplistic, however it would dictate unlimited spending on safety. Because no workplace can be absolutely safe, this approach would suggest that employment itself is unethical.

The costs of safety improvements inevitably will be considered. Some cost consideration is even in the interest of workers. Higher costs of production mean higher costs of products, which means less demand for products, so the costs of safety improvements will sometimes cost jobs. The more money spent on safety improvements, the less will be available for employee benefits or wage increases. Many workers have made clear that they will accept higher risk in return for a higher wage.

The ethical legitimacy of some cost consideration does not justify a disregard for worker safety, however. Human life and welfare is more than a pure matter of the balance sheet. Ethics does not limit safety improvements to those that are cost-effective for the employer. Interests of the worker and of society are also relevant.

The appropriate extent of safety improvements may depend on the circumstances of the employer. If the employer is flush with profits, it can afford and should institute more workplace safety. If safety enhancement is unaffordable, the employer could at lest inform its workers of the risks and help them take their own precautions against injury or disease.

International Occupational Safety Protection

Each nation has its own system to protect the health and safety of workers. Some foreign systems may go beyond U.S. protections. Most European nations, for example, required labeling of hazardous workplace chemicals long before the U.S. adopted its hazard communication standard. Great Britain's Health and Safety at Work Act of 1974 is similar to U.S. law. A British company was recently hit with a penalty of over $1.3 million for repeated violations that resulted in three deaths.

A key concern in international trade involves those countries with weak occupational safety and health laws. Some nations offer little legal protection to workers. Even nations with protective laws for workplace safety may do little enforcing of those laws.

Compliance with occupational safety laws and workers' compensation in the United States and other industrialized nations can be quite expensive. Consequently, a number of companies have moved production facilities to less developed nations that lack strict standards. There is considerable concern both for the welfare of the workers in these nations and for the jobs of American workers.

The International Labour Organization (ILO) of the United Nations, created in 1919, has established guidelines for worldwide occupational safety. The ILO has little power, however, for the enforcement of these standards and no real sanction authority. The ILO can only publicize noteworthy violations and encourage their correction.

The United States has taken steps in its trade legislation to encourage occupational safety. U.S. law specifies certain "internationally recognized worker rights." Among these rights are: "taking into account the country's level of economic development, acceptable conditions of work with respect to minimum wages, hours of work, and occupational safety and health."

The Office of the United States Trade Representative (USTR) reviews the practice of trading partners against this standard. If the USTR finds that a country is violating internationally recognized worker rights, the United States may declare an unreasonable trade practice. The USTR is then empowered to suspend trade agreement concessions or impose import fees or other restrictions, at the direction of the President.

The U.S. also may deny other trade opportunities. The USTR may suspend the Generalized System of Preferences that grants duty-free entry to the goods of certain less-developed nations. The U.S. may also cut off Overseas Private Investment Corporation insurance for such nations.

United States trade sanctions have not been widely used to protect worker rights such as health and safety. Sanctioned nations have been few, including Nicaragua, Romania, Chile, Ethiopia and Paraguay. The USTR has rejected numerous petitions to sanction other nations. Application of the law's provisions may depend more on generalized foreign policy objectives than on worker rights.

Questions and Case Problems

1. Manno Equipment was visited by an OSHA inspector. Manno's foreman asked to accompany the inspector on his trip throughout the Manno plant, but the inspector refused. After visiting the plant, the inspector issued a number of citations. Manno refuses to pay and claims that it was wrongfully denied its walkaround rights with the inspector. Manno contends that the evidence in the inspection should be inadmissible. Is Manno correct?

2. Sky Sailmakers runs a plant in which workers stitch sails together. Sky failed to provide guards for sewing machine needles, though workers had to move their hands within inches of the needle. A number of minor puncture wounds had resulted from the failure to provide guards. OSHA cited Sky Sailmakers for a violation and sought a penalty for willful violation of the law. Sky contended that its violation was de minimis and warranted no penalty. Should Sky Sailmakers be subject to a significant fine in this case?

3. An OSHA standard requires that workers wear hard hats for certain jobs. Seattle Stevedoring told its workers that they must wear the hard hats. The workers resisted wearing the hats, however, and Seattle Stevedoring was issued several citations. The company consistently insisted that the workers wear the hard hats, but the workers repeatedly took them off. Finally, OSHA issued a strict citation against Seattle Stevedoring for a willful violation of the act. Seattle Stevedoring appealed that it should not be blamed for its workers' refusal to wear the hats. Should Seattle Stevedoring be liable for a willful violation? [*Seattle Stevedoring Co.,* 8 O.S.H.C. 1240 (1980)].

4. Richard Lanno was a project engineer for Thermal Equipment Co., which manufactured pressure vessels for the aerospace industry. Lanno was sometimes required to proceed from his home directly to a job site and was on call at home after hours and on weekends. In order to answer these calls, Lanno needed the company truck, in which he carried tools. Thermal provided Lanno with the truck, gasoline money, and permitted him to use the truck for personal purposes. One day, Lanno left work and was driving home. He went out of his way to stop at a store. Before reaching the store, Lanno had an automobile accident. Was Lanno in the scope of employment at the time of the accident? [*Lazar v. Thermal Equipment Corp.,* 195 Cal. Rptr. 890 (1983)].

5. John Jacobs worked at a textile plant and complained to another worker that his back hurt when he performed certain lifting required by the job. The company doctor determined that Jacobs had strained his back muscles. Jacobs continued to work and the problem became worse. Not long thereafter, Jacobs died of cancer. Doctors found that the back strain had caused the cancer to spread more rapidly. Should Jacobs' widow be able to receive workers' compensation benefits in this case?

CHAPTER SIX

Accounting and the Law

KEY BACKGROUND

The essential background for this chapter on accounting and the law is found in Chapter 54 of *West's Business Law, Seventh Edition.* This chapter covers liability of accountants. Among the important points to remember from this chapter are:

- accountants' potential liability for breach of contract and negligence

- accountants' potential liability to non-client third parties

- accountants' potential liability under the federal securities laws

- rules for accountants' work papers and client communications

* * *

As the significance and complexity of financial transactions increases, so too does the role of accountants. Accounting firms are increasingly expanding their services into areas such as management consulting. Recent years also have seen an explosion of potential legal liability of accountants. More lawsuits were filed against accountants in the last fifteen years than in the entire previous history of the profession.

Malpractice Liability to Clients

The most traditional source of liability for accountants is to their clients for accounting malpractice or negligence. If a company hires an accountant to audit the company's financial condition and that accountant does a defective job, the accountant may be liable to the company for damages that it suffered from reliance on the inaccurate audit.

Much litigation results from accountants' performance of financial audits. Auditing typically involves rendering an opinion on the accuracy of a company's financial statements, including its balance sheet, its income statement, and its cash flow statement. The accountant tests these statements against general professional principles.

The most important of such principles are **Generally Accepted Auditing Standards** (GAAS) and **Generally Accepted Accounting Principles** (GAAP), a set of accounting methods for recording assets, liabilities, revenues and expenditures. GAAS and GAAP are derived from the principles set forth by a private organization, the American Institute of Certified Public Accountants (AICPA) and the Financial Accounting Standards Board (FASB).[1]

The traditional approach for malpractice liability to a client was under contract law for a violation of GAAS and GAAP. The accountant could be sued for breach of contract when an audit was negligently performed. The potential damages are relatively low in a contract claim and may be limited to the cost charged for the audit.

---

[1] Those in the field pronounce these initials as "fazbee."

In recent years, courts increasingly have found that accountants could be sued in tort, such as negligence, for malpractice to a client. Damages in tort may be significantly greater and could amount to millions of dollars.

Many tort cases allege simple negligence on the part of an auditor. Some cases go further and claim that the accountant engaged in fraud or gross negligence. For both contract and tort cases, the plaintiff client must prove that the accountant violated a legal duty.

Accountant's Duty

Accountants are in insurers of financial statement accuracy. Mere failure to report accurately a company's financial status, or failure to discover problems, does not automatically result in liability. The accountant will be liable for negligent failure to perform his or her duties.

Even in a tort case, the accountant's contract is a central source of his or her obligations. For example, suppose an accountant was employed to prepare income tax returns for a client. The accountant relied on client records that showed certain income to be taxable. The client later discovered that the income was not taxable and that they were owed a refund that the accountant failed to file to protect. In this case, the accountant was not liable because the agreement with the client provided that the accountant could rely on data provided by the company.[2]

The terms of contracts are not always clear. The accountant and the client will not always place the same interpretation on a contract term. Moreover, an accountant during the course of work may assume duties beyond those specified in the contract.

In addition, accountants have a generalized duty to fulfill the standards of their profession. Minimum standards are found in GAAS and GAAP. Accountants must also follow other standards set forth by the AICPA, FASB, and the Securities and Exchange Commission (SEC).

In some cases, accountants must go beyond the AICPA and other standards. There are some instances in which GAAP or other AICPA standards do not address a specific problem. In addition, some courts have found the GAAP standards to be inadequate and imposed higher standards on accountants.

An important factor in accountant liability is the presence or absence of qualifying or explanatory statements accompanying the accountants' report. If the accountant did not independently verify records supplied by the client, the accountant should include a qualifying statement to that effect.

An accountant's duties can go beyond the contract, and the accountant may have certain fiduciary duties to the client. An accountant always has the duty to perform with reasonable care and in good faith. An accountant entrusted with a client's funds is held to a high standard of care with respect to those funds.

Sources of Liability

Certain fact situations produce most malpractice lawsuits against accountants. The traditional sources of liability are a report that inaccurately reflects a client's financial condition and a failure to detect the **defalcations** (e.g., fraud, embezzlement) of the client's employees. More recently, accountants may be liable for failure to report on weaknesses in a company's internal control structure against fraud.

False representation of financial condition is a common source of liability. Suppose that a partnership's accountant audits the partnership and fails to note that one partner's contributions to the partnership were substantially overvalued. For example, suppose that a partner contributed used furniture and office equipment to the partnership offices and valued these materials too highly. The accountant may be liable for failure to discover and report this fact. Improper valuation of inventory is another source of liability.

There are now an increasing number of suits filed against accountants in connection with takeovers. When one company acquires another, the acquirer has sued the accountant for misstating the financial condition of the acquired company.

Accountants also are retained to investigate and discover **defalcations by a corporation's employees**. One such act occurs when a client's employee fraudulently falsified inventory valuations for the client. In such a situation, auditors must employ "professional skepticism" and seek out defalcations, though auditors are not expected to discover every conceivable instance of wrongdoing.

In an example case, an accountant failed to discover that well-established commodity prices did not

---

[2] *Lindner v. Barlow, Davis & Wood,* 27 Cal. Rptr. (Cal. App. 1963).

correspond with inventory valuations and that nearly half the freight rates listed were wrong. An employee was manipulating the books. The accountant was held to be liable for failure to discover the problem.[3]

Accountants are increasingly being sued for failure to report on weaknesses in the *client's internal structure to control defalcations* by employees. The internal control structure is the company's system to protect against errors finding their way into the company's financial statements. An internal control system should, among other things, ensure that transactions are reliably recorded in conformity with generally accepted accounting principles and that access to assets is limited by express management authorization. In 1988, the AICPA modified auditing standards to increase an auditor's responsibility for investigating, evaluating, and disclosing shortcomings in an internal control system.

In an unreported California case, an audit of a computer company failed to disclose that the company's internal controls were in disarray. Sometime after the audit, management discovered substantial unrecorded liabilities that resulted from the failure of internal controls. The company ultimately declared bankruptcy, and a jury found the accounting firm liable for $4 million.

Another common source of litigation is *tax preparation*. Many accountants are tax specialists, and individuals and companies rely on their accountants for tax preparation. Accountants may be sued for failure to use available deductions. Conversely, accountants may be sued for overclaiming deductions, which resulted in an IRS penalty assessment against the client.

Accountants were found liable in a recent case for failure to discover underpayment of federal taxes, which produced substantial damages causing the client's eventual bankruptcy.[4]

Contributory Negligence

When an accountant is sued for malpractice, the accountant often can claim that the client corporation should be unable to recover because the company was itself negligent. Suppose that a corporate officer was embezzling funds from a corporation.

An accountant failed to discover this embezzling in an audit. The accountant would argue that the company was itself negligent in not discovering the embezzlement and should not recover for the accountant's alleged negligence.

Most states use **comparative negligence**. This concept is discussed in Chapter 6 of *West's Business Law, Seventh Edition.* This rule would at least reduce the accounting firm's liability by the percentage of the client's negligence. In a recent case, an accountant was sued for failure to discover embezzlement by a client's employee. A court found that the accountant was liable, but that the client corporation's negligence was itself 80 percent responsible and reduced the accountant's liability accordingly.[5]

Suppose that Toy's, Incorporated, hired the AB&T accounting firm to conduct a financial audit. An employee of Toy's was diverting inventory for his personal profit and producing false records to cover it up. The AB&T firm did not rely on Toy's records, but conducted its own audit of inventory. AB&T failed to discover the employee's defalcation. While Toy's may have been itself negligent in permitting the employee theft, AB&T could not effectively use this as comparative negligence. Toy's negligence did not cause the accounting firm's erroneous report.

Other states provide for a broader comparative negligence defense. They hold that a client's own sloppiness in bookkeeping may be used by an accountant defendant, even if the accountant did not rely on the client's sloppy records. Florida, Minnesota, and Tennessee have adopted this more liberal approach to comparative negligence.

Accountants also may take advantage of another form of comparative negligence—the client's negligent reliance on an accountant's report. Suppose that an accounting firm submits a financial report and qualifies this report with a statement that it did not verify the underlying data supplied to the auditor. A client's reliance on the report may be negligent, because the client should have realized the limitations of the audit.

If the client's contributory negligence was foreseeable by the accountant, the defense may fail. For example, an accountant improperly prepared a tax

---

[3] *Lincoln Grain, Inc. v. Coopers & Lybrand,* 345 N.W.2d 300 (Neb. 1984).

[4] *Greenstein, Logan & Co. v. Burgess Marketing, Inc.,* 744 S.W.2d 170 (Tex. App. 1987).

[5] *Halla Nursery, Inc. v. Baumann-Firrie & Co.,* 438 N.W. 2d 400 (Minn. App. 1989).

return, which resulted in a penalty for the taxpayer. The accountant argued contributory negligence, because the taxpayer should have discovered the mistake. A court found the accountant liable, because it was foreseeable that the taxpayer would sign the prepared return without reading it and checking for errors.[6]

Unaudited Reports

In order to save costs, many companies hire accountants to perform unaudited reports. This type of investigation is much less thorough than a full financial audit. In an unaudited report, the accountant merely examines and compiles a company's published financial statements and then applies certain agreed-upon procedures to evaluate the statements.

An unaudited report is far more limited in its representations, but accountants may still be liable for inaccurate unaudited reports. The AICPA has adopted standards for unaudited reports that limit the scope of such reports and specifically states that such a review does not include an evaluation of the client's internal control structure.

The courts have not fully accepted the AICPA position, however, and have held accountants liable for unaudited reports. An accountant may be required to do more than it has contractually promised in the unaudited report. If the accountant happens to discover a defalcation or other problem, the accountant should report that fact, even if such a report is beyond the accountant's contract.

The following decision was a landmark in holding accountants liable for even unaudited reports.

---

[6]*Bick v. Peat Marwick and Main,* 799 P.2d 94 (Kan. App. 1990).

■ Case 6.1
Robert Wooler Company v. The Fidelity Bank
Superior Court of Pennsylvania, 1984
479 A.2d 1027

Background and Facts   *Robert Wooler Company employed a bookkeeper, Dona Raichle, who diverted 94 checks into a personal account of her own. Wooler had employed Touche Ross & Co. as its accounting firm to conduct unaudited services for the company. After this was discovered, Wooler sued the bank and Touche Ross for damages.*

The trial court found that the Touche Ross personnel had "failed to use reasonable care in being alert" and had "failed to make the necessary inquiries in accordance with reasonable professional standards." Nevertheless, that court dismissed the claims against Touche Ross, finding that the accounting firm had been improperly added as a defendant and had no duty to inquire into the client's system of internal controls in such an unaudited engagement.

WEIAND, Judge.

* * * *

Touche Ross's agreement to perform unaudited services was not a shield from liability if it failed to warn its client of known deficiencies in the client's internal operating procedures which enhanced opportunities for employee defalcations. Its agreement, in the absence of specific language relieving it from acts of negligence, did not relieve it from liability for ignoring suspicious circumstances which would have raised a "red flag" for a reasonably skilled and knowledgeable accountant. Thus, in 1136

Tenants' Corp. v. Max Rothenberg & Co., 36 A.D.2d 804, 319 N.Y.S.2d 1007, 1007-1008 (1971), aff'd. 30 N.Y.2d 585, 281 N.E.2d 846, 330 N.Y.S.2d 800 (1972) a New York court held that it was negligence for an accountant engaged to perform unaudited services to ignore suspicious circumstances and fail to inform the client of missing invoices, thereby enabling an employee's defalcations to go unnoticed.

And in *United States v. Natelli,* 527 F.2d 311, 320 (2nd Cir. 1975), cert. denied, 425 U.S. 934, 96 S.Ct. 1663, 48 L.Ed.2d 175 (1976), it was held that auditors preparing an unaudited financial statement in connection with a proxy statement for filing with the Securities Exchange Commission had a duty to investigate suspicious circumstances. Similarly, in *Blakely v. Lisac,* 357 F.Supp. 255, 265-266 (D.Or. 1972) it was held that an accountant preparing an "unaudited write-up" had to undertake at least minimal investigation of figures supplied and was not free to ignore suspicious circumstances. See also: *Ryan v. Kanne,* 170 N.W.2d 395, 404 (Iowa 1969) (accountant liable for negligence in preparing report of accounts payable even though statement unaudited and accountant expressly disclaimed knowledge that information was correct); *Bohhiver v. Graff,* 311 Minn. 111, 248 N.W.2d 291, 197-299 (1976) (accountants having unaudited engagement to bring insurance company's books "up to date" are liable for negligence in failing to examine books made available to them when such an examination would have disclosed the insurance company's insolvency).

When Touche Ross agreed to provide unaudited accounting services for Wooler, it undertook to exercise that degree of accounting skill possessed by other accountants in the community. Touche Ross's obligation required that its personnel be reasonably alert to internal control defects which were patently obvious. Witnesses for the Bank and the accountant agreed that Wooler's internal controls had been defective and had thereby increased the potential for defalcations by a dishonest employee. They agreed that such a danger is inevitably present when the same employee is responsible to post accounts receivable in a sales journal, to handle incoming receivables, and to record daily receipts of moneys received in settlement of accounts receivable. Raichle, it was agreed, performed all these duties for Wooler. There was evidence that on the occasions when Touche Ross sent an accounting employee to examine Wooler's books, that person worked in close proximity to Raichle and observed her perform these several functions. Expert witnesses uniformly expressed the opinion that an accountant possessing reasonable accounting skill would have been aware of the potential for theft inherent in Wooler's internal controls.

Decision and Remedy *The court reversed the lower court judgment and remanded the case for further proceedings.*

Liability to Non-Clients

The most controversial and significant issue in accounting law involves the liability of accountants to parties other than their clients. These third parties may have a greater stake in audit accuracy than does the client itself.

Suppose that Chemco is audited by the AB&T firm. Chemco's financial statements, approved by AB&T, suggest that the firm is financially healthy. Chemco obtains a large loan from CiuBank to expand overseas. CiuBank agrees to make the loan because the audited financial statements appear strong. Then it is discovered that the Chemco financial statements contained substantial errors, and Chemco declares bankruptcy. CiuBank stands to lose much of its money due to Chemco's bankruptcy. Should CiuBank be able to sue AB&T for accounting malpractice?

Creditors are a common third party that seeks recovery for accounting malpractice. The shareholders in an audited corporation are also third parties who may wish to sue accountants. Another foreseeable third party who might be injured by accounting malpractice is an insurance company.

The traditional rule of **privity**, however, held that only the company could sue for accounting negligence, and third parties had no remedy against an auditor. Chapter 54 of *West's Business Law, Seventh Edition,* discusses how the privity rule has been modified and how some third parties can now sue accountants.

The state courts are divided on the circumstances that enable third parties to sue for the simple negligence of accountants. Four different approaches are used: the substantial privity test, the Restatement test, the reasonable foreseeability test, and the balancing test. The applicable test will determine the liability of an accounting firm, such as AB&T, to third parties, such as CiuBank.

Substantial Privity Test

New York, the state that first abandoned the privity test, has adopted the substantial privity test to limit accountants' liability to third parties. The nature of this substantial privity defense was set forth in the leading case of *Credit Alliance v. Arthur Andersen & Co.*[7]

Credit Alliance established three tests that must be met before an accountant will be liable to a third party:

1. The accountants must have been aware that the audited reports were to be used for a particular purpose.

2. A known third party relied on the audited report for that purpose.

3. There must be some conduct by the accountants that linked them to the third party and demonstrates the accountants' awareness of the third party's reliance.

This test is highly protective of accountants. The key requirement is the third, linkage criterion. In our opening hypothetical example, AB&T probably would not be liable to CiuBank, unless CiuBank had gone directly to AB&T, mentioned the possible loan to Chemco, and inquired about the audited report. In addition, CiuBank would need to have contacted AB&T before the firm completed the audit.

Restatement Test

The Restatement (Second) of Torts Section 552 states that the accountant will be liable to "a person or a limited class of persons who the auditor can foresee as parties who will and [who] do not rely on the audited financial statements." This is also called the **actually foreseen test**. Many jurisdictions, including Pennsylvania and Ohio, have adopted the Restatement test.

Under the Restatement test, the accountant will be liable to parties whom the accountant knew that the client intended to influence with the audit report. This test has also been applied to unaudited financial statements.

Liability under this test will vary, depending on the nature of the third party. A future lender may well not have been foreseen by the accountant. Courts have suggested that a company's shareholders are by definition a foreseen class of plaintiffs, and accountants therefore will always be potentially liable to shareholders under the Restatement test.

Applying the Restatement test to the hypothetical example, AB&T might be liable. The accounting

---

[7] 483 N.E.2d 110 (N.Y. 1985).

firm would only be liable if it was aware that Chemco intended to use the audited financial statements to apply for a loan from CiuBank. AB&T would not be liable if it was unaware that Chemco planned to seek a loan from CiuBank based on the audited financial statements.

California historically held accountants to a broad standard of third party liability. A recent opinion reconsidered this position and cut back the potential liability.

Case 6.1
Bily v.
Arthur Young & Company
Supreme Court of California, 1992
834 P.2d 745

Background and Facts *In 1980, Osborne Computer Corporation was one of the fastest growing companies in the U.S. Osborne retained Arthur Young & Company to perform audits and issue reports on its 1981 and 1982 financial statements. Arthur Young issued "clean" audit opinions for both years. The company issued warrants to investors in exchange for direct loans or letters of credit, which warrants entitled acquirers to purchase stock at favorable prices in the event of a public offering of Osborne shares. By 1983, the company's financial performance faltered. Sales declined sharply, the public offering never materialized, and the company filed for bankruptcy in September 1983. Investors in the warrants sued Arthur Young, contending that its negligent audit reports caused their losses. A jury returned a verdict for plaintiffs of $4.3 million. After affirmance on appeal, the accountants appealed again to the California Supreme Court.*

LUCAS, Chief Justice.

* * * *

An auditor is a watchdog, not a bloodhound ... As a matter of commercial reality, audits are performed in a client-controlled environment. The client typically prepares its own financial statements; it has direct control over and assumes primary responsibility for their contents. ... Client control also predominates in the dissemination of the audit report. Once the report reaches the client, the extent of its distribution and the communications that accompany it are within the exclusive province of client management. Thus, regardless of the efforts of the auditor, the client retains effective primary control of the financial reporting process.

* * * *

Although the auditor's role in the financial reporting process is secondary and the subject of complex professional judgment, the liability it faces in a negligence suit by a third party is primary and personal and can be massive. The client, its promoters, and its managers have generally left the scene, headed in most cases for government-supervised liquidation or the bankruptcy court. The auditor has now assumed center stage as the remaining solvent defendant and is faced with a claim for all sums of money ever loaned to or invested in the client. Yet the auditor may never have been aware of the existence, let alone the nature or scope, of the third party transaction that resulted in the claim.

* * * *

Of the approaches we have reviewed, Restatement Second of Torts section 552, subdivision (b) is the most consistent with the elements and policy foundations of the tort of negligent misrepresentation. The rule expressed there attempts to define a narrow and circumscribed class of persons to whom or for whom representations are made. In this way, it recognizes commercial realities by avoiding both unlimited and uncertain liability for economic losses in cases of professional mistake and exoneration of the auditor in situations where it clearly intended to undertake the responsibility of influencing particular business transactions involving third persons.

Decision and Remedy *The court reversed the lower court judgment and remanded the case with instructions to direct judgment in favor of Arthur Young.*

Reasonable Foreseeability Test

The reasonable foreseeability test would hold accountants to be liable to any third parties that the auditors could reasonably foresee might rely on their report. This is the broadest test, under which the accountant is most likely to be found liable.

Wisconsin, New Jersey, and Mississippi employ the reasonable foreseeability test. The latter two states limit liability to third parties who have received the reports directly from the company audited.

In the hypothetical example, AB&T probably would be liable to CiuBank. It is certainly foreseeable that an audited company would need a bank loan. It is also foreseeable that any bank would rely on audited financial statements in deciding whether to give that loan.

Balancing Test

The balancing test is based on an earlier California decision. Under this test, the accountant's liability to third parties is based on a balancing of: (1) the extent to which the transaction was intended to affect the third party; (2) the foreseeability of harm to the third party; (3) the degree of certainty that the plaintiff suffered injury; (4) the closeness of the connection between the defendant's conduct and the injury suffered; (5) the moral blame attached to the defendant's conduct; and (6) the policy of preventing future harm.

Although California no longer relies on this balancing test, it has been adopted by other courts. In a North Carolina case, a company had accountants audit its financial statements and then forward them to Dun and Bradstreet for publication. A third party extended over two million dollars in credit to the company, in reliance on the Dun and Bradstreet report. The company went bankrupt, and the audited financial statements had substantially overstated the company's net worth. The court used the balancing test and held the accountants liable.[8]

The outcome of the above hypothetical example is not clear under the balancing test. The foreseeability of CiuBank's reliance, the certainty of its injury, and the closeness of the connection between the audit and the injury all suggest that AB&T could be liable. The first factor, the intent to influence CiuBank, might support AB&T's position.

Fraud or Gross Negligence

Accountant liability to third parties is broader in cases alleging fraud or gross negligence (extreme lack of care). New York courts, for example, have held that third party plaintiffs could not bring a negligence suit due to lack of substantial privity but could bring a fraud case on the same facts, even without substantial privity.

Fraud, of course, is an intentional tort and much more difficult to prove than negligence. Gross negligence is also more difficult to prove than simple negligence. To succeed in fraud, a plaintiff must show that the defendant accountant had actual knowledge of the erroneous records and failed to report it. If fraud is present, courts have suggested that an accountant may be liable to all injured third parties, even unforeseeable ones.

---

[8] *Raritan River Steel Co. v. Cherry, Beckaert & Holland,* 339 S.E.2d 62 (N.C. App. 1986).

Disclaimers

When accountants issue an audit, they customarily provide a certificate that may include qualifications or other disclaimers. The auditor might state, for example, that certain information is unverified. Such disclaimers have effectively protected accounting firms from liability.

In one case, a firm of public accountants was instructed not to audit the client company's accounts receivable or to adjust those accounts to reflect probable collectibility. The accountant followed these instructions and provided a certificate that reflected these limitations on its audit. When the accountant was sued by a shareholder who relied on its audit, the court held that the disclaimer protected the accounting firm.[9]

Disclaimers may be effective to avert negligence liability but will not protect an accountant from fraud claims. Because fraud is an intentional tort, an accountant could not rely on a disclaimer as a defense.

Although disclaimers can protect accountants from negligence liability, client firms will resist any qualifications on their audit. The presence of disclaimers makes it more difficult for the audited company to obtain financing based on the audit results. A recent study of 1800 audits found that only 9 percent had qualifications for uncertainties in results.

▄ Accountants and Confidentiality

An accountant conducting a full financial audit of a corporation may become aware of significant confidential information about the company. The key legal question is when accountants may be required to divulge confidential information acquired during the audit. Another important question is when accountants may be permitted to disclose such information.

There is no common-law accountant-client privilege comparable to the doctor-patient or attorney-client privilege against disclosure of confidential information. Twenty-four states have adopted statutes providing for some measure of accountant-client privilege. These states include Florida, Illinois, Michigan, and Pennsylvania. In addition to state laws, the AICPA ethics rules prohibit disclosure of confidential information obtained from clients.

While an accountant may be compelled to give confidential information in testimony, the accountant still has a duty not to disclose such information unless required. The accountant retains legal title to work records acquired in the audit but generally cannot disclose them to others without the client company's permission. The AICPA has established some limited exceptions to this rule.

In one case, an accounting firm provided bookkeeping services to a company and discovered certain cash flow problems. The firm then advised its other clients not to deal with the company. These other clients cancelled their contract with the original corporation, which went out of business. The accounting firm was found liable for breach of confidentiality.[10]

Confidentiality problems can arise in a number of circumstances. Suppose that Carolyn Gibson has a long-term successful accounting practice and is planning to retire and sell the practice to Tom Rousseau. Gibson must obtain client permission before giving past working papers to Rosseau.

AICPA provides exceptions to the confidentiality requirement: (1) when necessary to avoid violation of auditing standards and principles; (2) when necessary to comply with a legal command, such as a subpoena; and (3) when in connection with an AICPA inquiry or quality review.

Accountants currently face a disclosure dilemma when it appears that a client has committed fraud or other illegal acts. A new AICPA standard declares that accountants must sometimes breach confidentiality and publicly announce a client's fraud, even if that fraud was unrelated to the audit. The rule is vague, however, on the circumstances compelling disclosure.

This situation places accountants in something of a "Catch-22" position, as they are torn between the duties of confidentiality and those of disclosure. In one case, Fund of Funds purchased properties from John King. Arthur Andersen and Company was the auditor for Fund of Funds but also was the auditor for King. Fund of Funds discovered that the properties were overvalued. Arthur Anderson was found liable because it had not informed Fund of Funds of the information available to it from auditing King. This situation obviously presented a difficult conflict between the duties of confidentiality and disclosure.

---

[9] *Stephens Industries, Inc. v. Haskins & Sells,* 438 F.2d 357 (10th Cir. 1971).

[10] *Wagenheim v. Alexander Grant & Co.,* 482 N.E.2d 955 (Ohio App. 1983).

SEC Rules

Accurate accounting is critical to the fairness of stock and other transactions governed by the Securities and Exchange Commission. Consequently, Congress has provided the SEC with broad power to regulate the accounting profession. The SEC has not set detailed rules but has largely deferred to the private standard-setting bodies in the profession, such as FASB.

Disciplining Accountants

SEC Rule 2(e) provides that the Commission may punish accountants who practice before the SEC. Any accountant who prepares any filing or opinion filed with the SEC is deemed to practice before the Commission. SEC rules require so many filings by companies that virtually all accountants are deemed to practice before the SEC.

The SEC has stated that Rule 2(e) is not to be used to punish mere mistakes, or even negligence. Sanctions are limited to when the accountant (i) does not "possess the requisite qualifications to represent others, or (ii) [is] lacking in character or integrity or [has] engaged in unethical or improper professional conduct, or (iii) has willfully violated or willfully aided and abetted the violation of any provision of the Federal security laws."[11]

As a general rule, compliance with GAAS and GAAP will be sufficient for the SEC. The Commission may demand more, however. Moreover, the GAAS centrally calls for "judgment" by the accountant, and the SEC has questioned the judgment of accountants on issues such as how far to investigate a client's claims.

The accused accountant is granted procedural protection before the Commission. He or she has the right to timely notice of charges, representation by counsel, subpoena power, and cross-examination. Trial is generally before an impartial administrative law judge. The losing accountant may appeal to the full Commission.

If an accountant is found liable under 2(e), the Commission may deny, temporarily or permanently, the privilege of practicing before the Commission. During the 1980s, there were more than 50 administrative proceedings against accountants under Rule 2(e). Virtually all ended in consent agreements. In some cases, the accountants were merely censured, but some accountants were suspended from practice before the commission for as long as five years.

Opinion Shopping

The SEC is especially concerned with companies' opinion shopping among accountants. **Opinion shopping** occurs when a corporation to be audited retains a series of accountants, in hopes of finding one who will approve of management's position on financial statements.

To control opinion shopping, the SEC adopted item 304 of Regulation S-K. This rule requires certain disclosures whenever a corporation replaces its accountant. A change must be reported within fifteen days. The report must disclose any disagreement between the accountant and the company during the past two years. The discharged accountant must send a letter to the Commission confirming or denying the company's disclosure.

Civil Liability

The Securities Act of 1933 and the Securities Exchange Act of 1934 establish potential civil, or even criminal, liability for accountants. Section 11 prohibits misstatements of financial statements in connection with a securities registration. Section 10(b) generally prohibits any false or misleading statements made in connection with the sale of securities. The scope of these provisions is detailed in Chapter 7 on securities law and regulation. The application of these provisions to accountants is addressed extensively in Chapter 54 of *West's Business Law, Seventh Edition.*

In December 1995, Congress passed the Private Securities Litigation Reform Act (PSLRA), which affected accountant liability under the securities laws. One provision insulated accountants from damages. If outside accountant auditors become aware of an illegal act and inform the board of directors and ensure that the SEC is informed, the accountant will not be liable.

Other provisions of the PSLRA expanded potential accountant liability. New Section 10A of the law requires that audits of financial statements of public companies include "procedures designed to provide reasonable assurance of detecting illegal acts that would have a direct and material effect"

---

[11] 17 C.F.R. Section 201.2(e)(1).

on the statements' amounts. Moreover, once an accountant detects fraud, the statute contains a whistle-blowing provision that requires the accountant to inform the board of directors and ensure that the SEC is informed, unless appropriate remedial action is taken. Auditors are not directly liable to private parties for statements made in their section 10A reports, but the provision may be used by plaintiffs to establish liability under a duty to disclose.

RICO

Accountants have been held liable under the Racketeer Influenced and Corrupt Organizations Act, known as RICO. This law provides for conviction or civil penalties, with treble (triple) damages, whenever a party has engaged in a pattern of racketeering activity (e.g., commission of a series of securities-related crimes). The standards under RICO are set forth and detailed in Chapter 7 on securities law and regulation.

Because the issuance of a faulty audit report may violate the securities laws, plaintiffs may also sue under RICO. The Supreme Court has limited accountant RICO liability to instances when the accounting firm virtually controlled the audited entity.[12]

Management Consulting

Accounting firms have expanded their services to offer management consulting or management advisory services (MAS) to client corporations. These services now represent as much as a third of the income of major accounting firms. The law of management consulting is still quite unsettled. When accounting firms offer management consulting services, however, they create possible legal problems.

Independence

One of the foremost characteristics of an accountant is independence. Independence is vital to preserve both the reality and the appearance of integrity and honesty on the part of accountants. The U.S. Supreme Court has stressed that an accountant acts as a "disinterested analyst" who "maintain[s] total independence from the client at all times and … complete fidelity to the public trust."[13]

The SEC has issued guidelines for independence of accountants practicing before the Commission. These guidelines state that auditors may not engage in bookkeeping services for clients and that auditors cannot undertake jobs when the client owes a material amount of unpaid fees for prior jobs, among other requirements.

The AICPA also has standards for accountant independence. Among AICPA rules are stipulations that accountants cannot have any direct or material indirect financial interest in the client, that the auditor may not charge a contingency fee, and that the auditor should not loan money or accept loans from a client. AICPA Ethics Code Rule 101-B states that the accountant must not assume the role of an employee or of management of the client corporation. The supplementing statement, however, offers no examples of the activities that management consultants should avoid.

The growth of management consulting presents potential independence problems for auditors. Although a management consultant may not actually assume the role of an employee, the consultant will advise on the same decisions as ordinary management. There is a concern that an auditor is unlikely to question management consulting decisions previously made by the same accounting firm.

There is little regulation of the management consulting situation. The SEC adopted rules but then withdrew them and recently held that accounting firms could do consulting work through separate entities within the firm. The AICPA permits management consulting by accounting firms, so long as the consultant only advises and does not undertake final transactions on the part of the client.

Tort Liability

Management consulting may become a source of tort liability for accounting firms. Clients and injured third parties may be expected to sue for negligent or fraudulent management consulting. Few such cases have been brought, so the standards for liability are quite undefined.

Accountants have been sued for giving bad business advice. For example, an accountant

---

[12] *Reves v. Ernst & Young,* 113 S.Ct. 1163 (1993).

[13] *United States v. Arthur Young & Co.,* 465 U.S. 805, 817-18 (1984).

recommended to a partnership that it reorganize and liquidate one of the partnership's subsidiary corporations. The accountant was liable for failing to note the adverse effect this would have on the partnership's industrial revenue bond financing.[14] One recent case saw a consulting firm sued by a third party (the client's supplier of natural gas) when it advised a client not to pass on refunds that were allegedly due the supplier.

In another recent case, an accountant recommended that its client invest $59,000 with a seafood broker. The accountant was a shareholder, officer and director of the broker and made assurances to the client company. After losing its money, the client successfully sued the accountant. The court held that the accountant had a fiduciary relationship with the client and that the accountant's actions were unconscionable.[15]

None of these cases dealt specifically with management consulting, but they all illustrate how an accountant may be liable for giving business advice. The mixture of accounting and management consulting services creates a still undefined problem of liability.

---

[14] *The Billings Clinic v. Peat Marwick Main & Co.*, 797 P.2d 899 (Mont. 1990).

[15] *Dominguez v. Brackey Enterprises, Inc.*, 756 S.W.2d 788 (Tex. App. 1988).

Ethical Perspectives

Accounting Conflicts of Interest

As professionals, accountants should comply with a high ethical standard. A common ethical difficulty of accountants is the conflict of interest. A problematic conflict of interest arises whenever a person's ethical obligations conflict with that person's personal interests.

The most basic nature of the accountant's work seems to represent a conflict of interest. An accountant audits a company in order to present an accurate portrayal of its financial health to the public. Yet the company hires, pays, and potentially fires the accountant. A large company may pay between $1 and $6 million for an annual audit. An accounting firm is therefore somewhat beholden to the corporate entity that it should independently and fairly investigate.

The problem has become more pronounced because some accountants seemingly have favored their client's interests over fairness and accuracy. There are numerous cases in which a company received a clean bill of health in a financial audit and then promptly declared bankruptcy. This is especially true in the savings and loan industry.

Accountants have their own rules of ethics, which are intended to hold accountants to strict standards. The codes are necessarily worded vaguely, because so many different situations may arise. While such general codes may help improve the ethical environment, they cannot solve the problem of conflicts of interest.

Accountants are understandably wary about liability to third parties, because this opens firms to the potential for enormous damages. The very point of the accounting profession, though, is to render accurate and independent opinions that third parties can rely on.

Liability to third parties may therefore enhance the accountant's concern for ethical obligations and help counterbalance the inevitable concern for the corporate client's opinion.

The growth of management consulting services has created additional conflict of interest concerns. Management consulting business gives an accounting firm a greater stake in the client's business and also necessitates an auditor reviewing and second-guessing the decisions of the firm's own consulting practice.

Suppose a small company producing shoes lacks the knowledge to develop a computerized inventory system and hires a management consultant to do so. If the shoe company is later audited by the same firm, some charge that the auditors are unlikely to criticize their colleague's decisions. The AICPA disputes the existence of a problem, claiming that there is no substantial evidence that management consulting has impaired the independence of accountants. A U.S. Senate Committee, however, has concluded that auditors have subjugated themselves to clients in return for commitments from clients for profitable management consulting business.

Some suggest that a **Chinese Wall** could help ensure independence. This is a set of rules and physical office arrangements that prevent the communication of information within one company. Securities firms and law firms use this approach to guard against conflicts of interest.

While a Chinese Wall will not eliminate conflicts, it may mitigate them. An auditor will be more independent if the consultant is not a close coworker. The wall also could prevent auditors from knowing what the consultant recommended to the client corporation.

A more dramatic resolution would be to prohibit the same accounting firm from providing both auditing and management consulting services to a given company. This approach would largely eliminate any conflict of interest. Accounting firms argue, however, that the combined auditing and management consulting service is more efficient and enables them to offer a more informed service to the client.

International Perspectives

International Accounting Standards

Major U.S. accounting are global enterprises with dozens of foreign offices. The offices are closely tied together and accounting practice is increasingly international in scope. The accounting standards of the world's nations vary considerably, however.

U.S. accounting standards, for example, differ even from those in Canada in some significant respects. This fact has proved to be an obstacle to the full consummation of the United States-Canada free trade pact.[16] Asian standards differ from those in Europe, and there are significant differences among the nations of Europe. Some nations, such as Italy, do not even have a single authority for consistent accounting standards within that nation.

Different accounting standards not only complicate the efforts of accountants, they also have a significant impact on business operations. For example, the General Accounting Office has suggested that British and German companies have an advantage over U.S. companies in corporate acquisitions. U.S. accounting standards require the capitalization of goodwill costs and their amortization against future income. British and German standards permit writing off the costs against shareholder equity and thereby may avoid a decline in future earnings.

Different standards also complicate multinational stock offerings. At the present time, a company that wants to take advantage of such an offering must prepare financial statements according to the home country's accounting rules and must prepare additional statements for all the countries in which the offering will be made. This can be a costly procedure.

The International Accounting Standards Committee (IASC) has worldwide standards but these are voluntary and have had little practical impact. The IASC is attempting to adopt standards by the end of 1992 that will be made binding by governments. These standards apparently would be similar to the United States GAAP and would reduce the alternative accounting treatments permitted in financial statements. The European Community is also attempting to establish uniform community-wide standards and, ironically, this effort could derail the prospects for the IASC worldwide standards.

---

[16] A free trade pact is an agreement between governments that eliminates tariffs and other significant barriers to trade between the countries.

Questions and Case Problems

1. Arthur, an accountant, prepared the financial statements of the Velveteen Furniture Company. In preparing these statements, Arthur relied on Velveteen's inventory reports in preparation of the financial statements. The inventory report stated that the company's Lawrence warehouse was full of velour furniture. In fact, the warehouse was empty. A bank made a loan to Velveteen based on the collateral in the Lawrence and other warehouses, and the company eventually defaulted on the loan. The bank sues Arthur for negligence. Is Arthur liable to the bank?

2. Maple, an accountant, was employed by his wife to compile financial statements for her corporation and properly did so. His wife's corporation then became the target of an SEC investigation, and the government demanded that Maple provide all his working papers and documents in connection with his wife's business. Maple considers these papers to be confidential and refuses to provide them. Will a court compel Maple to provide the information demanded?

3. Lincoln Grain employed Coopers & Lybrand to audit its financial statements. The firm certified that Lincoln Grain had correctly valued the inventory of its Iowa division at approximately $2 million. In reality, the manager of this division had been embezzling money from the company and the division inventory had a value of only about $140,000. Lincoln Grain sued Coopers & Lybrand, claiming that the audit should have discovered its employee's defalcations and the failure to do so damaged the company. The firm defended on the grounds that Lincoln Grain was itself negligent in failing to discover the embezzlement. Is Coopers & Lybrand liable to Lincoln Grain on these facts? [*Lincoln Grain, Inc. v. Coopers & Lybrand,* 345 N.W.2d 300 (Neb. 1984)].

4. Fidler, the president of Witt Corporation, engaged Hanson, an accountant, to examine Witt's financial statements and issue a report for the annual stockholders' meeting, which would be held on March 31. The staff of Witt were slow in providing Hanson with information, however, and sometimes refused information. Hanson did his best and ultimately issued the report on April 4. Fidler refused to accept or pay for the report because it was no longer required. Hanson sued Witt to recover the fee for preparation of the report. Should Hanson be able to recover her fee?

5. A company retained Rothenburg, an accountant, to review its books. Rothenburg prepared a report that failed to discover or disclose very large defalcations by the company's employees. Rothenburg claimed that he was employed only to perform a "write up" of the plaintiff's books and records, and the company claimed that he was employed to conduct a regular audit. Rothenburg's worksheets indicate that he did in fact examine the company's bank statement, invoices, and bills. Should Rothenburg be liable to the company for negligent performance of services? [*1136 Tenants' Corp. v. Max Rothenburg & Co.,* 319 N.Y.S. 2d 1007 (1970)].

Chapter Seven

Securities Law and Regulation

Key Background

The essential background for this chapter on securities law and regulation is found in Chapter 43 of *West's Business Law, Seventh Edition,* and in Chapter 28 of *West's Legal Environment of Business, Third Edition.* These chapters cover corporations—financial regulation and investor protection and securities regulation. Among the important points to remember from this chapter are:

- the definition of a security
- the required contents of a registration statement
- the securities that are exempt form registration requirements
- the law restricting insider trading
- the law covering the regulation of investment companies

The reader will also benefit from familiarity with the duties of corporate directors and officers (in Chapter 41 of *West's Business Law, Seventh Edition*) and the Racketeer Influenced and Corrupt Organizations Act (in Chapter 7 of *West's Business Law, Seventh Edition*).

* * *

This chapter expands on the coverage of *West's Business Law, Seventh Edition,* and *West's Legal Environment of Business, Third Edition,* by providing additional detail on the definition of securities subject to regulation by the SEC, the requirements of securities' registration, the prohibition on insider trading, and liability under RICO. In addition, the chapter addresses other securities law issues, including liability under sections 11 and 12 of the 1933 Act, corporate liability for false and misleading disclosures, proxy regulations, and regulation of securities broker-dealers.

The Securities Act of 1933

The first substantial law for regulation of securities was the Securities Act of 1933. This law requires that securities be registered with the Securities and Exchange Commission. The registration must be accompanied by extensive disclosure of the nature of the securities being offered.

A threshold issue in securities regulation is the definition of the securities subject to regulation. Most people think of securities as shares of stock in a corporation, but the term is actually much broader and applies to many investment contracts. Creative finance professionals continue to invent new investment approaches. If the approach is not considered a security, considerable regulation and expense can be avoided. Failure to recognize that a new device should be considered a security, however, can have disastrous consequences in both civil and criminal liability. In the past, "many deals have been scuttled, parties held liable, and lawyers sued for failure...to recognize that a 'security' was present."[1] Consequently, understanding the definition of a security is of great importance.

The 1933 Act sets the groundwork for securities regulation, including the definition of "security" that may be covered. As discussed in *West's Business Law, Seventh Edition,* and *West's Legal Environment of Business, Third Edition,* the basic test for a regulated security is a transaction in which a person:

1. Invests.

2. In a common enterprise.

3. Reasonably expecting profits.

4. Derived primarily or substantially from others' managerial or entrepreneurial efforts.

Courts generally have interpreted this test broadly, to prevent evasion of the securities laws. A wide variety of investment contracts are covered by this definition. A plaintiff may claim that virtually any investment contract should be regulated as a security.

Many limited partnerships are considered securities under federal law. The SEC has said that participation in the sale of condominium units along with an arrangement to manage their rental is a regulated security. In a California case, the court held that the sale of memberships in a country club operated for profit should be considered a security.[2]

Some categories of investments are not covered by the definition of a security. For example, the test of a security requires a common enterprise, which implies a group of investors pooling their funds to share in a success or failure. Courts have found no security when there was only a single investor in a contract. Thus, suppose Kara Nash places her money with the Stevens, Jones investment firm or other brokerage to invest in securities. Is her contract with the brokerage itself a security? Because there is no common enterprise or pooled fund of investors, Kara's contract for placement of her money is not a security under the 1933 Act.

Other investments are not securities because they carry no expectations of profit. After release of the movie "Urban Cowboy," an entrepreneur marketed certificates representing one-millionth shares of a Texas longhorn steer. The SEC ruled that no security registration was necessary, because the certificates of ownership were mere novelties, and the certificate's purchasers had no expectation of profit from their purchase. While the entrepreneur certainly intended to profit from selling the "longhorn shares," the purchasers did not buy the certificates in hopes of their appreciation and resale for a profit. Also, when an investment is for personal use or consumption, it is not a security under the 1933 Act. Buying a health club membership or shares in a cooperative housing project in which to live is not a securities transaction.

The final test for a security is that the expected profits must derive from the managerial or entrepreneurial efforts of *others*. When an individual personally manages the investment, it is not a security. As a result, a general partner who helps manage the partnership has no security, but a limited partner who cannot participate in management usually does hold a security in a partnership. For the same reason, the holder of a franchise, such as a McDonald's outlet, holds no security, because he intends to profit from his own management efforts.

A 1990 Supreme Court decision slightly broadened the definition of a securities regulated by federal law. In that case, an agricultural cooperative sold $10 million in unsecured promissory notes. After the cooperative defaulted on the notes, the purchasers sought to recover for fraud under the securities laws. An appellate court held that the notes were not securities, but the Supreme Court reversed this decision. While these notes were not traded on any exchange, the court found that a note would generally be a security "if the seller's purpose is to raise money for the general use of a business enterprise or to finance substantial investments and the buyer is interested primarily in the profit the note is expected to generate." The Court was careful to hold that other notes, such as mortgages and consumer loans, would not be considered securities.

▬ Registration and SEC Review

When securities are issued, the issuer generally must file a registration statement with the SEC that makes certain disclosures about the issuer and the securities, including financial statements. For issuers who must register, the process is a detailed and costly one. The contents of this registration statement are well described in *West's Business Law, Seventh Edition,* and in *West's Legal Environment of Business, Third Edition.* This chapter will not repeat the contents but will elaborate the consequences of a defective registration of securities.

An organization planning to issue securities will require some time to prepare the detailed registration materials required by the SEC. The period during which these are being prepared is called the prefiling

---

[1] Marc Steinberg, *Understanding Securities Law* (1989), p. 15.
[2] *Silver Hills Country Club v. Sobieski*, 361 P.2d 906 (1961).

period. During this time, the issuer may not offer its securities for sale. The issuer cannot even publicize the planned future offering of securities—this is called "gun jumping."

In one well-known case, the owner of land in Florida sought to place it in a new corporation that would be financed through an offering of securities. During the prefiling period, the issuer put out press releases that described the new corporation and spoke of the potential value of the Florida properties. The publicity brought forth numerous purchasers, some of whom were disappointed when it turned out that the land had an undesirable location. The SEC sanctioned the issuer for gun-jumping.[3]

The prefiling period ends when the issuer submits its registration materials to the SEC. The 1933 Act provides twenty days for SEC review before the registration becomes effective. During this time, the SEC scrutinizes the proposed registration for completeness and accuracy. This is called the waiting period. During the waiting period, the issuer may begin to sell the securities through a prospectus. The contents of a prospectus are defined by section 10 of the Act. Most other written sales materials are prohibited during this period, however.

SEC Rule 134 does permit one special type of written sales material during the waiting period, called the "tombstone ad." Tombstone ads are those with very simple explanatory information, surrounded by a black border, which usually appear in publications such as the *Wall Street Journal*. Tombstone ads are limited to very basic information, such as the name of the issuer, the amount of securities being offered, a brief description of the company's business, the contemplated price of the securities, and the expected date of their issuance.

The number of new securities registrations is so great that the SEC cannot give close scrutiny to each. Registration statements by established companies may not be reviewed and their approval is often accelerated. New issuers generally receive closer examination of registration statements. After review, the SEC may demand more substantiation of claims or seek modifications in the issuer's financial statements. Even SEC acceptance of a registration statement does not constitute a legal finding of the statement's accuracy but simply permits the registration to become effective, allowing the sale of securities to proceed.

After the registration statement becomes effective, the issuer may begin to offer and sell the securities. The offeror can begin to use different forms of written sales literature but must generally still provide purchasers with a prospectus. In some circumstances, the issuer may use a shorter summary prospectus when making solicitations of sale.

Most major securities issuances are conducted through underwriters—organizations that specialize in placing securities with purchasers. Using underwriters helps guarantee that the offering will succeed. Underwriters usually agree to purchase all the offered securities at a discount and then resell them to investors or securities dealers. On other occasions, underwriters simply act as agents of the issuer, using their best efforts to place the offered securities. Underwriters' activities also are regulated by the SEC.

Exhibit 7-1 summarizes the restrictions on the sale of securities during the various stages of the registration process.

---

[3] *Carl M. Loeb, Rhoades & Co.* 38 S.E.C. 843 (1959).

Exhibit 7-1

Legal Restrictions During Registration Process

Prefiling Period	Waiting Period	Post-Effective Period
Offers to sell and sales prohibited	Oral offers allowed	Offers and sales allowed if prospectus provided
Some publicity of forthcoming offering allowed	Written offers by prospectus allowed	Summary prospectus allowed for solicitation
Negotiations with underwriter allowed	Tombstone Ad allowed	
	Other offers prohibited	
	Sales prohibited	

Section 11 Private Actions

If a false and misleading securities registration statement survives SEC review, and if a purchaser is injured by these false and misleading statements, the private purchaser may sue under section 11 of the 1933 Act. To make out a case under section 11, such a private plaintiff must always prove the following elements:

1. The existence of false statements or omissions in a registration statement when it becomes effective.

2. Materiality of those misstatements or omissions.

3. The plaintiff's reliance on the defective registration statement in purchasing the securities.

A plaintiff may sue even if she did not purchase the securities directly from the defendant issuer. For example, assume that Brighttex Corporation issues new securities with a registration statement. Antonio purchases these newly issued securities. Antonio then resells these securities to Margaret. If Margaret can show that the specific securities purchased were issued through a defective registration statement and that she relied on this registration statement when purchasing the securities from Antonio, she can sue Brighttex under section 11.

The issuing corporation, such as Brighttex, is not the only party who may be liable under section 11. The statute lists other potentially liable parties, including the directors of the issuer and principal executive officers of the issuer, as well as every underwriter and certain accountants, appraisers and other experts who prepared or certified a portion of the registration statement. Also potentially liable is anyone who "controls any person liable under section 11."

Defendants are liable only for "material" misstatements or omissions. The materiality of a misstatement or omission is critical to liability under this section of the securities laws, and this concept recurs throughout other sections. Materiality essentially means importance, and the courts will find information to be material if a reasonable investor would consider it important to the decision whether or not to buy a security, considered in the context of the total mix of available information. The determination of materiality is highly fact-specific, depending on close consideration of the disclosures in each disputed case.

The issuer of shares is strictly liable for any material omissions or misstatements in registration, even if the issuer had a good faith belief in the accuracy of the registration statement. Other defendants have the benefit of a due diligence defense. This defense protects those who performed a reasonable investigation and possessed a reasonable belief that the registration statement was complete and accurate. For these defendants, only negligent omissions or misstatements produce liability. Experts and inside directors are subject to a relatively high standard of diligence and accuracy, while outside directors and certain others may be subject to a lower standard of care.

Underwriters are considered experts who are held to high standards of diligence under section 11. Although underwriters may be unaware of the inaccuracies of the registration prepared by the issuer, they usually have access to the necessary information and the leverage required to force full disclosure. Consequently, underwriters must carefully scrutinize registration materials before participating in an offering. The law provides that even an underwriter is protected for "any part of the registration purporting to be made on the authority of an expert" such as a certified public accountant, so long as the underwriter had no reason to believe that the information was misleading.

Section 12 Private Actions

Section 12(1) of the 1933 Act provides straight forward relief to purchasers for a limited set of circumstances. If anyone offers or sells a security without an effective registration statement, she is liable to the purchaser for rescission or damages. The standard is strict liability, so a plaintiff need not show negligence, nor is there the same type of due diligence defense as under section 11. Defendants include those who offered or sold securities, which may include attorneys, investment bankers and others who were substantially involved in the sale.

Section 12(2) of the 1933 Act provides broad liability against anyone who makes a public offering of securities and makes omissions or misstatements with respect to a material fact. This misstatement or omission need not be made in the registration statement; section 12(2) also covers any other selling documents or even oral statements in connection with the sale of newly offered securities. Indeed, this section covers exempt securities that need not be registered. Potentially responsible defendants under section 12(2) include all "sellers"—those who actually sold the securities and some other parties who actively promoted the sale.

Under section 12(2), a plaintiff purchaser of securities must show a material misstatement or omission in connection with a sale in an initial issuance of securities, just as under section 11. The plaintiff must also allege the defendant seller's awareness of the misstatement, and the burden then shifts to the seller to demonstrate that he did not know of and could not reasonably have known of the inaccuracy.

Courts have increasingly applied the "bespeaks caution" doctrine to dismiss challenges under section 12(2). Virtually all prospectuses contain a section describing the risks of the investment, and the bespeaks caution doctrine holds that investors are thereby warned of risk and cannot complain of misleading omissions. A general risk warning is not a sufficient defense if specific materially misleading statements are made elsewhere in the prospectus, however.

While section 12 does not contain a specific due diligence defense, the seller normally can avoid liability by proving that it used reasonable care in the sale of securities. Courts have held that reasonable care depends on the circumstances of the offering. Sellers of a small, exempt offering of securities are held to a lower standard of care than those involved in major registered offerings. Section 12 damages are measured in the same manner as damages under section 11.

One controversial issue under section 12 involves which persons, other than the actual seller, are potential defendants. The Supreme Court recently established criteria for liability.

Case 7.1
Pinter v. Dahl
United States Supreme Court, 1988
486 U.S. 622

Background and Facts *Billie J. Pinter sold unregistered securities in oil and gas leases to Maurice Dahl. Dahl then touted the securities to friends, family and business associates and assisted them in subscribing to the securities, though Dahl received no commission. The venture failed, so Dahl and other purchasers sued Pinter for the unlawful sale of unregistered securities. Pinter counterclaimed against Dahl, claiming that he actively solicited the sales of others and should therefore share liability as a "seller" under section 12.*

The trial court granted judgment for plaintiffs and rejected Pinter's counterclaim against Dahl. The court of appeals affirmed, and specifically held that Dahl was not a seller under the terms of section 12 because he received no financial benefit. Pinter appealed to the Supreme Court. One key issue was whether Dahl was a potentially liable seller under section.

BLACKMUN, Justice.

* * * *

An interpretation of statutory seller that includes brokers and others who solicit offers to purchase securities furthers the purposes of the Securities Act–to promote full and fair disclosure of information to the public in the sales of securities. In order to effectuate Congress' intent that § 12(1) civil liability be *in terrorem*, see Douglas & Bates, 43 Yale L.J., at 173; Shulman, 43 Yale L.J., at 227, the risk of its invocation should be felt by solicitors of purchases. The solicitation of a buyer is perhaps the most critical stage of the selling transaction. It is the first stage of a traditional securities sale to involve the buyer, and it is directed at producing the sale. In addition, brokers and other solicitors are well positioned to control the flow of information to a potential purchaser, and, in fact, such persons are the participants in selling transaction who most often disseminate material information to investors. Thus, solicitation is the stage at which an investor is most likely to be injured, that is, by being persuaded to purchase securities without full and fair information. Given Congress' overriding goal of preventing this injury, we may infer that Congress intended solicitation to fall under the mantle of § 12(1).

Although we conclude that Congress intended § 12(1) liability to extend to those who solicit securities purchases, we share the Court of Appeals' conclusion that Congress did not intend to impose rescission based on strict liability on a person who urges the purchase but whose motivation is solely to benefit the buyer. When a person who urges another to make a securities purchase acts merely to assist the buyer, not only is it uncommon to say that the buyer "purchased" from him, but it is also strained to describe the giving of gratuitous advice, even strongly or enthusiastically, as "soliciting." Section 2(3) defined an offer as a "solicitation of an offer to buy…for value." The person who gratuitously urges another to make a particular investment decision is not, in any meaningful sense, requesting value in exchange for his suggestion or seeking the value the titleholder will obtain in exchange for the ultimate sale. The language and purpose of § 12(1) suggest that liability extends only to the person who successfully solicits the purchase, motivated at least in part by a desire to serve his own financial interests or those of the securities owner. If he had such a motivation, it is fair to say that the buyer "purchased" the security from him and to align him with the owner in a rescission action.

We are unable to determine whether Dahl may be held liable as statutory seller under § 12(1). The District Court explicitly found that "Dahl solicited each of the other plaintiffs (save perhaps Grantham) in connection with the offer, purchase, and receipt of their oil and gas interests." We cannot conclude that this finding was clearly erroneous. It is not clear, however, that Dahl had the kind of interest in the sales that make him liable as a statutory seller. We do know that he received no commission from Pinter in connection with the other sales, but this is not conclusive. Typically, a person who solicits the purchase will have sought or received a personal financial benefit from the sale, such as where he "anticipat[es] a share of the profits," *Lawler v. Gilliam*, 569 F.2d, at 1288, or receives a brokerage commission, *Cady v. Murphy*, 113 F.2d, at 990. But a person who solicits the buyer's purchase in order to serve the financial interests of the owner may properly be liable under § 12(1) without showing that he expects to participate in the benefits the owner enjoys.

Decision and Remedy   *The Supreme Court vacated the judgment of the court of appeals and remanded the case for a new trial.*

▬ The Securities Exchange Act of 1934

The Securities Exchange Act of 1934 expanded upon the 1933 Act and regulated the markets in which securities are traded. This law initiated regulation of the exchanges where securities are traded and also contained additional disclosure requirements, such as the prohibition on insider trading. Like the 1933 Act, the 1934 law focused upon full and accurate disclosure of material facts in connection with securities transactions.

▬ Insider Trading

Section 10(b) of the 1934 Act, as elaborated by SEC Rule 10b-5, prohibits fraud in connection with securities transactions, One leading form of prohibited fraud is insider trading, in which an individual who has secret inside information about a company uses that information to trade in the corporation's shares and profit from the secret inside information.

The traditional insider trading case was rather straightforward. It involved a true corporate insider, such as a chief executive officer, who became aware of some imminent development regarding his company. If the development were a good one, the insider would buy his company's shares, then the information would become public, increased demand for the shares would drive up their price, and the insider would reap the benefits of the shares' appreciation. If the development were a bad one, the insider would sell his shares in the company before the information became public, thereby avoiding a loss on the stock. This traditional approach is illustrated by the *Texas Gulf Sulphur* case in *West's Business Law, Seventh Edition*.

"Temporary insiders" working on a specific corporate transaction, may also be liable under section 10(b). Sometimes, a lawyer, accountant or other outsider will receive inside information about a corporation. Courts have held that these temporary insiders owe a duty not to take advantage of this information and profit from insider trading.

Recently, however, courts have grappled with the problem of total "outsiders" who trade on inside information. Occasionally, a person wholly outside a corporation may obtain inside information about the company. There is no absolute rule against outsiders using inside information to profit. Under some circumstances, however, such outsiders may be found in violation of insider trading laws. There are two leading theories whereby outsiders may be liable—the tipper/tippee theory and the misappropriation theory.

The tipper/tippee theory is designed to prevent insiders from indirectly profiting on inside information by "tipping" friendly outsiders with such information before it becomes public. The situation might develop as follows. Baker is an executive vice president of Microwave, Inc. Baker becomes aware that another company is planning to make a lucrative offer for the stock of Microwave at a higher price. Baker informs his banker, Prentice, of this still-secret development, in exchange for obtaining a low interest loan. The banker then buys stock in Microwave and profits when the offer is subsequently announced to the public. In this case, both Baker (the tipper) and Prentice (the tippee) are liable under section 10(b).

Not all stock tips are illegal, however. The requirements for tipper/tippee liability are strict. A tipper of information is only liable when the following conditions are met:

1. Disclosure of material insider information.

2. In violation of a legal or fiduciary duty not to disclose the information.

3. In expectation of some benefit in return.

There is no insider trading violation unless the tipper had some duty not to disclose, but most insiders do have such a duty not to disclose inside information about their own companies. Nor is there an insider trading violation if the tipper discloses the information without expectation of benefit in return. These limitations are illustrated in discussions in *West's Business Law, Seventh Edition*. Insider trading is not illegal unless it involves some breach of fiduciary duty.

The tippee may also be liable under section 19(b). Any tippee liability, however, is derivative of the tipper's liability. This means that a tippee can only be liable if the tipper is also liable. One leading case involved Barry Switzer, the former football coach at the University of Oklahoma. Switzer was lying down on the bleachers at a track meet when he inadvertently overheard another observer, G. Platt, mention an impending corporate sale to his wife. Switzer traded on and profited from the information. Switzer was not liable for insider trading, however. Mr. Platt was not an illegal tipper because he did not mean to be informing Switzer of the sale and thus could not have done so with expectation of benefit. Because Platt, the inadvertent tipper, was not liable, neither was Switzer.

If a tipper has violated the insider trading laws, however, the tippee may also be liable. When the tipper is potentially liable, the tippee is also liable whenever the tippee knew or should have known that the information received was material inside information. If the tippee has reason to know that the tip is secret information, she may not trade on the information. Thus, people may come upon nonpublic information and legally trade upon it, so long as they are reasonably unaware that the information is inside information or so long as an unlawful tipper is not involved.

Outsiders trading on inside information may also be liable under the misappropriation theory. This theory is an outgrowth of the *Chiarella* case in which a financial printer was found not liable for trading on inside information because the printer was not an insider of the corporation whose stock was traded. Use of the misappropriation theory might have convicted Chiarella. Under this theory, a person violates section 10(b) if he or she trades on material insider information that he or she misappropriated (stole) from another person or corporation. Thus, if an employee of the *Wall Street Journal* buys or sells stock based on inside information acquired through his work at the newspaper, he may be violating insider-trading law. This information is the property of the *Wall Street Journal* and the employee has misappropriated the information when he uses it for private personal gain.

Case 7.2
United States v. O'Hagan
United States Supreme Court, 1997
S.Ct

Background and Facts *Grand Metropolitan PLC retained the law firm of Dorsey & Whitney to represent the company in a potential tender offer for the Pillsbury Company. James O'Hagan was a partner of Dorsey & Whitney. He did not actively work on the representation of Grand Met but was aware of it and began purchasing shares and options on Pillsbury stock. After Grand Met publicly announced its tender offer, the price of Pillsbury stock rose dramatically. O'Hagan then sold his shares and options, for a profit of more than $4.3 million. The SEC then indicted O'Hagan and charged him with securities fraud in violation of §10(b). He was convicted at trial, but the Eighth Circuit Court of Appeals reversed the convictions, holding the misappropriation theory invalid. The SEC appealed to the Supreme Court.*

GINSBURG, Justice.

* * * *

Under the "traditional" or "classical theory" of insider trading liability, §10(b) and Rule 10b-5 are violated when a corporate insider trades in the securities of his corporation on the basis of material, nonpublic information. * * *

The "misappropriation theory" holds that a person commits fraud "in connection with" a securities transaction, and thereby violates §10(b) and Rule 10b-5 when he misappropriates confidential information for securities trading purposes, in breach of a duty owed to the source of the information. . . . In lieu of premising liability on a fiduciary relationship between company insider and purchaser or seller of the company's stock, the misappropriation theory premises liability on a fiduciary-turned-trader's deception of those who entrusted him with access to confidential information.

The two theories are complementary, each addressing efforts to capitalize on nonpublic information through the purchase or sale of securities. The classical theory targets a corporate insider's breach of duty to shareholders with whom the insider transacts; the misappropriation theory outlaws trading on the basis of nonpublic information by a corporate "outsider" in breach of a duty owed not to a trading party, but to the source of the information.

Decision and Remedy *The Court reversed the Eighth Circuit judgment and remanded for further proceedings consistent with the Court's opinion.*

Fraudulent Corporate Disclosures

Section 10(b) and Rule 10b-5 do more than simply prohibit insider trading—they outlaw any material fraudulent statements in connection with the purchase or sale of securities. For example, a corporation with publicly marketed shares might manipulate its financial records to conceal a quarterly loss or might artificially inflate its future earnings projections. In these cases, the company has violated section 10(b). Other SEC rules cover fraudulent statements made in certain specific contexts. For example, Rule 13e-3 prohibits deceptive statements made in the purchase of all publicly held shares of a company in a **going-private transaction**. Under these rules, a company is only liable for those misstatements that were made intentionally or recklessly, however.

Knowingly false statements may give rise to section 10(b) liability. In addition, companies may have a duty to speak, and a material omission may violate the section. When a company's officials speak on a topic, they must fully disclose material information or possibly be liable for a material omission. Thus, a company may have a duty to reveal bad news. Section 10(b) imposes potential liability for any of the following actions:

1. A false statement, such as lying about the amount of profits for the past year.

2. A true but misleading statement, such as reporting profits accurately but in a misleading context.

3. An omission, such as failure to disclose the unusual circumstances behind a year's profits.

A key to section 10(b) liability is the concept of materiality. A company is only liable if its false or misleading disclosure or omission is significant enough to be material. The commonly accepted test for materiality is whether the information would have significantly altered the "total mix" of information in the view of the hypothetical "reasonable investor."

There is an ongoing controversy over a company's obligation to disclose "soft" information. "Hard" information is that involving factual, objective information and generally must be disclosed. "Soft" information generally involves future predictions for the company, including corporate plans and forecasts. Generally, soft information need not be disclosed, but courts consider the issue on a case-by-case basis. Disclosure of soft information may be required, depending on issues such as "the qualifications of those who prepared or compiled it; ... its relevance to the stockholders' impending decision; ... and the availability to the investor of other more reliable sources of information."[4] On other occasions, a company may be liable under section 10(b) if it *does* disclose soft information that is not particularly reliable.

The Private Securities Litigation Reform Act of 1975 (PSLRA) created a safe harbor for certain forward-looking statements. The safe harbor is found in a new Section 27A in the 1933 Act and new Section 21A in the 1934 Act. Under these new sections, a company cannot be liable for such statements that prove inaccurate, so long as they are accompanied by meaningful cautionary statements identifying important factors that could cause actual results to differ from those projected. The safe harbor extends to press releases, oral statements, and many other communications but does not apply to forward-looking statements in initial public offering documents, tender offers, and certain other circumstances. Nor does the shelter apply to statements made in bad faith or without a reasonable basis.

Another controversial question is the responsibility of a company to deal with rumors about its stock. One particularly significant rumor would involve a potential merger of the corporation. In the following case, the Supreme Court set forth the standard for how the company can or must respond to rumors of a potential merger.

---

[4] *Flynn v. Bass Brothers Enterprises*, 744 F.2d 978, 988 (3d Circ. 1984).

Case 7.3
Basic, Incorporated v. Levison
United States Supreme Court, 1988
108 S.Ct. 978

Background and Facts Basic, Incorporated, was a publicly traded company manufacturing materials for the steel industry. In 1976, representatives of Combustion Engineering, Inc., began meeting with officers of Basic regarding a possible merger. During 1977 and 1978, Basic made three public statements denying that it was engaged in merger negotiations. On December 18, 1978, Basic issued a press release stating that it had been approached regarding a merger. On December 19, Basic's board of directors endorsed Combustion's tender offer to acquire Basic.

Max Levinson and others were Basic shareholders who held shares after the time of Basic's denial of merger negotiations, but who sold their shares before the merger announcement in December 1978. They contended that they sold their shares for an artificially low price, due to Basic's false and misleading denial of merger negotiations during this time. The shareholders sued for damages under section 10(b). The district court granted summary judgment for defendants, holding that the denials of merger negotiations were not material. The Sixth Circuit Court of Appeals reversed the summary judgment, and the Supreme Court took the case on writ of certiorari.

BLACKMUN, Justice.

* * * *

The application of this materiality standard to preliminary merger discussions is not self-evident. Where the impact of the corporate development on the target's fortune is certain and clear, the TSC *Industries* materiality definition admits straightforward application. Where, on the other hand, the event is contingent or speculative in nature, it is difficult to ascertain whether the "reasonable investor" would have considered the omitted information significant at the time. Merger negotiations, because of the ever-present possibility that the contemplated transaction will not be effectuated, fall into the latter category.

* * * *

Whether merger discussions in any particular case are material therefore depends on the facts. Generally, in order to assess the probability that the event will occur, a factfinder will need to look to indicia of interest in the transaction at the highest corporate levels. Without attempting to catalog all such possible factors, we note by way of example that board resolutions, instructions to investment bankers, and actual negotiations between principals or their intermediaries may serve as indicia of interest. To assess the magnitude of the transaction to the issuer of the securities allegedly manipulated, a factfinder will need to consider such facts as the size of the two corporate entities and of the potential premiums over market value. No particular event or factor short of closing the transaction need be either necessary or sufficient by itself to render merger discussions material.

As we clarify today, materiality depends on the significance the reasonable investor would place on the withheld or misrepresented information. The fact-specific inquiry we endorse here is consistent with the approach a number of courts have taken in assessing the materiality of merger negotiations. Because the standard of materiality we have adopted differs from that used by both courts below, we remand the case for reconsideration of the question whether a grant of summary judgment is appropriate on this record.

Decision and Remedy *The Court vacated the decision of the court of appeals and remanded the case for further proceedings consistent with this opinion.*

Only a purchaser or seller of securities may bring a section 10(b) action. This requirement significantly restricts the number of potential plaintiffs. Suppose that Cohenco puts out false and misleading information on its future prospects. Because of the information Mr. Shapiro decides *not* to purchase shares of Cohenco. Shapiro has no remedy because he was not a purchaser or seller of shares. Similarly, a shareholder who elects not to sell her shares because of information has no damages remedy under section 10(b).

In addition to the criminal penalties discussed in *West's Business Law, Seventh Edition,* and in *West's Legal Environment of Business, Third Edition*, section 10(b) also provides for a private civil action to recover damages from false or misleading disclosures. When a breach of section 10(b) has occurred, a purchaser or seller of securities may sue the responsible party for damages. Suppose Leon buys stock in Keefe & Associates for $50/share, based on unrealistic earnings projections put out by the company. When true information comes out, the price of the shares drops to $40/share. Leon could recover $10/share in a section 10(b) private action. Leon need not even prove that he personally read and relied upon the misstatement, because the law reflects a presumption that the general market has responded to the misinformation. This is generally called the "fraud on the market" theory.

In these cases, there can be an overlap between section 10(b) of the 1934 Act and sections 11 and 12 of the 1933 Act. Section 10(b) is often preferable for plaintiffs, because it is not limited to public offerings of new shares, it offers more potential defendants, and it may provide a longer statute of limitations.

The PSLRA contains provisions limiting corporate liability, such as the safe harbor for forward-looking statements discussed above. Other important provisions provide for reform of class action representation, a stay on discovery pending the resolution of a defendant's motion to dismiss, and a limitation of joint and several liability to cases of knowing violations of the law.

Proxy Regulations

Section 14 of the 1934 Act regulates the solicitation of proxies of companies required to register their securities. The term "proxy" is broadly defined to include any attempt by management to solicit the consent of their shareholders to corporate actions. As described in Chapter 43 of *West's Business Law, Seventh Edition*, shareholders possess certain election rights to select directors, modify corporate articles, and dictate some other corporate policies.

A proxy works as follows. Written proxy statements are sent by management to shareholders to obtain shareholder approval of management policies in an election. Shareholders who approve of management policies return a **proxy card** that authorizes management representatives to vote their shares at a shareholders' meeting. Those who disapprove may give a proxy card to a dissenting group who will vote the shares against management. Companies invariably send proxy solicitations in connection with their annual meeting, and the Act requires that these solicitations contain certain information specified by the SEC in Schedule 14A.

Proxy contests may arise, when some nonmanagement shareholder group seeks to elect a new slate of directors or to adopt some new corporate policy opposed by management. All participants in such an election contest must file a Schedule 14B with the SEC, requiring certain disclosures in proxy materials. The Schedule 14B must disclose the identity of the participants, the amount of their shareholdings, the nature of their involvement in the proxy contest and other relevant facts. The SEC scrutinizes these schedules to ensure that proxy disclosures are not materially false or misleading.

If a material misstatement or omission in a proxy solicitation slips past the SEC review, individual shareholders may sue. SEC Rule 14a-9 prohibits solicitation of proxies with statements that contain materially false or misleading information. Materiality is similar to the standard under section 10(b). In the proxy context, the test for materiality is whether the information has "a significant propensity to affect the voting process." If the shareholders win, they may overturn the results of the shareholder election, which was tainted by proxy materials containing material omissions or false statements.

Rule 14a-8 authorizes shareholders to make their own proposals for corporate governance at annual meetings. If a shareholder presents a proposal that is proper under the relevant state corporations statute, the company's management must include the proposal in the management's proxy statement, along with a brief statement of the shareholder's purpose for the proposal, so long as the proposal is received in adequate time for inclusion (usually 120 days before release of the management's proxy statement).

Shareholders can use this authority to submit proposals for both economic goals and political goals (such as requiring divestment from South African corporations). To be included in proxy materials, shareholder proposals cannot relate to the ordinary conduct of business but must involve some special action. For example, a shareholder proposal that a company should be put up for sale involves an exceptional transaction and must be included. Management may, however, oppose these proposals and present its reasons for opposition.

The Williams Act

In 1968, Congress passed the Williams Act, which amended the Securities Exchange Act of 1934. This Act regulated a newly developed means of taking over a corporation, known as a "tender offer." In a tender offer, some party makes an offer to a target company's shareholders to buy their stock in a company at some set price. For example, Paramount Communications, Inc. tried to take over Time, Incorporated, by making a public offer to all of Time's shareholders to buy their shares at $175/share. Tender offers, by definition, have certain characteristics, such as a public solicitation of public shareholders for a substantial percentage of the target's stock, usually at a significant premium over the prevailing market price.

There are differences among tender offers, however. The offeror may offer to buy all shares or only a percentage, and may offer cash for the shares or new securities. A successful tender offer is usually followed by a merger. The new owner uses majority control of the corporation to approve a merger of the company. Even those shareholders who did not sell in response to the tender offer may thus be compelled to relinquish their shares in a "second-step merger."

Congress passed the Williams Act because some tender offers were considered to be coercive and unfair. For example, some offerors made two-tier, front-end-loaded tender offers. In this type of offer, the acquirer offers a premium price for the first substantial percentage of shares tendered and a lower price for the remaining shares in a subsequent merger. For example, suppose Megacorp makes a tender offer for Minicorp. Megacorp might offer $125 per share in the first tier, for the first 67 percent of shares tendered. Assuming that this percentage of shares was tendered, Megacorp would then use its majority authority to merge the corporation and squeeze out the 33 percent of nontendering shareholders at a lower price in the second tier, such as $75 per share. Such offers tend to stampede shareholders into a quick acceptance of the offer, to avoid falling into the second tier and receiving a lower price. Today, most tender offers are not of this two-tier type, but many commentators still consider them to be coercive of shareholders.

A tender offer is usually preceded by quiet purchases of the target company's stock on the open market. Section 13 of the amended act and SEC Rule 13d-1 require that an individual or group of affiliated individuals must publicly declare when they have obtained more than five percent of the shares of certain corporations. These parties must file a Schedule 13D with the SEC, which requires disclosure of their identity, the number of shares they own, their purpose in buying the shares, and any plans they have for acquiring or altering the corporation's business, among other items. These requirements apply even if the person or group has no intent to make a tender offer.

If the purchaser goes forward and makes a tender offer for the corporation's shares, section 14 requires certain disclosures. Offerors must file a Schedule 14D-1 on the day the offer is commenced, and certain facts must be disclosed either in this Schedule or in the offer itself. Required disclosures include the name and background of the offeror, the source of financing for the tender offer, any plans for changes in the target's management, business or share marketability, and other facts. If disclosures are inadequate or misleading, the SEC and private parties may seek an injunction halting the tender offer.

The SEC recently adopted another regulation of tender offers in Rule 14d-10, known as the "all holders rule." This requires that a tender offer must be open to all a company's shareholders and that all shareholders have the opportunity to receive the same, best price. This rule prevents offerors from playing favorites in their tender offer and excluding certain shareholders from participation.

Section 14 also may require certain disclosures by the target corporation. Neither the target company nor its management can make any recommendation concerning a tender offer unless they file a Schedule 14D-9. Required disclosures are roughly similar to the Schedule 14D-1 and include disclosure of any negotiations with the offeror or a third party for a merger or corporate reorganization.

Rule 14e-2 also requires the management of the target company to respond to the tender offer within ten days by sending its shareholders a statement that recommends acceptance or rejection of the offer or expresses a position of neutrality on the offer. This statement must also provide reasons for management's position.

After a tender offer is commenced, shareholders must decide whether to tender their shares to the offeror or retain them. The Williams Act guarantees that shareholders must be given at least twenty business days to make this decision. Moreover, shareholders who tender their shares retain the right to withdraw their tender during the offering period before the offer closes. The Williams Act also contains a "best price" provision which guarantees all tendering shareholders the same, best price available. Thus, if an offeror raises its offer price during the offering period, the new higher price must be given even to shareholders who tendered prior to the increase. Section 14(e) of the Act also prohibits false and misleading disclosures and certain manipulative devices in connection with a tender offer.

Exhibit 7-2 summarizes the requirements of many of the most important SEC rules.

■ Regulation of Broker-Dealers

A broker is a "person engaged in the business of effecting transactions in securities for the account of others, but does not include a bank." A dealer is a "person engaged in the business of buying and selling securities for his own account." While broker-dealers are bound by various common law agency rules, the 1934 Act subjected them to additional regulation under federal securities law. Section 15(a) of that act requires a broker-dealer for nonexempt securities to register with the SEC. Broker-dealers are also regulated by private organizations, such as the National Association of Securities Dealers (NASD).

One important restriction on broker-dealers is the prohibition on **churning**. When brokers buy or sell stock for the accounts of others, they charge a small commission. The more transactions, the larger the total commission income. Churning is a practice of excessive trading to generate commissions, in which a broker advances his own interests at the expense of his client. In addition to violating the broker-dealer regulations of section 15(c)(1), churning has been held to violate section 10(b) and Rule 10b-5. The SEC may enforce these provisions, as may private plaintiffs injured by churning.

To prove churning, a plaintiff must first show that the broker controlled the client's account. In some accounts, a broker may trade without consulting the client in advance. This establishes the control element. Other factors, such as the client's inexperience with the market and particular trust in the broker, may also be used to establish this control element.

A plaintiff also must show excessive trading, which is a fact-specific, case-by-case determination. In addition to the frequency of trading, courts will consider the relative magnitude of the commissions generated to the size of the client's overall account. Courts may also look for "in and out trading" (selling and repurchasing the same security in a brief time period) and "cross trading" (shifting securities among accounts of different clients). Damages for churning typically include full restitution of all commissions received by the broker.

Another objectionable practice is called scalping—in which a broker-dealer purchases a company's securities for its own account and then recommends those shares to its clients, often reselling its own shares for a profit. Scalping can violate section 10(b) of the 1934 Act, because a broker's failure to disclose its purchases and resales to a client can be a material omission.

> **Exhibit 7-2**
>
> **Some Important SEC Rules and Schedules**
>
> **Rule 10b-5**
> Prohibits deceptive and manipulative practices in sale or purchase of securities
>
> **Schedule 13D**
> Statement of ownership that must be filed when person or group obtains more than 5% of class of company's securities
>
> **Rule 13e-3**
> Prohibits deceptive and manipulative practices in connection with going-private transactions
>
> **Rule 14a-9**
> Prohibits the solicitation of proxies that contain false or misleading statements or omissions
>
> **Schedule 14B**
> Statement that must be filed by all participants in a corporate election contest
>
> **Schedule 14D-1**
> Statement that must be filed by tender offeror, describing identity, financing, purpose of tender offer and plans for subject company
>
> **Rule 14d-9**
> Requires the subject company of a tender offer to disclose certain information
>
> **Schedule 14D-9**
> Statement that must be filed by subject company of tender offer, describing any arrangement or conflicts of interest with offeror, plus company's position on offer
>
> **Rule 14d-10**
> Requires that all shareholders have opportunity to receive the same "best price" in tender offer
>
> **Rule 14e-2**
> Requires that target management respond to shareholders within ten days of tender offer

Broker-dealers may also be liable for recommending stock purchases that are poorly suited to their clients. Brokers are expected to know their clients' needs and to investigate the securities they recommend. Certain high pressure sales tactics and cold-calling for securities sales, often called "boiler room operations," may also violate the duties of broker-dealers. The SEC requires that brokers find out certain minimum information about their client and about the recommended security before entering into a transaction.

In general, securities brokers are considered professionals and held to a higher degree of integrity in dealings with clients. The following case demonstrates the potential liability of brokers.

Case 7.4
Securities and Exchange Commission v. Ridenour
United States Circuit Court of Appeals, Eighth District 1990
913 F.2d 515

Background and Facts *Robert Ridenour was a very successful account executive in the institutional bond department of the brokerage firm of Dean Witter. Ridenour participated in over one hundred "matched trades" in which he would buy a security from a client, without informing the client that he was a purchaser. Then Ridenour would resell the same security at a profit to himself of over 90 percent. Sometimes he would resell the securities on the same day that he purchased them.*

The SEC filed a civil action against Ridenour for fraud. The district found that Ridenour had violated federal securities laws and ordered him to disgorge over $470,000 in his profits. Ridenour appealed.

LARSON, Senior District Judge. [sitting by designation]:

* * * *

The SEC acknowledges in its brief on appeal that in the usual bond transaction, a broker-dealer such as Ridenour does not owe a duty to those who are trading in bonds, because the dealer makes no representations about the price the dealer quotes, other than it is what the dealer is willing to pay. The SEC argues, however, that the issue in this case is not what the usual practice is but what Ridenour's relationship with his customers was. The district court agreed, finding that Ridenour was sophisticated and his clients were gullible: they relied on him to quote them the best available market price for the purchase and sale of securities because of the unique relationship of trust and confidence that Ridenour had developed with them over the years. As a result, the court concluded Ridenour had misused his relationship with his clients and had defrauded them in violation of federal securities laws.

* * * *

Ridenour's arguments that he need not register as a broker-dealer pursuant to 15 U.S.C.§ 78*o*(a)(1) are equally unavailing. It is undisputed that, during the period from 1979 to 1981, Ridenour engaged in a series of transactions involving municipal and corporate securities. We agree with the government that Ridenour's level of activity during this period made him more than an active investor. Ridenour attempted to obtain and keep a regular clientele for his "private" bond deals, which he negotiated out of his office at Dean Witter, albeit on his own behalf. We find no error in the court's conclusion that Ridenour was a broker-dealer, and that his failure to register as such violated section 15(a)(1) of the Securities Exchange Act, 15 U.S.C.§ 78*o*(a)(1).

Decision and Remedy *The court affirmed Ridenour's liability but reduced the amount to be disgorged by about $2000, due to an error in calculation by the district court.*

The Insider Trading and Securities Fraud Enforcement Act of 1988 placed additional obligations to detect insider trading on companies and especially upon securities broker-dealers. The law added a new section 15(f) to the 1934 Act, which established a compulsory surveillance system that enlists brokers in the enforcement against insider trading. This system requires each brokerage firm to implement procedures designed to detect insider trading by its employees. While the extensiveness of these procedures may vary with the size of brokerages, these organizations generally must establish written policies and procedures to prevent insider trading, control the flow of sensitive information and monitor their employees' trading.

The new Act also establishes liability for any organizations that are deemed "controlling persons." Controlling persons are companies, law firms, accountants and broker-dealers who presumably have control over their employees. The SEC now may bring an action for civil and criminal penalties against these parties who controlled any person who traded on insider information in violation of the law. To succeed in this action, the SEC must show either (1) that the controlling person knew or recklessly disregarded information that the controlled person was engaging in insider trading, or (2) that the controlling broker-dealer failed to maintain the newly required surveillance system and therefore failed to detect the insider trading. A liable control person can be fined up to $1 million or three times the profit from the insider trading, whichever is greater. The SEC may also prohibit a broker-dealer from using national securities exchanges.

RICO

In 1970, Congress passed the Racketeer Influenced and Corrupt Organizations Act (RICO), as discussed in Chapter 7 of *West's Business Law, Seventh Edition*. The primary purpose of this law was to prevent organized crime from further infecting the business world with illegal acts, such as fraud. RICO provided both criminal and civil penalties, and private citizens injured by racketeering activity may bring their own actions and recover triple their actual damages or obtain injunctive relief against responsible racketeers.

RICO was drafted very broadly and is increasingly employed in federal securities litigation. A company that violates section 10(b) will often find itself sued under RICO as well. Under the primary source of private RICO authority, a plaintiff must prove the following elements:

1. Defendant engaged in two or more predicate criminal acts.

2. Constituting a pattern of racketeering activity.

3. Thereby participating in an enterprise affecting interstate or foreign commerce.

4. Causing injury to the plaintiff's business or property.

Nothing in RICO is expressly limited to mobsters or organized crime, as that phrase is generally understood.

The first requirement of RICO liability is proof that a defendant engaged in two or more predicate criminal acts. In the securities context, these predicate acts take the form of violations of sections 10(b), 13(d), 14(e) or other provisions of the federal securities laws. Mail and wire fraud are also commonly alleged crimes in securities litigation. While the law requires proof of criminal acts, the Supreme Court has held that the defendant need not have actually been convicted of the alleged acts. Rather, a plaintiff need only allege that the defendant has committed two or more acts that meet the statutory definition of a crime.

A plaintiff also must allege that these acts constituted a "pattern" of racketeering activity. While courts are not entirely agreed on the definition of "pattern," plaintiffs generally must show that the predicate acts involved more than a single illegal scheme. Even a large number of criminal acts will not constitute a pattern of racketeering activity, if they involved only a single scheme over a short period of time. However, if defendants engage in criminal acts over a longer period of time, such as a year, courts have found a pattern of racketeering even where only a single illegal scheme was involved.

A plaintiff also must show that the defendant, through the pattern of racketeering, invests or otherwise participates in an enterprise. Enterprise is defined broadly as any individual or group of individuals "associated together for the common purpose of engaging in a course of conduct." The key here is proof of a continuing entity engaged in a common purpose. The enterprise must affect interstate or foreign commerce to be illegal, but only a slight effect is required.

RICO is increasingly used in the context of business transactions. The following case illustrates the breadth of RICO's potential application.

Case 7.5
Beauford v. Helmsley
United States Court of Appeals,
Second Circuit, 1989
865 F.2d 1386

Background and Facts *Harry Helmsley and others converted a New York apartment building, the "Parkchester," into condominium units. Helmsley offered these units for sale to the existing 8286 tenants and others. Some tenants purchased their units. Dissatisfied buyers sued and complained of the offering plan for the units. They alleged that the offering materials concealed the existence of serious structural defects in the building, the presence of asbestos materials, and the need for replacement of plumbing and electrical systems. Plaintiffs sued under RICO, claiming that the misstatements in the offering plan represented numerous independent instances of fraud.*

The district court dismissed plaintiffs' complaint. That court held that the plaintiffs had failed to prove a pattern of racketeering activity. The plaintiffs appealed and a panel of the Second Circuit Court of Appeals affirmed the dismissal. The case was then set for rehearing before the entire en banc panel of the Second Circuit, in order to clarify the scope of RICO law.

KEARSE, Circuit Judge.

* * * *

Within this framework, there is no question that the amended complaint in the present case adequately pleaded the RICO enterprise element. It alleged that there were two such enterprises: the partnership that sponsored the conversion, and all of the defendants in association with one another for the purpose of accomplishing the apartment sales. Each is within the statutory definition of enterprise. The more interesting question is whether the amended complaint adequately alleged a pattern of racketeering activity.

Our *Indelicato* analysis has persuaded us that a RICO pattern may be established without proof of multiple schemes, multiple episodes, or multiple transactions; and that acts that are not widely separated in time or space may nonetheless properly be viewed as separate acts of racketeering activity for purposes of establishing a RICO pattern. Thus, in *Indelicato*, we found that three acts of murder could constitute a RICO pattern even though there was proof of but one scheme, and even though the three murders, carried out virtually simultaneously, could not be viewed as separable episodes or transactions.

* * * *

In the present case, we conclude also that a RICO pattern may be adequately pleaded without an allegation that the scheme pursuant to which the racketeering acts were performed is an ongoing scheme having no demonstrable ending point. We reach this conclusion because nothing in the statute or the legislative history reveals an intent to require such an open-ended scheme. What is required is that the complaint plead a basis from which it could be inferred that the acts of racketeering activity were neither isolated nor sporadic. In *Indelicato*, we found the threat of continuity inherent in the criminal nature of the enterprise at whose behest the three related murders were committed. Were the same type of enterprise alleged here, we would have no difficulty in finding a sufficient allegation of the threat of continuity needed to show a pattern. When, however, there is no indication that the enterprise whose affairs are said to be conducted through racketeering acts is associated with organized crime, the nature of the enterprise does not of itself suggest that racketeering acts will continue, and proof of continuity or the threat of continuity of racketeering activity must thus be found in some factor other than the enterprise itself. We conclude that the amended complaint alleged sufficient other factors with respect to continuity to avoid dismissal for failure to allege a RICO pattern.

* * * *

In assessing the sufficiency of these allegations to show a pattern, we note first that § 1961(1)(B) defines racketeering activity, in pertinent part, as "any act which is indictable under ... section 1341 (relating to mail fraud)." and that each act of fraudulent mailing is separately indictable. Second, there can be no question that the thousands of alleged mail frauds here had the necessary interrelationship to be considered a pattern. All of the mailings were made to groups of persons related by either their tenancy in Parkchester apartments or their potential interest in purchasing such apartments. All of the frauds allegedly had the same goal, i.e., inflating the profits to be made by the defendants in the sale of the Parkchester apartments.

In sum, read with ordinary charity, the amended complaint alleged that on each of several occasions defendants had mailed fraudulent documents to thousands of persons and that there was reason to believe that similarly fraudulent mailings would be made over an additional period of years. These allegations sufficed to set forth acts that cannot be deemed, as a matter of law, isolated or sporadic. We conclude that the relatedness and continuity factors have been adequately revealed in the pleading and that the amended complaint did not fail to satisfy the pattern requirement.

Decision and Remedy *The Second Circuit vacated the previous circuit court opinion and the district court opinion. The case was remanded to the district court, so that the plaintiffs' case could proceed.*

RICO has been used by management seeking to resist a tender offer. For example, suppose that Megacorp purchases 5 percent of the shares of Minicorp and files a Schedule 13D. Minicorp may allege that Megacorp's Schedule 13D is false and misleading and therefore a violation of federal securities law. If Minicorp can find other instances of similar securities law violations by Megacorp, they can allege two or more predicate criminal acts that constitute a pattern of racketeering in violation of RICO. Minicorp will have a more difficult time, however, proving that a single tender offer would qualify as a pattern of racketeering. If Megacorp had engaged in similar takeovers in the past, this will support the evidence of a pattern.

Another securities law fact pattern invoking RICO could involve insider trading. If a group of individuals has participated in a pattern of insider trading, the victims of this pattern may sue for triple damages, which is more than they could recover under section 10(b) or other securities law provisions. RICO also offers other benefits to securities law plaintiffs. Some laws, such as mail fraud, have no private right of action for individuals' civil recovery of damages. A pattern of mail fraud, however, may enable private recovery under RICO. Other potential securities law plaintiffs may lack standing to challenge insider trading or corporate fraud under section 10(b), perhaps because they did not purchase or sell securities. These individuals may still be able to recover under RICO, which does not have the same requirements for standing.

Ethical Perspectives

Ethics and Insider Trading

Insider trading often is used as a textbook case of unethical behavior. Certainly, the secretive and manipulative use of improperly acquired inside information is ethically indefensible as well as illegal. Some experts argue, however, that insider trading by corporate officers and directors may be ethical.

The ethical analysis of insider trading begins with a consideration of which ethical duties may be violated by such trading. The first issue concerns duties of honesty and promise-keeping toward the insider's employing corporation. Unauthorized use of inside information is considered a breach of fiduciary duty to the corporation and its shareholders. Courts have analogized insider trading as a theft of inside information from the corporation, in order personally to profit.

The second concern with insider trading involves ethical duties toward other investors. Any time that an insider purchases stock, some other person or organization is selling that stock. Use of secret inside information may be considered a breach of an honesty duty toward the other party in the transaction.

The law of insider trading is primarily concerned with the first ethical issue. Insider trading is only illegal if it breaches some fiduciary duty. But what if the corporation authorized its insiders to trade on inside information? Some argue that authorized insider trading would violate no ethical duty and would actually improve the performance of corporations and the economy. They argue that authorized insider trading will provide executives with a greater incentive to increase the stock price of their corporation and will contribute to a more efficient securities market that employs all available information.[5] Others respond that authorized insider trading would corrupt the credibility of the stock market and only encourage executives to produce short-term swings in stock price.[6] Authorized insider trading may be ethical, but it may encourage unethical management by executives, in order to profit themselves. Also, is it ethical for a corporation to authorize its insiders to profit from secret information?

---

[5] *See* Carlton & Fischel, "The Regulation of Insider Trading," *35 Stanford L.* Vev. 857 (1983).

[6] *See* Cox, "Insider Trading and Contracting: A Critical Response to the 'Chicago School,'" 1986 Duke L. J. 628.

The law is less concerned with the effect of insider trading on third parties who buy or sell stock, but there are still ethical concerns. Suppose Susan is a long-standing shareholder in ChernoCorp and Edward is the president of ChernoCorp. Edward becomes aware of some development that will cause ChernoCorp stock to appreciate dramatically from $10/share to $20/share, once the development is publicly announced. So Edward enters the market and buys ChernoCorp shares from Susan. After the development is announced and the share price increases, Susan may feel cheated. She could argue that her long-term contribution to ChernoCorp's capital base means that she should receive the benefits of the company's success.

There are those who argue that Edward's trading is not at all unfair.[7] People often have special information when they make contracts. The buyer of a house may have information about the local housing market or future rental prospects that the seller lacks. This does not necessarily make the purchase of the house unethical. The free market seeks to encourage and reward parties who obtain information about the value of contracts. One author expressed this issue as follows: "Does morality really require that before I can deal with my indolent neighbor, I should communicate to him all my private plans, my long-sighted views of the future state of the market, my surmises — in short, all the results of that knowledge and address which have been the hard earned acquisitions of my own industry and activity?"[8]

The above theory has its own limitations. Sometimes, it is generally considered unethical to deal on certain forms of special knowledge. The car dealer who sells an automobile, knowing that the auto has a serious latent engine defect, is behaving unethically (and illegally) toward the purchaser. The doctor who uses specialized knowledge and position to recommend an unnecessary operation is also acting unethically toward the patient. The question is whether the specialized information of insider trading is the sort that is ethical to use in market transactions.

---

[7] *See* Lawson, "The Ethics of Insider Trading," 11 *Harvard J. of Law and Pub. Policy* 727 (1988).
[8] *Id.*

International Perspectives

The International Law of Insider Trading

International securities markets have grown dramatically in significance. More investors are diversifying their shareholdings by investments in Tokyo, Hong Kong, London, Paris and other markets. As a consequence, the international law of insider trading is a subject of increasing concern.

United States law on insider trading generally does not apply to foreign transactions. International laws on insider trading vary widely; in many nations there is no prohibition on insider trading. In Europe, for example, only three nations — Denmark, France and the United Kingdom—have meaningful prohibitions on insider trading. Moreover, the United Kingdom's law has strict limitations, lacks specific civil remedies, and is not frequently employed.

The European Community has adopted new rules to ban insider trading. The nations' finance ministers unanimously adopted a directive requiring all twelve member states to adopt and implement a "system aimed at assuring that people with access to confidential information regarding companies cannot use this information in the sale or purchase of securities." The directive also calls for a Community-wide enforcement system to penalize transnational trading. The directive suggests a prohibition on insider trading that is broader than that of U.S. law, but the effectiveness of the directive is dependent on its implementation by the Community's member states.

Japan regulates insider trading under its Securities Exchange Law. While Japanese law on insider trading roughly parallels U.S. law, there is much less enforcement of the law in Japan. By 1987, Japan's Ministry of Finance had brought only one formal proceeding to penalize insider trading. Enforcement has increased recently but is still much less frequent than in the United States.

United States law can affect the enforcement of insider trading prohibitions overseas. The insider trading prohibition has extraterritorial jurisdiction against foreign transactions in a security that is registered in the U.S. or traded on a U.S. exchange if the conduct has a direct and harmful impact on U.S. citizens. U.S. law also applies to transactions in foreign securities if the illegal insider-trading conduct occurs within the United States. The Insider Trading and Securities Fraud Enforcement Act, passed in 1988, gave the SEC greater enforcement authority over international transactions by U.S. investors buying foreign stocks. This law gave the SEC authority to conduct investigations in the United States on behalf of a foreign country, to assist in the prosecution of that nation's insider-trading laws.

Questions and Case Problems

1. Patrick earned an undergraduate degree in philosophy and then became a lawyer. He calls his friend Mike, a broker, to invest some of his lucrative lawyer salary. Mike realizes that Patrick has no idea how financial markets work and does extensive trading with Patrick's money without informing him of the details, which results in substantial commissions for Mike's brokerage firm. Patrick's wife, a finance major, begins to question Mike's decisions and motives. What must she show to successfully challenge Mike's pattern of trading?

2. Alright Company issued $1 million in preferred convertible stock after a long process of registration with the SEC. Upper management and the directors of Alright went out of their way to make sure that the information provided to the SEC was accurate and up-to-date. The stock issuance was a huge success at first but then plummeted. The embezzlement of a lower level employee had seriously undermined Alright's financial position. Upper management was unaware of this embezzlement at the time of the stock issuance, so it was not disclosed. Can a purchaser of Alright shares in the initial issuance recover for the false picture of Alright's financial status?

3. Ira Waldbaum was an insider of Waldbaum, Inc., who told his sister that the corporation was to be sold. She told her daughter, who told her husband, who told a friend, Robert Chestman. Chestman promptly purchased shares of Waldbaum, Inc., and profited enormously when the company was taken over. The SEC prosecuted Chestman for illegal insider trading. Is Chestman guilty of insider trading?

4. Burlington Northern made a hostile tender offer for 25 million shares of El Paso Gas Co. at $24 per share. The El Paso management opposed the offer but the company's shareholders tendered 25 million shares. Burlington, however, rescinded the tender offer under its terms and negotiated a deal with El Paso management. Under the deal, Burlington made another tender offer but for only 21 million shares. As a consequence, shareholders were unable to tender as many shares at the premium $24 per share price. These shareholders sued Burlington and El Paso under section 14(e) for defrauding them. Should the shareholders succeed with this claim? [*Schreiber v. Burlington Northern, Inc.* 472 U.S. 1 (1985)].

5. Nay worked for First Securities and encouraged individuals to invest in "escrow accounts" that were expected to have a high rate of return. In fact, he converted the funds to his own account and later committed suicide. The investors sought to recover their money, but First Securities was effectively bankrupt. The investors therefore sued the accounting firm for failure to conduct proper audits of First Securities. Do the investors have a good claim against the auditing firm under section 10(b)? [*Ernst & Ernst v. Hochfelder*, 425 U.S. 185 (1976)].

6. Ascor is a large corporation with extensive real estate holdings. In a prospectus associated with a new public offering of shares, Ascor reported its financial results and also had a section on investment risk. This section noted that all real estate owners were subject to the potentially great liabilities of Superfund, the hazardous waste cleanup statute. Gihann Patel purchased shares. Soon thereafter, she discovered that Ascor owned land that was on the Environmental Protection Agency's National Priorities List of the worse sites in America, and that cleanup would cost the company tens of millions of dollars. She sued Ascor, claiming the prospectus contained material omissions. Ascor defended with the bespeaks caution doctrine. How should the court rule?

CHAPTER EIGHT

Mergers and Acquisitions

Key Background

The essential background for this chapter on mergers and acquisitions is found in Chapter 42 of *West's Business Law, Seventh Edition* These chapters cover corporations—rights and duties of directors, managers, and shareholders; and corporations—merger, consolidation, and termination. Valuable background is also provided in Chapter 18 of *West's Legal Environment of Business, Third Edition,* which covers takeovers and mergers. Among the important points to remember from these chapters are:

- the fiduciary duties of corporate directors and officers
- the business judgment rule
- rights of shareholders in the corporation
- procedures for the merger of a corporation
- tender offers and target responses

* * * *

The 1980s saw an explosion of activity in corporate takeovers. Many individuals became wealthy by selling their shares in corporations or by purchasing all the shares of a corporation and selling off its assets for a profit. While the 1990s have already seen a decline in takeover activity, multibillion-dollar corporations are still being bought and sold.

The key legal issue on mergers and acquisitions involves the rights of shareholders. These rights are defined by the corporate laws of the states. Because most large U.S. companies are incorporated in Delaware, the Delaware state law is by far the most important and provides the focus for this chapter.

Mergers and acquisitions usually follow the same basic, though sometimes complex, factual scenario. This chapter begins by describing the basic factual setting for takeovers and then discusses how the law applies to these facts.

A Factual Scenario for a Takeover

The following facts represent a fairly typical takeover. Assume that Keggo is a fairly successful oil and mining company. Keggo is listed on the New York Stock Exchange, with two million outstanding shares that trade at about $25 per share. RBM Associates specializes in corporate acquisitions. RBM believes that Keggo's shares are significantly undervalued, because the natural resources owned by Keggo are themselves worth more than $25/share. Keggo becomes a target for takeover by RBM.

RBM would begin its takeover by purchasing Keggo stock on the open market. RBM probably would buy about 5 to 10 percent of Keggo's outstanding shares. RBM would next try to arrange financing (probably a loan) in order to purchase the remainder of Keggo's shares. RBM then would approach the Keggo board of directors and inquire about the possibility of a friendly takeover (with the board's approval). RBM might offer to pay $35/share for all of Keggo's outstanding shares, in cash or securities.

If RBM lacks financial resources to conduct the takeover, it may borrow virtually the entire cost of the takeover, which would make it a highly leveraged takeover. Such borrowing is available because Keggo's assets become **collateral** for the loan, if the takeover succeeds. This is called a **leveraged buyout** or **LBO**. The notes for this borrowing are sometimes called **junk bonds**, because they carry a relatively high risk of nonpayment. Newly acquired companies in LBOs have gone bankrupt and failed to pay off these bonds in full.

The Keggo board would evaluate the RBM offer, with the assistance of an **investment banker** and legal counsel. They might approve the offer as in the best interests of their shareholders. More likely, the board will reject the offer. They might believe that the offer is for an inadequate price or lacks adequate financing or interferes with Keggo's promising future business plans. All of these are legitimate reasons to oppose the RBM offer.

There is a risk, however, that the Keggo board of directors will fight the RBM offer for selfish reasons. The board probably contains several "inside directors," who are also officers of Keggo, such as the chief executive officer (CEO). These directors may fear the loss of their well-paying executive positions in the event of a takeover. To avoid the impression of self-interest, the Keggo board may appoint a special committee of outside directors, who are *not* employees of Keggo.

Once the Keggo board declines the friendly takeover, RBM may proceed in a "hostile" fashion. RBM can make a **tender offer**, which goes directly to all the Keggo shareholders and offers them $35 a share for all their stock. RBM will have to make several filings with the government in connection with the tender offer. The shareholders will have until a designated date to accept or reject this offer.

The Keggo board may recommend that its shareholders reject the offer, but the shareholders are likely to accept an offer that is $10/share over the market price. Therefore, the Keggo board may adopt defensive measures to fight off the takeover. The defensive measures may include the creation of a "poison pill" or a "lock-up" of Keggo's assets.

These defensive measures, which are discussed below, have the effect of making Keggo less attractive to RBM by making the takeover more expensive or less valuable. As a practical matter, they may render the RBM takeover impossible. Typical defensive measures can be eliminated at the board's discretion. Keggo's board may also seek out a **white knight** to take over the company and retain the officers.

RBM and other Keggo shareholders will probably sue Keggo and claim that the defensive measures are illegal. RBM may also raise its tender offer price to $40/share, if Keggo agrees to eliminate its defensive measures. If one of these approaches succeeds, RBM will go through with its tender offer. Perhaps 90 percent of Keggo's outstanding shares accept the tender offer.

Once RBM owns 90 percent of Keggo's shares, RBM runs the company. RBM, as the new majority shareholder of Keggo, will then adopt a **going private merger** plan. In the merger, the remaining 10 percent of Keggo shareholders must sell their Keggo shares, as Keggo is merged into RBM or its subsidiary. This second-step merger will probably be at the same $35-$40/share price as in the tender offer. The remaining minority shareholders will be required to sell their shares, and Keggo will become a wholly owned subsidiary of RBM. RBM can then run Keggo or sell off its assets for a profit, as they choose.

Directors' Duties

One of the key legal questions in mergers and acquisitions law involves the duties of directors. Many cases turn on whether the defensive measures adopted by the directors are legal. The defensive actions are illegal if they violate the directors' state law duties to the company's shareholders. The primary duties are those of loyalty and of due care.

Duty of Loyalty

Corporate directors owe a duty of loyalty to the corporation's shareholders, as fiduciaries of the shareholders' interests. This means that the directors must act in the best interests of the corporation and its shareholders and cannot act as directors in their own personal interests.

The duty of loyalty arises in a number of corporate contexts but is prominent in mergers and acquisitions. As described in the introductory scenario, the Keggo inside directors have a substantial financial self-interest in keeping their jobs. Yet they are charged with making decisions for the corporation. The Keggo directors might decide to reject the RBM offer for legitimate reasons, as not in the best interests of the Keggo shareholders. The Keggo directors might reach this same decision for improper reasons that violate their duty of loyalty, in order to keep their jobs.

Because directors could reach a given decision for either proper or improper reasons, it may be difficult for a court to determine whether the directors violated their duty of loyalty. Courts therefore must investigate the decision closely.

Duty of Due Care

Corporate directors also owe a duty of due care to their shareholders. This demands that the directors make careful, informed decisions for the corporation. In the takeover context, the most significant aspect of the duty of due care is the responsibility to investigate the facts before deciding.

The duty of due care means that directors must fully investigate an acquisition offer before making a decision about the offer. This typically means that the board should consult with investment bankers, attorneys, and other professionals regarding the offer. The duty of care may also compel directors to investigate all reasonable alternatives for the corporation. Directors should keep a full record of their investigation and the bases for their decision.

The directors' duty of care often arises when the directors accept a friendly takeover rather than a hostile one. Although the directors have a right to prefer one offer over another, they have the responsibility to investigate the preferred offer completely, to ensure that it is in the best interests of their shareholders.

The following case has quickly become the classic for alleged breaches of due care.

Case 8.1
Smith v. Van Gorkom
Supreme Court of Delaware, 1985
488 A.2d 858

Background and Facts *Trans Union Corporation's shares were trading at a low level (about $34 per share), and its management sought a merger to improve share value and to take advantage of tax credits that the company had accumulated. The board considered a management leveraged buyout (LBO) and concluded that they could probably borrow enough to offer around $55/share. On September 13, 1980, Jerome Van Gorkom, Trans Union's president, met Jay Pritzker, who was a "takeover specialist." Pritzker was interested in acquiring Trans Union, and Van Gorkom suggested a price of about $55/share.*

Pritzker brought a $55/share offer to Van Gorkom on September 18, who promptly called a board of directors meeting for September 20 but did not disclose its purpose. The directors heard a presentation from Van Gorkom describing the offer and stating that he considered the price fair. No investment banker was retained nor was any valuation effort made. The merger documents were not yet complete, but the directors went forward and approved the merger. Later that night, when the merger documents were ready, Van Gorkom signed them at a benefit for the opera, but he did not read them.

Shareholders of Trans Union sued to rescind the merger agreement, claiming that Van Gorkom and the other directors had breached their duty of due care. The trial court ruled for Van Gorkom, concluding that the board was informed and emphasizing that the merger offer was well in excess of the market price for Trans Union shares. The shareholders appealed.

HORSEY, Justice.

* * * *

The determination of whether a business judgment is an informed one turns on whether the directors have informed themselves "prior to making a business decision, of all material information reasonable available to them." *Id.*

Application of the [business judgment] rule of necessity depends upon a showing that an informed director did in fact make a business judgment authorizing the transaction under review. And, as the plaintiff argues, the difficulty here is that the evidence does not show that this was done. There were director-committee-officer references to the realignment but none of these singly or cumulative showed that the director judgment was brought to bear with specificity on the transactions.

Under the business judgment rule there is not protection for directors who have made "an unintelligent or unadvised judgment." *Mitchell v. Highland-Western Glass,* Del. Ch., 167 A. 831, 833 (1933). A director's duty to inform himself in preparation for a decision derives from the fiduciary capacity in which he serves the corporation and its stockholders. *Lutz v. Boas,* Del. Ch., 171 A.2d 38a (1961). ***Since a director is vested with the responsibility for the management of the affairs of the corporation, he must execute that duty with the recognition that he acts on behalf of others. Such obligation does not tolerate faithlessness or self-dealing. But fulfillment of the fiduciary function requires more than the mere absence of bad faith or fraud. Representation of the financial interest of others imposes on a director an affirmative duty to protect those interests and to proceed with a critical eye in assessing information of the type and under the circumstances present here.

* * * *

On the record before us, we must conclude that the Board of Directors did not reach an informed business judgment on September 20, 1980 in voting to "sell" the Company for $55 per share pursuant to the Pritzker cash-out merger proposal.

Our reasons, in summary are as follows:

The directors (1) did not adequately inform themselves as to Van Gorkom's role in forcing the "sale" of the Company and in establishing the per share purchase price; (2) were uninformed as to the intrinsic value of the Company; and (3) given these circumstances, at a minimum, were grossly negligent in approving the "sale" of the Company upon two hours' consideration, without prior notice, and without the exigency of a crisis or emergency.

As has been noted, the Board based its September 20 decision to approve the cash-out merger primarily on Van Gorkom's representations. None of the directors, other than Van Gorkom and Chelberg, had any prior knowledge that the purpose of the meeting was to propose a cash-out merger of Trans Union. No members of Senior Management were present, other than Chelberg, Romans and Peterson; and the latter two had only learned of the proposed sale an hour earlier. Both general counsel Moore and former general counsel Browder attended the meeting, but were equally uninformed as to the purpose of the meeting and the documents to be acted upon.

Without any documents before them concerning the proposed transaction, the members of the Board were required to rely entirely upon Van Gorkom's 20-minute oral presentation of the proposal. No written summary of the terms of the merger was presented; the directors were given no documentation to support the adequacy of $55 price per share for sale of the company; and the Board had before it nothing more than Van Gorkom's statement of his understanding of the substance of an agreement which he admittedly had never read, nor which any member of the board had ever seen.

* * * *

A substantial premium may provide one reason to recommend a merger, but in the absence of other sound valuation information, the fact of a premium alone does not provide an adequate basis upon which to assess the fairness of an offering price. Here, the judgment reached as to the adequacy of the premium was based on a comparison between the historically depressed Trans Union market price and the amount of the Pritzker offer. Using market price as a basis for concluding that the premium adequately reflected the true value of the Company was a clearly faulty, indeed fallacious, premise, as the defendants' own evidence demonstrates.

Decision and Remedy   *The Delaware Supreme Court reversed the lower court and held that the defendants had breached their duty of care. The case was remanded for proceedings to supply the shareholders a remedy for the breach.*

While it might seem obvious for directors to exercise due care and consult with relevant professionals, full investigation can be difficult in the context of mergers and acquisitions. The typical takeover develops very quickly and may demand board action within days, or even hours. Midnight meetings are not uncommon. The need for rapid decision making can create a problem under the duty of due care.

Business Judgment Rule

Directors of major corporations are frequently sued for violating their duties of loyalty and due care. The **business judgment rule** offers considerable legal protection to directors' decisions. This rule states that courts should not second-guess the business judgments of corporate directors, who are experts and better suited to making corporate decisions than are judges.

The business judgment rule usually shelters directors' decisions. If a shareholder sues corporate directors over a program of corporate expansion, for example, courts will defer to the business judgment of the directors. The directors are in the best position to determine whether expansion is in the best interest of the company.

Much takeover litigation centers around the application of the business judgment rule. If the rule applies, the directors' decision is virtually certain to be upheld. It is therefore critical for the challenger of the board of directors to find an exception to the business judgment rule.

One key exception to the business judgment rule occurs when directors have a personal interest in the decision. The courts will not defer to business decisions that appear to be in the self-interest of directors. If a business director gives a big corporate contract to his or her own company, courts may not apply the business judgment rule. Another important exception to the business judgment rule exists when the directors obviously have failed to investigate an important business decision.

Directors' Duties in Mergers and Acquisitions

For some time, courts applied the business judgment rule to directors' decisions regarding potential corporate acquisitions. In recent years, however, courts have recognized the potentially divided loyalties of directors and have limited the application of the business judgment rule in takeovers.

Now, courts in Delaware and elsewhere apply a two-part test to determine whether the business judgment rule should apply when directors seek to fight off a takeover, as Keggo did through the adoption of defensive measures in the opening scenario of this chapter. This is called the *Unocal* test, after the case that adopted the test.[1] This decision recognized the "omnipresent spectre" that defensive actions may be motivated by directors' personal interests.

Unocal first requires that directors show the presence of a *"threat"* to the corporation before defensive measures are authorized. Courts have found that several features of hostile takeovers may constitute such a threat. If a takeover is coercive, thereby denying shareholders a fair choice, a threat is present.

The "two-tier tender offer" is just such a coercive threat. A **two-tier tender offer** occurs when an acquirer, such as RBM, offers one price (e.g., $40/share) for the first group of shares tendered to the acquirer (such as the first 51 percent of Keggo shares). A different, lower price (e.g., $25/share) is offered for the remaining shares. When a tender offer is structured in this way, shareholders are coerced into accepting quickly, lest they fall into the second tier and receive much less for their shares.

Other features of a tender offer also may represent a threat to a target corporation, such as Keggo. For example, the acquirer might offer to pay for Keggo shares, not with cash but with shares or bonds in RBM or some other corporation. If these shares or bonds are not worth as much as RBM claims, the offer may be deemed to threaten the Keggo shareholders and justify defensive actions.

If a threat exists, the directors also must satisfy the second part of the *Unocal* test. This requires that the defensive action be *proportional* to the threat. The defensive measure may not be greater than the threat presented by the takeover. The larger the threat, the more extensive the defensive measures that will be allowed.

If the directors' action passes both parts of the *Unocal* test, the business judgment rule will protect the directors' decision to adopt the defensive measures. If the *Unocal* test is not met, the court will not use the business judgment rule but will evaluate the directors' decision itself to determine whether it is truly in the best interest of the shareholders.

Courts usually will uphold the initial adoption of defensive measures under the *Unocal* test. This is because defensive measures can buy time for the directors so that the shareholders may find a better deal. Defensive measures can delay a takeover, so that the company's directors can seek out other acquirers. If other companies are interested in acquiring Keggo, the directors can induce a bidding war, or auction, that will yield a higher price for its shareholders.

Even where the initial adoption of the defensive measures is lawful, courts may find that continuation of the defensive measures violates the *Unocal* test. Suppose that Keggo's directors try to induce an auction but no other companies are interested in bidding for Keggo. At this point, the RBM offer may appear to offer the most value to Keggo shareholders, and the directors will have a more difficult time proving a threat that justifies continuation of the defensive measures.

Specific Defensive Measures

Courts have evaluated the lawfulness of the adoption and continuation of various types of defensive measures. It is important to understand how all of these defensive tactics operate and when they can be used.

One of the most common defensive tactics is a **shareholder rights plan**, often called a **poison pill**. This might involve Keggo's directors giving each of its shareholders one "right" for each share. This right would give the shareholder a valuable bond or cash or stock options at a below-market price. The effect of the rights plan is to give much of the company's wealth directly to its existing shareholders, thereby making the remaining company assets much less valuable to an acquirer.

The typical rights plan is a **flip-in poison pill**. This means that the rights are not actually granted until a person buys a high percentage (e.g., 20 percent) of Keggo's stock. Shareholders therefore do not receive the rights unless a takeover is well on the way to success. In this way, the rights plan does not interfere with the unacquired company. A company could also adopt a **flip-over poison pill**. This is a plan that gives Keggo's shareholders some rights in any acquiring company, such as RBM. This enables Keggo shareholders to receive not only the tender offer price but also shares in RBM at a below-market price.

The following case addresses the lawfulness of a poison pill and other defensive measures.

---

[1] *Unocal Corp. v. Mesa Petroleum Co.*, 493 A.2d 946 (Del. 1985).

Case 8.2
Paramount Communications Inc., v. QVC Network, Inc.
Supreme Court of Delaware, 1993
637 A.2d 828

Background and Facts *Paramount Communications, Inc. and Viacom Inc. reached a merger agreement on September 12, 1993. QVC Network sought to acquire Paramount and initiated a tender offer on October 21, 1993 at a much higher price than in the Viacom merger. Paramount had in place a shareholder rights plan ("poison pill") and other measures to deter takeovers, but was waiving the application of this plan with respect to Viacom. In addition, the merger agreement with Viacom contained a "no shop" provision that impeded Paramount's ability to negotiate with QVC or others regarding a better price for Paramount's shareholders. After some discussions, Paramount decided to proceed with the Viacom merger, suggesting that the companies were a better fit than Paramount and QVC. QVC filed this action to enjoin the Viacom tender offer and prevent the selective waiver of defensive measures to favor Viacom. the Delaware Chancery Court found for QVC and issued an order enjoining application of the poison pill so as to favor Viacom. Paramount and Viacom appealed.*

ORDER

* * * *

The obligations of the Paramount directors included the duties (a) to be diligent in examining critically the Paramount-Viacom transaction and the QVC tender offers; (b) to act in good faith; (c) to summon, and act with due care on, all material information reasonably available, including information necessary to compare the two offers to determine which of these transactions, or an alternative course of action would provide the best value available to the stockholders; and (d) to negotiate actively and in good faith with both Viacom and QVC to that end.

* * * *

These duties necessarily implicated various issues, including the questions of whether or not those provisions and other aspects of the Paramount-Viacom transaction (separately and in the aggregate): (a) adversely affected the value provided to the Paramount stockholders; (b) inhibited or encouraged alternative bids; (c) were enforceable contractual obligations in light of the directors' fiduciary duties; and (d) in the end would advance or retard the Paramount directors' duty to secure for the paramount stockholders the best value available under the circumstances.

The Paramount defendants contend that they were precluded by certain contractual provisions, including the "no-shop" provision, from negotiating with QVC or seeking alternatives. Such provisions, whether or not they are presumptively valid in the abstract, may not validly define or limit the directors' fiduciary duties under Delaware law or prevent the Paramount directors from carrying out their fiduciary duties under Delaware law, when selling control. To the extent such provisions are inconsistent with those duties, they are invalid and unenforceable.

Since the Paramount directors had already decided to sell control, they had a duty to continue their search for the best value available to the stockholders.

* * * *

Decision and Remedy *The court affirmed the Chancery Court ruling and remanded for proceedings consistent with the order. The opinion triggered a new round of open and more equal bidding between Viacom and QVC. In the end, Viacom had the highest bid and acquired Paramount, but at a price significantly higher than that in the original merger agreement.*

Roughly similar to a poison pill is a **restructuring**. A corporate restructuring usually involves the target company taking on substantial debt through borrowing and then distributing a substantial cash dividend to its shareholders or repurchasing a significant portion of its shares. This approach makes shareholders happier with the incumbent management and also makes the newly debt-laden company less attractive to the acquirer. A repurchase also removes shares from circulation for potential acquisition by the acquirer.

In 1985, Turner Broadcasting System, Inc., announced a highly leveraged tender offer for CBS for $175/share in junk bonds. CBS responded by offering to repurchase 21 percent of its own stock for $40/share cash and $110/share in bonds. This substantially increased CBS total debt, in order to pay for the repurchase. Turner challenged the restructuring, but a court upheld the CBS actions as offering more value to its shareholders.[2]

Another common defensive tactic is the search for a **white knight**. A white knight is another person or company who would acquire Keggo but leave Keggo's management in place. White knights are often good for shareholders because they may bid up the takeover price but may be bad for shareholders if the board of directors shows favoritism to the white knight and accepts a lower offer from a white knight.

Takeovers are very costly, even to attempt, and the Keggo board in our chapter's opening scenario might have to provide inducements to a potential white knight. One inducement is a **no-shop clause**, in which Keggo promises not to seek out other acquirors to bid against the white knight. Keggo also might offer a **hello fee** (an upfront payment to the white knight to obtain an offer) or a **goodbye fee** or **break-up fee** (an agreement to pay the white knight's expenses if the white knight's efforts to acquire the company fail).

When a white knight is unavailable, a company may use a **white squire**. A white squire lacks the resources to buy the company in its entirety but can purchase a substantial number of the company's shares. Keggo would sell its **treasury shares** (those owned by the company) or issue new shares to a white squire, which would promise not to tender the shares to RBM. This would make it more difficult for RBM to acquire the percentage of shares necessary to take over Keggo. To interest a white squire, Keggo probably will have to sell shares to the white squire at a discount below market price or offer other inducements.

Another defense tactic is the **lock-up**, which often operates in tandem with the white knight. In a lock-up, the company contracts to sell some asset to a third party (such as the white knight) at a below-market price. Lock-up agreements usually "flip-in," after an acquirer exceeds a certain percentage of shares in the target company.

A lock-up usually involves the company's **crown jewels**. Crown jewels are the especially valuable assets of the target corporation. Consider a diversified consumer products company. One division of this company may be especially profitable, supporting the other divisions. This profitable division is probably the target of the acquirer, who may sell off the less profitable divisions. If the target, such as Keggo, locks up a sale of the profitable division, or crown jewels, in the event of a takeover, Keggo becomes much less attractive to an acquirer such as RBM.

Courts tend to be skeptical of lock-ups, which seem primarily designed to favor some outside party, with little direct benefit to shareholders. The Delaware courts have suggested that a lock-up could be legitimate if it served to attract an outside party into the bidding for the company, thereby driving up share prices.

Another defensive tactic is the creation of an **employee stock option plan**, or **ESOP**. This is where the company issues its own shares to a plan in which its employees can participate in ownership, through stock options. The theory behind an ESOP is that the company's employees will be much less likely to tender their shares to an acquirer such as RBM. Many takeovers have resulted in massive layoffs, as the acquirer strives to make the company more efficient and pay off its debts. For this reason, employees may refuse to sell their shares in order to protect their jobs.

The Delaware courts have been favorable toward the ESOP approach, especially if it does not make a takeover impossible. Polaroid Corporation created a large ESOP in response to a takeover threat. The court upheld the ESOP because: (1) Polaroid had planned for some years to create a smaller ESOP, (2) the ESOP has corporate benefits

---

[2] *Turner Broadcasting System, Inc. v. CBS, Inc.*, 627 F.Supp. 901 (N.D. Ga. 1985).

such as improved employee morale, and (3) the ESOP created only a substantial, but not an insurmountable, barrier to a takeover.[3]

The Keggo directors might also decide to adopt **golden parachutes** for the company's officers and directors. Golden parachutes are lucrative severance arrangements. If the officers are fired after a takeover, they obtain a right to receive a substantial payment, such as two years' salary. If the costs of the golden parachutes are substantial in proportion to the size of the target company, they may deter a takeover. Some argue in favor of golden parachutes, however, noting that they help remove the self-interest of officers in opposing a takeover. Courts have been more skeptical of golden parachutes that were adopted when a takeover was already underway.

Some companies have sought to protect themselves from takeover through amendments to their certificate of incorporation or bylaws, sometimes called **shark repellents**. For example, a company might require a **supermajority vote** of shareholders to approve a merger or other significant corporate action. Keggo might adopt a bylaw requiring an 80 percent shareholder vote before a merger could be approved. This would force acquirers to obtain 80 percent of Keggo's shares (rather than 50 percent) before gaining control of the company.

Another structural provision to frustrate takeovers is the adoption of staggered terms for directors. This provision means that only a fraction of the board of directors is elected annually, and incumbent directors may stay in office and control the corporation for years. Of course, if the acquirer obtains enough shares, it may repeal the rule providing for the staggered terms.

Courts have generally upheld shark repellent structural policies, especially if these policies were approved by a vote of the company's shareholders. This is especially true if the policies are adopted in advance, when no tender offer for the company is pending. Courts are more skeptical if the policies are adopted when a specific acquirer has expressed interest and a takeover seems imminent.

A Delaware court struck down a shark repellent that would have required a sixty-day waiting period before a potential acquirer could have full use of its newly purchased shares. The court emphasized that the bylaw was adopted by the board of directors when a takeover was already proceeding and was adopted without getting the consent of their shareholders.[4]

One of the most dramatic defensive measures is a **management buyout (MBO)** or **self tender**. This occurs when a group of the directors and officers of the target corporation put together their own offer to buy the corporation. These individuals will usually require some financing assistance from a third party, such as a white knight. Management's self tender then competes with the acquirer's tender offer for control of the target company. The possibility of self-interested dealings is especially obvious in the case of an MBO.

If management itself cannot initiate a takeover, it can complicate takeover efforts with a share repurchase. Such a repurchase takes shares off the market for an acquirer and may concentrate shareholdings in friendly hands. The Delaware Supreme Court recently approved such a repurchase that increased the bloc of shares held by management, so long as the repurchase did not preclude an acquisition and was within the range of reasonable defensive measures.[5]

"Just Say No"

Directors can often justify defensive measures as a means to get a higher price for their shareholders. Removable defensive measures can induce an acquirer to raise its tender offer price or attract competing bidders. It may be more difficult to justify defensive measures if the board desires to "just say no"—to fight off any acquisition and continue business as usual.

It can be legal to "just say no." Directors have no duty to sell their corporation or even to maximize the short-run value for their shareholders. Directors can maintain that continuing the business is in the long-run interest of shareholders.

The Delaware courts recently decided a critical "just say no" case, in *Paramount Communications, Inc. v. Time, Inc.*[6] Time and Warner Communications planned a merger, because the two

---

[3] *Shamrock Holding, Inc. v. Polaroid Corp.*, 1 M&A Law Rep. 1250 (1989).

[4] *Datapoint Corp. v. Plaza Securities Co.*, 496 A.2d 1031 (Del. 1985).

[5] *In re Unitrin, Inc. Shareholders Litigation*, 651 A.2d 1361 (Del. 1995).

[6] 15 *Del. J. Corp.* L. 700 (1990).

companies fit well together and promised successful operations. Paramount then made a tender offer for Time. Time maintained its poison pill and restructured the merger with Warner. Time took on debt and undertook a friendly takeover of Warner. This made it impossible for Paramount to proceed with its tender offer to acquire Time.

Paramount sued Time, claiming that Time had denied its shareholders a chance to sell their shares. The court agreed that Paramount offered Time's shareholders more immediate cash than did the restructuring and merger. The court nevertheless upheld Time's actions, because the board was furthering a business plan that offered greater long-run benefits to shareholders of the merged Time/Warner corporation.

Auction Duties

Shareholders typically want an auction of their company, because a bidding war promises the best price for their shares. Corporate directors do not have a generalized duty to auction off their company, however, but may choose to attempt to run the company profitably. Once the directors decide that the shares in the corporation should be sold, the directors do assume a duty to get the best possible price for their shareholders, usually through an auction.

The auction duty was defined by the Delaware courts in *Revlon, Inc. v. MacAndrews & Forbes Holdings, Inc.*,[7] and is usually called the *Revlon*

---
[7] 506 A.2d 173 (Del. 1986).

duty of directors. Revlon sought to fight off a takeover sponsored in part by MacAndrews & Forbes, by use of a poison pill, a white knight, a lock-up of the crown jewels, and other tactics. The court approved Revlon's initial defensive measures, including the poison pill, as a valuable tool to maximize the value of its shares. After Revlon found a white knight, however, the court held that the company showed improper favoritism for the white knight's offer. *Revlon* stands for the position that, once the directors decide to sell the corporation, they must conduct some sort of auction to obtain the highest bid for their shareholders. The board cannot selectively maintain defensive measures against some but not all bidders.

Delaware courts have applied the *Revlon* duty to any sale of control of a corporation. Suppose that the directors of a corporation want to agree to a friendly takeover by an acquirer. The directors cannot simply accept the friendly takeover but must investigate the possibility of obtaining a higher offer by seeking out competing acquirers.

The courts have not interpreted *Revlon* to always require a formal auction of the company. Thus, directors need not publicly announce the sale of the company and set a date for final and best offers. Rather, a company need only explore the market for possible interested acquirers.

The legal difficulties of conducting an auction and attempting to maximize value for shareholders are illustrated in the following decision. This case was heard in federal court but applied the corporate state law of Delaware.

■ Case 8.3
Samjens Partners I v. Burlington Industries, Inc.
United States District Court for the Southern District of New York, 1987
663 F. Supp. 614

Background and Facts Samjens Partners I owned about 13 percent of the stock of Burlington Industries, Inc., and on May 6, 1987, made a tender offer for Burlington at $67/share. Burlington's board of directors rejected this offer as inadequate. The Morgan Stanley Group, Inc., subsequently expressed interest in a friendly takeover of Burlington.

After Burlington threatened a self tender, Samjens increased its price to $72/share on May 15. On May 20, Burlington and Morgan agreed to merge, with Morgan offering $76/share for all shares of Burlington. Burlington agreed to suspend its self tender, if Morgan's tender offer succeeded. Burlington also agreed to a *"no shop" clause promising not to seek competing bidders and a $25 million "break-up fee" for Morgan, should its tender offer fail. The board refused to pay Morgan a $7 million "hello fee."*

The board recommended that its shareholders accept the Morgan offer. On May 28, Samjens raised its offer price to $77/share. Shortly thereafter, Morgan raised its offer to $78/share. Samjens sued Burlington to obtain a preliminary injunction against any merger between Burlington and Morgan. Among the main claims brought by Samjens, it alleged that the Burlington directors violated their fiduciary duties to shareholders by favoring the Morgan bid and conducting an unfairly biased auction of the company.

KRAM, U.S. District Judge.

* * * *

The negotiations with Morgan lasted for two days. The Board members read the merger agreement carefully and went through it with outside counsel. The price the Board secured from Morgan was $76 per share, $4 per share higher than the highest outstanding bid.

The Board negotiated strictly with Morgan about the other terms of the agreement. It rejected the $7 million hello fee. The Board was not happy with the break-up fee, but after investigating it, the Board realized that such a fee was standard, and that the amount of the fee was fair and within the normal range. The Board also realized that Morgan would back out of the deal without the fee, and justifiably decided to agree to it. The Board also insisted on changing the no-shop clause to a "window-shop" clause. The new clause allows the Board to look at other bids, but not solicit them. If the Board sees a higher bid, it can accept it.

The merger agreement is not so onerous as to end the auction or exclude other bidders. The break-up fee and related expenses total approximately 2 percent of the value of the company, leaving other parties free to bid. There is also no auction-ending lock-up agreement. In fact, the merger did not end the auction: in response to the merger, Samjens increased its bid to $77, and Morgan has responded with a bid of $78. Thus, the merger agreement has increased the value to the shareholders by $6 per share, and Samjens has hinted that it might make a higher bid.

The evidence also indicates that the Board reached all of its decisions after thorough consultation with its financial and legal advisors. Its decisions were based on reasonable and thorough investigations, and its conclusions were justifiable and in good faith. The Board did not rush. Its investment bankers solicited bids over an eight-day period. When the Board was assured that Morgan's bid was the best, it pursued its negotiations with Morgan over a two-day period. The Board fulfilled its duty of care in the takeover contest, and its decision is entitled to the protection of the business judgment rule.

In short, if the procedure the Board followed and the merger agreement it approved were not protected by the business judgment rule, the Court doubts that any merger agreements would ever be allowed in the context of takeover contests. This case indicates that this would be detrimental to shareholders. The merger agreement approved in this case has resulted, so far, in an increase of $6 per share in the price that will be paid to shareholders.

Plaintiffs' version of how the auction should have been conducted is unrealistic and ignores a number of important factors. First, the Board was operating under time pressure caused by Samjens. The Samjens offer was to expire on June 3. Thus, when the board met on May 29, it had only two weeks to find an alternative to an inadequate bid. Morgan was the only party ready to make a bid, all the other parties needed additional time. Second, although Morgan might have been Burlington's white knight, it was not Burlington's patron saint. Morgan was involved in negotiations with Burlington because it was an opportunity to make money. Thus, it wanted a response to its bid quickly, it wanted compensation for the risk it was undertaking in typing up its capital, and it did not want to serve as a "stalking horse" and have its bid shopped around. In light of this, however, the Board spent two days negotiating the merger agreement, and bargained vigorously with Morgan.

* * * *

Decision and Remedy *The court found that Samjens was unlikely to succeed on the merits of its claim and therefore denied its motion for a preliminary injunction.*

State Anti-Takeover Statutes

State governments have passed a series of laws to make corporate takeovers more difficult. The first set of anti-takeover laws ran into constitutional problems. The primary constitutional problem is in the supremacy clause of the United States Constitution, which preempts state laws that conflict with federal laws.

The federal government adopted the Williams Act to regulate tender offers (discussed in the chapter on securities law and regulation). This act required extensive disclosure on the part of tender offerors and created procedural rules for such offers.

Some early anti-takeover statutes were deemed contrary to the Williams Act, and therefore unconstitutional. Courts held that the Williams Act purposefully allowed for tender offers, when properly regulated. Tender offers gave shareholders the right to sell their shares for a premium price. If the anti-takeover statutes made tender offers virtually impossible, they contradicted the purpose of the Williams Act. Anti-takeover laws could also unconstitutionally interfere with interstate commerce, if they sought to regulate companies incorporated in other states.

States responded by passing a new type of anti-takeover law, called **control-share acquisition statutes**. Delaware passed such a control-share acquisition law. This approach has been found to be constitutional.

Delaware's control-share acquisition law operates as follows. The statute is triggered by an acquirer's purchase of a control share, statutorily defined as 15 percent or more of a company's stock. The statute prohibits the control shareholder from voting its shares to force a second-step merger of the corporation for three years unless certain conditions are met.

A second-step merger can be conducted if the acquirer obtains 85 percent or more of the company's shares or the board of directors and two-thirds of the remaining shareholders authorize the acquirer to do so. This statute makes it more difficult for an acquirer to take control of a corporation. Takeovers are still possible, though, if the acquirer makes a good enough offer to obtain 85 percent of the shares. They are also possible if the acquirer offers a good enough deal in the second-step merger to obtain the approval of two-thirds of the remaining shareholders.

The Delaware statute also provides for a company's directors to decide on its application to their corporation. The directors may decide that they want to facilitate a takeover of their company and make the statute inapplicable. This action may improve the market value of the company's shares.

The Pennsylvania anti-takeover statute was tested when a board accepted a two-tier friendly tender offer and rejected a significantly higher offer from another bidder. The friendly acquirer had promised to preserve the positions of incumbent management. The court found that the new law granted the board great discretion to act in the interests of the corporation as a whole, not necessarily the shareholders. Hence, the court upheld the board's action.

LBOs, MBOs, and Second-Step Mergers

Leveraged buyouts, or LBOs, involve an acquirer's borrowing much of the money necessary to undertake an acquisition. In one recent year, there were over three hundred LBOs with a total acquisition value of more than $40 billion. Federal tax laws actually encourage the use of borrowed money to acquire a corporation.

A substantial number of LBOs are management buyouts, or MBOs. MBOs may be a defensive response to an outside takeover threat or may simply involve a desire by a company's directors and officers to own the company that they manage.

As in most takeovers, the MBO involves a second-step merger, adopted after the acquirer obtains a controlling number of shares. This merger, which eliminates all minority shareholders, takes the company private (under the complete ownership of the acquirer). The success of the second-step merger is often crucial to the acquirer. The merger enables the acquirer to reap all the benefits of the takeover, without sharing these benefits with the remaining minority shareholders.

The key legal problem involves the fairness of the price offered in the second-step merger. As the controlling shareholder can force the merger on minority shareholders, there is a danger that the acquirer will provide an unfairly low price to the minority. Under state law, the controlling shareholders has a duty of fairness to minority shareholders. The duty is especially great in an MBO, given the directors' fiduciary duties to their shareholders.

To help ensure the fairness of the second-step merger consideration, directors usually obtain a valuation of the company from an outside banker, called a **fairness opinion**. The content of this opinion must be fully disclosed to minority shareholders. Simple use of an investment banker may be insufficient, however, and courts have encouraged companies to submit the price to a vote for approval by minority shareholders or to create an independent negotiating committee of directors that are not participating in the MBO.

There is no procedural recipe to guarantee fairness, however. The following case reviewed the fairness of a second-step merger that did obtain a fairness opinion and approval by a majority of minority shareholders.

Case 8.4
Weinberger v. UOP, Inc.
Supreme Court of Delaware, 1983
457 A.2d 701

Background and Facts *Signal Companies, Inc., was interested in acquiring UOP, Inc., and initiated a 1975 tender offer at $21/share. The tender offer succeeded, and Signal acquired 50.5 percent of UOP's shares. In 1978, Signal decided to acquire the remaining 49.5 percent of UOP shares in a second-step merger. A valuation study for Signal by Arledge-Chitiea concluded that UOP would be a good investment at any price up to $24/share. Signal decided to pay about $20 or $21 per share for the remaining shares of UOP. UOP's chief executive officer, who was recently appointed by Signal, found this price to be fair. The market price of UOP's shares was $14.50/share.*

On February 28, 1978, Signal announced the planned merger. The UOP directors retained Lehman Brothers to provide a fairness opinion on the proposed price. On March 6, Lehman brothers opined that $20 or $21/share was fair. The boards of Signal and UOP both met that day and approved the merger. The merger was submitted to a vote of UOP shareholders, who overwhelmingly favored the merger.

Dissenting UOP shareholders filed suit to challenge the fairness of the merger. The trial court held that the terms of the merger were fair and ruled for the defendants. The shareholder plaintiffs appealed.

MOORE, Justice.

* * * *

A public policy, existing through the years, and derived from a profound knowledge of human characteristics and motives, has established a rule that demands of a corporate officer or director, peremptorily and inexorably, the most scrupulous observance of his duty, not only affirmatively to protect the interests of the corporation committed to his charge, but also to refrain from doing anything that would work injury to the corporation, or to deprive it of profit or advantage which his skill and ability might properly bring to it, or to enable it to make in the reasonable and lawful exercise of its powers. The rule that requires an undivided and unselfish loyalty to the corporation demands that there shall be no conflict between duty and self-interest.

Given the absence of any attempt to structure this transaction on an arm's length basis, Signal cannot escape the effects of the conflicts it faced, particularly when its designees on UOP's board did not totally abstain from participation in the matter. There is no "safe harbor" for such divided loyalties in Delaware. When directors of a Delaware corporation are on both sides of a transaction, they are required to demonstrate their utmost good faith and the most scrupulous inherent fairness of the bargain.

* * * *

The structure of the transaction, again, was Signal's doing. So far as negotiations were concerned, it is clear that they were modest at best. Crawford, Signal's man at UOP, never really talked price with Signal, except to accede to its management's statements on the subject, and to convey to Signal the UOP outside directors' view that as between the $20-$21 range under consideration, it would have to be $21. The latter is not a surprising outcome, but hardly arm's length negotiations. Only the protection of benefits for UOP's key employees and the issue of Lehman Brothers' fee approached any concept of bargaining.

As we have noted, the matter of disclosure to the UOP directors was wholly flawed by the conflicts of interest raised by the Arledge-Chitiea report. All of those conflicts were resolved by Signal in its own favor without divulging any aspect of them to UOP.

This cannot but undermine a conclusion that this merger meets any reasonable test of fairness. The outside UOP directors lacked one material piece of information generated by two of their colleagues, but shared only with Signal.

True, the UOP board had the Lehman Brothers' fairness opinion, but that firm has been blamed by the plaintiff for the hurried task it performed, when more properly the responsibility for this lies with Signal. There was no disclosure of the circumstances surrounding the rather cursory preparation of the Lehman Brothers' fairness opinion. Instead, the impression was given UOP's minority that a careful study had been made, when in fact speed was the hallmark, and Mr. Glanville, Lehman's partner in charge of the matter, and also a UOP director, having spent the weekend in Vermont, brought a draft of the "fairness opinion letter" to the UOP directors' meeting on March 6, 1978 with the price left blank. We can only conclude from the record that the rush imposed on Lehman Brothers by Signal's timetable contributed to the difficulties under which this investment banking firm attempted to perform its responsibilities. Yet, none of this was disclosed to UOP's minority.

Decision and Remedy *The Delaware Supreme court reversed the trial court judgment for defendants and remanded the case for further proceedings to establish a fair price for the plaintiff shareholders.*

Courts have occasionally considered the motive of the majority shareholders in forcing the merger. In one case, the majority shareholders adopted a going-private merger in order to eliminate a lawsuit brought against them by minority shareholders for earlier breaches of duty. The court found that this action violated the duty of fair dealing.[8]

State corporation law also provides shareholders with the right of **appraisal** in these second-step mergers. If a shareholder believes that the consideration offered is unfair, the shareholder can dissent by voting against the merger and then going to court for an appraisal of the fair value of the shares. The appraisal remedy, however, is both costly and risky. The court could value the shares at less than the merger consideration.

Federal Regulation of Takeovers

While most significant regulation of takeovers occurs under state corporations laws, federal laws also regulate aspects of the process. The 1968 Williams Act establishes rules for tender offers, which require filings with the Securities and Exchange Commission for the disclosure of key information to shareholders. The requirements of the Williams Act are discussed in detail in the preceding chapter on securities law and regulation.

---

[8] *Merritt v. Colonial Foods, Inc.*, 505 A.2d 757 (Del. Ch. 1986).

Federal antitrust laws can also affect mergers and acquisitions. The government through the Federal Trade Commission (FTC) can prohibit mergers that substantially injure competition. Thus, the FTC might sue to halt a takeover of Pepsi-Cola by Coca-Cola, or vice versa. The authority for this regulation is found in the Clayton Act. The restrictions of antitrust law are discussed in detail in Chapter 47 of *West's Business Law, Seventh Edition* and in Chapter 26 of *West's Legal Environment of Business, Third Edition.*

One additional antitrust law, the Hart-Scott-Rodino Antitrust Improvements Act of 1976, is uniquely applicable to takeovers. This law can apply to an acquisition in which one party (either the acquirer or the target) has sales or assets of at least $100 million and in which the other party has sales or assets of at least $10 million. Unless one of the Act's technical exemptions applies, the acquiring party must file information on the acquisition with the Federal Trade Commission.

After the filing, the Hart-Scott-Rodino Act then imposes a waiting period for the acquisition. In the case of a cash tender offer, this waiting period is fifteen days. In other types of acquisitions, the waiting period is thirty days. During this waiting period, the FTC or the Department of Justice considers the potential anti-competitive effects of the takeover. The acquisition cannot proceed until the waiting period elapses or the government expressly authorizes the takeover.

Ethical Perspectives

Stakeholder Rights

A current ethical controversy involves the rights of a corporation's **stakeholders** in a takeover. Stakeholders are persons such as the corporation's employees or those holding the company's bonds. Sometimes, the entire community surrounding a major manufacturing plant is considered a stakeholder.

The ethical problem arises in the following situation. Suppose that Keggo, the natural resource company, is trading at about $25/share. RBM makes a takeover offer at $50/share. RBM's offer is highly leveraged, however, and if RBM succeeds in the takeover, Keggo's stakeholders are likely to suffer. RBM may sell off plants and equipment in order to pay off their debt. The new company may go bankrupt. Employees may lose their jobs, and bondholders may lose much of the value of their investments, as the company loses its ability to pay off its debts.

This is not an uncommon situation. A takeover may appear to be an excellent deal for a company's shareholders but a threat to the company's stakeholders. What are the board's ethical duties to the stakeholders?

Corporate law makes the board of directors into fiduciaries for the corporation's shareholders. the directors are legally required to manage the company in the best interest of the shareholders. Traditional corporate law would prohibit the directors from considering the interests of stakeholders and force them to act only in the interests of shareholders.

This traditional approach has received considerable criticism. Some states have amended their corporate laws specifically to authorize directors to consider the interests of stakeholders in their management decisions. This action only permits directors to consider stakeholders, however, and does not dictate the nature of that consideration.

Although the traditional rule may seem somewhat harsh, there is justification for considering only shareholder interests. The shareholder owns the company, after all. The capitalist system generally lets persons sell their property for their own interests. This rule promotes economic efficiency by placing property into the hands of those who value it the most and can best profit from it.

Advocates of takeovers argue that they make corporations more efficient and help the economy overall. While some individual stakeholders may suffer the loss of jobs, a more efficient economy should provide more-than-compensating benefits.

Even such takeover advocates must concede that the system has not worked perfectly. Some takeovers have created enormous profits for a few, while bankrupting companies and throwing thousands out of work. The junk bonds created in LBOs have played a significant role in the collapse of some banks, costing the government billions in bail-out costs for the depositors.

There is a strong ethical argument for considering stakeholder interests. The company has made something of a promise to bondholders. In order to borrow money, the company must assure lenders that they will be repaid. While a company may not have made such a promise to its employees, layoffs cause undeniably severe financial harm to families. While shareholders must retain the right to sell their shares, the board of directors arguably should prefer takeover offers that keep the company running, even at some loss of profit to shareholders.

≡ International Perspectives

Foreign Takeover Laws

Foreign companies often present promising takeover opportunities. Purchase of a Japanese or European company can provide a United States company with a valuable entry point into a large foreign market. The laws of most foreign nations, however, make mergers and acquisitions somewhat more difficult than in the U.S.

In Japan, there are thousands of corporate acquisitions every year, but the vast majority of these are friendly takeovers. Although Japan allows for hostile takeovers, few are conducted. Part of the difficulty in a Japanese hostile takeover is cultural. The Japanese business culture considers hostile takeovers to be almost unethical and stigmatizes the acquirer. Even should the takeover succeed, the acquirer will suffer in future business relations with other Japanese companies.

Japanese law also affects takeover prospects. Japan's federal law on tender offers is similar to the United States' Williams Act, but contains a provision that requires a ten-day advance notice for a tender offer. This limits the speed and flexibility of the acquirer. In addition, Japanese law does not provide for the second-step merger even after a tender offer succeeds. Many Japanese companies have placed their shares with other companies who act as white squires in most takeover attempts.

The various nations of the European Community (EC) still have differing laws affecting mergers and acquisitions. As a rule, takeovers are more difficult than in the United States. In most European countries, the directors have a wide scope of allowable defensive actions to fend off a hostile takeover. French law restricts defensive measures after a takeover bid has been announced but generally permits such actions in advance of a bid. Italy allows directors a broad range to adopt defensive actions and permits compulsory second-stage mergers only if the acquirer obtains 90 percent of the company's shares. In the Netherlands, the target's employees have the legal power to prevent its acquisition.

The United Kingdom is an exception to the difficulty of European takeovers. Acquisitions, even hostile ones, are relatively common in the U.K. The applicable Code on Takeovers and Mergers was adopted privately by the securities industry and not government legislation. This Code is dedicated to the protection of shareholder interests and limits defensive measures taken without shareholder approval. The Code also regulates takeover offers. Under the Code, any person who acquires 30 percent or more of a company's shares, must offer to acquire all the remaining shares at the highest price paid for the company's shares within the prior twelve months. In some circumstances, the acquirer must offer to pay cash (rather than securities) for minority shares.

There are currently proposals for a new EC Directive to harmonize takeover laws throughout the European Community. Current and future opportunities are particularly great in the European Community (EC). In the interim, U.S. corporations are buying companies in Europe. The EC Treaty facilitates international banking by requiring member states partially to deregulate banking and better enable international mergers.

Questions and Case Problems

1. Trusts holding 30 percent of the stock in Anderson Clayton were about to expire. Seeing a takeover opportunity, a group of bidders announced an interest in acquiring all the Anderson Clayton stock at $54 per share. The Clayton board of directors then made a two-tiered self tender offer for 65 percent of the company's stock at $60 per share, plus the sale of shares to an ESOP. The group of acquirers argued that the two-tiered self tender was an unlawful defensive measure that prevented shareholders from making a choice between competing acquirers. Should a court enjoin the self tender? [*AC Acquisition Corp. v. Anderson Clayton & Co.*, 519 A.2d 103 (Del. Ch. 1986)].

2. Nuclear Company was a small corporation that had two million shares outstanding. About 20 percent of these shares were held by Nuclear's officers and directors. Armco approached the Nuclear directors and offered to buy the company for $25 per share, based on the report of a financial adviser. Armco made this proposal as a friendly takeover and promised to retain Nuclear's officers in their positions. The Nuclear directors, who were also officers, believed that the takeover would facilitate the company's expansion and voted to approve a merger agreement with Armco. Minority shareholders in Nuclear sued the directors, claiming that they had breached their fiduciary duty in not seeking other offers. Did the directors breach their fiduciary duty?

3. Grand Metropolitan made a tender offer for all shares of Pillsbury at $63 per share in cash. The Pillsbury board decided that this price was inadequate, based on the report of an independent financial adviser, and adopted defensive measures. This included adoption of a poison pill, the spin-off of the company's Burger King subsidiary, and the sale of some of its other restaurant properties. Grand Metropolitan complained that these defensive measures made its takeover either impossible or unprofitable and sued to enjoin the implementation of these measures. Are the Pillsbury defensive measures a lawful response to a takeover threat? [*Grand Metropolitan PLC v. Pillsbury Co.*, 558 A.2d 1049 (Del. Ch. 1988)].

4. Universal Foods adopted a poison pill. Not long thereafter, Amanda Acquisition made a highly leveraged tender offer for all shares of Universal at $30.50 per share in cash. The Universal board simply rejected the offer and refused to redeem the poison pill, stating that it was in the company's best interest to remain independent. They also claimed that the tender offer contained false and misleading statements about Universal's prospects and the characteristics of the offer. Amanda sued to compel Universal to redeem the poison pill. Should the court require the redemption of the pill? [*Amanda Acquisition Corp. v. Universal Foods Corp.*, 708 F.Supp. 984 (E.D. Wis.), *aff'd on other grounds*, 877 F.2d 496 (7th Cir. 1989)].

5. After observing unusual activity in its stock, the board of directors of TW Services adopted a poison pill. Soon thereafter, SWT Acquisition made a tender offer for 31.5 percent of TW's stock at $29 per share. The offer was subject to a condition that the offer be approved by the TW board of directors. The TW board of directors considered the price to be unfair and refused to take any action. SWT asked a court to enjoin the TW poison pill and reconsider its offer. Should the court provide SWT its requested relief? [*TW Services, Inc. v. SWT Acquisition Corp.*, 14 Del. J. Corp. Law 1169 (Del. Ch. 1989)].

6. Joe Frasca is the President and Chairman of the Board of Directors of Ajax Corporation and holds shares in Baker, Inc. The President of Baker, Scott Pollard, approaches Joe and suggests a friendly acquisition of Ajax, promising Joe continued employment. After examining financial data, Joe concludes that the merger is in the best interests of Ajax and agrees to a binding merger agreement. Charles Company subsequently expresses interest in acquiring Ajax at a higher price than offered by Baker. Joe refuses to negotiate with Charles, because he believes that Baker is a better "fit" for the company and because the merger agreement with Baker precludes him from considering takeover discussions with others. An Ajax shareholder sues Frasca and seeks to halt the friendly merger. How should this case be resolved?

Chapter Nine

Insurance Law

Key Background

The essential background for this chapter on insurance law is found in Chapter 52 of *West's Business Law, Seventh Edition*. This chapter also covers insurance law. Among the important points to remember from this chapter are:

- the features necessary for a beneficiary to have an enforceable insurable interest

- central features of insurance contracts and their coverage

- the many types of insurance available in the marketplace

* * *

Insurance coverage has enormous importance for modern businesses. Today's companies are subject to enormous liability under a variety of laws involving product liability, employment law, and standard torts such as negligence. An enormous source of future liability is in environmental law.

A judgment under the above laws may amount to millions of dollars, including punitive damages. Such a judgement may bankrupt an otherwise successful company. The ability to insure against the risk of such judgement is therefore important to all industries.

In addition, insurance companies themselves represent an important business sector. Insurance is a multibillion-dollar enterprise, with its own risks. Insurance law helps balance the interests of insurers and insured, so that effective insurance protection remains available.

Insurance Coverage Issues

Among the most common insurance cases today are disputes over the coverage of insurance policies. When an insured company suffers a loss, it is likely to claim that the insurance company may maintain that the loss is outside the policy's coverage. The policy itself may not expressly address the issue.

This section discusses the standards for determining coverage, particularly the "reasonable expectations" doctrine. It also discusses certain exclusions from coverage, and applies the standards to the most significant contemporary issue—insurance coverage of hazardous waste and pollution liabilities.

Reasonable Expectations Doctrine

An insurance policy is a contract, and, like other contracts, its terms are interpreted according to the intent of the parties. most insurance contracts are considered **contracts of adhesion**, however. This means that the insurance company has written the contract itself and presented it to the insured, with little opportunity for negotiation over contract terms. In this circumstance, the courts focus primarily on the intent of the insured party.

The **reasonable expectations doctrine** was developed to protect the insured. In the United States around 1800 fire insurance companies would issue policies through form contracts that contained unclear provisions. If a fire occurred, the large insurance companies would employ a battery of lawyers to dispute coverage, and individual policyholders had a difficult time recovering. Courts therefore developed the reasonable expectations doctrine.

Courts interpreting insurance contracts emphasize the "reasonable expectations" of the insured party. The court analyzes the insurance contract with an eye to what the insured party thought it was obtaining. A closely related doctrine is called the **ambiguity doctrine**. This states that any ambiguous, or unclear, policy provisions are to be construed against the insurance company and in favor of the insured.

A leading case under the reasonable expectations doctrine involved an Iowa store that purchased a "Mercantile Burglary and Robbery Policy." The policy provided burglary protection for the insured's warehouse, but specifically limited protection to cases in which the burglar left "visible marks" of entry on the outside of the building. The warehouse was robbed by a burglar who entered through a Plexiglass door and left no visible marks. The Iowa Supreme Court held that the insurance company nevertheless was required to compensate for the burglary losses. The court stressed that the limitation to cases of "visible marks" was "buried" in the definitions section of the insurance policy and that a reasonable person would expect the policy to cover this episode.[1]

Some victims of drive-by shootings claimed that they should be covered under uninsured motorist insurance that extended to injuries resulting from the "use" of a car. While some lower court decisions have found coverage, the Virginia Supreme Court recently denied coverage. The court found that gunshots fired from an automobile did not constitute "use" of the car, as that term was intended.[2]

The reasonable expectations of the insured party often arise from the insurance company itself. Statements by insurance agents may create reasonable expectations in coverage, even if the policy itself is contrary.

A slightly different circumstance concerns a provision in an insurance policy that is somewhat ambiguous in its coverage. If a provision is ambiguous, courts generally will enforce that provision for the benefit of the insured party, under the reasonable expectations doctrine.

Even a perfectly clear term may be ambiguous in its application. For example, a woman was covered by her husband's automobile insurance policy as a "family member." She separated from her husband and continued to drive the car. After she suffered an accident, the insurance company denied coverage, contending that she lived at another site and was no longer a covered family member. A court held that she was covered, under the reasonable expectations doctrine.[3]

The reasonable expectations rule does not mean that the insurance company always loses. Rather, the rule places the burden on the insurance company to inform its policy holder of the true scope of the policy, including its limitations. When unexpected events occur that arguably fall within the policy, the insured will get the benefit of a presumption of coverage.

The key question in coverage is the intention of the parties to the insurance contract. The following recent case illustrates how clear intentions can override even the presence of an ambiguous contract.

---

[1] *C&J Fertilizer, Inc. v. Allied Mutual Insurance Co.*, 227 N.W.2d 169 (Iowa 1975).

[2] *Lexie v. State Farm Mutual Automobile Insurance Company*, 469 S.E.2d 61 (Va. 1996).

[3] *Gordinier v. Aetna Casualty and Surety Co.*, 742 P.2d 277 (Ariz. 1987).

Case 9.1
Aromin v. State Farm Fire & Casualty Company
United States Court of Appeals, Eleventh Circuit, 1990
908 F.2d 812

Background and Facts *W.R. Matix was involved in a violent streetside fight with his girlfriend. Thomas Aromin drove up to assist, and Matix and Aromin began to argue after Matix's girlfriend left the scene. Matix then shot Aromin in the groin from six feet away and caused Aromin to become a paraplegic, with damages of approximately $1 million. Matix was insured by State Farm Fire & Casualty Company under a personal liability umbrella* *policy. Aromin demanded payment of his damages from State Farm, which refused. Aromin then sued to recover. Both sides moved for summary judgement.*

HOEVELER, District Judge.

* * *

Matix was insured by State Farm under a personal liability umbrella policy at the time of the shooting. The insurance policy provides that it will cover, in its section labeled "personal injury:"

a. bodily injury, sickness, disease, shock, mental anguish or mental injury.

b. false arrest, false imprisonment, wrongful eviction, wrongful detention, malicious prosecution or humiliation.

c. libel, slander, defamation of character or invasion of rights or privacy.

d. assault and battery.

By express terms, therefore, the insurance policy appears to extend coverage for assault and battery, the intentional tort complained of in this case. The policy also proclaims, however, that it will not provide coverage:
[I]f you intend to cause the personal injury or property damage. We will not apply this exclusion if:

a. you were acting in good faith to protect people or property; and

b. your actions were not fraudulent, criminal or malicious.

The state court found that the insured was not acting in good faith to protect people or property and that his actions were not negligent, but were criminal in nature. The parties do not contest this finding.

Discussion Under Florida law, if the provisions of an insurance contract conflict, the contract must be resolved to afford maximum coverage. *Nu-Air Mfg. Co. v. Frank B. Hall & Co.*, 822 F.2d 987 (11th Cir.1987). If the two provisions in the instant policy—one covering assault and battery, the other excluding coverage for intentional torts—are found to conflict, the court must resolve the question of which provision prevails.

On the other hand, it is a cardinal principle of construction that, if reasonably possible, no part of a contract should be taken as eliminated or stricken by some other part. *Burton v. Travelers Ins. Co.* [341 Mich. 30], 67 N.W.2d 54, 55 (MI 1954). The insurer argues that the terms of its contract do not conflict because coverage extended only to the civil torts of assault and battery, not to criminal conduct. The insurer explains that civil battery—covered under the policy—requires only the general intent to cause a harmful or offensive contact, resulting in a non-consensual contact, whereas the intentional injury exclusion applies to those situations where the actor intended to cause the specific result.

* * * *

While State Farm included coverage for "assault and battery" in its list of covered circumstances, it is equally clear and without ambiguity that it intended to exclude coverage where the insured..."intended to cause the personal injury..." and that the exclusion would *not* apply where the actions were not "...criminal or malicious." That the exclusion applies to the circumstances of this case seems quite clear. The question remains, though, what of the coverage for assault and battery. Assistance in finding the answer is provided by reference to the *Appelstein* case. ***Note also part (a) of the section describing the inapplicability of the exclusion. Where one is acting in "good faith" to protect people or property, the exclusion does not apply. While the apparent conflict in the described provisions seems to create a tension in interpretation that tension is more apparent than real. There can, no doubt, be circumstances where one is charged with an assault (threatened battery) and battery (an uninvited touching or contact) where the insured intended no harm under the circumstances. Clearly, in this case, the act was criminal (the shooting of another at close range) and the injury (or even death) intended. The coverage afforded by the policy should not and does not apply under such circumstances.

Decision and Remedy *The court granted summary judgment for the defendant insurer.*

Policy Exclusions

Most insurance policies contain some general exclusions of coverage. These include exclusion of damages that the insured expects at the time of the contract and preexisting conditions applicable to the insured.

Expected or Intended Clause

Comprehensive insurance policies generally afford no coverage for damages that the insured party expected to occur or intended to occur. Thus, a company cannot take out a policy to protect against a harm that is almost sure to happen.

For example, a county operated a landfill in which various types of waste were dumped. The landfill was required to pay damages for the release of pollutants and sought insurance coverage for these payments. A court denied coverage, because the landfill company was aware of the pollution problem years before the insurance policy and still continued its dumping practices. Coverage was therefore excluded under the policy's expected or intended clause.[4]

In determining whether a risk was expected or intended, most courts use an objective standard. This means that the court does not look to the actual knowledge of the insured party. Instead, the court considers whether a reasonable person in the position of the insured would have expected this type of damage to occur.

It is important to note that awareness of a possible future harm does not deny insurance coverage. The very act of insurance suggests recognition of the possibility of damage. Courts invoke the expected or intended clause to deny insurance coverage only when there is a "substantial probability" or a "substantial certainty" of the occurrence of damages.

Loss-in-Progress Clause

Insurance policies generally exclude coverage for a preexisting condition or a "loss-in-progress." Thus, suppose Doug Murray visits his doctor, and she diagnoses him as suffering from lung cancer. Doug then runs next door and takes out a cancer insurance policy. The insurance company probably need not make payments on Doug's lung cancer costs, because it was a preexisting condition at the time of insurance.

In one recent case, a company purchased property that contained hazardous waste and purchased a comprehensive insurance policy covering the property. Soon thereafter, the insured was sued for cleanup expenses on the property. Insurance coverage for the lawsuit was denied, because evidence showed that the company had commissioned an investigation of the property that informed it of the exact nature of the pollution problem at the site. The damages, therefore, were part of a known loss-in-progress that was excluded from insurance coverage.

---

[4] *County of Broom v. Aetna Casualty & Surety Co.*, 540 N.Y.S.2d 620 (N.Y. App. Div. 1989).

■ Insurer's Duty to Defend

Most liability policies give the insurer both the right and obligation to take over the defense of the case. Suppose that Anna Charnes is involved in an automobile accident with Henry Wong. Henry is injured in the accident and sues Anna, who has automobile liability insurance coverage. Anna's insurance company would take over the claim against her, to settle or to defend in court.

What if the insurance company refuses to defend Anna in this case, for any reason? Anna will have a case against the insurance company for breach of its duty to defend her. In the case of Henry's action against Anna, the insurance company's duty to defend is rather clear, assuming she had a standard policy. In a pollution case, when the insurer has an argument against coverage, the duty to defend would be less clear.

The general rule is that a duty to defend arises based upon the allegations in the complaint against the insured. If the complaint's allegations fall within the policy's coverage, the insurer has a duty to defend. Courts have tended to resolve doubts in favor of the insured.

Thus, if a complaint contains allegations both inside and outside of coverage, the insurer assumes a duty to defend. Uncertainty about coverage may also establish the duty to defend. Some courts have required the insurer to investigate the complaint to seek out claims that would be covered.

The broad interpretation of the duty to defend can be illustrated by example. Suppose that Richard Glaser has a comprehensive insurance policy for his shop. A customer, Lynne Salbu, enters the shop and is injured by a fall. She sues Glaser and claims assault and battery. Glaser's insurance contract excludes intentional torts, such as assault and battery. The facts alleged by Salbu, however, suggest potential liability in negligence, which *is* covered by the insurance policy. Glaser's insurance company will have a duty to defend, even though the alleged assault and battery is outside the policy's coverage.

The following decision illustrates how an insurance company's duty to defend may be broader than its ultimate responsibility under a policy containing a pollution exclusion clause.

■ Case 9.2
Avondale Industries, Incorporated v. Travelers Indemnity Company
United States Court of Appeals, Second Circuit, 1989
887 F.2d 1989

Background and Facts *Avondale Industries is in the business of building and repairing ships. In the course of this work, it removed certain wastes from the ships, temporarily stored them, and then shipped them to a recycling facility. The recycling facility suffered leaks that necessitated government cleanup. The government sued Avondale for part of the costs of this cleanup. Private parties also sued for damages from the wastes.*

Avondale sought to recover its cleanup cost liability from its insurance company. The insurance policy contained a pollution exclusion that denied coverage for pollution liability unless it resulted from a "sudden and accidental" release. The insurer denied coverage under this exclusion. Avondale sued for a judicial determination that the insurance company had a duty to defend both the government and private claims against the company. A district court ruled for Avondale.

CARDAMONE, Circuit Judge.

* * * *

An insurer's duty to defend and to indemnify are separate and distinct, and the former duty is broader than the latter. * * * The duty to defend rests soley on whether the complaint in the underlying action contains any allegations that arguably or potentially bring the action within the protection purchased. *Technicon,* 74 N.Y.2d at 73, 544 N.Y.S.2d 531, 542 N.E.2d 1048. So long as the claims alleged against the insured rationally may be said to fall within the policy coverage, the insurer must come forward and defend. *Id.*

New York courts have held, in addition, that an insurer seeking to avoid its duty to defend bears a heavy burden. "[B]efore an insurance company is permitted to avoid policy coverage, it must ... establish[] that the exclusions or exemptions apply in the particular case, and that they are subject to no other reasonable interpretation." *Seaboard*, 64 N.Y.2d at 311, 486 N.Y.S.2d 873, 476 N.E.2d 272; see also *Neuwirth v. Blue Cross & Blue Shield*, 62 N.Y.2d 718, 476 N.Y.S.2d 814, 465 N.E.2d 353 (1984) (mem.) (citations omitted). To avoid the duty therefore the insurer must demonstrate that the allegations in the underlying complaints are "soley and entirely" within specific and unambiguous exclusions from the policy's coverage. See *International Paper*, 35 N.Y.2d at 325, 361 N.Y.S.2d 873,320 N.E.2d 619.

Consequently, Travelers can be excused from its duty to defend only if it can be determined as a matter of law that there is no possible basis in law or fact upon which the insurer might be held to indemnify Avondale. See, e.g., *Vila Charlotte Bronte, Inc. v. Commercial Union Ins. Co.*, 64 N.Y.2d 846, 848, 487 N.Y.S.2d 314, 476 N.E.2d 640 (1985) (mem.). A comparison must be made *de novo* between the allegations contained in the complaint or underlying action and the terms of the policy.

* * * *

Examining the allegations of the underlying Louisiana complaints it appears that Avondale is one of 70 named defendants. The allegations charge all the defendants with "insufficient" containment measures; with "generating" hazardous waste; with "knowledge" of the presence of toxins; with culpability for "escape" of hazardous materials. None of these conclusory assertions "clearly negate" the possibility that discharge or escape was "sudden and accidental."

Decision and Remedy   *The court affirmed the ruling that the insurer had a duty to defend both actions.*

If an insurance company breaches its duty to defend, it may be subject to several types of damages. First, the insurer must pay all costs and attorney's fees incurred by the insured in his or her own defense. Second, the insurer may be required to pay any judgment or settlement by the insured in the case. Third, the insurer may be liable for additional damages caused by its refusal to defend, such as mental anguish on the part of the insured.

▬ Wrongful Treatment of Claimants

Many contemporary cases involve allegations that an insurance company has wrongfully treated the claims made by an insured. These were traditionally called "bad faith actions." Increasingly, though, insurance companies may be found liable even in the absence of real bad faith on their part.

Many jurisdictions consider the wrongful denial of insurance benefits to be a distinct tort cause of action. Other jurisdictions consider the wrongful denial to be a breach of contractual duties to deal in good faith. Even the latter jurisdictions tend to allow punitive damages.

There are several sources of these wrongful treatment actions. These include: (i) failure to investigate claims sufficiently before claims denial; (ii) purposeful and unjustified delay in payment; and (iii) refusal to settle a claim against the insured within the policy limits.

Some of these wrongful treatment claims may be brought by the insured party itself and are called "first party claims." Others may be brought by another party, called "third party claims." Third party claims arise when the third party has a right to recover on insurance. In the automobile accident case discussed above, Henry is a third party seeking to claim against Anna's insurance.

Some first party claims involve improper denial of claims. These usually involve a claim that the insurance company denied a claim after an insufficient investigation of the claim's merits. If a company denies coverage without conducting a thorough and honest investigation of the claim, it may be liable. In some unfortunate cases, an insurance company will deny coverage to get leverage over the claimant for an advantageous settlement of the claim.

In one case, a California woman took out a disability insurance policy and was assured of lifetime benefits should she be permanently disabled. Thereafter, she suffered a stroke that left her permanently disabled. The insurance company made payments for two years. Then, the company discovered that the woman had made trips to church and also made monthly trips to visit her doctor. The company claimed that she was not disabled and discontinued the benefits payments. She sued the company on grounds that she was disabled and recovered both actual and punitive damages.[5]

Potential damages from wrongful denial of benefits is illustrated by another California action, in which the owner of a laundromat was seriously injured on the job and required extensive medical care. After the insurance company denied payment, the plaintiff sued because he was ejected from two hospitals, denied surgical services, exhausted all his personal assets, lost his business, had his utilities disconnected, had his credit ruined, and had his wheelchair repossessed. He obtained essential surgery only by tricking a third hospital into accepting him on a weekend, before they could check for his coverage.[6] He eventually received $75,000 in actual damages but no punitive damages. In another case, a court awarded $740,000 in punitive damages against an insurance company that sought to exploit the plight of a paralyzed insured.

Refusal to pay a claim, of course, is not necessarily improper. Some claims are uncovered by an insurance policy. The company has an obligation simply to investigate a claim and pay those that fall within the scope of the insurance policy.

Insurers have also been held liable for unjustified delay in paying claims. For example, an insurer may fail a frivolous appeal of a judgment of its liability to delay payment or coerce settlement from a needy insured. If the delay of payment is without any justification, the insurer may be liable for damages in addition to the liability under the policy.

Another claim against insurance companies is failure to settle claims. The difficulty with settlements can be illustrated by example. In the automobile accident discussed above, suppose that Henry sued Anna for $200,000. Anna had $100,000 worth of automobile liability insurance. After a period of time, Henry approached the insurance company and offered to settle for $100,000. This settlement would be in Anna's interest, because she would have no liability over and above the insurance. The settlement is not in the insurer's interest, however. Because the settlement offer was for the policy limit, the insurer is normally better off taking its chances at trial.

Courts have held that insurers have a responsibility to initiate settlement negotiations. They have also held that the insurer must accept a settlement offer that is reasonable under the circumstances. The company must consider the interests of the insured and not merely its own interests.

Amoco Corporation, a large oil company, sued Lloyds of London, after the insurer failed to settle or take other action to resolve a claim that Amoco had installed defective pipes. Amoco lost one of the cases and was liable for $39 million. Amoco argued that Lloyds committed bad faith and obtained an award of over $340 million against Lloyds in compensatory and punitive damages.

Some courts have granted damages for emotional distress resulting from an insurer's refusal to settle a case, based on the theory that insurance is for the peace of mind of the policyholder. Courts in some states, including California, have limited emotional distress recovery to cases in which the insured suffered some independent harm to person or property. For example, if an insured's car was repossessed or the insured lost a job, she would have suffered independent property harm and be able to recover damages for mental distress.

The results of bad faith claims have depended in part on the type of insurance. Claims are more likely to succeed for medical insurance. Very few states have recognized claims for bad faith handling of workers' compensation insurance claims, however. Even California courts, which pioneered the bad faith insurance claims cases, have refused to recognize such claims under workers' compensation.

Policyholders also have legal obligations. A small business told its independent insurance agent to obtain additional insurance coverage, but the agent failed to do so. After the business suffered a loss in excess of policy limits, it filed suit against the agent for breach of contract and tort. The court

---

[5] *Wetherbee v. United Insurance Co. of America*, 71 Cal. Rptr. 764 (1968).

[6] *Silberg v. California Life Insurance Co.*, 521 P.2d 1103 (Cal. 1974).

threw out the claim, because the plaintiff was at fault for failing to read the policy.[7]

Wrongful Nonrenewal of Policy

Insurance policies govern a specific term of time. When the time is up, the insurance policy lapses unless it is renewed. Ordinarily, the insurance company has a right to choose not to renew a policy for a given insured. In some circumstances, though, an insurer may be liable for wrongful nonrenewal even if the insurer has a contract option not to renew. Some state laws require that an insurer have a good reason not to renew certain types of policies.

The presence of a wrongful nonrenewal action depends largely on the type of insurance policy in question. Automobile liability insurance, for example, is of broad public concern because many states require such insurance in order to drive legally. Many states have passed laws that prohibit nonrenewal of automobile insurance policies without good reason.

In one interesting case, a seventy-four-year-old man had a perfect driving record for nearly fifty years. He then received one speeding violation (for driving 54 mph in a 20 mph zone). He then had an accident at an intersection, but no traffic citation was issued. After the insurance policy refused to renew his policy, he sued and won a judgment that the nonrenewal had been unjustified under a state statute.[8]

For fire insurance and other forms of property insurance, however, insurance companies have great discretion in deciding whether to renew a policy. Several insurers have been sued for refusing to renew policies in inner-city areas. Courts generally have upheld this business decision, unless it was racially motivated.

Some states, such as Pennsylvania, have statutes that limit nonrenewal of property insurance to cases of good cause. In one instance, a business policyholder obtained a German Shepherd dog for security, and the insurer cancelled its policy. A court held that this was not good cause, even if the presence of the dog increased the insurance risk slightly.[9]

Wrongful refusal to renew has also occurred in policies for professional liability insurance. Insurance coverage under a malpractice policy, for example, is usually on a "claims made" basis. Thus, the insurer becomes potentially responsible for claims made during the term of the insurance policy.

In one case, an engineering firm had a malpractice policy. The firm worked on a mine that suffered an explosion during the policy period, but no claims were filed immediately. Fearing that claims eventually would be filed for the explosion, the insurer refused to renew the policy. A court held that this was wrongful to avoid liability for an accident that occurred during the policy term.[10]

In addition to the above common law actions, most states have passed an Unfair Insurance Practices Act or an Unfair Settlement Practices Act. These laws prohibit insurance companies from refusing to settle or taking other unfair actions toward an insured. In most states, these laws do not create a private right to action. Thus, the insured party cannot sue for a violation of the statute. Only the state Commissioner of Insurance can sue to enforce the law in these states.

Under a typical state law, the Commissioner has the authority to investigate alleged unfair practices and hold hearings. If wrongful dealing is found, the Commissioner may assess fines and penalties or even revoke a company's license to sell insurance in the state. State Commissioners have undertaken relatively few enforcement actions, however.

Insurance Company Defenses

The purpose of insurance is to protect insureds from certain consequences, such as fire, for which they pay premiums. As a result, when a fire occurs, the insurance company generally has an obligation to pay the insured. There are some defenses for insurance companies even for risks covered by the policy. If the policyholder sets the fire, for example, the insurance company need not compensate him or her.

Two such defenses are often raised by insurance companies. The first is that the insured party made some misrepresentation to the insurance company in order to obtain coverage. The second is that the insured failed to give timely and proper notice of the problem to the insurance company.

---

[7] *General Insurance of Roanoke, Inc. v. Page*, 464 S.E.2d 343 (Va. 1995).

[8] *Sentry Insurance v. Brown*, 424 So.2d 780 (Fla. App. 1982).

[9] *Lititz Mutual Insurance Co. v. Commonwealth*, 401 A.2d 606 (Pa. 1979).

[10] *Heen & Flint Associates v. Travelers Indem. Co.*, 400 N.Y.S.2d 994 (1977).

Application Misrepresentations

When individuals or businesses apply for insurance coverage, they will be required to fill out a questionnaire that includes questions about their past losses. The insurance company will base its decision to enter a contract on the answers to these questions.

If a person has a history of traffic violations, medical problems, or past excessive claims, he or she may be unable to obtain insurance. If the person is aware of this problem, he or she may be tempted to lie on the application in order to obtain coverage. If a person lies on an application for automobile insurance, obtains coverage, and then gets into an accident, the insurance company may attempt to deny coverage for the accident, due to the misrepresentation in the application.

The issue of application misrepresentation is complicated because often a third party is the beneficiary of the insurance coverage. If Robin lies on an automobile liability insurance application and runs over Juan with a car, Juan is the payee on the policy. Juan did not lie to the insurance company and will claim that the company should pay for his damages.

Insurance companies do not want to pay claims resulting from application misrepresentation, and most policies contain language similar to the following:

We do not provide coverage to an insured who has

a. intentionally concealed or misrepresented any material fact or circumstance; or

b. made false statements or engaged in fraudulent conduct relating to this insurance.

Even with this language, the insurance company may be liable to injured third parties.

To avoid coverage, the insurance company must demonstrate that the misrepresentation is material. This means that the company must show that it would have refused coverage if it had known the true facts on an honest application. The insurance company must also show that it actually relied on the application misrepresentations.

Suppose that a chain smoker of cigarettes applied for a health insurance policy. On the application, the person lied and claimed that he never smoked cigarettes. A court would probably find this misrepresentation to be material and deny coverage for the costs of later medical care for emphysema or lung cancer.

If a misrepresentation is material, the insurer may declare the policy void and avoid payments. It is important to realize that the misrepresentation must be material to the issuance of the policy but need not be material to the actual claim made, in order to void the policy. This issue is presented in the following recent case.

Case 9.3
New York Life Insurance Company v. Johnson
United States Court of Appeals
Third Circuit, 1991
1991 WL 2064

Background and Facts In 1986, Kirk Johnson took out a $50,000 life insurance policy on himself and named his father, Lawrence Johnson, as beneficiary. In the application for the policy, Kirk Johnson stated that he never smoked cigarettes. In fact, he had smoked since 1973 and was then smoking about ten cigarettes per day. Had the insurance company known the true facts, it would have offered a policy but at much higher premiums. In 1988, Kirk Johnson died from an AIDS-related disease unrelated to his cigarette consumption. The insurance company investigated the claim and refused to pay on the life insurance policy, due to misrepresentation in the application. The company offered to refund the premiums paid, but Lawrence Johnson refused this offer.

Lawrence Johnson sued to recover on the policy. A district court held that the statements about smoking were material misrepresentations but refused to void the policy altogether. The court *used the insurance company's rate schedules to determine the additional premiums that Kirk Johnson would have paid if he had honestly disclosed his smoking habit. The court then deducted this amount from the policy value and awarded Lawrence Johnson the difference. The insurer appealed.*

DEBEVOISE, District Judge.

* * * *

In the present case disclosure of the true facts about Kirk Johnson's smoking practices would be caused New York Life to have demanded higher premiums and thus the misrepresentations were material.

One would have expected that application of this well recognized Pennsylvania law to the undisputed facts would have required a declaration that the policy was void ab initio [from the beginning]. However, the district court noted that in Pennsylvania this law typically had been applied in the context of misrepresentations about the state of one's medical condition or health background and had never been applied in the context of a misrepresentation about smoking habits. The additional question was posed, therefore, whether under Pennsylvania law a material misrepresentation in the smoking context called for the severe remedy of voiding the policy or whether some lesser remedy would be appropriate.

* * * *

The logic of the district court's opinion would require abrogating the void ab initio rule not just in smoking misrepresentation cases but in all misrepresentation cases where, if the true facts were known, the insurance company would have issued a policy at a higher precisely ascertainable rate exception to the void ab initio rule. The relevant inquiry is whether the misrepresentation is material. Although not decided in the smoking context, Pennsylvania cases uniformly hold that a policy will be void ab initio if issued as a result of a misrepresentation whether the truth would have resulted in no policy being issued or whether the truth would have resulted in the policy being issued with a higher premium.

* * * *

Thus the Courts of Appeals for the Second and Fourth Circuits, the District for the Southern District of Florida, and the courts of New York and Oregon have held that a misrepresentation as to smoking habits in an application for insurance relieves the insurer of liability on the policy. There is every reason to conclude that the same result would prevail in Pennsylvania if and when the question is presented.

While a court might sympathize with a beneficiary who does not receive the proceeds of a policy obtained by the insured's fraud, there are strong reasons of pubic policy supporting the rule which we believe prevails in Pennsylvania. If the only consequence of a fraudulent misrepresentation in a life insurance application is to reduce the amount paid under the policy, there is every incentive for applicants to lie. If the lie is undetected during the two-year contestability period, the insured will have obtained excessive coverage for which he has not paid. If the lie is detected during the two-year period, the insured will still obtain what he could have had if he had told the truth. In essence, the applicant has everything to gain and nothing to loose by lying. The victims will be the honest applicants who tell the truth and whose premiums will rise over the long run to pay for the excessive insurance proceeds paid out as a result of undetected misrepresentations in fraudulent applications.

Decision and Remedy *The court reversed and remanded the case for the entry of a judgement that the policy was void.*

An insurance company may also be required to show that the misrepresentation was made knowingly and in bad faith. If the insured party simply misunderstood the application and made an "honest misrepresentation," the insurer would be required to pay.

Even if an insured party made material and intentional misrepresentations, the insurance company may still be liable to make insurance payments to an injured third party. This is under a theory of the insurer's duty to investigate the statements in the application.

In one case, an insured party made numerous significant misrepresentations about his past driving record in an insurance application. An accident victim of the insured sought to recover, but the insurance company refused to pay. A court found the insurance company to be liable because the "quasi-public" character of automobile liability insurance created a duty on the insurance company to "conduct a reasonable investigation of insurability."[11]

Thus, an insurance company cannot simply rely on the truth of the answers in its application questionnaire. The company must make some reasonable investigation of the answers' accuracy, if the insurer wants to rely on material misrepresentations to avoid coverage.

Failure of Notice

Insurance policies typically require that the insured make prompt notice of the existence of facts that create an insurance claim, as well as the claim itself. A typical comprehensive general insurance policy would contain language such as the following:

> You must see to it that we are notified as soon as practicable of an "occurrence" which may result in a claim. Notice should include:
>
> 1. How, when and where the "occurrence" took place.
>
> 2. The names and addresses of any injured persons and witnesses.
>
> 3. The nature and location of any injury or damage arising out of the "occurrence."

In addition to requiring notification of such a potential liability-inducing "occurrence," policies also require prompt notification of any claim made against the insured that might trigger insurance coverage. In addition, the insured party must cooperate with the company in investigation of the claim.

Timely notice is important to insurance companies for a variety of reasons. First, it facilitates thorough investigation of potential and actual claims. Second, notice enables the insurer to maintain sufficient reserves to pay losses.

In many cases, an insured party fails to make prompt notice under such policy provisions, especially the notice of the "occurrence" itself. The insurance company may then seek to avoid coverage for lack of timely notice. Failure of notice alone, however, does not absolve the insurer of responsibility to pay.

Many jurisdictions require that the insurer demonstrate that it suffered some prejudice from late notice, before denying coverage. This means that the company must show that the lateness of notice caused it some damage, such as impeding full investigation of the occurrence.

Suppose that a company reached a settlement with the Environmental Protection Agency to pay for environmental cleanup at its facility and only then notified its insurance company. The insurance company could be required to pay for the cleanup costs, unless it could show that the settlement terms were worse than those the insurance company could have negotiated itself.

Some states will deny coverage for lack of timely notice even in the absence of prejudice. Recent decisions in New York and Kentucky denied insurance coverage when an insured waited over two years to notify the insurance company and did not require the insurance company to demonstrate that it suffered some prejudice from late notice.

Even if notice is not late under the policy, its timing may influence an insurer's obligation, as illustrated in the following opinion.

---

[11] *Barrera v. State Farm Mutual Automobile Insurance Co.*, 79 Cal. Rptr. 106 (1969).

Case 9.4
Great American Insurance Company v. Aetna Casualty and Surety Company
Supreme Court of Hawaii, 1994
876 P.2d 1314

Background and Facts *Mitsui & Co., Inc. supplied steel used for the construction of a stadium in Hawaii. In 1982, the state filed suit against Mitsui and others for allegedly defective steel. One of its insurers, Great American Insurance Company accepted the defense of the case. Over the next several years, the company incurred over $300,000 in legal defense costs. In 1987, Great American discovered from Mitsui that Aetna Casualty and Surety Company had insured Mitsui for part of the relevant period. Great American promptly notified Aetna. Very soon after this, the case settled. Great American then sued Aetna for a contribution to the defense costs incurred between 1982 and 1987. Aetna said it was not liable because it had not received notice, but Great American argued that Aetna had suffered no prejudice. This question was certified to the Supreme Court of Hawaii.*

MOON, Chief Justice.

* * * *

Here, it is undisputed that prior to Aetna receiving notice of the lawsuit on February 11, 1987, Mitsui had been served with the complaint in July 1982 and presumably knew by its records that Great American and Aetna had been its insurers during periods potentially relevant to allegations within the complaint. Despite the availability of coverage for defense costs, Mitsui voluntarily chose to retain its own counsel until it tendered its defense to Great American on December 1, 1983, after incurring approximately $77,500 in legal fees. Upon accepting Mitsui's defense… Great American repeatedly requested names of Mitsui's other insurers. However, it was not until January 9, 1987 that Mitsui disclosed to Great American that Aetna had insured Mitsui…of paramount significance is that the information regarding Aetna's identity as Mitsui's insurer from April 1976 to April 1978 was a matter of public record as a result of Mitsui's answers to interrogatories filed on December 22, 1983, over three years before Aetna received notice of the lawsuit. Considering the totality of circumstances, we hold, as a matter of law, that Mitsui waived any claim against Aetna based on its duty to defend up to February 11, 1987 when Aetna received notice.

* * * *

Decision and Remedy *The court answered the trial court's certified questions by holding that Aetna had no duty to contribute to defense costs incurred prior to its receipt of notice regarding the underlying action.*

Wrongful Issuance of Life Insurance

In addition to wrongfully denying insurance renewal, some insurers have been held liable for wrongfully issuing life insurance policies. This problem arises when a person takes out an insurance policy on the life of a second person and then murders that person in order to recover the insurance proceeds. In this circumstance, an insurance company may be liable to the victim's heirs for encouraging the murder.

In order to recover on a wrongful issuance of life insurance claim, the heirs of the murder victim must first show that the company was somehow negligent in issuing the policy. This might be due to the company's failure to investigate the relationship between the parties. The heirs must also show that the murder was foreseeable to the company.

In one case, a company was liable because it had some notice of the beneficiary's murderous intentions, an investigation would have uncovered that the insured was worth much more to the beneficiary dead than alive, the murdered insured's lack of consent to the issuance of the policy, and the financial inability of the beneficiary to make premium payments for any extended period of time.[12]

In an older case, a son took out a $200 life insurance policy on his mother and then killed her for the insurance proceeds. The court held that the company was not liable because it was unforeseeable that he would murder his mother for such a small insurance payment.[13]

The cases of wrongful issuance of life insurance are not frequent, but damages can be great when they arise. More significantly, this doctrine illustrates an important broad principle of insurance law—that insurers have a significant responsibility to investigate facts surrounding a policy and to deal with affected parties in good faith.

---

[12] *Life Insurance Co. v. Lopez,* 443 So.2d 947 (Fla. 1983).

[13] *Holloman v. Life Insurance Co.,* 7 S.E.2d 169 (S.C. 1939).

■ Ethical Perspectives

Insurance and the AIDS Crisis

Acquired immune deficiency syndrome (AIDS) is an enormous public health problem. The disease currently causes thousands of deaths per year and costs billions of dollars annually. The insurance industry faces a difficult problem in dealing with the AIDS crisis.

To the best of current knowledge, AIDS begins through infection with a human immune deficiency virus (HIV). For many people infected with HIV, the disease slowly destroys their immune system of resistance to other diseases. The person is then highly susceptible to other fatal diseases. Some HIV-infected individuals, however, may never suffer from advanced stages of AIDS.

The insurance industry has been reluctant to provide insurance for individuals with AIDS or even those with a potential exposure to HIV. These individuals are considered to be relatively likely to make large claims for medical costs.

Insurance companies have been criticized for denying coverage to a group of those who need it most (AIDS patients). The entire point of insurance is to share risks by taking relatively small premium payments from large groups of people and redistributing much of that money to a smaller group of people who are unfortunate enough to suffer an insured occurrence, such as a serious disease requiring extensive medical care. Naturally, though, insurance companies want to take in as much money as possible and pay out as little as possible.

Insurers respond to this criticism by noting that they operate in the free market and must be able to make a profit. Insurance companies typically discriminate against high-risk groups, by charging them more for insurance. The potential costs of AIDS crisis. The typical AIDS patient requires up to $150,000 a year in medical treatment and total annual medical costs of the disease are approximately $8 billion.

Insurance companies certainly do not have enough profits to enable them single-handedly to pay the costs of the AIDS crisis. Their only alternative, in order to provide AIDS coverage, is to increase insurance premiums substantially. Yet many Americans would object to paying much higher premiums, and some Americans would be unable to pay the premiums.

The insurance companies clearly have a legitimate concern. In general, companies do not have an ethical duty to do business with a particular person. Without insurance, however, AIDS victims are more likely to die sooner for lack of care. AIDS victims need care and at least some insurance practices may be unethical or discriminatory.

Suppose that an insurer denies coverage to individuals who have tested positive for HIV. This policy is likely to discourage voluntary testing for AIDS, thereby frustrating society's ability to respond to the problem. Some companies require a test for HIV before they will issue a policy. This procedure risks public exposure of AIDS sufferers, who may consequently suffer discrimination in housing, employment or even health care.

Still further problems are presented when insurance companies use general categories to avoid insuring potential AIDS victims. For example, a company might refuse to insure individuals who live in certain high-risk inner-city areas, many of whom are members of minorities.

In general, insurance companies base their decisions on actuarial information on populations that are likely to suffer covered occurrences. This process is often reasonable, fair and efficient. But there is nothing sacred about this process, which must remain subject to ethical concerns for fairness.

International Perspectives

Insurance and Europe

Insurance, like most areas of business, is increasingly becoming global. Insurance also is one of America's advanced service sectors that offer particular promise in international competition. The combined nations of Europe may be the world's largest market for insurance products. Consequently, this area is of great interest to insurance companies.

Historically, some European nations have made it difficult for U.S. insurance firms to enter their market. Other countries, including France, had such an elaborate system for foreign insurance companies that direct entry became inefficient. The unification of the European Community promises to break down some of these barriers to American insurance companies.

The Commission of the European Communities has already begun to lay the groundwork for a joint insurance market through a number of directives to member states. The first critical European directive is known as Directive 73/239, which provides for "the coordination of laws, regulations and administrative provisions relating to the taking-up and pursuit of the business of direct insurance other than life insurance."

Directive 73/239 establishes procedures for the formal "authorization" of insurance companies in Europe. Authorization involves a demonstration of solvency, an agreement to keep certain records in the country, a certification of its plan of business, and the designation of an authorized agent within the country. Authorization still must be sought from the appropriate authority of the individual European member state.

Directive 73-239 also contains protections to prevent individual nations from arbitrarily denying or delaying foreign applications for authorization. Denials must contain a statement of precise reasons for that action, and any delay of over six months enables the company to appeal to a court.

Other directives also have been adopted to facilitate the licensing of insurance agents and brokers, giving some credit to the licensing of other nations. Other directives provide coordination for co-insurance operations.

To date, the opening up of European insurance markets has shown substantial progress and continues to advance. Less progress has been made in the life insurance market, however, which remains a problem because a majority of U.S. insurance companies focus in this area. Individual country regulation remains predominant in life insurance. Establishing other insurance operations may provide a toehold for future continent-wide progress in life insurance.

Questions and Case Problems

1. Jim was a homosexual male who had several relationships over the course of a year. he applied for medical insurance, and the form asked if he was a practicing homosexual. Jim was offended by this question and answered it "no." He received the insurance coverage. Subsequently, Jim contracted AIDS and there after required extensive medical treatment. The insurance company refused to pay for the treatment, and Jim sued the company for wrongful denial of benefits. The company's defense was Jim's application misrepresentation of his sexual preference. Should the company succeed in its misrepresentation defense to insurance coverage?

2. Ms. Poling was a retired state worker who had group health insurance administered by the Wisconsin Physicians Service. The policy provided reimbursement for skilled care but not for custodial care. She was hospitalized with Parkinson's disease and Alzheimer's disease. The insurance company initially denied coverage on the grounds that her care was custodial. her physician informed the company that her care was clearly skilled in nature and included occupational therapy. The company continued to refuse to pay, now contending that there was no expectation that the occupational therapy could rehabilitate her. Does Ms. Poling have a good claim against the insurance company? [*Poling v. Wisconsin Physicians Service*, 357 N.W.2d 293 (Wis. Ct. App. 1984)].

3. Wellstone, Inc., was a small corporation owned almost entirely by the Mondale family, but Wellstone had a few outside shareholders. Members of the Mondale family served on the board of directors. Wellstone had an insurance policy covering its directors and officers. One of the outside shareholders brought an action of breach of fiduciary duty against the directors of Wellstone, and the insurance company refused to provide coverage of the lawsuit. The claim sought millions in damages and could bankrupt the company. The directors eventually settled the case for $50,000, and the company than sued their insurance company to recover this sum, plus emotional distress damages. Assuming that the insurance company's coverage denial was wrongful, should the company's stockholders be allowed to recover damages for emotional distress?

4. A man drowned in a municipal swimming pool, and his survivors sued the city for damages. The city was insured, and the city's insurance company defended the action. A jury eventually awarded $350,000 in damages to the survivors. The insurance company first sought a new trial and then appealed this decision to a higher court. The company offered a settlement of less than half the jury verdict. Although the survivors were financially needy, they refused this offer. Some time later, the insurance company and the claimants settled for $300,000. The survivors then brought an additional suit against the insurance company for bringing the appeal and refusing to settle earlier in hopes that financial pressure would force the survivors into a bad settlement. Should the insurance company be liable for delaying the settlement unnecessarily? [*Coleman v. Gulf Insurance Group*, 226 Cal. Rptr. 90 (Cal. 1986)].

5. Mr. Brown was 74 years old. He received a speeding ticket, and his insurance company then notified him that they would not renew his policy. He appealed to them, and they agreed to renew his policy in light of his 49-year tenure with the company. Mr. Brown was then involved in a traffic accident at an intersection, but no citation was issued. Although there was a state law prohibiting nonrenewal of a policy for a single accident for a policyholder of five years or more, the company refused to renew Brown's policy. Brown sued the company for wrongful nonrenewal of his policy. Should he succeed with this claim?

6. An insurance application inquired whether applicants drank to "excess", and the insured answered in the negative. In fact, the insured drank a great deal but had never been formally diagnosed as having a drinking problem. After he was diagnosed with cirrhosis and subsequently died, the insurance company sought to avoid payment on grounds of misrepresentation on the application and sought summary judgment. How should the court rule? [*Coolspring Stone Supply, Inc. v. American States Life Insurance Co.*, 10 F.3d 144 (3d Cir. 1993)].

Chapter Ten

Real Estate Finance and Liability

Key Background

The essential background for this chapter on real estate finance and liability is found in Chapters 50 and 51 of *West's Business Law, Seventh Edition,* and Chapter 25 of *West's Legal Environment of Business, Third Edition.* These chapters cover real property and landlord-tenant relationships. Among the important points to remember from these chapters are:

- the nature of ownership interests in real property
- deeds and other methods of transfer of ownership in real property
- land use controls applicable to real property
- legal rules governing the lease of property

* * *

The ownership of land, generally referred to as **real property** or **real estate**, historically has held great importance, both financially and psychologically. Many of today's largest financial transactions involve real estate. Urban property, such as an office building, periodically sells for many millions of dollars. Individual homes do not sell for so high a price, but the cumulative value of residential sales is enormous.

Real estate business is as closely associated with the law as any business. Detailed legal rules govern most real estate transactions, even relatively small ones. In addition to the common law, states have adopted a significant number of statutes that regulate the real estate business.

This chapter selects three broad categories of the law as it relates to real estate. The first section covers the law and the financing of real estate purchases, a matter of great importance to banks as well as to other businesses. The second section addresses the leasing of real estate for commercial purposes. The final section discusses the growing importance of fraud claims in real estate transactions.

Real Estate Finance

Most real estate developments, ranging from a small single-family home to a multimillion-dollar high-rise office building, require borrowed financing in the form of a **mortgage**. A bank loans the funds necessary to construct a building or to purchase an existing building. The bank retains a security right in the property as **collateral** for this loan. If the borrower fails to make payments, the bank can take steps to assume ownership of the property.

Mortgage loan funds currently come from a variety of sources. Commercial banks and Savings and Loan Associations are traditional sources. Tax laws have encouraged the development of Real Estate Investment Trusts, in which investors pool their money to make real estate loans.

The real estate finance market has become increasingly complex. Once, a home buyer would take out a loan with a local banker and the mortgage would be held by the bank for its 30-year duration. Monthly payments would be made to the local bank.

Today, there is a thriving secondary market in mortgages. The original lending bank will sell the mortgage (the right to receive monthly payments) to another institution. This permits banks to exchange the uncertain rights to future payments for immediate funds.

A wide variety of legal issues arise in mortgage lending, including securities laws, environmental laws, and other seemingly unrelated regulations. This section discusses three important legal issues—government regulation of mortgaging, legal restrictions on mortgage provisions, and rules for foreclosure in the event of mortgage default.

Some government regulations constrain the mortgage process. The Real Estate Settlement Procedures Act of 1974 mandates that a lender make certain disclosures to home buyers, such as the amount of closing costs. Loans are also regulated by the Truth-in-Lending Act, which is discussed in Chapter 46 of *West's Business Law, Seventh Edition*.

Mortgage Terms

Most mortgage terms are set by the lender and are not subject to negotiation. Often borrowers may not understand the full significance of such mortgage terms. Many borrowers have sued under state law, claiming that certain terms of the mortgage are unfair and should be held to be invalid. These challenges have often involved provisions that require the entire mortgage to be paid off ahead of the term, prohibitions on paying off the mortgage early, and penalties for late payment.

A significant legal controversy arose over mortgage clauses that permit the lender to accelerate the debtor's full payment of the principal before the loan term is complete. An important type of loan acceleration provision is the **due-on-sale** clause found in many home mortgages. These clauses accelerate the time for payment of the full mortgage principal when the property is sold.

Suppose that Frank takes out a 30-year home mortgage. After seven years, Frank sells the house to Sharon. Sharon may wish to assume the mortgage payments of Frank. If the mortgage contained a due-on-sale clause, however, she could not do so. The bank would insist that Frank pay off the original mortgage upon the sale of the house, and Sharon would have to obtain a new mortgage.

For a time, some state courts held that such due-on-sale clauses were invalid. In the 1980s, however, federal statutes and judicial decisions clearly established the validity of due-on-sale clauses in home mortgages.

Today, some borrowers still challenge due-on-sale conditions. The main argument is that the due-on-sale clause was not clear in the original mortgage. If the mortgage was ambiguous, it will be construed against the lender and the court may find the clause inapplicable.

In addition, some acceleration clauses may still be challenged as unconscionable in special circumstances. If the clause permits arbitrary acceleration without reason and this right is abused, a court may refuse to enforce an acceleration clause.

Another dispute arose over mortgage clauses with **prepayment prohibitions**. This is the converse of the acceleration clause. A homeowner may find herself with a surplus of cash and may desire to pay off the mortgage ahead of its full term. A lender, though, may refuse to permit such prepayment. Alternatively, the mortgage may impose financial penalties for prepayment.

A lender may have sound financial reasons for opposing prepayment. Banks profit from interest received on loans that they make and their future lending and other practices are based on their expected future income. Prepayment can cost a bank or other lender those expected future profits.

Prepayment restraints may create serious difficulties for a borrower, however. Suppose now that Frank wants to sell his house to Sharon, but she refuses to assume his mortgage terms (perhaps interest rates have dropped significantly). If Frank cannot prepay his original mortgage, he may be unable to sell the house. Frank might sue the lender by claiming that the prepayment prohibition unfairly prevents him from selling the property.

Conflicts over prepayment are relatively common in loans. The resolution of a conflict can be more difficult if the contract fails to mention prepayments and the parties' dispute escalates, as in the following case.

Case 10.1
Poommipanit v. Sloan
Court of Appeals of Nebraska, 1993
510 N.W.2d 542

Background and Facts In 1979, Pairote and Somchit Poommipanit entered into a real estate contract with Dewey and Diane Sloan to purchase an apartment complex. The Poommipanits agreed to pay $480,000, structured with a $50,000 down payment and the balance to be paid in installments over twenty years. The contract was silent as to prepayment. In 1988, the Poommipanits offered to prepay the balance of the contract and demanded conveyance of title to the property. After Sloan refused, the Poommipanits ceased making installment payments. Sloan then declared the purchasers in default and sought repossession of the property. After a trial, the court found that the Poommipanits had a right to prepay the contract and directed Sloan to convey the premises. Sloan appealed and continued to seek ejectment of the Poommipanits from the property.

CONNOLLY, Judge.

* * * *

The principal issue in this case is whether a purchaser-vendee of an installment real estate contract is entitled to compel the seller-vendor to accept prepayment of the contract balance where the contract is silent on the matter of prepayment. * * * We adopt the majority rule and hold that where an installment real estate contract does not contain a provision permitting prepayment, the vendee-purchaser cannot force the vendor-seller to accept prepayment on the contract.

* * * *

... ejectment of a vendee may be granted as a remedy for violating the terms of a land contract only where the equities of the particular case justify such a disposition, where the property is of less value than the contract price, and where such a procedure would not offend against justice and equity ... At the time the dispute arose in the case at bar, Poommipanits had already paid Sloan over $200,000, which is nearly half of the total purchase price. An order of forfeiture and ejectment would allow Sloan to keep the money already paid by Poommipanits and leave Poommipanits with no interest in the real estate. While it is true that Poommipanits may have violated the terms of the contract by defaulting on monthly installment payments... we find that the equities of the case do not warrant a forfeiture by Poommipanits of their interest in the real estate at issue.

Decision and Remedy The court reversed the judgment ordering Sloan to accept prepayment on the contract but affirmed the judgment dismissing Sloan's claim for forfeiture and ejectment.

Suppose that a loan contains both an acceleration clause and a prepayment prohibition. The acceleration clause would permit the lender to take advantage of higher interest rates by calling in the loan and requiring refinancing. The prepayment prohibition prevents the borrower from comparably taking advantage of lower interest rates. One court found this combination to be invalid.[1]

State statutes also restrict prepayment prohibitions. New Mexico has a law prohibiting such clauses. More common are state laws that require full disclosure of such clauses to borrowers.

Late Payment Fees

Most mortgages have specific fees charged for late mortgage payments. These fees are often quite significant and more substantial than may seem justified by the lateness of the payment. For example, a

---

[1] *Wisconsin Ave. Associates, Inc. v. 2720 Wisconsin Ave. Cooperative Assoc.*, 441 A.2d 956 (D.C. App. 1982).

borrower who makes a payment three weeks late may be required to pay a late fee that is the equivalent of three months of interest.

Borrowers have challenged these late payment fees in mortgages. Some courts have found these fees to be invalid. Many decisions have characterized the late fees as an attempt at imposing **liquidated damages** for breach of contract. These damages are discussed in Chapter 20 of *West's Business Law, Seventh Edition*. Because the fees seem excessive and because actual interest is readily calculable, some courts have found the late payment fees to represent a **penalty clause** in the contract, which courts will not enforce.

Other courts have struck down late payment charges as a violation of the state usury laws (which set maximum interest rates allowable). The effective interest rate charged on the late payment may exceed the maximum permitted under state usury laws.

Default and Foreclosure

Recent years have seen an increase in defaults on mortgage payments and resulting **foreclosures** by lenders. This is a procedure in which the lender takes ownership of the property, after the borrower proves unable to keep up the required payments on the loan.

The first important legal issue is whether there has been a default. A single late payment does not qualify as default. After a borrower has repeatedly missed payment deadlines, however, or has failed to pay altogether, the lender will use an acceleration clause to make the full debt come due. Most mortgages permit acceleration if the borrower fails to keep up payments.

If the lender chooses to accelerate the debt payment, it is generally required to notify the borrower of this decision. The borrower may waive this right to notification, however.

Assuming that the borrower cannot pay off the loan, the lender can then institute foreclosure on the property. Many states provide the borrower with a **redemption right**. If the borrower can obtain the money to pay off the mortgage within a certain period of time (usually six months), the foreclosure is canceled.

When foreclosure goes forward, it is governed by the terms of the mortgage deed of trust and by state law. The mortgage deed may provide for power-of-sale foreclosure, which enables the lender to act unilaterally. If the mortgage does not authorize direct sale, the lender must go to court for judicial foreclosure.

In foreclosure, the borrower puts the property up for sale and uses the proceeds to pay off the loan. both power-of-sale and judicial foreclosure are governed by state statutes. In Texas, for example, the debtor must be notified three weeks before the foreclosure sale and the sale must be by an auction at the local county courthouse during a certain time period.

The foreclosure auction must be conducted impartially, in an attempt to get the highest price for the property. Suppose that Reiner Kutor defaults on a $200,000 loan for a residence. If the property sells for $250,000, more than the loan balance, the $50,000 surplus is paid to the borrower, Kutor. If the property sells for only $150,000 or less than the loan balance, the lender can attempt to get a $50,000 **deficiency judgment** against Kutor to make up the difference.

The foreclosure system and deficiency judgments have a significant problem. Often, the only bidder at a foreclosure auction is the lender. In these circumstances, the lender can obtain the property at auction for a low price (even below fair market value) and obtain a large deficiency judgment against the borrower. The following case reflects this problem.

■ Case 10.2
Savers Federal Savings & Loan Association v. Reetz
United States Court of Appeals, Fifth Circuit, 1989
888 F.2d 1497

Background and Facts *Horst and Kathleen Reetz obtained a $6.3 million note from Savers Federal Savings & Loan Association. The note was secured by two deeds of trust for two parcels of real estate. The note was payable in monthly installments, but the Reetzes soon fell into default on the note, and Savers accelerated the note. The Reetzes were unable to pay and the property was put up for sale at a judicial foreclosure auction.*

At the foreclosure sale, Savers purchased the parcels of property for $4 million. Savers then sought a deficiency judgment against the Reetzes for the balance of the note. The Reetzes filed a response in which they claimed that the fair market value of the property was $8 million and that they should owe no deficiency judgment. The court found no irregularity in the auction procedures and entered a deficiency judgment for Savers for more than $3 million. The Reetzes appealed.

GARWOOD, Circuit Judge.

* * * *

We conclude under controlling and long-established Texas law that where there has previously been a valid nonjudicial deed of trust foreclosure on real property securing a debt, the amount to be credited on the debt for deficiency judgment purposes is the amount received at the foreclosure sale; that inadequacy of the consideration received on the foreclosure sale cannot alone invalidate an otherwise valid deed of trust nonjudicial foreclosure on real estate; that in order for inadequacy of consideration to have that effect, there must also be some irregularity in the foreclosure which caused or contributed to cause the real property to be sold for a grossly inadequate price; and that all these rules are fully applicable where the creditor is the purchaser at the foreclosure.

* * * *

Thus Texas nonjudicial foreclosure sales of real estate under deed of trust powers have for approximately a century been conducted pursuant to special, structured and formal statutory scheme calling for public sales between 10:00 a.m. and 4:00 p.m. of the first Tuesday in each month preceded by three weeks' public notice. This statutory scheme, by its own terms, applies only to real property sales. The amendments to the statute in 1975, 1983-84, and 1987 preserved the basic scheme, but added specific provisions designed to enhance the fairness of the sale, the likelihood there would be public bidders, and the protection of debtors in respect to deficiency actions. These amendments were made well *after* the Texas Supreme Court's decisions in *Tarrant Savings Ass'n* and *Maupin* (and, except for the 1975 amendments, after *Musick*) which held that gross inadequacy of price (absent and irregularity in the sale contributing thereto) was not a basis on which to set aside a real estate deed of trust foreclosure, even thought the creditor was the purchaser, and that if the sale were valid, the foreclosure sales price, rather than the then market price, constituted the proper amount to credit on the debt for deficiency judgment purposes, again even though the creditor was the purchaser at foreclosure. Accordingly, the Texas legislature may be deemed to have found that the rules applied in those cases were appropriate components of a proper scheme for regulating real estate nonjudicial foreclosures, and consequent deficiency claims, which did not need to be changed except in the specific respects addressed by the amendments. *Cf. Coastal Industrial Water Authority v. Trinity Portland Cement,* 563 S.W.2d 916, 918 (Tex. 1978); *Kennedy v. Hyde,* 682 S.W.2d 525, 529 (Tex. 1984). Subsequent judicial abrogation of the settled rules which furnished the legal context on the basis of which the legislature may be presumed to have acted in amending the statute would constitute an unwarranted upsetting of the overall balance which the legislature struck.

Decision and Remedy *The court affirmed the district court judgment to Savers.*

A majority of states restrict deficiency judgments in some manner. Most jurisdictions impose strict notice requirements and time limits for deficiency judgments. Other laws are even more restrictive. California prohibits deficiency judgments in power-of-sale foreclosures. Other states also prohibit deficiency judgments when the mortgage was for the purchase of residential real estate.

The above discussion assumes that the bank is the only lender on the property. Foreclosure is more complex when the real property is encumbered with more than one lender. For example, suppose that Kutor had construction workers do extensive building on the property. If he failed to pay the workers, they have a mechanic's lien on the property. They, too, will seek proceeds from the foreclosure sale.

Commercial Leasing

Most retail stores and offices do not own the building in which they are located. Instead, they lease the property from a building owner, often a real estate developer, and pay rent on the space. The commercial leasing process is of great economic significance and productive of many legal disputes. The market for commercial leases has been volatile, and parties have often tried to escape the terms of certain leases.

Several legal issues are of recurring importance in commercial leasing. This section discusses the presence of an **implied warranty of suitability** of the commercial lease, the material breaches of a lease that permit a party to avoid the lease, the rules for determining abandonment of lease rights, and the tort of wrongful interference with a commercial lease.

Warranty of Suitability

A tenant in a commercial lease may be disappointed in the quality of the facilities provided. If so, the tenant may attempt to avoid the lease or escape rental payments by contending that the space provided breached the lessor's implied warranty of fitness or suitability.

Traditional common law provided the tenant with no implied warranty of the property's quality, except those expressly stated in the lease contract. Increasingly, courts have adopted an implied warranty of habitability for residential leases (the premises must be in a livable condition). Some courts have extended this implied warranty to commercial leases.

Suppose that a group of doctors leases space in a commercial development for their practice. After moving in, the air conditioning breaks down, the water supply is irregular, the electricity cuts off frequently, and little maintenance or janitorial service is provided. The doctors would try to escape their lease under an implied warranty of suitability.

Some states have refused to imply a warranty of suitability in commercial leases. They rely on a position that commercial tenants have sufficient bargaining power to provide *express* contractual protections for themselves. Recent decisions in Massachusetts, Missouri, Ohio, Iowa and other states have found no implied warranty in commercial leasing.

Other states, however, have found an implied warranty of suitability. Precedents in California, New York, New Jersey and Louisiana recognize at least some such implied warranty of suitability. In one case, a parking and automobile storage garage leased space in a building. The roof of the building was in disrepair, chunks of concrete fell onto the floor, large quantities of rainwater leaked in and damaged cars, and the garage suffered frequent electrical failures. A court found that this was a breach of the lessor's implied warranty.[2] In contrast, courts have found that a leaky bathroom roof in an office does not breach an implied warranty of suitability.

The following recent decision represents an important extension of the implied warranty of suitability in a state that had not previously recognized the warranty.

---

[2] *Reed v. Classified Parking System*, 232 So.2d 103 (La. App. 1970).

Case 10.3
Davidow v. Inwood North Professional Group—Phase I
Supreme Court of Texas, 1988
747 F.2d 373

Background and Facts *Inwood North Professional Group—Phase I leased commercial space to Joseph F. Davidow, M.D., for use as a medical office. Davidow entered into a five-year lease agreement that required him to pay approximately $880 per month. The lease obligated Inwood to provide air conditioning, electricity, hot water, janitor and maintenance services, light fixtures, and security services.*

After moving in, Dr. Davidow began experiencing problems. The air conditioning did not work properly, causing temperatures to rise above 85 degrees. The roof leaked after a rain, which resulted in stained tiles and mildewed carpets. Pests and rodents often infested the office. Hallway lights were not replaced, so hallways were dark. Cleaning and maintenance and hot water were not provided. The parking lot was constantly filled with trash. Several burglaries and acts of vandalism occurred.

Fourteen months before the lease expired, Dr. Davidow moved out and refused to make further payments. Inwood sued for unpaid rent, and Davidow counterclaimed. After a trial, a jury ruled for Davidow and awarded him $9300 in damages. The court of appeals reversed the trial court judgment, holding that there was no implied warranty of suitability and that Inwood's breaches did not justify Davidow's total breach of the lease contract. That court awarded Inwood damages for unpaid rent and attorney's fees. Davidow appealed.

SPEARS, Justice.

* * * *

In the past, this court has attempted to provide a more equitable and contemporary solution to landlord-tenant problems by easing the burden placed on tenants as a result of the independence of lease convenants and the doctrine of *caveat emptor.* See, e.g., *Kamarath v. Bennett,* 568 S.W.2d 658 (Tex. 1978); *Humber v. Morton,* 426 S.W.2d 554 (Tex. 1968). In *Kamarath v. Bennett,* we reexamined the realities of the landlord-tenant relationship in a modern context and concluded that the agrarian common-law concept is no longer indicative of the contemporary relationship between the tenant and landlord. The land is of minimal important to the modern tenant; rather, the primary subject of most leases is the structure located on the land and the services which are to be provided to the tenant. The modern residential tenant seeks to lease a dwelling suitable for living purposes. The landlord usually has knowledge of any defects in the premises that may render it uninhabitable. In addition, the landlord, as permanent owner of the premises, should rightfully bear the cost of any necessary repairs. In most instances the landlord is in a much better bargaining position than the tenant. Accordingly, we held in *Kamarath* that the landlord impliedly warrants that the premises are habitable and fit for living. We further implicitly recognized that the residential tenant's obligation to pay rent is dependent upon the landlord's performance under his warranty of habitability. *Kamarath,* 568 S.W.2d at 660-61.

When a commercial tenant such as Dr. Davidow leases office space, many of the same considerations are involved. A significant number of commentators have recognized the similarities between residential and commercial tenants and concluded that residential warranties should be expanded to cover commercial property.

* * * *

It cannot be assumed that a commercial tenant is more knowledgeable about the quality of the structure than a residential tenant. A businessman cannot be expected to possess the expertise necessary to adequately inspect and repair the premises, and many commercial tenants lack the financial resources to hire inspectors and repairmen to assure the suitability of the premises. * * * Additionally, because commercial tenants often enter into short-term leases, the tenants have limited economic incentive to make any extensive repairs to their premises. Consequently, commercial tenants generally rely on their landlords' greater abilities to inspect and repair the premises. *Id.*

* * * *

There is no valid reason to imply a warranty of habitability in residential leases and not in commercial leases. Although minor distinctions can be drawn between residential and commercial tenants, those differences do not justify limiting the warranty to residential leaseholds. Therefore, we hold there is an implied warranty of suitability by the landlord in a commercial lease that the premises are suitable for their intended commercial purpose. This warranty means that at the inception of the lease there are no latent defects in the facilities that are vital to the use of the premises for their intended commercial purpose and that these essential facilities will remain in a suitable condition. If, however, the parties to a lease expressly agree that the tenant will repair certain defects, then the provisions of the lease will control.

Decision and Remedy   *The court reversed the portion of the appellate court judgment that had denied damages to Davidow.*

Material Breaches of Contract

Commercial tenants should have legal protection even in those states that fail to recognize an implied warranty of suitability. Most commercial lease contracts contain **covenants** in which both parties to the contract make certain promises. For example, the tenant promises to pay rent and the landlord promises to provide quality facilities.

A breach of a lease covenant gives rise to remedies against the breaching party. A breach does not necessarily permit the other party to terminate the lease, however. Rather, only a "material" or "substantial" breach permits rescission of the lease. The tenant or landlord can then avoid its obligations under the lease.

The law of material breaches has been of economic significance. Suppose that a developer leases space in an office building to an accounting firm for 25 years at $30 per square foot. After a few years, rents escalate dramatically. The developer could now get over $75 per square foot for the space. The accounting firm is two weeks late in its rent payment. Does this permit the developer to cancel the lease and find a better-paying tenant?

Section 241 of the Restatement (Second) of Contracts provides a series of standards for determining whether such a breach of lease terms is sufficiently material to terminate the lease. These standards are:

a. The extent to which the injured party was deprived of the benefit reasonably expected.

b. The extent to which the injured party can be adequately compensated for the damages.

c. The extent to which the party failing to perform will suffer from forfeiture.

d. The likelihood that the party failing to perform will cure the failure.

e. The extent to which the behavior of the party failing to perform comports with standards of good faith and fair dealing.

These standards were applied in a recent case. A tenant was using office space to operate a mailorder business but inadvertently failed to obtain a certificate required by the government. The lease had a provision permitting termination if the tenant used the property for any "unlawful purpose." The lessor therefore sought to rescind the lease arrangement.

A court held that the lease could not be rescinded. The court noted that the landlord had failed to act for two years after discovering the problem, that the tenant had not acted willfully or in bad faith, that the tenant eventually cured the breach, and that the landlord was acting in bad faith, trying to get rid of the tenant for economic reasons.[3]

Some tenants have claimed landlords committed a material breach by "double-leasing." For example, if a lessor leases a small parking lot for the use of one office and then leases the same lot for another office, the first office may seek rescission. This has been found to be material so long as the lot was insufficient for the parking needs of both offices.

Lessees may also avoid a contract due to the landlord's failure to provide services. Lack of heat, air conditioning or electrical power may represent a material breach, unless the problem was infrequent.

Another problem arises over noncompetition covenants. Suppose that a shopping center developer leases space to a drug store. Ivy Drug accepts the lease only after the developer promises not to lease any other space to competing drug stores. Then the developer has trouble leasing space and breaks the covenant, leasing other space to Laurel Drugs. Is this breach sufficiently material that Ivy Drug can break the original lease? A court would probably say yes.

Many cases involve breaches by tenants and attempts by lessors to break a lease. Nonpayment or late payment of rent is a common problem. A court found a material breach when a tenant failed to pay rent three months during one year. Chronic late payment has also been found to be a material breach. If a landlord consistently accepts late payments without protest, however, it may waive the right to terminate the lease.

Late payment of a single month's rent, especially if it is only days late, will generally not be held a material breach. In one case, a court found that even a two-month delay in rent payment was not material in the context of a 15-year lease. The court reasoned that a small interest payment could fully compensate the landlord.[4]

In some cases, such as a shopping center, the landlord takes its rent payments in a percentage of the tenant's profits rather than in a flat fee. In these instances, a landlord may terminate a lease if the tenant fails to take actions necessary to make profits. If a tenant movie theater consistently shows low-profit, unpopular films, for example, the lessor might terminate the lease.

Other material breaches by tenants have been found when the tenant fails to pay taxes or utility bills as required in the lease, when the tenant fails to make repairs or keeps the premises in poor condition, when the tenant makes unauthorized physical modifications to the property, and when a tenant violates a covenant prohibiting subleasing the property.

Abandonment

The issue of whether a tenant has "abandoned" the leased property has legal significance. If so, the landlord can enter the property and terminate the lease, if it desires. Abandonment by a tenant may be necessary to protect its interests in a **wrongful construction eviction claim**. This occurs when a tenant complains that the landlord made the space uninhabitable and sues the landlord for damages.

A finding of abandonment requires acts by the tenant suggesting abandonment plus other evidence of an intention to abandon the property. The key issue is the intent of the tenant.

Mere breach of the lease is insufficient to constitute abandonment. Suppose that AJ Spirits leases property for a liquor store. AJ cannot get a liquor license and stops making payments on the lease. AJ informs the landlord that it is seeking someone with a license to operate the store. The developer cannot claim that AJ abandoned the lease. The developer's only remedy would be to argue that nonpayment was a material breach justifying rescission.

Nonpayment may be evidence of abandonment, however. If a tenant stopped paying, had no employees or property present on the leased premises, and failed to communicate with the landlord, abandonment may be found. Courts will also consider whether the tenant kept a key to the property, although other facts are also relevant.

When a tenant removes its furniture and other property from the leased space, abandonment is strongly suggested. This would not be abandonment, though, if the tenant were merely freeing up the space for an authorized subtenant.

---

[3] *Entrepreneur, Ltd. v. Yasuna*, 498 A.2d 1151 (D.C. App. 1985).

[4] *57 E. 54 Realty Corp. v. Gay Nineties Realty Corp.*, 335 N.Y.S.2d 872 (1972).

If abandonment does occur, the landlord may consider the lease terminated or may permit the premises to remain vacated and then seek to recover rent from the tenant. A tenant that abandons leased space can then sue for constructive eviction.

In one case, a shopping center entered a ten-year lease with a retail store. At the time of the lease's commencement the store owners did not move in for years and the center leased the space to another store. Mall construction had been delayed, however, and the mall was not fully completed. A court found no abandonment by the original tenant, because the delay in occupying the space was due to the construction delays.[5] The shopping center developer remained liable on the original lease.

Wrongful Interference with Lease

Suppose that Kalbin & Orman, lawyers, have a long-term office space lease in the First Plaza building. Other lawyers may greatly desire this space and try to interfere with Kalbin & Orman's lease commitment. Or the Congress Square office building may be desperate for tenants and try to induce Kalbin & Orman to break the lease and move to their space. These actions may constitute wrongful interference with a lease contract.

Wrongful interference with contracts in general is discussed in Chapter 7 of *West's Business Law, Seventh Edition,* and in Chapter 13 of *West's Legal Environment of Business, Third Edition.* In a case for wrongful interference with a commercial lease, a plaintiff must meet five requirements:

1. The existence of a binding lease.

2. The alleged wrongdoer's knowledge of the lease.

3. Its intentional causation of breaking the lease.

4. Without sufficient justification.

5. Resultant damages.

Possible liability also exists for interference with an expected lease that is not yet finalized.

In one case, a tenant had a ten-year oral commercial lease with a lessor. A competing building caused the tenants to breach their contract by making repeated visits to their leased property and offering inducements to move. The lease with the original lessor was unenforceable because it was not in writing. Nevertheless, the court enabled the original lessor to sue the new lessor for wrongful interference with contract.[6]

Competition among commercial lessors is legal. Suppose that the First Central office building advertises for new tenants from existing buildings. The building promises six months' free rent and to pay the last month's rent that the tenant owed its previous lessor. This is considered fair competition and not wrongful interference.

Other cases deal with interference with the tenant's rights in a lease. In one recent case, a small business operated a combination gas station and grocery store in leased property. The gasoline tanks and pumps were independently owned by an oil company. The oil company then locked the gas pumps (even though the store owed it no money) and suggested that the lessor evict the business. The court held that the oil company had wrongfully interfered with the lease contract.[7]

Several additional factors are relevant to the interference cases. First is the issue of fair competition. both lessors and lessees have a right to seek out the best deal available and advertise for business. Competition becomes tortious when a party singles out a specific lease and seeks to induce a party to break that lease.

Second, where the lease is a prospective one, the relative certainty of the leasing is crucial. If parties are merely negotiating a lease, third parties have a right to jump into the negotiations and offer a better deal.

Real Estate Fraud

As real estate transactions become increasingly important and costly, fraud claims have multiplied. There may be no more actual fraud in real estate transactions than there is in other types of business, but the high stakes make litigation more likely. Courts also have tended to adopt especially strict disclosure requirements for real estate sales, which makes fraud claims easier to prove.

The basic requirements for a fraud claim are the same in real estate as in other contracts and include:

---

[5] *Fera v. Village Plaza, Inc.*, 218 N.W.2d 155 (Mich. App. 1974).

[6] *Daugherty v. Kessler,* 286 A.2d 95 (Md. 1972).

[7] *Fossett v. Davis,* 531 So.2d 849 (Ala. 1988).

1. A misstatement of material fact.

2. The misstatement is made intentionally or with reckless disregard for the truth.

3. Reasonable reliance on the part of the other party.

4. Damages caused due to the reliance on the misrepresentation.

Fraud arises in many different situations in real estate sales. One frequent issue is whether the allegedly false statement was a fact (which may be fraud) or a mere prediction or opinion (which generally is not fraud).

Suppose that a seller of residential property describes it as "high and dry" on a promotional document. After sale of the property, the buyer discovers that the basement floods every time it rains in the area. The seller may argue that "high and dry" is too nonspecific to represent an assertion of fact. Some courts have held that this type of language is a statement of fact sufficient to constitute fraud, if incorrect.

In another disputed action, the seller's agent informed the purchasers of condominiums that the wooded land behind the building would remain undeveloped. In fact, she was aware that the community planned a playground for this site, which was eventually constructed. The seller argued that the playground was not built at the time of the statement and the statement was a prediction not a fact. The court disagreed and found fraud.[8]

Another common issue is whether a false statement is material enough to constitute fraud. Was the nature of the false statement really significant enough to affect the buyer's decision?

The materiality issue arises in cases where a seller has misrepresented the cost of heating or cooling the property to be sold. In one case, the seller of an apartment building informed the buyer that the electric and heat cost was $4000. The actual cost had been $5400 in the most recent year. The court held that this disparity was material—the difference could cause a temporary net loss that could ruin the buyer's investment plans.[9]

The following case presented an unusual issue of materiality and also presented the question of when silence (failure to disclose facts) could constitute fraud.

---

[8] *Boykin v. Hermitage Reality,* 360 S.E.2d 177 (Va. 1987).

[9] *Levy v. Bendetson,* 379 N.E.2d 1121 (Mass. App. 1978).

Case 10.4
Reed v. King
California Court of Appeals
Third District, 1983,
193 Cal. Rptr. 130

Background and Facts *Dorris Reed purchased a house from Robert King for $76,000. King and his real estate agents were aware that a woman and her four children had been murdered in the house ten years earlier. They did not inform Reed of this fact, however. They did inform Reed that the house was fit for an elderly lady living alone. After the transaction, Reed learned of the house's history from a neighbor. She claims that the house is only worth $65,000 and sued to rescind the sale and for damages. The trial court dismissed Reed's action, and Reed appealed.*

BLEASE, Judge.

* * * *

Accordingly, the critical question is: does the seller have a duty to disclose here? Resolution of this question depends on the materiality of the fact of the murders.

In general, a seller of real property has a duty to disclose: "where the seller knows of facts materially affecting the value or desirability of the property which are known or accessible only to him and also knows that such facts are not known to, or within the reach of the diligent attention and observation of the buyer, the seller is under a duty to disclose them to the buyer." [Italics added; citations omitted.] (*Lingsch v. Savage,* supra, 213 Cal.App.2d at p.735.) This broad statement of duty has led one commentator to conclude: "The ancient maxim caveat emptor ('let the buyer beware.') has little or no application to California real estate transactions."

* * * *

Whether information is of sufficient materiality to affect the value or desirability of the property... depends on the facts of the particular case." (Lingsch, supra, 213 Cal.App.2d at p. 737.) Materiality "is a question of law, and is part of the concept of right to rely or justifiable reliance." (3 Witkin, Cal. Procedure (2d ed. 1971) Pleading, @ 578, p. 2217.) Accordingly, the term is essentially a label affixed to a normative conclusion. Three considerations bear on this legal conclusion: the gravity of the harm inflicted by nondisclosure; the fairness of imposing a duty of discovery on the buyer as an alternative to compelling disclosure, and its impact on the stability of contracts if rescission is permitted.

* * * *

The murder of innocents is highly unusual in its potential for so disturbing buyers they may be unable to reside in a home where it has occurred. This fact may foreseeably deprive a buyer of the intended use of the purchase. Murder is not such a common occurrence that buyers should be charged with anticipating and discovering this disquieting possibility. Accordingly, the fact is not one for which a duty of inquiry and discovery can sensibly be imposed upon the buyer.

Reputation and history can have a significant effect on the value of realty. "George Washington slept here" is worth something, however physically inconsequential that consideration may be. Ill-repute or "bad will" conversely may depress the value of property. Failure to disclose such a negative fact where it will have a foreseeably depressing effect on income expected to be generated by a business is tortious.

* * * *

Whether Reed will be able to prove her allegation that the decade-old multiple murder has a significant effect on market value we cannot determine. If she is able to do so by competent evidence she is entitled to a favorable ruling on the issues of materiality and duty to disclose. Her demonstration of objective tangible harm would still the concern that permitting her to go forward will open the floodgates to rescission on subjective and idiosyncratic grounds.

Decision and Remedy   *The court reversed the lower court's dismissal of Reed's claim.*

An allegedly fraudulent statement about future profitability was found to be immaterial in a case where a person purchased land with car wash facilities. Evidence showed that the purchaser was only interested in tax advantages of ownership and evidence on an overclaim of taxable income was therefore not material to the purchaser.[10]

---

[10] *Jackson v. Fontenot Building, Inc.,* 314 So.2d 516 (La. App. 1975).

Silence as Fraud

Still another important issue is whether the seller had a duty to disclose certain facts. This arises where everything said by the seller was perfectly honest, but the seller failed to inform the buyer of some hidden problem in the property. This can be constructive fraud due to the seller's silence in the face of a duty to disclose.

Water problems are relatively common in real estate. Sellers have been found liable in constructive fraud for failing to disclose that the property was in a flood zone, for failing to disclose a known erosion problem, for failing to disclose periodic water leakage problems, for failing to disclose a defective roof over the property, and for failing to disclose foundation or septic tank problems.

To recover for fraud, however, a purchasing plaintiff must show a reasonable reliance on the seller's statement. Suppose that Claire Serice, a home-seller, failed to tell Mike Kirk, a potential buyer, that her basement had water problems. When Mike visits the home during an open house, he is taken to the basement where there is a pool of water in a corner, but he asks no questions about it. On these facts, Mike had no reasonable reliance on Claire's failure to disclose the problem, because it was obvious from reasonable inspection of the property.

Broker Liability

Purchasers of land increasingly are suing the real estate broker in the sale for fraud, as well as the seller. In many cases, the broker has "deeper pockets" than the seller and is better able to pay a damages judgment.

Over 80 percent of real estate sales involve the use of one or more brokers, who bring the buyer and seller together and help negotiate the contract. As a legal matter, the broker almost always represents the seller, even if the broker was working with the buyer throughout the negotiations. The broker is paid by the seller out of the purchase price. Some buyers are now paying brokers themselves, so that the broker represents their interests, rather than representing those of the seller.

As the seller's agent, the broker's central responsibilities are to the seller. As a result, courts traditionally held that the broker had no fiduciary duty to purchasers. Now, most courts hold that a broker has some fiduciary duties to the purchaser, however, and may certainly be sued for fraud.

States have passed a variety of laws governing broker duties to purchasers. Almost all states have passed disclosure laws, requiring all brokers to disclose whom they represent. Some states, such as Colorado, have created the position of "transaction broker," which is not an agent for either party but simply facilitates agreement. Other states have replaced common law with statutory duties. In Georgia, for example, brokers have some specific statutory duties to all parties in the transaction.

Fraud by the broker has been found in a variety of situations, including when the broker inaccurately described zoning restrictions on property, and when the broker misrepresented condominium units as "outstanding investments' and "luxurious" although the broker knew the units to be of substandard quality.[11]

To prove fraud against a broker, the purchaser must meet the same legal standards as for a case against the seller. In the case of brokers, it may be more difficult for a plaintiff to show that the broker was aware that a representation was false, however. Brokers generally get their information on property from the seller and may unwittingly make false representations.

Although an unintentional false statement cannot be fraud, a broker might still have some liability for negligent misrepresentation. If the broker should have known that the information was unreliable, the broker may be liable for negligent misrepresentation. According to one ruling, the real estate broker must "employ a reasonable degree of effort and professional expertise to confirm or refute information from the seller which he knows, or should know, is pivotal to the transaction from the buyer's perspective."[12]

A broker may also have liability in constructive fraud for failing to mention latent defects in the property. Some decisions have simply required brokers to disclose those defects that are "reasonably discoverable."

---

[11] *Cooper v. Jevne,* 128 Cal. Rptr. 130 (1976).

[12] *Tennant v. Lawton,* 615 P.2d 1305 (Wash. App. 1980).

Ethical Perspectives

AIDS Disclosure and Residential Real Estate

A current controversy in both law and ethics concerns the extent to which sellers or real estate brokers must disclose that residents of a property for sale were infected with the virus that causes acquired immune deficiency syndrome ("AIDS") and may have died from the complications of the disease. Some argue that brokers have an ethical duty to disclose this fact. Others argue that brokers have an ethical duty *not* to disclose this fact.

The problem arises due to the following facts. First, many people are extremely fearful of contracting AIDS and seek to avoid any contact with the virus. Second, the actual risks of contracting AIDS from a house owned by an AIDS victim are essentially nonexistent.

Those who argue for a duty to disclose emphasize the importance of honesty and the buyer's right to make his or her own decisions. Ordinarily, ethics commands full disclosure of any information that would be material to a buyer. Buyers should not be "tricked" into purchasing property through nondisclosures.

This ordinary rule respects the individual rights of each human being to make his or her own choices. Even if a choice might seem irrational to others, each person has a right to make his or her own decisions and accept the consequences of those decisions. The contrary position is authoritarian.

While there are good reasons for fully informing buyers, there are exceptions to this rule. For example, federal civil rights laws prohibit discrimination in housing and in contracts, and a broker would not be required to disclose that a seller was African-American, even if that fact were significant to a prejudiced potential purchaser.

The AIDS context creates countervailing concerns. An irrational fear of contacting AIDS from a house may seriously harm AIDS sufferers. Such AIDS sufferers may be unable to sell their homes when it becomes financially necessary.

Disclosure of AIDS seems to discriminate against those who have already suffered greatly. Moreover, disclosure may also serve to enable discrimination against homosexuals. The very fact of disclosing the problem may reaffirm the public's inaccurate perceptions about the risks of AIDS and perpetuate unfair and false stereotypes about the disease and its victims.

The law has dealt with this problem by holding that a broker must answer honestly if a buyer asks about whether the previous owner had AIDS. This seems consistent with the ethical requirements of honesty. The law has *not* imposed a duty on brokers to disclose AIDS if unasked, however. This leaves the disclosure choice to ethics, rather than law.

International Perspectives

Foreign Investment in U.S. Real Estate

Foreign investment in United States real estate remains a controversial issue. When a huge Japanese company bought 51 percent ownership of Rockefeller Center in New York, a hailstorm of concern and criticism resulted. Many opposed foreign purchases of U.S. land.

Foreign investment is important to the real estate industry, however. With the decline of the dollar's value against foreign currencies, foreign investors became attracted to U.S. real estate. Maintenance of this foreign interest may be crucial to finding future buyers and maintaining real estate values. Many foreign investors work with U.S. investors in joint ventures for purchase of real property in this country.

The International Investment Survey Act of 1976 requires reporting of foreign purchases of certain United States assets. When a foreign person acquires a 10 percent or greater interest in a U.S. business enterprise, that enterprise must file a form BE-13 within 45 days of the acquisition transaction. The definition of a business enterprise also encompasses real property. An exception exists for purchases of less than 200 acres.

When filing is required, form BE-13 calls for information on the identity of the parties, the percentage ownership of the parties, and certain financial projects, among other information. In addition, the new owners must make annual periodic reports on the property in a form BE-605.

If these reports are not filed, or if filing is late, the company is subject to a civil penalty of up to $10,000, and individuals may be imprisoned for up to one year. The law is enforced by the Department of Commerce, which has been relatively tolerant of late filings so far.

Purchases are also subject to the Foreign Investment in Real Property Tax Act of 1980. This law also imposes reporting requirements on foreign purchases of land and creates special tax rules requiring immediate withholding of a percentage of profits at the time of the transaction. The federal government places additional reporting requirements on foreign purchases of U.S. farm property under the Agricultural Foreign Investment Disclosure Act of 1978.

Questions and Case Problems

1. A real estate broker told prospective buyers that a home could be heated for "a little over a hundred dollars a year." In fact, a defect in the house's boiler meant that the house could not be heated at all. After purchasing the house and discovering the defective boiler, the buyers sued for misrepresentation by the broker. The broker stated that she was simply speaking of the energy efficiency of the house and was unaware of a defect in the heating system. Should the broker be liable to the buyers? [*Spargnapani v. Wright,* 110 A.2d 82 (D.C. App. 1954)].

2. A property owner placed an advertisement in the paper that read: "Home and income ... Be sure to see this 8-family dwelling on 90 ft. corner lot." A purchaser bought the land with the intent to rent out the eight units in the building. A local zoning ordinance, however, precluded renting out all the units. The purchaser complained that the advertisement was fraudulent by implying that the entire building could be leased. Was the advertisement fraudulent? [*Emily v. Bayne,* 371 S.W.2d 663 (Mo. App. 1963)].

3. The buyers of a building had a mortgage that prohibited them from prepaying more than 10 percent of the mortgage debt in any single year. The buyers later complained that they were unable to refinance the property in order to obtain access to their equity for use in other investments. They argued that the mortgage clause was an invalid restraint on their access to their own equity. The lender resisted prepayment, and the buyers went to court. Should the court order the lender to permit prepayment of the mortgage loan? [*Hartford Life Ins. Co. v. Randall,* 583 P.2d 1126 (Ore. 1978)].

4. A survey of California state-licensed savings and loan associations (S&Ls) found that a majority (113) of the institutions charged between 1 and 10 percent of the monthly payment for delinquent payments on loans. Twenty-one S&Ls charged one percent of the balance, and eleven charged a flat fee of about five dollars. Coast & Southern charged two percent of the total loan balance per year for the period of delinquent payment. A borrower who paid off a loan late complained that this charge was excessive and an unlawful penalty. Should the court uphold the S&L's late fee? [*Garrett v. Coast & Southern Federal Savings and Loan Ass'n,* 108 Cal. Rptr. 845 (1973)].

5. A commercial building rented space in a long-term lease to a pharmacy and granted the pharmacy an exclusive right to engage in this business in the building. Years later, the building owner leased a floor of the building to a medical group that operated its own pharmacy on the premises. The pharmacy sought to get out of the lease for the building. Was the rental of space to the medical group a material breach that enabled the pharmacy to break its lease on the building? [*Medico-Dental Bldg. Co. v. Horton & Converse,* 132 P.2d 457 (Cal. 1942)].

6. Tenants of an apartment building sued their landlord alleging a breach of the implied warranty of habitability. This was based on the presence of uninvited people, including drug dealers in common areas of the building and the landlord's failure to take action to eject such persons. Has the landlord violated the implied warranty? [*Doe v. New Bedford Housing Authority,* 417 Mass. 273 (1994)].

Chapter Eleven

Bank Regulation and Liability

Key Background

The essential background for this chapter on bank regulation and liability is found in Chapter 28 of *West's Business Law, Seventh Edition.* This chapter covers checks and banking and lender liability. Among the important points to remember from this chapter are:

- the duties of banks to customers
- federal regulation of banking deposits
- liability of lenders under contract law
- liability of lenders under tort law

* * *

The traditionally technical subject of banking has found its way onto the front pages of today's newspapers. Unfortunately, this reflects the troubles of banking, not its successes. As more and more banks face financial woes, banking has become increasingly intertwined with the legal system.

Legal structures have been important to banking since the first United States bank (the Bank of North America) was incorporated by the Continental Congress in 1781. Nineteenth-century American banks were subject to a variety of laws, but the legal system was broadly restructured during the Great Depression, after thousands of banks failed. The Federal Deposit Insurance Corporation ("FDIC") provided protection for depositors and set regulations for banks. Other laws restricted the types of financial activities in which banks could engage.

Many of the Depression-era laws remain critical to banking regulation. There are over 10,000 commercial banks in the United States, and virtually all of them belong to the FDIC insurance and regulation system. Banks remain subject to detailed regulation under other laws as well. Recent years have seen increased bank liability under various doctrines of lender liability.

Other depository institutions, such as savings and loan associations (S&Ls), are closely related to banks and have suffered enormous problems in recent years. This chapter will focus on bank regulation and liability, because banks are the most economically significant institutions, but much savings and loan regulation roughly parallels that of banks.

Bank Regulation

Banks are regulated by several agencies. The FDIC regulates practices of all its member banks (which include all nationally chartered banks and most state-chartered banks). The Federal Reserve Board has supervisory authority over these banks and also regulates bank mergers, consumer credit protection laws, bank holding companies, and other issues. The Board also has some authority over nonmember banks to protect industry stability. States also have banking commissions that regulate their own banks. All regulation begins with the decision of the federal government or a state government to grant a banking charter.

Bank Regulatory Supervision

Once a bank is chartered it becomes subject to a variety of regulations. The bank probably belongs to the FDIC system. This insurance is required for national banks and many state banks to enter the system in order to provide the assurance necessary to attract depositors. The FDIC presently insures deposits of up to $100,000 per account.

Because the FDIC does not want to be liable under this insurance, much of its regulation is directed toward preventing the failure of its member banks. A bank can fail when it makes loans to parties who cannot make payments (called "nonperforming" loans). If losses on nonperforming loans outstrip the bank's capital reserve, the bank may go into bankruptcy.

Every bank has some nonperforming loans. The key to solvency is to minimize the amount of these nonperforming loans and retain sufficient capital reserves to account for such loans. The federal government places specific limitations on banking activities to protect the solvency of banks.

One important regulation involves **lending limits**. Under law, a bank can loan no more than 15 percent of its capital stock and surplus to any single person or entity. Some exceptions to this limit exist, but it is designed to require diversification of lending in order to reduce risks.

Suppose that the Capital Bank has a capital stock and surplus of $100 million. The American Railway Co., a long-standing reliable bank customer, approaches Capital for a loan of $20 million in order to purchase new cars and upgrade their facilities. This would exceed the bank's lending limit. The bank could still make the loan if it could show that the extra 5 percent was secured by readily marketable collateral. The bank would have to demonstrate that railroad cars securing the loan were readily marketable.

The law used to restrict the amount of lending that was secured by real estate. A 1982 law removed much of this restriction, and consequently nonperforming real estate loans have become a major problem for banks.

Other regulations involve **transactions with affiliated banks**. As a rule, a bank cannot loan more than 10 percent of its capital stock and surplus to a single affiliated bank. Banks are prohibited from loaning more than 20 percent of their capital stock and surplus to all their affiliates combined.

Insider lending is also regulated. **Insider lending** is when a bank makes loans to its officers, directors, or to shareholders owning more than 10 percent of its voting stock. Insider lending is not prohibited, but specific approval requirements exist for loans to insiders that exceed a certain amount (e.g., 5 percent of capital surplus).

The FDIC also establishes *minimum capital ratios* for banks. These ratios require that a bank maintain a specific percentage of capital to its total assets. The minimum capital ratio now required is 3 percent. Additional capital requirements exist for banks that have a significant number of riskier loans.

The FDIC can also threaten to terminate deposit insurance coverage for banks that engage in unsafe or unsound practices or violate laws or regulations. To do so, the FDIC must provide the bank with notice of the intent to terminate and allow the bank 120 days to correct the problem. This period may be shortened to twenty days if necessary. If the problem is uncorrected, the bank must be provided with a hearing in order to defend itself.

The FDIC also has control over the ownership of insured banks. The Change in Bank Control Act of 1978 ("CBCA")[1] provides that a federal banking agency can disapprove a bank acquisition or change in control that is considered contrary to the public interest. The following decision illustrates an application of this power.

---

[1] 12 U.S.C. section 730q.

Case 11.1
Sletteland v. Federal Deposit Insurance Corporation
United States Court of Appeals
District of Columbia Circuit, 1991
924 F.2d 350

Background and Facts *The Sletteland family has controlled the Pigeon Falls State Bank since the 1920s. In the spring of 1988, George Sletteland, the bank's principal owner and chairman of the board of directors, was removed from his position by an FDIC order. The FDIC forbade him from further involvement in the bank, including the voting of his shares in directors' elections. George Sletteland then signed an agreement with his son, Peter Sletteland, already a bank director, giving Peter control over 41 percent of the bank's stock.*

The FDIC issued a notice disapproving of Peter's acquisition. Peter Sletteland objected, and a three-day trial was held before an administrative law judge ("ALJ"). The ALJ agreed with the FDIC that Peter lacked the competence and experience to warrant approval of the change in control of the bank. The FDIC adopted the ALJ's conclusions, and Peter appealed to federal court.

GINSBURG, Circuit Judge.

* * * *

The FDIC determined that, because of Petitioner's youth, inexperience, and tenuous financial status, the change in control application should be disapproved. The record shows that at the time Petitioner filed for the change in control, he was only twenty-six years old. He had spent a total of three and a half years at three universities but had not earned a degree. He had not studied finance or banking, and his only banking experience consisted of summer employment as a teenager at another Wisconsin bank in which his father had an interest. More recently, Petitioner had worked for one year at a mens-wear boutique, and then had conducted an interior decorating business operating out of a spare bedroom in his apartment.

* * * *

The CBCA contemplates that financial regulatory agencies have the authority to deny approval of a change in control application when the proposed acquisition shows the potential for future problems. Thus, the Act allows an agency to disapprove an application if "the effect of the proposed acquisition ... may be substantially to lessen competition," or if "the financial condition of any acquiring person is such as might jeopardize the financial stability of the bank." See 12 U.S.C. § 1817 (j)(7)(B), (C) (emphasis added). Similarly, the Act instructs that an agency may disapprove a change in control where "the competence, experience, or integrity of any acquiring person ... indicates that it would not be in the interest of the depositors [or the public]." See 12 U.S.C. § 1817 (j)(7)(D) (emphasis added). This prescription requires the agency to make a predictive judgment, tied to supporting evidence, about problems that might result from the change in control. In light of Petitioner's youth, lack of a college degree or other relevant educational background, and limited work experience, we are satisfied in this case that there is substantial evidence "indicat[ing]" that Petitioner's "competence, experience, or integrity" rendered the proposed acquisition not in the best interest of the Bank's depositors or the public.

Decision and Remedy *The court affirmed the FDIC's ruling.*

Director Liability

A bank director who fails to comply with statutes or regulations may be held personally liable for this failure. If a director undertakes a "knowing" violation of the law, he or she may be sued by regulatory agencies or by individual bank shareholders who have suffered damages.

For example, if a director assents to loans that exceed the federal lending limits, the director may be liable for resultant losses suffered by the bank. Directors recently received some legal protection in these claims. After an administrative law judge held directors liable for violating lending limits, a court overturned the ruling and found that directors could only be held liable in a court of action.[2]

Bank directors may be sued even if they did not directly participate in the violation. A court approved an FDIC action that removed two directors who were aware of, but did not personally engage in, unlawful lending practices made by another director. The court found that the nonparticipating directors had a duty to prevent such transactions.[3]

Bank directors can also be liable whenever they engage in unsafe and unsound banking practices. Unsafe and unsound practices include failure to maintain an adequate cash reserve, failure to diversify the bank's loans, or making loans without sufficient precautions.

A director may be liable for irresponsible conduct or even the failure properly to monitor bank activities. In one case, a bank director was held personally liable for more than $1.4 million. The court found that the director had invested the bank's funds irresponsibly and continued to do so even after the bank suffered losses.

Bank directors and officers can be liable to make restitution for improperly acquired funds. The following decision demonstrates this authority.

Bank directors may even be criminally liable. Most state laws make it a felony for a bank director to make a false entry in the books or statements of a bank. Directors may be guilty of a misdemeanor for other actions, including a false statement about insurance of a bank's deposits.

In January 1997, the U.S. Supreme Court considered the scope of bank director liability under state and federal law, in *Atherton v. Federal Deposit Insurance Corporation*.[4] The Court held that federal law provides a liability "floor" of "gross negligence," which supplants easier state standards of simple negligence. States may, however, create their own stricter standards for bank director liability.

Federal regulatory agencies also have power to remove an officer or director of a bank. This authority can be exercised if the director or officer has violated a law or regulation, has breached his or her fiduciary duty, or has engaged in any unsafe or unsound banking practice. Removal requires notice and a hearing for the director.

---

[2] *Larimore v. Comptroller of the Currency*, 789 F.2d 1244 (7th Cir. 1986).

[3] *Brickner v. FDIC*, 747 F.2d 1198 (8th Cir. 1984).

[4] 117 S.C. 666 (1997).

Case 11.2
Hoffman v. Federal Deposit Insurance Corporation
United States Court of Appeals
Ninth Circuit, 1990
912 F.2d 1172

Background and Facts *Alaska Continental Bank ("ACB") began encountering financial difficulties in 1986. Harold Hoffman was the president of the bank. The FDIC and state regulators informed Hoffman in May 1988 that they considered ACB to be technically insolvent and that it should be sold. Hoffman was told to be a caretaker of the bank in the interim and maintain the bank's assets as well as possible.*

Among the actions taken by the ACB board of directors was to buy out the balance of Hoffman's employment contract with the bank, because he declared that he would resign as of June 10,

1988. The cost of this buyout was over $61,000. The FDIC concluded that Hoffman was "bleeding off" the bank's assets and initiated an administrative proceeding. The Administrative Law Judge approved a cease and desist order entered by the FDIC that required Hoffman to make restitution of the buyout of his salary. Hoffman appealed.

FERNANDEZ, Circuit Judge.

* * * *

A. *The Authority to Issue the Cease and Desist Order*

Hoffman claims that the FDIC had no authority to order him to make restitution of the $61,796.48 payment he received for his contract. We disagree.

There can be no doubt that the FDIC has authority to issue a cease and desist order if it finds that an institution has engaged in an unsafe or unsound practice. 12 U.S.C. § 1818(b)(1).

It has been said that an unsafe or unsound practice is one " 'which is contrary to generally accepted standards of prudent operation, the possible consequences of which, if continued, would be abnormal risk or loss or damage to an institution, its shareholders, or the agencies administering the insurance funds' " and that it is a practice which has a "reasonably direct effect on an association's financial soundness." *Gulf Fed. Sav. & Loan Ass'n v. Federal Home Loan Bank Bd.,* 651 F.2d 259, 264 (5th Cir.1981), *cert. denied,* 458 U.S. 1121, 102 S.Ct. 3509, 73 L.Ed.2d 1383 (1982). Self-dealing has been identified as an unsafe or unsound practice because of the conflict it creates between the interests of the institution and the interests of an individual. *First National Bank of Lamarque v. Smith,* 610 F.2d 1258, 1265 (5th Cir.1980); *Independent Bankers Ass'n of America v. Heimann,* 613 F.2d 1164, 1168 (D.C. Cir. 1979), cert. denied, 449 U.S. 823, 101 S. Ct. 84, 66 L.Ed.2d 26 (1980). Those cases turn on the principle that breaches of fiduciary duty by bank officials are inherently dangerous and cannot be considered safe. Cf. *Federal Sav. & Loan Ins. Corp. v. Molinary,* 889 F.2d 899, 903-04 (9th Cir. 1989).

As the FDIC board pointed out, during a time when Hoffman and ACB's board knew that they were supposed to be acting as caretakers of a bank that was rapidly declining, they decided to divert some of its assets in a way that could not help but cause detriment to the shareholders and other creditors of the bank. Evidence before the ALJ and the FDIC indicated that Hoffman was cashed out because the bank was about to close. The terms were favorable to Hoffman; they amounted to prepayment of his salary to the end of his contract—December 2, 1988—although it was rather obvious that he would not be working that long. This would raise eyebrows under the best of circumstances; the FDIC properly determined that it was considerably more dubious under the circumstances of this case. Even if there are cases in which the FDIC and the courts should countenance the idea that a breach of fiduciary duty is not an unsafe or unsound practice, this is not one of those cases.

Decision and Remedy *The court affirmed the FDIC's order.*

Failing Banks

In addition to the specific regulations described above, federal agencies conduct generalized bank examination and supervision in an attempt to avoid bank failures. This system is intended to prevent bank failures and alleviate the consequences when failure does occur. The FDIC considers a bank's capital adequacy, asset quality, management ability, earnings performance, and liquidity. Then banks are rated on a scale of 1 to 5.

A rating of "1" is best and reflects a very sound bank. A rating of "3" suggests a potential problem bank, and regulators will keep an eye on its practices to prevent further deterioration. A rating of "4" is a serious problem bank and that requires immediate action. A rating of "5" is lowest and reflects a bank that is likely to fail even with rescue measures (these banks are sometimes called "zombies").

Suppose that the Second National Bank made a significant number of large real estate loans, whereupon the local real estate values collapsed. Second National may have low capital adequacy (due to nonperforming loans), poor asset quality (its loans may not be paid off), and correspondingly low earnings performance. The above factors may also call into question the bank's management capabilities.

If the FDIC found the bank to be "unsafe or unsound" it could then step in to attempt to save Second National from its management practices. The FDIC has great influence because it can threaten to terminate the bank's insurance unless the bank agrees to certain reform measures. The FDIC may also obtain a cease-and-desist order from an administrative law judge that compels certain corrective actions.

The FDIC might force changes in management practices on Second National, including tougher standards for making loans, cutbacks on bank overhead expenses, seeking additional capital from private sources or the Federal Reserve, and even the suspension and removal of bank officers and directors.

Procedural protections are required for final cease-and-desist orders. The regulatory agency must serve notice on the bank and provide for a hearing after at least a month. Violation of a cease-and-desist order is punishable by a $1000-per-day fine.

Bank Closures

If a bank is insolvent, or failing, the FDIC may seek to shut down the bank before further deterioration occurs. The FDIC lacks authority to close a bank directly. The FDIC can use its authority to terminate insurance coverage to impel the bank to close, however. The Comptroller of the Currency, which charters banks, also has the authority to close them down.

The FDIC takes over as the receiver of a failed bank. As receiver, it manages the bank in order to preserve as much equity as possible. It may also liquidate the assets of the bank and distribute them to creditors. The FDIC pays off depositors from the bank's funds or from its insurance fund. In the past, over 99 percent of bank depositors have been repaid in full.

As receiver, the FDIC also is subrogated to the bank's legal claims against others. The FDIC may attempt to obtain damages from the bank's directors, officers or other parties who contributed to the failure.

The FDIC often tries to save a failed bank through a **purchase and assumption transaction** ("P&A"). In a P&A, a successful bank agrees to assume the liabilities of the failed bank in exchange for the assets of the bank. The FDIC pays cash to the successful bank to make up for any excess of liabilities over assets.

The FDIC's powers over failed banks are complicated by the ability of a company to declare bankruptcy and place itself under the jurisdiction of a bankruptcy court. The complexity of the situation is illustrated by the failure of First RepublicBank Corporation in Texas.

First RepublicBank was a holding company with forty-one subsidiary banks. The FDIC provided $1 million in emergency assistance to the subsidiary banks in order to reassure depositors. The FDIC then sought out a buyer for the subsidiary banks. The FDIC found NCNB Corporation as a purchaser.

The Comptroller of the Currency then shut down First RepublicBank's subsidiary banks and sold then to NCNB. The next day, First RepublicBank itself filed for bankruptcy. The FDIC sought to recover from First RepublicBank itself for allegedly diverting hundreds of millions of dollars from the subsidiary banks (by overextracting dividends and purchasing property at less than fair market value). The bankruptcy filing helped protect First RepublicBank from these claims.

FIRREA

Congress provided bank regulators with broad new powers in the Financial Institutions Reform, Recovery and Enforcement Act of 1989 ("FIRREA"). While much of FIRREA was intended to correct crises in the savings and loan industry, FIRREA's provisions also affect other banking institutions.

FIRREA expanded the enforcement powers of the FDIC and other regulatory agencies. FIRREA makes clear the authority to issue cease-and-desist orders to restrict the growth of the banking institution, rescind agreements or contracts, and force parties to make restitution for losses caused by an officer or director of the bank.

FIRREA also modified the authority of the FDIC to collect monetary penalties. If a bank or officer violates a law, regulation or FDIC agreement, it is subject to a fine of up to $5000 per day of violation. If the violation is part of a pattern of misconduct or causes a significant loss to the institution, the fine may be up to $25,000 per day. Knowing misconduct that causes a substantial loss is punishable by fines of up to $1,000,000 per day.

FIRREA contains a provision (section 212(k)) that states that a director or officer of an insured bank may be personally liable for "gross negligence." This standard is higher than that of many states, which permit director and officer liability for simple negligence. Defendants have argued that the federal law preempts the state laws and means that they are liable *only* for gross negligence. This issue is highly litigated and unresolved, but the majority of courts have ruled against the defendant officers and directors on this point.

Other Bank Regulations

There are a myriad of detailed bank regulations. In addition to the broad supervisory authority of the FDIC and other regulatory agencies, specific regulations limit banks in the areas of branch banking, bank holding companies, bank mergers, and depositor privacy.

Branch banking has historically been a regulatory controversy. This is the ability of a bank to establish branches in other geographic areas. Government policy dating back to the nineteenth century has limited the ability of a bank to establish branches in other states, or even in other counties.

Recent years have seen some liberalization of branch banking, with many states permitting branch banks. State laws vary, however. Massachusetts allowed branch banking but only with other New England states. Many states, such as Illinois, permit reciprocal branch banking, i.e. with banks from states that permit Illinois banks also to establish branches.

Bank holding companies also are regulated under the Bank Holding Company Act of 1956. Some corporations sought to evade branch banking restrictions by creating holding companies controlling many different banks in different states. The 1956 Act largely prevents this action.

Bank holding company acquisitions are limited to preserve competition in banking. Banks are also restricted in their ability to participate in insurance, securities and other riskier financial transactions. Bank holding companies are also restricted in these activities.

Bank mergers raise many of the same antitrust concerns as mergers of other corporations but are subject to special legislation in the bank Merger Act of 1960. This law requires the written consent of the Comptroller of the Currency or other federal supervisory agency whenever an insured bank seeks to acquire another insured bank.

In 1989, the Comptroller refused to permit St. Croix Valley Bancshares, Incorporated, to acquire the Stillwater Bancorporation, Incorporated. Federal officials were concerned that the resulting bank would not be adequately capitalized.

Traditional antitrust concerns are also present in bank mergers. Courts have halted horizontal mergers among competing banks in a given market. Courts have been more willing to permit mergers that extend competition into new geographic areas.

Federal regulations also protect the financial privacy of bank depositors. The Fair Credit Reporting Act of 1970 limits the use and release of credit reports. A bank must have a proper purpose for requesting credit information and must inform the customer if it takes any adverse action based upon the credit report.

Federal banking agencies adopted **real estate lending standards** on December 31, 1992. This rule requires that every bank adopt a written policy for appropriate limits on granting real estate loans, which were the source of many bank failures in the 1980s. The requirements of this rule are quite detailed and include the following:

- establishment of real estate appraisal and evaluation programs
- management monitoring techniques, including reports to the bank's board of directors
- presumptive loan to value limits for various categories of loans (65% for raw land, 80% for commercial construction, etc.)
- specific documentation and verification of borrower financial statements

These regulations admit of no exceptions based upon the bank's overall soundness.

Lender Liability

Lender liability is not only one of the most significant issues in banking law, but is among the most significant issues in all business law. In one recent year, six of the ten largest jury verdicts against defendants were in lender liability cases. Several lender liability cases resulted in verdicts in excess of $100 million.

Common Law Sources of Lender Liability

A primary source of lender liability is found in the loan contract. A lender may be liable for breach of contract or for promissory estoppel, even in the absence of a binding contract.

In addition to specific duties created in a contract and by contract law, the lender is subject to a duty of good faith and fair dealing with the borrower. This very general duty requires that the lender deal honestly and fairly with the borrower.

Another source of lender liability is tort law. The lender may be liable for the torts of fraud, duress, interference with business relationships, or an emerging tort of breach of fiduciary duty.

Contexts of Lender liability

Banks face lender liability in certain recurring contexts that call for caution. These include preliminary loan negotiations, extension of credit, and loan terminations.

Banks may find themselves liable in loan applications and commitments. In the course of negotiating a loan, a bank may make certain promises to a prospective borrower. That borrower may seek to hold the bank to its "gentlemen's agreement" or negotiating promises, even in the absence of a firm binding loan contract. A bank may be liable to provide credit based on its conduct in such negotiations.

In one important case, a company negotiated a loan of $6 million and obtained a commitment letter. In finalizing the loan, the lender added a new condition that the borrower refused to accept. The loan fell through, and the company was forced into bankruptcy. The lender was held liable for a breach of good faith.[5]

Banks can also be liable for negligent handling of loan applications. Where a bank solicits loan applications but fails to process them promptly, the bank is subject to liability. Suppose that Capital Bank negotiates a loan with Hallstrom, Inc. Capital receives a loan application and promises to process the application within two months and lock in a favorable interest rate. If the bank negligently fails to do so, it may be liable.

Banks have also been held liable for the termination of lines of credit extended to regular customers. In one case, a bank terminated a $1 million line of credit with borrowers. The borrower demonstrated that the bank wrongfully terminated the borrower due to inaccurate rumors of organized crime involvement in the borrower's business. A court granted the borrower $15 million in damages, including punitive damages.

Another source of liability is loan termination. Banks can be found liable for wrongfully accelerating a loan and demanding full payment without sufficient cause. In one case, a borrower was consistently late in payments, but the bank took no action. Finally, after a payment was again late, the bank called in the loan and demanded full payment. This destroyed the borrower's business. The court found the lender liable, because the latest payment was only one day late and because the bank had previously accepted late payments without penalty.[6]

---

[5] *999 v. CIT Corporation,* 776 F.2d 866 (9th Cir. 1985).

[6] *Sahadi v. Continental Illinois National Bank and Trust Company of Chicago,* 706 F.2d 193 (7th Cir. 1983).

Banks also have been found liable for refusal to release security interest in property. In one significant case, a bank extended two loans to one party, for $1.5 million and for $185,000. The smaller loan was secured by a deed of trust on a piece of land. After the second loan was paid off, the bank refused to release its security interest in the land, hoping to use it as collateral against the larger loan. This prevented the borrower from using the land to obtain further financing and ultimately caused the borrower's bankruptcy. A jury held the bank liable for over $9 million in actual damages and $50 million in punitive damages.[7]

Another source of lender liability arises out of **participation agreements**. This is where two or more banks jointly extended credit to the same borrower. One bank is considered the lead lender and administers the loan.

Suppose that Second State Bank wants to make a loan to a local developer but cannot fund the entire loan itself. Second State then presents the loan to other banks for their participation. If Second State exaggerates the credit-worthiness of the borrower, other participating banks may sue Second State, as lead lender, if a problem arises. The lead lender and other participants also may be liable to borrowers.

Banks may also be liable for negligent loan administration. Failure to properly post loan payments to a borrower's account has been the basis for lender liability. Other banks have been held liable for failing to obtain insurance as agreed.

Lenders are more frequently found liable under a combination of the above circumstances. Lenders are not always liable for borrowers' problems, however, as demonstrated by the following decision.

---

[7] *Robinson v. McAllen State Bank*, 48 BNA Banking Rptr. 1004 (Tex. Dist. Ct. 1987).

■ Case 11.3
Greenway Investments General Partnership v. Signet Bank/Maryland
United States Court of Appeals
Fourth Circuit, 1993
991 F.2d 789

Background and Facts *Perry & Sons, Inc. was in the plumbing supply and service business and began experiencing financial difficulties. In May 1990, Signet Bank/Maryland extended Perry a $2.5 million revolving line of credit under a loan and security agreement. This agreement provided that if Perry defaulted, the bank could at its election, without notice, accelerate the loan and take possession of the collateral. In December, Perry Supply and Signet agreed to reduce the line of credit to $1.75 million but extend an additional $150,000 loan, evidenced by a promissory note requiring monthly interest payments. After Perry fell into technical default, its owners met on March 6, 1991 with Michael Mahon, an assistant vice president of Signet. The Perrys claim that Mahon promised not to call the loan, though he disputes this. On March 7, Mahon heard that the Perrys would file for bankruptcy and promptly froze their operating account and notified them that the bank was accelerating the loan. On March 13, Perry Supply filed for bankruptcy, allegedly because their operating account was frozen. The company then sued Signet for breach of the contractual covenant of good faith, fraud, and other counts. The district court ruled for Signet and plaintiffs appealed.*

PER CURIAM.

* * * *

... "the duty of good faith merely obligates a lender to exercise good faith in performing its contractual obligations; it does not obligate a lender to take affirmative actions that the lender is clearly not required to take under its loan documents." ... It follows that the duty of good faith does not obligate a lender to refrain from taking actions it is permitted to take under its loan documents. Signet did nothing more than pursue its contractual rights in response to Perry Supply's default, and did not violate its duty of good faith.

* * * *

[The court next considered the fraud claim based upon Mahon's alleged promise at the March 6 meeting.] Mahon maintained that because he learned from the call that Perry Supply was on the verge of declaring bankruptcy, he did not have the option of keeping his promise; he had to freeze the operating account and call the loan immediately to protect the Bank's interests. Perry Supply alleged no facts to establish clearly and convincingly that Mahon intended not to keep his promise at the time he made it.

Decision and Remedy   *The court affirmed the dismissal of plaintiff's complaint.*

Statutory Sources of Lender Liability

In addition to general principles of common law, lenders are susceptible to liability under certain federal and state statutes.

A common statutory source of lender liability is under the federal *securities laws*. A lender that buys or sells stock based on nonpublic information acquired from a borrower can be liable for insider trading. The most relevant securities law provisions are those that prevent fraud. A lender may also be liable for securities fraud when the lender has participated in preparing documents that are misleading or false.

Lenders are usually not directly liable under securities laws because they do not control the corporation selling the securities. Lenders may be liable, however, for aiding and abetting a securities law violation. Aiding and abetting lender liability has the following three elements:

1. Some person committed a violation of securities laws.
2. The lender was aware of playing a role in an activity that was unlawful.
3. The lender knowingly and substantially assisted the violation.

A lender is not liable for aiding and abetting a securities law violation simply by making a loan to a corporate violator. A lender is subject to liability for taking a more active role. Suppose that the First National Bank's appraisers provided inflated real estate appraisals to DevelopCo., which were published in a prospectus for issuing new securities. First National could be liable for aiding and abetting a securities law violation.

Another statutory source of lender liability is found in the environmental laws, especially the Comprehensive Environmental Response Compensation and Liability Act of 1980 ("CERCLA"), which is discussed in Chapter 14 on environmental liability. This law requires landowners, among others, to pay the costs of cleaning up hazardous waste problems on their property.

Lenders become potentially liable under CERCLA when they take property in a foreclosure proceeding. Lenders can also be liable if they participate in the management of a company that owns a hazardous waste disposal site.

Congress in 1996 provided some relief from CERCLA lender liability, in The Asset Conservation, Lender Liability, and Deposit Protection Act of 1996, which is discussed in Chapter 14 below.

A third source of statutory lender liability is the antitrust laws. Banks are potentially liable under the general antitrust laws for such violations as price fixing, group boycotts, and other anticompetitive activities.

In 1970, Congress passed a specific antitrust law to governing banking practices, in the Bank Holding Company Act Amendments. These amendments contain three major prohibitions on lender actions:

1. A prohibition on a Bank's extending credit conditioned on the borrower's willingness to obtain some additional service from the bank.
2. A prohibition on a bank's extending credit conditioned on the borrower's providing some additional credit or service for the bank.
3. A prohibition on a bank's extending credit conditioned on the borrower's not dealing with some competitor of the bank.

The borrower can sue for damages to enforce these provisions. Triple damages are provided under the act.

In a leading case, a bank agreed to loan money to a corporation on the condition that stock in the corporation be transferred to one of the bank's other customers. A court held that this violated the Act's prohibition on demanding additional services in exchange for credit.[8]

Mortgage Lender Liability

Lending for new homes creates different and significant sources of lender liability. Many residential mortgages are held by savings and loan institutions, but banks and life insurance companies also have a significant share of the home lending market.

The special problem of mortgage lenders is illustrated by the following scenario. Paul Barro obtains a loan to build a new house. After the house is built, Paul discovers serious defects in the house that destroy its value. Paul might sue the construction company that built the house, but suppose that the construction company lacks the funds to pay Paul's damages. Paul may sue the lender to recover the damages from his defective home.

Contract Liability

A contract between a lender and a home purchaser takes the form of a loan agreement that sets forth the basic terms of the mortgage. For its own protection, a bank will usually make provisions for inspections of the property during the construction process and provisions for surveys of the property. Borrowers have used these provisions as a source for lender liability.

Suppose that Paul's construction loan had a provision for periodic inspections by his lender. The bank made these inspections but either did not discover the defect or did not disclose it. Courts may permit Paul to recover from the bank. Paul will lose, however, if the contract or other evidence demonstrates that the inspections were intended only for the benefit of the bank and not of the borrower.

A second mortgage liability problem involves claims against the borrower by third parties. In order to protect their collateral, lenders obligate themselves to ensure that no third parties have security interests in the property. For example, construction companies may have a **mechanics' lien security interest** in the house until they are paid.

In one case, a lender agreed to ensure that the property was not encumbered by mechanics' liens. The general contractor who built the house was not paid and recorded a lien against the property. The borrower had to pay off the general contractor and sued the bank for damages. A court found the lender liable because it had assumed a duty to protect the mortgaged real estate from third-party liens.[9]

Lenders may also be liable for assuming a duty to survey property under construction. In one case, a builder had much of the house built, when it was discovered that two feet of the garage were on the property of an adjacent owner. The bank had not procured a survey. The borrowers had to tear down the garage and rebuild it. A court found the lender was not liable, though, because the lender had not promised to obtain a survey at any particular time in the construction process.[10]

---

[8] *Swerdloff v. Miami National Bank*, 584 F.2d 54 (5th Cir. 1978).

[9] *Prudential Insurance Co. v. Executive Estates, Inc.*, 309 N.E.2d 1117 (Ind. App. 1978).

[10] *Mosley v. Perpetual Savings & Loan Association*, 227 S.E.2d 163 (N.C. App. 1976).

Negligent Misrepresentation

A borrower may recover from a mortgage lender for negligent misrepresentation, if the lender failed to use reasonable care in informing the borrower of information. Negligent misrepresentation may involve a failure to inform the buyer of construction defects, as well as other material facts.

In one leading case, the borrowers contracted to purchase a home, conditioned on securing a mortgage. A lender conducted a negligent appraisal of the value of the home and approved the mortgage application. After moving into the house and discovering significant structural defects, the buyer sued the lender for negligently misinforming him of the home's value. The court found that the lender negligently performed the appraisal and that the buyer relied on the negligent appraisal in purchasing the property. The lender was liable for the buyer's damages.[11]

Indirect Lender Liability

Under some circumstances, a lender may be liable to a home buyer, even if the lender did not make the loan to purchase the home. This arises when a lender makes a loan to a large developer who builds an entire subdivision. The developer then markets individual houses to buyers. Some dissatisfied buyers have sued the lender, after the developer proved insolvent.

Courts have held lenders to a duty to indirect purchasers, depending upon their involvement in the subdivision development. In the first significant case, which arose in California, buyers of a home suffered serious damages because the house was built on adobe soil that could not support the home's foundation as constructed. After the developer suffered financial problems, the lender was held liable to the home purchasers because it retained the right of first refusal on mortgages to home buyers, had the right to inspect and control construction work, and obtained profits from the development over and above its interest payments.[12]

In a subsequent case, California courts held that a lender was not liable for defective development. The court emphasized that the lender did nothing more than provide funds for development for interest and took no additional profit.[13] Other states are divided over whether lenders may be indirectly liable to home buyers.

---

[11] *Larsen v. United Federal Savings & Loan Association,* 300 N.W.2d 281 (Iowa 1981).

[12] *Connor v. Great Western Savings & Loan Association,* 447 P.2d 609 (Cal. 1968).

[13] *Bradler v. Craig,* 79 Cal. Rptr. 401 (1969).

Ethical Perspectives

An Ethical Duty to Loan?

A general principle of our free enterprise system is that each businessperson has a right to decide which contracts to enter. Like others, a banker has a right to decide which loans to make. The law places only limited restrictions on this right, such as a prohibition on racial discrimination in lending decisions.

Despite the prohibition on racial discrimination, studies have shown that blacks and other minorities are denied loans far more often than are whites. People who want to borrow for construction in minority communities generally have more difficulty obtaining loans than people in more affluent, white communities.

Some bankers explain that this statistical disparity has nothing to do with discrimination. They note that blacks applying for loans may have less income or a poorer credit history. They also note that properties in minority communities are less marketable and therefore riskier for lenders. These are, of course, legitimate and nondiscriminatory reasons for loan denial.

But might bankers have an ethical responsibility to relax their lending rules somewhat for minority communities? Loan denials may create a self-reinforcing spiral of poverty in such communities. If builders cannot obtain loans to renovate these communities, the existing buildings will deteriorate further and more affluent individuals will move to wealthier areas. This will in turn make the minority community worse and make it even more difficult to get future development loans. An inability to obtain financing can damage a community.

A banker might recognize an ethical duty to clients but respond that he or she is not in business to help poor people. The business of a bank is to make a profit, and bad loans will only undermine the bank, endanger its shareholders and depositors and perhaps harm the greater community. The banker would contend that it is the government's responsibility to help poorer or minority communities.

There are no clear-cut ethical duties for a banker's social responsibility to a community. No one would argue that a bank must make a risky loan to an individual simply because he or she wants to build in a minority community. But the bank could take some action to assist these communities.

Most banks, like other corporations, acknowledge some need to benefit their communities. For example, many banks contribute money to local charities, which may include help for the poor or may include donations to the local symphony or art museum. Bankers should carefully consider the nature of their contributions.

A bank might consider making its contribution in the form of loans to minority communities. The bank might even make these loans at low interest rates. Providing development financing is especially suited to banks, which may uniquely possess the ability to facilitate development. Other institutions can donate money to other causes. Furthermore, the bank may discover that these loans prove to be profitable. The bank can find trustworthy minority developers who benefit both their community and the bank, by paying off the loan.

International Perspectives

U.S. Banks in Europe

Since the end of World War II, United States banks have been very successful in international markets. After the nations of the European Community (EC) united in a single economic market on December 31, 1992, the banking opportunities became enormous. These nations have a combined population of over 330 million people and a combined gross national product in excess of $4 trillion. U.S. banks will strive to compete for a portion of this market.

To seize the financial opportunities of the emerging European market, U.S. banks must understand the new legal rules for banking in Europe. The EC's first banking directive, in 1977, prohibited discrimination among member European states. The second banking directive established standards for foreign banks seeking to do business in Europe.

The key to banking in Europe is governmental reciprocity. The ability of a U.S. company to establish a bank in Europe, or to purchase an existing bank, is dependent upon the ability of a European bank to undertake similar actions in the United States. While the U.S. generally does not discriminate against the establishment of foreign banks in this country, U.S. law does place significant restrictions on banking activities. There is some concern that U.S. banks operating in Europe may face similar restrictions.

In 1989, EC officials stated that U.S. banks operating in Europe would have all the same rights as European banks, but this assurance was not legally binding. Once a bank obtains a single license, it will be authorized to provide a wide range of products and services in all the member states of the EC. Assuming that U.S. banks are able to establish branches in Europe, the banks then must understand the banking regulations of the EC.

The EC will not abolish all member country regulation of banking practices. The EC has prohibited discrimination against banks outside the country and has also created a uniform system for certain essential supervisory standards.

The second EC banking directive creates a framework for minimum capital standards for banking. Individual member states may apply for even higher minimum capital standards for banking in their country.

The EC will exercise control over major shareholders of banks. A bank must inform the relevant authorities of the identity of any more-than-10-percent shareholders, and the authorities may disapprove such shareholders, whom they believe would not provide safe and sound banking management.

The second directive also provides for community-wide controls on accounting and control mechanisms. This includes the adoption of minimum solvency rations, requiring banks to limit lending to a certain multiple of their capital reserves. Many of these rules will be administered by member states, but the administration must conform to community-wide standards.

Questions and Case Problems

1. The Bank of Edwardsville loans Stapleton Construction Company $60,000 for the purchase of new equipment over a two-year period. The principal will be allotted to Stapleton in $15,000 increments every six months. Under the terms of the agreement, the Bank of Edwardsville is required to advance the funds so long as Stapleton maintains certain carefully specified financial ratios. The contract contains a covenant that obliges both parties to a duty of good faith and fair dealing in the contract's performance. Stapleton fails to meet the financial ratios after the second allotment of money and the bank refuses to lend further. Can Stapleton recover the remaining $30,000 from the original agreement?

2. The Santa Fe Apartments Project was developed and built with financing from the sale of tax exempt bonds issued by the Salt Lake County Housing Authority. Commonwealth Savings facilitated the financing by issuing a Letter of Credit to Zions Bank (the trustee for the bondholders), guaranteeing repayment of the principal and interest on the bond loan to the Housing Authority bondholders. In return, Commonwealth received a Letter of Reimbursement from Santa Fe and a loan fee. In 1986, Santa Fe entered into an agreement to sell the project to Castleglen, in which Castleglen assumed the obligations of the loan documents. Castleglen had trouble servicing this debt and was declared in default. Castleglen sued Commonwealth, claiming that telephone conversations with the officers of Commonwealth promised that it would not be found in default. Commonwealth was then put into receivership due to insolvency. The government sought to recover from Castleglen in default. Can the government recover from Castleglen, in light of the telephone promises by the Commonwealth officers? [*Castleglen, Inc. v. Commonwealth Savings Association*, 728 F. Supp. 656 (D. Utah 1989)].

3. Target Corporation is a longstanding client of MegaBank, as is the Raider Company. One day, the general manager of the Raider Company comes to MegaBank and seeks a loan in order to conduct a hostile takeover of Target Corporation. The bank approves the loan, and the officers and directors of Target become extremely distressed. Target sues MegaBank for violation of the bank's fiduciary duties. Should Target succeed on this claim?

4. Sunshine State Bank is a state-chartered institution located in South Miami, Florida. The Corona family, including Rafael, Ray, and Ricardo, acquired the bank in 1978. Since acquiring control, each of the Coronas has served as an officer and director of Sunshine. In 1983, the FDIC conducted an examination of the bank and reclassified $30 million of the bank's loans to more doubtful recovery categories. About 47 percent of the loans were adversely classified and this amounted to 581 percent of Sunshine's total equity capital and reserves. The FDIC also found numerous violations of law in the bank's procedures. In 1984, the FDIC removed Rafael, Ray, and Ricardo Corona from their roles as bank directors and officers and forbade them from participating in banking activities at FDIC insured institutions. Was the FDIC action lawful? [*Sunshine State Bank v. FDIC*, 783 F.2d 1580 (11th Cir. 1986)].

5. Amidst a deep recession, Gallagher Equipment Company needed to obtain additional capital to retool their outdated machinery. Gallagher negotiated a loan with The Bank of Logan on January 15 for $500,000. On January 15, the prime rate is 9 percent, and Logan promises to process the application within a month to enable Gallagher to obtain a favorable interest rate. The loan processing became delayed, however, and on February 17, the Federal Reserve Board caused interest rates to increase by one percent. When Logan granted the loan on February 22, the interest rate was 10 percent. Gallagher sues Logan for the costs of the extra point of interest. Can Gallagher succeed on this claim?

6. John Posey and Danny Watkins planned to open a sporting goods store and took out loans of $134,000 for this purpose. They claimed that a bank vice president promised them additional loans as necessary. The store never turned a profit, and the bank refused to make further loans. Posey and Watkins sued the bank alleging fraud and breach of contract due to the alleged promises to provide financing. After the store went bankrupt, they claimed that this was due to the bank's actions and sought damages accordingly. Should plaintiffs recover damages for the failure of their store? [*The Bank of Shaw v. Posey*, 573 So.2d 1355 (Miss. 1990].

Chapter Twelve

Unfair Competition

Key Background

The essential background for this chapter on the law of unfair competition is found in Chapter 7 of *West's Business Law, Seventh Edition,* and in Chapter 13 of *West's Legal Environment of Business, Third Edition.* Among the important concepts to remember from this chapter are:

- wrongful interference with a contractual relationship
- wrongful interference with a business relationship
- trademark infringement
- disparagement

The reader will also benefit from familiarity with the requirements of the Robinson-Patman Act, discussed in Chapter 47 of *West's Business Law, Seventh Edition,* and in Chapter 26 of *West's Legal Environment of Business, Third Edition.*

* * *

Capitalism relies on competition to function properly and efficiently. Such competition may often be fierce, with competitors vigorously cutting prices to capture a larger market share. Economic theory generally suggests that the fiercer the competition, the better the system works. Some particularly fierce types of competition, however, are considered to be unfair. The law prohibits certain defined types of unfair competition.

There is no clear-cut test for what makes competition unfair. Certain categories of actions, though, are clearly illegal. The unfair trade practices discussed in this chapter include intentional interference with contracts or business expectations, trade disparagement, trademark infringement, and predatory pricing under antitrust law.

Wrongful Interference with Business

It may be unlawful for a company to interfere with the business relations of another business, especially a competitor. The relevant tort claims are wrongful interference with contractual relations and wrongful interference with business expectation.

Suppose that Cherno and Flood are competing to obtain a government contract to produce armored vehicles. To compete for the contract, Cherno requires electronic equipment produced by Shriver, and Cherno contracts to obtain the equipment. Then Flood pays Shriver to break the contract with Cherno, in order to get the government contract for itself. Flood has wrongfully interfered with the Cherno/Shriver contract and is liable for the tort of intentional interference with contract.

The tort of intentional interference with a contract has three essential elements:

193

1. Plaintiff has a valid contract with another party.

2. Defendant knows that this contract exists.

3. Defendant acts intentionally to cause the third party to breach the contract with plaintiff in order to advance the defendant's own economic interests or with some other wrongful purpose.

The first requirement is that an actual contract exist before a party may be liable for interference. If the underlying contract is void for *illegality,* there can be no liability for inducing its breach. A defendant may be liable, however, for interfering with a contract that is *unenforceable.* For example, an oral contract for land will not be enforceable due to the Statute of Frauds, which requires a writing. Wrongfully interfering with such an unenforceable oral contract, however, will expose a party to liability.

The second requirement, that the defendant be aware of the contract, is necessary because this is an *intentional* tort. If a defendant is unaware of the contract, it will not be liable. It is not necessary for a plaintiff to prove that a defendant knew all the details of the contract, however. The plaintiff need only prove that the defendant was aware of facts that should put it on notice of the presence of a contract.

Under the third requirement, that the defendant intentionally induce the breach, the plaintiff need not prove that the defendant acted with **malice** toward the plaintiff. The plaintiff must show self-interest or some improper motive or methods, however. The plaintiff also must show that the defendant *caused* the breach of contract.

Consider the following scenario. Michael Nassau has a contract to purchase all the shares of Acomp, Inc., for $15 per share. The chief financial officer of Acomp then approaches Anna Bayardo and asks her to pay $18/share. Anna agrees and acquires Acomp. Michael does not have a good case against Anna because (a) she was unaware of the Nassau/Acomp contract and (b) she did not induce the breach of contract but merely accepted an offer from Acomp.

A company may be liable for intentional interference with contracts even if the actions that it takes are within its legal rights. For example, one company owned a quarry that had only a single access road to market. A railroad company often blocked this access road and prevented the quarry operator from delivering his product on time. Although the railroad had a perfect legal right to park its cars anywhere on its track, a court found the railroad company liable for intentional interference with contract. The court found that the railroad's actions in blocking the road were malicious and had no valid business purpose.[1]

Businesses are increasingly bringing actions for intentional interference with contracts. Not all interferences with contractual relationships are wrongful, however. Some persons have a privilege to interfere with contracts. Corporate officers are generally privileged to cause their company to breach a contract. This is sometimes called the **manager's privilege.**

Manager's privilege means that an officer can lawfully breach a contract, if to do so is in the best interest of the employing company. Suppose that the Glaser Company has a contract to buy a tractor manufacturing plant from Salbu, Inc., for $5 million. Ms. Winslett, a financial officer of Glaser, does some research and discovers that the manufacturing plant is full of hazardous wastes and is worthless. She persuades Glaser to breach the contract. Winslett will not be liable to Salbu, Inc., for intentional interference with contractual relations. Glaser may still be liable to Salbu, however, for breach of contract.

The manager's privilege is not absolute. A manager is only privileged to induce a breach of contract when the manager is acting for the best interests of the employing company. If the manager is acting out of self-interest, he or she can still be liable for intentional interference with contract.

In one recent case, a corporate employee was fired and sued two vice presidents of the company. He alleged that they had him fired because his success was a threat to their position. The court found that the employee had stated a valid claim, because the vice presidents' alleged actions were entirely selfish and not motivated by the general interest of the corporation.[2]

Another important defense is **fair competition**. Some acts may induce a breach of contract, yet be perfectly proper. For example, low prices or effective advertising may attract customers away from competitors. These acts, however, are considered fair competition and are therefore lawful.

---

[1] *St. Louis S.F.R. Co. v. Wade*, 607 F.2d 126 (5th Cir. 1979).

[2] *Presto v. Sequoia Systems*, 633 F.Supp. 1117 (D. Mass.

Although a valid, underlying contract is necessary for the tort of wrongful interference with contract, a business could sue for wrongful interference with business expectations, even in the absence of a contract. While a contract is not essential for this tort, there must be some reasonable certainty of business for a defendant to be liable. A plaintiff has the burden to prove a reasonable probability that, but for the wrongful interference, the business relationship would have been realized. Plaintiff need not prove a certainty of such business, however.

Interference with business expectations is also an intentional tort. Consequently, the plaintiff must show that the defendant had knowledge of the plaintiff's business expectancy. A plaintiff also must show that the defendant intentionally interfered with the business expectancy.

The following case shows the facts that give rise to a claim of wrongful interference with business expectancy and the standards applied by courts.

Case 12.1
Leigh Furniture & Carpet Co. v. Isom
Supreme Court of Utah, 1982
657 P.2d 293

Background and Facts *The owner of Leigh Furniture agreed to sell his furniture business to Richard Isom. Leigh also owned the building where the furniture store was located and agreed to provide Isom with a ten-year lease on the first floor store and an option to buy the entire building, once Isom finished paying for the business. Sometime thereafter, Leigh wanted to sell the entire building but was unable to do so because of Isom's lease. Leigh and his wife began making demands on Isom, repeatedly visited the store, disrupted operations, and filed lawsuits against Isom. Isom sought to take on a partner and pay off the purchase price to Leigh, but Leigh refused to approve the partner or accept the purchase price.*

Isom filed a counterclaim in one of Leigh's lawsuits, claiming intentional interference with contract and business expectancy. Soon thereafter, Isom went bankrupt and claimed that this was due to Leigh's harassment. A jury ruled for Isom and awarded him compensatory and punitive damages. Leigh appealed.

OAKS, Justice.

* * * *

There was ample evidence that Isom had business relationships with various customers, suppliers, and potential business associates, and that Leigh, the former owner of the business, understood the value of those relationships. There was also substantial competent evidence that the Corporation, through Leigh, his wife, and his bookkeeper, intentionally interfered with and caused a termination of some of those relationships (actual or potential). Their frequent visits to Isom's store during business hours to confront him, question him, and make demands and inquiries regarding the manner in which he was conducting his business repeatedly interrupted sales activities, caused his customers to comment and complain, and more than once caused a customer to leave the store. Driving away an individual's existing or potential customers is the archetypical injury this cause of action was devised to remedy.

Other actions by which the Leigh Corporation imposed heavy demands on Isom's time and financial resources to the detriment of his ability to attract and retain customers and conduct the other activities of his business included: numerous letters of complaint, Leigh's demand for an audit of Isom's books and inventory during the busy holiday season, his continued threats to cancel the contract and sell the building and business to another buyer, his refusal to pay the contracted share of the heating bills or the cost of repairing the furnace and the store's broken window, his refusal of the tendered payment of the balance due under the contract, and his suit for repossession, termination, and injunction. Leigh's refusals also prevented Isom from consummating potentially advantageous business associations with Hunter, with Talbot, and finally with Applegate, all experienced retailers able to contribute expertise and additional capital to Isom's business.

Taken in isolation, each of the foregoing interferences with Isom's business might be justified as an overly zealous attempt to protect the Corporation's interests under its contract of sale. As such, none would establish the intentional interference element of this tort, though some might give rise to a cause of action for breach of specific provisions in the contract or of the duty of good faith performance which inheres in every contractual relation. Even in small groups, these acts might be explained as merely instances of aggressive or abrasive — though not illegal or tortious — tactics, excesses that occur in contractual and commercial relationships. But in total and in cumulative effect, as a course of action extending over a period of three and one-half years and culminating in the failure of Isom's business, the Leigh Corporation's acts cross the threshold beyond what is incidental and justifiable to what is tortious. The Corporation's acts provide sufficient evidence to establish two of the elements in the definition of this tort: an intentional interference with present or prospective economic relations that caused injury to the plaintiff.

Decision and Remedy *The court affirmed the jury verdict for Isom.*

Courts often focus on the existence of improper motives of business methods in claims for wrongful interference with business expectations. When one business defendant acts with a malicious purpose—only to destroy another business—courts will find the defendant liable. Similarly, the use of force or threats to scare off potential customers of a rival is considered wrongful.

For example, Sportsmen's Boating Corporation ran a fishing charter, called the Mijoy. For potential customers to reach the Mijoy, they had to pass by the dock of a competing charter, called the Blackhawk. The Blackhawk's employees would direct the Mijoy's prospective customers to their own boat and would falsely state that the Mijoy was full that day or was not sailing. A court found that the Blackhawk's owners were liable for wrongful interference with a business expectancy.[3]

As a general rule, a person will not be liable for negligent interference with business. Suppose that a rock group, called The Hot Shots, is to play a lucrative concert at a local opera house. Then a local citizen, Janet Claire, negligently starts a fire that burns down the opera house. She will not be liable to The Hot Shots for the concert's cancellation (though, of course, she may be liable for damages to the opera house).

---

[3] *Sportsmen's Boating Corporation v. Hensley,* 474 A.2d 780 (Conn. 1984).

Trademark Infringement

A great deal of modern litigation involves the alleged infringement of a company's **trademark**. A legally valid trademark is protected from copying by competitors. The courts also protect "trade dress," which is the distinctive visual appearance of a product. For example, a new soft drink business could not sell its product in a can that used Coca-Cola's distinctive colors and pattern and certainly could not call the product "Coke." Traditional common law protected trademarks, and Congress passed the Lanham Act to provide statutory protection.

The first essential requirement in a trademark action is that the plaintiff possess a **valid trademark**. Some product names cannot be used as valid trademarks, often because they are generic. A **generic trademark** is one that identifies the type of product rather than the producer. Thus, a company cannot trademark "Shampoo" brand shampoo. Miller Brewing was not allowed to trademark "light" or "lite" for their low-calorie beer, because the word simply described the color and other characteristics of the beer.[4]

Even a perfectly good trademark can become generic over time. Long ago, the name aspirin was a defensible trademark for a pain reliever. People began using the name aspirin, however, for any brand of this particular type of pain reliever. The name aspirin became generic and today any company can market this type of pain reliever and call its product aspirin. Loss of a trademark in this way is called "genericide." The trademark "thermos" also became generic for an insulated bottle product.[5]

Another requirement for a valid trademark is that it not be misleading. Suppose that a company markets a perfume that it calls "Maid in Paris." If the perfume did not come from Paris, this title would be unprotected in trademark. Seat covers made from manmade artificial components could not obtain a valid trademark in the term "Love Lamb" seat covers. "Durango" tobacco was not protected in trademark because it did not come from the tobacco-producing region of Durango in Mexico.

To be a valid trademark, a mark must be distinctive and not misleading. The most distinctive marks are called "fanciful." These trademarks are often made-up words and have no innate connection to the product. For example, "Kodak" is a fanciful name for cameras and film, because nothing about the word Kodak suggests a connection with those products.

Another category of protected trademarks are those that are "suggestive." These **suggestive trademarks** suggest some of the characteristics of the product. For example, "Coppertone" suntan lotion suggests the benefit of the product. The same would be true of "Penguin" brand refrigerators.

The most difficult area of trademark protection involves "descriptive" marks. This is a name that merely describes the product sold. For example, "Chap Stik" lip balm simply describes a stick for chapped lips. "Newsweek" describes a weekly newsmagazine. Descriptive marks can receive trademark protection but not as easily as for fanciful or suggestive marks. The concern is that descriptive marks can unfairly restrict a competitor's ability to name its product.

A similar analysis applies to trade dress. One cannot get protection in a basic or functional shape, such as a cylinder. Unusual shapes of packaging may be protected. The distinctive bottle of "Pinch" brand Scotch was held to be protectable in trademark. Similarly, in most cases a company cannot get trademark protection in a color. Nutrasweet recently tried to prevent other artificial sweeteners from using a blue package, but lost. Distinctive combinations and designs of colors, though, are certainly protected.

To help ensure that a trademark is protected, a company can register a mark with the U.S. Patent and Trademark Office. Registration is not required —an unregistered trademark is protected to the extent that it was actually used. Registration has some important benefits, though. First, registration protects the mark throughout the entire United States rather than just the geographic region of use. Second, after a mark has been registered for five years, its validity cannot be challenged.

The government will grant a registration in a trademark if it is considered distinctive, not misleading, and not confusingly similar to trademarks that were previously registered. Competitors may oppose issuance of the registration. A registration lasts for ten years and may be renewed by the user.

---

[4] *Miller Brewing Co. v. G. Heileman Brewing Co., Inc.*, 561 F.2d 75 (7th Cir. 1977).

[5] *King-Seeley Thermos Co. v. Aladdin Industries, Inc.*, 321 F.2d 577 (2d Cir. 1963).

If a trademark is registered by the government, it is presumptively valid. Until five years have elapsed, the validity of the trademark may be challenged by a competitor. Even a registered trademark will be unprotected if a court finds it to be generic or misleading.

Even an unregistered trademark is protected by the law, but only to the extent that it is used. Suppose a company markets "Texas Redhot Salsa" in the states of Texas and Louisiana. That company has a protected trademark in those two states, but another company could come along and sell "Texas Salsa" in the other 48 states. Also, unregistered trademarks do not become incontestable after five years.

Protection of a descriptive or unregistered trademark requires proof of **secondary meaning**. Secondary meaning is found when a trademark is associated with a particular maker's product, rather than all products of a type. "Newsweek" has a secondary meaning because it is associated with a particular magazine and not every weekly newsmagazine.

The presence of a secondary meaning is a factual question that may be resolved by surveys asking consumers whether they associate the descriptive trademark with a particular maker's product. Courts also consider other factors. These factors include the length and exclusivity of past use of the mark, the amount of advertising expenditures employed to create the secondary meaning, and unsolicited coverage of the trademark in the media.

Likelihood of Confusion If a company possesses a valid trademark, its competitors cannot use that mark. The company does not have an exclusive right to use the trademark, however. The second key requirement of a trademark infringement action is proof of a *likelihood of confusion*. Trademark law is primarily for the protection of consumers and only prohibits uses that are likely to confuse consumers about a product's origin.

Use by a direct competitor will generally create a likelihood of confusion. When another party takes your valid trademark exactly and puts it on identical goods sold in the same geographic area, proof of likelihood of confusion is easy. Most cases are not quite this easy.

Most competitors will not copy a trademark exactly but will modify it at least slightly. This is not a defense against trademark infringement, however. Marketing the "Cup-O'-Cola" could violate the "Coca-Cola" trademark because the two marks sound very much alike. In one case, a court found that "Tornado" wire fencing violated the established trademark in "Cyclone" wire fencing.[6]

In making the determination of infringement due to substantial similarity, courts consider the intent of the second user (called the "junior user"). Thus, if the mark is highly descriptive and the junior had good reason for use of a similar mark, the court will find no infringement. Suppose one company had a trademark in "Cool Menthol" cough lozenges. A junior user might be allowed the use of "Soothing Menthol-Flavored" cough lozenges.

On the other hand, if it appears that the junior user is purposefully trying to copy the senior user's mark, courts will find likelihood of infringement. If a company seeks to market "KooKoo Cola," courts are likely to conclude that the company's intent is to confuse customers and take them away from "Coca-Cola."

A junior user may be able to trade on another's mark if it is a parody. By its nature, a parody does not attempt to confuse the customer, as explained in the following decision.

---

[6] *Hancock v. American Steel & Wire Co.*, 203 F.2d 737 (C.C.P.A. 1953).

■ Case 12.2
Jordache Enterprises, Inc. v. Hogg Wyld, Ltd.
United States Court of Appeals,
Tenth Circuit, 1987
828 F.2d 1482

Background and Facts *Jordache is the fourth-largest blue jeans manufacturer in the United States and has a distinctive pocket design. The pocket has "jordache" written in white with a gold horse's head superimposed over the lettering. A New Mexico company, Hogg Wyld, Ltd., began marketing designer blue jeans in large sizes for bigger women. Their jeans were marketed under the name "Lardashe" and had their own distinctive pocket design.*

Their design had "Lardashe" written on the pocket and had a brightly colored pig's head and hooves peering over the pocket.

Jordache sued Hogg Wyld for trademark infringement. The district court, after a bench trial, found no likelihood of confusion between the two brands of jeans and therefore no trademark infringement. Jordache appealed.

TACHA, Circuit Judge.

* * * *

The similarity between the marks in appearance, pronunciation of the words used, translation of the designs used, and suggestion or meaning is the first factor to consider in determining whether there is a likelihood of confusion. The district court found that the Jordache mark and the Lardashe mark are not confusingly similar. Appellant argues that the court employed an improper legal construction of "suggestion" or "meaning" in reaching this result. Even if we were to reject this argument, appellant would have us hold the finding of no similarity to be clearly erroneous.

Trademarks may be confusingly similar if they suggest the same idea or meaning. For example, this court has held that a trademark consisting of an overflowing stein with the words "Brew Nuts" conveys the same meaning as a trademark consisting of the words "Beer Nuts." *Beer Nuts II,* 805 F.2d at 926. The district court in the present case found that "the two marks suggest dissimilar images or concepts."

* * * *

The "deliberate adoption of a similar mark may lead to an inference of intent to pass off goods as those of another which in turn supports a finding of likelihood of confusion." *Beer Nuts II,* 805 F.2d at 927. "The proper focus is whether defendant had the intent to derive benefit from the reputation or goodwill of plaintiff." *Sicilia Di R. Biebow & Co. v. Cox,* 732 F.2d 417, 431 (5th Cir. 1984); *accord* Restatement of Torts § 729 comment f at 594-95 (1938). A conscious choice of a mark similar to a mark already established in the marketplace usually supports a finding of a likelihood of confusion "because the court presumes that [the alleged infringer] 'can accomplish his purpose: that is, that the public will be deceived.'" *Beer Nuts I,* 711 F.2d at 941 (quoting *AMF Inc. v. Sleekcraft Boats,* 599 F.2d 341, 354 (9th Cir.1979)).

Given the unlimited number of possible names and symbols that could serve as a trademark, it is understandable that a court generally presumes one who chooses a mark similar to an existing mark intends to confuse the public. However, where a party chooses a mark as a parody of an existing mark, the intent is not necessarily to confuse the public but rather to amuse.

Decision and Remedy *The court affirmed the district court's finding of no likelihood of confusion and therefore no trademark infringement.*

Noncompeting Goods Another common problem involves noncompeting goods. Suppose that a company begins selling "Kodak" toothpaste. There is no likelihood of confusion among customers in this case. Consumers will not confuse toothpaste with cameras. This is why so many companies can have common names, such as "Acme."

A likelihood of confusion may arise when products are different, but similar. This is often called the **related products rule** and recognizes that a trademark holder might want to expand the use of its trademark into related areas. In a classic case, the "Yale" trademark for locks and other hardware was unlawfully infringed by a junior user's attempt to market "Yale" flashlights and batteries.[7]

Several tests are used by the court to determine the likelihood of confusion. The court considers whether the "ordinary" consumer is likely to be confused but recognizes that purchasers of some products, such as very expensive products, are likely to be more "sophisticated" and are less subject to possible confusion.

Several other factors also are relevant to a finding of likelihood of confusion. These include the strength of the mark (its distinctiveness and fame in the market) and the relative good faith of the junior user. The owners of "Playboy" magazine were able to halt the use of "Playboy" to sell dune buggies, because a court found that the junior user wanted to trade on the magazine's goodwill to promote the sale of its dune buggies.

Courts also consider the degree of similarity (in appearance, sound, etc.) and a concept called "bridging the gap." **Bridging the gap** means the likelihood that a senior user would want to use its trademark to enter the product market of the junior user. In the Yale locks case, it was likely that the senior user would want to bridge the gap and market its own Yale flashlights.

Trademarks are generally unprotected from parodies. As a result, a company might print up a satirical newspaper called the "Off the Wall Street Journal." This parody would be legal under trademark law.

Abandonment A trademark, even a registered one, may be lost through nonuse. If the owner does not use the trademark in selling goods, it will be deemed abandoned. Under the Lanham Act, nonuse for two years is considered evidence of abandonment that enables others to use the trademark for their own goods.

Antidilution Statutes

Trademark law protects against consumer confusion about the source of goods but offers no protection against noncompeting uses. Antidilution laws provide some protection against such copying. Most states have antidilution laws, and in 1996, Congress passed the Federal Trademark Dilution Act.

Antidilution laws protect "famous" trademarks and may extend to famous trade dress, such as a uniquely shaped bottle. Antidilution laws do not require evidence of consumer confusion. They offer protection in the following circumstances:

1. When a use of another's trademark causes a loss of uniqueness or individuality

2. When a use of another's trademark tarnishes the reputation of that mark.

Consider a company with a unique trademark, such as Polaroid cameras. An antidilution law will protect Polaroid from noncompeting uses of its trademark. If an appliance repair service attempts to call itself Polaroid, the camera company may halt such use, which may hurt the individuality of the camera trademark or damage the reputation of the mark.

Antidilution statutes provide protection when a noncompeting product uses a prestigious trademark in a less-than-wholesome context. For example, a poster company copied the Coca-Cola design for a poster stating "Enjoy Cocaine." A court held that this use tarnished the Coca-Cola trademark and was illegal under the New York antidilution law.[8]

The antidilution laws also provide some protection against parodies of established trademarks. Parody is protected by First Amendment freedom of speech, however, and therefore may be allowed even when they could dilute or tarnish a trademark, as illustrated by the following decision.

---

[7] *Yale Electric Corp. v. Robertson*, 26 F.2d 972 (2d Cir. 1928).

[8] *Coca-Cola Co. v. Gemini Rising, Inc.*, 346 F.Supp. 1183 (E.D.N.Y. 1972).

Case 12.3
L. L. Bean, Inc. v. Drake Publishers, Inc.
United States Court of Appeals, First Circuit, 1987
811 F.2d 26

Background and Facts *L. L. Bean, Inc., is the trademark for that company's catalog and other sales of clothing products. Drake Publishers, which owns High Society magazine, published a parody of the catalog in its October 1984 issue. This involved a two-page article called "L. L. Bean's Back-To-School-Sex-Catalog" and featured pictures of nude models in sexually explicit positions using products "that were described in a crudely humorous fashion."*

L. L. Bean sued under the Maine antidilution statute, among other claims. The district court granted Bean summary judgment on the antidilution claim, because the catalog had tarnished the company's reputation. The court entered an injunction prohibiting further publication or distribution of the Sex Catalog parody. Drake Publishers appealed.

BOWNES, Circuit Judge.

* * * *

Parody is a humorous form of social commentary and literary criticism that dates back as far as Greek antiquity. "The rhapsodists who strolled from town to town to chant the poems of Homer," wrote Issac D'Israeli, "were immediately followed by another set of strollers — buffoons who made the audiences merry by the burlesque turn which they gave to the solemn strains." I. D'Israeli, *"Curiosities of Literature, quoted in* D. MacDonald, *Parodies: An Anthology from Chaucer to Beerbohm-and After* 562 (1960). The Oxford English Dictionary defines parody as "[a] composition in which the characteristic turns of thought and phrase of an author are mimicked to appear ridiculous, especially by applying them to ludicrously inappropriate subjects." Chaucer, Shakespeare, Pope, Voltaire, Fielding, Hemingway and Faulkner are among the myriad of authors who have written parodies. Since parody seeks to ridicule sacred verities and prevailing mores, it inevitably offends others, as evinced by the shock which Chaucer's *Canterbury Tales* and Voltaire's *Candide* provoked among their contemporaries.

* * * *

***the dilution injury stems from an unauthorized effort to market incompatible products or services by trading on another's trademark. The Constitution is not offended when the antidilution statute is applied to prevent a defendant from using a trademark without permission in order to merchandise dissimilar products or services. Any residual effect on first amendment freedoms should be balanced against the need to fulfill the legitimate purpose of the antidilution statute. See *Friedman v. Rogers,* 440 U.S. 1, 15-16, 99 S.Ct. 887, 896-897, 59 L.Ed.2d 100 (1979). The law of trademark dilution has developed to combat an unauthorized and harmful appropriation of a trademark by another for the purpose of identifying, manufacturing, merchandising or promoting dissimilar products or services. The harm occurs when a trademark's identity and integrity—its capacity to command respect in the market—is undermined due to its inappropriate and unauthorized use by other market actors. When presented with such circumstances, courts have found that trademark owners have suffered harm despite the fact that redressing such harm entailed some residual impact on the rights of expression of commercial actors. See, *e.g., Dallas Cowboys Cheerleaders v. Pussycat Cinema, Ltd.,* 604 F.2d 200 (plaintiff's mark damaged by unauthorized use in content and promotion of a pornographic film); *Chemical Corp. of America v. Anheuser-Busch, Inc.*, 306 F.2d 433 (5th Cir. 1962), *cert. denied*, 372 U.S. 965, 83 S.Ct. 1089, 10 L.Ed.2d 129 (1963) (floor wax and insecticide maker's slogan, "Where there's life, there's bugs," harmed strength of defendant's slogan, "Where there's life, there's Bud"); *Original Appalachian Artworks, Inc. v. Topps Chewing Gum*, 642 F.Supp. 1031 (N.D.Ga.1986) (merchandiser of "Garbage Pail Kids" stickers and products injured owner of Cabbage Patch Kids mark); *D.C. Comics, Inc. v. Unlimited Monkey Business*, 598 F.Supp. 110 (N.D.Ga. 1984) (holder of Superman and Wonder Woman trademarks damaged by unauthorized use of marks by singing telegram franchisor); *General Electric Co. v. Alumpa Coal Co.*, 205 U.S.P.Q. (BNA) 1036 (D.Mass.1979) ("Genital Electric" monogram on underpants and T-shirts harmful to plaintiff's trademark); *Gucci Shops, Inc. v. R.H. Macy & Co.*, 446 F.Supp. 838 (S.D.N.Y.1977)(defendant's diaper bag labelled "Gucchi Goo" held to injure Gucci's mark); *Coca-Cola Co. v. Gemini Rising, Inc.*, 346 F.Supp. 1183 (E.D.N.Y.1972) (enjoining the merchandise of "Enjoy Cocaine" posters bearing logo similar to plaintiff's mark).

While the cases cited above might appear at first glance to be factually analogous to the instant one, they are distinguishable for two reasons. First, they all involved unauthorized commercial uses of another's trademark. Second, none of those cases involved a defendant using a plaintiff's trademark as a vehicle for an editorial or artistic parody. In contrast to the cases cited, the instant defendant used plaintiff's mark solely for noncommercial purposes. Appellant's parody constitutes an editorial or artistic, rather than a commercial, use of plaintiff's mark. The article was labelled as "humor" and "parody" in the magazine's table of contents section, it took up two pages in a one-hundred-page issue; neither the article nor appellant's trademark was featured on the front or back cover of the magazine. Drake did not use Bean's mark to identify or promote goods or services to consumers; it never intended to market the "products" dislayed in the parody.

Decision and Remedy *The court reversed the summary judgment for Bean and remanded the case for district court implementation of the order.*

Disparagement

Disparagement is a traditional common law tort involving false statements about a business. Disparagement is similar to defamation of a person's reputation, but disparagement involves a business's reputation or that of its products. Disparagement involves (i) a disparaging statement, (ii) that is false, (iii) that was made with an intent to harm the plaintiff's business; and (iv) causes special damages.

Unlawful disparagement may be done by competitors. Suppose one fast food restaurant chain publishes advertisements stating that a competing chain uses horse meat in its hamburgers. Assuming the claim is untrue, this would be disparagement.

Noncompetitors, such as consumers, may also be liable for disparagement. In a classic case, the entertainer Arthur Godfrey stated that the producers of a cheap ukulele that he disliked "should be jailed." The court ruled that this statement qualified as actionable disparagement.[9]

Some disparaging statements may be protected by the freedom of speech of the First Amendment. A critical movie review, for example, will not be actionable disparagement. In a recent case, the magazine *Consumer Reports* criticized the quality of a company's audio speakers. The company sued for disparagement but lost, because the criticism was protected by the First Amendment.[10]

---

[9] *The Harmonica Man, Inc. v. Godfrey*, 102 N.Y.S.2d 251 (1951).

[10] *Bose Corp. v. Consumers Union of U.S., Inc.*, 466 U.S. 485 (1984).

To recover for disparagement, a plaintiff must show "special damages" in the form of monetary losses resulting from the disparaging comments. Courts generally require a plaintiff to prove a specific amount of sales lost due to the disparagement. This is often difficult. A plaintiff also may obtain an injunction ordering the defendant to cease its disparagement.

In 1989, Congress revised the Lanham Act to provide federal statutory protection from disparagement. The new law prohibits any misrepresentations about the "nature, characteristics, qualities" of "goods, services or commercial activities" in "commercial advertising or promotion."[11] This law does not appear to require proof of special damages or even a defendant's knowledge of falsity.

Under both common law and the revised Lanham Act, a statement must be false to constitute disparagement. A true statement of fact, or an opinion, is thus legal and not disparagement.

▬ Robinson-Patman Act

The Robinson-Patman Act addresses **price discrimination**—in which one company sells an identical product at different prices to different customers. Suppose Ranch Produce sold 100 bushels of peaches to May Grocery for $2000. On the same day, in the same city, Ranch sold 100 bushels of identical quality peaches to June Grocery for $1500. This is price discrimination and may be considered a form of unfair competition. The Robinson-Patman Act does not prohibit all price discrimination, but only when the practice injures competition.

Section 2(a)

The basic case of illegal price discrimination under section 2(a) of the Robinson-Patman Act has the following required elements:

1. A person engaged in interstate commerce.
2. Discriminated in price between different purchasers.
3. For commodities of like grade and quality.
4. The effect was substantially to lessen competition.

---

[11] 15 U.S.C. Sec. 1125(a).

The first requirement, of **interstate commerce**, will almost always be met. The second requirement, of price discrimination, is also quite straightforward. This simply requires proof of differing purchase prices between two purchasers. The Act does require a purchase and does not apply to rentals.

The third requirement, that the commodities be of like grade and quality, is more complex. The Act is limited to commodities, or tangible objects, and is generally inapplicable to services. Defining "like grade and quality" can sometimes be difficult. What if identical goods are sold in different packages under different brand names? The Supreme Court has held that such goods are of "like grade and quality" and satisfy the third test.

Most Robinson-Patman Act litigation deals with the fourth requirement, that the price discrimination must substantially lessen competition. One form of lessened competition is in **primary line competition**, between the seller and his competitors.

Price discrimination could lessen primary line competition in the following way. Suppose that Argon computers has a large percentage of the nation's market for large computers. Argon sells its computers for $12,000. A small Florida company, named Xenon, begins selling competing large computers in Florida for $11,000. Argon then sells its large computers in Florida for only $9000 and thereby drives Xenon out of business. This is **predatory pricing** which constitutes an injury to primary line competition.

Price discrimination also is illegal if it lessens **secondary line competition**. This is competition among the buyers of the product. Suppose Argon sells its large computers to ITT Systems for $11,000 and sells the same computers to ITT's competitor, ABS Computing, for $13,000. The price difference may lessen the ability of ABS Computing to compete with ITT. If so, the price discrimination would illegally lessen secondary line competition.

A substantial lessening of competition is necessary for price discrimination to be illegal under the Robinson-Patman Act. Much price discrimination (e.g., different fares for airline seats) does not substantially lessen competition in goods and is therefore legal.

The Supreme Court has created a standard that makes it difficult to prevail under the Robinson-Patman Act, as illustrated in the following decision.

Case 12.4
Brooke Group Ltd. v. Brown & Williamson Tobacco Corporation
Supreme Court of the United States, 1993
113 S.Ct. 2578

Background and Facts *In 1980, the Brooke Group (then called Liggett) pioneered the economy segment of the cigarette market with "black and white" generic cigarettes. By 1984, the generics constituted 4% of domestic cigarette sales, and Liggett held 97% of this share. Another large producer, Brown & Williamson, introduced its own black and white cigarette in that year. Brown & Williamson matched Liggett's prices and beat them by offering greater volume discounts and rebates. Liggett responded by increasing its own rebates. On five occasions, Liggett sought to beat the rebates offered by Brown & Williamson, and on each occasion Brown & Williamson beat Liggett's cuts. By the end of this series, Liggett maintains that Brown & Williamson was selling its cigarettes at a loss. Liggett filed a complaint under section 2(a) of the Robinson-Patman Act, alleging predatory pricing. A jury awarded Liggett $49.6 million in damages, but the district court overruled the jury and granted judgment notwithstanding the verdict. The Fourth Circuit Court of Appeals affirmed, and Liggett appealed to the Supreme Court.*

KENNEDY, Justice.

* * * *

Liggett contends that Brown & Williamson's discriminatory volume rebates to wholesalers threatened substantial competitive injury by furthering a predatory pricing scheme designed to purge competition from the economy segment of the cigarette market. This type of injury, which harms direct competitors of the discriminating seller, is known as primary-line injury.

* * * *

Even an act of pure malice by one business competitor against another does not, without more, state a claim under the federal antitrust laws; those laws do not create a federal law of unfair competition or "purport to afford remedies for all torts committed by or against persons engaged in interstate commerce."

* * * *

Evidence of below-cost pricing is not alone sufficient to permit an inference of probable recoupment and injury to competition. Determining whether recoupment of predatory losses is likely requires an estimate of the cost of the alleged predation and a close analysis of both the scheme alleged by the plaintiff and the structure and conditions of the relevant market. * * * In certain situations—for example, where the market is highly diffuse and competitive, or where new entry is easy, or the defendant lacks adequate capacity to absorb the market shares of his rivals and cannot quickly create or purchase new capacity—summary disposition of the case is appropriate.

Decision and Remedy *The court affirmed the judgment in favor of Brown & Williamson.*

Defenses

The Robinson-Patman Act contains important defenses to price discrimination claims under section 2(a). The most important defenses are cost justification and meeting competition.

Cost justification enables Argon to sell at a lower price to Customer A than Customer B if the costs of selling to Customer A are correspondingly less than selling to Customer B. If Argon must bear higher shipping costs for Customer B, Argon may charge Customer A proportionally less to account for those costs. In a similar way, quantity discounts may be justified by lower production costs for large orders.

The meeting competition defense enables a seller to reduce prices selectively to meet lower prices by competitors. In a previous example, Argon sold its computers nationwide for $12,000, and Xenon entered the market in Florida selling a comparable computer for $11,000. The meeting competition defense would enable Argon to lower its prices in Florida to $11,000 to meet the Xenon price. In such a case, Argon may only meet the competitor's price, however, and may not offer a lower price.

Sections 2(d) and 2(e)

Sections 2(d) and 2(e) of the Robinson-Patman Act address a different form of discrimination among customers. These sections prohibit a seller from offering promotional payments, services or facilities to one buyer, without offering comparable opportunities to other competing buyers. The restriction only applies to customers in competition. Significantly, these sections do not require proof of injury to competition, as under section 2(a).

Some examples of illegal promotional discrimination would be a company that grants credit card charge privileges to some but not all buyers, or a company that accepts the return of unsold merchandise from some but not all buyers. If a seller offers some favorable service to one buyer, it must make a similar service available to other competing buyers, on "proportionally equal" terms.

Suppose that Borax, Inc., manufactures and sells a brand of laundry detergent. In Denver, Borax detergent is sold by a chain of grocery stores and another chain of discount department stores. If Borax provides a special service or allowance to the grocery stores (e.g., coupon reimbursement), Borax must provide the same service on proportionately equal terms for the department stores.

The only affirmative defense under these sections is the meeting competition defense. The cost justification defense is not available. The "proportionally equal" language, however, will enable a seller to tailor the promotional services to the amount of goods purchased. Thus, if a seller provides a certain amount of free advertising for large buyers, the seller need not provide the same total amount of free advertising to smaller buyers.

State Laws

Every state now has a statute prohibiting deceptive trade practices, often called a "little FTC act." These laws were primarily designed to protect consumers, but most of these laws also permit businesses to recover damages from unlawful business practices. These laws generally prohibit companies from employing unfair business practices.

The state deceptive trade practices acts vary but have certain common elements. First, the definition of "unfair" or "deceptive" conduct proscribed by the laws is generally broad. Therefore, the acts cover many business torts, including interference with business expectations, predatory pricing, disparagement and fraud.

The state laws offer particular benefit to plaintiffs because they typically provide for supracompensatory damages. A successful plaintiff can thus recover two or three times its actual damages (called double or treble damages) under the deceptive trade practices legislation.

The state laws go beyond business torts and may even reach an "opportunistic" or "bad faith" breach of contract. An unfair breach of contract might involve a party's dishonest interpretation of a contract term or strategic refusal to perform the contract in an attempt to extract additional consideration from the other party.

In one modern case, a soft drink distributor had a dispute with its supplier, a bottling company. The distributor refused to pay over $60,000 that it owed until the bottler provided additional delivery service. A court held that this withholding of due payments was "a form of extortion" to force the bottler to deliver more product, when the bottler had no contractual obligation to do so. The court, therefore, found a violation of the deceptive trade practices act and granted the bottler triple damages of over $180,000, plus attorneys' fees.

Twenty-three states have statutes prohibiting predatory pricing by selling below cost. These laws go beyond the federal antitrust laws by striving to protect small local retailers threatened by national chains. In 1993, Wal-Mart Stores, Inc. was held liable for nearly $300,000 by an Arkansas court under that state's predatory pricing law.

Opportunistic Behavior and Business Transactions

The law of unfair competition reflects an attempt by government to prohibit certain unethical business practices. In this area, there is considerable overlap between legal requirements and ethical dictates. But is the law alone sufficient to uphold business ethics in competition? Some argue that the law has gone too far in promoting business ethics.

A key contemporary concern of both the law and ethics is "opportunistic" business behavior. Opportunism is "crafty" business behavior that uses every available tool to promote the self-interest of the business.

Consider the following example of opportunistic behavior. Plasco Company makes toys and other items out of plastics. Plasco is a major company that has good relations with the retail outlets that sell its products. Plasco has a long-standing relationship with Petrox Company to supply the raw plastics necessary to make Plasco's toys. Petrox is bound by contract to provide all Plasco's plastic requirements throughout 1990. In August 1990, Petrox refuses to supply more plastic to Plasco unless Plasco agrees to a 25 percent increase in price for the plastic.

The law would enable Plasco to sue Petrox for breach of contract. Such a lawsuit, however, would be costly and prolonged. Moreover, the lack of plastic could prevent Plasco from making toys for the Christmas season. This could poison Plasco's goodwill with retailers. Plasco may have no economically efficient alternative but to give in to Petrox's demand for a price increase.

To some, the demand by Petrox for a price increase was unfair and tantamount to blackmail. They would argue that Petrox did not use good faith in its business dealings. Reliance on suppliers' good faith is arguably critical to the effective functioning of the free market. Petrox clearly violated the principle of promise-keeping.

To others, including some economists, Petrox did nothing wrong. Petrox simply used its position in the marketplace to make a good deal. Under this view, Plasco has only itself to blame for its predicament, which resulted from *undue reliance* on a single supplier. The free market depends, to a degree at least, on each company's ability to look out for its own interests. Plasco is not a small uneducated business or consumer and should be expected to protect itself.

The choice between these views says much about one's perspective on business and free enterprise. But the choice is not always so clear-cut. Suppose that Petrox demanded the increase because its raw materials costs had risen unexpectedly and substantially. Without the increase, Petrox might have been required to sell at a loss or even go bankrupt. In such a case, would Plasco have been unethically "opportunistic" in insisting on the price set in the original contract?

The ethical issues in this case may not be easy. This makes it even more difficult for the law to define unfair competition. Some argue that the law should set a few clear-cut rules against fraud and leave the difficult cases for business ethics and the functioning of the market. Otherwise, lawsuits could be used opportunistically. But can we count on businesses to behave ethically in the absence of legal requirements?

International Perspectives

Trademark Protection and Grey Market Goods

The international law of trademarks is "territorial" in nature. This means that a registered trademark only protects a company in the country of registration. If Plasco uses or registers its name as a trademark in the United States, no other company can use the mark in this country. Some other company, however, could market Plasco products in the countries of South America, unless Plasco takes steps to register its trademark in those nations as well.

In addition, registering a trademark in the U.S. may not even provide exclusive control over the trademark in this country, due to grey market goods. The problem is illustrated by the following scenario. Vivimax produces cameras overseas. Americam pays for the exclusive right to market Vivimax cameras in the U.S. and obtains the U.S. trademark rights to Vivimax. Americam maintains a line of retail shops that sell Vivimax cameras. Then ImpoCam begins buying Vivimax cameras overseas, importing them to the U.S., and selling them in U.S. stores. This is known as the "grey market." These cameras are Vivimax-made and identical to the ones sold by Americam. The legal question is whether Americam can use its U.S. trademark rights in Vivimax to prevent ImpoCam from selling Vivimax goods in this country.

The legal rights of a United States trademark holder against grey market importers is of great significance. Studies suggest that one-third of all cameras sold in this country are grey market cameras. The grey market is also significant in other product lines and the total grey market sales may exceed $10 billion. Because of currency fluctuations, grey market importers may be able to sell the product for less than the U.S. distributor and trademark holder.

Section 526 of the Tariff Act of 1930 provides some protection to the U.S. trademark owner. This section enables the United States Customs Service to bar the importation of trademarked goods, unless the domestic trademark owner consents. The Customs Service regulations, though, permit third parties to import identically trademarked goods when "the foreign and domestic trademark or trade name owners are parent and subsidiary companies or are otherwise subject to common ownership or control."[12] Section 526 may therefore provide little protection to domestic subsidiaries

---
[12] 19 C.F.R. section 133.21(c)(2).

of foreign manufacturers. In addition, Customs Service enforcement of section 526 is short of perfect.

Section 526(c) provides a private right of action to United States trademark owners against grey market importers. The U.S. owner must prove that the grey market imports cause a likelihood of consumer confusion, however. Some courts have held that if the grey market goods are genuine (the same quality goods from the same manufacturer), there is no possibility of harmful consumer confusion. This interpretation seriously undermines protection for U.S. trademark owners.

Questions and Case Problems

1. A very widely known chef, Henri Panglod, fed up with life in the big city, signed a contract in October with a little restaurant in the suburbs called La Vie. La Vie was in the process of renovations and wouldn't be ready for business until April of the next year. In May (with construction still not complete at La Vie), La Vie's chief suburban competitor, The View, solicited Panglod, offering him twice the salary and a quiet apartment nearby. The chef agreed with The View and began cooking for that restaurant. La Vie sued The View, seeking the cost of finding a new chef and their lost profits from losing Panglod. Should La Vie win and be able to recover these damages?

2. A drug company, Ives Laboratories, manufactured the prescription drug cyclandate under the brand name "Cyclospasmol." The company's patent on this drug had expired. Another drug company, Darby Drug, manufactures a generic form of cyclandate and advertises that its drug is similar to Cyclospasmol. Ives produced its Cyclospasmol in red and blue capsules, which were associated with the drug by physicians. Darby Drug also used red and blue capsules for its new generic competitor. Ives sued for trademark infringement. Does Darby's packaging violate the trademark of Ives? [*Ives Laboratories, Inc. v. Darby Drug Co., Inc.,* 455 F.Supp. 939 (E.D.N.Y. 1978); 697 F.2d 291 (2d Cir. 1982)].

3. Warner Brothers produced a television series entitled the "Dukes of Hazard," which featured an automobile called the "General Lee." The car was orange and emblazoned with a confederate flag. Gay Toys manufactured a toy car patterned after the "General Lee." Warner Brothers sued Gay Toys for trademark infringement. Gay Toys defended that the design and appearance of the "General Lee" was functional and therefore unprotectible. Should Warner Brothers succeed against this defense? [*Warner Brothers, Inc. v. Gay Toys, Inc.,* 724 F.2d 327 (2d Cir. 1983)].

4. Benzo gasoline was a company's special product containing a coal derivative. Another company, which was a competitor and sold White Rose gasoline, published a pamphlet stating that Benzo gasoline was harmful to automobiles and urged its readers to buy White Rose, "an honestly made gasoline." The only service station that marketed Benzo gasoline sued the producers of White Rose for disparagement. Should Benzo be able to recover on this claim? [*National Refining Co. v. Benzo Gas Motor Fuel Co.,* 20 F.2d 763, *cert. denied,* 275 U.S. 570 (1927).

5. Borden Co. produced milk under both its own name brand and under other private labels. Milk sold under the Borden label was priced higher than milk sold under the other private labels. The Federal Trade Commission claimed that all the milk produced by Borden was the same, so the different prices constituted illegal price discrimination under the Robinson-Patman Act. Are the milk products of "like grade and quality" so that the price differential would violate the Robinson-Patman Act? [*FTC v. Borden Co.,* 383 U.S. 637 (1966)].

6. Emerson Tiller was a senior vice president of the Security State Bank, and Jay Koehler was one of his management employees with an at will employment contract. Both became smitten with India Prentice, recently hired as a teller. Jealous of the amount of time that Jay was spending with India, Emerson fired Jay from his position at the bank. Jay sues Emerson for wrongful interference with contract. Who should win and why?

Chapter Thirteen

Advertising Law

Key Background

The essential background for this chapter on advertising law is found in Chapter 45 of *West's Business Law, Seventh Edition,* and Chapter 23 of *West's Legal Environment of Business, Third Edition.* These chapters cover consumer protection law. Among the important points to remember from this chapter are:

- determination of "unfair or deceptive acts"
- remedies for deceptive advertising
- Federal Trade Commission enforcement procedures

* * *

Virtually every major company in the United States advertises its goods or services. Moreover, advertising itself is big business. Total billings of advertising agencies in the United States are approximately $50 billion. This sum does not even include the amount spent on advertising by companies that do their own advertising and do not employ specialized agencies.

This chapter focuses on the legal issues dealing with advertising itself. Specifically, the chapter discusses First Amendment rights of advertisers, rules prohibiting deceptive advertising, regulation of comparative advertising, and advertising misappropriation claims. Other advertising issues are discussed in chapters on unfair competition (trademark protection, disparagement) and communication laws (tort liability).

First Amendment Rights of Advertisers

The First Amendment to the U.S. Constitution guarantees free speech. For many years, advertising was considered "commercial speech" and was unprotected by the First Amendment's guarantee of freedom of speech. The Supreme Court began to extend some First Amendment protection to advertising in the 1960s and in 1976 the court held that a purely commercial advertisement had some First Amendment protection from government regulation.

The Court first recognized the First Amendment protection for commercial speech in *Virginia State Board of Pharmacy v. Virginia Citizens Consumer Council.*[1] Virginia had a law that prohibited pharmacists from advertising the prices of prescription drugs for sale. The Supreme Court held that this law was an unconstitutional violation of the First Amendment.

The Court protected commercial speech under the First Amendment in the interest of consumers. The rights of the speaker, in this case an advertiser, were not so important as the interest of the listener,

---
[1] 425 U.S. 748 (1976).

or consumer. The Court held that consumers had a strong interest in price comparisons in order to save money. The consumers' interest justified First Amendment protection for advertisements.

While advertising has some protection under the First Amendment, the free speech rights of advertisers are not as great as those of political speakers, for example. Government may constitutionally prevent false or misleading advertisements. The Supreme Court also has held that Puerto Rico could prohibit advertisements for casino gambling on the grounds that such ads could increase crime and disrupt the island's moral and cultural patterns.[2] The government could not regulate political speakers on these grounds.

Because the government has greater flexibility in regulating commercial speech, it is necessary to define commercial speech and distinguish it from more protected forms of speech. The distinction is especially difficult for "advertorials," which are paid advertisements that take an editorial stand on significant public issues.

In one case, the R.J. Reynolds Tobacco Company took out advertorials claiming that cigarettes were not proven to cause heart disease. The Federal Trade Commission staff tried to halt the Reynolds ads as false and misleading, but Reynolds claimed that the advertorials were political speech protected by the First Amendment.

The Supreme Court has given guidance regarding what speech may be regulated as commercial. Commercial speech usually has the following three characteristics: (a) it is in the form of a paid advertisement; (b) it refers to a specific product; and (c) it is motivated by economic gain. Although the Reynolds ad did not refer to a specific product, the Commission held that it was commercial speech, and Reynolds eventually reached a settlement agreeing not to make such claims in "advertorials."

Commercial speech that is false or misleading has no First Amendment protection. Truthful advertising, however, is protected speech but may still be regulated if necessary. In order to regulate commercial speech, the government must prove three elements:

1. The government must have a substantial legitimate interest that it is protecting.

2. The restriction of speech must directly advance the government interest.

3. The restriction of speech must be reasonably related to achieving the government interest.

On the first test, the courts have recognized many legitimate government interests in restricting speech as indicated by the Puerto Rico case discussed above. On the second test, the government must show that its advertising restrictions will actually be effective in advancing the government's interest.

The third test requires that the government not restrict advertising more than necessary. Some states have sought to prohibit advertising by lawyers, out of concern that lawyer advertising could deceive potential clients. Courts have held that an absolute prohibition on lawyer advertising is unconstitutional. States can adopt more limited regulation of lawyer advertising in order to prevent deception.

The application of these tests to a government regulation of commercial speech is illustrated in the following case.

---

[2] *Posadas de Puerto Rico Associates v. Tourism Company of Puerto Rico,* 106 S. Ct. 2968 (1986).

■ Case 13.1
National Funeral Services, Inc. v. Rockefeller
United States Court of Appeals, Fourth Circuit, 1989
870 F.2d 136

Background and Facts West Virginia passed a law regulating "pre-need funeral contracts," those sold for persons still living. The law required all sellers of such services be licensed by the state. The law also prohibited "in-person and telephonic solicitation of prospective purchasers in nursing homes, hospitals, and private residences, as well as the solicitation of relatives of persons near death."

National Funeral Services, Inc. ("NFS") argued that the restrictions on solicitation were an unconstitutional interference *with its freedom of speech. A district court held that the law was constitutional and NFS appealed.*

KISER, District Judge, Sitting by Designation

* * * *

Turning to the facts of this case, the state has not contended that appellant's solicitations were in any way fraudulent or misleading. Therefore, I must conclude that appellant's speech is legitimate commercial speech, which is protected by the first amendment.

Likewise, I have no difficulty in concluding that the government interests furthered by these restrictions are substantial. The most obvious of these interests is the protection of consumers from overreaching and high pressure sales tactics of this most unique product. W.Va.Code § 47-14-10(e)(1983). Directly speaking, the subject of these contracts is funeral arrangement; indirectly speaking, their subject is death—the death of the buyer, or one close to him. This topic is obviously one charged with emotion and one fraught with the potential for overreaching by solicitors. In promulgating the funeral rule, FTC noted that the extremely sensitive nature of this subject in part necessitated its regulation.

* * * *

The next inquiry is whether this ban directly advances these interests. The potential for fraudulent overreaching in the sale of these contracts is at its greatest when the consumer is confronted by a salesman:

Unlike a public advertisement, which simply provides information and leaves the recipient free to act upon it or not, in-person solicitation may exert pressure and often demands an immediate response, without providing an opportunity for comparison or reflection. The aim and effort of in-person solicitation may be to provide a one-sided presentation and to encourage speedy and perhaps uninformed decision making...

* * * *

Unlike direct mail solicitations that can be readily distinguished and easily discarded, a recipient of telephone solicitation must answer the phone to determine who is calling, and must risk an uncomfortable confrontation to rid himself of the solicitor. Further, it is beyond dispute that this most sensitive product makes an uninvited telephone call even more upsetting, especially when it invades the privacy of the home. In the words of one commentator, "[t]he telephone is an instrument with a unique capacity to intrude. Note, *Give Me A Home Where No Salesmen Phone: Telephone Solicitation and the First Amendment,* 7 Hastings Const. L.Q. 129. Thus, like in-person solicitation, telemarketing poses a very real threat to the privacy of a consumer's home. Consequently, because I conclude that telemarketing is in many ways analogous to in-person solicitation, I believe that the state's prohibition of it furthers the state's interests.

* * * *

In making this determination, a court should view the anti-solicitation statute as a whole. West Virginia has demonstrated that two substantial interests underlie this statute, the protection of its people from fraud and the protection of its people's privacy. To further these interests, the legislature has restricted appellant's speech in a few special situations that it identified as particularly prone to these problems—when the consumer is in a hospital, in a nursing home, confronted by the death of a loved one, or in the privacy of his own home. *W.Va.Code,* § 47-14-10 (1983). Similarly, the legislature has prohibited only two limited forms of speech that it felt posed special threats to the state's interests—uninvited in-person solicitation and telemarketing. Out of this scheme, appellant challenges only the state's restraint on in-home solicitation. I find it to be constitutional.

Decision and Remedy *The court upheld the constitutionality of the West Virginia statute.*

In 1996, the Supreme Court confirmed its commitment to free speech protection in *44 Liquormart v. Rhode Island.*[3] Rhode Island law had prohibited vendors and the news media from publishing the price of alcoholic beverages, in advertisements or otherwise. The Court struck down the law, finding the state's interest in promoting "temperance" inadequate as a justification. There was no evidence that the law significantly affected alcohol consumption.

▬ Federal Trade Commission Regulation

In 1938, the FTC was given specific authority to regulate trade practices. The Commission's authority to control "unfair methods of competition" was soon used against deceptive advertising. Since that time, the FTC has adopted rules and undertaken enforcement actions against advertising that the Commission considered to be false or misleading.

Procedures

FTC enforcement begins with an investigation by the Commission's staff. If the FTC believes that advertising is deceptive, the staff draws up a complaint and tries to settle the dispute without a hearing. If settlement proves impossible, the FTC staff prosecutes its complaint in a hearing before an administrative law judge ("ALJ"). This hearing is much like a civil trial, but the ALJ is not a true judge but an employee of the FTC.

If there is a trial, and the advertiser wins the case before the ALJ, the matter is over—the FTC has no authority to appeal the decision. If the FTC wins the administrative hearing, the advertiser can appeal the decision to the Commission and a federal circuit court of appeals.

While deceptive advertising claims may involve a full trial before the ALJ and appeal to federal court, the vast majority of cases are settled by consent decree. This occurs when the FTC and the advertiser reach an agreement on some remedy that usually involves halting the advertisement. A consent order is published for public consideration and does not become final until 60 days after it is signed by the parties.

The FTC has been less active against deceptive advertising in the last decade, but continues to focus on what are sometimes called "outlaw" industries. These include weight-loss promoters, baldness remedies, land speculators, and residential siding companies. The Commission also is especially concerned with safety issues. The Commission enforced the law against a company that advertised a fire mask as effective in helping escape from home fires. This advertisement was deceptive for its failure to disclose that the mask did not protect against carbon monoxide, a common cause of death in fires.[4]

Deceptive Advertising

The FTC has adopted rules and made decisions regarding what sort of advertisements are considered illegally deceptive. When determining whether an advertisement is deceptive, the FTC does not base its judgment on the response of a knowledgeable person. Instead, the Commission decides whether a significant number of consumers, including unsophisticated consumers, actually will be deceived. One court decision emphasized that the law was made for the protection of "that vast

---

[3] 116 S.Ct. 1495 (1996).

[4] *In re Emergency Devices, Inc.,* 102 F.T.C. 1713 (1983).

multitude which includes the ignorant, the unthinking and the credulous."[5]

A company marketed a product called "Rejuvenescence" and advertised the cosmetic with the claim that it would make skin younger. After the FTC disputed this claim, the company responded that no consumer would reasonably believe that the product actually would reverse the aging process. The court held for the FTC because the advertisements would be deceptive to naive consumers.

The FTC has a relatively low **burden of proof** in deceptive advertising cases. The Commission does not have to prove that the advertiser intentionally set out to deceive customers. The Commission need not even prove that customers were in fact misled. The Commission need only show that an advertisement is "likely to mislead."

While the FTC may protect the gullible consumer, it only protects those consumers who act reasonably under the circumstances. When a company claimed that its product was "invisible," the Commission held that the claim was not deceptive. No consumer could act reasonably in relying on the claim that the product was literally invisible. Likewise, the Commission has written that pastry need not be actually made in Denmark to be called a "Danish." Advertisers may also claim that their product is "perfect," because no consumer would rely literally on such a claim.

Many different types of advertising claims may be deceptive. The Commission has held specific types of practices to be illegally deceptive. These include clear falsehoods, false testimonials, misleading omissions, and unsubstantiated claims.

First, some advertisements contain claims that are literally false. A company was liable for advertising "antiques" when the products were not old enough to qualify as antiques. Another advertiser was liable for promoting "caffeine free" coffee that actually contained caffeine.

False testimonials are unlawfully deceptive. If a celebrity claims that he or she uses a product, it must be true. Suppose that Chanel advertises that Tom Selleck uses a new brand of cologne. Chanel must show that Selleck actually used the cologne at the time of his endorsement.

An advertising claim may also be misleading for failing to disclose a material fact. Suppose that a Taiwanese manufacturer of shirts omits to disclose that its product was made overseas. In the past, the Commission has held that goods of foreign origin must disclose that they were not made in the United States.

False implications of expertise are also misleading. The FTC has found advertising deceptive when a company's name included the words "institute" or "laboratories," but the company had no scientific personnel. A company deceptively referred to its salespersons as "trained qualified food consultants" when they had received only one week of training given by the company.

Good faith honesty is not a defense to a deceptive advertising challenge. Unlike common law fraud, the FTC need not prove an advertiser's knowledge of the falseness of the claim or an intent to deceive. The Commission need only show that the advertising had a tendency to deceive consumers.

The FTC also requires that companies substantiate advertising claims, particularly those claims that are scientific in nature. Advertising statements such as "studies prove" must be supported by substantiation. If a company claims that its muffins help control cholesterol and prevent heart attacks, the company must have good evidence to substantiate the truth of this claim.

Most deceptive advertising claims do not involve an absolute untruth or lack of substantiation. Many claims are true but still deceptive. For example, the Ford Motor Company ran an advertisement claiming that the Ford LTD was quieter than a glider in flight. The FTC complained that the advertisement was unlawfully misleading, because a glider in flight is actually quite a noisy environment. In one interesting case, a bread manufacturer was held to have practiced deceptive advertising. The manufacturer stated that its bread had fewer calories per slice than other brands. While true, the reason was that its bread was sliced thinner.[6]

Remedies

If the FTC finds that a company has engaged in deceptive advertising, the Commission has several remedies that it may enforce. The most typical remedy for the FTC is the cease-and-desist order. This

---

[5] *Charles of the Ritz Dist. Corp. v. FTC*, 143 F.2d 676 (2d Cir. 1944).

[6] *Bakers Franchise Corp. v. Federal Trade Commission*, 302 F.2d 258 (3d Cir. 1962).

order forbids future use of the deceptive advertisement. A company violating a cease-and-desist order is liable for up to $10,000 per violation.

Every appearance of the illegal advertisement is considered a violation. In one decision, *Reader's Digest* ran a sweepstakes promotion that the FTC prohibited as deceptive. The company still sent out 18 million pieces of mail containing the sweepstakes promotion. The FTC claimed 18 million violations of its order. A court imposed $1.75 million in penalties against Reader's Digest (the maximum potential penalty was about $180 billion).

If a cease-and-desist order is considered inadequate, the FTC may require corrective advertising. This means forcing the company to use its own advertising to correct its previous deceptive claim. Warner Lambert Co. advertised the mouthwash Listerine as effective in preventing the common cold. In truth, there was no significant evidence supporting this claim. The Commission ordered Warner Lambert to state in future advertising that: "Listerine will not help prevent colds or sore throats or lessen their severity."

The following case describes a Commission finding that advertising was false and deceptive and an order that a company take some corrective action.

Case 13.2
Removatron International Corporation v. Federal Trade Commission
United States Court of Appeals, First Circuit, 1989
884 F.2d 1489

Background and Facts *Removatron International Corporation sells a product to deal with unwanted hair. Most hair removal mechanisms are either temporary or involve electrolysis, which is painful and can leave scars and pits on the skin. Removatron's project involves tweezers and a machine that emits radio frequency energy that, the company claims, destroys the cells that cause hair to return. Among the advertising claims made by Removatron was that it caused permanent hair removal.*

The Federal Trade Commission staff brought a claim against Removatron, and an administrative law judge issued a cease-and-desist order. The judge found that Removatron's claims were insufficiently substantiated and deceptive. The judge also ordered that Removatron include a disclaimer in future advertising. Removatron appealed to the full FTC, but the Commission approved the lower decision in large part. Removatron then appealed to federal court.

BOWNES, Circuit Judge.

* * * *

Petitioners advertise their product mainly in the beauty industry trade magazines. Sales are made after a series of telephone calls, mailings of literature, and meetings. The machine costs about $4,000. During the sales process, the purchasers are told that the machine will not work for everyone and that permanent removal will only be obtained after several treatments. Women who wish to be treated by the machine are given much the same information in written or oral form by the machine owner or operator. The written information is provided by petitioners who also provide purchasers with advertisements to place in local print media. Treatments cost approximately $35 per hour.

Rather than rehash all the evidence about petitioners' advertising, we present only a few typical samples of the types of claims made by petitioners. The petitioners stated that with Removatron treatments, hair removal can be "permanent" and unwanted hair will no longer be a problem; the ads also stated the machine is "effective" and an "alternative to electrolysis." The advertising also included statements that the machine has been "clinically tested and endorsed" and "clinically tested and shown superior." The ads also claimed that the FCC approved petitioners' product.

* * * *

***Petitioners defend their advertising claims on three grounds.

First, they argue that they never claimed that their machine would produce permanent hair removal for all people all the time. It is irrelevant that petitioners never claimed 100% efficacy; the common-sense reading of the ads is that the machine will permanently remove hair for most people most of the time.

Second, petitioners contend that their ads and sales pitches qualified their permanency claims in two ways: (1) the machine would not work on everyone, and (2) permanent removal could only be obtained after several treatments. As a part of this argument, they assert that the only relevant audience is the beauty industry since that is to whom they advertised and marketed their product. We reject the contention that the relevant audience is only the beauty industry. While it is true that petitioners placed their ads in trade magazines, it is also true that their sales personnel provided brochures and other information to purchasers who were then instructed to provide these materials to potential clients. Furthermore, petitioners provided advertising to purchasers who would then place it in local print media. The relevant audience thus includes potential purchasers and customers of purchasers ***.

* * * *

Finally, petitioners argue that the words "clinically tested" do not mean, and would not be taken by a reasonable person as meaning, "supported by rigorous scientific tests." Petitioners claim that "clinical" evidence merely means that a product has been used successfully in a clinical setting, while "scientific" evidence means that actual well-controlled studies had been performed. Regardless of any actual differences there may be between "clinical" and "scientific" evidence, petitioners have offered no basis for us to find that lay people would make such a fine distinction.

Decision and Remedy *The court upheld the FTC Order against Removatron and issued an injunction against its violation.*

One remedy that the FTC may lack is an order to pay damages. The Commission has sought to require a company to make restitution to purchasers of products that were deceptively advertised. A federal court held that the FTC had no authority to require such payments, though some companies have obeyed FTC orders to reimburse their customers. The Commission also has required companies to recall products or provide customers with revised product instructions to correct deceptive messages.

Comparative Advertising

Comparative advertising is a technique in which a company compares its product with that of a competitor. By comparison, the company tries to demonstrate its superiority and even seize customers of the competitor. The FTC believes that comparative advertising provides valuable information and encourages its use.

Advertisers increasingly employ comparative advertising. Pepsi-Cola and Coca-Cola have engaged in a series of taste tests, each purporting to show that their cola tasted better than that of their rival. Over the past two decades, comparative advertising has increased from 7 percent of all ads to nearly 50 percent.

Comparative advertising is controversial because so many comparative claims are questionable. Both Pepsi-Cola and Coca-Cola claimed that unbiased taste tests proved that their respective products tasted better. With such directly conflicting claims, one of these advertisements was presumably deceptive.

FTC Action The FTC may challenge comparative advertising as unlawfully deceptive. Comparative product demonstrations may be misleading. In one case, a company compared its floor wax to rival products in a demonstration. The demonstration did not follow the directions of the rival product, however, and the rival therefore appeared inferior. The FTC found that this comparison was unlawfully deceptive.[7]

Even fair and true comparative advertising has been found deceptive by the FTC. A manufacturer of razor blades ran a commercial showing greatly magnified pictures of its blades and those of its competitor, after five shaves. The pictures showed greater corrosion on the blades of the competitor. The FTC held that this advertisement was unlawfully deceptive because the greater corrosion had no material effect on shaving effectiveness or safety.[8]

Lanham Act Private Remedies

The 1946 Lanham Act enables private companies to sue for false or misleading comparative advertising. Section 43(a) of the Lanham Act permits private parties to sue if they have been somehow injured by deceptive ads. This section permits private actions for "any false or misleading description of fact ... in commercial advertising or promotion" that "misrepresents ... goods, services, or commercial activities."

Originally, the Lanham Act only prohibited false statements about the advertiser's own product. The 1988 Trademark Law Revision Act strengthened section 43(a) to prohibit false statements about the competitor's product as well.

---

[7] *In re American Home Products Corp.*, 83 F.T.C. 579 (1972).

[8] *In re Eversharp, Inc.*, 77 F.T.C. 686 (1970).

Suppose that Federal Airlines runs television commercials claiming "our planes are safer than those of Confederated Airlines." Confederated Airlines believes that this advertisement is false and misleading. Confederated could file a complaint with the FTC, but this action would be time-consuming and would depend on FTC initiative. Confederated could also sue Federal in court under section 43(a) of the Lanham Act.

Courts have held that private section 43(a) actions on comparative advertising have five required elements:

1. The defendant's comparative advertising made false statements about its own product or the plaintiff's product.

2. The comparative advertising actually deceived or had the tendency to deceive a substantial segment of their audience.

3. This deception is material and likely to influence the purchasing decisions of the audience.

4. The defendant put the falsely advertised goods in interstate commerce.

5. Plaintiff was or is likely to be injured by the deceptive comparative advertising.

All these elements must be present for a section 43(a) case to succeed.

In such a Lanham Act case, the plaintiff (Confederated) has the burden of proof to show that the defendant's (Federal) advertising was deceptive. Confederated would have to show that Federal's planes were not safer than the Confederated planes.

The plaintiff also must prove that consumers were deceived by the advertisements or probably would be deceived. If false statements in advertising were made intentionally, some courts will presume deception, so the plaintiff need not prove it. If Federal's statement is false, Confederated probably could show deception.

While a plaintiff such as Confederated must prove deception, it need not prove that all customers are deceived by an advertisement. Courts have been satisfied with evidence that as little as 10 to 15 percent of consumers were deceived.

Confederated next must prove that the deception was so significant, or material, that it would influence consumer decisions. Plane safety is so important that it would surely be material. Confederated also will have an easy time showing that Federal is in interstate commerce. The remaining requirement would be for Confederated to show that it was injured.

An increasing number of companies are suing as plaintiffs under section 43(a), claiming that competitors' comparative ads were deceptive. The comparative advertisement need not expressly name the plaintiff's product to warrant an action.

One leading case was brought by The Coca-Cola Company, which owns Minute Maid orange juice. Coca-Cola sued Tropicana for misleading comparative advertising. Tropicana orange juice ads said that Tropicana juice was "pure, pasteurized juice as it comes from the orange." The ads also showed an actor squeezing orange juice directly into a Tropicana carton. The Tropicana ads did not refer to Minute Maid by name, but implied that competitive products were not so fresh.

The court ruled for Coca-Cola, finding the Tropicana ads unlawfully deceptive. Tropicana orange juice, like most packaged juices, is pasteurized and frozen and does not come straight from fresh oranges. In addition, Coca-Cola presented evidence that surveyed customers were in fact deceived into believing that Tropicana juice came straight from fresh oranges. The court granted an injunction halting future broadcasts of the Tropicana advertisements.[9]

Most plaintiffs seek some sort of injunction against their competitors' deceiving comparative advertisements. A plaintiff ordinarily seeks a prompt preliminary injunction to stop the ads. To obtain such an injunction, the plaintiff need not prove that the public was actually deceived but need only show a likelihood of deception. Deception is presumed if the comparative advertisements are literally false.

In a leading case, the manufacturer of Tylenol sued the manufacturer of Anacin. Anacin ran a television commercial claiming to be superior in pain relief and reduction of inflammation. A court ruled that the two pain relievers were equal, so the Anacin advertisement was misleading. The court enjoined further presentations of Anacin's commercial.[10]

An injunction will compel the defendant to remove the deceptive advertisement as soon as possible. This action may be expensive. For example, a defendant may be required to modify its billboard advertising. In one case, the Noxell Corporation was forced to discontinue shipments of its Clean Lash mascara, because the packaging on the product deceptively claimed that the mascara was uniquely waterproof.[11]

Some competitors now receive money damages under section 43(a) of the Lanham Act. Damages are more difficult to obtain than an injunction. To get damages, a plaintiff must show that customers actually were deceived by the misleading ads. Moreover, a plaintiff may be required to show that it has lost profits as a result. It is difficult to prove the amount of lost profits caused by comparative advertising.

Section 35 of the Lanham Act provides some assistance to plaintiffs in damage actions. That section permits plaintiffs to recover their own lost profits, the wrongfully obtained profits of the deceptive advertiser, and the costs of litigation. In addition, section 35 permits up to triple these damages to punish the deceptive advertiser.

In the leading damages case, U-Haul sued Jartran, claiming that Jartran misleadingly claimed that U-Haul had inferior trucks and was more expensive. These advertisements misstated the cost of U-Haul renting and printed a misleading picture of the two companies' trucks. The court found unlawful deception and awarded U-Haul $40 million in damages. The court found that it would cost U-Haul $13.6 million in advertising to correct Jartran's misleading ads. The court added $6 million of Jartran's profits and multiplied this amount under section 35 due to Jartran's willful deception.[12]

Comparative advertising battles can become bitter, especially in the over-the-counter remedy markets. These fights have led to several Lanham claims, such as the following case.

---

[9] *Coca-Cola, Inc. v. Tropicana Products, Inc.*, 690 F.2d 312 (2d Cir. 1982).

[10] *American Home Products v. Johnson & Johnson*, 577 F.2d 160 (2d Cir. 1978).

[11] *Maybelline Co. v. Noxell Corp.*, 643 F. Supp. 294 (E.D. Ark. 1986).

[12] *U-Haul, Int'l v. Jartran, Inc.*, 601 F. Supp 1140 (D. Ariz. 1984), aff'd, 793 F.2d 1034 (9th Cir. 1986). Ironically, Jartran had received a prestigious "Gold Effie" advertising award for the commercial that the court later found deceptive.

Case 13.3
Johnson & Johnson-Merck Consumer Pharmaceuticals Company v. Rhone-Poulenc Rorer Pharmaceuticals, Inc.
United States Court of Appeals, Third Circuit, 1994
19 F.3d 125

Background and Facts *Johnson-Merck produces and markets Mylanta Double-Strength, an antacid. Rorer produces competing product, Extra Strength Maalox Plus. Rorer commercials for ESMP declared the product to be "the strongest antacid there is." Johnson-Merck filed a Lanham Act case claiming that this statement misled consumers into believing that ESMP was a superior product and states that its sales suffered accordingly. After a hearing, the district court concluded that Johnson-Merck had failed to meet its burden of proof that the ad was misleading and held for Rorer. Johnson-Merck appealed.*

SCIRICA, Circuit Judge

* * * *

The district court's conclusion that neither in vitro nor in vivo tests provides any basis for either antacid manufacturer to claim that its product is more effective at relieving symptoms is well supported, and neither party contests it. The dispute is over whether Rorer caused consumers to think that ESMP was more effective at relieving symptoms by making misleading claims of superior relief in its commercials, thereby violating the Lanham Act.

* * * *

We hold that it is not sufficient for a Lanham Act plaintiff to show only that the defendant's advertising claims of its own drug's effectiveness are inadequately substantiated under FDA guidelines; the plaintiff must also show that the claims are literally false or misleading to the public.

* * * *

Both the earlier Mylanta advertising and the Maalox advertising have tried to exploit the consumer confusion the FDA feared between the effects of ANC tests (laboratory studies of antacid strength) and symptom relief. The advertisements tout the ANC strength, promise symptom relief, and invite consumers to make the connection. Although there is evidence of intent to mislead, it is of a kind regrettably pervasive throughout the antacid industry and does not reach the egregious proportions that would warrant a presumption shifting the burden of proof.

Decision and Remedy *The court held that Johnson-Merck had not provided persuasive survey data that the advertising had actually mislead the public and affirmed the decision in favor of Rorer.*

Plaintiffs do not always succeed under section 43(a). In *Mennen Co. v. Gillette Co.*, complaining of misleading comparative shaving ads, the court dismissed the complaint as a "competitive ploy" by the plaintiff.[13] Haagen-Daz ice cream sued the manufacturers of Frusen Gladje ice cream, alleging that Frusen Gladje's name misled consumers into believing that the ice cream had a Scandinavian origin. The court rejected the complaint because Haagen-Daz used the same marketing ploy.[14]

Most Lanham Act misleading advertising claims have been brought by competitors, but some are being filed by consumers. Early decisions permitted these lawsuits, but recent cases have held that consumers have no standing to sue under section 43(a). When a consumer complained that a gasoline falsely promised "more power and quicker acceleration," the case was thrown out by a court holding that the law's purpose was the protection of commercial interests, not purchasers.[15]

Private Regulation of Advertising

Private organizations also regulate deceptive advertising, and much private regulation focuses on comparative advertising. Indeed, until 1972, two national television networks refused to accept comparative advertising. While networks now accept comparative ads, they regulate the content of comparative advertising. Exhibit 13-1 shows the NBC standards for accepting such commercials.

The advertising industry itself employs self-regulation through the National Advertising Division (NAD) and the National Advertising Review Board (NARB). These organizations were created in 1971 to promote truth in advertising. In its first year, the NAD/NARB heard nearly 2000 complaints of unfair advertising. More recently, the NAD has handled about 100 cases per year.

NAD/NARB decision making is much like that of a court. A company or the Better Business Bureau first files a complaint of unfair advertising with the NAD, and the NAD then demands substantiation of the complaint and investigates the facts. If the NAD considers the advertisement unfair, it requests modification or removal of the ad. NAD standards are much like those used by the FTC. Approximately two-thirds of the NAD cases are found to involve deception or lack of substantiation. NAD decisions are officially reported, much like judicial decisions.

One recent NAD decision involved comparative advertising for peanut butter. Bama Peanut Butter ran newspaper ads that stated:

> Peanut butter lovers say "You Can't Beat Bama! Jif Can't! Skippy Can't! In recent taste tests in the South, boys and girls who love peanut butter found Bama Peanut Butter unbeatable!

Bama's taste tests had shown that the product was as good as all its competitors' overall average, but customers preferred the flavor of one of Bama's competitors' products. The NAD ruled against Bama and held that the advertisement was a misleading description of the taste tests.

An NAD decision may be appealed to a five-member panel of the NARB. The NARB decision is final. Although the NAD/NARB process has no legally binding effect, its decisions have always been followed. This process has some limits. The NAD/NARB generally reviews national advertising and often provides no remedy against misleading local commercials. Moreover, no money damages can be awarded.

Advertising Misappropriation

An advertiser may be liable for misappropriation if it uses the name or picture of a person in advertising without obtaining permission. Misappropriation is sometimes considered a form of invasion of privacy and at other times is simply considered the unauthorized taking of a person's or a company's goodwill right to publicity.

For example, a portable toilet company marketed its products under the name "Here's Johnny." Johnny Carson sued the company for misappropriation and won. The court held that a "celebrity's legal right of publicity is invaded whenever his identity is intentionally appropriated for commercial purposes."[16] In another case, a television game show was liable for using the pictures of a past winner in advertisements without permission.

---

[13] 565 F. Supp. 648 (S.D.N.Y. 1983), aff'd, 742 F.2d 1437 (2d Cir. 1984).

[14] *Haagen-Daz, Inc. v. Frusen Gladje, Ltd.*, 493 F. Supp. 73 (S.D.N.Y. 1980).

[15] *Serbin v. Ziebart Intern. Corp.*, 11 F.3d 1165 (3d Cir. 1993).

[16] *Carson v. Here's Johnny Portable Toilets, Inc.*, 698 F.2d 831 (6th Cir. 1983).

Exhibit 13-1

National Broadcasting Co., Inc., Department of Broadcast Standards
Comparative Advertising Guidelines

NBC will accept comparative advertising which identifies directly or by implication, a competing product or service. As with all other advertising, each substantive claim, direct or implied, must be substantiated to NBC's satisfaction and the commercial must satisfy the following guidelines and standards for comparative advertising established by NBC:

1. Competitors shall be fairly and properly identified.

2. Advertisers shall refrain from disparaging or unfairly attacking competitors, competing products, services or other industries through the use of representations or claims, direct or implied, that are false, deceptive, misleading or have the tendency to mislead.

3. The identification must be for comparison purposes and not simply to upgrade by association.

4. The advertising should compare related or similar properties or ingredients of the product, dimension to dimension, feature to feature, or wherever possible be a side-by-side demonstration.

5. The property being compared must be significant in terms of value or usefulness of the product or service to the consumer.

6. The difference in the properties being compared must be measurable and significant.

7. Pricing comparisons may raise special problems that could mislead, rather than enlighten, viewers. For certain classifications of products, retail prices may be extremely volatile, may be fixed by the retailer rather than the product advertiser, and may not only differ from outlet to outlet but from week to week within the same outlet. Where these circumstances might apply, NBC will accept commercials containing price comparisons only on a clear showing that the comparative claims accurately, fairly and substantially reflect the actual price differentials or retail outlets throughout the broadcast area, and that these price differentials are not likely to change during the period the commercial is broadcast.

8. When a commercial claim involves market relationships, other than price, which are also subject to fluctuation (such as but not limited to sales position or exclusivity), the substantiation for the claim will be considered valid only as long as the market conditions on which the claim is based continue to prevail.

9. As with all other advertising, whenever necessary, NBC may require substantiation to be updated from time to time, and may re-examine substantiation, where the need to do so is indicated as the result of a challenge or other developments.

Courtesy of National Broadcasting Company, Inc. © 1982 National Broadcasting Company, Inc. All rights reserved.

Rules against misappropriation are especially strict for advertising. A newspaper could lawfully use a photograph of Donald Trump in connection with a relevant news story on troubled businesses. But if the same newspaper uses a photograph of Donald Trump in an advertisement for the newspaper, the newspaper may be liable for misappropriation.

A company may unlawfully misappropriate a person's identity, even if it does not physically use the person in an advertisement. The following case involves the practice of "sound-alikes" in commercials.

Case 13.4
Midler v. Ford Motor Company
United States Court of Appeals, Ninth Circuit, 1988
849 F.2d 460

Background and Facts Ford Motor Company and its advertising agency, Young & Rubicam, Inc., devised a "Yuppie Campaign" to sell the Ford Lincoln Mercury with commercials that tried to make an emotional appeal to yuppies. The campaign would use songs, including one by Bette Midler. Midler refused to perform the song for Ford. Young & Rubicam then sought out a backup singer for Midler. The backup singer was told to "sound as much as possible like the Bette Midler record."

The commercial never used the name or picture of Midler, but many people believed that she was singing in the commercial. Midler sued for misappropriation. The district court ruled in favor of Ford on a motion for summary judgment. Midler appealed.

NOONAN, Circuit Judge.

* * * *

When Young & Rubicam was preparing the Yuppie Campaign it presented the commercial to its client by playing an edited version of Midler singing "Do You Want to Dance," taken from the 1973 Midler album, "The Divine Miss M." After the client accepted the idea and form of the commercial, the agency contacted Midler's manager, Jerry Edelstein. The conversation went as follows: "Hello, I am Craig Hazen from Young & Rubicam. I am calling you to find out if Bette Midler would be interested in doing …? Edelstein: "Is it a commercial?" "Yes." "We are not interested."

* * * *

Why did the defendants ask Midler to sing if her voice was not of value to them? Why did they studiously acquire the services of a sound-alike and instruct her to imitate Midler if Midler's voice was not of value to them? What they sought was an attribute of Midler's identity. Its value was what the market would have paid for Midler to have sung the commercial in person.

A voice is more distinctive and more personal than the automobile accoutrements protected in *Motschenbacher.* A voice is as distinctive and personal as a face. The human voice is one of the most palpable ways identity is manifested. We are all aware that a friend is at once known by a few words on the phone. At a philosophical level it has been observed that with the sound of a voice, "the other stands before me." D. Ihde, *Listening and Voice* 77 (1976). A fortiori, these observations hold true of singing, especially singing by a singer of renown. The singer manifests herself in the song. To impersonate her voice is to pirate her identity. See W. Keeton, D. Dobbs, R. Keeton, D. Owen, *Prosser & Keeton on Torts* 852 (5th ed. 1984).

> We need not and do not go so far as to hold that every imitation of a voice to advertise merchandise is actionable. We hold only that when a distinctive voice of a professional singer is widely known and is deliberately imitated in order to sell a product, the sellers have appropriated what is not theirs and have committed a tort in California.

Decision and Remedy   *The court reversed the summary judgment against Midler and remanded the case for a trial.*

Incidental use of a person's name or picture is legal, however. Thus, a clothing advertisement might contain a picture of a busy New York street. Individuals who were incidentally present on the street would not have a good case for misappropriation.

In addition, some highly public persons may be unable to sue for misappropriation. For example, a court held that a company could market "Franklin D. Roosevelt cigars" without obtaining permission from the then-President. An All-American football player, who had deliberately sought and received widespread publicity, was denied any recovery for a brewing company's football schedule calendar that contained the name and likeness of the player.[17]

Unlawful misappropriation was found when a women's medical center used a physician's name and picture in the center's annual calendar. The calendar was distributed as a solicitation of patients, and the doctor had not given his permission for use of his likeness.

Advertisers may use pictures of public events. For example a performer at the enormous free rock concert Woodstock complained when a movie producer used a picture of his performance to promote a movie. The court held that the matter was of public interest and legally used in the advertisement. Famous quarterback Joe Namath of the New York Jets complained when *Sports Illustrated* used a picture of him in action as part of their advertisement for subscribers. The court held for *Sports Illustrated*, because pictures of a football game could be used for advertising.

Even legitimate use of public pictures may be wrongful misappropriation when the advertiser falsely suggests that the pictured individuals endorse their product. If *Sports Illustrated* had used a picture of Joe Namath *and* had also suggested that he recommend that fans subscribe to the magazine, the unauthorized endorsement could constitute misappropriation.

Advertising Negligence

If a person is injured by an advertised product, he or she may sue the product manufacturer for negligent advertising. Some smokers, who suffer from lung disease, now are suing tobacco companies, claiming that the advertising for cigarettes suggested that the product was safe.

A negligent advertising claim must meet the traditional requirements of negligence. Thus, a plaintiff must show that the advertiser breached a duty of due care. A careless misrepresentation of product safety would breach the advertiser's duty of due care. One child's parents bought a toy pistol that was advertised as "totally harmless." Later, the pistol emitted flames that set fire to a Santa Claus costume that the child was wearing. A court held that the manufacturer could be liable for negligent advertising.

In another case, a detergent manufacturer claimed that its product was safe enough to put in your eye. A purchaser accidentally rubbed her eyes with detergent and eventually became blind. The detergent contained a chemical that was known to be dangerous to eyes. A federal court held that the injured purchaser could recover for advertising negligence.[18] The false claim breached the defendant's duty of due care.

If advertising is unlawfully false and deceptive under the FTC Act, the plaintiff can use **negligence *per se*** (a legal presumption of negligence). Violation of a statute is considered automatically to be a violation of a duty of due care. A deodorant producer claimed in ads that the product could not

---

[17] *O'Brien v. Pabst Sales Co.*, 124 F.2d 167 (5th Cir. 1941).

[18] *Hardy v. Procter & Gamble Mfg. Co.*, 289 F.2d 124 (5th Cir. 1954).

cause an allergic skin reaction. This advertisement was found deceptive under a Massachusetts statute, and a plaintiff succeeded in an advertising negligence claim.

A plaintiff in an advertising negligence case also must show that the negligence was the proximate cause of the plaintiff's injuries. In one proximate case, a victim of a mugging sued the manufacturer of mace. She had purchased mace, based on a statement that it would cause "instantaneous incapacitation." The plaintiff was able to recover for advertising negligence because she bought the mace in reliance on this claim and because she used the mace without the desired effect.

Suppose that an auto manufacturer advertises a car with the claim that it is inexpensive, gets excellent gas mileage, and has unbreakable safety glass. A woman buys the car because it gets excellent gas mileage. Then she is in an accident in which the car's glass shatters and injures her. She will be unable to recover because she did not purchase the car in reliance on the advertising claim of unbreakable safety glass.

In addition to negligence, an advertiser may be liable for fraud. This would occur when false advertising claims are made knowingly and with an intent to deceive consumers. In one recent case, a medical clinic that performed abortions sued a pro-life organization that ran a "Help Clinic" that counseled pregnant women. The medical clinic argued that "the Help Clinic, through false and deceptive advertising and related activity, misleads persons into believing that abortions are conducted at the clinic with the intent of deceptively luring those persons to the clinic to unwittingly receive anti-abortion propaganda." The court agreed and awarded the medical clinic $23,500 in compensatory damages and $5500 in punitive damages.[19]

---

[19] *Fargo Women's Health Organization, Inc. v. FM Women's Help and Caring Connection,* 444 N.W.2d 683 (N.D. 1989).

Ethical Perspectives

Social Responsibility in Advertising

Most advertising is intended to persuade large groups of people to purchase a product. Some argue that this intent is unavoidably manipulative and dishonest toward its audience. For these advocates, advertisers always try to trick the public into buying products that they don't need.

Others, including economists, see great social value in advertising. They contend that advertising provides essential information to potential customers. Because of advertising, consumers can make a more informed choice of products.

The existence of advertising is, of course, a fact of life. Even its advocates concede, however, that some advertising is unethically misleading. Historically, the focus was on truth in advertising, and the government regulates the content of commercials to ensure that it is not misleading.

Recently, an ethical controversy has arisen over advertising's effects on society, regardless of whether it is true. This controversy has been most pronounced in the advertising of "sneakers" or athletic shoes. Several advertising companies have mounted very successful campaigns for sneakers such as Nike's "Just Do It" campaign using the famous athlete, Bo Jackson.

The sneaker ads may have been too successful. Some allege that these advertisements were targeted at poor minority males in the nation's central cities. The ads have in fact made certain expensive brands of sneakers into status symbols in many inner cities. This, in turn, has spawned violence over the sneakers. *Sports Illustrated* ran a story entitled "Your Sneakers or Your Life" that chronicled a series of fatalities in fights over the possession of sneakers.

At first glance, it seems difficult to blame the sneaker advertisers for these deaths. The critics argue, however, that the advertisers improperly targeted "young black males as buyers, through the use of seductive, macho-loaded sales pitches presented by black stars."[20] Many of these youths, of course, cannot afford to pay for a pair of $100 sneakers. They also argue that the phrase "Just Do It" has a special meaning in the inner city—do whatever is necessary, without moral qualms.

To what extent should an advertiser anticipate and consider the social consequences of its advertising? And is it proper to target advertising to a group that does not need or cannot afford a product? Nike expressed concern over the misinterpretation of its advertisements but continued to run them.

---

[20] "They Know Bo," *N.Y. Times Magazine,* November 11, 1990, p. 48.

International Perspectives

International Advertising

International advertising is difficult because of language and cultural differences among nations. The cross-national regulation of advertising further complicates global promotion efforts. There is no uniform international code for advertising. Instead, advertising content is regulated by individual nations, and these regulations vary considerably.

Consider advertising in the People's Republic of China. The Chinese require that advertising be "true, wholesome, clear and understandable." This highly subjective standard is enforced by a series of penalties ranging from criticism to monetary fines to the revocation of a license to do business.

In Great Britain, there is no national agency such as the United States FTC to regulate advertising. Rather, advertising is primarily regulated in a voluntary private system through the British Code of Advertising Practice. This Code requires that advertising be "legal, clean, honest, and truthful" and specifically regulates testimonials, scientific claims, and comparative claims.

The regulation of comparative advertising is particularly controversial and inconsistent, even within Europe. Comparative advertising is essentially prohibited in Switzerland and Finland, allowed with substantiation in Italy, and prohibited if considered denigrating in Austria, Belgium and Sweden. In Spain, advertisers can compare their brands only against other brands that they own. As a consequence, some companies register fictitious brand names and then favorably compare their product with the fictitious brand.

In Germany, comparative advertising must be universally true. Thus, a potato chip marketer was prohibited from advertising its brand as having 40 percent less fat because this claim was not true as opposed to every other brand of potato chip on the market. The chip may have had 40 percent less fat than average but did not have 40 percent less fat than all other brands. The European Economic Community has been attempting to develop a uniform advertising code but thus far has been unable to do so.

Questions and Case Problems

1. Both Thrill and Dynamics manufacture electric tools designed for the home consumer market. Thrill complains that Dynamics conducted a multimedia promotional campaign in which it explicitly named and showed Thrill products. These advertisements made certain factual statements in comparative and absolute terms concerning the qualities and relative performance of its own products and those of Thrill. These statements asserted that Dynamics products had greater durability than those of Thrill but used older, now obsolete Thrill products for the comparison. Thrill complains that the statements have caused loss of customers, decreased goodwill and dilution of its trademark. Can Thrill recover under the Lanham Act?

2. Ms. Hanberry purchased a pair of shoes that were advertised as containing the "Good Housekeeping Consumers' Guaranty Seal." Later, she was crossing her kitchen's vinyl floor, and the soles of the shoes became slick, causing her to slip and fall. She sued the producer of the "Good Housekeeping Seal" for negligently advertising that the products carrying the seal were "good ones." Should Ms. Hanberry recover?

3. A well-known packaged goods company started a new advertising campaign for one of its shampoo products. The campaign claimed that its shampoo gave people's hair more body and bounce than a competing product. The competitor sued over the advertisement, claiming that the ad was false and misleading. The parties disputed whether claims about the "body and bounce" of hair were really factual and whether they could be misleading. Who should prevail in this action? (*Vidal Sassoon, Inc. v. Bristol Myers Co.,* 661 F.2d (2d Cir. 1981).

4. A manufacturer of a consumer pain relief product ran the following advertisement:

"New Un-Burn actually anesthetizes nerves in sensitive sunburned skin.

Un-Burn relieves pain fast. Actually anesthetizes nerves in sensitive sunburned skin.

* * * New Un-Burn contains the same local anesthetic doctors often use *** I'll tell you what I like about Un-Burn. It's the best friend a blonde ever had! *** It stops sunburn pain in * * * less time than it takes me to slip out of my bikini. That's awfully nice to know when you're the sensitive type."

The Federal Trade Commission brought an action claiming that this advertisement was false and misleading. What must the company show to defend its ad? [*In re Pfizer, Inc.* 81 F.T.C. 23 (1972)]

5. Absolut Vodka developed a unique and effective advertising campaign. The campaign focused on the name Absolut as evidence of purity and substantially increased the company's share of the vodka market. A new vodka, imported from the Soviet Union, called itself Icy Vodka. This company began running an advertising campaign that was based on the slogan, "Try Icy, It's Absolutely Vodka." Is this advertising campaign lawful?

6. A manufacturer produced a perfume with a label that said: "If you like OPIUM you'll love OMNI." The slogan appeared prominently on the box top. Inside the box was a card stating that "OPIUM is a registered trademark of Parfum and is not associated in any manner with [this product]." OPIUM's manufacturer filed suit, claiming that the product was misleading and would confuse consumers. Who should prevail? [*Charles of the Ritz Group v. Quality King Distributors, Inc.*, 636 F. Supp. 433 (S.D.N.Y. 1986)].

Chapter Fourteen

Environmental Liability

Key Background

The essential background for this chapter on environmental liability is found in Chapter 46 of *West's Business Law, Seventh Edition,* and in Chapter 24 of *West's Legal Environment of Business, Third Edition.* These chapters cover environmental protection. Among the important points to remember from this chapter are:

- leading federal environmental statutes, including the Clean Air Act, Clean Water Act, Superfund, and others

- liability for damages under common law

- liability for damages under federal statutes

- the costs of compliance with or violation of environmental law

* * *

In the 1990s, business will spend tens of billions of dollars annually on environmental protection. This new item on the balance sheet deserves careful attention. Avoidance of environmental liabilities and efficient compliance may become critical to the success of many businesses.

Businesspersons in most industries must respond to the requirements of a long list of environmental laws. One particular law, the Comprehensive Environmental Response, Compensation and Liability Act of 1980 (known as "CERCLA" or "Superfund") creates the liability of greatest concern to businesses.

This chapter begins by outlining the details of CERCLA's operation. The chapter then goes on to analyze the application of CERCLA and other environmental laws to business transactions and business operations. It also considers the increasing application of criminal liability to corporate officers and directors for violations of environmental laws.

CERCLA/Superfund

Government and industry in the United States are spending billions of dollars to clean up hazardous wastes under the authority of CERCLA. Knowledge of CERCLA is important because of its potentially enormous liability and because this liability is not limited to the obvious "guilty" parties who unsafely dumped hazardous wastes.

CERCLA liability may apply to businesses who did not participate in hazardous wastes production or disposal and who may be wholly unaware of the presence of hazardous wastes on their properties. The act also applies to any disposal of hazardous wastes, not just large dumps.

Suppose Ervin Computer Company takes its leftover bottles of solvents to Consolidated Wastes for disposal. Consolidated then buries them in a very small pile on vacant property. In this circumstance, Ervin could be liable for substantial costs of cleanup.

Application of CERCLA

CERCLA is triggered any time there is a "reasonable basis to believe there may be a release or threat of release of a hazardous substance" or any other pollutant that may endanger public health. Courts have interpreted these terms very liberally, making the law's application quite broad.

Most responses involve hazardous substances. The law defines "hazardous substance" as any substance regulated under certain sections of the Clean Air Act, the Federal Water Pollution Control Act, and other federal environmental lists. Hundreds of substances are deemed hazardous substances. Although the term hazardous waste implies heavy industry to many individuals, even "white collar" office jobs use hazardous substances (for cleaning, in office machines, etc.).

A recent article by environmental attorneys recently noted the breadth of Superfund:

> While it may be a slight overstatement to declare that everything is a hazardous substance, the exceptions are narrow and few. And it is perhaps only slightly more of an overstatement to say that any site in the United States is a potential CERCLA site.[1]

A release means any escape of a hazardous substance into the environment. This can include leakage on the disposal site itself; there is no requirement of potential human exposure. A threatened release is even broader and requires no actual escape of hazardous substances. The court in one case found a threatened release simply because the wastes were not in proper containers and the region's annual rainfall created a potential for leaching of wastes into the groundwater.[2]

Once a release or threatened release triggers the application of CERCLA, the government may enter a site and remove the hazardous substances and clean up the surrounding area. The government may then sue various responsible parties to recover its cleanup costs. CERCLA also authorizes the government to order private parties to clean up the hazardous conditions themselves. In addition to cleanup costs, CERCLA allows the government to sue private parties for any damages to natural resources (e.g. fish kills) that result from hazardous waste releases.

Private parties also may choose to clean up a hazardous waste site. For example, the current owner of land may need to eliminate hazards before developing the property. In such a case, the private landowner may clean up the site and then sue other responsible parties to recover at least a portion of its cleanup costs.

These cleanup costs are usually quite substantial. Hazardous substances must be carefully handled and removed to a well-run disposal site. The average cleanup cost for a disposal site is $25 million, and costs for even a relatively small disposal site will run into the millions of dollars. The government has claimed for billions of dollars in cleanup costs for a single large waste site. The Office of Technology Assessment has estimated that total cleanup costs for all sites may exceed $600 billion or fully 10 percent of the total annual output of the United States.

Responsible Parties

Under CERCLA, several different parties may be liable. The law's liability extends to: (1) the current owner and operator of the site; (2) anyone who formerly owned the site at the time of hazardous substance disposal; (3) the generators of the wastes who arranged for its disposal; and (4) the transporters of the wastes.

The generators of hazardous wastes, such as Ervin Computer, can be liable under virtually any circumstances. In one case, the owners of waste PCB oil (oil contaminated with a highly toxic substance) arranged with a transporter for disposal. Rather than safely disposing of the contaminated oil, the transporter sprayed and thereby contaminated over two hundred miles of rural roadsides in North Carolina. The waste generator was held liable for the costs of correcting this contamination.[3]

In addition, once a generator's waste is taken to a given site, the generator may be liable for any and all cleanup costs at that site. Many leaking hazardous waste sites have produced a "toxic soup," in which it is impossible to identify the source of the

---

[1] Anderson & Taylor, "Representing Buyers," 3 *Nat. Resources and Env't* 3 (1988).

[2] *Con-Tech Sales Defined Benefit Trust v. Cockerham*, 698 F. Supp. 1249 (E.D. Pa. 1988).

[3] *United States v. Ward*, 618 F. Supp. 884 (E.D.N.C. 1985).

leaking substances. As a consequence, CERCLA requires only proof that the generator's hazardous wastes were sent to a site.

Owner and operator liability is also broad. The current owner of land including a CERCLA site will be liable, even if the owner were entirely blameless or even unaware of the presence of a hazardous waste problem. This application is evidenced in the following decision.

Case 14.1
Tanglewood East Homeowners v. Charles-Thomas, Inc.
United States Court of Appeals, Fifth Circuit, 1988
849 F.2d 1568

Background and Facts *A residential subdivision was built upon a site formerly owned by the United Creosoting Company. That company operated a wood-treatment facility and deposited toxic creosote waste in pools on the property. The property was later acquired by real estate developers. After the wastes were discovered, the homeowners complained about the waste and further development ceased.*

The homeowners sued the developer, the bank lender for the development, construction companies, and real estate agents, seeking to compel cleanup for the site and pay their costs. The cleanup would cost millions of dollars. The defendants filed a motion to dismiss, claiming that they were not responsible parties under CERCLA. The district court denied the motion, and the lender brought this appeal of that ruling.

POLITZ, Circuit Judge.

* * * *

Appellant maintains that under § 9607(a)(1), the only owner and operator who discharged hazardous materials was the United Creosoting Company, who abandoned the site in 1972. We find nothing in the wording of § 9607(a) to exclude present owners of properties previously contaminated. We join our colleagues of the Second Circuit in concluding that the structure of the statute removes any doubt. Section 9607(a)(2) expressly applies to past owners and operators who contaminate their surroundings; it is therefore manifest that § 9607(a)(1) applies to current owners of adulterated sites. See *New York v. Shore Reality Corp.*, 759 F.2d 1032 (2nd Cir. 1985). We hold that § 9607(a)(1) imposes strict liability on the current owners of any facility which releases or threatens to release toxic substance.

* * * *

Finally, appellant maintains that CERCLA was intended to cover only persons actually engaged in the chemical/hazardous materials industry and those engaged in business which generated such materials. It vigorously contends that the legislation was not meant to impose chilling liability on the defendants' businesses: banking, real estate, construction, and development.

* * * *

We are persuaded beyond peradventure that a determination of the specific businesses and activities covered by CERCLA is beyond the pale of a 12(b)(6) motion. That remains for another day.

Decision and Remedy *The Court affirmed the district court judgment refusing to dismiss the complaint.*

A former owner of property is also liable if the ownership occurred at the time that the wastes were disposed. The former owner need not have participated in or known of the disposal to be liable.

Suppose that Roberta Serota has large landholdings in Louisiana and leased this land to a variety of tenants, including an oil company. During the lease, the oil company disposed of hazardous wastes on the land. Serota then sold the land to the oil company. If the government later cleans up the land, the government may recover their cleanup costs from Serota. This is true even if Serota was not involved in the operations of the tenant oil company and exercised no managerial control over the property at the time of disposal.

Owner and operator liability extends even further. The bank who loaned money for a real estate purchase may become liable under CERCLA, especially if the purchaser defaults on the loan and the bank takes over the property. This is called lender liability.

Congress relaxed the standards of CERCLA lender liability in the Asset Conservation, Lender Liability, and Deposit Insurance Protection Act of 1996. Under this law, lenders are not liable for cleanup costs unless they exercise decision-making control over environmental compliance at the property, exercise overall management of the property including decision making on environmental cleanup, or exercise responsibility for substantially all of the operational functions of the property. A lender who merely forecloses on property and does not participate in its management prior to foreclosure is not a potentially liable owner and operator. The law also limits the liability of fiduciaries. The statute created a safe harbor for fiduciaries by specifying certain actions that could be taken without causing personal liability.

In addition, a parent corporation may be liable for land owned or operated by a subsidiary corporation. Gulf, a large conglomerate, owned Bunker Hill Company, among many other subsidiaries. Bunker Hill owned a hazardous waste facility that became liable for CERCLA cleanup costs. A court held that Gulf could itself be liable for these costs because it controlled and monitored Bunker Hill's management. The court also noted that Bunker Hill was undercapitalized and probably unable to pay the cleanup costs itself.[4]

Liability Standards

The liability standards under CERCLA are quite strict. The act provides for strict liability, which requires no showing of negligence or other culpability. Indeed, the government need not even show that the defendant's actions caused the need for cleanup. The government need only link the defendant with the site (e.g., the defendant sent wastes to the site at some time in the past).

Liability under CERCLA is often joint and several. This means that each responsible party is potentially liable for all the costs at a given site. Suppose that Ervin Computer Company had its wastes taken to a specific hazardous waste site. Ervin's wastes represented 1 percent of all the hazardous wastes at the site. After cleanup, Ervin may be liable for 100 percent of cleanup costs.

In the above example, Ervin may sue the site owner and the generators of the other 99 percent of wastes for contribution to these costs. If these other generators are unidentifiable or bankrupt, however, Ervin may be required to pay the full cleanup bill.

Moreover, Superfund is *retroactive*, applying to wastes disposed long before the act was passed in 1980. As a consequence, a company may be liable in 1991 for wastes disposed in the 1950s, even if those wastes were disposed according to state-of-the-art disposal techniques of the time.

Defenses

Defenses to CERCLA liability are few and narrow. Statutory defenses are available for releases due to what the law considers an act of war or an act of God (such as a massive flood). These defenses are of little use in most cases.

CERCLA also provides a defense for releases that are due to the actions of third parties, but even this defense is very narrow. The defense applies only if the release was caused solely by a third party and if the defendant had no contractual relationship with that third party. The defendant also must show that it took precautions to prevent the foreseeable acts of third parties.

The third party defense might be available if the owner of a hazardous waste site took great care, but vandals broke into the site and spilled the wastes. Even in this circumstance, the owner would be required to show it took appropriate precautions against such vandalism. The most common application of this defense is known as the **innocent purchaser defense**, which is discussed in the following section.

---

[4] *Idaho v. Bunker Hill Co.*, 24 Env't Rep. (BNA) 1160 (N.D. Cal. 1986).

Environmental Liability in Business Transactions

Virtually every business transaction carries a risk of environmental liability. Suppose that Amco Lines purchases a fleet of trucks from CrossCountry Co. for $500,000. In connection with the truck purchase, CrossCountry agrees to throw in its trucking terminal and garage with an appraised value of $300,000. This may seem like a good deal, but suppose that the terminal building contains soil contaminated from waste oil or underground petroleum storage tanks. Perhaps the building contains asbestos materials. Amco may have set itself up for multimillion-dollar liability by taking possession of the terminal.

The nature and extent of liability will depend on the type of acquisition. A purchase of assets results in possible liability under CERCLA and other environmental statutes. A purchase of the stock of a company may cause even greater environmental liability.

CERCLA Liability

In today's legal environment, no one should purchase land without first checking for the presence of hazardous wastes. As noted above, an innocent landowner may bear substantial liability for past actions on the site. A 1986 survey found that environmental liability in real estate transactions was the foremost concern of corporate facility planners.

The purchaser of real estate may attempt to protect itself from future CERCLA liability with contractual provisions. The purchaser may demand that the seller provide a warranty that there are no hazardous wastes on the site. Alternatively, the sale may contain a "hold harmless" clause in which the seller agrees to indemnify the buyer for any future hazardous waste cleanup costs. Such an indemnification provision should be as specific as possible.

Contractual protection is of limited value, however. A party cannot contract away its responsibilities to the government. Therefore, the government can still recover all its cleanup costs from the purchaser of the land. The contract merely enables the purchaser to sue the seller for these costs. This remedy is only good if the seller is still in existence and sufficiently solvent to afford the costs.

A more promising opportunity for buyers of land is CERCLA's **innocent purchaser defense**. Congress recognized the potential unfairness of CERCLA liability and in 1986 created a defense for innocent purchasers. The defense is limited, though, and ignorance of a problem is not sufficient for "innocence" under CERCLA.

To take advantage of the innocent purchaser defense, the buyer of land must show that it "did not know and had no reason to know" that hazardous substances were on the property. To have "no reason to know" the buyer must show that it conducted "all appropriate inquiry into the previous ownership and uses of the property consistent with good commercial or customary practice in an effort to minimize liability."[5]

Suppose that Kaplan, Inc., wishes to purchase manufacturing facilities, including a refinery, that might contain hazardous waste. To take advantage of the innocent purchaser defense, Kaplan, Inc., must conduct "environmental due diligence." Government mortgage authorities (such as "Fannie Mae") have established guidelines for what this due diligence should include. At minimum, the buyer should conduct a title search to identify all past owners. The buyer also should search government records for past environmental violations at the site, inspect the site carefully, and interview employees at the site. If any of these steps suggest problems, the buyer probably should undertake chemical testing of suspect areas.

If Kaplan conducts this environmental due diligence and uncovers no problems, it can take advantage of the innocent purchaser defense. This means that Kaplan will not be liable for cleanup costs. If a problem arises, however, Kaplan will be required to allow EPA onto its land to clean up the site. This cleanup activity could still cost Kaplan profits from the use of its land.

The innocent purchaser defense has so far been of little assistance to defendants. The following decision involves a case in which the defense was rejected.

---

[5] 42 U.S.C. Sec. 4601(f)(35)(B).

Case 14.2
United States v. A & N Cleaners and Launderers, Inc.
United States District Court, Southern District of New York, 1994
854 F. Supp. 229

Background and Facts The United States government incurred costs in cleaning up a site after the release of hazardous substances from real estate owned in part by the Berkmans. The Berkmans purchased the property in 1979 and were aware that a dry cleaning business had been located on the site. Not long after the purchase, state and federal environmental officials sought access to the site to check for hazardous substances. The Berkmans granted access but did not question the officials. The government sued the Berkmans to recover its cleanup costs, and they invoked the innocent landowner defense.

SWEET, District Judge

* * * *

To qualify as an innocent landowner under CERCLA § 101 (35) (A), one must have undertaken "all appropriate inquiry into the previous ownership and uses of the property, consistent with good commercial or customary practice" at the time of transfer...In deciding whether a defendant has complied with this standard, courts consider any specialized knowledge or expertise the defendant has, whether the purchase price indicated awareness of the presence of a risk of contamination, commonly known or of the presence of contamination at the property, and the ability to detect such contamination by appropriate inspection.

* * * *

Were the Berkman defendants to have had a clear, intelligible mandate from Congress or the EPA regarding the investigation they should have conducted prior to purchasing the property and the monitoring that they should have conducted since its purchase, it is doubtful that they would be before the court at this time. By imposing a standard of diligence which the government itself can neither meet nor define, CERCLA has imbued the conduct of business with unnecessary peril, and has made the current defendants liable for our collective failure to fashion a reasonable response to the problems of chemical contamination.

Decision and Remedy The court ruled that the Berkman defendants were not entitled to rely on the innocent purchaser defense.

Other Environmental Laws

The purchaser of land must also be concerned with other environmental statutes. If a purchaser such as Kaplan is acquiring a refinery for its own use, Kaplan will need to be concerned with the environmental compliance of these facilities. A refinery must obtain pollutant discharge permits under the Resource Conservation and Recovery Act and air pollution permits under the newly amended Clean Air Act. These are only a few of the many environmental permits that may be required.

If Kaplan's newly acquired facility lacks these permits, the refinery may be unable to operate. A refinery that cannot operate is obviously of dubious value. If it does operate, Kaplan will become subject to civil fines and possibly criminal penalties. Kaplan may upgrade the refinery with pollution control devices necessary to obtain permits, but these improvements could cost hundreds of thousands of dollars. The permit may also limit a facility's hours of operation and production rate.

Even if a purchaser obtains land for future industrial development of new facilities, the buyer still has environmental law concerns. Many environmental laws restrict the use of land and prevent its profitable development. If property contains wetlands (similar to swamps), it is strictly regulated. In many circumstances, all development is prohibited on wetlands. This could render the property virtually worthless to the purchaser.

Both federal and state authorities also protect groundwater resources by restricting development. Many types of building programs may be outlawed under these restrictions. Regulations under the Clean Air Act can prohibit new construction in geographic regions that already have excessive air pollution levels.

If land contains the habitat for a plant or animal in danger of extinction, the Endangered Species Act may prohibit development. The golden-cheeked warbler was recently declared an endangered species. This listing will prevent landowners in certain areas of Texas from cutting down trees on their land.

Purchase of Securities

The above discussion has assumed that the purchaser bought only assets. If a purchaser buys an entire existing company (such as in a hostile takeover), the purchaser has even greater potential environmental liability.

In an asset acquisition, the purchaser's liability will be limited to future government actions specific to the on-site assets acquired. In a securities acquisition, the purchaser will succeed to all the liabilities of the acquired company, including past liabilities. The purchaser may also be liable for disposal of wastes off-site.

Suppose Kaplan buys all the stock of Chin Associates. Thirty years ago Chin may have sent asbestos wastes to a disposal site thousands of miles away. If the waste site is cleaned up on 1992, Chin would be liable as a generator, and Kaplan would succeed to this liability. This is true even though Kaplan had nothing to do with the asbestos wastes and never assumed ownership of the disposal site.

The existence of **successor liability** is dependent on corporation law principles discussed in Chapter 42 of *West's Business Law, Seventh Edition*. A complete stock purchase or merger will invoke successor liability. Even a purchase of assets may invoke the broader successor liability if the purchaser continues the seller's business and retains the same personnel.

Seller's Liabilities

The above discussion has been concerned with the liability of purchasers, but sellers have a different set of concerns. The sale of assets can produce later environmental liability, as illustrated by the following example.

Suppose that Kaplan produces some hazardous wastes at its manufacturing facility and disposes them on-site. Kaplan is very careful to comply with the best waste management practices available at the time and the wastes are carefully contained. Then the Zepp Corporation makes a lucrative offer to purchase the land.

Kaplan may desire to sell the land, but it can not escape the potential liability. Even if Kaplan sells the land, it is potentially responsible for future CERCLA cleanup costs. Kaplan owned and operated the land at the time of hazardous waste disposal. If Zepp is an irresponsible manager, the well-maintained Kaplan waste disposal site may degenerate and leak hazardous substances. Kaplan will be liable for cleanup costs in this case.

Kaplan, therefore, has a strong incentive to ensure that any purchaser, such as Zepp, will maintain the land carefully. There is no guarantee, however, that Zepp will not resell the land to another party, who may be irresponsible. Kaplan's only guarantee of protection is to keep the land itself and maintain it carefully and indefinitely.

A seller of land may obtain contractual protection against future liability. The contract of sale could require the buyer to indemnify the seller for later liability that is the fault of the buyer. These provisions do not protect the seller from liability to the government, but they enable the seller to sue the buyer to recover its liabilities to the government. The seller is dependent on the buyer's solvency in order to recover, however.

A seller of land may be directly liable to the buyer in tort or contract law. If a seller conveys hazardous waste-contaminated property and fails to disclose the fact, the buyer may sue for fraud. This could enable the buyer to rescind the contract and recover its purchase price. To avoid this risk, the seller should conduct its own environmental due diligence and make full disclosure of risks to the purchaser.

Individual Liability for Environmental Violations

Traditionally, a violation of an environmental statute imposed penalties on the responsible corporation. This approach was criticized because some corporations would simply violate the laws and pay the resulting fines or might even declare bankruptcy. There is a trend toward holding corporate officers, directors, and even shareholders liable for a company's environmental violations.

In some cases, an individual businessperson may become personally liable for cleanup costs under CERCLA. Individual liability is particularly likely for closely held nonpublic corporations.

In a key case, the president and principal shareholder of a closely held corporations was individually liable under CERCLA. The court emphasized that the president was "responsible for the entire operation" and involved in "basically every facet" of its activities. The president was therefore liable as an owner and operator of the site.[6]

Such total control is not necessary for liability. The following recent decision distinguishes the sorts of executive actions that can produce individual liability under CERCLA.

---

[6] *United States v. Mottolo*, 605 F. Supp. 898 (D.N.H. 1984).

Case 14.3
Riverside Market Development Corp. v. International Building Products
United States District Court,
Eastern District of Louisiana, 1990
Civ. A. No. 88-5317; 1990 WL 72249

Background and Facts *International Building Products, Inc. ("IBP"), purchased a National Gypsum Company plant in 1981 and continued to manufacture asbestos cement products. A shopping center development wanted to purchase the site for $3.4 million. The site require cleanup, which was undertaken by the purchaser.*

The purchaser then sought to recover cleanup costs from IBP and two individual officers of the corporation, Gerard von Dohlen and T. Gene Prescott. Prescott and von Dohlen moved to dismiss the complaint against them, arguing that they were not responsible parties under CERCLA.

WICKER, District Judge.

* * * *

When IBP purchased the National Gypsum plant, Prescott and von Dohlen were the sole shareholders: Prescott held eighty-five percent (85%) of the stock and served as Chairman of the Board; von Dohlen held fifteen percent (15%) of the stock and served as President. From March 1981 through December 1983, von Dohlen also served as Chief Executive Officer. In 1984, other shareholders invested in IBP. Prescott lived in New York and visited the New Orleans facility only on one to three occasions per year during the time that IBP owned the plant: (1) annual Christmas Party; (2) attendance at a meeting for an Erectors' Association, some of whose members used products from the plant and (3) brief visit with executive personnel.

* * * Von Dohlen testified that Prescott was principally the source of money.

* * * Von Dohlen further explained that as an IBP officer, Prescott reviewed financial statements regularly. "During meeting of officers, he consulted with me or other people but that's about it."

> * * * The Court finds no evidence that Prescott was an operator of the asbestos manufacturing facility within the meaning of CERCLA.
>
> As to von Dohlen, however, the Court finds that a genuine issue of material fact exists as to whether or not he was an "operator" under CERCLA.
>
> Unlike Prescott, von Dohlen spent forty percent (40%) of his time in New Orleans. He testified that from March 1981 through December, 1984, he spend ten percent (10%) of his time each month at the New Orleans factory.
>
> * * * Although he states in his affidavit that his major duties involved sales, he testified earlier that he was occasionally involved in the actual day-to-day operations of the factory, that he may have operated some of the machines himself from time to time in order to solve problems in manufacturing processes, and that he was actually out on the plant floor supervising at other times.
>
> * * * Ray Plauche confirmed that through 1984, von Dohlen had an office at the plant, and was at the plant "almost every week—for all practical purposes, three weeks out of the month."
>
> Other evidence shows that when IBP bought the plant from National Gypsum, von Dohlen wrote the cover letter and signed IBP's application for an identification number from the Louisiana Hazardous Waste Management Program for Tchoupitoulas facility. (Plaintiffs' Exhibits 6 and 7.) Also on March 15, 1983, the State of Louisiana sent a warning letter to von Dohlen, as president of IBP, stating that an inspection revealed that a "container of hazardous waste was not marked with required information" and giving IBP thirty (30) days to correct the violation.
>
> **Decision and Remedy** *The Court granted Prescott's motion to be dismissed from the case but permitted the claims against von Dohlen to go forward to trial.*

Even the officers of large publicly held corporations are possibly liable under CERCLA. A person can be liable as a generator if he or she arranged for the disposal of hazardous substances. An officer directly involved in decision making for waste disposal was found personally liable under this provision.[7] The court emphasized that the officer personally participated in the wrongful conduct.

▀ Compliance and Criminal Liability

In 1981, the Environmental Protection Agency formed the Office of Criminal Enforcement, and the Department of Justice created their Environmental Crimes Unit. Since that time, there have been over 600 environmental criminal indictments and over 450 guilty pleas or convictions. These have resulted in over $25 million in fines and about 300 years in jail sentences. The average guilty defendant was sentenced to slightly over one year.

Most major environmental statutes contain criminal liability provisions. After the massive Alaskan oil spill from their tanker, the *Exxon Valdez*, Exxon was charged with criminal violations of five different federal statutes. Individual officers have also been charged.

RCRA

Perhaps the most common source of environmental criminal liability is the Resource Conservation and Recovery Act, known as RCRA. RCRA governs

---

[7] *United States v. Northeastern Pharmaceutical and Chemical Co., Inc.*, 810 F.2d 726 (8th Cir. 1986).

present and future disposal facilities, transporters, and generators of wastes.

The primary tool of RCRA is the creation of a "cradle-to-grave" manifest system. This system requires that records must be maintained for all hazardous wastes from their creation ("the cradle") to their disposal ("the grave"). The generator of the wastes must identify and label them and furnish information about their contents to those who transport, store or dispose of the wastes. The manifest system permits the wastes to be identified and tracked throughout their existence.

RCRA also creates detailed regulations for the ongoing disposal and treatment of hazardous wastes. Government regulations establish detailed technical requirements for treatment or disposal. Permits must be obtained from EPA for disposal. Some especially hazardous wastes may not be disposed on land.

RCRA's first set of criminal sanctions apply to anyone who knowingly causes disposal at an unpermitted facility, makes false representations to the EPA, transports wastes without a manifest, or fails to file records required by the Act. A conviction under any of these provisions is a felony punishable by a fine of up to $50,000 per violation and imprisonment for between two and five years.

RCRA's second set of criminal penalties applies to anyone who knowingly violates the above standards and "knows at the time that he ... places another person in imminent danger of death or serious bodily injury."[8] An individual violator of this "knowing endangerment" provision is subject to a fine of up to $250,000 and up to fifteen years in prison. A corporation may be fined up to $1 million for violating this provision.

A company was convicted under the "knowing endangerment" provision when it exposed its employees to toxic chemicals without sufficient protection. Some of the employees became seriously ill and all had an increased risk of cancer. The court ordered the defendant to establish a $950,000 trust fund for the employees, ordered the company to pay $440,000 in fines, and placed the company on probation. Probation conditions included the payment of over $2 million in waste cleanup costs.[9]

To obtain a conviction under the key section of RCRA, the government must show that a person or corporation: (1) knowingly; (2) transports or disposes or treats or stores; (3) a hazardous waste; (4) without a permit or in violation of a permit. The key issue in most cases is whether the violation was "knowing."

The term "knowing" does not necessarily mean that the defendant was aware that a crime was committed, however. The following decision involved criminal liability on the part of a supervisor who may have been unaware of potential liability.

---

[8] 42 U.S.C. Sec. 6928(e).

[9] *United States v. Protex Industries, Inc.*, 874 F.2d 740 (10th Cir. 1989).

Case 14.4
United States v. Hoflin
United States Court of Appeals,
Ninth Circuit, 1989
880 F.2d 1033

Background and Facts *Douglas Hoflin was the director of the Public Works Department for Ocean Shores, Washington. In this position he was in charge of waste paint left over from road maintenance and sludge removed from the kitchen of the city golf course. He instructed an employee to haul the paint drums to the sewage treatment plant and to bury them. Some of the drums were crushed in the process of disposal, and the waste was then covered with sand.*

Neither the sewage treatment plant nor the city had a permit for the disposal of hazardous wastes. EPA became aware of the leaking paint drums and had him indicted for disposing of hazardous waste without a permit. A jury found Hoflin to be guilty. Hoflin appealed, claiming that he believed that the city had a permit to dispose of waste and that he was not "knowing" in his disposal without a permit.

THOMPSON, Circuit Judge.

* * * *

Hoflin's challenge to his conviction on Count II focuses on subsection (2)(A) of 42 U.S.C. § 6928(d) (1982). Section 6928(d) provides in pertinent part:

(d) Criminal penalties

Any person who-

....

(2) *knowingly* treats, stores or disposes of any hazardous waste identified or listed under this subchapter either-

(A) without having obtained a permit under section 6925 of this title....; or

(B) in *knowing* violation of any material condition or requirement of such permit;

....

shall, upon conviction, be subject to [fines, imprisonment or both]. (emphasis added).

42 U.S.C. § 6928(d)(2)(A) and (B).

It is Hoflin's position that "knowingly" in subsection (2) modifies both subsections (A) and (B). Under this interpretation, knowledge becomes an essential element of the crime defined by section 9628(d)(2)(A), and Hoflin could not be convicted on Count II without proof that he knew no permit had been obtained. He correctly points out that the jury was not given an instruction to this effect. This argument requires us to interpret section 6928(d)(2)(A) and decide whether knowledge of lack of a permit is an essential element of the crime the statute defines.

* * * *

Had Congress intended knowledge of the lack of a permit to be an element under subsection (A) it easily could have said so. It specifically inserted a knowledge element in subsection (B), and it did so notwithstanding the "knowingly" modifier which introduces subsection (2). In the face of such obvious congressional action we will not write something into the statute which Congress so plainly left out.

Finally, our conclusion is consistent with RCRA's goals and the treatment Congress gave "knowledge" in 42 U.S.C. § 6928(d)(2)(A) and (B) to achieve these goals. The statute requires knowledge of violation of the terms of a permit under subsection (B) but omits knowledge that a permit is lacking as an element of disposing of hazardous waste without a permit under subsection (A). There is nothing illogical about this. Knowledge of the location of hazardous waste, from its generation through its disposal, is a major concern of RCRA. *See* 1976 U.S.Code Cong. & Admin.News 6264. Those who handle such waste are, therefore, affirmatively required to provide information to the EPA to know who is handling hazardous waste, monitor their activities and enforce compliance with the statute. On the other hand, persons who handle hazardous waste materials without telling the EPA what they are doing shield their activity from the eyes of the regulatory agency, and thus inhibit the agency from performing its assigned tasks. We hold that knowledge of the absence of a permit is not an element of the offense defined by 42 U.S.C. § 6928(d)(2)(A).

Decision and Remedy *The court affirmed Hoflin's conviction.*

In another case, a defendant claimed that he was unaware that the disposed waste was hazardous. The court rejected this defense holding that the defendant should have known that waste containing paints was potentially hazardous and should have investigated proper disposal.[10]

Clean Water Act

The Federal Water Pollution Control Act, frequently known as the Clean Water Act, also contains criminal sanctions. This law sets maximum standards for the discharge of pollutants into the water. While EPA has not yet adopted standards for every industry, all polluters must obtain a permit that regulates their discharges. Some companies discharge pollution into publicly owned treatment works (such as a sewer system), which clean water for household use. EPA has set pretreatment standards for these dischargers, which require them to clean up their discharges somewhat.

The Clean Water Act makes it a crime to discharge any pollutant into a publicly owned treatment work in violation of a pretreatment standard or to discharge any pollutant into the waters of the U.S. without a permit. This is not a strict liability standard, but the government must show that the defendant was at least negligent in violating the standard.

A conviction for a negligent violation of the Clean Water Act can result in a misdemeanor fine of up to $25,000 per day of violation and imprisonment for up to one year. If the law is violated knowingly, the resulting conviction would be a felony punishable by a fine of up to $50,000 per day and/or imprisonment of up to three years. The Clean Water Act also has a "knowing endangerment" provision, like RCRA's, that provides for a fine of up to $250,000 and imprisonment for up to fifteen years for discharges of pollutants into the water.

Clean Air Act liability is not limited to large industries discharging highly toxic chemicals. In one recent prosecution, a fruit juice company pleaded guilty to twenty-one counts of violating the Clean Water Act for unlawfully disposing of cranberry peelings and acidic waste water.[11]

Clean Air Act

The Clean Air Act was broadly amended in 1990 to expand the restrictions on air pollution and also expand the penalties for violation of these restrictions. A key change in the 1990 amendments was to require permits for tens of thousands of "major sources" that discharge hazardous pollutants into the air. The law also calls for strict new regulations on these emissions.

The new permit program requires the states to adopt programs to grant these permits. To obtain a permit, a source must have a compliance plan to ensure that the source will abide by all federal regulations. The source also must periodically certify that it is complying with the rules.

The 1990 amendments also changed criminal penalties for violating the Clean Air Act from misdemeanors to felonies. A knowing violation of the permit provision can mean imprisonment for up to five years. Negligent emissions of hazardous air pollutants in excess of standards can be punished by imprisonment for up to a year, and the new Clean Air Act also contains a knowing endangerment provision that parallels those of RCRA and the Clean Water Act.

An asbestos removal company violated EPA regulations and dropped asbestos-containing materials to the ground causing a cloud of released asbestos. The company was ordered to pay $50,000

---

[10] *United States v. Hayes Int'l Corp.*, 786 F.2d 1499 (11th Cir. 1986).

[11] *United States v. Ocean Spray Cranberries, Inc.*, 19 Env't Rep. (BNA) 1781 (D. Mass. 1988).

Exhibit 14-1

Penalties Imposed on Businesses that Violate Federal Environmental Laws

Statute	Highest Penalty	Average Penalty
CERCLA	$15,550	$7,295
Clean Air Act (stationary sources)	$600,000	$69,000
Clean Water Act	$1,540,000	$57,000
Resource Conservation and Recovery Act	$2,778,000	$43,300
Safe Drinking Water Act	$125,000	$11,500
Toxic Substances Control Act	$615,650	$13,563

in fines. The foreman in charge was sentenced to 90 days in jail and three years probation.[12]

Other Laws

Many other federal laws also impose strict burdens on business and contain criminal penalties for their violation. The Federal Insecticide, Fungicide and Rodenticide Act regulates pesticides through labeling requirements and other means and contains criminal liability for businesspersons, even if the individuals lack direct knowledge of the violation. Wildlife protection statutes, such as the Endangered Species Act and the Migratory Bird Treaty Act, also contain criminal sanctions for knowing and unlawful destruction of protected animals or plants.

In 1990, EPA collected over $40 million in fines under environmental laws. Exhibit 14-1 provides a measure of the penalties imposed on business under a selected group of environmental statutes.

[12] *United States v. DAR Construction, Inc.*, Env't Rep. (BNA) 21 (S.D.N.Y. 1989).

Ethical Perspective

Export of Hazardous Wastes

As expensive requirements for waste disposal mount in the United States, more companies are seeking to export their hazardous wastes to other nations. American companies now export 160,000 tons of hazardous waste per year. Most of these exports go to poorer nations with less regulation, often in Africa.

There is little legal limitation on hazardous waste exports. RCRA does require that a company file an "acknowledgment of consent" with EPA for hazardous waste exports. This is to ensure that the foreign nation is knowingly accepting the wastes.

Many argue that the export of hazardous wastes is unethical. These wastes may cause great harm to the environment and to humans if they are improperly disposed. Critics contend that the wastes are exported specifically because the disposal requirements of many foreign nations are weak and insufficient to protect the environment.

The export of hazardous waste is sometimes justified by reference to the responsibility to shareholders to make a profit. Some argue that U.S. rules are too strict and unduly restrict our businesses. This justification has not been especially persuasive because the responsibility not to do significant harm should outweigh profits in circumstances such as this.

Another justification focuses on the consent of the foreign nation. In the typical circumstance, the exporter pays the foreign nation to accept the wastes. As a consequence, some argue that any attempt to restrict the waste exports, on ethical grounds or otherwise, is paternalistic and insulting to other nations. They contend that the governments of these countries need the money and should be given the right to decide whether to take the wastes.

A shortcoming in this argument involves the limitations of foreign governments. Some of these governments are undemocratic and insufficiently concerned about the welfare of their citizens. Other governments lack the resources and expertise to appreciate the danger of the wastes and to ensure their safe disposal. Exporters may use their greater knowledge and influence to trick these governments into unwise decisions.

Critics contend that many foreign governments are simply incapable of protecting their own interests. In one circumstance, however, the government of Sierra Leone dramatically rejected a payment of $25 million to accept the wastes from a U.S. company. It is noteworthy that this rejection occurred only after the deal became public and the government faced extensive adverse publicity.

There is undeniable ethical merit in allowing sovereign foreign nations to make decisions for themselves about accepting hazardous wastes. Before this becomes a justification for export, however, the foreign consent must be fully informed. The exporter may, therefore, have an ethical duty to ensure that the foreign nation fully understands the nature of the hazardous wastes and the risks that they present. The company also should assist the nation in providing for the safe disposal of the wastes.

International Perspectives

Foreign Environmental Regulations

Few areas of international law are expanding faster than that governing the environment. Foreign trade agreements, such as the North American Free Trade Agreement, now commonly contain provisions for environmental protection. National laws are also burgeoning.

European environmental laws are increasing and can have important implications for exporters. For example, Germany enacted an important law governing product packaging. The first regulated area under this law is "transport packaging," which governs any material used to protect the product during its transit to the retailer. Under the law, the manufacturer or importer and retailer are responsible for "taking back" any transport packaging. These parties also must ensure that the packaging does not find its way into public waste disposal, which generally means recycling.

Retailers must "take back" secondary packaging, those materials used for advertising the product (such as cartons of blister packs). Retailers may take it back at the time of sale or permit the consumer the opportunity to return the packaging to the point of sale without charge. Retailers must also supply containers and signs to encourage such recycling.

In addition to Germany, other European countries, such as Austria and the Netherlands, have similar laws for electronic products. These laws require sellers to take back used electric or electronic equipment and parts from consumers. Manufacturers are required to take back the parts from retailers. Similar laws are under consideration for other products, including automobiles.

Questions and Case Problems

1. EPA cleaned up a spill of trichloroethylene at the site of a textile plant, Stamina Mills, that was a subsidiary of Kayser-Roth Corporation. Soon thereafter, Stamina was dissolved. Kayser-Roth had owned a majority of the shares in Stamina Mills, and EPA sought to recover its cleanup costs from Kayser-Roth, as an owner and operator of the site. Kayser-Roth controlled the operations of Stamina Mills, including many budgetary details. For example, Kayser-Roth had to approve any capital expenditure greater than $5000 by Stamina. Kayser-Roth claimed that Stamina was the owner and operator of the site and that Kayser-Roth should not be liable. Should Kayser-Roth be held liable for cleanup costs? [*United States v. Kayser-Roth Corp.*, 910 F.2d 24 (1st Cir. 1990)].

2. A bank loaned funds to Swainsboro Print Works, secured by the company's accounts receivable and its plant and equipment. Swainsboro's financial condition deteriorated, and the bank foreclosed on some of the company's equipment. The bank also took a role in managing Swainsboro in an attempt to protect its interest.

EPA subsequently found toxic chemicals on the site of Swainsboro's plant and spent $400,000 in cleanup costs to remove them. Given Swainsboro's fragile economic condition, EPA also sued the bank for cleanup costs. Should the bank be liable for these cleanup costs? [*United States v. Fleet Factors Corp.*, 901 F.2d 1550 (11th Cir. 1990)].

3. A worker for Ortho Pharmaceutical claimed that, while working for the corporation, he was exposed to chemicals that caused him to suffer a reduced sperm count and loss of sexual appetite, among other injuries. He sued the company and its officers and directors in tort for personal injury damages. He claimed that the company and its officers improperly failed to warn him of the risks of work. An officer sought to dismiss the claim. Should the officer be individually liable for the worker's injuries? [*Cruz v. Ortho Pharmaceutical Corp.*, 691 F.2d 902 (1st Cir. 1980)].

4. Friendly Chemical Corp. is intent on "green marketing." The company believes that it can reduce costs and increase revenues by being scrupulous in protecting the environment. Every corporate policy is dedicated in part to environmentalism. Friendly sought to expand to a new site. Before doing so, Friendly hired an expert to examine the site for any signs of hazardous substances. The expert reported that the site was "clean," so Friendly purchased the site. Later, hazardous wastes were discovered, EPA cleaned up the site, and the agency charged Friendly with cleanup costs. Friendly resisted payment, fearing damage to its reputation, as well as to its pocketbook. Should Friendly be liable for cleanup costs at this site?

5. John Stimkorb was the manager of a hazardous waste disposal facility. After an extremely heavy rainfall, Stimkorb ordered his employees to pump rainwater that had accumulated in the site and direct it into a ditch. Because the rainwater had come into contact with hazardous wastes, EPA prosecuted Stimkorb criminally under RCRA. Stimkorb argued that the rainwater was not a hazardous substance and that no harm was done to the environment. Is Stimkorb guilty?

6. Catellus Corporation sold used automobile batteries. These batteries were no longer useful to power cars but had value because of the lead they contained. After the lead was extracted, the batteries were disposed. The government cleaned up a site containing the batteries and brought a CERCLA cleanup cost recovery action against Catellus, contending that the company had arranged for disposal or treatment of the batteries and was thus a liable party. How should the court rule? [*Catellus Dev. Corp. v. United States*, 828 F. Supp. 764 (N.D. Cal. 1993)]

CHAPTER FIFTEEN

Health Care Law

KEY BACKGROUND

Health Care is at the center of many of today's greatest legal and moral controversies, including abortion, the right to die, the epidemic of drug abuse, and AIDS. Health-care administrators and providers are daily confronted with these difficult "life-and-death" questions and subject to potential legal liability for their decisions.

Health care is also a large and rapidly growing sector of the economy. The health-care industry accounts for well over 10 percent of the nation's gross national product and employs over 8 million persons. Many of the most important legal issues in health care are much more mundane than the above controversies. These less prominent issues, however, may be economically, medically, and legally more important.

This chapter focuses on the everyday issues of health care, such as government regulation of the health-care industry. The chapter also concentrates on the perspectives of the hospital, rather than of the individual doctor, though hospitals and doctors share many of the same legal concerns.

Government Regulation of Health Care

For most of this century, only state governments actively regulated health-care professionals. States maintained boards charged with licensing and disciplining physicians to ensure quality care. These boards have been overwhelmed with their workload and their effectiveness has been criticized.

The federal government's involvement in health-care regulation began in 1965 with the enactment of Medicare and Medicaid. These laws funded health care for the poor and the elderly and reimbursed health-care professionals for their reasonable costs of care. The costs of Medicare and Medicaid quickly got out of hand.

A portion of the high costs of Medicare and Medicaid was due to advanced technology and increased demand for medical services. Another portion of the cost, estimated at over $1 billion per year, was estimated to be due to physician abuse of the process and overcharging the government.

Suppose that a person covered by Medicare came to a doctor for treatment. The doctor was aware that the individual was backed by unlimited resources. If the doctor undertook procedures that were medically unnecessary, he or she would be compensated, and there was no institution to check the process. Some doctors would even bill the government for care that was not rendered. Over 50 million Americans have some coverage under Medicare and Medicaid, and these programs have tens of billions of dollars of federal funding. The potential for abuse was enormous.

PROs

Congress took steps to control the costs of Medicare and Medicaid. In 1982, Congress passed the Peer Review Improvement Act, which established a **peer review organization** (PRO) system. Under this program, a board of peer physicians reviews healthcare services to determine if they are "reasonably and medically necessary,"[1] and of proper quality.

Suppose that a PRO decides that a doctor's treatment decisions are incorrect or unnecessary. The PRO cannot take direct enforcement action against the doctor but can recommend that payment be denied under Medicare or Medicaid. The care recipient may then become personally liable for the costs, but most beneficiaries of the government programs lack the funds or private insurance to pay.

The PRO can also recommend that the Office of the Inspector General (OIG) of the Department of Health and Human Services (HHS) take enforcement action against the doctor. The OIG can issue fines or suspend the doctor from participation in Medicare and Medicaid.

A doctor may appeal the PRO decision and is entitled to due process in review of the appeal. The doctor is entitled to be represented by counsel, cross-examine witnesses, and present his or her own expert witnesses at a hearing. The hearing is conducted before an arbitrator or panel of disinterested experts.

Some doctors have even sued the physicians serving on the PRO over their decisions. In one case, a doctor serving on a PRO participated in revoking the hospital surgical privileges of another physician. The sanctioned doctor sued the PRO physician under antitrust law and received a multi-million-dollar verdict.[2] The court found that the PRO was used to enable the physician to monopolize the local market for surgery.

Health Care Quality Improvement Act

Congress sought to correct some of the problems with PROs in 1986 under the Health Care Quality Improvement Act (HCQIA). This law was intended to encourage physicians to identify and discipline other doctors who were incompetent or dishonest.

One important provision of HCQIA is its provision of partial legal immunity for peer review. If peer review is conducted in compliance with government standards, the reviewing physician, the hospital, and other participants in the process are immunized from liability. Immunity protects these participants from many actions but does not extend to civil rights cases or cases brought by the U.S. Attorney General.

Another key provision of HCQIA is its creation of a national databank on possible malpractice. Hospitals are required to report certain information to the databank. First, a hospital must report any payment made in court or in settlement of a medical malpractice claim. Second, a hospital must report any episode in which a physician is sanctioned for improper practice. Failure to report is subject to a $10,000 fine per instance.

HCQIA also requires hospitals to request information from the databank. Any time that a hospital considers granting clinical privileges to a new physician, dentist or licensed health-care practitioner, it must request reported information from the databank. The hospital also must request such information every two years for individuals who maintain privileges at the hospital's facilities.

If a hospital fails to request information, it becomes subject to greater malpractice liability in any future cases. The hospital is much more likely to be liable for failure to investigate the quality of its physicians. This source of liability is discussed below.

Reimbursement Controls

HCQIA and other federal statutes also changed the system of physician reimbursement in the 1980s. Traditionally, the system had reimbursed doctors for their reasonable costs of care, based on the actual costs incurred. Under the new system, there are predetermined reimbursement rates for care of many common medical problems.

This change significantly altered the incentive structure of doctors. Under the old system, doctors had an incentive to provide an excess of care in order to obtain added reimbursement. Under the new system, doctors have an incentive to provide an insufficiency of care. Doctors can profit only to the extent that their actual costs of care are less than the predetermined reimbursable amount.

Reimbursement is typically set through **Diagnosis-Related Groups** (DRGs). DRGs break down common medical needs into over 460 separate

---

[1] 42 U.S.C. Sec. 1320c-3(a)(1)(A).

[2] *Patrick v. Burget,* 108 S.Ct. 1658 (1988).

categories and the care required for treatment of each category of medical need. Reimbursement schedules are then established for the categories of care.

The schedules for reimbursement proved to be extraordinarily complex. One court characterized them as something that "only legislators and accountants can appreciate."[3] For some categories, the reimbursable amount set by the government seems too low and discourages the provision of even necessary medical care.

The new structure puts some physicians and hospitals in a difficult situation. They retain a duty to provide proper care to patients or face malpractice liability. The actual costs of such care, however, may exceed the reimbursement obtainable from the government. This means that the care provider may effectively have a legal duty to lose money. Physicians remain ultimately responsible, however, for their patients and cannot put the burden off on insurers, as illustrated by the following case.

---

[3] *American Medical Association v. Bowen*, 857 F.2d 267, 269 (5th Cir. 1988).

Case 15.1
Wickline v. State
California Court of Appeals, 1986
228 Ca. Rptr. 661

Background and Facts   Lois Wickline, a married woman in her mid-forties, received physical therapy treatment for problems with her back and legs. She was admitted to Van Nuys Community Hospital and treated by a specialist on peripheral vascular surgery, Dr. Gerald E. Polonsky. Polonsky diagnosed her condition as a form of arteriosclerosis that required surgery. Ms. Wickline was covered by the state insurance system, known as Medi-Cal. Medi-Cal authorized the surgery and ten days of hospitalization for treatment.

On January 7, 1977, Polonsky undertook surgery and replaced part of Ms. Wickline's central artery with a synthetic graft. Later that day, she required additional surgery to remove a blood clot. During her recovery from these operations she suffered a great deal of pain and experienced hallucinating episodes. Five days later, Dr. Polonsky performed further surgery to relieve spasms in her blood vessels. Wickline was scheduled to be released on January 16, but Dr. Polonsky concluded that she would require eight days of additional hospitalization. This required submitting an additional form to Medi-Cal. Medi-Cal rejected reimbursement for this extension but authorized an additional four days of hospitalization.

Wickline's condition remained stable in the four additional days of hospitalization, until January 21. While recognizing that she still faced some danger, Dr. Polonsky discharged her from the hospital on January 21, when Medi-Cal funding expired. After several days at home, Wickline began experiencing great pain in her leg, which also became discolored. On January 30, she was readmitted to the hospital as an emergency patient. Her circulation problems could not be surgically corrected, so her leg was amputated above the knee. Had she remained in the hospital, amputation might not have been necessary.

Wickline sued several defendants for damages, including Medi-Cal. After a jury ruled for Wickline, Medi-Cal appealed.

ROWEN, Associate Justice.

* * * *

Title 22 of the California Administrative Code section 51110, provided, in pertinent part, at the relevant time in issue here, that: "The determination of need for acute care shall be made in accordance with the usual standards of medical practice in the community."

The patient who requires treatment and who is harmed when care which should have been provided is not provided should recover for the injuries suffered from all those responsible for the deprivation of such care, including, when appropriate, health-care payors. Third party payors of health care services can be held legally accountable when medically inappropriate decisions result from defects in the design or implementation of cost containment mechanisms as, for example, when appeals made on a patient's behalf for medical or hospital care are arbitrarily ignored or unreasonably disregarded or overridden. However, the physician who complies without protest with the limitations imposed by a third party payor, when his medical judgment dictates otherwise, cannot avoid his ultimate responsibility for his patient's care. He cannot point to the health care payor as the liability scapegoat when the consequences of his own determinative medical decisions go sour.

There is little doubt that Dr. Polonsky was intimidated by the Medi-Cal program but he was not paralyzed by Dr. Glassman's response nor rendered powerless to act appropriately if other action was required under the circumstances. If, in his medical judgment, it was in his patient's best interest that she remain in the acute care hospital setting for an additional four days beyond the extended time period originally authorized by Medi-Cal, Dr. Polonsky should have made some effort to keep Wickline there.

* * * *

This court appreciates that what is at issue here is the effect of cost containment programs upon the professional judgment of physicians to prescribe hospital treatment for patients requiring the same. While we recognize, realistically, that cost consciousness has become a permanent feature of the health-care system, it is essential that cost limitation programs not be permitted to corrupt medical judgment. We have concluded, from the facts in issue here, that in this case it did not.

Decision and Remedy *The court reversed the judgment against Medi-Cal.*

The new reimbursement system of DRGs apparently has significantly reduced the costs of federally insured medical care. Some observers fear, however, that the system has caused some patients to be refused and others to receive insufficient medical attention.

The government also maintains enforcement mechanisms under Medicare and Medicaid. Medicare fraud is a crime. In addition, the government may discontinue the payment of benefits to facilities that fail to comply with federal requirements.

Health Insurance Portability and Accountability Act

The Health Insurance Portability and Accountability Act of 1996 placed new restrictions on health insurance providers. The law applies to "group health plans" and "health insurance issuers." The new portability requirements limit the extent to which such plans and issuers may impose preexisting conditions exclusions on participants or beneficiaries. The Act prohibits a plan from discriminating based on health-related status, such as a disability or genetic makeup. As a consequence, a plan or issuer may not create eligibility rules or charge higher premiums to individuals based on their health status.

▬ Malpractice

More and more individuals are suing physicians for malpractice, to the point that one may consider the system to be in "crisis." The costs of malpractice insurance have skyrocketed and, sometimes, insurance is wholly unavailable. Reducing malpractice liability is a central concern for health care providers.

Standards of Malpractice Liability

Primary malpractice liability usually lies with the treating doctor. It is well-established that physicians owe a very high level of care, described as a fiduciary duty, to their patients. If a physician breaches that standard of care, he or she may be liable in malpractice.

A leading source of malpractice liability is failure to diagnose or treat. Suppose that Patrick Kelly has a skin discoloration on his leg and consults a dermatologist. The doctor examines the skin, diagnoses the problem as a rash, and prescribes an ointment. Patrick later discovers that the problem is skin cancer. The delay in diagnosis may cause Patrick to suffer painful treatment or even death. In this case the dermatologist may be liable for malpractice.

Another source of liability is inappropriate treatment. Suppose that the physician accurately diagnoses the problem but provides some treatment recently found to be ineffective. Or the physician may prescribe a treatment to which the patient is allergic, causing greater medical problems.

The above categories are the most common sources of malpractice liability, but many other potential problems exist. For example, doctors have been found liable for failing to disclose their findings to patients, for breaching the patient's right of confidentiality, or for failing to provide adequate treatment facilities and support staff. A recent decision found a doctor potentially liable for failure to inform a rape victim of the availability of a "morning-after pill" that could avert pregnancy.

A key issue in malpractice litigation is the standard of care to which doctors are held. Historically, the standard of care was a local one. A Montana physician, for example, would have a different standard of care than a doctor in Los Angeles. Today, the standard of care is considered to be uniform nationwide, and all doctors are held to the same high standard.

The standard of care is usually that recommended in expert treatises on medical care and in medical journals. Each case is unique, however, and the malpractice case often comes down to a "battle of experts." Each side in the case will present medical experts attacking or defending the quality of care provided. The jury is left with the decision.

In one case, a plastic surgeon performed silicone implantation for breast enhancement. After the surgery, the patient suffered a series of complications, including soreness, inflammation, hematomas (collections of blood under the skin) and physical disfigurements. She sued the doctor for malpractice. Evidence demonstrated that the doctor's surgical technique was taught to him at a prestigious college of medicine and was used by many plastic surgeons in the area. Other evidence showed, however, that the technique was no longer recognized or accepted by experts. The court held that the doctor had violated the "reasonable and prudent" physician standard, even though many other doctors continued to use this practice.[4]

One defense for physicians is the "honest error in judgment" rule. Physicians typically do not guarantee the success of a treatment regime. If a physician made a good faith treatment judgment that turned out badly, courts are reluctant to second-guess the decision.

Another possible defense is a "good samaritan" statute. Physicians who are responding to an emergency situation without a fee arrangement are freed from liability under good samaritan statutes in most states.

The patient's informed consent may also be a defense under malpractice. Suppose that a certain diagnostic procedure presents a 1 in 100,000 chance of a serious allergic reaction in patients. The doctor should inform the patient of this risk and obtain written consent from the patient to conduct the procedure. If the patient is fully and fairly informed of the risks, the patient normally cannot win a malpractice claim in the event that he or she suffers the allergic reaction.

To recover under malpractice, patients also must show that they were damaged by the improper treatment. Even use of an unwise and negligent treatment does not produce liability unless damages can be traced to that treatment. This is a particular problem in cases of advanced cancer. In these cases, the patient might well have died even with optimal medical treatment.

A doctor may also escape liability if the damages are due to the contributory fault of the patient. If a patient violates a doctor's orders, this may represent contributory negligence. Patient's fault may also be present when the patient incorrectly discloses information to the doctor. A doctor considering a prescription may ask if the patient is taking any nonprescription medication, and the patient may erroneously answer no. A doctor should not be liable for an adverse drug reaction that results from the combination of prescription and nonprescription drugs.

Many states have passed laws to limit malpractice liability. Some states limit punitive damages and noneconomic damages (mental anguish), while others restrict attorneys' fees. Total malpractice liability remains enormous, however.

---

[4] *Henderson v. Heyer-Schulte Corp.*, 600 S.W.2d 844 (Tex. App. 1980).

Hospital Liability

An important legal question is the extent to which a hospital should be liable for the malpractice of doctors who practice within the hospital. This issue has great practical significance. Seventy-five to 80 percent of malpractice actions arise out of treatment in hospitals. Malpractice recoveries may exceed the insurance coverage of individual physicians and, therefore, plaintiffs seek recovery from hospitals.

Under traditional common law, most hospitals were exempt from liability in these circumstances. Nonprofit hospitals received **charitable immunity**, which meant that they could not be vicariously liable for the acts of even their employees.

Now, charitable immunity seldom protects hospitals. The potential **vicarious liability** of hospitals for malpractice of doctors is generally governed by principles of agency law, as set forth in Chapter 34 of *West's Business Law, Seventh Edition.*

Under these agency law principles, hospitals will generally be liable for the acts of physicians who are employees of the hospital. Most doctors who practice in hospitals, however, are not employees. Instead, the doctors are **independent contractors** who make arrangements for use of the hospital's facilities.

As a general rule, a hospital will not be liable for the torts of an independent contractor. In certain circumstances, though, the hospital will be liable. Courts increasingly apply **ostensible agency liability** on the theory that hospitals hold themselves out to patients as providers of care through the services of a doctor.

Determination of hospital liability under ostensible agency is highly fact-specific. Consider the following decision. A patient was treated by radiologists at a hospital and suffered damages from overexposure to radiation. She sued the hospital for damages. An appellate court reversed summary judgment for the hospital and held that the hospital was potentially liable.[5] In reaching this result, the court considered the fact that the radiologists were located on the main floor of the hospital, and that patients had to enter through the hospital's main entrance and pass through doors labeled "X-ray department." The court also stressed that there was no dress code to distinguish the independent contractor doctors from hospital personnel. The hospital was potentially liable even though the doctors provided all their own equipment and the hospital received no payments for radiation treatments provided.

Other courts have been somewhat less strict in holding hospitals liable. A recent Montana case held that a hospital was not liable for the malpractice of a resident radiologist.[6] That case stressed the rural nature of the area, where virtually all radiologists practiced in hospitals. The issue of vicarious liability is of great concern to hospitals, especially because hospitals have little control over the independent contractor doctors who practice on their premises.

The key question in assessing hospital liability is whether the patient considered himself or herself a patient of the hospital or recognized that the hospital was merely the site of treatment by a doctor. Courts have considered the following factors in deciding whether to assign liability to a hospital:

- Whether the physician had a private practice outside the hospital.

- Whether the patient came to the physician through the hospital or through an outside practice.

- The extent to which the physician received compensation or supplies from the hospital.

- The nature of the physician's staff privileges at the hospital.

- Whether the physician was administrator or stockholder of the hospital.

None of these factors alone is crucial; they are simply considered by courts, along with other evidence. To help insulate themselves from liability, hospitals can insist that independent contractor physicians wear distinguishing badges or dress and post notices that alert patients that the doctor is not an employee.

Hospitals are even more likely to be found liable for malpractice by nurses. Nurses are hospital employees. Nurses also have a professional standard of care. Nurses must effectively carry out the orders of physicians.

Suppose that a nurse employee of a hospital is directed to check a patient's vital signs every thirty minutes and notify the physician if the patient's con-

---

[5] *Sztorc v. Northwest Hospital,* 496 N.E.2d 1200 (Ill. App. 1986).

[6] *Milliron v. Francke,* 793 P.2d 824 (Mont. 1990).

dition appeared to deteriorate. The nurse fails to do so, and the patient dies. The hospital will be liable as the employer of the nurse who committed malpractice.

Nurses must also exercise their own medical judgment. A nurse may have a duty to violate a physician's orders, if he or she knows those orders to be unsafe. Suppose a physician erroneously orders medication that a nurse knows would harm a patient. If the nurse gives the medication, the injured plaintiff would have a strong malpractice case. Nurses have a general duty to supervise patients and inform physicians of any material change in the condition of patients. The hospital may be liable under any of these circumstances of nursing malpractice.

▰ Hospital Direct Liability

Hospitals may also be directly liable to patients of independent contractor physicians under a theory of corporate negligence. Such negligence may exist when a hospital negligently permitted an unqualified doctor to practice. This is especially likely if the hospital failed to avail itself of the HCQIA databank in investigating the physician's qualifications.

Hospital liability may be predicated on violation of some recognized standard. Many hospitals have bylaws to govern physicians who practice at the hospital. A violation of these bylaws may produce liability. In addition, the Joint Commission on Accreditation of Hospitals ("JCAH") sets minimum standards for hospital review of physician actions. Violation of these standards may be considered negligence. For example, the JCAH demands that hospitals provide drug monitoring services to avoid adverse drug interactions.

Hospital liability is not limited to negligent hiring. If a hospital has notice of a physician's incompetence, it should deny the use of its facilities to that physician. Otherwise, the hospital may be liable for negligence.

In one case, a patient in a hospital underwent surgery that was improperly conducted and caused the patient serious harm, including the loss of a kidney. The patient recovered damages from the hospital, which knew or should have known of the surgeon's incompetence and still provided operating room facilities. In this case, the hospital had been sued in two prior cases when the physician conducted the same type of surgery. [7]

Hospitals may also be liable for failure to supervise and monitor doctors who practice at the hospital. Although the hospital may have no direct control over treatment in individual cases, the hospital can monitor the general quality of the physician. The JCAH standards require that a hospital have an ongoing quality assurance program to monitor and evaluate the quality of patient care provided by doctors.

A hospital is not liable for all instances of malpractice that occur on its premises. Hospital liability is broad, however, as illustrated in the following decision.

---

[7] *Purcell v. Zimbalman*, 500 P.2d 335 (Ariz. App. 1972).

▰ Case 15.2
**Francisco v.
Hartford Gynecological
Center, Inc.**
Superior Court of Connecticut, 1994
No. CV92-0513841

Background and Facts *Lori Francisco suffered injuries while undergoing intravenous anesthesia at the Hartford Gynecological Center. She sued the responsible nurse and the Center itself for malpractice for her injuries. The Center moved for summary judgment on claims against it, contending that the nurse was an independent contractor, so the hospital was not vicariously liable for her malpractice.*

CORRADINO, Judge.

* * * *

The cases have set forth several reasons for applying the doctrine of apparent authority to a hospital or medical center in this type of situation.

(1) The center here agreed to perform certain surgical procedures for the plaintiff. No patient in the plaintiff's situation would assume anything else but that someone performing a necessary medical intervention to accomplish that procedure was anything else than an employee of the center that had agreed to perform the agreed upon procedure ....

(2) When a patient agrees to have a surgical procedure performed at a hospital or medical center, she has a right to rely on the reputation of the hospital as opposed to any particular health professional who may have a contract or perform particular services for the hospital ....

(3) A person enters a hospital or goes to a medical center for a wide range of services rather than treatment by a particular health professional ....

(4) Public outrage would surely follow an announcement by a medical center or hospital "that it regards all staff doctors as completely independent professionals, conducts no supervision of their performance and takes no interest in their competence."

Decision and Remedy *The court denied the center's motion for summary judgment, because plaintiff had sufficiently alleged apparent authority.*

Hospitals can also be liable for products they supply. Hospitals typically provide medical devices and drugs for patients of doctors that practice in the hospital. Devices must be properly maintained, and a hospital may be strictly liable if they are defective. Hospitals have also been liable for failure to have necessary equipment (e.g., portable oxygen supply) available. With respect to drugs, hospitals may have their own duty to warn patients of potential side effects, in addition to the duty of the prescribing doctor.

▰ Patient "Dumping"

According to a subcommittee of the House of Representatives, William Jenness suffered a serious automobile accident and was rushed to a nearby hospital. Though facilities were available, the hospital asked for $1000 advance deposit, which he could not provide. He was therefore transferred to a public hospital, where he had to wait four hours for an operating time. During this time, he bled to death.[8]

This example illustrates a pressing health concern, known as "patient dumping" or medical nonpractice. The example is by no means an unusual one. Approximately 250,000 patients every year are refused emergency treatment by hospitals, according to congressional estimates. A study in Chicago found that nearly 10 percent of patients transferred away by emergency rooms died, as opposed to 4 percent among those treated promptly.

When a patient is turned away from a hospital, there usually is some alternative. The patient typically is taken to a public hospital that accepts all patients, regardless of ability to pay. These hospitals are often overburdened, however, and unable to provide prompt quality care.

There are several causes of the patient dumping problem. Eighty-seven percent of the time, dumping is due to the patient's lack of insurance. Over 30 million Americans lack private health insurance. Budget cuts during the 1980s removed millions from coverage under Medicare and Medicaid. Changes in federal reimbursement reduced hospital profits that previously were used to cover care for the uninsured.

When a hospital turns away a desperately needy patient, it seems cruel. But hospitals must receive payments of the expensive care they provide or the hospitals may risk bankruptcy. One

---

[8] *Equal Access to Health Care: Patient Dumping: Subcomm. on Human Resources and Intergovernmental Relations to the House Comm. on Government Operations,* H.R. Rep. No. 531, 100th Cong., 2d Sess. at 6-7 (1988).

hospital administrator bluntly noted: "We don't expect Safeway or A&P to give away free food for people who can't afford it."[9] In some circumstances, however, the law may compel hospitals to provide medical care to the uninsured.

Common Law

Under traditional principles of common law, a hospital or doctor owed no duty of treatment. Historic negligence law imposed no duty of rescue, and this principle extended to health care providers.

Courts in a number of states, however, have created some duty to render care. In some states, courts have held hospitals liable for providing full care, once they initiate any care. If a hospital emergency room admits a person as a patient, the hospital may have assumed a duty of care and can no longer turn away that person.

A Delaware court suggested that a hospital may have a duty to provide care when a patient relies upon the hospital's custom of furnishing emergency services. A few states have gone further and held that hospitals have a duty to provide care in cases of emergency.

About half the states have passed statutes that impose some obligation on hospitals to provide emergency care. Even in these states, the laws may provide no private damages remedy for persons who are turned away from emergency rooms. In addition, most of the laws are rather vague regarding the circumstances and extent of the hospital's duty.

Comprehensive Omnibus Budget Reconciliation Act

In 1986, Congress passed the Comprehensive Omnibus Budget Reconciliation Act (COBRA). Although this legislation was primarily concerned with the federal government's budget, it also contained a small provision that requires hospitals to provide care in emergency rooms.

COBRA applies to all hospitals that both have emergency care departments and that participate in the Medicare reimbursement program. This includes the majority of hospitals.

Under COBRA, the hospital must provide a medical examination for any person who requests one. This examination is used to determine whether the person is suffering from an "emergency medical condition" or is in "active labor" in pregnancy. If so, the hospital must provide the person with necessary treatment (called "stabilization") or transfer the person within the requirements of COBRA. The following case reflects the scope and application of COBRA.

---

[9] *Washington Post,* June 30, 1985, at A14.

■ Case 15.3
Cleland v. Bronsons Health Care Group, Inc.
United States Court of Appeals,
Sixth Circuit, 1990
917 F.2d 266

Background and Facts *The Clelands took their fifteen-year-old son to the Bronsons Methodist Hospital emergency room, complaining of cramps and vomiting. He was examined by a doctor, who diagnosed the problem as influenza and discharged the boy. Cleland was actually suffering from intussusception, a serious intestinal disease. Less than twenty-four hours later, he suffered cardiac arrest and died.*

The parents brought this suit under COBRA, claiming that their son had been improperly dismissed from the emergency room. The district court dismissed their claim, and the parents appealed.

BOGGS, Circuit Judge.

* * * *

[The court first held that COBRA was not limited to discharges based upon the patient's inability to pay.]

However, Congress did limit the cause of action provided by the Act to only those who did not receive an "appropriate" screening or who were not "stabilized" before being transferred or discharged. In attempting to interpret those ambiguous phrases, we can look to legislative history, along with other aids to construction.

"Appropriate" is one of the most wonderful weasel words in the dictionary, and a great aid to the resolution of disputed issues in the drafting of legislation. Who, after all, can be found to stand up for "inappropriate" treatment or actions of any sort? Under the circumstances of the act, "appropriate" can be taken to mean care similar to care that would have been provided to any other patient, or at least not known by the providers to be insufficient or below their own standards. Plaintiffs essentially contend that "appropriate" denotes, at a minimum, the full panoply of state malpractice law, and at a maximum, includes a guarantee of successful result.

In one sense, in hindsight, the screening provided in this case could scarcely be called appropriate. The patient came in, he had a condition that was at least conceivably ascertainable by medical science, the condition was not ascertained, and he died within twenty-four hours. At the same time, there is not the slightest indication that this outcome would have been any different for a patient of any other characteristics. Had his sex, race, national origin, financial condition, politics, social status, etc., been anything whatsoever, as far as can be gleaned from the complaint, the outcome would have been the same. Under these circumstances, we hold that the complaint simply fails to allege any inappropriateness in the medical screening in the sense required by the Act.

The same reasoning applies to stabilization, though with even greater force. To all appearances, the plaintiff's condition was stable. He was not in acute distress, neither the doctors nor the patient or his parents made the slightest indication that the condition was worsening in any way or that it presented any risk that might become life-threatening, or that it would worsen markedly by the next day.

Again, in hindsight, any stability was quite short-run. The patient died. However, neither the normal meaning of stabilization, nor any of the attendant legislative history or apparatus, indicates that Congress intended to provide a guarantee of the result of emergency room treatment and discharge.

* * * *

We can think of many reasons other than indigency that might lead a hospital to give less than standard attention to a person who arrives at the emergency room. These might include: prejudice against the race, sex, or ethnic group of the patient; distaste for the patient's condition (e.g., AIDS patients); personal dislike or antagonism between the medical personnel and the patient; disapproval of the patient's occupation; or political or cultural opposition.

If a hospital refused treatment to persons for any of these reasons, or gave cursory treatment, the evil inflicted would be quite akin to that discussed by Congress in the legislative history, and the patient would fall squarely within the statutory language. On the other hand, if, as appears to be the case here (and as is not contradicted in the pleading), a hospital provides care to the plaintiff that is no different than would have been offered to any patient, and, from all that appears, is "within its capability" (that is, constitutes a good faith application of the hospital's resources), the words "appropriate medical screening" in the statute should not be interpreted to go beyond what was provided here.

Decision and Remedy. *The court affirmed the district court's dismissal of this claim.*

After determining that emergency treatment is necessary, COBRA permits a hospital to transfer a patient under some circumstances. Transfer is allowed only when (1) the receiving facility has adequate space and qualified personnel for treatment; (2) the receiving facility agrees to accept and treat the patient; (3) the transferring hospital provides all necessary medical records; (4) the transfer is performed by qualified personnel with appropriate equipment; and (5) the transfer meets other requirements necessary for patient safety.

COBRA is violated whenever a hospital refuses treatment to an emergency patient or transfers the patient without compliance with all federal requirements. If COBRA is violated, hospitals (but not physicians) are strictly liable for damages to the patient or others harmed by the violation. Hospitals who receive patients dumped in violation of COBRA may also sue the transferring hospital for their costs.

In addition to private damages, COBRA provides for civil monetary penalties of up to $50,000 per violation. The government also may suspend Medicare payments for hospitals that willfully or negligently violate the statute.

Antitrust Liability

In addition to all the legal issues specific to the health care industry, hospitals and other providers are subject to more general requirements. For example, the health care industry must abide by federal labor laws, if employees seek to unionize, and must abide by federal antidiscrimination laws in employment decisions. For the health care industry, probably the most important of these general requirements is antitrust law. The basic provisions of antitrust law are set forth in Chapter 47 of *West's Business Law, Seventh Edition*, and in Chapters 26 and 27 of *West's Legal Environment of Business, Third Edition*.

Health-care professionals are part of a very large and lucrative industry. As in any business, some individuals or hospitals may abuse their position to seek excess profits. In some circumstances, a hospital or other care provider may even attain a monopoly over a segment of the health-care market. The medical profession is subject to antitrust laws, just like other industries.

Many antitrust cases are brought under Section 1 of the Sherman Act. This section proscribes contracts, combinations or conspiracies in restraint of trade. Many hospital actions may be subject to Section 1 challenges.

Staff Privileges

Approximately half of all antitrust litigation in health care involves the denial of staff privileges. A doctor who is refused an opportunity to practice at a hospital may sue and claim that the denial violates antitrust laws.

Suppose that York Hospital is the largest hospital in town. Jane Forsythe has a contract to provide radiological services for hospital patients, and she is also a stockholder in the hospital. Jim Walcz seeks permission to offer radiological services in the hospital. After consulting with Jane Forsythe, the hospital rejects Walcz's request. This may violate antitrust laws by permitting Jane to control the largest local market for radiological services.

Exclusive staff arrangements are not always illegal. In a recent decision, a local hospital had an exclusive contract with one physician to perform all pathological tissue analysis. The court rejected an antitrust challenge to this arrangement, because the hospital had no financial interest in the pathologist's practice and because the hospital did not have sufficient local market power to restrain competition in pathology.[10] The following decision further analyzes this situation.

---

10 *Steuer v. National Medical Enterprises,* 672 F. Supp. 1489 (D.S.C. 1987).

Case 15.4
Todorov v. DCH Health Care Authority
United States Court of Appeals, Eleventh Circuit, 1991.
821 F.2d 1438

Background and Facts DCH is the largest general hospital in the Tuscaloosa, Alabama area. Alexandre Todorov is a member of the DCH medical staff with privileges to practice neurology. He then applied for the privilege to perform radiological services in the form of CT scans of the head to detect neurological damage. CT scans were currently performed by the hospital's radiology staff.

DCH denied Todorov's request to perform CT scans on his patients. This was based on the judgment of the hospital's credentials committee. Two physicians advised the hospital that Todorov lacked the competence to administer CT scans. Both physicians were current DCH radiologists. Todorov appealed the denial to the hospital Hearing Panel. This panel concluded that Todorov was competent to perform CT scans but made no recommendation on his application.

The hospital's executive committee heard presentations from Todorov and the credentials committee. The executive committee then denied his application because it did not want to establish a precedent of granting radiology privileges to nonradiologists. It feared that this could make organization and scheduling of radiology chaotic and would drive staff radiologists away from the hospital. The committee also expressed concern that Todorov might have difficulty complying with hospital reporting requirements.

Todorov brought this action against the hospital and its radiologists. He made a number of antitrust claims, including that the hospital and radiologists conspired to deny him privileges, in violation of Section 1 of the Sherman Act. The district court granted the defendants' motions for summary judgment. Todorov appealed.

TJOFLAT, Chief Judge.

* * * *

DCH could have fostered competition among the radiologists—and thus its potential for further profits—by granting Dr. Todorov, and, eventually, other nonradiologists, privileges to practice in its radiology department, but it chose not to do so. At first blush, DCH's decision appears to be anticompetitive and against its own self-interest—and therefore supportive of Dr. Todorov's argument that the hospital conspired to help the radiologists maintain their super competitive profits. Dr. Todorov, however, does not explain why the hospital would want to act this way; he simply concludes that it did.

We have searched the record for a possible, and reasonable, explanation as to why DCH would deliberately act against its own economic interest, and find none. What we find, instead, is that DCH denied Dr. Todorov's application for privileges to foster competition and to serve its own economic interest.

The principal reason DCH's board of directors gave for rejecting Dr. Todorov's application for privileges was to preserve the efficient operation of the hospital's radiology department. The board thought that if it granted Dr. Todorov privileges it would invite a flood of similar applications from nonradiologists, and as more of these physicians performed their own radiological procedures, the radiology department would become unmanageable—experiencing scheduling delays, increased operation and upkeep costs, and an overall decrease in the quality of service. This, in turn, would impair the department's ability to turn a profit. DCH thus claims, in effect, that its board decided that the competitive benefits the hospital's radiology department would gain—from greater efficiency—by denying Dr. Todorov privileges outweighed the additional revenue the department might generate—from a greater volume of business—by granting Dr. Todorov privileges.

Dr. Todorov claims that this procompetitive reason for denying him privileges is a mere pretext. According to Dr. Todorov, the board was not seeking to maintain a competitive edge in the market for the provision of CT scans, but acted only to further the radiologist's economic interest in preserving their super competitive profits.

Dr. Todorov bears the burden of proving that DCH's board of directors was willing to act against the hospital's economic interest simply to further the goals of the radiologists. He has failed to meet this burden.

Decision and Remedy *The Court affirmed the dismissal of Todorov's complaint.*

Antitrust regulation of staff privileges creates problems for doctors. As discussed above, hospitals have a duty to ensure that staff privileges are only granted to capable doctors or they risk negligence liability. Rejection of requests for staff privileges may produce antitrust liability, however. The HCQIA immunized peer review actions from antitrust liability to help alleviate this conflict.

Health care providers have some quality-of-patient-care defense to antitrust challenges. Denial of staff privileges to unqualified physicians will be legal even if it restricts competition. To use the patient care defense, a defendant must show that concern for patients' welfare was their dominant concern, that the concern was objectively reasonable, and that the disputed practices were necessary to protect the quality of patient care.

Health Maintenance Organizations

Americans increasingly use Health Maintenance Organizations (HMOs) for medical care, and these institutions have additional antitrust problems. Thus, one HMO had an exclusivity clause to preclude its primary care physicians from working for any other HMO plan. A court held that this arrangement would not raise health care costs and was legal under the rule of reason.[11] Physicians have also sued, because an HMO refused to deal with them, but HMOs have so far prevailed in these actions. One group of physicians settled an antitrust case after they joined together to negotiate fees with an HMO, which caused two HMOs to leave the market.[12]

Given the increased prominence of Health Maintenance Organizations (HMOs) in providing health care, injured patients have sought to sue them for malpractice. In most states, courts have held that HMOs are not potentially liable defendants in malpractice actions. The state of Texas recently passed legislation making HMOs potentially liable.

Mergers

Hospital mergers are increasingly common. A record number of hospitals are closing down in current financially difficult times, ninety-six in one recent year. New Medicare payment systems endanger providers. Surviving hospitals have increasingly sought to combine to strengthen themselves financially. Mergers are a concern because hospital service markets are often highly concentrated. Many locales have only a few hospitals.

In addition to Section 1 of the Sherman Act, hospital mergers can be challenged under Section 7 of the Clayton Act. This law makes mergers illegal if they produce an overly concentrated market with a substantial impact on interstate commerce. These laws apply to nonprofit hospitals as well.

Hospital mergers present unique circumstances for the law. In defense of mergers, they may improve patient care. In contrast, hospitals may find it especially easy to collude and raise charges because most patients do not pay for hospital services themselves.

One defense to antitrust attack is the **failing company defense**. This permits mergers when one company is about to go out of business. The theory is that a merger will not cause increased market concentration if one company was failing anyway.

---

[11] *U.S. Health Care v. Healthsource,* 1992-1 Trade Cas. (CCH) P69,697 (D.N.H. 1992).

[12] *Minnesota v. Mid-Minnesota Associated Physicians,* 1991-2 Trade Cas. (CCH) P69,531 (D. Minn. 1991).

Ethical Perspectives

The Value of Human Life

Many health-care cases present serious ethical problems. A majority of the most central problems regard the value of human life. The very idea of placing a financial value on human life is ethically controversial.

Some argue that human life is sacred and, therefore, priceless. It is difficult for anyone to say that someone else should die because it is not worth the cost of saving his or her life. Health care has traditionally operated under this sort of assumption. Medical knowledge and technology have advanced enormously over recent decades. Much of this innovation is extremely costly to use. Nevertheless, hospitals will spend enormous amounts of money to save a single life.

In the future, hospitals increasingly must confront the issue of whether such large expenditures are ethically (or legally) required. In fact, there are ethical reasons for limiting the expenditures employed to save lives.

Inevitably, lifesaving resources are limited. When a hospital devotes millions of dollars to some highly advanced cardiac-care technology, those dollars are unavailable for other health care facilities. Hospitals could save many more lives by devoting increased resources to prenatal care and emergency rooms and fewer resources to *life-extending* technologies.

In this circumstance, there may be an ethical duty not to spend money to save lives in certain ways. Arguably, some hospitals are now behaving unethically. Hospitals have spent huge resources on advanced technology to care for patients with insurance that will compensate the hospitals. Many poor mothers in need of prenatal care, however, lack insurance. When hospitals spend large amounts of money on advanced technology, this may reflect concern for profit as much as concern for human life.

This issue has arisen in the area of "right to die." When a patient is in a permanent vegetative state, the patient's family may prefer that life-sustaining technology be turned off. Some hospitals have gone to court and argued that their ethics commanded that the patient be kept alive.

In the future, we may confront even more difficult questions. There is already one case in which a hospital is seeking to disconnect life-sustaining technology when the patient's family wants the patient to be kept alive. In this case, the hospital was not being reimbursed for its expenses. This may seem callous of the hospital, but remember that its resources might be transferred to uses that will save other lives.

As technology advances, the problem will only get worse. We may soon be able to keep many persons alive indefinitely. To resolve these questions, we must consider the meaning of life itself. There is more to life than just its prolongation. Ethics may not demand that we always preserve life as long as technically possible.

International Perspectives

AIDS and International Health Care

The health-care industry is less international than many other businesses. One cannot export medical services in the same manner as cars. Nevertheless, health-care services are increasingly crossing national boundaries. The high level of U.S. health-care technology makes this area a promising one for export.

The international health-care community has begun to deal with the global epidemic of acquired immune deficiency syndrome ("AIDS") and its relationship with health-care workers. The World Health Organization ("WHO") of the United Nations has begun to set forth regulations and recommendations in this area. Individual nations are also adopting policies in this area.

Health-care workers are at risk of contracting AIDS from their patients due to the potential transference of blood during surgery and other health-care operations. Regardless of how they contracted AIDS, these health-care workers present some risk of communicating the disease to their patients. Health-care workers also are at the front line of society's AIDS protection policies.

WHO has adopted standards for testing patients for AIDS and for counseling those who have tested positive for the disease. The Organization has adopted general recommendations for the protection against AIDS in the course of the care of patients. WHO generally lacks the authority, however, to impose rules on member nations. WHO does maintain a clearinghouse on important AIDS information for the benefit of physicians in all countries.

Many nations have rules that protect the confidentiality of those suffering from AIDS. The Council of Europe has adopted recommendations to this effect. Statutes in many countries, including Australia, China, Spain, Sweden, and Panama, also protect this confidentiality interest. Numerous other nations also provide confidentiality protection for patients who test positive. These may prevent doctors from informing other health-care providers that a prospective patient has AIDS.

Some physicians have refused treatment for patients with AIDS infections. The American Medical Association, the General Medical Council of the United Kingdom and the French National Council of the Association of Physicians have adopted policies against this practice, directing doctors to provide treatment. Other nations have no limitations on denial of treatment.

Another issue of concern is AIDS-infected health-care workers. To date, nations have not demanded AIDS testing of health-care workers and have not demanded that patients be informed that their care provider has AIDS. There is increasing public pressure, however, to adopt such requirements.

Questions and Case Problems

1. Blue Shield Insurance had substantial market power in private health insurance, possessing about 60 to 80 percent of the market. Ocean State Insurance was a small company competing with Blue Shield in Rhode Island. Blue Shield adopted a policy under which they would not pay participating physicians any more than the lowest amount that they had accepted from Blue Shield's competitors. As a rule, Ocean State paid its participating physicians less for a given act. The Blue Shield policy caused many physicians to drop out of the Ocean State coverage, in order to obtain the higher average reimbursement rates provided by Blue Cross. Ocean State sued Blue Shield under both Sections 1 and 2 of the Sherman Act. Should Ocean State win? [*Ocean State Physicians Health Plan, Inc. v. Blue Cross & Blue Shield of Rhode Island,* 1988-2 Trade Cas (CCH) P68,161 (D.R.I. 1988)].

2. A doctor attending an infant patient left orders that she be given Lanoxin. The nurse felt that the order was unclear about the administration of the drug and contacted two doctors, who told her that there was no concern. She did not contact the attending physician and went ahead and administered the drug by injection. The dosage, when given by injection, was lethal, and the patient subsequently died. The infant's survivors sued the hospital for malpractice. Should the hospital (the nurse's employer) be liable? [*Norton v. Argonaut Insurance Company,* 144 So.2d 249 (La. App. 1962)].

3. An independent physician took biopsy samples from both breasts of a woman, in order to check for breast cancer. Before sending the samples for pathological analysis, the physician directed the nurse to place samples from both breasts in a single container. The nurse questioned this direction, but the physician told her to proceed as directed, so the nurse did so. The pathologist found one of the samples to be malignant. Because the samples had been mixed together, both of the woman's breasts were removed in mastectomy, though only one was malignant. Later, after she discovered the above facts, she sued the hospital for malpractice. Should the hospital (the nurse's employer) be liable in this case? (*Variety Children's Hospital v. Osle,* 292 So.2d 382 (Fla. App. 1974)

4. Maria Pedroza was pregnant and under the care of Ben Bryant, who was on the staff of Skagit Valley Hospital. She visited Dr. Bryant at his private office, however, and not at the hospital. In her eighth month of pregnancy, she began developing complications and became comatose. She was admitted to the hospital where she was under the care of another doctor. Her child was successfully delivered by emergency cesarean section, but Maria Pedroza died. Her survivors sued the hospital claiming that Dr. Bryant had been negligent in his care of Maria and that the hospital had been negligent in granting staff privileges to Dr. Bryant. The hospital defended that Dr. Bryant was an independent contractor and that she did not even visit him in the hospital. Should the hospital be liable in this case? [*Pedroza v. Bryant,* 677 P.2d 166 (Wash. 1984)].

5. A hospital had a policy of referring patients only to doctors who had been members of the hospital's medical staff for at least five years. A doctor, who had no patients referred to him, sued the hospital, claiming that this practice violated Section 1 of the Sherman Act. The hospital defended that it had a right to establish rules on patient referrals, and that the hospital allowed the plaintiff doctor to use its facilities when necessary. Did the hospital violate Section 1? [*Cooper v. Amster,* 645 F. Supp. 46 (E.D. Pa. 1986)].

6. Sycamore Municipal Hospital treated its active staff physicians as independent contractors and did not pay them salary, expenses, social security taxes, insurance, or other benefits. Physicians took regular rotation in the hospital's emergency room. Jack Giblet suffered pain in his chest and arrived at the emergency room and was seen by a physician, who prescribed medication. Within the day, Gilbert had died of a heart attack, and his survivors sued for malpractice. The hospital contended that it was not vicariously liable. Should the hospital receive summary judgment?

Chapter Sixteen

Sports and Entertainment Law

KEY BACKGROUND

Sports and other forms of public entertainment, such as motion pictures and sound recordings, have become a large part of our nation's economy. As this economic sector has grown, so have legal disputes. The legal issues raised in sports and entertainment law are often common problems of contracts, antitrust, intellectual property, etc. The sports and entertainment context of a dispute, however, can have a significant effect on its resolution. Special rules may apply in sports and entertainment law.

Sports Law

The law of sports covers a broad range of issues and situations, ranging from professional basketball (where the average salary exceeds $600,000) to amateur high school soccer. Sports has become big business—the four major team sports (baseball, basketball, football and hockey) have over a billion dollars a year in gross revenues. Over $1.3 billion is spent by all types of companies in promoting sports events. An increasing number of lawsuits have accompanied this business. As any reader of the sports pages is aware, legal controversies are prevalent in the sporting world.

Private Regulatory Bodies

A rather unusual circumstance of sports law is the presence of private regulatory bodies that set rules for events. In *amateur* sports at the university level, the best-known body is the National Collegiate Athletic Association (NCAA). Smaller schools are governed by the National Association of Intercollegiate Athletics (NAIA) and other groups of schools, such as junior colleges, have other ruling organizations.

These private organizations have their own governance structures in which member schools participate. The NCAA adopts rules governing recruiting, admissions, financial aid, and eligibility for participating schools. Basic policies are set at a national convention of all member schools and then administered by a governing council and committees.

Most NCAA rules are aimed at protecting the amateur status of its "student-athletes." Detailed recruiting rules prohibit offering gifts to prospective athletes, arranging loans and providing reduced cost services or housing. Other, more technical, rules limit the number of campus visits and off-campus contact that a recruit may take. The rules also prohibit a recruit from being interviewed on a university coach's radio or television program.

The NCAA recently adopted a Draconian "death penalty" rule. The death penalty applies if the school has twice committed major rules violations within a single five-year period. The NCAA can then ban participation in the sport subject to the latest violation for up to two years. The death penalty also eliminates athletic scholarships and recruiting activities in that sport. Southern Methodist University twice committed recruiting violations and received the death penalty, which temporarily abolished its football program.

Some NCAA rules are quite controversial and have been challenged in court. The primary legal basis for challenging an NCAA rule is found in the antitrust laws. Antitrust laws are discussed in Chapter 47 of *West's Business Law, Seventh Edition*, and prohibit monopolies and certain combinations of competitors.

The NCAA rules may be challenged under the Sherman Act. Section 1 of the Sherman Act prohibits anticompetitive combinations, such as price fixing. Section 2 of the Sherman Act prohibits monopolization of a product market. Because the NCAA is a combination of competing schools and has a monopoly on a large segment of the sports market, potential antitrust problems are obvious.

Although the NCAA is itself a nonprofit organization, courts have found it subject to the antitrust laws. In so holding, courts have distinguished between "commercial" and "noncommercial" actions of the NCAA. The NCAA rules that limited television coverage of college football were considered a commercial action. The Supreme Court struck down these NCAA restrictions as an unlawful combination in restraint of trade.[1] NCAA regulations to protect amateurism, however, are usually considered noncommercial. A hockey player, who had been paid for hockey in the past, challenged an NCAA rule prohibiting him from playing college hockey. The court ruled for the NCAA because the rule was noncommercial in nature.[2] Courts are reluctant to apply antitrust law to noncommercial rules of the Association. Cheerleaders and alumni of Southern Methodist University sued the NCAA to challenge the death penalty for their football program but lost.

Even noncommercial rules can have a significant effect on individuals. The following case involves a recent challenge to NCAA eligibility rules.

---

[1] *NCAA v. Board of Regents of the University of Oklahoma*, 468 U.S. 85 (1984).

[2] *Jones v. NCAA*, 392 F. Supp. 295 (Mass. 1975).

Case 16.1
Banks v. National Collegiate Athletic Association
United States District Court for the Northern District of Indiana, 1990
Case No. S90-394

Background and Facts *Braxton Banks entered the University of Notre Dame in 1986 on a football scholarship worth approximately $16,000 per year. Banks played three years as a fullback for Notre Dame and missed one season because of injury. As a consequence, he was eligible for the professional draft but also had a year of collegiate eligibility remaining. An NCAA rule stated that any player who entered the professional draft would no longer be eligible for collegiate football. Banks decided to enter the draft and signed a required form that included the statement: "I HEREBY IRREVOCABLY RENOUNCE ANY AND ALL REMAINING COLLEGE ELIGIBILITY I MAY HAVE." After performing poorly in tryouts, Banks was not chosen in the draft. He sought to return and play for his final year at Notre Dame but was barred by the NCAA rule. Banks filed suit against the NCAA and Notre Dame, claiming that the NCAA rule violated section 1 of the Sherman Act. He moved for a preliminary injunction ordering the defendants to allow him to compete for Notre Dame.*

MILLER, United States District Judge.

* * * *

The NCAA is a private, voluntary, unincorporated association of approximately 1,017 members, consisting of colleges and universities (including

Notre Dame), conferences and associations, and other education institutions. According to the NCAA constitution, the NCAA's purpose is to promote intercollegiate athletics in the United States and to maintain amateur intercollegiate athletics "as an integral part of the educational program and the athlete as an integral part of the student body and by so doing, retain a clear line of demarcation between intercollegiate athletics and professional sports." Approximately 187 colleges that play intercollegiate football are members of the NCAA. It is the dominant association of colleges and universities that engage in intercollegiate athletics.

* * * *

What the NCAA and its member institutions market in this case is competition itself—contests between competing institutions. Of course, this would be completely ineffective if there were no rules on which the competitors agreed to create and define the competition to be marketed. A myriad of rules affecting such matters as the size of the field, the number of players on a team, and the extent to which physical violence is to be encouraged or proscribed, all must be agreed on, and all restrain the manner in which institutions compete. Moreover, the NCAA seeks to market a particular brand of football—college football. The identification of this "product" with an academic tradition differentiates college football from and makes it more popular than professional sports to which it might otherwise be comparable, such as, for example, minor league baseball. In order to preserve the character and quality of the "product," athletes must not be paid, must be required to attend class, and the like. And the integrity of the "product" cannot be preserved except by mutual agreement; its effectiveness as a competitor on the playing field might soon be destroyed. Thus, the NCAA plays a vital role in enabling college football to preserve its character, and as a result enables a product to be marketed which might otherwise be unavailable. In performing this role, its actions widen consumer choice—not only the choices available to sports fans but also those available to athletes—and hence can be viewed as procompetitive.

* * * *

In sum, it is clear that the NCAA is engaged in two distinct kinds of rule making activity. One type…is rooted in the NCAA's concern for the protection of amateurism; the other type is increasingly accompanied by a discernible economic purpose…. The NCAA sanctions at issue here are clearly of the former variety. Because the sanctions evince no anticompetitive purpose, are reasonably related to the association's central objectives, and are not overbroad, the NCAA's action does not constitute an unreasonable restraint under the Sherman Act.

Decision and Remedy *The court denied the preliminary injunction sought by Banks, because he had little likelihood of success in his case.*

Another legal controversy surrounds the methods of enforcement of NCAA rules. Enforcement is run by the NCAA Committee on Infractions, which is made up of college faculty members. The Committee investigates alleged violations, makes factual determinations, and when appropriate penalizes the member institution in violation of NCAA rules.

Several cases have been brought claiming that the NCAA enforcement procedure violates due process of law (the guarantee of procedural fairness contained in the United States Constitution). Jerry

Tarkanian, head men's basketball coach at the University of Nevada at Las Vegas, brought a due process action challenging his suspension for recruiting violations. The due process clause only protects individuals against government action, however. Tarkanian lost his case because the Supreme Court considered the NCAA to be a private organization to which the due process clause does not apply.[3]

The NCAA is subject to government rules for private organizations. The NCAA adopted a random drug testing program for college athletes to detect use of illegal drugs and performance-enhancing drugs, such as steroids. A 1990 California state court decision held that this drug testing program violated the state constitution of California, which guarantees a right of privacy from even nongovernment organizations. Although the binding legal effect of this decision is limited to California, the ruling may force the NCAA to restructure its entire drug testing program.

Professional sports also are governed by private regulatory organizations, such as the National Basketball Association (NBA) and the National Football League (NFL). These professional groups of teams are more clearly commercial, and the antitrust laws are more frequently applied to their actions than to the NCAA.

One key sports antitrust issue involves the concept of free agency. Most sports leagues had some rule that binds players to their existing teams (sometimes known as a **reserve clause**) and that prohibits players from selling their services to the highest bidder (known as **free agency**). Player demands and lawsuits have eliminated the *absolute* reserve clause. Most professional leagues now permit partial free agency to players but place some restrictions on their rights to switch teams.

Suppose that Jose Canseco of the Oakland Athletics baseball team has an excellent year. He may believe that he can substantially increase his salary by creating a bidding war for his services. Perhaps he believes that he could make more money if he played in New York or Los Angeles. Largely because of the antitrust laws, Major League Baseball permits Canseco some opportunity to shop his services. This opportunity is restricted, however, by detailed rules that define limited times in their career when players can seek free agency.

Even baseball players' limited free agency rights have been undermined by the owners. The owners allegedly conspired not to seek other teams' free agents, in order to avoid bidding up player salaries. As a result, many free agents received no offers and had to re-sign with their existing team. After the players challenged the owners' collusion, an arbitrator ruled that the league owed over $100 million in damages to the free agent players.

Several types of professional sports league rules have been found to violate the antitrust laws. When the Oakland Raiders sought to move their franchise to Los Angeles, they were prohibited by a vote of the National Football League. The Raiders ignored this vote and eventually won an antitrust case against the NFL, permitting them to move the franchise.[4] Other courts have struck down a league's reserve clause that prevents players from being free agents and offering their services to other teams. Major league baseball, however, is partially exempt from the antitrust laws under a 1922 U.S. Supreme Court decision.

In one dramatic case, the United States Football League (USFL) successfully proved that the National Football League was an unlawful monopoly, but the USFL received only $1.00 in actual damages. The jury theorized that the USFL would have gone out of business anyway, regardless of the NFL's monopolistic practices.

Antitrust laws apply to more than just sports leagues. The U.S. Supreme Court has found that boxing promoters violated the antitrust prohibition on monopolization. A small group of promoters acquired exclusive rights to the fights of all four leading contenders for the heavyweight title, and exclusive promotion rights for title bouts in many classes. They used this power to sign up all leading contenders. The Court held that the promoters violated sections 1 and 2 of the Sherman Act.[5]

Most professional players are represented by a union. The players' unions bargain with the team owners over pay and other league policies. If a policy, such as the draft, is subject to collective bargaining between the league's owners and a players'

---

[3] *National Collegiate Athletic Association v. Tarkanian*, 488 U.S. 179 (1988).

[4] *Los Angeles Memorial Coliseum v. National Football League*, 726 F.2d 1381 (9th Cir. 1984).

[5] *International Boxing Club, Inc. v. United States*, 358 U.S. 242 (1959).

union, the courts will respect the labor agreement. This is the labor exemption to the antitrust laws. When players' unions recognize and provide for practices such as the draft or restrictions on free agency in labor agreements, the antitrust laws will not be used to prohibit the agreements.

Professional sports has witnessed considerable strife, as the 1994 baseball season was shut down. Players have sought to strengthen their negotiating position with owners by claiming that league rules violate the antitrust laws, but this claim is undermined by the existence of collective bargaining agreements that sanction the rules. The following decision addresses a challenge to such rules.

Case 16.2
National Basketball Association v. Williams
United States District Court for the Southern District of New York, 1994
857 F. Supp. 1069

Background and Facts *In the 1970s, professional basketball players filed suit to challenge certain National Basketball Association (NBA) rules, including the annual draft of players. The parties ultimately settled, and the terms of this settlement were incorporated into a collective bargaining agreement. This agreement provided for a modified draft. In the 1980s, the collective bargaining agreement was again modified to provide for a salary cap that limited the total salaries of players to a certain percentage of revenues. This collective bargaining agreement expired by its terms in 1994. The league went to court and sought a judgment that the draft, the salary cap, and other provisions did not violate the antitrust laws. The players counterclaimed, alleging that these provisions did violate the antitrust laws. A key question was whether the challenged provisions were still protected by the labor agreement exception to the antitrust laws.*

DUFFY, District Judge.

* * * *

The labor arena is one with well established rules which are intended to foster negotiated settlements rather than intervention by the courts. The league and the players have accepted this "level playing field" as the basis for their often tempestuous relationship, and we believe that there is substantial justification for requiring the parties to continue to fight on it, so that bargaining and the exertion of economic force may be used to bring about legitimate compromise… antitrust immunity exists as long as a collective bargaining relationship exists and labor law remedies are available.

* * * *

This does not mean that the players are "stuck" with these provisions forever. Certainly, they can attempt to bargain these provisions away—including exerting economic pressure by means of a strike. Or, the players may request decertification of the [National Basketball Players Association] as a collective bargaining agent. I do not mean by this ruling to encourage the players to decertify their union so that they may bring an antitrust claim. But, decertification is certainly an option the Players have.

Decision and Remedy *The court granted the teams' declaratory judgment that the college draft, salary cap and other provisions did not violate the antitrust laws.*

Other than the antitrust laws, there is little government control over the practices of professional sports organizations. Sports organizations are not government bodies but are voluntary groups. As a result, the government generally lets the leagues make their own rules for the game.

This principle is illustrated by the Pete Rose case, when the Commissioner of Baseball, A. Bartlett Giamatti, disciplined Rose for gambling on major league games. Rose claimed that the Commissioner was biased against him and sued. A federal court rejected Rose's case, noting that the Major League Agreement gave the Commissioner extraordinary power to take whatever action was necessary "in the best interest of baseball."[6]

Sports Agents

Not long ago, most professional athletes negotiated their own contracts with a team's general manager. Now, these athletes are virtually all represented by an agent for contract negotiations. Agents are usually lawyers or business professionals who may also represent the athlete in all his or her business dealings, such as advertising and promotions.

One of the most remarkable scandals involved sports agents Norby Walters and Lloyd Bloom, who operated as World Sports & Entertainment, Inc. Walters and Bloom paid hundreds of thousands of dollars to sign up college athletes for future representation. Among these athletes were two basketball players from the University of Alabama. When this professional representation was discovered, the NCAA required Alabama to return over $250,000 to the NCAA that the university had received from a post-season tournament appearance.

The University of Alabama sued Walters and Bloom for over $3 million for the tort of intentional interference with a contractual relationship. In addition, Alabama indicted Walters and Bloom for criminal violations of the state Deceptive Trade Practices Act. Both cases were ultimately settled when Walters agreed to pay the University of Alabama $200,000.

Seventeen states now have specific laws regulating sports agents. The most prominent and comprehensive law is the California Athlete Agent Statute. This law requires all sports agents to register with the state's labor commissioner. The agent also must place a $25,000 bond with the labor commissioner to cover potential liability. The agent must retain all records of transactions with and for the athlete represented. The California law also regulates the content of contracts between agents and athletes for fairness and prohibits certain conflicts of interest. This law provides both civil and criminal penalties for its violation.

In addition to new state laws, sports agents are bound by all the traditional common law rules of agency. The most important of these is the command that the agent always act in the interest of the principal (athlete), and not for selfish motives. Several athletes have sued their agents for damages but with only limited success. The agents have often lacked the assets to pay off even a meritorious claim. Several NFL players alleged that Probus Management, Inc., defrauded them of $150,000, but the company had no assets to attach.

Agents have also sued athletes for breach of contract. If the contract is legitimate, this is a standard contract claim as judged by traditional common law rules. Walters and Bloom sued a professional football player who took their money while in college in exchange for future representation. The player later hired another agent to represent him as a professional. The court rejected Walters and Bloom's breach of contract case, however, on the grounds that both parties knew their original agreement to be "fraudulent and wrong."[7]

Sports Torts

More and more cases are being brought for tort damages that arise out of a sporting event. Most of these cases involve injury to spectators, and a high proportion of spectator injury cases involve spectators who were hit by baseballs while watching a game. What is the duty of a team owner to protect spectators from injury in such a case?

Spectator cases Team owners do have a legal duty to provide a protective screen for the baseball spectators in seats most at risk of harm (those behind home plate). With this exception, the traditional rule held that most spectators have assumed the risk of being injured by a ball. Courts have found that most spectators are aware of the risk of being struck by a baseball and accept that risk when they attend a

---

[6] *Rose v. Giammatti*, 721 F.Supp. 906 (S.D. Ohio 1989).

[7] *Walters v. Fullwood*, 675 F.Supp. 155, 164 (S.D.N.Y. 1987).

game and sit in unscreened seats. One recent case held that the New York Mets were not liable to a spectator, sitting behind the first base dugout, who was struck by a foul ball.

In some cases, spectators have had more success in recovering damages for their injuries. A baseball spectator was allowed to proceed with his case against the Atlanta Braves, after being injured by a foul ball tipped over the screen. The court reasoned that the screen may have been negligently defective. Another court found that the Pittsburgh Pirates could be liable to a spectator who was struck during batting practice while she was standing on a stadium walkway. The court in that case noted that the walkway was unprotected and forced spectators to turn their attention away from the field.

Professional teams are also potentially liable to spectators for other sources of harm. The Milwaukee Braves were held liable to a sixty-nine-year-old fan who was trampled by other spectators scrambling for a foul ball.[8] The court reasoned that a stadium usher might have protected the fan but was absent from his assigned station at the time.

Another case was brought by a Notre Dame football spectator who was injured by two drunk men while she was on her way to her car in the stadium parking lot. She sued Notre Dame for failure to provide security protection for fans. The appellate court permitted her case to proceed because Notre Dame was well aware of the drinking that went on at "tailgate" parties in the area and should have taken action to protect their fans.

The Los Angeles Dodgers were found potentially liable for providing inadequate medical care to an injured fan. A spectator was struck unconscious by a foul ball. The doctor employed at the Dodgers" emergency medical station advised the fan that he was not seriously injured and should return to his seat. Four days later, the spectator died of a brain hemorrhage. The court held that if the doctor were guilty of malpractice, the Dodgers could be guilty as the doctor's employer.[9]

A sports organization may also be liable to an injured passerby. In one instance, a golf course used a public waterway as a water hazard. When a wayward golf ball struck a boater in the eye, the course owners were held liable for the injuries.[10]

Athlete cases Sometimes even the participants in sporting events will sue for their injuries. Usually, a court will find that a participant has consented to the risk of injury. For example, a football quarterback can hardly sue a linebacker for a hard tackle.

Players cannot recover for injuries suffered within the rules of the game. Nor can players recover for negligent actions by other players. A player may be able to recover for injuries from intentional actions of other players that were outside the legal rules of the game.

Probably the most-publicized case involved Rudy Tomjanovich of the basketball Houston Rockets. His face was shattered by an unprovoked punch delivered by an opposing player during a game. A jury awarded Tomjanovich over $3 million in damages. The fight in this case was wholly unrelated to the game.

A more controversial case involved Dale Hackbart, a defensive back for the NFL's Denver Broncos, who sued the Cincinnati Bengals and one of that team's players. While Hackbart was down on the field, Charles "Booby" Clark struck him in the back of the head with a forearm. No penalty was called. Hackbart suffered a serious neck fracture injury. The district court ruled for the Bengals, but an appellate court reversed. The Tenth Circuit Court of Appeals ruled that a football player does not consent to violence that is not within the rules of football. That court held that Clark's actions could constitute assault and battery.[11]

Mere negligence by another athlete will not support liability, however. There are several horse racing cases in which jockeys have sued on the basis that careless riding by other jockeys caused injury. In these cases, courts have held for defendants and found that a jockey assumes the risk of careless riding or "jockey error" by other participants in the race.

Jockeys and race car drivers have recovered on occasion against the owner of a racetrack, when the track itself created a danger. The owner of a sports facility has a duty to exercise reasonable care to

---

[8] *Lee v. National League Baseball Club*, 89 N.W.2d 811 (Wis. 1958).

[9] *Fish v. Los Angeles Dodgers Baseball Club*, 128 Cal. Rptr. 807 (1976).

[10] *Kirchoffner v. Quam*, 264 N.W.2d 203 (N.D. 1978).

[11] *Hackbart v. Cincinnati Bengals*, 601 F.2d 516 (10th Cir. 1979).

prevent foreseeable injury to the sports participants. Many facility owners now require race car drivers to sign a waiver and release assuming the risk of injury and promising not to sue the owner. Thus, when a stock driver was injured due to a defect in the track, he could not recover because he signed a release in which he agreed not to sue.[12]

Many of the athlete tort cases involve the sport of hockey, as the following case illustrates.

Several athletes have sued their teams for providing inadequate medical care. Most sports teams maintain their own trainers and team doctors to care for injured players. There have been several scandals when a team and its doctor unsafely urged an athlete back into a game and aggravated an athlete's injury. A pitcher for the Philadelphia Phillies baseball team sued when the team physician gave him massive doses of pain-killing drugs so that he could continue pitching. He argued that the high doses caused his subsequent mental illness.[13] Players also have successfully sued the manufacturers of sports equipment (such as football helmets) for defective products that contributed to an injury.

▬ Entertainment Law

Entertainment law primarily involves motion pictures and television, though it may also include popular books, artistic works, and other forms of art or popular entertainment. Entertainment law presents important issues of contracts and copyright protection. Unique issues of artists' rights are also present in the entertainment business.

Entertainment Contracts

Entertainment contracts are governed by traditional rules of contract law, as set forth in Chapters 12 through 20 of *West's Business Law, Seventh Edition*. The unique context of the entertainment industry, however, presents special contract problems. This is true for several reasons. When an actor or a musician first signs a contract, he or she is typically unknown to the public. Consequently, the artist may receive relatively little compensation. Such unknown artists may become "overnight successes." This situation enables record and film companies to make enormous profits from an artist's work, yet pay the artist little. Moreover, many artists are not well informed about their legal rights.

To help protect themselves in transactions, most artists hire an agent or management company. The artist must make a contract with the agent. Normal practice in the music business provides an agent with a commission of 10 percent to 25 percent of the artist's gross receipts from recordings, plus expenses. The agent also generally receives exclusive rights to represent the artist.

---

[12] *Lee v. Beauchene*, 337 N.W. 2d 827 (S.D. 1983).

[13] *Bayless v. Philadelphia National League Club*, 579 F.2d 37 (3d Cir. 1978).

▬ **Case 16.3**
Parker v. Centre Group Limited Partnership
United States Court of Appeals,
Fourth Circuit, 1995
70 F.3d 1262

Background and Facts *Jeffrey Parker played hockey for the Hartford Whalers. While playing a game against the Washington Capitols, he was checked into the boards. The boards are covered by a metal standard that is designed to hold in place the plexiglass panels surrounding most of the ice. In one section of the rink, there are no plexiglass panels, in order to allow press photographers to take clear pictures. Parker hit the metal standard in this section, where there was no plexiglass. He suffered a career-ending injury. Parker sued the owner of the facility, the teams, and the National Hockey League, among others. The district court granted summary judgment for the defendants, holding that Parker had assumed the risk of this happening. He appealed to the Fourth Circuit.*

PER CURIAM.

* * * *

There is little doubt that Parker knew of the danger, appreciated it, and voluntarily encountered it. First, Parker had played hockey since he was five years old and had played professionally since 1986. Second, Parker knew of the roughness involved in hockey because he had been injured many times. Indeed, on one previous occasion, Parker had been injured after hitting a metal standard in a penalty box. Third, Parker had played at the Capitol Centre in two previous games, and on those occasions, the photographers' box was not shielded by the protective plexiglass. Fourth, before the game in question, Parker undoubtedly was on the ice during the Whalers' pre-game warm-up drills. * * * Fifth, the photographers' box was directly across from the teams' bench area, an area which itself was not shielded by plexiglass. Finally, Parker's injury occurred late in the game. Under these circumstances, we have no doubt that a person of normal intelligence in Parker's position would have discovered the absence of the plexiglass shield in front of the photographers' box and would have understood the risk of being checked into the padded, metal standard. By deciding to participate as a player in the hockey game, Parker voluntarily chose to accept the risk.

Decision and Remedy   *The court affirmed the district court's grant of summary judgment.*

While agents are hired to represent and protect the artist, it is not uncommon for artists to sue their agents. In one case, the widow of Jim Croce, a singer and songwriter, sued their agent for negotiating a bad contract on their behalf. She complained because their agent was also an officer of the publisher and production company with whom the Croces signed. As a result, she claimed an improper conflict of interest. The court found that the contract was not unconscionable (unlawfully unfair), because the Croces were aware of the agent's representation of both sides in the contract. Mrs. Croce did receive some damages. The court held that the agent breached his duty to the Croces when he failed to advise them to hire another independent counsel to evaluate the contracts.

Many performing artists are represented by a union, the American Federation of Television and Radio Artists (AFTRA) which regulates the relationship between the agency and the performer. AFTRA has developed standard agency contracts that are regularly used. Exhibit 16-1 contains some key portions of the AFTRA agency contract for performers working under AFTRA's jurisdiction, including singers.

The artist or agent negotiates a contract with the production company. For a musician, the contract provides a royalty for sales of the record to be produced. The usual royalty rate for a new artist is about 8 percent. This rate often increases for sales above a specified number, such as 500,000 records. Musicians with a record of success often can negotiate a better royalty rate, as high as 17 percent.

Contracts with production companies often limit royalties in other ways. A certain percentage of the receipts from record sales is deducted for packaging. In addition, royalties may be paid on only 90 percent of records sold to stores (to account for returned records). Suppose that a musician sells 1 million records at $8.98 apiece. The basis for royalty calculation could be reduced 10 percent for packaging costs and another 10 percent under the

90 percent rule. The actual royalties would be about 65 cents per album and total royalties would come to $650,000. This total is not all profit. Many contracts provide that the performer must bear the costs of producing the recording. The performer's agent may also take a percentage of the royalties.

Another provision in the typical recording contract permits the company to renew the contract at its option. In this way, the company can benefit for many years. If the performer's record fails to sell, the company does not renew the contract. If the performer's record is a success, the company renews the contract and keeps the rights to produce the artists in the future under the terms of the original contract.

It is not uncommon for performers to be dissatisfied with their contract rights, especially after an initial success. The performer has a binding contract, however, and cannot market his or her services to other record companies. The performer may simply refuse to produce additional records.

If a performer refuses to perform, the company's remedies are somewhat limited. The company usually cannot collect damages, because there is no way of knowing the success of the potential future records that the artist refuses to produce. The company also cannot compel the performer to record. This would be specific performance, which normally is not granted in personal service contracts. No person can use contract law to require personal service performance. Often, the company's best available remedy is to get an injunction. This injunction would prohibit the artist from performing for any other company.

Suppose that a new performing group, called Caress, signs an exclusive contract with CBS Records for a low royalty rate. The first album produced by Caress is an enormous success. CBS probably has an option to renew the contract for many years and to keep selling future Caress records, under the original royalty agreement. Caress discovers that MCA Records will offer the group a much better royalty rate for future albums. Caress then refuses to produce more records for CBS in order to get out of the contract. CBS cannot force Caress to record. CBS can probably get an injunction preventing Caress from recording for MCA or any other company.

Such an injunction can be a powerful weapon for recording companies. If Caress wants to make records, it will have to abide by its contract with CBS. If Caress wants to make money from its music and collect royalties, it will be bound to the deal that it made with CBS.

California law provides some protection for artists such as Caress. The law contains a "minimum compensation" requirement for such injunctions. The minimum compensation requirement provides that CBS must guarantee Caress a minimum of $6000 per year, in order to utilize its right to an injunction. If this guarantee is not present, CBS cannot get an injunction, and Caress can sign with MCA or some other recording company that offers a better royalty rate than in the original contract.

California's minimum compensation law was successfully used by Redd Foxx, a comedian. Mr. Foxx was a struggling comedian performing in nightclubs when he signed a contract to produce comedy records at a royalty rate of only 2 to 3 percent. When his records were a success, Foxx sought to get out of his contract and refused to perform. The company sought an injunction, preventing Foxx from making records for anyone else. The court denied the injunction, because Foxx's contract did not entitle him to a minimum guarantee of $6000 per year. This was true even though Foxx actually had received more than $6000 per year in royalties.[14]

In another case, the singer Teena Marie signed a contract with Motown to produce her first record. After producing four successful records, Teena Marie wanted out of her contract. After learning of her intent to perform for another company, Motown invoked a contract clause providing her with $6000 per year and sought an injunction prohibiting her performance for a competitor. The court ruled for Teena Marie, holding that the company must guarantee her $6000 per year in the *original* contract and could not simply retain the option to pay her that sum at some later date.[15]

California law provides a second route for artists to escape production contracts. The law states that a personal service contract cannot be enforced after seven years from the date that service began. This prevents production companies from extending their renewal option on performers' contracts beyond seven years.

---

[14] *Foxx v. Williams*, 244 Cal. App. 2d 223 (1966).
[15] *Motown Record Corporation v. Brockert*, 160 Cal. App. 3d 123 (1984).

Exhibit 16-1

American Federation of Television and Radio Artists
Standard AFTRA Exclusive Agency Contract under Rule 12-B

THIS AGREEMENT, made and entered into at _____, by and between _____, hereinafter called the "AGENT," and _____, hereinafter called the "ARTIST."

Witnesseth:

1. The Artist employs the Agent as his sole and exclusive Agent in the transcription, radio broadcasting and television industries (hereinafter referred to as the "broadcasting industries") within the scope of the regulations (Rule 12-B) of the American Federation of Television and Radio Artists (hereinafter called AFTRA), and agrees not to employ any other person or persons to act for him in like capacity during the term hereof, and the Agent accepts such employment. This contract is limited to the broadcasting industries and to contracts of the Artist as an artist in such fields and any reference hereinafter to contracts or employment whereby the Artist renders his services, refers to contracts or employment in the broadcasting industries, except as otherwise provided herein.

2. The Artist agrees that prior to any engagement or employment in the broadcasting industries, he will become a member of AFTRA in good standing and remain such a member for the duration of such engagement or employment. The Artist warrants that he has the right to make this contract and that he is not under any other agency contract in the broadcasting fields. The Agent warrants that he is and will remain a duly franchised agent of AFTRA for the duration of this contract. This paragraph is for the benefit of AFTRA and AFTRA members as well as for the benefit of the parties to this agreement.

3. The term of this contract shall be for a period of _____, commencing the _____ day of _____ 19 _____ (Note—The term may not be in excess of three years.)

4. (a) The Artist agrees to pay to the Agent a sum equal to _____ per cent (not more than 10%) of all moneys or other consideration received by the Artist, directly or indirectly, under contracts of employment entered into during the term specified herein as provided in the Regulations. Commissions shall be payable when and as such moneys or other considerationation are received by the Artist or by anyone else for or on the Artist's behalf.

(b) Any moneys or other consideration received by the Artist or by anyone for or on his behalf, in connection with any termination of any contract of the Artist on which the Agent would otherwise be entitled to receive commission, or in connection with the settlement of any such contract, or any litigation arising out of such contract, shall also be moneys in connection with which the Agent is entitled to the aforesaid commissions; provided, however, that in such event the Artist shall be entitled to deduct arbitration fees, attorney's fees, expenses and court costs before computing the amount upon which the Agent is entitled to his commissions.

This exhibit represents only a portion of the complete document. Printed with permission from AFTRA.

Copyright

The most significant legal benefit available to successful artists, directors, writers, and other creative individuals is the law of copyright. The owner of an entertainment product's copyright has control over the use of that product and can sell the rights to that product. The details of copyright law are set forth in Chapter 9 of *West's Business Law, Seventh Edition,* and in Chapter 15 of *West's Legal Environment of Business, Third Edition.*

Most entertainment vehicles can be copyrighted. The law permits copyright of original expressions that are fixed in some medium (e.g., written down, tape recorded, filmed). Literary works, musical works, films, photographs and most forms of art can be copyrighted. An author also can receive a copyright in a particular compilation, such as a collection of essays or songs (e.g., a "Best of …" compilation).

Copyright law provides great control to the owner of a copyright. The owner, however, is not necessarily the creative artist. Many entertainment products are in the category of "work for hire." In this system, the directors, screenwriters, and other participants in producing a movie assign all their rights to the production or distribution company, in exchange for compensation (a flat fee or a percentage of profits). The copyright of a work for hire belongs to the employer of the creative artist. The production or distribution company reaps the financial benefits of copyright ownership and the artist receives whatever the employment agreement provides.

In many cases, the production contract will specify that any product is a work for hire, belonging to the employer. If the contract does not specify these rights, the employer's ownership depends on whether the work is prepared by an employee in the scope of employment or is specially commissioned for the employer. To qualify as a work for hire, the company must actively supervise production or at least retain control over those who produce the work. Otherwise, the creative artist controls the copyright in the product.[16]

Gilbert is a free-lance photographer and writer who prepares travel articles for magazines. Gilbert prepares an article on Barbados and sells the article to *Travel & Leisure* magazine. Because Gilbert is a free-lancer, he retains the copyright in this article, unless the copyright is transferred to the magazine in a written contract. If he were a staff writer, however, the copyright would belong to the magazine.

The owner of a copyright in an entertainment work has broad power over the use of that work. The owner has exclusive rights to publish, sell, and rent the work. The owner also has exclusive rights to performance and display of the work. The owner controls the right to make derivative works (such as making a movie from a copyrighted book). The owner also has the right to control and prevent copying of the entertainment work by others.

The copyright protects the owner against unauthorized copying and sale of the work. Thus, if a counterfeiter makes unauthorized copies of videotapes and sells them to the public, the owner's copyright has been violated, and the owner can sue for damages. In addition to actual damages from lost sales, the Act provides for statutory damages (like punitive damages) of $50,000 per violation.

In a recent case, a company made unauthorized recordings of several record albums, including "Breezin" by George Benson and "Bat Out of Hell" by Meatloaf. The plaintiff record company had difficulty proving damages, because it could not determine the number of counterfeit records sold by the defendants. The court awarded the plaintiff all the defendants' profits from the illegal sale, which exceeded $42,000. In the alternative, plaintiffs could accept statutory damages under the Copyright Act of $50,000 for each record that was unlawfully copied, totaling in excess of $1.4 million.[17] Obviously, plaintiffs chose the greater sum.

Unlawful copying of copyrighted works is not limited to underground counterfeiters. For example, Joseph Schlitz Brewing Company was found liable for using "The Theme from Shaft" in a beer commercial, without obtaining permission from the copyright holder.

Most copyright problems do not involve literal copying of an entire work or entertainment, however. More typically, the owner of a copyright in a work of entertainment sues for a work that is very similar to the copyrighted original. The copyright is violated only if the new work by the defendant is "substantially similar" to the plaintiff's original.

---

[16] *Community for Creative Non-Violence v. Reid*, 490 U.S. 730 (1989).

[17] *RSO Records, Inc. v. Peri*, 596 F. Supp. 849 (S.D.N.Y.

The "substantially similar" test is used to determine whether the second work was copied from the first. If the works are extremely similar, a court will infer that the second work must have been copied. Courts also consider proof that the defendant had access to the original work before producing the second work.

The copyright owners of the song "He's So Fine" sued George Harrison for his best-selling song, "My Sweet Lord." The court ruled for the original copyright owners, because Harrison's song was "strikingly similar."[18] The court did not hold that George Harrison intentionally copied the earlier song. Unintentional or "subconscious" copying also produces copyright liability.

Given the limited number of melodies and common lyrics, songwriters are often subject to copyright infringement claims. The following case illustrates the scrutiny that a court must give to such claims.

---

[18] *Abkco Music, Inc. v. Harrisongs Music, Ltd.*, 722 F.2d 988 (2d Cir. 1983).

Case 16.4
Siskind v. Newton-John
United States District Court for the Southern District of New York, 1987
No. 84 Civ. 2634

Background and Facts *In 1980, Laura Taylor Siskind wrote a song entitled "Take Another Chance on Love." She registered a copyright at that time. Siskind produced several songs, including "Take Another Chance on Love" to submit to The Entertainment Company ("TEC"). Steve Lukather played guitar on a different song, entitled "Paradise." In 1983, Lukather, singer Olivia Newton-John, and other artists composed the song "Take A Chance" for performance by Newton-John and John Travolta. "Take a Chance" was used in a motion picture. Siskind filed suit against Newton-John, Lukather, the record company, and others, claiming that "Take a Chance" infringed her copyright in "Take Another Chance on Love."*

To show access, Siskind alleged that Lukather may have heard "Take Another Chance on Love" after it was submitted to TEC on the tape on which he had performed "Paradise." Lukather stated that he never heard this tape. Defendants moved for summary judgment to dismiss Siskind's complaint. Given the weak evidence of access, the court focused on the similarity of the two songs.

GRIESA, Judge.

* * * *

Plaintiff's claim relates to the chorus of her song, which she alleges was copied in the chorus of defendants' song. The choruses are only portions of the songs, and they are the only portions about which there is any claimed similarity or copying.

In plaintiff's song the chorus appears for the first time after Verse 1. The lyrics of the chorus are:

> Take a chance, take a chance; Take another chance on love. Take a chance, take a chance; Take another chance on love.

This is followed by Verse 2, after which there is a repetition of the chorus. Then comes Verse 3. The song concludes with the chorus repeated twice and a fade.

Defendants' song commences with Verses 1 and 2, followed by the chorus:

> Take a chance, take a chance. Shall I take another chance on love?
> Take a chance, take a chance. Shall I take another chance on love?
> When it feels so right; When I'm safe and warm inside? Take [a] chance and fall tonight.

After this comes Verse 3. The song concludes with the chorus repeated twice and then a fade.

The verses of the two songs are entirely different. However, as the quoted material indicates, the lyrics of the first four lines of defendants' chorus are the same as the lyrics of plaintiff's chorus, except that the words "Shall I" appear at the beginning of the second and fourth lines of defendant's chorus. Defendants argue that the words and phrases in these choruses are commonplace, and as such have appeared in various popular songs other than those of the parties to this action. Defendants cite songs with the titles "Take a Chance," "Take a Chance on Love," and "Take Another Chance." However, no other song has been found with the precise arrangement of the phrases as contained in the songs in the present case.

* * * *

As to the music, the melodies are entirely different. The limited rhythmic similarities relate to the rhythm of the words and do not indicate copying of plaintiff's rhythm. To the extent that there are similarities in harmonic progressions, it is a matter of standard or usual harmonic progressions, something which does not indicate copying. In any event, it is the melody which is the most important feature of the music, and the melodies in plaintiff's and defendants' works are quite different.

Decision and Remedy *The court granted summary judgment for defendants and dismissed Siskind's complaint.*

In one case, an underground comic book used characters created by Walt Disney, including Mickey Mouse. In the underground comic, the Disney characters took drugs and engaged in "bawdy" behavior. Defendants argued that their comic should be legal, as a parody. The court held that defendants had substantially infringed Walt Disney's copyright in the characters because of the great similarity of the drawing of the characters and their names.[19]

Not all copying is illegal. The copyright act permits individuals to make "fair use" of a copyrighted work. Courts consider four factors in deciding whether the use of a copyrighted work is fair:

1. The purpose of the use (educational use is broader, commercial use is more restricted).

2. The nature of the copyrighted work (entertainment works of great creativity are especially protected).

3. The amount and substantiality of the portion of the copyrighted work used.

4. The effect of the use on the market for the copyrighted work (if the use does not hurt sales of the work, the use is more likely to be considered fair).

These standards are applied on a case-by-case basis to determine whether copying is fair use. Copying a small portion of a use for personal or educational purposes will be legal. Copying larger amounts for commercial use is more problematic.

Some rap musicians "sample" previous recordings, which means they copy portions or all of previously recorded works and speak over the music. Roy Orbison brought a copyright action when the

---

[19] *Walt Disney Productions v. Air Pirates*, 581 F.2d 751 (9th Cir. 1978).

group 2 Live Crew sampled his song "Oh, Pretty Woman" and substantially changed the lyrics. The case ultimately went to the U.S. Supreme Court, which unanimously held that the sampling was a fair use necessary to give "breathing space" to constitutionally protected speech.[20]

Compulsory Licensing

In general, copyright law permits the copyright owner to license the use of the work at its discretion. Thus, the owner of a novel, such as *Gone with the Wind*, can license a movie studio to make a film of the book for an agreed-upon fee. Or, an author will enable a book company to produce and sell a copyrighted work, in exchange for royalty payments.

Although most copyright holders can refuse to license their works to others, the Copyright Act creates compulsory licensing for musical recordings that have been distributed. This means that a record can be played on the radio, or on a jukebox, without requiring specific permission from the copyright holder. The law provides a specific royalty payment for these uses. The present royalty rate is five cents per recording or 0.95 cents per minute of playing time, whichever is greater.

Trademark, Misappropriation, and Unfair Competition

In addition to the copyright, the producer or owner of an entertainment work has protection under the law of trademark, misappropriation, and unfair competition. These issues are discussed in more detail in Chapters 11 and 12 of this book. Some expressions, such as the title of a movie or the name of a group, are too short to obtain full copyright protection. While titles are not protected in copyright, they may be protected under other sources of law.

The law of trademark protects against copying of trademarked names and figures, such as Superman. The law of misappropriation prevents persons from profiting from the unauthorized use of the name and identity of others, such as celebrities. The tort of unfair competition generally protects against unfair trade practices. The requirements of these actions are discussed in more detail in Chapter 11 of this book.

DC Comics, Inc., claimed trademark protection in the comic book character Aquaman, an underwater hero, who fights the forces of evil with his female companion, Mera, and his loyal, walrus-like companion, Tusky. CBS showed a cartoon television series featuring Manta, an underwater hero, accompanied by Moray, his female companion, and Whiskers, a walrus-like companion. DC Comics sued for infringement of trademark and misappropriation of their characters, and a jury awarded nearly $400,000 in damages. The appellate court overturned the damages award, because DC Comics had not proved that the television show had caused financial loss to DC Comics. The court found some damages resulted from a television cartoon on "Superstretch" that copied the comic books' "Plastic Man" character.[21]

Movie companies have also sued to protect the titles of their films from use in the movies of others. George Romero produced "Night of the Living Dead" and "Dawn of the Dead." He sued another movie company that produced a film entitled "Return of the Living Dead." The court found that Romero's titles were protected and granted an injunction against the use of the title "Return of the Living Dead" for a competing movie.[22] A famous 1950s musical group, called "The Platters," also won an injunction preventing another group from calling itself the "New Century Platters."[23]

Misappropriation can involve using the name or likeness of a celebrity to promote a product, without the celebrity's authorization. Cher gave a journalist from *Us* magazine an exclusive interview but then obtained the magazine's agreement not to use the interview. The journalist sold the interview to *Forum* magazine and others. *Forum* ran the interview and engaged in substantial advertising, which used Cher's name and picture and which stated that Cher endorsed *Forum* (a *Penthouse* magazine). Cher sued for misappropriation and won

---

[20] *Campbell v. Acuff-Rose Music, Inc.*, 62 U.S.L.W. 4169 (1994).

[21] *DC Comics, Inc. v. Filmation Associates*, 486 F. Supp. 1273 (S.D.N.Y. 1980).

[22] *Dawn Associates v. Links*, 23 U.S.P.Q. 831 (N.D. Ill. 1978).

[23] *The Five Platters, Inc. v. Purdie*, 419 F. Supp. 372 (D. Md. 1976).

$269,000 in damages. While *Forum* had a legal right to publish the interview, they improperly implied that Cher endorsed their magazine.[24]

Artist's Rights

The laws of copyright, trademark, etc., provide strong rights for those artists who have retained the ownership rights in their works of entertainment. Most significant entertainment works, however, are works for hire, in which the artist has given over copyright and other protection to an employing company. What, if any, rights does the creative artist retain in the entertainment product?

The law of some European countries, such as France, provides artists with "moral rights" over the creative product, even after the economic rights have been assigned to a corporation. These moral rights enable an artist to prevent others from modifying his or her work, for example. The United States generally does not recognize moral rights for artists.

U.S. law does grant some limited rights to even those artists who have lost copyright control over their creative works. The Directors Guild of America has a labor agreement that permits directors to consult in the final editing of their movies.

Other rights are provided by law. California law requires that a movie give proper credit to actors and other participants in a motion picture. California law also protects works of fine art (painting, sculpture, etc.) from mutilation, destruction, negligent framing, and other damage by even the owner of the art.

Giving proper credit is critical to motion picture performers and other artists and this issue has been the subject of much litigation. Actors have even sued over the size of the type in their credit on a movie poster. Credit requirements are often included in contracts with performers. One actor won nearly $2 million in damages when he was promised "fourth-star billing" on a movie but received only alphabetical billing, which placed his name much lower than fourth.

United States law generally provides the artist little control over the final product of a work for hire. This issue became controversial with the development of "colorization." The colorization process enables the owner of a black-and-white film to add color and display the film in color. While directors have complained that colorization improperly altered their films, the law generally permits colorization or other alterations by the copyright owner.

Some limited measure of artists' rights may be found in United States law. The following case involves a comedy group that successfully sued over the modification of its work.

---

[24] *Cher v. Forum International, Ltd.*, 692 F.2d 634 (9th Cir. 1982).

Case 16.5
Gilliam v. American Broadcasting Companies, Inc.
United States Court of Appeals, Second Circuit, 1976
538 F.2d 14

Background and Facts *The comedy troupe known as Monty Python produced a series of thirty-minute programs telecast by the British Broadcasting System (BBC). The BBC's agreement gave it the right to rebroadcast Monty Python's programs overseas. ABC reached an agreement to do two ninety-minute specials on American television. ABC significantly edited the British programs to make time for commercials and to eliminate skits that were considered to be offensive.*

After the first ABC special, Monty Python sued to halt the edited broadcast of their skits. They claimed that ABC's editing violated its contract with the BBC and mutilated their programs. A district court agreed with Monty Python on the substance of their claims but refused to enjoin ABC's broadcast of the second special, because ABC could suffer a great financial loss from an injunction issued just a week before the broadcast was planned. The district court judge did require ABC to broadcast a disclaimer stating that Monty Python disassociated itself from the special. Monty Python appealed.

LUMBARD, Circuit Judge.

* * * *

Since its formation in 1969, the Monty Python group has gained popularity primarily through its thirty-minute television programs created for BBC as part of a comedy series entitled "Monty Python's Flying Circus." In accordance with an agreement between Monty Python and BBC, the group writes and delivers to BBC scripts for use in the television series. This scriptwriters' agreement recites in great detail the procedure to be followed when any alterations are to be made in the script prior to recording of the program. The essence of this section of the agreement is that, while BBC retains final authority to make changes, appellants or their representatives exercise optimum control over the scripts consistent with BBC's authority and only minor changes may be made without prior consultation with the writers. Nothing in the scriptwriters' agreement entitles BBC to alter a program once it has been recorded. The agreement further provides that, subject to the terms therein, the group retains all rights in the script.

These cases cannot be distinguished from the situation in which a television network broadcasts a program properly designated as having been written and performed by a group, but which has been edited, without the writer's consent, into a form that departs substantially from the original work. "To deform his work is to present him to the public as the creator of a work not his own, and thus makes him subject to criticism for work he has not done." In such a case, it is the writer or performer, rather than the network, who suffers the consequences of the mutilation, for the public will have only the final product by which to evaluate the work. Thus, an allegation that a defendant has presented to the public a "garbled," distorted version of plaintiff's work seeks to redress the very rights sought to be protected by the Lanham Act, 15 U.S.C.A. § 1125(a), and should be recognized as stating a cause of action under that statute. See *Autry v. Republic Productions, Inc.*, 213 F.2d 667, 101 U.S.P.Q. 478 (9th Cir. 1954); *Jaeger v. American Int'l Pictures, Inc.*, 330 F.Supp. 274, 169 U.S.P.Q. 668 (S.D.N.Y.1971), which suggests the violation of such a right if mutilation could be proven.

During the hearing on the preliminary injunction, Judge Lasker viewed the edited version of the Monty Python program broadcast on December 26 and the original, unedited version. After hearing argument of this appeal, this panel also viewed and compared the two versions. We find that the truncated version at times omitted the climax of the skits to which appellants' rare brand of humor was leading and at other times deleted essential elements in the schematic development of a story line. We therefore agree with Judge Lasker's conclusion that the edited version broadcast by ABC impaired the integrity of appellants' work and represented to the public as the product of appellants what was actually a mere caricature of their talents. We believe that a valid cause of action for such distortion exists and that therefore a preliminary injunction may issue to prevent repetition of the broadcast prior to final determination of the issues.

Decision and Remedy *The Second Circuit also found that ABC had violated copyrights retained by Monty Python. The court ordered the district court to enter an injunction barring ABC's broadcast of the second special.*

Tort of Incitement

Some victims of violent attacks have sought to sue television or motion picture producers for their injuries. These plaintiffs sue under a theory that the on-screen violent actions of actors incited real world persons to reenact the program or movie, causing harm to the victim.

In the first important incitement case, a Florida couple sued CBS, ABC and NBC, claiming that their son had become addicted to television violence. They alleged that "TV intoxication" caused their son to murder an eighty-three-year-old woman. The parents referred to no particular program but complained of television violence in general. The court ruled against the parents, because they could not cite specific programs that incited their son to violence.[25]

Since the Florida case, numerous incitement claims have been brought against television stations, motion picture producers, rock-and-roll groups, and others. While these claims have generally failed, the decisions suggest that future plaintiffs could possibly recover for incitement. In a California case, a young girl was horribly raped in a unique manner similar to that shown on a television program the previous night. She sued NBC and an appellate court held that the plaintiff had stated a legitimate claim.[26] The jury ultimately ruled for NBC, finding no incitement to violence, but the court opened the door for potential future liability for entertainment programming.

---

[25] *Zamora v. Columbia Broadcasting System*, 480 F. Supp. 199 (S.D. Fla. 1979).

[26] *Olivia N. v. National Broadcasting Co.*, 74 Cal. App. 3d 383 (1977).

▬ Ethical Perspectives

Sports Agents and Ethics

In hearings before the United States Congress, sports agents were described as "sleazoid" and "slime." These agents have been at the center of legal and ethical scandals, some of which are described above. One additional controversy involved Paul Palmer, once an All-America running back at Temple University. While a senior at Temple University in 1986, Palmer received a $5000 loan and monthly cash payments from sports agents Norby Walters and Lloyd Bloom. After Palmer became a professional player, this arrangement was disclosed. Temple forfeited its 1986 victories and erased all the records that Palmer had achieved while at the school. Walters and Bloom represented Palmer in his professional contract and persuaded Palmer to invest nearly a third of his $450,000 signing bonus in a "credit repair" business. Bloom did not actually invest this money but instead used it to cover his personal expenses, including the lease on a Rolls-Royce, his personal credit cards, and his ex-wife's rent. Palmer saw no benefit from this money.

Examples such as Paul Palmer's, which involve blatant disregard of duties of honesty, loyalty, and promise keeping, clearly involve unethical conduct on the part of sports agents. Recognizing that these examples of dishonesty and corruption were tarnishing the image of some good and honest sports agents, a group of agents formed the Association of Representatives of Professional Athletes (ARPA). The ARPA then adopted a code of ethics for its members.

Membership in ARPA and its ethical code is voluntary. Some athletes have begun insisting that their representation contract specify that the agent will conform to the ARPA code of ethics. Other athletes use screening committees of trusted friends to interview agents and help select an honest representative for the athlete.

While the ARPA ethical code is a step forward, it does not settle ethical problems. The code prohibits representation by an agent who lacks "competence ... in a particular area." This provision is important, because in the past anyone could be a sports agent. As a consequence, athletes have been represented by a dry-cleaning manager, a caterer, and a dentist. The ARPA code does not define "competence," however, so its benefits are not certain. The code also prohibits excessive fees, conflicts of interest by agent, and the disclosure of the client's confidential information.

Although the code is a step forward and might prevent the worst excesses of past sports agents, it fails to deal with some important ethical questions confronting sports agents. A common problem involves the ethical duties of agents when negotiating a representation deal with a college or high school athlete. Ordinarily, we expect each party to a contract to look out for his or her own interests.

In a perfect free market, an agent would have a right to make his own best deal with an athlete. It would be the athlete's own fault if the deal were an unfair one. Many of today's young athletes, though, are naive or undereducated. Tragically, even some athletes who graduated from college may be unable to read the English language. Is it realistic to expect such athletes to be able to protect their own interests when dealing with an agent?

The way that sports agents have structured their contracts creates a recurring problem. Suppose that a rookie signs an initial professional contract for $25,000 a year for two years, with a $10,000 bonus. The agent will take $6000, or 10 percent of $60,000, which is the total contract value. Then, the rookie doesn't make the squad and never receives the two years of $25,000 salary. The only money received by the athlete was the $10,000 signing bonus, and the agent took 60 percent of that money, leaving the athlete with only $4000.

The above situation is often legal, because the contract provides for its distribution of revenues, but is the agent's action ethical? Of course, the athlete is the one who signed the contract and failed to make the professional team. But the agent may still have some ethical duty of fairness in negotiating the contract. Perhaps the contract itself is inherently unfair, or perhaps the agent should at least disclose the future financial risk to the athlete. What ethical duties should an agent have in negotiating contracts? Will the acceptance of high ethical standards hurt an agent's financial success?

International Perspectives

International Marketing of Motion Pictures

Foreign distribution of U.S. motion pictures has become big business. The motion picture industry contributes over $1 billion per year to a positive trade balance for this nation. Nearly half of all profits in the motion picture industry derive from foreign distribution of films.

While international film distribution is clearly a success, substantial legal problems interfere with even greater profits. One major problem is the copyright protection provided by foreign nations. A United States copyright directly protects the owner only for U.S. distribution. In foreign distribution, a producer may be required to acquire a special copyright for a foreign nation.

To ease the problem of establishing international copyright protection, over fifty nations, including the United States, have joined in the Universal Copyright Convention (the Berne Convention). Under this Convention, member nations must recognize a United States copyright as protecting the owner of the copyright. The extent of protection, though, is determined by each country. Suppose that a United States producer gets a U.S. copyright and distributes a film in France. The French will recognize the U.S. copyright but will provide only that protection afforded to a French copyright. The U.S. company is still dependent on the strength of foreign copyright protection. The Convention does have a provision requiring that member states provide for "adequate and effective" protection of copyrights.

Other international conventions and agreements also protect copyrights in international law. This international law, including the Universal Copyright Convention, does not provide fully effective protection for motion picture rights. Virtually all nations (even those not members of the Convention) provide for copyright protection, but in practice these laws may not be enforced. Some nations provide insufficient penalties for copyright infringement.

U.S. motion picture companies have lost substantial potential profits from unauthorized performances and even piracy of films, such as from unauthorized reproduction and sale of video-cassettes. The film industry estimates that 50 percent of potential videotape revenues in Japan is pirated, resulting in an annual loss of over $250,000 in producers' receipts.

While piracy may never be totally eliminated, U.S. companies can take legal steps to reduce the financial impact of such piracy. Producers and distributors should ensure that they understand the specifics of foreign copyright laws. This can help the U.S. company structure its contracts and distribution arrangements to better protect its copyrights. One company, for example, will not grant a foreign company theatrical exhibition rights for its motion pictures unless the company also agrees to buy the videocassette rights as well.

Joint industry action can also help. A trade association of motion picture companies sent representatives to nations in South American and Latin America to work with their governments in preventing film piracy. While some foreign governments were uncooperative, others actively enforced the laws by raiding the pirates' production facilities. An industry source estimates that this program reduced piracy by 50 percent in Brazil and Mexico and by lesser percentages in other nations.

Questions and Case Problems

1. A grade school gym teacher at a private school took her class of thirty-five students out to the playground for a game of "dodgeball." Kaye Fidler, who was very bright, had skipped several grades and was much smaller and less coordinated than the other students. She was unable to avoid a ball thrown at her head and suffered a severe concussion during the game. Fidler sues the teacher and the school for these injuries. Should Fidler be allowed to recover?

2. A new female singer, Latomma, grew up on the music of Madonna and believes that she is the most talented musician and performer around. Latomma therefore decides that she must dress and act like Madonna. Therefore, she patterned her personal dress and style very closely after Madonna's. Latomma, who is a performer of heavy metal music, signed a five-year record contract and went out on tour. Madonna sued Latomma for misrepresentation. Should Madonna succeed in this action?

3. On May 23, 1979, a young boy was watching "The Tonight Show" when a stunt man was performing. The stunt man did a simulated hanging of Johnny Carson on the show, and Carson survived without any injury. Before the simulated hanging, the guest stated: "Believe me, it's not something that you want to go and try.... I happen to know somebody who did something similar to it, just fooling around, and almost broke his neck." After watching the show, the young boy, who was a regular viewer of the show, apparently tried the stunt and hanged himself to death. The boy's parents sued NBC. Should they be able to recover for the death of their son? [*DeFillippo v. National Broadcasting Co.*, 446 A.2d 1036 (R.I. 1982)].

4. Margaret Landon entered into an agreement with a studio to sell the motion picture rights to her book entitled *Anna and the King of Siam*. The agreement was that the studio would give her credit appropriate to "her contribution to the literary material upon which such motion pictures shall have been based." The studio had full editorial control in using Landon's book. The studio produced a series of thirteen films for television, and the film credits stated that they were based on Landon's work. Landon sued the studio, claiming that the films abandoned the theme of her work and that the credit injured her privacy and literary reputation by making a serious work appear frivolous. If she is correct about suffering damages, should she succeed in this lawsuit? [*Landon v. Twentieth Century-Fox Film Corp.*, 384 F. Supp. 450 (S.D.N.Y. 1974).

5. The Kingsmen were formed in 1962 and recorded a demo tape of the song entitled "Louie, Louie." The lead vocalist on this tape was Jack Ely, who left the group in 1964, before the song became popular. The entire group disbanded in 1967. Sometime later, a record company hired Ely to rerecord "Louie, Louie" for a collection of songs, and the record jacket stated that it included rerecording by the original artists, and mentioned the name, The Kingsmen. The Kingsmen sued the record company, because Ely was the only one of the original Kingsmen to rerecord the song. Should The Kingsmen succeed in this case? [*Kingsmen v. K-Tel International, Ltd.*, 557 F. Supp. 178 (S.D.N.Y. 1983)].

6. Larry Ford was waterskiing on a narrow channel and was skiing barefoot and backward. Ford was experienced and had skied in this manner and in this area many times. The boat was being driven by Jack Gouin. While waterskiing, Ford got too close to the bank and was struck by an overhanging tree limb, causing him severe head injuries. He could not see the limb because he was facing backwards. Ford sued Gouin for negligence in driving the boat. Who should prevail? [*Ford v. Gouin*, 266 Cal. Rptr. 870 (Cal. Ct. App. 1990).

Chapter Seventeen

Hospitality Management Law

▬ Key Background

The most important legal issues in hospitality management involve some of the most basic legal principles. One important issue is negligence, which may occur when a hotel is liable for carelessly allowing its guests to be injured. Agency law is also involved when an employer hotel is liable for the acts of its employees. Standard contract law controls several legal issues, such as reservations.

While the basic legal standards of these negligence and contract cases are straightforward, their application in hospitality management may be different because of the special guest-innkeeper relationship. This chapter goes through each of these issues in turn, highlighting the potential liability of hotel and restaurant owners.

▬ Guest-Innkeeper Relationship

The laws governing hotels and similar establishments evolved through the common law. The common law developed rules that placed particular legal burdens on what were then called "innkeepers." The law generally required that innkeepers were required to provide accommodations to all travelers who were able and willing to pay for them. The common law also provided that the innkeeper would be strictly liable for the loss of guests' property brought into the inn.

Since the adoption of these traditional common law rules, the federal and state governments have passed a number of statutes affecting the legal responsibilities of innkeepers. While some of these statutes imposed additional responsibilities on innkeepers, many of the laws have limited the potential common law liability faced by innkeepers.

The special rules only apply when there is a **guest-innkeeper relationship**. Finding this special relationship is, therefore, an essential threshold matter. The term "inn" or "hotel" is defined very broadly by the law to cover those who provide temporary, furnished lodging facilities for the general public and usually provide food service.

The guest-innkeeper relationship is a contractual one, dependent on the intent of the parties. If a person enters a hotel merely to dine at the restaurant, she will not be subject to the rules of the guest-innkeeper relationship. If she intends to spend the night after finishing her dinner, however, she becomes a guest.

Most controversies arise over when the guest-innkeeper relationship commences and terminates. Suppose that a guest gives his luggage to a doorman upon entering the hotel lobby. His luggage is then lost. The claim is made that the person had not yet registered and was not yet a guest subject to the special guest-innkeeper relationship. A court disagreed, saying that the acceptance of luggage was an ordinary incident to the guest-innkeeper relationship and fell within it.[1]

---

[1] *Korr v. Thomas Emery's Sons, Inc.*, 93 N.E.2d 781 (Ohio 1949).

In another case, a woman asked a hotel bellboy to take her bags to the taxicab area after she checked out. When she came to the cab area, the bags and the bellboy were both missing. One court held that she was no longer within the guest-innkeeper relationship.[2] Some courts have disagreed with this latter case.

Responsibility for the Safety of Guests

A key legal issue in hospitality management is the hotel's responsibility to protect the personal safety of its guests. The general rule is that a hotel is not an insurer of its guests' safety. As a result, hotels will be liable for injuries only when they (or their employees) are negligent in causing the injury. The special guest-innkeeper relationship, though, may mean that a hotel is held to a higher standard of care than under ordinary negligence law.

Liability under negligence, detailed in Chapter 6 of *West's Business Law, Seventh Edition*, and Chapter 12 of *West's Legal Environment of Business, Third Edition*, has standard requirements. To win under negligence, a person must show that the defendant had a duty of due care, negligently breached that duty, and that the negligence was the proximate cause of the person's injuries.

Some cases fit the standard pattern of negligence. For example, suppose that a hotel has a swimming pool that is outfitted with a diving board. Because the diving board was poorly maintained and the water was too shallow, a guest seriously injures herself. The hotel will be liable in negligence for the guest's injuries.

The following case expresses the extent of duty owed by those in the hospitality management industry.

---

[2]*Spiller v. Barclay Hotel*, 327 N.Y.S.2d 426 (1972).

Case 17.1
Becker v. Club Las Velas
United States District Court for the Southern District of New York, 1994
94 Civ. 2412

Background and Facts *Phyllis and Andrew Becker learned of a Mexican resort, Club Las Velas or "CLV," through marketing by a New York-based corporation, The Hotel Company. The Beckers vacationed at CLV in Cancun. While kayaking in a lagoon adjacent to the resort, their kayak was struck from behind by a power boat. The Beckers suffered serious injuries, including permanent quadriplegia for Phyllis. They sued both CLV and the Hotel Company for their damages. The Hotel Company moved to dismiss all claims against it.*

KEENAN, United States District Judge

* * * *

This court finds that, while plaintiffs have adequately pleaded a claim for negligence as to CLV, it has failed to do so as to The Hotel Company.

* * * *

Here, plaintiffs have successfully alleged such a claim against CLV. First, plaintiffs have alleged that CLV owed them a duty of care to protect them from injury as a result of dangerous conditions at the resort. In addition, plaintiffs have alleged that CLV breached that duty in a variety of ways, including, *inter alia,* failing to warn plaintiffs of the danger, failing to train plaintiffs in use of resort equipment, failing to provide a lifeguard, and failing to provide adequate rescue facilities.

* * * *

The claims for breach of implied warranty of safety and fraudulent misrepresentation apparently rest on statements made in CLV brochures distributed by The Hotel Company that allegedly promoted the activity of kayaking in the lagoon surrounding CLV. Distribution of literature, without more, is not sufficient to create liability on The Hotel Company's part for activities that were out of their control and occurred several thousand miles away.

Decision and Remedy *The court dismissed all claims against The Hotel Company but permitted plaintiffs to proceed with their case against CLV.*

Rooms

A hotel generally has a responsibility to provide safe premises for its guests. This means that bathrooms should be functioning and safe. Lighting should be adequate. Furniture, such as beds and chairs, must be safe for ordinary, foreseeable uses. In one case, a hotel was liable after a boxer injured his hand before a fight when a venetian blind collapsed on it.[3]

A hotel may also be liable in negligence for the preventable acts of others. In one famous case, the entertainer Connie Francis was raped while staying at a hotel. The rapist had entered the room through a sliding glass door that could not be effectively locked. Ms. Francis was awarded $2.5 million, because the hotel negligently failed to provide safe lodgings.[4] After appeal, the parties settled for a payment of $1.475 million.

The Connie Francis case shows how hotels can be liable for criminal acts that occur on their premises. The following decision is a more recent analysis of this cause of action.

---

[3] *Messina v. Sheraton Corportion of America*, 291 So.2d 829 (La. 1974).

[4] *Garzilli v. Howard Johnson's Motor Lodges, Inc.*, 419 F. Supp. 1210 (E.D.N.Y. 1976).

■ Case 17.2
Crinkley v. Holiday Inns, Inc.
United States Court of Appeals
Fourth Circuit, 1988
844 F.2d 156

Background and Facts *Sarah and James Crinkley were guests at the Holiday Inn in Concord, North Carolina. In the two weeks preceding their stay, guests at several area motels had been robbed by a group called the "Motel Bandits." The motel decided not to hire additional security guards but continued its program to encourage law enforcement personnel to frequent the premises by "offering a free snack tray and discount meals in the restaurant."*

Shortly after the Crinkleys checked into their room, an armed man burst inside and beat, bound and gagged James Crinkley. Sarah was threatened, bound and gagged. The robbers took their property, including her engagement ring. Eventually, Sarah Crinkley escaped her bonds and called the front desk for help.

After the police arrived, the Crinkleys were rushed to an area hospital. Mr. Crinkley suffered a broken jaw and multiple bruises. Ms. Crinkley suffered a personality change after the assault, becoming "fearful, anxious and withdrawn." A psychiatrist diagnosed her as a victim of post-traumatic stress disorder. Some fourteen months after the assault, she suffered a heart attack.

The Crinkleys sued the Holiday Inn-Concord, alleging that the hotel was negligent for failing to provide adequate security, which was the proximate cause of their injuries. The jury returned a verdict awarding Sarah Crinkley $400,000 in damages and James Crinkley $100,000. The Holiday Inn appealed.

PHILLIPS, Circuit Judge.

* * * *

To provide that the special duty of care created by the circumstances was breached, the Crinkleys relied primarily on the testimony of an expert in hotel-motel security, Kenneth Prestia.

Prestia testified that security at the Holiday Inn-Concord was inadequate in several respects. The motel had widespread access from several directions, a security problem exacerbated by the fact that the front desk did not provide employees with a view of all points of access. Existing fencing was of inadequate height to adequately deter access to the premises and there were no "no trespassing" signs around the perimeter. He opined that these obvious physical measures have a deterrent effect on crime by conveying the impression that the motel maintained a heightened security posture, and that their absence therefore increased the risk of criminal activity on the premises.

Prestia also opined that there were inadequacies apart from these physical measures. The motel had not instituted a formal security plan specifically tailored to the premises and did not employ security patrols. Prestia testified that security patrols are again particularly important where there is widespread access to the motel and limited observation from the employees. On this same point, he noted that more security patrols could be added during a period of higher crime activity or an increased threat of crime, a measure that could be taken by hiring off-duty law enforcement personnel.

* * * *

Under the less stringent test which we understand the North Carolina cases to apply, there was sufficient evidence to support the jury finding of proximate causation. The jury was entitled to accept the expert Prestia's opinions that criminals typically assess the risk of apprehension presented by the security measures in place, frequently by on-site surveillance of practices; and that the measures taken on the premises here in issue would not have acted as an effective deterrent. Having accepted this conclusion, the jury could reasonably have inferred—though surely it need not have—that the Crinkleys' assailants were indeed emboldened by the lax security measures to come on the premises, size up the situation, and plan their assault. The fact that it took some time to get the Crinkleys into their room supports the inference that the assailants were aware that security patrols were not in place.

* * * *

Decision and Remedy *The court affirmed the trial court judgment and award for the plaintiffs.*

Hotels also may be liable for failing to accommodate the needs of children as guests. In one case, an eight-month-old infant fell from a standard adult bed against hot radiator pipes and injured himself. The hotel was found liable for failure to furnish a baby crib, and the family was awarded $56,000.[5]

Common Areas

In addition to providing safe rooms, hotels also must make common areas safe. There is a long line of cases in which hotels were liable for malfunctioning elevators or hazardously maintained stairways. Restaurants are another source of potential liability. In one case, a careless waiter preparing cherries jubilee sprayed rum on a diner's shirt and then accidentally ignited it. A court awarded $80,000 for the plaintiff's burns.[6] Swimming pools are another common source of injury and liability for hotels.

A somewhat more difficult question involves guests who are injured while entering or leaving a hotel. The general rule is that a hotel is not obligated to provide a porter or doorman to assist the guests. If such a doorman is provided, however, the hotel will be liable for his negligent actions. If a doorman injures a plaintiff trying to leave a car, the hotel may be liable.

Other cases involve guests who were assaulted and injured while in a hotel parking lot. A hotel is not necessarily liable in these cases because it is not really the cause of the injuries. If, however, the parking lot were especially dangerous (e.g., without sufficient lighting) and if previous guests had been recently assaulted in the same parking lot, the hotel may be found liable for negligent failure to protect its guests.

An important doctrine is *per se* **negligence**. This doctrine states that if the defendant hotel violates a law, it will automatically be deemed to be negligent for injuries that result. In one recent case, a hotel pool attendant sought to adjust the pH balance of the pool. Because the feeder system was inoperative, the attendant simply dumped soda ash into the pool, which made it quite cloudy. This violated state rules for pool maintenance. After a guest drowned, unseen because of the pool's cloudiness, the hotel was found to be negligent *per se*.[7]

Defenses

Hotels may take advantage of the traditional defenses to a negligence action. One important defense is **comparative negligence** (when the plaintiff was negligent in his or her actions, contributing to the injury). Suppose that a 300-pound man stands on a tiny stool in order to adjust the room's thermostat temperature. The stool collapses and the man is injured. Comparative negligence would be a good defense for the hotel.

Another defense is **assumption of risk**. If the injured guest sees a risky course of action and still voluntarily takes it, the guest cannot recover. A guest was staying at a hotel in the French Quarter of New Orleans during Mardi Gras. Spurred on by the raucous crowd below, the guest climbed on a balcony railing and "mooned" the crowd. The guest then fell to the street and was seriously injured. The court directed a verdict for the hotel, because the plaintiff had assumed the risk.[8]

Suppose that a hotel posts a sign at its pool stating: "No Lifeguard on Duty. Swim at Your Own Risk." A poor swimmer enters the water and drowns. The guest will probably be found to have assumed the risk. There might be a different result, however, if the pool were unusually and unforeseeably hazardous or if some state law required hotels to provide lifeguards at pools when they are open to hotel guests.

Duty of Rescue

As a general rule of negligence law, a person has no duty to rescue another and cannot be liable for failure to rescue. A duty of rescue may arise, however, when the persons are in a special relationship with one another. The guest-innkeeper relationship creates at least some duty to rescue guests in danger.

Suppose that a guest enters the hotel's bar and drinks for an hour or two. Then, on the way to the bathroom, the guest falls down a stairway and seriously injures himself. The bartenders laugh at this

---

[5] *Seelbach, Inc. v. Cadick,* 405 S.W.2d 745 (Ky. 1966).

[6] *Young v. Caribbean Associates, Inc.,* 358 F. Supp. 1220 (V.I. 1973).

[7] *First Overseas Inv. Corp. v. Cotton,* 491 So.2d 293 (Fla. 1986).

[8] *Eldridge v. Downtowner Hotel,* 492 So.2d 64 (La. 1986).

Exhibit 17-1

State Limits on Liability in Hotels

State	Limit	State	Limit
Alabama	$300	Montana	$500
Alaska	$300	Nebraska	$300
Arizona	$500	Nevada	$750
Arkansas	$300	New Hampshire	$1000
California	$500	New Jersey	$500
Colorado	$5000	New Mexico	$1000
Connecticut	$500	New York	$500
Delaware	Total	North Carolina	$500
Florida	$1000	North Dakota	$300
Georgia	$100	Ohio	$500
Hawaii	$500	Oklahoma	$300
Idaho	$500	Oregon	$300
Illinois	$500	Pennsylvania	none given
Indiana	$600	Rhode Island	$500
Iowa	$100	South Carolina	$300
Kansas	$250	South Dakota	$300
Kentucky	$300	Tennessee	$300
Louisiana	$100	Texas	$50
Maine	$300	Utah	$250
Maryland	$300	Vermont	$300
Massachusetts	$1000	Virginia	$500
Michigan	$250	Washington	$1000
Minnesota	$300	West Virginia	$250
Mississippi	$500	Wisconsin	$300
Missouri	none given	Wyoming	none given

event and fail to call for medical assistance. The bar, and the hotel that owns it, may be liable for failure to rescue the guest.

Responsibility for Guest's Property

The common law made a hotel strictly liable for any loss of a guest's property through theft, loss, or otherwise. The hotel's defenses were limited to unusual circumstances, such as what the law considers an act of war or an act of God (e.g., tornado, flood). Today, all states have passed laws that limit the strict liability of hotel owners.

The state laws significantly limit the liability of the hotel industry for lost or stolen property. Exhibit 17-1 lists the maximum liability of hotels that comply with state laws. Although the limits vary by state, most are rather low.

The state statutes preserve some strict liability for the loss of clothing and necessary travel items, but limit liability for jewelry, large sums of money, and other items considered to be valuables. All states also place an absolute monetary limit on the hotel's liability, usually at a rather low level. A hotel must meet certain statutory requirements, however, before it can take advantage of these limits on liability. If the hotel fails to meet these requirements, it will remain strictly liable for guests' losses of property.

Posting

The **posting** requirement means that guests must be made aware of their inability to recover for the loss of their valuables. This is customarily done through a card placed in the guest's room. The law requires that such posting be sufficiently conspicuous that a guest should reasonably be aware of the limits. Placing the notification of limited liability on the guest's registration statement on a very small card on the dress is insufficiently conspicuous.

The contents of the posting also must accurately state the limitations on the hotel's liability. Posting an accurate description of the law on a guest room door, on a normal-sized piece of paper, has been found to be sufficient. Some laws, such as that of New York, also require posting in common areas.

Providing a Safe

Most of the state laws that limit the innkeeper's strict liability require that the hotel must provide a safe for their guests' valuables. The safe must be available to guests at all reasonable times. Some states require that the safe be available for twenty-four hours a day. The law generally protects the hotel, even if the valuables are stolen from the safe.

There are no clear-cut rules on the type of safe that is required for hotels. Some statutes specify that the safe must be fireproof. In a New York case, guests at a Manhattan luxury hotel had in their possession an extensive jewelry collection worth $1,000,000. The guests delivered their jewelry to management for deposit in safe-deposit boxes provided by the hotel. The safe-deposit boxes were contained in an ordinary room. After thieves broke in and stole the jewels, the guests sued. The court held that the hotel's safe may have been insufficient as a matter of law.[9] Had the safe been found sufficient, the guests could have recovered only $500.

Hotels may contractually agree to provide greater protection to their guests for valuables deposited in their safe. Under this procedure, guests first must declare the value of the property they place in the safe. Some hotels will refuse to insure or even accept valuables that exceed a certain value.

In addition, hotels may waive the protection of the liability limitation statute. Charging guests to insure their valuables is one example of such a waiver. Courts also may find a waiver when a hotel employee simply promises guests that the hotel will be responsible for their valuables. Consequently, it is crucial to inform employees of the hotel's practices.

Defining Valuables

Because the hotel's liability for valuables is limited, the definition of a valuable becomes important in many cases. Large amounts of money, very costly jewelry, negotiable instruments, and precious stones clearly qualify as valuables.

Disputes arise over how much money a guest should keep in his or her room and over whether functional jewelry must be deposited in a safe. Most courts have held that watches are utilitarian and are not valuables. As a consequence, the hotel will be liable for watches stolen from guest rooms. In a Washington decision, however, a court held that a watch worth $3685 was a valuable, and the guest was unable to recover for its theft from his room.

Property in Transit

A recurring problem in hospitality management law is the responsibility of hotels for valuables and other property during the time shortly before check-in or during and after check-out. As described above, the hotel's potential liability begins as soon as the parties have formed an intent to establish a guest-innkeeper relationship.

Guests at a New York hotel paid their bill and checked their luggage with a bellhop for a few hours. Unknown to the hotel, the bags contained jewelry worth over $60,000. When the guests returned, the valuable jewels were missing. The court held that the hotel's liability was limited because the retention of the luggage was a service provided for its guests, even though they had checked out.[10]

---

[9] *Goncalves v. Regent International Hotels, Ltd.*, 460 N.Y.S. 2d 750 (1983).

[10] *Salisbury v. St. Regis-Sheraton Hotel*, 490 F.Supp. 449 (1980).

Automobiles

Eighty-five percent of all guests arrive at a hotel driving an automobile. The automobile is considered neither a "valuable" with limited liability nor "personal property" for which the hotel remains strictly liable. If a guest's automobile is stolen, the hotel's liability will depend on circumstances.

The liability of hotels for guests' loss of automobiles is usually determined under the law of **bailment**. An excellent background discussion on the general law of bailments can be found in Chapter 49 of *West's Business Law, Seventh Edition*.

There are three different legal types of bailment. A gratuitous bailment is one in which the bailee (the person taking control of the car) does so without any benefit. In a gratuitous bailment, the bailee is held to a low standard of only slight diligence. An exceptional bailment is one by which the hotel takes possession of the car solely for the hotel's benefit. In this case, the hotel will be held to a standard of very high diligence.

Most automobile cases will involve mutual-benefit bailments. The guest benefits from the ability to garage the car, and the hotel benefits by providing a service to attract guests and for which they may charge. In such a mutual-benefit bailment, the bailee is held to a standard of ordinary diligence. All bailments contain a promise to return the property to the guest on demand and to no one else.

In a Tennessee case, a guest turned his car over to a hotel bellboy to park in the hotel's lot. Later in the day, the bellboy returned to the lot, took the car for a joyride, and smashed it. Although the hotel may not have been directly negligent in this case, it was liable for permitting the car to be taken by someone other than the bailor (guest).

A bailment may also exist for the personal property that guests leave in the automobiles turned over to the hotel. To avoid this situation, many hotels state that they have no responsibility for any goods left in the automobile. The hotel may still be liable if its employees knowingly and explicitly accept responsibility for the goods.

A bailment exists when the hotel's employees take custody of the car and park it themselves. A bailment may also exist when the guest parks the car in a garage and receives a ticket from an attendant. A bailment will not exist, if the guest parks the car on the street outside the hotel.

Negligence and Intentional Torts

State laws clearly limit the liability of hotelkeepers sued for the traditional common law of strict liability. States are divided, however, on whether the limitations on liability protect the hotel from damages based on negligence. Many major jurisdictions, including California, New York, Florida, and Illinois apply the limited liability even to negligence.

It seems clear that the liability-limiting statutes will not apply to intentional torts by the hotel or its employees. The following case illustrates how a hotel may be liable for the intentional tort of conversion.

■ Case 17.3
Bhattal v.
Grand Hyatt-New York
United States District Court,
Southern District of New York, 1983
563 F. Supp. 277

Background and Facts *Upon arriving at the Grand Hyatt in New York, the Bhattals turned their luggage, including valuables, over to the hotel bell captain. The luggage included pearls and other valuables worth $250,000. After checking into their room, the Bhattals went out to visit the city. On returning to their room that evening, they found their luggage missing.*

Apparently, the hotel computer erroneously instructed hotel employees to take the Bhattals' luggage from their room to JFK International Airport, along with the luggage of an aircraft crew who had been staying in the Bhattals' room at the hotel. The luggage was then placed on an airplane to Saudi Arabia. The Bhattals' bags were never recovered.

The Bhattals sued the hotel for the loss of their property worth $250,000 and for emotional distress damages. The hotel defended *by using the New York statute limiting innkeeper liability for valuables.*

BRIEANT, Judge.

* * * *

Here, defendant's employees entered plaintiffs' locked room, without plaintiffs' permission or knowledge, and removed their luggage, commingled it with the luggage of the Saudi Arabian aircraft crew members and placed it on a bus headed for Kennedy Airport. The Court infers that if the luggage was not stolen at Kennedy Airport, it arrived in Saudi Arabia and was eventually stolen by a Saudi thief who still had the use of at least one good hand. In this instance, the intentional acts of the defendant clearly constituted conversion under New York law.

Sections 200 and 201 of the New York General Business Law were adopted in the middle of the nineteenth century to relieve an innkeeper from his liability at common law as an insurer of property of a guest lost by theft, caused without negligence or fault of the guest. These statutes and the cases cited thereunder by the defendant extend to the situation where there is a mysterious disappearance of valuable property, either as a result of a theft by an employee of the hotel—or a trespass or theft by an unrelated party, for whose acts the innkeeper is not responsible. The statutes are also intended to protect the innkeeper from the danger of fraud on the part of a guest in a situation where the property said to have disappeared never existed at all, or was taken or stolen by or with the privity of the guest.

* * * *

The reason for providing a hotel safe in compliance with [Section] 200 and the reason for limiting a hotel's liability under [Section] 201 is to protect against just such situations. When a hotel room is let to a guest, the innkeeper has lost a large measure of control and supervision over the hotel room and its contents. While housekeeping and security staff can enter the room at reasonable hours and on notice to any persons present therein, essentially, for most of the time at least, property of a guest which is present in a hotel room can be said to be under the exclusive dominion and control of the hotel guest, rather than the innkeeper.

We have been cited to no case extending the limited immunity provided by statute against the common law liability of innkeepers, where the liability sought to be founded on the innkeeper was based on the exercise of unlawful dominion and control by the innkeeper himself, or his agents and employees acting in the course of their employment; as contrasted with mysterious disappearances due to causes unknown, or criminal acts of third parties or employees acting for themselves rather than for the employer. As noted above, it was only for the latter class of cases that the statutes granted immunity.

Decision and Remedy *The court ruled for plaintiffs on their property claim and scheduled a hearing to determine its value.*

Liability for Refusing or Evicting Guests

Under the traditional common law, innkeepers were required to accept all guests. Limited exceptions existed for circumstances such as the unavailability of rooms. The hotel might also refuse a person who is seriously intoxicated, suffering from a contagious disease, or disorderly. The hotel could also refuse a guest who was unable or unwilling to pay for the room. A restaurant could also deny service to customers for these reasons.

Federal law expressly prohibits rejecting guests on the basis of their race or sex. State laws may go further. For example, New York law prohibits hotel discrimination on the basis of handicap, marital status, and other conditions.

A refused guest may sue the hotel for wrongful refusal. The guest would be required to show that the hotel lacked a reasonable basis to refuse lodging. If the guest wins, the damages may be quite limited, such as the cab fare to another hotel. Some guests have sued for embarrassment and mental anguish resulting from the hotel's refusal, but most states do not recognize these damages in a wrongful refusal case.

In unusual circumstances, damages may be greater. If alternative hotel accommodations are unavailable, and the guests were compelled to sleep in their automobiles, a court could find more substantial actual damages and even punitive damages.

The innkeeper also has the right to evict guests with sufficient reason. Eviction for failing to pay a hotel bill is authorized. If the guest agreement provides for a specific period of stay, the hotel may also evict guests who overstay that period. A hotel also may evict those who have contagious diseases, or who are committing crimes or being disorderly, or who violate hotel regulations.

A guest can also sue for wrongful eviction, much like wrongful refusal. Some courts have awarded mental distress damages in wrongful eviction cases. Cases have even awarded punitive damages against the hotelkeeper for **wrongful eviction** when the plaintiff can show (1) a wrongful act that was (2) performed intentionally, (3) with malice or gross disregard of rights, and (4) with willfulness.

The method of eviction is also important. Hotels customarily lock the guests out of their rooms and may deny them access to their baggage. This is ordinarily a lawful means but its reasonability depends on the circumstances. A hotel could not prevent a guest from obtaining necessary medication contained in his or her luggage. Hotels may even use some force to evict guests but should take care not to employ unreasonable, excessive force.

Reservations

Many hospitality management conflicts involve a guest's reservations. The traditional common law rules did not provide for reservations. Today, most experienced travelers make reservations in advance. Yet many of these travelers either cancel their reservations or never show up at the hotel. As a consequence, many hotels overbook their rooms, taking more reservations than they can accommodate. Problems arise when a hotel cannot honor its reservations.

The legal status of reservations depends in part on whether they may be considered a contract. There will generally be an offer and an acceptance when a guest makes reservations, and a number of courts have held that reservations represent a binding contract. The law allows few excuses for breach of this contract, though impossibility (e.g., a fire destroying the hotel) would be an excuse.

A guest with a reservation who is refused a room may thus sue for breach of contract. A guest may also sue if he or she receives a room that is inferior to the quality of the room reserved.

Some states also have passed statutes regulating overbooking. In Florida, for example, when a guest makes a deposit with the reservation, the hotel must provide a room. If space is unavailable, the hotel must make every effort to find alternate accommodations for the guest, must refund the deposit, and is liable for a fine of up to $500 per guest.

Most guests denied rooms do not sue the hotel. This may be due to the availability of alternative hotels and the high costs of litigation. Some guests have sued, however, and have claimed substantial damages for emotional distress. Punitive damages are generally unavailable in breach of contract claims. The following decision analyzes the damages available for failure to honor reservations.

Case 17.4
Dold v. Outrigger Hotel
Supreme Court of Hawaii, 1972
501 P.2d 368

Background and Facts *Mr. and Mrs. Dold made a confirmed reservation with the Outrigger Hotel in Hawaii. The reservation was confirmed with the Dolds' American Express Card and a guarantee to pay for one night. When the Dolds arrived, the Outrigger was overbooked, and the hotel referred them to the less expensive Pagoda Hotel. These referrals were common and the Outrigger made a profit on them.*

The Dolds sued the Outrigger for breach of contract and for breach of innkeepers' duty. The Dolds sought damages for mental distress and punitive damages. The trial judge held that the Dolds could recover the mental distress but not for punitive damages. The jury awarded the Dolds $600. They appealed the denial of the possibility of punitive damages.

KOBAYASHI, Justice.

* * * *

The question of whether punitive damages are properly recoverable in an action for breach of contract has not been resolved in this jurisdiction.

In the instant case, on the evidence adduced, the trial court refused to allow an instruction on the issue of punitive damages but permitted an instruction on the issue of emotional distress and disappointment.

In a case involving a similar pattern of overbooking of reservations the court in *Wills v. Trans World Airlines, Inc.,* 200 F.Supp. 360 (S.D.Cal. 1961), stated that the substantial overselling of confirmed reservations for the period in question was a strong indication that the defendant airline had wantonly precipitated the very circumstances which compelled the removal of excess confirmed passengers from its flights.

* * * *

We are of the opinion that the facts of this case do not warrant punitive damages. However, the plaintiffs are not limited to the narrow traditional contractual remedy of out-of-pocket losses alone. We have recognized the fact that certain situations are so disposed as to present a fusion of the doctrines of tort and contract. Goo, supra, 52 Haw. at 241, 473 P.2d at 567. Though some courts have strained the traditional concept of compensatory damages in contract to include damages for emotional distress and disappointment (*Kellogg v. Commodore Hotel,* 64 N.Y.S.2d 131 (Sup.Ct. 1946), we are of the opinion that where a contract is breached in a wanton or reckless manner as to result in a tortious injury, the aggrieved person is entitled to recover in tort. Thus, in addition to damages for out-of-pocket losses, the jury was properly instructed on the issue of damages for emotional distress and disappointment.

Decision and Remedy *The court affirmed the judgment of the trial court.*

Larger damages, including punitive damage awards, can result if the hotel has willfully insulted or abused the guest. This action could involve intentional infliction of emotional distress or defamation.

A New York doctor and his wife, who was recovering from surgery, made reservations for a three-week stay at a Caribbean hotel. They missed the first night because of a snowstorm that prevented plane travel. When they arrived, the hotel denied them a room for more than two nights. The doctor and his wife were unable to find alternative accommodations and were unable even to get on a plane flight back to New York. Eventually, they had to fly to another island and book a ship back home. A jury awarded them $15,000 in damages, though they eventually settled for $6,000.[11]

Damages may be much greater in the circumstances of a convention or group travel. A travel agent promoted a group tour of Hawaii and featured a specific hotel for its customers. Although the hotel

---

[11] *Scher v. Liberty Travel Service,* 328 N.Y.S. 2d 386 (1971).

had confirmed reservations, it refused to honor them. In an unreported decision, a jury awarded the travel agent over $150,000 in damages for harm to their reputation. Another decision awarded approximately $70,000 in damages when a Las Vegas hotel failed to honor a tour group reservation.[12]

When reservations are a contract, they also bind the guest. If the guest fails to arrive, or checks out before the assigned date, the guest may be liable to the hotel. A traveler unable to abide by a reservation should promptly inform the hotel of this fact. Under contract rules, the hotel is bound to attempt to rent the room to another. If the hotel is successful, it has suffered no damages and must refund any deposit to the traveler.

If the guest does not honor the reservation and makes no effort to inform the hotel, the hotel could treat the deposit as its damages. If there was no deposit, the hotel will have to sue the guest for non-performance. The small amount in question generally makes such litigation pointless. For conventions or group bookings, however, the hotel may benefit from suing over the failure to honor reservations.

In practice, most reservations are made over the telephone and guaranteed by giving the hotel a credit card number. The hotel usually tells the guest a deadline by which to cancel the reservation (usually the day before). If the guest fails to show up and did not inform the hotel by the stated deadline, the hotel may charge the guest's credit card for the cost of one night's stay.

Rights of Guests

In addition to the above rights to sue for dishonor of reservations, property loss, and personal injury, guests have some specific common law rights in hotels. Two such traditional rights are those of courtesy and privacy.

Longstanding precedent requires that an innkeeper treat a guest in a respectful and courteous manner. A guest may sue if subjected to uncivil and abusive treatment at the hands of the hotel employees. Such behavior may give rise to damages for mental distress or loss of reputation.

A guest also has some right of privacy in a hotel room. As a consequence of this rule, the hotel has a duty not to allow third parties access to its guests' rooms. The right is not absolute, however, and the innkeeper retains a right of access to the room. Occasional entries are allowed as necessary for the discharge of the duties of maids, etc.

The hotelkeeper also may enter a guest's room due to a suspicion of criminal activity. The hotelkeeper is not a government agent and is not bound by the requirements of a warrant prior to a search. In addition, the hotelkeeper may request police accompaniment on such an entry to investigate possible criminal behavior, but any police search is limited in the absence of a warrant.

If the entry is instigated by the police, however, the guest retains constitutional protection against warrantless search and seizure. Although the hotelkeeper may use a master key to provide the police access to a guest room, the hotel cannot consent to the search on behalf of the guest. The police must abide by constitutional limits that prohibit unreasonable searches and most warrantless searches. Once the person is no longer a guest of the hotel (e.g., his reserved stay is over), the person may lose these privacy protections.

Rights of Innkeepers

Much of this chapter has focused on the rights of guests, but hotels have rights as well. The paramount right of the innkeeper is the right to be compensated.

The right of compensation is essentially one of contract law. The hotelkeeper has a legal right to whatever price the parties agreed upon. Many hotels use standard rates, and there may be some confusion about the agreed-upon price for the rooms. To avoid this problem, many states have enacted laws that require innkeepers to post their rates and charges in every guest room and in certain common areas. The hotel may also charge for extra services (such as telephone calls) but must inform the guest of this charge in advance.

Because hotels deal with travelers from many distant points, the hotels may have an especially difficult time enforcing the duty of compensation. To help ameliorate this problem, state law has created the *innkeeper's lien*.

The innkeeper's lien essentially provides that the hotel has a right to all the goods that the guest brings into the hotel, up to the value of the charges due the hotel. The lien covers virtually all kinds of

---

[12] *Cardinal Consulting Co. v. Circo Resorts, Inc.*, 297 N.W. 2d 260 (Minn. 1980).

property (including automobiles and securities left in a safe-deposit box) and enables the innkeeper to take possession of a guest's luggage, for example, pending payment of the guest's bill.

The lien arises as soon as the guest arrives and any charges are incurred. The hotel loses its lien as soon as it voluntarily delivers these goods to the guest. The guest's payment of the bill also ends the lien.

In addition to the hotel's civil remedies, every state has passed a law that makes it a crime to defraud an innkeeper. As an example, Massachusetts law provides for a maximum of two years in prison for defrauding an innkeeper of more than $100 in goods and services and also allows an innkeeper to detain persons that they reasonably believe to have committed such a fraud. Because fraud is a criminal act, a conviction under these laws required proof of intent to defraud on the part of the guest.

The hotel also has the right to establish reasonable rules for the establishment. The most controversial hotel rules involve those that bar non-guests from the premises. A hotel may exclude "undesirables," such as known criminals. Hotels may also exclude solicitors, even including religious groups that are soliciting members or contributions.

Licensing and Regulation of Hotels

Most cities and states require a license to operate a hotel. State and local building codes also generally require permits or certificates of occupancy before a hotel may operate. Hotels may also require licenses for specific activities such as food and liquor service. Failure to obtain the proper license will prevent the hotel from charging guests. In addition, a license may be revoked if the hotel operates unlawfully.

Many state and local hotel regulation statutes require the hotels to maintain guest registers and keep them for up to three years. The register may be used as an investigatory tool for law enforcement. Private persons may also want to examine the register, but the hotel should obtain the guest's consent before permitting such an examination.

Hotels are also affected by credit regulations. The federal Truth-in-Lending Act requires that hotels provide credit card customers with information on the procedures for disputing billing charges of the hotel. State laws can prevent a hotel from doing a credit check on a guest without first informing the guest and later informing the guest of any adverse outcome of the check.

Various public health and safety laws also govern hotels. Building codes regulate the manner in which buildings may be constructed and operated. Rules applicable to hotels may be especially strict with respect to maximum capacity regulations and required exits.

Hotels also are subject to many federal, state and local fire safety requirements. After the disastrous MGM Grand Hotel fire in Las Vegas in 1981, the county adopted a stringent code for high-rise hotels that required that sprinkler systems be installed in every room and in all exit corridors. Many states and localities require smoke detectors throughout hotels. Violation of these codes can invoke criminal penalties against the hotel or its owner.

Public health laws further regulate other aspects of hotel management. State laws set cleanliness standards for hotel linens and towels and may even prescribe the number of these items that must be provided guests. Hotel swimming pools are highly regulated in many jurisdictions.

Licensing and Regulation of Restaurants

Food and alcohol service is extensively regulated by states and municipalities. Federal and state rules attempt to prevent service of unwholesome food. Civil law also applies to these cases. A woman at a Bermuda hotel sued when she ate a croissant that contained slivers of glass, which caused bleeding when she swallowed it.

Alcohol service is licensed by the states. These licensing laws generally restrict the hours of sale, require maintenance of certain books and records, and prohibit service of alcoholic beverages to intoxicated persons or minors.

Many states also have **dram shop laws**, which statutorily authorize a suit against a server of alcohol. Under these laws, if a person is injured by a drunken person, the injured individual may sue the bar or restaurant that caused the drunkenness. The dram shop laws do not make the bar strictly liable. Most of these dram shop laws limit liability to injuries resulting from the sale of alcohol to a person who is visibly intoxicated or known to be a habitual drunkard.

A new generation of laws imposes additional requirements on restaurants. Many states and localities now require restaurants to maintain a nonsmoking section. Some states require owners to post diagrams or instructions on how to aid a choking victim. A number of states have **truth-in-menu laws** prohibiting the misrepresentation of the identity of food items offered.

Hotel and restaurant owners also must comply with a myriad of more general government regulations. Significant examples of these include employment laws, antitrust laws, consumer protection laws, trademark laws, tax laws and others. These laws are discussed elsewhere in this book, in *West's Business Law, Seventh Edition,* and in *West's Legal Environment of Business, Third Edition.*

Ethical Perspectives

Ethics and Overbooking

Overbooking occurs when the hotel makes more reservations than it has rooms available. At first glance, overbooking seems unethical. If a guest with a reservation must be turned away, the hotel has violated an obligation of promise keeping. The hotel may also greatly inconvenience the guest, because alternative accommodations may be unavailable, inferior, too costly, or in an inconvenient location.

A case can be made for overbooking. Consider the Concord Resort Hotel in the Caribbean. The Concord may know from experience that only 80 percent of the guests who make reservations actually arrive at the hotel. While in theory the Concord might sue the remaining 20 percent for breach of contract, it is too costly to pursue the responsible parties in courts all over the world.

Suppose that the Concord does not overbook and never reserves more than 100 percent of its rooms. This means that, on average, the Concord will be 20 percent unoccupied. The lowered occupancy rate will mean that the Concord will have to charge guests a higher rate in order to make a profit. If the Concord overbooked, the hotel could maintain a higher occupancy rate and charge less or offer better services. Everyone, including the average guest, would be better off with overbooking.

In a situation such as that of the Concord, the mere act of overbooking should not be considered unethical. This is especially true if the Concord is careful in its overbooking and does not exceed 115 percent of capacity. If so, very few, if any, reserved guests should be denied a room. The overbooking simply compensates for the guests who fail to keep their reservation.

There remains an ethical problem, however, on those occasions when a greater-than-expected number of reserved guests arrive and some must be turned away for lack of rooms. The Concord has broken its promise to these potential guests and may have caused them harm.

Perhaps the Concord should adopt a policy of providing extensive assistance to reserved guests who cannot be accommodated. The Concord could itself arrange alternate rooms of equal or superior quality. The Concord might itself make up any difference in cost or provide special services to these individuals. In addition to helping fulfill the hotel's ethical responsibilities, these practices should breed good will.

The hotel probably has one other ethical obligation. It should inform potential guests of its practice of overbooking at the time that they make a reservation. In this way, the guests better understand the risks they take, even after reserving a room.

International Perspectives

International Hospitality Management Law

International travel is a multibillion-dollar business. Hospitality management law largely depends on the law of the nation in which the hotel is located. For example, if a British tourist brings securities worth $100,000 and has them stolen from his or her hotel room, New York law will limit the guest's recovery to $500. If a New York tourist loses $100,000 in securities at a London hotel, however, the hotelkeeper will be strictly liable for *all* of his or her damages. There are some common themes in international hospitality management law, however.

As to guests' loss of property, the common law nations of the British Commonwealth make the hotel strictly liable for the losses. European civil law nations (such as Germany, France and Italy) also provide for strict innkeeper liability, but these nations have adopted liability limitations similar to those in the United States.

With respect to personal injuries, most nations (including the United States, the United Kingdom, and Italy) adopt a negligence standard for innkeeper liability. Some countries, such as Germany, hold the innkeeper strictly liable for injuries to guests caused by defects on the premises.

On the issue of reservations, hotels in popular destinations (such as the Caribbean and Europe) typically require significant advance deposits and therefore tend to do less overbooking. When overbooking does occur and a reserved guest is turned away, these nations provide little recourse for the guest. Germany is an exception, making overbooking illegal and subject to significant monetary penalties.

The International Institute for the Unification of Private Law (UNIDROIT) has adopted a Draft Convention on the Hotelkeeper's Contract in an attempt to make international hospitality management law consistent. Although this Convention has not yet been adopted, its terms offer some guidance on a possible future international law of hospitality management.

The UNIDROIT Convention would impose strict liability on the hotelkeeper for property losses but would limit liability for valuables to an amount within the range of 500 to 1000 times the daily room rate, if the hotel posts this limit and provides a safe. The Convention makes the hotel liable for injuries caused by its negligence but permits the hotel to limit its liability in other circumstances. The Draft Convention would also make the hotelkeeper liable for any damage that a guest may suffer because of the hotel's failure to honor reservations.

Questions and Case Problems

1. The assistant manager of the Hyatt Regency was given a briefcase (closed but unlocked) that was found in the main lobby. He opened the briefcase to search for identification and found a wallet plus large bundles of money. When a person came to claim the briefcase, the manager demanded identification, and the individual said that his identification was in his wallet. The conversation became agitated, and the manager paged the hotel's security personnel, who were off-duty police officers. The security personnel opened the briefcase to get out the wallet and discovered a bag of marijuana. The guest was arrested and claims that the discovery of the marijuana was the result of an illegal search. Should the court exclude the marijuana as the result of an illegal search? [*Berger v. State*, 257 S.E.2d 8 (Ga. 1979)].

2. The Roosevelt Motor Lodge had forty rooms on the ground level. After showering, a woman guest of the lodge left the window open, covered only by a screen that could not be locked. An intruder broke into her room through the open window, raped her, and stole some of her property. She sued the motor lodge for damages from her injuries. Should she recover from the lodge? [*Brewer v. Roosevelt Motor Lodge*, 295 A.2d 647 (Me. 1972)].

3. Robert, a business student seeking a job, was running late for a hiring reception being given by a company. He gave his car keys to the valet for parking after taking off his class ring and putting it into the glove compartment. Rushing into the reception room, Robert tossed his new cashmere overcoat on top of a rack that the hiring company had placed outside the reception room. After the reception, Robert returned to the coat rack to discover that his coat was missing. When he obtained his car from valet parking, he found that his ring was missing. Robert sued the hotel for the loss of his coat and his ring. Should he be able to recover from the hotel?

4. Andrea, a sales representative, was running late for her plane to her next sales destination. Running off the elevator, she flagged a bellboy to take her bag, which contained her presentation and samples. When she came out to the taxi stand, she discovered that her bag was missing. She sued the hotel for the loss of her bag. Should the hotel be held responsible for Andrea's damages?

5. Members of the Jehovah's Witnesses religion entered the Endicott Hotel and went down the hotel's corridors knocking on doors. They sought to give hotel guests literature on their religion. Contributions were not actively solicited but were encouraged and accepted. They conducted this activity as quietly as possible. The hotel manager had received no complaints but nevertheless asked the Jehovah's Witnesses to cease their activities. They invoked their constitutional rights and refused to leave the hotel. The hotel than called the police, which forcibly evicted the Jehovah's Witnesses. After they attempted to re-enter the hotel, they were arrested and prosecuted for disorderly conduct. Was the eviction proper and are the Jehovah's Witnesses guilty? [*People v. Thorpe*, 101 N.Y.S.2d 986 (1950)].

6. James Sperka was a guest at a Holiday Inn in Florida that was adjacent to the Gulf of Mexico. After a couple of drinks, Sperka went into the ocean and dived into what appeared to be deep water. In fact, he dived into a concealed sandbar and was rendered quadriplegic. Sperka sued Holiday Inn for failure to warn him of the hazard. Was Holiday Inn liable on these facts? [*Sperka v. Little Sabine Bay, Inc.*, No. 92-2449 (Fla. App. 1994)].

CHAPTER EIGHTEEN

Communications Law

KEY BACKGROUND

Mass communications form a substantial portion of the modern United States economy. Newspapers, television, radio and other media do a growing, multibillion-dollar business. Moreover, the effects of these media influence political campaigns and individual lives. A special area of law has grown up around mass communications. Television and radio broadcasts are regulated by the Federal Communications Commission (FCC). In addition, all media are affected by potential liability arising from their entertainment and news reports.

Federal Communications Commission Regulation

The federal government's regulation of mass communications began early in the twentieth century with rules for the use of wireless radio by ships at sea. The need for broader regulation became clear with the first commercial radio broadcast on November 2, 1920. The government's limited authority was unable to avoid chaotic interference on radio airwaves. Some rule was necessary to allocate frequencies for broadcasters.

Congress responded to this need by passing the Federal Communications Act of 1934. This law created and empowered the Federal Communications Commission. Originally, the Commission allocated frequencies for the exclusive use of licensed broadcasters but concerned itself little with broadcast content. In 1939, however, the World Series was broadcast by the Mutual Broadcasting System. Communities that lacked an affiliate of Mutual were denied any radio coverage of the series. The resultant outcry prodded the Commission to expand its regulation into issues of market power and broadcast content.

The modern FCC is organized into a number of bureaus. The two most significant bureaus are:

1. Mass media—dealing with commercial broadcasting and cable radio and television.

2. Common carrier—dealing with telephone, telegraph, facsimile and related communications.

Other bureaus deal with other communications applications, such as the private radio, which regulates police and industrial band transmissions. Each bureau has unique powers over its own special type of communications.

In general, the FCC has a very broad grant of regulatory authority. The preamble to the 1934 Act states that the Commission shall regulate communications "as public convenience, interest, or necessity requires." This has been interpreted to permit regulation when the "public interest" so dictates.

Spectrum Allocation

One of the most important powers of the FCC is the allocation of broadcast spectrum among the various

297

types of communication. Television or radio stations broadcast at a given frequency (actually a number of electromagnetic oscillations per second). There is a continuum, or spectrum, of possible frequencies for communications. Because the length of the spectrum is limited, the FCC must apportion the spectrum among the various types of communications.

Under its "block" allocation system, the Commission estimates the amount of spectrum required for a particular communications service and accordingly devotes a portion of the spectrum for that service. Thus, the Commission allocates a certain portion of the spectrum for AM radio, FM radio, VHF television, UHF television, private radio services, and other uses. This allocation is to respond to the public's need for these varied types of communications.

The FCC has been criticized for being slow to respond to public needs for new communications services. In response, the Commission increasingly uses "flexible use" allocation. For example, the Commission has taken a portion of the UHF television band and permitted its use for land mobile communications (e.g., cellular car phones). The use of this spectrum in any given locality will depend in part upon the market demand for the competing services.

Licensing

Another critical role for the FCC is in the licensing of stations to broadcast at a given frequency. An FCC license is a legal requirement for broadcasting. License holders also must have their license renewed periodically (seven years for a radio license, five years for a television license). Most broadcast licenses are quite lucrative and there is often intense competition for this right to broadcast. The FCC conducts a hearing among competitors and uses a defined list of criteria to select which applicant will receive the desired license. These criteria are listed in Exhibit 18-1 and summarized below.

Licensing standards Some of the standards for licensing a broadcast station are straightforward. For example, a licensee must be a *citizen* of the United States. If the licensee is a corporation, no more than 25 percent of its ownership may be foreign. Another standard is that the applicant make a *technical showing* of qualifications. The applicant thus must show that it intends to broadcast with equipment approved by the Commission and operate within the FCC's technical rules for broadcasting. A third standard is *financial qualifications*. An applicant must have the capital necessary to construct and operate the proposed station or to continue its operations if a renewal is being requested.

Exhibit 18-1

Criteria for Broadcast Licenses

- Citizenship
- Showing of technical qualifications
- Showing of financial qualifications
- Good character
- Diversity of ownership
- Minority ownership
- Ascertainment of community needs
- Programming quality

Other licensing standards are less clear and subject to greater dispute among applicants. For example, the applicant must have **good character**; a license applicant is likely to be denied if he or she has been convicted of a felony, especially if that conviction involved fraud. This is not an absolute bar to ownership, however. One applicant was granted a license even though he had a past conviction for running guns to Israel.[1] The FCC also considers the applicant's candor and honesty in the application process.

Diversity of media ownership is also a standard used in broadcast licensing decisions. The Commission has rules to prevent any single entity from dominating media outlets in a community. These rules impose three restrictions:

1. No single entity can own more than one station in the same service (e.g., television) in one single community.

2. No single entity can own more than twelve AM radio stations, twelve FM radio stations, and twelve television stations (a total of thirty-six) within the United States.

3. The owners of daily newspapers may not own AM radio, FM radio, or television stations in the community served by the newspaper.

Even if these rules are met, the Commission will still make comparative judgments of diversity among competing applicants in choosing which applicant should receive the license.

The Commission also considers **minority ownership** in granting broadcast licenses. Minority-owned applicants get some preference in licensing. Minority owners receive an "enhancement." If Station A and Station B are otherwise equal, but Station A is owned by African Americans, A is likely to receive the license. In addition, all stations must undertake affirmative action programs so as better to represent minority groups among the station's officers and managers, technicians and salespersons.

In addition to the minority ownership preference, the FCC prohibits licensees from practicing racial discrimination in employment. The following case illustrates an application of this rule.

---

[1] *Las Vegas Television, Inc.*, 14 R.R. 1273 (1957).

■ **Case 18.1**
Florida State Conference of Branches of the NAACP v. Federal Communications Commission
United States Court of Appeals, District of Columbia Circuit, 1994
24 F.3d 271

Background and Facts *Pasco Pinellas Broadcasting Company operates two radio stations in Florida. When its licenses for renewal were up in 1988, it confronted opposition from the NAACP under the equal employment opportunity rule. Pasco had hired 58 employees in the past year, all of them white. The Commission granted Pasco only a short-term renewal and imposed an $18,000 forfeiture along with reporting requirements to enable the FCC to gauge its progress in equal employment opportunity compliance. The NAACP petitioned for review of this order, claiming that the FCC should have conducted a full hearing into its claims that license renewal should be denied.*

SILBERMAN, Circuit Judge.

* * * *

Pasco sought to excuse its employment record by explaining that it encountered difficulties in attracting minority applicants. The bulk of the minorities ... lived 25 miles away in the Tampa-St. Petersburg environs, separated from the station by inadequate highways and a lack of public transportation. The company's salaries, moreover, were said to be significantly lower than stations in the urban area, so it was difficult to attract anyone from those areas given the long and difficult commute.

* * * *

We do not agree with petitioners that the case before us presents such actual evidence of discrimination that would oblige the Commission to proceed to a hearing. Here we are not faced with a conspicuous departure of minorities en masse nor is there any evidence even suggesting that qualified minority applicants were refused employment. Only one minority applied for a position during 1987-88 ... Pasco's explanation for its difficulties in attracting minority employees, moreover, are neither self-contradictory nor suspicious.

* * * *

The Commission did not ignore Pasco's inadequate affirmative EEO program ... Accordingly, the Commission fined Pasco $18,000 and, perhaps more significantly, granted Pasco only a short-term renewal under more onerous reporting requirements—keeping Pasco, as it were, on a short leash.

Decision and Remedy *The court affirmed the Commission's decision.*

The final criteria for choosing a licensee are **community ascertainment** and **programming**. Potential broadcasters must familiarize themselves with the needs and problems of the community they seek to serve. Then, the applicant must propose programming that is responsive to the local needs. While programming standards were greatly relaxed during the 1980s, the broadcaster still must demonstrate that its programming will be in the "public interest." The FCC has denied a license renewal due to defamatory and racist programming.

Hearings The FCC will hold a contest hearing and seek to determine which applicant best meets the above criteria. In such a hearing, the parties can present the case for their application, as opposed to the other applications. No one standard is clearly more important than others. The Commission's choice is based on which applicant will provide the "best practicable service" to the public.[2]

A station that is up for license renewal is often awarded **renewal expectancy**. This is a bonus for existing stations and may enable them to keep their station, even against challengers with somewhat better applications. Renewal expectancy was adopted to encourage stations to invest more in quality service and because incumbents have a proven track record.

Renewal expectancy is not automatically granted for an incumbent station, however. The station must demonstrate that it has engaged in quality programming. The following case discusses the requirements of license renewal.

---

[2] 1 F.C.C.2d 393 (1965).

■ Case 18.2
Monroe Communications Corporation v. Federal Communications Commission
District of Columbia Circuit Court of Appeals, 1990
900 F.2d 351

Background and Facts *Video 44 sought a renewal of its license to operate station WSNS-TV in Chicago, Illinois. Monroe Communications Corporation challenged for the right to the license. Video 44 had converted the traditional television station to a subscription television service. Video 44 transmitted various nationally syndicated programs, including a substantial number of adult films that contained nudity and offensive language.*

An Administrative Law Judge at the FCC ruled that the license should be awarded to Monroe. On appeal, the FCC overturned the judge and ruled that Video 44 was entitled to the renewal expectancy benefit. The Commission also held that the renewal expectancy was sufficient to outweigh any advantages of Monroe's application. The Commission refused to consider allegations that Video 44 had obscene and indecent programming. Monroe appealed this FCC ruling to federal court.

SENTELLE, Circuit Judge.

* * * *

An incumbent applicant may be entitled to a renewal expectancy if its performance during the preceding license term has been "substantial," meaning "sound, favorable and substantially above a level of mediocre service which might just minimally warrant renewal." *Cowles II*, 86 F.C.C.2d at 1006 (quoting *Cowles Florida Broadcasting, Inc.*, 62 F.C.C.2d 953, 955-56 (1977). In deciding whether to award a renewal expectancy, the Commission focuses on non-entertainment programming broadcast by the station, including news, public affairs, and public service announcements. See, *e.g.*, *Radio Station WABZ, Inc.*, 90 F.C.C.2d 818, 840-42 (1982), *aff'd sub nom. Victor Broadcasting, Inc. v. FCC*, 722 F.2d 756 (D.C.Cir. 1983). A licensee is expected to ascertain and respond to community needs and problems in its non-entertainment programming in order to earn a renewal expectancy.

* * * *

Had the Commission properly weighted the station's performance following its conversion to STV format, it may well not have awarded Video 44 a renewal expectancy. The Commission found that through the full final year of its license term Video 44 offered .08 percent news, 2.57 percent public affairs, and only 5.84 percent other non-entertainment programming. *Video 44 III*, 4 F.C.C. Rcd. at 1210. These figures place Video 44 near the bottom of the pack, relative to other Chicago stations, in terms of news, public affairs, and other non-entertainment programming. By the very end of its license period, Video 44 had scaled back its non-entertainment programming to five hours per week and had discontinued local production. Given that the license expectancy analysis focuses on the incumbent licensee's responsiveness to the ascertained problems and needs of its community, *Simon Geller*, 90 F.C.C.2d at 271, the Commission was arbitrary in awarding Video 44 a renewal expectancy in light of record evidence of a strong downward trend in Video 44's responsiveness to community needs in the form of news and non-entertainment programming.

Decision and Remedy *The court remanded the case to the FCC and directed the Commission to consider the downward trend in Video 44's non-entertainment programming and the evidence of obscene broadcasts.*

Sometimes, a party may argue that no application should be licensed for a new station. For example, in *Federal Communications Commission v. Sanders Bros. Radio Station*,[3] a station owner opposed a new broadcast station in a city by arguing that local advertising could not support more stations. The Supreme Court held that the Commission could consider the community's ability to support another station but emphasized that the Act was intended to protect the public, not the revenues of incumbent licensees.

The public also may participate in licensing proceedings and petition for the denial of a license to a particular broadcaster. In 1966, a federal court ruled that African Americans in Mississippi had a right to challenge the license renewal of a station in Jackson for biased and unfair programming.

The FCC has considerable discretion in the licensing process and has been criticized for arbitrariness. One interesting case involved a noncommercial FM radio station in Seattle that was up for license renewal. The station devoted some programming to the 1960's "counterculture" including programs by Lenny Bruce, William Kunstler and others. The FCC criticized the station's broadcast of occasional obscene words. The FCC granted only an abbreviated one-year license renewal. Unsurprisingly, the station eliminated its unconventional programming and eventually obtained a standard seven-year renewal.

In 1971, the FCC became concerned about the lyrics of popular songs that allegedly glorified the use of drugs. The Commissioner provided stations with a "do-not-play" list of objectionable songs, including "Lucy in the Sky with Diamonds" by the Beatles and "Mr. Tambourine Man" by Bob Dylan. The Commission soon revoked this list in response to public outcry.

Broadcasting Regulations

The FCC has adopted a series of rules to regulate broadcasting programs. Regulation of mass media program content obviously raises First Amendment issues. The Supreme Court has granted the FCC considerably constitutional authority over programming, however. This is based on the theory that the broadcast spectrum is limited, or scarce, and the government has a right to control its use.

Equal time One broadcasting programming rule is the equal time rule. This provides that a station that permits a candidate for office to use the station must also provide an equal opportunity for all other candidates for that office.

The equal time rule applies only when a candidate personally appears on a program. The use also must be significant. For example, suppose that Martha Sobel, a candidate for attorney general, makes a three-second introduction to a program on which her supporters appear and urge her election. Because Ms. Sobel herself appeared for such a brief time, the equal time rule would not be invoked for her competitors.

The FCC has several exceptions for its equal time rule. The rule does not apply when a candidate appears in a bona fide newscast or in live coverage of bona fide news events, including political conventions. Under the latter rule, a station can broadcast a privately sponsored debate between candidates as a news event, without having to give equal time to candidates who did not participate in the debate.

The exemptions to the equal time rule have provoked litigation at the FCC and in court over the type of programs exempt. The following case involves a debate over the definition of an exempted "bona fide newscast."

---

[3] 309 U.S. 470 (1940).

Case 18.3
In Re Request of Oliver Productions, Inc.
Federal Communications Commission, 1989
4 F.C.C. Rcd 5953

Background and Facts *Oliver Productions, Inc. is the producer of a show called "The McLaughlin Group." This show involves a debate among a panel of political commentators. A typical program consists of four to six issues discussed by the panel. Each issue is usually introduced by a videotaped newsclip. These newsclips occasionally contain an interview with or speech by a candidate for political office. Oliver Productions sought a Commission ruling that the program was a "bona fide newscast" and exempt from the equal time requirements of the Communications Act. In November 1988, the FCC's Mass Media Bureau ruled that the program was a bona fide newscast.*

In December 1988, the Telecommunications Research and Action Center ("TRAC") filed a petition for review with the full Federal Communications Commission. TRAC argued that the McLaughlin Group was not a bona fide newscast that could be exempted from the equal time provisions of the Communications Act.

By the Commission.

* * * *

Although the legislative history is vague as to the meaning of "newscast," it does emphasize a congressional intent to increase news coverage of political campaigns, to give broadcasters great deference in making reasonable news programming judgments, and to give the Commission flexibility and discretion in interpreting the exemptions and in applying them to particular program formats in order to further the basic purpose of increased political information to the public. As the court stated in affirming the Commission decision to exempt debates and press conferences:

> In creating a broad exemption to the equal time requirements in order to facilitate broadcast coverage of political news, Congress knowingly faced risks of political favoritism by broadcasters, and opted in favor of broader coverage and increased broadcaster discretion. Rather than enumerate specific exempt and nonexempt uses, Congress opted in favor of legislative generality preferring to assign that task to the Commission.

Chisholm v. FCC, 538 F.2d 349, 366 (1976).

* * * *

9. We believe the Bureau was correct in its finding that the "news reporting segments" of "The McLaughlin Group" satisfy the criteria necessary for the newscast exemption under Section 315 (a) (1). Regarding the "bon fide" requirement, there is no information before the Commission to indicate that the "news reporting segments" are selected for reasons other than their genuine news value or are designed to advance or harm any particular candidacy.

* * * *

Thus, the Bureau correctly stated that as long as the brief reports of current news stories on "The McLaughlin Group" are distinct segments and the purpose is not to advance or harm any candidacies, those segments should be accorded the bona fide newscast exemption. We also agree with the Bureau that its ruling was consistent with the statutory objective of increasing the news coverage of political campaign activity.

Decision and Remedy *The Federal Communications Commission held that the Bureau's decision was correct and denied TRAC's petition.*

While stations may be compelled to provide equal time for candidates, they are not allowed to censor or even regulate what candidates say. Some Georgia stations sought to withhold spot announcements by a local candidate who proclaimed himself a "white racist" and spoke demeaningly of African Americans. The Commission ruled that the stations could not boycott the material.[4]

FCC rules also require stations to provide political candidates with "reasonable access" to their stations' broadcasts. While stations have some flexibility regarding what access is reasonable, the Commission requires that time be offered on a basis comparable to that offered commercial advertisers. Suppose that station WRES decides that short ten-second political advertisements are misleading to voters and refuses to carry them. This restriction is unlawful if WRES permits ten-second advertisements for commercial products. Stations cannot impose significantly stricter rules for political ads.

For many years, the FCC also used the "Fairness Doctrine" to regulate broadcasting. This required that broadcasters provide balanced coverage of controversial public issues and campaigns. In 1987, the Commission abolished this rule on the grounds that it conflicted with the First Amendment. Congress has sought to reinstitute the Fairness Doctrine but has not yet succeeded.

A final broadcast programming standard prohibits "obscene" or "indecent" programs. The definition of obscenity or indecency depends in part on whether children are likely to be part of the program's audience. Even if children are not expected to be part of the audience, questionable programming must be preceded by a warning to listeners.

Except for the above circumstances, the FCC generally avoids control over programming. For example, the Commission generally does not concern itself with a station's format. In the 1970s, the owner of a Chicago station wanted to change its format from classical music to rock-and-roll. A citizen group petitioned the FCC to halt this change, but the Commission refused to intervene in this type of dispute.

Common Carrier Regulation

A second major form of FCC communications regulations involves common carriers. The Supreme Court has defined a common carrier as one that "makes a public offering to provide [communications facilities] whereby all members of the public who choose to employ such facilities may communicate or transmit intelligence of their own design and choosing."[5] The best known common carriers are the telephone and telegraph systems.

The key legal principle of a common carrier is that it provides service to everyone on an equal basis. Accordingly, a common carrier exercises no control over the content of the messages that it transmits. Thus, the phone company does not regulate the content of telephone conversations.

The Federal Communications Commission exercises very little content over messages transmitted over common carriers. The Commission does prohibit the advertising of cigarettes over any

---

[4]*Letter to Lonnie King*, 36 F.C.C.2d 635 (1972).

[5]*Federal Communications Commission v. Midwest Video Corp.*, 440 U.S. 689, 701 (1979).

common carrier. The Commission also has regulated "dial-a-porn" services to prevent their access to minors. Obscene or fraudulent telephone calls are also illegal.

The primary FCC regulation involves the duties and liabilities of common carriers. The Communications Act imposes a duty on common carriers to provide service to any party "upon reasonable request."[6] The common carrier also must provide this service at rates that are "just and reasonable" and without "unreasonable preference or advantage" to any party using the carrier.[7] The FCC regulates common carriers by requiring them to submit "tariffs" to the Commission for approval. Tariffs are schedules of rates and rules for offering service. The commission also regulates mergers and prohibits foreign ownership of common carriers in the United States.

New Communications Technologies

In recent decades, entrepreneurs have developed many new and innovative communications technologies. The most prominent of these, cable television, is now regulated closely by the FCC. The Commission is still developing its response to other innovative technologies.

Cable Television

The first cable television transmission occurred in 1950, when the industry was intended to provide broadcast services to rural areas. Before long, the industry realized the potential of providing multichannel service in urban areas. More than 80 percent of U.S. households have access to cable service and over 50 percent actually use cable. Cable television advertising revenues have surpassed 1 billion dollars and operating revenues exceed 11 billion dollars.

After hesitating for years, the FCC adopted regulations for cable television service, treating it as something of a hybrid of broadcast and common carrier. The most significant feature of cable television is that the television signal enters the home on a cable (like a telephone line) and does not use the broadcast spectrum.

In 1984, Congress adopted the Cable Communications Policy Act to provide a comprehensive regulatory system of cable television. This law gave the FCC specific power to regulate cable and treated the technology much like a broadcasting service. The regulatory system for cable differs from that for broadcast services, however.

Franchising First, a local cable television system does not require an FCC license but must obtain a franchise. These franchises are granted by a state or local government, not the FCC. A franchise is somewhat like a broadcast license and typically lasts between ten and twenty years, depending on local rules. The 1984 Act limits the franchising powers of the local government, however.

The 1984 Act established specific standards and procedures for local governments to use in franchise renewals to protect existing franchise holders. In a franchise renewal hearing, the local agency can consider only four factors—(1) how the cable operator has complied with the terms of the franchise; (2) the quality of cable service provided; (3) the operator's financial and technical ability to provide future services; and (4) the operator's proposal for meeting future community needs and interests.

Access channels The Cable Act permits franchise authorities to require cable operators to provide channels for public access. These channels must be reserved for "public, educational or governmental use." This permits members of the local public to produce programming that is carried on the cable system via the access channels. A typical access program might broadcast the local city council meeting. States also require an opportunity for locally produced programming. Rhode Island, for example, requires each cable system to provide at least seven separate channels for public access. Cable systems also must provide facilities for people to produce this programming.

The 1984 law also required that channels be leased for commercial access. Any cable system with more than thirty-five channels must set aside at least 10 percent of its channels for lease. A common use of these channels is the video shopping program. These leased channels are not like common carriers, however. The cable operator can consider

---

[6] 47 U.S.C. Section 201(a) (1982).

[7] 42 U.S.C. Section 201(b), 202(a) (1982).

the use of the channel in rate setting and can exercise some content control over the leased channels.

Obscenity and indecency The Cable Act made it illegal to transmit obscenity over a cable system. Guilty parties can be jailed for up to two years and fined up to $10,000. Cable operators also are required to market "lockboxes" to subscribers, which enable them to prevent certain channels from being used, unless a code is entered.

Subscriber privacy Another provision of the 1984 Cable Act concerns the privacy rights of cable subscribers. The law prohibits cable operators from collecting personally identifiable information about its subscribers, without consent. An exception was made to this rule when necessary to provide cable service or to detect unauthorized use of cable. Cable subscribers have a right of access to all personally identifiable information collected. Cable privacy laws also have been passed by a number of states, including California, New York, Illinois, and Wisconsin.

Equal employment opportunity The Cable Act established policies to ensure equal employment opportunity in cable companies. The Act not only prohibits discrimination but also requires that operators establish a program to ensure equal opportunity. The law also requires cable operators to file an annual statistical report with the FCC indicating their success in assuring equal opportunity. Employees who believe that they have suffered discrimination at the hands of a cable operator may file a complaint with the FCC for investigation.

Cable regulation was furthered by the Cable Television Consumer Protection and Competition Act of 1992, passed over the veto of President George Bush. The law recognized that virtually all local cable television services (about 99%) had monopoly power and established rate regulation on such services. The law's objective is to determine what rates would be charged in a competitive marketplace and limit monopoly services to those rates. While sponsors promised great consumer savings, a significant minority of cable subscribers saw their rates increase. The law also restricted equipment leasing rates and installation charges.

The 1992 act also contained "must carry" rules, which required cable operators to negotiate for and carry the signals of local broadcast networks. Cable systems claimed that this rule violated their First Amendment rights, but the U.S. Supreme Court disagreed.[8] The Court did remand the rule to the FCC to demonstrate that the rule was necessary to prevent undue financial hardship to broadcasters.

The 1992 Act also had other restrictions. Operators must carry public, educational, and governmental (PEG) television programming. The law also required cable operators to set aside channel capacity for programmers who want to lease channel capacity.

Multipoint Distribution Service

Multipoint Distribution Service (MDS) is primarily useful to rural citizens who have no cable service and who can receive few broadcast transmissions. Approximately one million households have no access to television and millions more can receive only one or two broadcast channels in their home (without a satellite dish antenna). The FCC made channels available for MDS transmission to these citizens.

MDS consists of a microwave transmitter broadcasting on a microwave frequency. The signal is picked up by an antenna and then converted to a frequency compatible with an individual television set. MDS is sometimes called "wireless cable." MDS transmission is on a common carrier basis. As a result MDS services are not subject to content regulation, such as the equal time requirement.

MDS is a direct competitor with cable, in urban as well as rural areas. MDS has advantages over cable because it is less regulated and not subject to local franchising requirements. MDS can carry no more than thirty channels, however, and has not expanded as fast as cable television.

Telecommunications Act of 1996

Congress sought to comprehensively adapt traditional telecommunications regulation to the context of new technologies. The 1996 Act was fundamentally deregulatory in nature. Federal, state, and local regulation of telecommunications was eliminated or

---

[8] *Turner Broadcasting System, Inc. v. Federal Communications Commission,* 114 S.Ct. 2445 (1994).

restricted, and steps were taken to enhance a competitive market in telecommunications services.

The most significant aspect of the new law was the creation of competition in local telephone and cable television markets. While long considered natural monopolies, these markets could be made competitive by leasing physical equipment. The law requires equal and reasonable access to these facilities. To encourage competition, Congress removed restrictions on the businesses in which phone companies could operate. Long-distance phone companies can compete to offer local calling services, and vice versa. The advent of competition reduces the need for government rate regulation, which is to be phased out.

The 1996 law stops well short of total deregulation. Congress was also concerned with universal service and worried that the free market might ignore rural areas or public interest organizations. The Act created a Federal-State Joint Board on Universal Service to ensure that telecommunications services remained available when essential to education or public safety. Other provisions require that carriers provide affordable access to rural health care providers, schools, and public libraries.

The 1996 Act also made changes in broadcast regulation. Cross-ownership rules were eased, enabling a single company to own many more radio and television stations. The law also provided for FCC licensing of advanced television services and afforded television operators flexibility to use their allocated spectrum for certain non-broadcasting services.

Communications Law and the First Amendment

All communications services have some protection from the First Amendment's guarantee of freedom of speech and of the press. The extent of this First Amendment protection depends on the type of communications service.

Print communications, such as newspapers and magazines, receive the highest level of First Amendment protection. Virtually no content regulation of print media is constitutional. For example, newspapers need not provide the public with access to space in the paper. The government may, however, prevent obscene materials even in the print medium.

Broadcast radio and television receive less First Amendment protection than does the print medium. This is because the spectrum for radio and television signals is scarce and controlled by the government. Consequently, the government may consider broadcast content in licensing space on the spectrum. The Supreme Court has held that the rights of listeners take precedence over the First Amendment rights of broadcasters.[9]

The extent of First Amendment protection for cable television is still uncertain. It seems clear that cable operators have First Amendment rights at least as strong as those of broadcasters and perhaps as strong as that of newspapers. Several content regulations on cable television have been struck down in court as contrary to the First Amendment.

The U.S. Supreme Court in 1997 affirmed First Amendment rights on the Internet. The 1996 Telecommunications Act contained a title called the Communications Decency Act that prohibited the transmission of "indecent" material to persons under the age of eighteen. Given the nature of the internet, no provider could ensure that its pages were not accessible to those underage. The Court held that the law was overbroad in preventing access to adults.[10]

Some First Amendment issues are common to all forms of mass media. The most significant First Amendment issues relate to news broadcasting or publication. Prominent controversies include reporter's privilege and news gathering rights.

Reporter's Privilege

When obtaining news, many reporters promise their sources confidentiality. Reporters believe that keeping sources secret is essential to getting controversial information out of the sources. When the news involved a criminal case or civil litigation, however, a court may subpoena the reporter and demand the identity of the source.

Even in the face of a subpoena, many reporters have refused to disclose their source. One Los Angeles reporter wrote an article regarding the

---

[9]*Red Lion Broadcasting Co. v. FCC*, 395 U.S. 367, 390 (1969).

[10]*Reno v. American Civil Liberties Union*, No. 96-511 (1997).

1970 Charles Manson multiple murder trial and reported that one defendant had confessed. The government subpoenaed the reporter, but he refused to disclose his source, and he was jailed for forty-six days.

Reporters argued that source confidentiality was a fundamental part of the freedom of the press protected by the First Amendment. This issue reached the Supreme Court in a series of cases. The Court recognized that there was a First Amendment interest at stake but refused to recognize an absolute privilege for reporters not to reveal their sources.

Courts are more willing to recognize a reporter's privilege in the context of civil litigation. For example, a reporter for the *Saturday Evening Post* published a major article on racial discrimination in the sale of houses in Chicago. A group of citizens sued for damages from this discrimination and sought the reporter's source. While the reporter was sympathetic to their cause, he refused to disclose the identity of his source. A federal court held that he need not reveal his source, to avoid a "chilling effect" on the willingness of sources to come forward.[11]

Reporters have received less protection in criminal cases. Many courts use a three-part test and hold that a reporter must disclose a source if:

1. There is a reason to believe that a reporter has information relevant to a specific violation of the law.

2. There is no preferable alternative way to obtain this information.

3. The prospector or defense has a "compelling and overriding interest" in the information.

When these three facts are present, a reporter normally will be legally compelled to disclose the identity of a source. Many reporters still will refuse to identify their sources and go to jail for contempt of court.

In addition to First Amendment protection for reporters, at least twenty-six states have passed "shield laws" that protect reporters from a requirement to disclose their sources. Few of these shield statutes are absolute, however. For example, some laws protect only sources of information that are actually broadcast or published. Other statutes protect only the reporter, personally. If the source's identity is known to the station owner, the owner may be required to disclose the source.

Newsgathering Rights

The mass media often claim that they have a First Amendment right to gather news, as well as to broadcast news. Reporters may demand access to government meetings or facilities in order to report on them. The courts have recognized a First Amendment right of newsgathering, but it is not an absolute right.

The government generally may not provide discriminatory access to information. A federal court in Iowa has ruled that the police department cannot show its records to one newspaper and deny them to others. A federal court in Hawaii held that a mayor could not deny access to his press conferences to a reporter whom the mayor disliked.

Federal and state laws provide journalists with broad access to government records and meetings. Laws may not permit such broad access to other government facilities or operations, however. The government may seek to deny reporters access to a prison or to a judicial trial, for example.

Many cases have considered the rights of the press to cover trials. In general, the press and the public both have a right to attend criminal or civil trials. The state of Massachusetts had a law that prohibited access to rape trials in which the victim was a minor, to protect the minor's privacy. The Supreme Court held that this law was unconstitutional, because the First Amendment right outweighed the state's interest in protecting the victim.[12]

Another case that reached the Supreme Court involved a television station seeking access to a county jail. The county provided only monthly guided tours of the jail and prohibited private access to individual inmates. The Supreme Court ruled in favor of the government and held that the press had

---

[11] *Baker v. F & F Investment*, 470 F.2d 778 (2d Cir. 1972).

[12] *Globe Newspaper Co. v. Superior Court*, 457 U.S. 596 (1982).

no special right of access to prisoners.[13] An Oklahoma decision also denied the press a right of access to a nuclear power plant.

Another controversial issue involves the right of press access to accident scenes. In the leading case, a photographer of the *Newark Star-Ledger* took dramatic pictures of the victims of an automobile accident. The police arrived and told the photographer and other members of the public to withdraw from the scene. The photographer refused to leave, was arrested, and was eventually convicted. He argued that the conviction violated his First Amendment rights, but the New Jersey Supreme Court upheld the conviction.

Mass Media Liability

Potential civil liability is a major concern of broadcasters, newspaper publishers and others involved in mass communications. Traditionally, the media have been subject to liability for the torts of defamation and invasion of privacy. More recently, the media were made subject to suit for a general doctrine of media malpractice for negligent and inaccurate reporting.

Defamation

Defamation is a tort consisting of a false communication that injures a person's reputation. The basic elements of a defamation case are set forth in Chapter 6 of *West's Business Law, Seventh Edition*. Defamation law is a particular concern of the mass communications industry.

A controversial recent case involved CBS and its 1982 documentary on the Vietnam War. This documentary suggested that General Westmoreland was involved in a conspiracy to underestimate enemy strength in the war. Westmoreland sued for over $100 million in defamation damages, and the case received enormous publicity. Ultimately, the parties settled and CBS paid no money damages.

The first requirement of a defamation case is that the defendant make a **defamatory statement**, something that would injure the plaintiff's reputation. If the mass media inaccurately report that a person was a criminal, the report would be defamatory. The media must use great precision in reporting on crimes. Suppose that a local politician is stopped for drunk driving. The press report that the politician was charged with drunk driving. If the politician was not actually arrested, but only warned, the press have reported inaccurately and committed defamation.

One common misunderstanding is that the word "alleged" protects the press from defamation. Thus, a television news broadcast may refer to a source alleging that a person is a murderer. This may still be defamatory if the defendant is innocent. The television station is reporting some source that alleges the defendant to be guilty. If the source is wrong, the station is also potentially liable for defamation.

Simple carelessness can produce defamation liability. In the 1970s, *TV Guide* took an item submitted from a talk show that included the question "From Party Girl to Call Girl?" *TV Guide* changed the question mark to a period. For this and other reasons, a jury found that the magazine had misleadingly implied that a guest was a prostitute and awarded over $250,000 in damages.[14]

Photographs also may be defamatory. A magazine of the trucking industry ran an article on bankruptcy in the industry. The article was accompanied with a picture of a trucking firm named Drotzmann's. Drotzmann sued, claiming that the photo misleadingly implied that his successful firm was going out of business. A jury awarded Drotzmann $245,000 in damages, though an appellate court reversed on procedural grounds.[15]

A second requirement of a defamation action is *publication*. Because defamation protects reputation, a successful action requires that the defamatory statement be communicated, heard, and believed. Damages will be in part proportional to the size of the audience. For this reason, the mass media, which reach millions, are particularly at risk from defamation actions.

Defamation also permits actions for republication of defamatory statements. Suppose a politician accuses a rival of theft of government funds. If a

---

[13] *Houchins v. KQED*, 438 U.S. 1 (1978).

[14] *Montandon v. Triangle Publications, Inc.*, 45 Cal. App. 3d 938 (1975).

[15] *Drotzmann's, Inc. v. McGraw-Hill, Inc.*, 500 F.2d 830 (8th Cir. 1974).

radio station reports on this accusation, the radio station may be liable for republishing a defamatory statement.

Truth is a defense to defamation. If a communications outlet publishes true facts that injure a person's reputation, the outlet will not be liable. A true but misleading story may produce liability, however. A Memphis newspaper reported that a Ms. Newton shot a Ms. Nichols when she found Ms. Nichols together with Mr. Newton in the Nichols' home. The paper did not report that three others also were present. The newspaper was found liable because it created a misleading impression of an adulterous affair between Ms. Nichols and Mr. Newton.[16]

In addition, the press has a broader defense of qualified privilege when the plaintiff is a public figure. In these circumstances, the plaintiff must show that the untrue statement was published with malice or with reckless disregard for the truth. An innocent falsehood is protected.

The media have the qualified privilege only when the allegedly defamed plaintiff is a public figure. A publicly elected official, such as a governor or representative, is clearly a public figure. Most celebrities are public figures. Courts have held Johnny Carson, Carol Burnett and William F. Buckley, Jr., to be public figures in all contexts. A former University of Georgia football coach also was held to be a public figure.

Individuals who themselves have created a public controversy are also considered public figures. Say that an environmental activist calls a press conference to report on hazardous conditions at a nuclear power plant. The media report on the press conference but also on the activist's allegedly fraudulent past behavior. The activist will be considered a public figure for purposes of this controversy.

If the plaintiff is a public figure, even some false and defamatory statements are protected. The plaintiff must show that the defendant was unusually careless in checking the facts of the story or intentionally committed defamation. The mass media get some special consideration under this standard. For example, the courts realize that newspapers and television stations have pressure from short deadlines and may not be able thoroughly to check out every story. If a story is from an apparently reliable source, the press usually will not be liable even if the story proves to be false.

The defenses provided the press may be overcome if actual malice can be shown. In such a case, the media are subject to multimillion-dollar liability. The following case reveals the risks of running a controversial news story.

---

[16] *Memphis Publishing Co. v. Nichols,* 569 S.W. 2d 420 (Tenn. 1978).

Case 18.4
Brown & Williamson Tobacco Corporation v. Jacobson
United States Court of Appeals
Seventh Circuit, 1987
872 F.2d 1119

Background and Facts *Walter Jacobson, a prominent newscaster in the Chicago area, delivers a nightly feature known as "Walter Jacobson's Perspective." One evening's broadcast focused on tobacco industry advertising practices. The program was prepared by Michael Radutzky, a researcher. Jacobson said that a "confidential" federal report indicated that Viceroy cigarettes were targeting their ads at the youth. The federal report actually discussed a marketing proposal by Marketing and Research Counselors, Inc. ("MARC"). Although MARC's report did discuss a campaign aimed at young potential smokers, Viceroy explicitly rejected this approach.*

Viceroy's parent company sued Jacobson and his employer, CBS, Inc., for defamation. A jury found the defendants liable and entered an award of $3 million in compensatory damages and

$2.05 million in punitive damages. The district court judge then reduced the compensatory award to $1.00 but upheld the punitive damages. Both sides appealed this ruling.

BAUER, Chief Justice.

* * * *

The attitude of most knowledgeable and disinterested persons toward the tobacco industry is certainly negative; at least it has been negative for the past decade. In such an atmosphere, it becomes difficult to imagine how the tobacco people can be libeled. The bashing of the industry by government and private groups has become a virtual cottage industry. This case, however, demonstrates that general bum raps against the whole tobacco industry are different from a specific accusation of skullduggery by a specific company or person. And this case involves some very specific statements against a very specific company in the tobacco industry.

* * * *

Jacobson then reached the portion of his Perspective that the jury and the district court found libeled Brown & Williamson:

The cigarette business insists, in fact, it will swear up and down in public, it is not selling cigarettes to children; that if children are smoking (which they are, more than ever before), it's not the fault of the cigarette business. Who knows whose fault it is, says the cigarette business.

That's what Viceroy is saying. Who knows whose fault it is that children are smoking? It's not ours. Well, there is a confidential report on cigarette advertising in the files of the federal government right now, a Viceroy advertising [sic]. The Viceroy strategy for attracting young people (starters, they are called) to smoking.

"For the young smoker a cigarette falls into the same category with wine, beer, shaving, or wearing a bra," says the Viceroy strategy. "A declaration of independence and striving for self-identity. Therefore, an attempt should be made," says Viceroy, "to present the cigarette as an initiation into the adult world, to present the cigarette as an illicit pleasure, a basic symbol of the growing-up maturity process. An attempt should be made," says the Viceroy slicksters, "to relate the cigarette to pot, wine, beer, and sex. Do not communicate health or health-related points."

Brown & Williamson put forth evidence that it adhered vigorously to the Cigarette Advertising Code, which bars advertising to persons under 21. In addition to adhering to the Code, Brown & Williamson took the additional step of establishing a detailed procedure to ensure that its advertising agencies did not use models who either were or appeared to be younger than 25. When undertaking advertising campaigns that involved the distribution of samples, Brown & Williamson required the individuals distributing the samples to sign statements promising not to distribute cigarettes to people under 21.

Decision and Remedy *The court affirmed the jury's finding of liability. The court also affirmed the punitive damages award and held that Brown & Williamson should receive $1 million in actual compensatory damages.*

The media may also have a **privilege** against defamation actions in limited circumstances. Broadcast stations have an absolute privilege for broadcasts by politicians. The press also has an absolute privilege when reporting the proceedings of many government bodies, including the courts, the United States Congress, state legislatures, and even local councils. This privilege can be lost, however, if the reportage is inaccurate or malicious.

The press is also privileged for reports of **opinion** or **parody**. Defamation only extends to a false report of facts. When an author called William F. Buckley, Jr., a "fascist," the court found that this term was an opinion, not a fact. A parody, such as a political cartoon, is also protected against defamation challenge.

Defamation cases are of great concern to the media, even if they ultimately win the cases. The cost of litigation can be substantial. A widely publicized defamation can also hurt the public reputation of a broadcaster. In the Westmoreland case described above, CBS spent over a million dollars in legal expenses, and the network's reputation suffered from publicity surrounding the case.

Invasion of Privacy

A second tort of concern to the communications industry is invasion of privacy. News and entertainment stories may cover facts that the stories' subjects consider to be private. The nature of an invasion of privacy claim is discussed in Chapter 6 of *West's Business Law, Seventh Edition*.

One type of invasion of privacy claim involves the public disclosure of embarrassing private facts. *Time* magazine ran an article on a woman with a rare disease that caused her to lose weight, no matter how much she ate. They also printed a picture of her in the hospital and referred to her as a "starving glutton." The court found the magazine liable for invasion of privacy.[17]

An important defense to this type of invasion of privacy claim is **newsworthiness**. The media have a privilege to public information of legitimate news interest to the public. Moreover, courts often defer to the media's judgment that an item is newsworthy.

Events involving crimes or fires are usually considered newsworthy. Unusual skills or actions are also newsworthy. *Sports Illustrated* published an article about a surfer, describing how he would purposefully injure himself, in order to collect insurance, so he could spend time surfing. The article also reported the he ate insects and dived down flights of stairs. The court rejected the surfer's invasion of privacy claim, holding that the unusual practices were legitimately newsworthy.[18]

The newsworthiness defense has no clear-cut dimensions. Public interest alone is not enough to make an item newsworthy, but such interest is relevant. The following case illustrates the complex of factors affecting the determination of newsworthiness.

---

[17] *Barber v. Time, Inc.*, 159 S.W. 2d 291 (Mo. 1942).
[18] *Virgil v. Sports Illustrated, Inc.*, 424 F. Supp. 1286 (S.D. Cal. 1976).

■ Case 18.5
Sipple v. Chronicle Publishing Company
California Court of Appeals
First District, 1984
154 Cal. App. 3d 1040;
201 Cal.Rptr. 665

Background and Facts *In September 1975, Sara Jane Moore attempted to assassinate President Gerald Ford. Oliver Sipple, an ex-Marine, was in the surrounding crowd and grabbed Moore's arm as she was firing a gun. Sipple was hailed as a hero for his protective action. Many news articles about the episode mentioned that Sipple was a prominent member of the San Francisco gay community.*

Sipple filed an action for invasion of privacy against the newspapers that reported his sexual preference. He claimed that the articles caused his family to learn for the first time of his homosexual orientation. The trial court granted summary judgment for the defendants. Sipple appealed.

CALDECOTT, P.J.

* * * *

As referred to above, our courts have recognized a broad privilege cloaking the truthful publication of all newsworthy matters. Thus * * * our Supreme Court stated that a truthful publication is protected if (1) it is newsworthy and (2) it does not reveal facts so offensive as to shock the community notions of decency. While it has been said that the general criteria for determining newsworthiness are (a) the social value of the facts published; (b) the depth of the article's intrusion into ostensibly private affairs; and (c) the extent to which the individual voluntarily acceded to a position of public notoriety. The cases and authorities further explain that the paramount test of newsworthiness is whether the matter is of legitimate public interest which in turn must be determined according to the community mores. As pointed out in *Virgil v. Time, Inc.,* supra, 527 F.2d at page 1129: " 'In determining what is a matter of legitimate public interest, account must be taken of the customs and conventions of the community; and in the last analysis what is proper becomes a matter of the community mores. The line is to be drawn when the publicity ceases to be the giving of information to which the public is entitled, and becomes a morbid and sensational prying into private lives for its own sake, with which a reasonable member of the public, with decent standards, would say that he had no concern.' "

* * * *

In the case at bench the publication of appellant's homosexual orientation which had already been widely known by many people in a number of communities was not so offensive even at the time of the publication as to shock the community notions of decency. Moreover, and perhaps even more to the point, the record shows that the publications were not motivated by a morbid and sensational prying into appellant's private life but rather were prompted by legitimate political considerations, i.e., to dispel the false public opinion that gays were timid, weak and unheroic figures and to raise the equally important political question whether the President of the United States entertained a discriminatory attitude or bias against a minority group such as homosexuals. Thus appellant's case squarely falls within the language of Kapellas in which the California Supreme Court emphasized that "when, [as here] the legitimate public interest in the published information is substantial, a much greater intrusion into an individual's private life will be sanctioned."

* * * *

Appellant's contention that by saving the President's life he did not intend to enter into the limelight and become a public figure, can be easily answered. In elaborating on involuntary public figures, Restatement

Second of Torts section 652D, comment f, sets out in part as follows: "There are other individuals who have not sought publicity or consented to it, but through their own conduct or otherwise have become a legitimate subject of public interest. They have, in other words, become 'news.' ... These persons are regarded as properly subject to the public interest, and publishers are permitted to satisfy the curiosity of the public as to its heroes, leaders, villains and victims, and those who are closely associated with them. As in the case of the voluntary public figure, the authorized publicity is not limited to the event that itself arouses the public interest, and to some reasonable extent includes publicity given to facts about the individual that would otherwise be purely private."

Decision and Remedy *The court affirmed the lower court's grant of summary judgment.*

Another form of invasion of privacy is intrusion into areas in which a person has a reasonable expectation of privacy. If the press uses electronic snooping devices or secret recording devices, this may represent unlawful intrusion. Overzealous harassment may also be unlawful. Jacqueline Onassis successfully sued a photographer for constantly following her and taking pictures.

Still another form of invasion of privacy is misappropriation. This occurs when the press uses a picture of a person for commercial purposes. If *Playboy* magazine takes a newsphoto of a man reading *Playboy* and uses it for promotion, the magazine may be liable for misappropriation of the subject's likeness. To be safe, a magazine should always obtain permission for republication of pictures in advertising materials.

Media Malpractice

Individuals are increasingly bringing actions against the media for inaccurate or negligent reporting of the facts. These claims are lumped under the heading "media malpractice."

Some plaintiffs have sued the press for inaccurate reporting, even if it is not defamatory. One investor sued over an inaccurate description of corporate bonds in which he then invested. The court dismissed this claim for fear of "chilling" or deterring reporting. Courts have permitted a plaintiff to sue the government for a negligent weather forecast, though, and some fear that the press could be subject to similar liability.

Other individuals have sued the media for failure to investigate statements, especially those made in advertisements. In one case, *Soldier of Fortune* magazine published an ambiguous advertisement that turned out to be a solicitation by a "hit man" who would kill under contract. The family of a murder victim sued the magazine for failure to investigate the advertisement. A jury returned a verdict of $9.4 million against the magazine. Courts have yet to award liability for nondefamatory news articles under this duty to investigate.

Still another source of potential media liability is the infliction of emotional distress, as discussed in Chapter 6 of *West's Business Law, Seventh Edition*. *Cinema X* magazine described Terry Clifford as an "aspiring erotic actress" and placed her name under a nude photograph of someone else. Clifford received a number of "loathsome and horrifying calls" that interrupted her work and gave her nightmares. She sued the magazine and received $10,000 in damages.[19]

The press also has been found liable to its sources. One campaign worker gave the press information about a rival candidate under a promise of confidentiality. The newspaper later revealed the source. The source sued the paper and initially received a $700,000 judgment.

---

[19] *Clifford v. Hollander*, 6 Med. L. Rptr. 2201 (N.Y. Civ. Ct. 1980).

Ethical Perspectives

Free Press vs. Fair Trial

Several ethical controversies arise out of the media's coverage of criminal investigations and prosecutions. The media generally recognize an ethical obligation to their viewership or readership and to society as a whole. This obligation takes the form of investigating and publicizing the true facts on matters of great public interest. But what should the media's ethical responsibility be toward the subjects of their reporting, e.g., a criminal defendant? The duties here are not so clearly recognized.

A problem arises when media coverage may prejudice a defendant's right to a fair trial. The classic case arose in Ohio in the 1950s, when a relatively prominent doctor, named Sam Sheppard, was accused of murdering his wife. Newspapers headlined the story. A front page editorial questioned: "Why Isn't Sam Sheppard in Jail?" He was arrested the next day.[20] All but one of the jurors had heard about the case in the media, and two had heard a radio story that Sheppard had fathered an illegitimate child. The judge accepted the jurors' word that they would be uninfluenced by the press reports. Dr. Sheppard was convicted. He spent twelve years in jail and went through a series of appeals before the United States Supreme Court reversed his conviction. The Court found that the extensive publicity had denied Sheppard's right to a fair trial before an impartial jury.[21]

Press coverage of criminal trials also raises privacy questions. The press may have a legal right to publish the names of crime victims, but is it ethical to do so? A Florida court dismissed a rape victim's privacy case against a television station but admonished the station for its "insensitivity" in publishing her name.[22]

These cases involve a balancing of the public's need or right to know information against a lone individual's right to a fair trial or personal privacy. A major criminal trial is surely newsworthy, but the media may have some ethical duty of fair coverage. In the case of crime victims, one can reasonably question whether the public's right to know the victim's identity is particularly newsworthy. This is a situation in which a privacy interest might outweigh the public right to know facts.

Some maintain that the media should not make these ethical judgments because their only responsibility is to their readers or viewers. This attitude has provoked a backlash against the press, however, and may even yield more government regulation of the news media. In some states, journalists have entered into voluntary agreements with judges and prosecutors regarding the nature of pretrial publicity in criminal cases.

---

[20] Kent Middleton & Bill Chamberlin, *The Law of Public Communication* 386 (1988).

[21] *Sheppard v. Maxwell*, 384 U.S. 333 (1966).

[22] *Doe v. Sarasota-Bradenton Television Co.*, 436 So. 2d 328 (Fla. App. 1983).

The communications industry increasingly is adopting its own ethical codes of conduct. A landmark 1947 report by the Commission on Freedom of the Press declared that press freedom "can only continue as an accountable freedom" and that the constitutional rights "will stand unaltered [only] as its moral duty is performed."[23] This report provoked considerably reflection by the media.

The Society of Professional Journalists adopted a code of ethics that declares its "overriding mission" as protecting the "public's right to know of events of public importance and interest." The code criticizes journalists who use their position "for selfish or other unworthy motives." The code goes on to recognize an obligation to report with "intelligence, objectivity, accuracy, and fairness." Other press organizations have comparable codes of conduct.

The journalists' codes recognize ethical duties in media coverage, but the true significance of the codes is unclear. Most codes emphasize the public's right to know, rather than the rights of individuals covered in the press. The temptation to sensational coverage remains great. After all, dramatic and controversial headlines sell newspapers.

---

[23] Commission on Freedom of the Press, *A Free and Responsible Press* (1947), p.18-19.

■ **International Perspectives**

Cross-Border Broadcasting

Television and radio signals are unaffected by national borders. A signal broadcast from one nation may be received by citizens of a neighboring nation. This is sometimes called a spillover signal. Sometimes, cross-border broadcasting is intentional, as has been the case with Radio Free Europe's broadcasts into communist nations. Such spillover broadcasting has on occasion become politically controversial.

The significance of cross-border broadcasting from traditional television and radio stations was a limited and localized problem. These broadcasts can travel only within a line of sight from the transmitter. The advent of new technologies, however, will increase the conflict of spillover broadcast signals. A single DBS satellite, for example, could theoretically broadcast to 40 percent of the world's surface.

Governments have a variety of reasons for concern with spillover signals. Some governments fear that foreign transmissions could destabilize their governments. Others are concerned that foreign broadcasts will undermine the national culture or moral sensibility. Still other governments are concerned for the integrity of their nation's language.

International controversies over DBS have already begun. A Japanese DBS station recently began broadcasting and its signals were picked up by individuals in South Korea. The South Korean government vehemently protested to the Japanese government, but the protests were essentially ignored.

An individual nation can itself do little about its citizens' reception of spillover broadcast signals. A government could ban individuals from owning satellite dishes, but many governments are developing their own DBS systems. If satellite dishes are allowed, it is practically impossible to prevent reception of signals originating in foreign nations. As a result, any regulation of spillover broadcasting will largely be a matter of international law.

In 1982, the United Nations General Assembly adopted a resolution that required nations to consult with each other about the effects of DBS spillover. The resolution has little legally enforceable effect, however. Moreover, most nations with DBS broadcast capability voted against the resolution.

DBS spillover is particularly significant in Europe, where many economically and technologically advanced nations are in relatively close geographic proximity. Within the twelve-nation European Community, the Single European Act protects DBS transmissions. This law prevents any member nation from discriminating against services that originate in another member nation. Television and radio broadcasts qualify as protected services under the act. Many European nations are not part of the official European Community, however. Switzerland, for example, is located in the midst of the Community's nations, but is not itself a member nation.

There is no globally applicable, clear-cut international law to apply to spillover broadcasting. Some argue that these broadcasts are a form of pollution that should be subject to international environmental law.

Regional organizations may regulate DBS transmissions. In Europe, for example, the European Human Rights Convention recognizes freedom of speech as a right. However, the Convention recognizes limitations on this right where necessary for national security, territorial integrity, public safety, the prevention of disorder and crime, the protection of health and morals, the protection of the reputation and rights of others, the prevention of the disclosure of information received in confidence, and maintaining the authority and impartiality of the judiciary. Obviously, free speech will not receive complete legal protection under these potentially broad exceptions.

Broadcasters also must beware of potential liability from cross-border signal transmissions. Beaming a signal into a foreign country may subject the broadcaster to the jurisdiction of a foreign court and the application of foreign laws. Foreign liability for defamation generally tends to be stricter than in the United States. Spillover broadcasting can subject the communications industry to new sources of international liability.

Questions and Case Problems

1. A Utah state statute made criminal the distribution of pornographic or indecent materials by wire or cable. Indecency was defined as including nude figures. A national cable broadcaster challenged the constitutionality of the statute. Utah defended by noting its rights to regulate cable transmissions and its concern for minors viewing cable programs. Is the state statute constitutional? [*Home Box Office, Inc. v. Wilkinson,* 531 F. Supp. 987 (D. Utah 1982)].

2. Preferred Communication, Inc., was organized to operate a cable television system in Los Angeles. Preferred sought to obtain leases allowing it to install cables on utility poles owned by the city utilities. The utilities refused to grant leases until Preferred had a cable franchise from the city. Los Angeles would not grant Preferred a franchise but required the company to go through its competitive franchising process. The city effectively limited access to a given area of the city to a single cable operator, even though utilities are capable of accommodating multiple operators. Preferred claimed that this system was unconstitutional. Does the Los Angeles policy violate the First Amendment rights of Preferred? [*City of Los Angeles v. Preferred Communications, Inc.,* 106 S.Ct. 2034 (1986)].

3. Dale Barshak was caught selling cocaine and heroin to grade school children in the small town of Bellington, Illinois. Dale was charged with selling illegal drugs and held in the county jail to await trial. The law enforcement officials have kept all details about the case, including Dale's identity, a secret. The press increasingly is hounding the police for details about the case, however, and Barshak's defense attorney is nervous that publication of the details of the case could compromise his client's right to a fair trial. The press go to court seeking an order compelling the police to disclose the facts of the case, and Barshak's attorney responds with a motion to prevent any out-of-court statements about the case. What should the court do?

4. Hutchinson was a research scientist who received over $500,000 in federal grants to research aggression in animals. U.S. Senator William Proxmire gives a "Golden Fleece" award for wasteful government spending. Proxmire selected Hutchinson for this "award" and issued a press release and newsletters publishing the details of Hutchinson's allegedly wasteful research. Hutchinson sued Proxmire, claiming that the senator had distorted the substance of his research and defamed him. Hutchinson's research had received little publicity prior to Proxmire's announcement. Is Hutchinson a public figure who must prove actual malice to succeed in his defamation claim? [*Hutchinson v. Proxmire,* 443 U.S. 111 (1979)].

5. *Hustler* magazine published a parody about the Reverend Jerry Falwell entitled "Jerry Falwell talks about his first time." The parody involved incest and portrayed both Falwell and his mother as drunk and immoral. The parody contained a small disclaimer of truth at the bottom of the page. Falwell is widely known throughout the nation and is considered a public figure for defamation purposes. Falwell could not succeed for defamation, however, because no one would have believed the parody. Falwell sued and won for intentional infliction of emotional distress. *Hustler* appealed claiming that recovery for emotional distress in this case violated their First Amendment rights. Should a court overturn Falwell's damages for emotional distress? [*Hustler Magazine, Inc. v. Falwell,* 485 U.S. 46 (1988)].

6. The Federal Communications Commission adopted rules requiring that operators provide access channels sufficient that any member of the public could transmit programs over cable. Operators were required to accept such access programs on a first-come, nondiscriminatory basis and could exercise no control over the content of access programming. Cable operators complained that these rules unfairly transformed them into a common carrier and violated their First Amendment rights. Are these rules lawful? [*Federal Communications Commission v. Midwest Video Corporation,* 440 U.S. 689 (1979)].

Chapter Nineteen

Government Contracts

Key Background

Many government functions are carried out through contracts with private companies. If the Department of Defense wants to procure a new fighter jet, the Department will contract with some private defense company to produce the jet. Government contracts are responsible for many billions of dollars of business.

Every significant agency of the federal government awards private contracts, which can range from the most complex missile system to the most mundane catering operation. The procedures for awarding contracts can be rather complex, with numerous legal requirements. The most important requirements are discussed below.

This chapter also addresses the substantial problem of government contract fraud and its punishment. The chapter deals with the uniform, national law of federal government contracts and not with state and local government contracts that are governed by the law of the appropriate jurisdiction. State and local government contract law tends to be quite similar to federal laws.

Types of Contracts

Many federal agencies award contracts for many different services, but there is great commonality in the basic types of contracts granted. The government awards two basic types of contracts, called fixed price contracts and cost reimbursement contracts.

Fixed Price Contracts

In a **fixed price contract**, the total amount due to the contractor is set in advance. The contractor must first complete the contract and then will be paid the fixed price provided in the contract. The actual cost of performing the contract is irrelevant. The fixed price contract (when adhered to) protects the government from cost overruns and enables the private contractor to increase profits by increasing efficiency.

Many private contractors have insisted on a modified fixed price contract, however, to avoid risk. This is the **fixed price contract with economic price adjustment**. A typical fixed price with economic price adjustment would permit the contractor to recover payments in excess of the fixed price, if the costs of labor or material increase during the time of contract performance.

The nature of the adjustment depends on what is provided in the contract with the government. For example, a contract could provide for price adjustment based on some market index. Suppose Norco has a contract with the government to produce tanks. Norco might offer a fixed price, plus an adjustment based on fluctuations in the price of steel or other raw materials.

Cost Reimbursement Contracts

The **cost reimbursement contract** provides payment to the contractor of all costs of contracting plus an added fee. In these contracts, the contractor must provide an estimate of costs, called target costs. If costs exceed the predicted estimate, however, the government must pay for the cost overrun. The contractor is obliged to notify the government of cost overruns in order to recover.

The standard cost reimbursement contract provides little incentive for private parties to be efficient in carrying out the contract and has the potential for defrauding the government. As a consequence, the government has tried to develop incentive clauses in cost reimbursement contracts.

The **cost plus incentive fee contract** offers greater profits for private parties that can keep costs low. Payments are based on a comparison of actual costs with the initial target costs estimated in the proposal. If actual costs exceed the target costs significantly, the contractor receives a smaller additional percentage fee for profit. If actual costs remain low, below even the target cost, the contractor receives a larger additional percentage fee. The incentive fee also may be based on the quality of the contractor's performance.

Incentive contracts may reduce the problems of fraud on the government, but a risk remains. One concern is that contractors will artificially inflate their target cost estimate, as well as actual costs. For example, a company could intentionally overestimate labor costs in its original proposal. Incentive contracts do not protect against this type of fraud.

Contract Formation

The legal rules for making a binding contract with the government are much like the rules for purely private contracts, as set forth in Unit Two of *West's Business Law, Seventh Edition*, and Chapters 9 and 10 of *West's Legal Environment of Business, Third Edition*. The contract requires an agreement with mutual assent, consideration and other requirements of contract. The procedures for government contracts are slightly different.

The government usually initiates the process by publicizing its interest in contracting and issues a solicitation for offers. The solicitation sets forth the specifications of the items to be bid on. The content of the solicitation is very important—the government can select a contractor based only on the criteria set forth in the solicitation.

In response to the solicitation, interested private parties then must make an offer, typically using a required government form. For some procurement, companies submit sealed bids which are to be opened at a specified date. In other procurement, the government negotiates the terms and attempts to obtain a better deal. Offers become irrevocable once the government opens the sealed bids or awards a contract.

The government accepts the preferred bid by signing the offer form submitted by the private party. The standard offer form gives the government sixty days from bid-opening or receipt of proposals to accept. In other cases, the government has a "reasonable time" in which to accept an offer. As in private contracts, the government's acceptance must be unambiguous. In one case, government notification that an offer was "selected as the lowest responsive bid" did not qualify as an acceptance.[1] The intention to accept the contract must be absolutely clear.

The government may give a conditional acceptance. Here, the government would accept the offer with some condition, such as the future availability of funds to pay for the contract. The government may have a good faith duty to attempt to provide funds. If the condition fails, however, neither side would be bound to the contract.

The government also may be bound by an **implied-in-fact contract**. A contract may be implied-in-fact from the actions of the parties. In one case, the government awarded a contract for the production of armor-plated gun carriage parts. The government was to furnish the basic armor plate which was manufactured into the parts in the contract. After the contract was completed, the company asked the government to remove the surplus armor plate, but the government failed to do so. After eleven years, the contractor billed the government for storage costs. A court found that the government was required to pay these costs, due to an implied-in-fact contract.[2]

In private transactions, a party may also be liable in **quasi-contract**. A quasi-contract may arise when one party confers a benefit upon another and justice requires compensation. Courts have consistently held that the government cannot be liable in

---

[1] *DeMatteo Construction Co. v. United States*, 600 F.2d 1384 (1979).

[2] *Algonac Manufacturing Co. v. United States*, 428 F.2d 1241 (1970).

quasi-contract. In such a case, a party is dependent on the good will of the government to provide a benefit.

Contracting Requirements

The government has a series of requirements that must be met before it will grant a contract. First, the contractor must demonstrate to the government that it is qualified to fulfill the contract. Second, the government has rules for competition in contracting.

Contractor Qualifications

Before giving any contract, the government must determine that the prospective contractor is qualified. The government first considers the contractor's responsibility. This includes an evaluation of the contractor's ability to perform the contract, which involves the following factors:

1. Adequacy of financial resources to perform.

2. Ability to comply with the government's delivery schedule.

3. Possession of necessary production, construction and technical equipment and facilities.

4. Possession of necessary management, accounting and other technical skills.

5. A historic record of satisfactory performance.

In addition to the responsibility qualification, potential contractors also must demonstrate a satisfactory record of *integrity and business ethics*. Submission of false documents, for example, may disqualify a prospective government contractor. Irresponsible contractors may be barred from all federal contracts, as discussed below.

Competition

The government has several procedures for selecting contractors. The Competition in Contracting Act requires "full and open" competition for government contracts and provides two primary methods for granting contracts: (i) the sealed bid procedure or (ii) negotiated procurement, which is sometimes called competitive proposals.

Sealed bid procedures are best used for contracts where price competition is paramount. In this procedure, the government solicits offers and sets a deadline by which time bids must be submitted. Once the deadline passes, the government conducts a public opening of all the bids.

To select the winning bid, the government first must make a finding of responsiveness. The bid must conform to the solicited specifications sought by the government. If a nonresponsive defect is minor, the bid will be considered as long as the contractor is deemed responsible. If the bid contains a material nonconformity with the solicitation, the bid must be rejected. This is true even if the bidder expresses a willingness to correct the bid.

A material nonconformity might be the offer of a significantly different product or service from that solicited. Thus, the government rejected an offer to furnish a drill with a torque capacity of 6000 ft-lbs at 27 rpm instead of the solicited capacity of 5800 ft-lbs at 50 rpm.[3] Material nonconformity could also be a failure to agree to the government's desired delivery schedule or presentation of a bid that is indefinite and ambiguous regarding the cost or quality of the products to be provided.

The government then evaluates the responsive bids in order to award the contract. The key evaluation involves price, and the government is to select the lowest-cost bid. Because bids may provide for differing payment schedules, the determination of the lowest-cost bid may require financial analysis. Once this determination is made, the government publicly announces the award.

Negotiated procurement may be used where non-price factors are significant in awarding a contract. The negotiated procurement procedure is often controversial and the source of most claims of fraud.

Under negotiated procurement, the government solicits offers but usually with less detail than under sealed bidding. Contractors then submit proposals that must include cost and pricing data. The government must seek out proposals from the maximum number of qualified sources. Then, government representatives conduct written or oral discussions with the contractors. In the course of these discussions, proposals are often modified. The government awards the contract based on price and on non-price factors, such as technical capability.

---

[3] *Mobile Drilling Co.,* Comp. Gen. Dec. B-216989 (1985).

Negotiated procurement leaves government officials with discretion in awarding the contract. The government official must use the following evaluation factors:

1. Technical and management ability (such as experience, facilities, and quality of proposal design).

2. Contract amount (the compensation sought by the contractor).

3. Other costs to the government (for example, if the government must bear certain transportation costs under the proposal).

4. Responsibility factors (as discussed above).

The government uses varying procedures to evaluate the above factors and weight them against one another.

The government's solicitation should provide contractors some description of its weighting process. In one recent case, the government granted a contract to a bidder whose offer was 27 percent higher than that of another bidder. This resulted because the government gave 91 percent weighting to technical ability and only 9 percent weighting to contract amount. The award was reversed under protest, because the government insufficiently weighted cost and because the government did not disclose its unequal weighting of factors in its initial solicitation.[4]

The Competition in Contracting Act directs the choice of the proposal with the lowest overall cost to the government but permits consideration of other factors. Moreover, it may sometimes be difficult to determine the lowest cost proposal. In pure fixed-price contracts, the lowest cost proposal will be clear, but in a cost reimbursement contract, costs can only be known after they are already incurred by the contractor and billed to the government. The relative importance of price and quality should be set forth in the government's solicitation.

The negotiated procurement process has been controversial and is the source of hundreds of protests every year. The government is permitted to conduct discussions with competing contractors but must be careful not to show favoritism in the bidding process. When the government has given only one of the bidders valuable inside information, courts have overturned a contract award to the favored bidder.

When the government improperly conducts a negotiated procurement, the contract may be canceled and the government may be liable for the costs of the private parties engaged in the bidding. This principle is illustrated by the following decision.

---

[4] *Video Ventures, Inc.*, B-240016 (1990).

■ Case 19.1
QualMed, Inc. v. Office of Civilian Health and Medical Program of the Uniformed Services
United States District Court for the District of Colorado, 1996
934 F.Supp. 1227

Background and Facts *The Civilian Health and Medical Program of the Uniformed Services (CHAMPUS) conducted a negotiated procurement for medical services for military dependent care in Hawaii and California. The initial contract was given to Aetna Government Health Plans, Inc. and was challenged by QualMed, Inc. The GAO sustained the protest, CHAMPUS undertook reprocurement, and the contract was won by QualMed. QualMed intended to use Value Behavioral Health (VBH), a subsidiary of Value Health, Inc. (VHI), as a subcontractor. Another subsidiary of VHI, Lewin-VHI was a consultant that had a central role in evaluating the competing bidders. Other bidders protested this award, and the GAO also sustained this protest and terminated the QualMed contract. The GAO found no actual evidence of bias but held that the "Chinese Wall" created within VHI to separate Lewin from VBH during the bidding was insufficient to counteract the appearance of impropriety. QualMed appealed this finding. Both sides moved for summary judgment.*

DANIEL, District Judge.

* * * *

In the case at hand, QualMed argues that the GAO's decision contained no meaningful analysis of the conflict of interest issue ... I do not agree. First the GAO found that an [organizational conflict of interest] OCI did exist in QualMed's proposal since, given the relationship between Lewin and VBH, Lewin was "potentially unable to render impartial assistance or advice"...

* * * *

The GAO rejected CHAMPUS' determination that a Chinese Wall arrangement would be satisfactory for resolving the conflict and that, "due to the absence of financial or other pressure on the individual Lewin-VHI evaluators, the 1994 plan mitigated Lewin-VHI's [OCI]." The GAO held that these conclusions were unreasonable since the conflict at issue related to "potentially impaired ability" which could not be resolved through a "Chinese Wall" arrangement ... Further, the GAO explained why, regardless of the 1994 plan, the OCI simply could not be mitigated. This was due to the significant dollar value of the VBH subcontract, the historical role of Lewin in the procurement, and the subjective nature of the evaluation of probable health care costs in which Lewin was involved.

Decision and Remedy *The court granted the motion for summary judgment against QualMed on its challenge to the GAO.*

Other practices also are forbidden in negotiated procurement discussions. The government may not use "auction techniques," such as informing one bidder of the price bid by other bidders. Nor can the government help a bidder by pointing out weaknesses resulting from the bidder's lack of diligence in preparing the bid.

Other than competitive bidding is statutorily limited to defined circumstances when a competitive bidding process is unfeasible. This is sometimes called **sole source contracting**, because the government negotiates with only one source. For example, no competitive bidding is required when only one contractor can fulfill the government's needs. In one case, the government needed a certain quality of scanning microscope, and only one company made a microscope of the necessary quality.

Other than competitive bidding also may be used when there is an unusual and compelling urgency to accept a bid imminently. In other cases, sole source contracting was allowed to ensure that new supplies would be compatible and interchangeable with existing supplies. Whatever the reason, the agency must provide a detailed justification for use of less than competitive bidding.

The law of government purchases was simplified in the Federal Acquisition Streamlining Act of 1993. This law governs federal purchases of commercial products. The primary purpose of the law was to direct agencies not to establish rigid design requirements or specifications for their purchases. Rather, proposals should simply state the need in terms of function and performance of the product.

Collateral Policies

Government contracts are not always given to the lowest bidder or the most qualified potential contractor. Congress has adopted a series of collateral policies to be considered in grant awards. These include a small business preference, a domestic preference, and an affirmative action preference.

Small Business Preference

Congress has authorized several programs to encourage the award of government contracts to small businesses. The definition of a "small" business depends on a company's number of employees or average annual receipts. The standards for a small business vary, however, for different classes of business and are set by the Small Business Administration.

Congress has directed that small businesses receive a "fair proportion" of government contracts but has declined to set a percentage quota for what proportion would be fair. Some agencies use "set asides," where the agency reserves a portion of contract awards for only small businesses. Contracts for less than $10,000 are presumptively reserved for small business. Larger proposals may be set aside for small business only if there is a reasonable expectation that at least two responsible small businesses will present competitive offers for the contract.

While small business cannot perform many large government contracts, the government encourages a large prime contractor to subcontract with small business when possible. For contracts in excess of $500,000 the large contractor's proposal must include a plan for granting subcontracts to small business.

Another small business preference occurs in the case of equally low bids in a sealed bidding process. To "break the tie" in bidding, the agency must award priority to small businesses that operate in areas where there is a labor surplus. The second tie-breaker is for small businesses in any area.

Domestic Preference

The Buy American Act established a general preference for acquisition of domestic products whenever possible. For unmanufactured articles in government contracts, the law requires generally that they be "mined" or "produced" in the United States. For manufactured articles supplied in government contracts, the article must be manufactured in the United States and more than 50 percent of its component parts must have been mined, produced, or manufactured in the United States.

The Buy American Act contains certain exceptions enabling the purchase of foreign items. If the cost of United States-produced items is "unreasonable," the contractor may use foreign-produced items. Under federal regulations, domestic cost is unreasonably high if it is more than 6 percent higher than foreign cost. If, however, the U.S. manufacturer is a small business, its costs are considered unreasonable only if they exceed foreign cost by 12 percent or more.

Affirmative Action Preference

The government also grants a contract preference to businesses owned and controlled by socially and economically disadvantaged persons. This preference primarily extends to businesses that are more than 51 percent owned by members of minority groups.

This preference is under the Small Business Administration, which seeks to identify qualified minority businesses and match them with available contracts. Contracts may be awarded to a minority-owned business, even if that company is not the lowest bidder. In addition, for contracts exceeding $500,000, the potential contractor must include a plan describing its intent to subcontract with minority-owned businesses.

Contract Challenges

The losing bidder in a government contract award has the ability to challenge the government's decision, if the bidder believes that it was treated unfairly. There are a variety of procedures and forums to make such a protest. The vast majority of these protests fail, however.

The losing bidder may protest the award to the government officer who decided the contracting or to the officer's superiors within the agency. The agencies have broad discretion regarding the procedures that they may use to evaluate such protests and the responses they choose.

If the losing bidder wants to take a formal protest outside the agency, the primary method used is to file the protest with the Comptroller General of the General Accounting Office (GAO) or with the General Services Board of Contract Appeals (GSBCA). Any losing bidder is an interested party and has **standing** to file such a protest.

Both the GAO and the GSBCA review the contract award to determine if it violated any statute or regulation. The General Services Board conducts a full evidentiary trial with opportunity for discovery and reverses those decisions that are unreasonable.

By contrast, the GAO has a greater presumption of the agency's correctness and decides based on the submission of written reports by the protesting party and the agency. The GAO also provides much less opportunity for **prehearing discovery**, such as taking **depositions** of government officials. The costs of protesting to the GAO may be less, but the prospects for success are somewhat greater in the GSBCA.

Both the GAO and the GSBCA consider the same specific grounds for granting a protest, such as simple arbitrariness or unreasonability. In one case, International Business Machines Corporation and ViON Corporation both bid on a contract for supply of direct access storage devices. IBM's bid was lower, but the contract was awarded to ViON, which had a lower failure rate for the devices. IBM presented statistical evidence to the GSBCA, proving that there was no statistically significant difference in failure rates, so the board granted IBM's protest.[5]

Another ground for protest exists when the agency evaluates the bids on bases different from those set forth in the solicitation. In one recent case, the government solicitation said that certain subfactors (cost, experience, etc.) were to be weighted equally. When granting the award, the government gave one subfactor three times greater weight, and the GSBCA overturned the contract award for inconsistency with the solicitation.[6]

Parties may also protest whenever illegitimate prejudices enter the award process, as exemplified by the following case.

---

[5] *International Business Machines Corp.*, GSBCA No. 8959-P (1987).

[6] *Severn Companies, Inc.*, GSBCA No. 9344-P (1988).

Case 19.2
Latecoere International, Inc.
v.
U.S. Department of the Navy
United States Court of Appeals, Eleventh Circuit, 1994
19 F.3d 1342

Background and Facts *The Navy issued a request for proposals for the design, construction, and maintenance of G-Tolerance Improvement Program Training Systems (G-TIP), with specifications. Five firms submitted proposals, and the initial review found that Latecoere International, Inc. had the best submission. Environmental Tectonics Corporation's (ETC) submission was unsatisfactory. The Assistant Secretary of the Navy questioned granting the contract to a French company, even though the U.S. has an agreement with France not to use local preference rules against French companies. After a second round of proposals, ETC was now deemed satisfactory, but Latecoere was still unanimously deemed the best. Fearing "political heat," the Navy awarded the contract to ETC, and Latecoere protested. A district court granted summary judgment for ETC, and Latecoere appealed.*

CARNES, Circuit Judge.

* * * *

As the following evidence demonstrates, bias against Latecoere infected the decision not to award it the contract:

(1) Michael McDonald, senior procurement analyst for the Assistant Secretary of the Navy attacked a note to the G-TIP clearance memorandum that stated that an award to a French company could be a "political hot potato [sic]" and asked, "[d]on't we have to apply Buy American factors?"

(2) Assistant Director Frank Ford admitted that, while meeting with the Training Center's officials to discuss the G-TIP clearance memorandum, he stated that an award to a French company could present political problems.

* * * *

(7) The selection process initially identified Latecoere's proposal as the one offering the best technical performance and best value, but after politics, the nationalities of the offerors, and "Buy American" factors were articulated, the same process moved inexorably and irrationally toward selection of an inferior-rated, but politically safer, domestic corporation (ETC).

* * * *

The original selection authority, Daniel Rowley, had chosen Latecoere, warning in a selection decision document that the proposals of ETC and two other domestic corporations were "unacceptable" and that awarding the project to an unacceptable offeror, such as ETC, would risk the loss of human lives.

Decision and Remedy *The court reversed the grant of summary judgment for ETC and remanded to district court for consideration of Latecoere's summary judgment motion.*

Another basis for protest is that the solicitation contains unnecessary requirements. In another recent case, a protester claimed that a government solicitation for disk drives had minimum conditions on failure frequency that exceeded the government's needs and thereby restricted competition in bidding. The Board agreed, granting the protest because the performance requirement in the solicitation was not justified by the agency's needs. The agency could consider the criterion as a factor but should not have set such a high minimum for acceptability.[7]

If a protest succeeds, the GAO lacks authority to reverse the agency's contract award. The GAO *can* compel the agency to suspend the award temporarily and can recommend that the agency terminate the contract and reconsider competing proposals. The General Services Board has the power to revoke a contract award but has substantial discretion in making this decision. The Board could find that a contract award was contrary to law but still permit it to take effect.

In addition to the administrative remedies described above, a protesting bidder may also file a complaint in federal district court. A district court will only reverse a contract award when the award has no rational basis or involves a clear violation of a statute or regulation. The district court has broad remedial power and can enjoin, or prohibit, the protested contract award.

Contractors have increasingly sued the government for breach of an implied-in-fact contract to treat bids honestly and fairly. In an important 1995 case, the government sought to steer a contract to a favored bidder. After a competitor submitted the low bid, government officers informed their favored bidder of the difference and called for a new round of offers. The competitor won the new round also, with an even lower bid. After discovering the facts, the competitor sued to reform its contract and recover the price in the original bid. The Federal Circuit held that the government's action was plainly illegal but denied relief, because the government also had a legitimate reason for conducting the second round of bidding.[8]

---

[7] *Memorex Corp.*, GSBCA No. 7297-P (1985).

[8] *Labarge Products, Inc. v. West*, 46 F.3d 1547 (Fed. Cir. 1995).

Contract Administration

Once a contract is awarded, the contractor begins performing the contract, and the government monitors this performance. This is to ensure that performance is timely and up to specifications. The government may also monitor the costs of performance in order to avoid overcharges in cost reimbursement contracts.

In general, the interpretation of government contracts and rules for discharge of government contracts roughly parallel the rules for private contracts. Thus, if performance is inadequate, the government need not pay out on the contract. As in private contracts, the contractor must be given some opportunity to cure defective performance and recover on the contract. The contractor also will be able to obtain at least a partial payment if it has substantially performed the contract.

One important characteristic of government contracts that differs from most private contracts is the **changes clause**. This gives the government the right to insist on changes in contract work during the course of performance of the contract. The government may change characteristics of the goods or services under the contract and may also change the quantity demanded or the time of performance. The changes clause also enables the private contractor to propose changes to the government, which may permit more efficient performance.

The changes clauses require that government change orders must be in writing. Many government-ordered changes impose extra costs on the contractor. In this event, the contractor can make a claim for an "equitable adjustment" in the negotiated contract price. This claim must be filed with a court or the relevant agency within thirty days of the time of the change order. The tribunal then adjusts the contract price to provide the contractor with fair compensation for the change required by the government.

There is another important provision that is special to government contracts, called **termination for convenience**. This unique authority, contained as a condition in government contracts, permits the government to terminate the contract at any time. After termination for convenience, the contractor can recover only costs incurred and profits attributable to work that is *already* done.

The government may terminate for convenience any time that termination is "in the Government's interest." Termination for convenience is most commonly used when the government no longer needs the goods or services under contract. A contractor can avoid a termination for convenience only if the termination is arbitrary, in bad faith, or independently violates some law. For example, in one case a court enjoined a termination for convenience because the termination would violate a federal law requiring an environmental impact statement for a federal project.[9]

The right to terminate for convenience is also limited by the rules of contract law. The following case established this principle.

---

[9] *National Helium Corp. v. Morton,* 455 F.2d 650 (10th Cir. 1971).

■ Case 19.3
**Torncello v.
United States**
United States Court of Claims, 1982
681 F.2d 756

Background and Facts *Plaintiff was the president of Soledad Enterprises which received a government contract for grounds maintenance and refusal removal at Navy facilities near San Diego. The pest control portion of the contract specified a price of $500 per call. After the contract was entered, the Navy decided that this price was too high and did not use Soledad for pest control. Instead, the Navy used a competing bidder, who offered a lower price, but who had been rejected in favor of Soledad in the original bidding.*

Soledad files suit in the Armed Services Board of Contract Appeals. The Board found that the Navy may have committed a breach, but the availability of termination for convenience justified the government's action. Although the government did not give notice of the termination for convenience, the Board held that it was a constructive termination. Soledad appealed to the Court of Claims.

BENNETT, Judge.

* * * *

We are not holding here that the government cannot settle with contractors on those contracts that the government needs to settle. The termination for convenience clause is a valuable and important aspect of federal procurement. It has a long history and is founded solidly on Corliss of 1876. Nor are we holding that the government cannot draft for itself some method of exculpation so long as it also binds itself to something that will support the contract. We hold in this opinion only that the government may not use the standard termination for convenience clause to dishonor, with impunity, its contractual obligations.

In the case before us, the Navy had accepted Soledad's bid and had executed a contract knowing that another bid was lower. This contract bound the Navy to give to Soledad all of its pest control needs at the six housing projects covered. The Navy could not just walk away from this promise without making a mockery of the contract. It is nothing more than basic contract law that a power to terminate must be limited in some meaningful way, as measured by the requirement of consideration. The government has argued that there are no limits on its power to invoke termination for convenience. However, since the government's convenience terminations procedures (giving notice and paying for services rendered), at least as applied to this case, also put no sufficient limits on the government, its unrestricted use of the clause cannot be correct.

Decision and Remedy   *The court granted Soledad's motion for summary judgment and remanded the case for further proceedings for damages for the breach of contract.*

▬ Contractor Fraud

Contractor fraud is a major concern of the government. Scandals, such as the infamous $500 screwdriver or toilet seat, have caused government officers to attempt to crack down on overcharges. Congress has passed several laws in an attempt to halt contractor fraud.

The most prominent fraud is of a type known as **defective pricing**. Defective pricing occurs when the contractor's bid contains inaccurate and inflated estimates of its costs, thereby providing the contractor a hidden extra profit. This generally occurs in cost reimbursement contracts, though it may also exist in fixed-price contracts with adjustment. A 1988 report by the Defense Contract Audit Agency found that 47 percent of all contracts investigated contained overpricing.

Truth in Negotiations Act

The Truth in Negotiations Act, as amended in 1986, requires all prime contractors and subcontractors to provide the government with cost and pricing data that they certify to be "accurate, complete and current." Cost and pricing data includes virtually all costs relevant to performing a contract, including costs such as computer time.

Under the Act, cost and pricing data must be submitted on Standard Form 1411 or its equivalent. The contractor also must explain the significance of this data to the government whenever necessary.

The contractor must execute a Certificate of Cost or Pricing Data, which formally certifies to the accuracy, completeness and currency of the data submitted.

To succeed in a claim under the Truth in Negotiations Act, the government must have relied on the defective pricing in the contract. Regulations create a presumption of government reliance on this information, and the contractor has the burden of proof to show that the government did not so rely.

The Truth in Negotiations has no requirement of fraudulent intent. A contractor can violate this act, even if the defective pricing submitted to the government was accidental or innocent in nature.

The Truth in Negotiations Act applies to all government contracts that exceed $100,000. If the winning contractor's original pricing data is later found to be inaccurate, incomplete, or noncurrent, the government is entitled to a price adjustment of the amount that the price was overstated, plus any related overhead, profit, or fee.

Some contracts are exempted from the Truth in Negotiations Act. The first important exemption exists when there is "adequate price competition" for a contract. Adequate price competition occurs when there are two or more responsible offerors for a contract, and they compete independently for a contract to be awarded to the offeror submitting the lowest price. Another exemption exists when the price submitted is established in a catalog or privately negotiated market price.

False Claims Act

Defective pricing and other forms of contractor fraud are covered by the False Claims Act (FCA). Congress amended this law in 1986 to enhance the government's ability to prosecute fraud. This Act "piggybacks" on other statutes: A false certification of pricing data under the Truth in Negotiations Act would also be a false claim prohibited by the FCA.

The False Claims Act makes it illegal to submit a false claim to any government agency. A "claim" exists any time that a contractor submits a bill for recovery on a government contract, and each invoice or voucher is a separate claim.

The False Claims Act prohibits the *knowing* submission of a false claim for payment from the government. The 1986 amendments to the act defined the term "knowing" to mean that the claimant has actual knowledge of the falsity of the information underlying the claim, acts in deliberate ignorance of the truth or falsity of the information, or acts in reckless disregard of its truth or falsity. The FCA does not extend to innocent mistakes.

The False Claims Act provides significant civil penalties for its violation. The government can recover triple its actual damages, a $5000 to $10,000 penalty per false claim, and the costs of the lawsuit. A contractor can reduce its potential damages, however, by promptly disclosing any false claims that it has made and cooperating with the government investigation.

Qui Tam Actions

Qui tam actions are suits brought by private citizens against contractor fraud under the FCA. A private person who becomes aware of fraud, often an employee of the contractor, can file a suit against the fraud. The private prosecutor in a qui tam suit can recover a percentage of the government's recovery. Successful private plaintiffs can recover up to 30 percent of the government's damage award, plus attorneys' fees and expenses of the lawsuit. This is sometimes called a "bounty-hunter" provision. Government employees cannot use the qui tam recovery authority.

After a qui tam complaint is filed, the government has sixty days in which the Attorney General can take over the private action. The government is most likely to take over an action when the stakes are high and the case is strong. Alternatively, the government can permit the private plaintiff to attempt to enforce the law and recover an award. In recent years, hundreds of qui tam suits have been filed.

Criminal Fraud

Fraud on the government is a crime, and government contractors have been convicted of filing false statements and making false claims. Both individual employees and the corporation itself may be found guilty of crimes. Some prosecutions have been under generalized criminal statutes against mail fraud, wire fraud, or conspiracy.

The Criminal False Statements Act is a specific law that penalizes any person who knowingly and willfully submits false material statements to the government or who knowingly and willfully conceals or covers up such a falsification. A conviction under the Criminal False Statements Act requires proof of the following five elements:

1. The submission of a statement.
2. The submitted statement was intended to bear a relation to some matter under the jurisdiction of a federal agency.
3. The statement was material (significant).
4. The statement was false.
5. The party submitted the statement knowing it to be false.

Government contracts necessarily involve the submission of statements relating to the jurisdiction of a federal agency. Unlike a false claim, the statute prohibits all fraudulent statements, even if they do not involve a direct claim for money from the government. If the statement affects the awarding of a contract or the amount to be paid on the contract, it is likely to be found to be material. Knowingly false statements by contractors often fall within the statute.

In a recent case, a NASA contractor had to modify contract performance under a changes clause order and submitted its increased costs to the government. The contractor certified that its costs were accurate but was aware that the costs were significantly inflated over their actual costs. The defendants were convicted under the Criminal False Statements Act.[10]

Congress also has passed the Criminal False Claims Act, that covers any claims for federal money that are false or fraudulent. The general requirements are similar to the Criminal False Statements Act and this law requires a knowing or willful violation but is limited to actual claims on the government. A violation of either the false statements or the false claims act is punishable by maximum fines of up to $250,000 for individuals and $500,000 for corporations per violation. Defense contractors can be fined up to $1 million per violation. Individual violators may be sentenced to prison for up to five years.

Exhibit 19-1 compares and contrasts the requirements and penalties of the major laws regulating contractor fraud.

▇ Suspension and Debarment

Suspension or debarment is a drastic sanction undertaken by a federal agency, which prohibits a company or individual from receiving government contracts. A **suspension** is temporary (pending an investigation) and can last no longer than eighteen months, while a **debarment** is a final judgment that can last for a time period of years, as specified by the government. Both actions essentially involve a finding that the contractor lacks the responsibility necessary for government contracting. The government now suspends hundreds of contractors every year.

Because many companies are highly dependent on government contract work, suspension or debarment can be a crushing sanction. Suspension and debarment cannot be used as "punishment" for fraud, but can be imposed when in the "public interest." This standard, though, is a vague one.

Suspension is usually triggered by a contractor's indictment for a criminal offense. An agency advises the contractor, and the suspension takes effect immediately to disqualify new contracting. The contractor has an opportunity to submit a rebuttal in response to the notice. The agency may grant the contractor a hearing, but need not always do so. if the contractor is found innocent, the suspension is lifted. If the contractor is found to lack the necessary responsibility, the agency may impose a debarment. A debarment by one federal agency precludes a company from contracting with any federal executive agency.

The federal regulations list several causes that will justify a debarment order. One such cause is a lack of business integrity, as evidenced by a conviction of fraud or other crimes. Debarments have been based on violations of civil rights laws, antitrust laws, and environmental laws. Another cause is a willful violation of the terms of existing government contracts. For example, in one case a contractor was debarred for three years for construction of a building foundation that violated minimum state building code requirements, which the contractor knew or should have known.[11]

Debarment is not inevitable, even if a company has been convicted of a crime that justifies debarment. A company can always argue that "unusual circumstances" justify a decision not to bar the company. The following case illustrates the application of this principle.

---

[10] *United States v. White*, 765 F.2d 1469 (11th Cir. 1985).

[11] *Donald Schutte*, AGBCA 77-189.

Exhibit 19-1
Requirements and Penalties of Contractor Fraud Laws

	Truth in Negotiations	False Claims Act	Criminal False Statement Act	Criminal False Claims Act
ACTION	Submission of inaccurate, incomplete or noncurrent data	Making of false claim	Making material false statement	Making of false claim
INTENT	None required	Knowing false submission or disregard for truth	Knowing and willful submission	Knowing submission
RELIANCE	Required	Not required	Not required	Not required
REMEDY	Refund of overstatement	Triple damages plus $5,000 to $10,000 penalty per false claim	Up to $1 million penalty & 5 years imprisonment	Up to $1 million penalty & 5 years imprisonment

---

Case 19.4
Federal Food Service, Inc. v. Donovan
United States Court of Appeals for the District of Columbia Circuit, 1981
658 F.2d 830

Background and Facts *Federal Food Service was in the business of furnishing mess services to military installations around the country. A Department of Labor investigation found that Federal Food Services had violated the terms of the Service Contract Act by occasionally failing to pay employees their required holiday overtime pay and back pay. The law provides that violators of this Act are debarred from all government contracts for three years, unless the Secretary of Labor finds that unusual circumstances warrant removal from the debarment list.*

After an administrative law judge found Federal Food Service guilty of violating the Service Contract Act, the company appealed the debarment order, alleging unusual circumstances. Federal Food Service appealed to the Secretary of Labor, who affirmed the debarment. The debarment had a "catastrophic impact" on the company's business, so Federal Food Service sought a court ruling that the debarment was inappropriate.

NICHOLS, Judge.

* * * *

In *Washington Moving and Storage Co.,* No. SCA-168, March 12, 1974, the Secretary established the following guidelines by which "unusual circumstances" should be judged:

> Whether "unusual circumstances" are present in a case within the meaning of the Act must be determined on the basis of the facts and circumstances of the particular case. Some of the principal factors which must be considered in making this determination are whether there is a history of repeated violations of the Act; the nature, extent, and seriousness of

past or present violations; whether the violations were willful, or the circumstances show there was culpable neglect to ascertain whether certain practices were in compliance, or culpable disregard of whether they were or not, or other culpable conduct (such as deliberate falsification of records); whether the respondent's liability turned on bona fide legal issues of doubtful certainty; whether the respondent has demonstrated good faith, cooperation in the resolution of issues, and a desire and intention to comply with the requirements of the Act; and the promptness with which employees were paid the sums determined to be due them.

* * * *

In the instant case, after finding appellants were responsible for a deficiency of $3,328.35—an amount less than one-fifth of 1 percent of the contract values and in a labor intensive business, no doubt almost as low a ratio compared to total payrolls—the ALJ ostensibly applied the *Washington Moving* guidelines. The ALJ found that there was no evidence the violations were willful or deliberate and that appellants cooperated with the extensive and complex investigation of the case except for one unexplained instance at the Norfolk location. Payments were made fully and promptly even though substantial amounts had to be estimated through no fault of appellants. Previous violations in the past were not substantial and did not result in debarment because of unusual circumstances.

The vital finding which most influenced the ALJ and the district court was that "proper management would have precluded the continuing occurrence of these widespread underpayments." This is an important finding in view of the small ratio of violations to value of contracts (and to total payrolls, presumably) and the absence of consideration—admitted at oral argument—of offsetting over-payments. Large underpayments might be res ipsa loquitur of improper management. There are no facts in the record to refute the judicial belief that no rational precautions could reduce violations to absolute zero. In the instant case there was no showing in the record to support the ALJ's findings of what proper management would have accomplished in these premises and it was bald assumption. The ALJ cited to no testimony of management experts or of prevalent business practices to establish what practices appellants should have followed and did not. Certainly, contractors could hire an army of bookkeepers, accountants, and supervisors to insure no underpayments would occur, and perhaps most needful to all, lawyers at each location. Such a practice, however, would elevate the cost of operation to a level to endanger the future of appellants' type of business as a source of employment

Decision and Remedy *The court reversed the Secretary of Labor's ruling and remanded the case to district court with directions to vacate the debarment.*

Ethical Perspectives

Government Contracts and Corporate Codes of Ethics

Contractor fraud involves lying to and stealing from the federal government and is rather obviously unethical. Yet such fraud is fairly widespread. Unlike some areas of the law, government agencies attempt to enforce business ethics in contracting. The federal acquisition regulations specifically require that a government contractor maintain a satisfactory record of integrity and business ethics.[12]

A 1986 Presidential commission, known as the Packard Commission, reported on the extensiveness of defense contractor fraud and urged that contractors adopt and enforce corporate codes of ethics. The Commission also promulgated Defense Industry Initiatives on Business Ethics and Conduct. These initiatives established six guiding principles:

1. Each company will have and adhere to a written code of business ethics and conduct.

2. The company's code establishes the high values expected of its employees ... each company will train its employees concerning their personal responsibilities under the code.

3. Each company shall create a free and open atmosphere that allows and encourages employees to report violations of its code to the company without fear of retribution for such reporting.

4. Each company has the obligation to self-govern by monitoring compliance with federal procurement laws and adopting procedures for voluntary disclosure of violations of federal procurement laws and corrective actions taken.

5. Each company has a responsibility to each of the other companies in the industry to live by standards that preserve the integrity of the defense industry.

6. Each company must have public accountability for its commitment to these principles.

Forty-six major defense contractors agreed to adopt and enforce these initiatives.

The defense contracting industry has been at the forefront of the move to employ ethical codes, and a survey by the Ethics Resource Center found that 92 percent of defense contractors have adopted a corporate code of ethics. Some companies have implemented codes of ethics in response to government demands.

The defense industry certainly illustrates that the adoption of a code of ethics is insufficient to ensure ethical behavior. Contractor fraud is still appallingly frequent. Some of the ethical codes are themselves deficient, and there are shortcomings in communicating the codes to employees and enforcing the ethical precepts found in the code.

Nevertheless, the government believes that such codes are valuable. The Defense Department regulations virtually insist that a contractor adopt a written code of ethics and an ethics training program for employees. The Department of Justice has adopted guidelines that consider the existence of a corporate code and training program in the decision of whether to prosecute a company for criminal fraud. The presence of a corporate code can also help a company avoid or shorten a debarment ruling.

---

[12] 48 C.F.R. section 9.104-1 (1988).

> **International Perspectives**

International Government Contracting

Competing for government contracts in foreign nations can be extremely lucrative. Government contracts in the European Community (EC) exceed $700 billion. South Korea recently has agreed to open over $500 million of government contracts for competition by foreign firms. Many countries, however, reserve government contracts for domestic firms. U.S. companies currently have about $5 billion in contracts in Western Europe.

An international Procurement Code has been adopted in connection with the General Agreement on Tariffs and Trade (GATT). The GATT Procurement Code has been signed by twenty-three nations, including all twelve members of the European Community, Japan, and the United States. The Code covers contracting by a nation's central government but does not extend to regional, state or local contracting.

The GATT Procurement Code is intended to open government contracting to international competition. Consequently, the Procurement Code restricts "buy national" laws, such as the Buy American Act. The U.S. Buy American Act does not apply to procurements covered by the Code, with respect to companies from other countries that have signed the Code. The Procurement Code also establishes rights and procedural obligations in government procurement.

The GATT Procurement Code is still limited, however, to a relatively small amount of government contracting. The Code does not cover contracting in the sectors of telecommunications, heavy equipment, transportation, and energy utilities. The Code's application is also limited to only some government agencies. Approximately 10 percent of the European Community's procurements are covered by the GATT Code. Seventy-five percent of European government contracts are granted to domestic companies on the basis of bidding specifications tailored for the national firm.

The United States government increasingly uses our trade laws to attempt to open overseas government procurement markets. Title VII of the Omnibus Trade Act of 1988 authorizes the president to close federal procurements to suppliers in any country that discriminates against U.S. companies. Section 301 of the Trade Act of 1984 permits the president to retaliate against unfair trade practices.

Section 301 was applied when Oslo, Norway, bid a contract for electronic tool booth equipment. After an American company won the bidding, the Norwegian Transportation Minister intervened and gave the contract to a Norwegian supplier. The U.S. threatened to apply section 301, and Norway agreed to compensate the U.S. company.

The U.S. has threatened to use the section 301 or Title VII against Japan. Japan has a $300 billion total construction market, and U.S. firms have about $430 million in total construction contracts and $85 million in government contracts. The U.S. claims that Japanese companies use *dango,* a procedure by which they rotate winning bids among themselves and exclude foreign companies. Trade officials are still trying to negotiate a resolution to this dispute.

Questions and Case Problems

1. Bay Cities Services had a contract with the Navy to provide service that had been issued on a sole-source basis. When the Navy sought an extension of the contract, it requested cost and pricing data, but the company refused to supply such information. The Navy then solicited a new contract on a competitive basis and excluded Bay Cities from even competing for the contract due to their refusal to supply the requested information. Only one company submitted a proposal, which the Navy accepted. Bay Cities sued over their exclusion from the contract. Should the General Accounting Office uphold the exclusion of Bay Cities from contracting? [*Bay Cities Services, Inc.*, B-239880 (1990)].

2. The Army Tank Division Command solicited a contract for forklifts, and its proposal stated that "cost [is] of primary importance and is worth significantly more than technical, and somewhat more than technical, logistics/MANPRINT, and production capability combined." The contracting official was directed to make an award to the offeror whose proposal was "most advantageous and offers the greatest value." Later, the Command official awarded the contract to an offeror who was not the low price offeror. The lowest price offeror claimed that the contract award violated the Request for Proposals and should be overturned and granted to the low price offeror. Should a court overturn the contract award? [*BMY, a Division of HARSCO Corp.*, 693 F. Supp. 1232 (D.D.C. 1988)].

3. Cutler-Hammer, Inc., contracted with the U.S. Air Force to design, develop, and manufacture an electronic reconnaissance system to be carried in aircraft. The contract price was over $24 million and contained a defective pricing clause. The government sought a reduction in the total contract price when it discovered that Cutler-Hammer had disclosed a subcontractor's bid of $406,445 for a component lens and had not disclosed another subcontractor bid of $91,260 for the lens. Cutler-Hammer responded that the lower subcontractor's bid was so low that it was not a plausible offer. Should the government be able to obtain a cost reduction due the Cutler-Hammer's failure to disclose the low subcontractor bid? [*Cutler-Hammer, Inc. v. United States*, 416 F.2d 1306 (Ct. Cl. 1969)].

4. An aircraft manufacturer negotiated a $10.5 million fixed price contract with the U.S. Air Force to develop and produce an electronic Malfunction Detection and Recording System to be installed in B-52 aircraft. A subsequent audit discovered that a subcontractor had overstated material and labor costs by $234,623. The Air Force demanded a refund of this amount from the general contractor aircraft manufacturer. The company defended that it was unaware of the overcharge and bore no fault. Should the company be required to refund money to the government? [*Lockheed Aircraft Corp. v. United States*, 485 F.2d 584 (Ct. Cl. 1970)].

5. The Defense Logistics Agency solicited contracts for pediatric cystourethroscope kits. The solicitation required the kits to contain three different scope devices to examine certain internal body organs. A company's proposal was for kits that contained two different scope devices. After that company was awarded the contract, a losing bidder protested that the proposal did not match the solicitation. The winning bidder then promised to supply kits with three scope devices at the same price as in its original offer. The protester persevered. Should the General Accounting Office accept the modified proposal and uphold the contract award? [*Circon Acme*, B-231108 (1988)].

6. The Navy sought to purchase navigational radar systems for training at its electronic school. These systems had to be identical to that already available at the school, so the Navy did not engage in competitive bidding but relied on its earlier source. The Navy then amended the solicitation to purchase additional different systems for use in ship construction and overhaul. A protester claimed that this modification required a new proposal and competitive bidding, but the Navy suggested that a separate contract would be too costly. Should the protest succeed?

Chapter Twenty

Legal Representation of Business

▬ Key Background

Effective use of legal representation is increasingly important to business success. Every business action is potentially subject to a plethora of common law principles or regulatory requirements. The successful businessperson must be able to maneuver through this legal web, avoiding sources of liability. Legal problems lie at the doorstep of many failed businesses.

Many businesses perceive legal representation purely in terms of liability avoidance. They see potential liability for the negligent actions of employees or from manufacturing violations of environmental laws, or from any number of similar rules. Lawyers may be used preventatively to avoid sources of liability or in defense at a trial.

Some businesses use lawyers affirmatively, even as a profit center. The owner of patents must use lawyers to protect rights in those patents and obtain possibly lucrative royalty arrangements. Other businesses use lawyers to enforce their valuable rights in contracts or to sue in tort when they have been injured.

Moreover, virtually all businesses employ lawyers even when no lawsuit is present. Lawyers are important in negotiating and drawing up contracts for companies and for advising companies on their general legal rights and responsibilities.

Law is very important to contemporary business practice. A survey of recently appointed chairmen of boards of directors found that over 70 percent of these business leaders believed that business law education was important to a career in business management. Businesses in America spend over $25 billion every year for legal services.

Given the significance of legal problems, the modern businessperson must understand how to use the law, and lawyers, wisely. Quality legal representation can save a business (or gain a business) millions of dollars. Equally important is the need to understand how to use lawyers efficiently. Legal representation is expensive and a legal victory may become an economic loss, as legal fees and expenses mount.

This chapter discusses several key issues in the legal representation of business. First, the chapter considers the relationship of a business and its lawyers, and the rights of the businessperson. This includes the nature of the attorneys' duties toward clients and the rights and responsibilities of clients. Second, the chapter discusses business approaches to legal matters, such as litigation strategies.

▬ Attorney-Client Relationship

When a person or a business retains legal counsel, it also obtains certain defined benefits in the **attorney-client relationship**. An attorney has a responsibility of great fidelity to the interests of the client. This is true regardless of whether the attorney is advising the client or litigating in court on the client's behalf.

A critical question in many cases is whether the parties have an attorney-client relationship. When a lawyer purchases a car, for example, she would be acting simply as a regular citizen and no attorney-client relationship is created. The following recent decision illustrates the process of identifying the protected attorney-client relationship.

■ Case 20.1
Sheinkopf v. Stone
United States Court of Appeals,
First Circuit, 1991
No. 90-1838

Background and Facts *In 1987, the Omni Group was formed as a joint venture to develop real estate. Warren Sheinkopf was invited to join the venture by David Saltiel, a partner in the Boston law firm of Nutter, McLennen & Fish. Sheinkopf invested $100,000 in Omni. Saltiel organized the venture out of his law office and told Sheinkopf that many of his other clients were participating in the venture. Omni's projects ultimately failed, and Saltiel eventually entered personal bankruptcy. As a result, Sheinkopf lost his entire investment and suffered additional liability as a guarantor on several mortgages.*

Sheinkopf then "dove toward the deepest pocket in sight" and sued John Stone and other partners in the Nutter firm. Sheinkopf claimed that he relied on Saltiel's legal advice in investing and this constituted a breach of fiduciary duty by Saltiel in the course of an attorney-client relationship as an agent of the Nutter firm. The district court held that no attorney-client relationship existed and therefore granted summary judgment to defendants. Sheinkopf appealed.

SELYA, Judge.

* * * *

Human beings routinely wear a multitude of hats. The fact that a person is a lawyer, or a physician, or a plumber, or a lion-tamer, does not mean that every relationship he undertakes is, or can reasonably be perceived as being, in his professional capacity. Lawyers/physicians/plumbers/lion-tamers sometimes act as husbands, or wives, or fathers, or daughters, or sports fans, or investors, or businessmen. The list is nearly infinite. To imply an attorney-client relationship, therefore, the law requires more than an individual's subjective, unspoken belief that the person with whom he is dealing, who happens to be a lawyer, has become his lawyer. If any such belief is to form a foundation for the implication of a relationship of trust and confidence, it must be objectively reasonable under the totality of the circumstances. We agree with the court below that this threshold was not crossed in the instant case. A reasonable businessman in Sheinkopf's shoes might have assumed that Saltiel had become his real estate guru, his business partner, his investment adviser, or even his fugleman—but no reasonable businessman would have assumed, on these facts, that Saltiel had become his attorney.

Appellant's assertion that such a relationship came into being rests on little more than his subjective belief, bolstered by his recollection of a general conversation, unanchored in time or place, concerning his desire to avoid personal liability in the Omni venture and Saltiel's assurance that he would "protect" appellant. We find nothing in such an exchange, however construed, suggesting that Saltiel (himself an investor in, and organizer of,

Omni) thereby became appellant's attorney or agreed to furnish legal advice. At the very most, the comment was ambiguous, consistent with the role of either a legal or an investment adviser.

Decision and Remedy *The court affirmed the grant of summary judgment against Sheinkopf.*

When an attorney-client relationship does exist, the attorney assumes certain responsibilities. The American Bar Association has developed a Code of Professional Responsibility to guide an attorney's duties to the client. Among the "canons" of conduct for lawyers are:

- A lawyer should preserve the confidences and secrets of a client.

- A lawyer should exercise independent professional judgment on behalf of a client.

- A lawyer should represent a client competently.

- A lawyer should represent a client zealously within the bounds of the law.

These canons are elaborated by more specific ethical considerations and disciplinary rules governing attorneys.

Not every lawyer lives up to his or her duties every minute of the time. A client does have a right to count on a lawyer's responsibility, and this right is legally enforceable in a variety of circumstances.

Attorney-Client Privilege

The **attorney-client privilege** provides that confidential communications between a client and an attorney are protected from disclosure. The attorney-client privilege belongs to the client—the client can generally prevent disclosure regardless of the attorney's desires. If an attorney, for some reason, chose to testify in violation of the privilege, the evidence would be inadmissible in court, and the attorney would be subject to sanctions.

The attorney-client privilege exists in order to encourage frank discussions between the attorney and the client. The client is less likely to be honest with an attorney if the client believes that its communication may be turned against it. Honest attorney-client communications enable the attorney better to represent the client's interests. In contrast, the privilege denies the courts' access to relevant evidence.

The Corporate Client

The attorney-client privilege is relatively straightforward in representation of an individual, such as a criminal defendant. The privilege becomes more complex if the attorney is representing a corporation.

This issue is an important one—corporations are commonly sued and need effective legal representation. Suppose that a company is sued for violation of an environmental regulation. The corporate counsel needs to know the true facts surrounding the alleged violation (for defending the case or for settling it). A corporation needs the assurance of the privilege of confidentiality for communications with its attorney.

The Supreme Court conclusively settled the issue of whether the attorney-client privilege protected corporations. The Court emphasized the importance of the privilege, noting that "[i]n light of the vast and complicated array of regulatory legislation confronting the modern corporation, corporations, unlike most individuals, 'constantly go to lawyers to find out how to obey the law.'"[1]

Communications with Corporate Agents

Of course, a corporation cannot itself communicate with attorneys but must speak through its agents (directors, employees, etc.). There remains a question of which communications are protected by the privilege. Some courts held that the privilege was limited to communications by the "control group," high corporate officers and directors.

---

[1] *Upjohn Co. v. United States*, 449 U.S. 383, 392 (1981).

The Supreme Court rejected the control-group limitation on attorney-client privilege and extended it more broadly, writing:

> Middle-level—and indeed lower-level—employees can, by actions within the scope of their employment, embroil the corporation in serious legal difficulties, and it is only natural that these employees would have the relevant information needed by corporate counsel if he is adequately to advise the client with respect to such actual or potential difficulties.[2]

The Supreme Court adopted a "subject matter" test that applies the privilege to the communications of any employee, so long as the communication relates to the employee's corporate duties and the communication is made at the direction of a higher level corporate officer. This decision applied only in federal courts, however, and some states continue to use the control group test.

Even communications with former corporate employees may fall within the attorney-client privilege. Several courts have held that a privilege applies to communications between a corporation's attorney and the corporation's former employees, if the discussion relates to matters taken in the course of the past employment relationship.

Suppose that Lance Bihalik was a vice president of Techtron in 1987 but subsequently moved on to another corporation. While working for Techtron, Bihalik helped prepare documents for the company's issuance of stock. Techtron shareholders sue the company for false and misleading statements in connection with the stock issuance. Techtron's defense attorney may discuss the issue with Bihalik, and the contents of this discussion may be privileged. The plaintiff shareholders may, however, themselves question Bihalik and obtain evidence for their case.

Courts also have suggested that a corporation's attorney-client privilege can apply to communications with nonemployee insiders. Techtron may have brought in an outside accounting firm to prepare materials for its share offering. Communications between Techtron's attorneys and its accountants may also be covered by the privilege, though this issue is not conclusively settled.

Officer's Right to Privilege

If a corporation has a privilege when its officers communicate with its attorneys, do the officers have a privilege in these communications? This issue is also an important one, because the government is increasingly seeking *individual* liability of corporate officers, as well as of the corporation itself.

A key case involved a Securities and Exchange Commission investigation into the actions of a corporation and its employees. The court held that employees theoretically could claim the attorney-client privilege but only in limited circumstances. The court ruled that the individual employees would be required to show:

1. That they made clear to the lawyer that they were seeking advice in their individual personal interest.

2. That the lawyer communicated to them in their personal capacity.

3. The substance of the communication did not involve the employees' official duties.[3]

Seldom will individual employees be able to meet this test and take advantage of the privilege themselves. Most employees remain dependent on their corporation to invoke the attorney-client privilege.

Exceptions to Privilege

These are exceptions to the attorney-client privilege for both corporations and individuals. In some cases, a client may have the protection of the privilege and then lose it.

The attorney-client privilege is limited to confidential communications. If a client fails to keep the communications confidential, there is no privilege. If a corporate director discusses a case with an attorney and then describes this discussion at a large luncheon meeting, the privilege may be lost. In addition, a client may always waive the privilege and permit disclosure of the communications.

Another significant exception to the privilege exists where the communication does not involve legal advice. Corporate attorneys are often business counselors, and some attorneys have independent

---

[2] *Id.* at 391.

[3] *In re Grand Jury Investigation*, 575 F.Supp. 777 (N.D. GA. 1983).

positions in a business. If a corporate president discusses a matter with his attorney and seeks business advice, rather than legal advice, the communication is not covered by the privilege.

Another problem with the attorney-client privilege exists when the attorney's duty of confidentiality would force him or her to engage in fraud. Model Rule 8.4(c) of professional responsibility creates in lawyers an obligation not to engage in dishonesty, fraud, deceit, or misrepresentation. In such circumstances, a lawyer should withdraw from representing the client.

The following recent decision details the requirements that must be proved for a party to take advantage of the attorney-client privilege.

Case 20.2
Helman v. Murry's Steaks, Inc.
United States District Court for the District of Delaware, 1990
728 F. Supp. 1099

Background and Facts Gloria Helman and her mother were shareholders in Murry's Steaks, Inc. ("MSI"). MSI subsequently merged with another company, and Helman and her mother were paid cash for their shares in MSI. Helman brought this suit complaining that MSI and individual officers of the company withheld material information regarding MSI's business in order to get Helman and her (now deceased) mother to sell their MSI shares for less than their true value.

At the closing in which MSI purchased the shares, John Cogar attended in representation of Ms. Helman and her mother. The price was renegotiated and the parties later undertook a second and final closing. MSI sought to depose Cogar and question him about his discussions with Helman. The six discussions in question all occurred after the first closing, and Cogar did not bill Helman for this advice. Helman and Cogar resisted this testimony as protected by the attorney-client privilege. MSI moved the court to compel this testimony, arguing that no attorney-client relationship existed.

LONGOBARDI, Chief Judge.

* * * *

The privilege applies only if (1) the asserted holder of the privilege is or sought to become a client; (2) the person to whom the communication was made (a) is member of the bar of a court, or his subordinate and (b) in connection with this communication is acting as a lawyer; (3) the communication relates to a fact of which the attorney was informed (a) by his client (b) without the presence of strangers (c) for the purpose of securing primarily either (i) an opinion on law or (ii) legal services or (iii) assistance in some legal proceeding, and not (d) for the purpose of committing a crime or tort; and (4) the privilege had been (a) claimed and (b) not waived by the client.

* * * *

Defendants rely on *United States v. Wilson*, 798 F.2d 509 (1st Cir. 1986) for the proposition that the Plaintiff was not a client of Cogar's. In *Wilson*, the court held that where the defendant had not stated his desire to obtain legal services from the attorney, and the attorney testified that he did not give any legal advice to the defendant, and the defendant was not billed by the attorney, a memo written by the defendant to the attorney was not protected by the attorney/client privilege because the defendant was not, nor sought to become a client. *Id.* at 513. Although in the present case the Plaintiff was not billed for the services rendered by Cogar, it is evident from the deposition testimony of both the Plaintiff and Cogar that the Plaintiff was seeking legal advice. Thus, the present case is distinguishable from *Wilson*. Further, the Third Circuit has stated that unless the communication is in furtherance of some crime or fraud or the privilege has been waived, "communications with an attorney are privileged when they concern 'legal advice of any kind... sought ... from a professional legal advisor in his capacity as such.'" Matter of Grand Jury Empanelled Feb. 14, 1978, 603 F.2d 469, 474 (3rd Cir.1979) (quoting J. Wigmore, Evidence s 2292 at 554 (1961), quoted in *United States v. Costanzo*, 625 F.2d at 468. The essence of whether one communicating with an attorney is a "client" depends upon whether that person is seeking legal advice not whether there is a payment of a fee or an execution of a formal contract.

Decision and Remedy   *The court ruled that MSI was not entitled to depose Cogar regarding the discussions in question.*

The privilege also does not apply when the communications are for the purpose of committing a crime or a fraud, when the attorney has an ethical obligation to disclose the communication (e.g., in order to prevent a client's perjury in court), and when the attorney acquired the information through his or her own research from outside third parties or even from business records.

Work Product Privilege

A separate protection is found in the **work product privilege**. This privilege means that lawyers need not disclose the contents of materials that they prepare in the course of pursuing a case or defending a client.

When an attorney is preparing a defense, he or she typically will do extensive analyses of both the facts and the law of the case. A good attorney will prepare honest analyses, but these may be embarrassing to a client, as the attorney may find potential liability for the client. The work product privilege protects against disclosures of these analyses.

Unlike the attorney-client privilege, the work product privilege historically was for the benefit of the attorney, who theoretically could waive the privilege and incriminate the client. Courts now may permit the client to claim the benefit of the work product privilege as well.

The work product privilege was also historically limited to litigation and applied only to trial preparation activities of lawyers. Standard corporate counseling was excluded from the privilege. The lawsuit need not have been filed, however, and the privilege applies to documents prepared for possible future litigation. Some states, such as California, have extended the work product privilege to counseling in the course of contract litigations, even if litigation is not imminent.

Legal Representation of the Corporation

As noted above, attorneys have ethical duties to represent the interests of their clients zealously and competently. If a lawyer fails to do so, the client may sue the lawyer for malpractice. When a lawyer is representing a corporation, however, the obligations of loyalty may become unclear.

Conflict of Interest

Attorneys who represent corporations may be put into difficult positions. The interests of the corporation as an entity are difficult to separate from the interests of its constituent parts. Nevertheless, the attorneys' Code of Professional Responsibility states:

A lawyer employed or retained by a corporation or similar entity owes his allegiance to the entity and not a stockholder, director, officer employee, representative, or other person connected with the entity. In advising the entity, a lawyer should keep paramount its interests and his professional judgment should not be influenced by the personal desires of any person or organization.[4]

The interests of the corporate entity are not easy to find, however. There is a natural tendency for corporate attorneys to identify themselves with the officers and directors who hired the attorneys.

A lawyer may violate duties, however, by identifying too closely with a corporate officer. The officer may have a conflict of interest with the corporation as a whole. In this case, the lawyer may have a duty to side with the corporation, even to blow the whistle on the director and seek his or her ouster. If a lawyer fails to do so, the corporation may sue the lawyer for breach of ethical duties.

The Securities and Exchange Commission ("SEC") has sought to require lawyers to play a greater role in supervising corporate governance and to be more aggressive in exposing and fighting self-interested actions of officers and directors. The SEC has sued lawyers for failing to go over the heads of the directors and inform shareholders of false and misleading information issued by the corporation.

Officers and directors may also seek to retain the corporation's lawyer to represent them in their individual capacities. In such cases, the lawyer must be careful that the individual interests of the officers and directors do not conflict with the interests of the corporation. If a lawyer is representing both the corporation and individual officers and if a conflict arises, the lawyer may be disqualified from representing *either* side in the dispute.

The identity of clients in a corporate context can easily become confused, as indicated in the following decision.

[4] Ethical Consideration 5-18.

Case 20.3
Waggoner v. STAAR Surgical Company
United States Court of Appeals for the Ninth Circuit, 1993
991 F.2d 1501

Background and Facts Thomas Waggoner was a cofounder and president of STAAR Surgical Company. Elliot Lutzker was counsel for STAAR. After the company confronted financial problems, Waggoner expressed a willingness to guarantee over $6 million in corporate debt in exchange for preferred stock providing voting control over the company. Waggoner consulted with Lutzker in this transaction, and Lutzker made assurances about Waggoner's rights. After the board of directors resolved not to continue takeover negotiations with Chiron, it was discovered that Waggoner was continuing negotiations. At an emergency meeting, the board terminated Waggoner. Waggoner then used his power as shareholder to name a new board and removed the other directors. In the ensuing litigation, Waggoner lost his position and much of his stock ownership in STAAR, because the issuance of shares in connection with the loan guarantee was unlawful. Waggoner then filed an action against Lutzker, claiming that he was liable for malpractice in structuring the share issuance. Lutzker defended that he could not be liable in malpractice to Waggoner, because Waggoner was not his client. The district court ruled for Lutzker on summary judgment, and Waggoner appealed.

SNEED, Circuit Judge.

* * * *

Despite Waggoner's allegations, the intent and conduct of the parties supports the district court's finding that Waggoner and Lutzker were not in an attorney-client relationship. As noted above, it is undisputed that Lutzker informed everyone at the board meeting ... that Lutzker was only present as counsel for STAAR * * * Waggoner's counsel at the Delaware trial made a point of establishing that Lutzker was STAAR's corporate counsel in response to allegations by the other directors that Lutzker had not acted appropriately on behalf of the board. He pointed out that: Lutzker had been described as corporate counsel by virtually all the directors; the directors sought his counsel about filing a bankruptcy petition; and Lutzker prepared the minutes of board meetings even after Waggoner purportedly removed them as directors.

* * * *

Unless the attorney for a corporation or partnership affirmatively assumes a duty toward an officer or partner, the lawyer is not liable to a partner or director who relied on his advice. In the instant case, Lutzker's duty as counsel for STAAR lay with the corporation, not with its officers and directors individually. In addition, the record reveals no sign that Lutzker affirmatively adopted Waggoner as a client during the transfer of preferred stock.

Decision and Remedy *The court affirmed the district court's grant of summary judgment to defendant.*

Malpractice

Clients may sue their attorneys for legal malpractice. Malpractice is a distinct tort, but this action may also take the form of a breach of contract action, assuming that the client and the attorney have a contract.

To maintain a malpractice action, the client first must show that there was an attorney-client relationship. Payment of fees to an attorney is generally sufficient to establish such a relationship, unless evidence indicates that the services rendered by the attorney were not legal in nature. In general, a client can sue only his or her own attorney for malpractice and cannot sue an opposing party's attorney.

The second requirement of a malpractice action is proof that the attorney failed to exercise ordinary legal skill and knowledge. Some courts use a "locality" standard and hold the attorney to the ordinary standard of skill found in the lawyer's community. A New York attorney, therefore, might be held to a different standard than that for a Nebraska attorney.

The third and most difficult requirement of a malpractice action is proof of damages. Suppose that Cole Corporation hires a lawyer to sue its competitor Hanom Corporation for unlawful monopolization. Cole's attorney fails to use ordinary skill, and the case is dismissed. If Cole sues its attorney, it must prove that it would have won the antitrust case against Hanom, had it had proper representation. Otherwise, Cole suffered no damages from the malpractice. It may be difficult for a plaintiff to show that it would have prevailed in the initial action.

Various legal errors may produce malpractice actions. Some of the traditional sources of malpractice are: (i) failure to file a claim before the statute of limitations runs out; (ii) failure to sue all the proper defendants; and (iii) failure to raise a legal defense. All these represent fairly clear-cut circumstances of malpractice.

An increasingly important area of malpractice litigation involves the settlement of lawsuits. As discussed in the following section, lawyers are being sued for negligently conducting settlement negotiations.

Settlements

Over 90 percent of lawsuits are settled without going to trial. Settlement saves legal costs and avoids risks. Many parties leave the substance of settlement negotiations to their attorneys, who understand the law and the client's relative prospects.

Although the lawyers often conduct the settlement negotiations, the client retains ultimate control over the decision to settle (unless the client has expressly delegated this control to the attorney). An attorney-client relationship does not give the lawyer the power to settle the case.

A lawyer has specific duties when conducting settlement negotiations. First, the lawyer must exercise ordinary skill and knowledge in the conduct of settlement negotiations. This includes the investigation of the details of any settlement offers. Second, the lawyer must communicate settlement offers to the client, to enable the client to make a choice of whether to accept the offer. This generally should be done in writing.

A number of lawyers have been held liable for negligently settling or failing to settle cases. The following decision provides an example of such a case.

Case 20.4
Smiley v. Manchester Insurance & Indemnity Company of St. Louis
Supreme Court of Illinois, 1978
375 N.E.2d 118

Background and Facts *The underlying lawsuit arose when Charles Toney's car crossed the center line of the road and struck a vehicle in which Roy Smiley, Byron Emanuel, and the Arnolds were riding. Smiley was seriously injured and Emanuel was killed, as was Toney. The Arnolds suffered relatively minor injuries. Toney had been poor, having only assets of an insurance policy with Manchester Insurance & Indemnity Company for $20,000 per accident. Plaintiff's attorney, Bernard Reese, sought to settle for this amount, but the insurance company refused. Reese then sued Toney's estate for $50,000 for Smiley and $100,000 in wrongful death damages for Emanuel. The Arnolds threatened suit for their minor injuries.*

Manchester assigned the case to William Knight and encouraged him to seek a settlement. The company authorized Knight to settle all claims arising from the accident for $20,000; $17,000 for the Smiley and Emanuel claims and $3000 for the possible claims of the Arnolds. Reese sought $10,000 each for Smiley and Emanuel. Knight refused and made no counteroffer.

After a trial, a jury returned an award of $25,000 for Smiley and $50,000 for Emanuel's estate. The insurance company paid $10,000 to each, the maximum policy limits. Reese then sued Manchester for the remaining $55,000 on a claim of bad faith refusal to settle. A court declared that Manchester was liable for $35,000. Manchester then sued Knight for negligently failing to settle the initial claim for $20,000. A jury returned a verdict for Knight, but an appellate court overturned this holding and found Knight liable for negligence. Knight appealed.

RYAN, Justice.

* * * *

It is clear that an attorney is liable to his client only when he fails to exercise a reasonable degree of care and skill; he is not liable for mere errors of judgment. (*Brown v. Gitlin* (1974), 19 Ill.App.3d 1018, 313 N.E.2d 180; *Dorf v. Relles* (7th Cir. 1966), 355 F.2d 488.) In viewing the evidence in this case most favorably to Knight, we must affirm the decision of the appellate court that as a matter of law he failed to act as a reasonable and skillful attorney in the area. The uncontroverted evidence at trial shows that as early as November 1967 he was instructed to attempt settlement with all of the claimants. He never contacted the Arnolds nor did he every discuss settlement with their attorney, Clifford Stoner, testifying that he had not been hired to handle their claims. The undisputed evidence also shows that on June 18, 1968, Knight was expressly authorized to settle the Smiley and Emanuel claims for $17,000 and to reserve $3,000 for the Arnolds. In spite of this authority, he never offered any amount to settle the claims, nor did he disclose his authority to Reese or to the trial judge. On June 24, 1968, at the start of the trial when Reese asked if there was any offer and renewed his demand to settle the cases for policy limits, Knight replied "no comment." Even if we accept Knight's testimony that he only had $17,000, his complete inaction when he had knowledge of the seriousness and probable liability of the claims clearly did not comport with the actions of a reasonable attorney. In addition, the evidence shows that Knight had the complete file, including the adjuster's report of Reese's plan to sue in an attempt to collect any judgment in excess of policy limits. His failure to make even a token offer on the record constituted strong proof of bad faith in support of the claim for recovery of the excess. Even if Reese would not have accepted $17,000 in settlement, such an offer would at least support a claim by Manchester of a good faith attempt at settlement. Attorney Ohlson also testified that even if Knight only had $17,000 authority, he had not acted reasonably in failing to offer it.

Decision and Remedy *The court affirmed the finding that Knight was negligent and remanded the case for a trial on damages.*

▄ Document Retention and Destruction

Corporate documents are an enormously significant part of most litigation. After a plaintiff files an action, the plaintiff makes **discovery requests** to go through the defendant's document files. Attorneys may scour many file cabinets' worth of files including millions of documents, in hopes of finding a single key document that will support their action. Sometimes, the plaintiff's attorney may find a "smoking gun" document, in which some employee of the defendant virtually confesses that the defendant engaged in illegal activity.

Companies also must be concerned about the documents retained in private files. A company settled a case for hundreds of millions of dollars, after the plaintiff found a "smoking gun" document in the possession of a retired employee that he kept at home in his personal files.

A company's policy on *retention of documents* can thus have a significant bearing on its ultimate liability. Obviously, companies have reasons to keep documents on hand to preserve a record of past decisions and inform future decisions. In most cases, however, it is lawful for companies to destroy most of their documents. Companies today are far more likely to have a formal program to destroy documents systematically.

A systematic program is important to a lawful document destruction program. It is important that document destruction be a matter of a company's ordinary course of business and not a selective destruction of potentially incriminating documents.

It is also unlawful to destroy documents even in a systematic program if those documents are potential evidence in a lawsuit. Once a company is sued, document destruction related to the suit must halt. Indeed, a company must cease document destruction as soon as it is placed on notice of a potential lawsuit against it. Failure to abide by these rules can result in substantial sanctions against a corporation.

When a company has documents in its possession, it must provide them to an opposing party who makes a relevant request for the documents. In a 1991 case, a company promised to turn over relevant documents but then intentionally failed to do so. A judge found that the company had obstructed justice and ordered the company to pay $2.98 million in sanctions. The company's attorneys were fined $300,000 for their participation in the obstruction of justice.

Management of Legal Affairs

Legal issues are so important to companies that most major businesses have separate legal departments. The management of legal issues involves many of the same business decision-making principles as do more traditional business decisions. Wise decision making involves an understanding of the legal context, however.

In-House vs. Outside Counsel

Traditionally, when a company ran into legal trouble the company called upon an outside law firm to help resolve the difficulty. Most companies thereby developed long-standing relationships with particular law firms that handled the companies' business.

Using law firms is rather expensive, however, as many attorneys bill at high hourly rates. Companies discovered that many routine legal tasks could be handled more cheaply "in-house." The company would hire full-time lawyers as employees of the company in order to handle these tasks.

Companies are making increased use of in-house counsel to cut costs. The number of in-house counsel is growing at a rate twice as fast as for outside counsel. Over 90 percent of business consumer affairs legal problems are handled by in-house counsel. Two-thirds of litigation practice, however, is handled by outside counsel, and a much higher percentage of complex litigation is handled by outside counsel.

A business must decide how much of its legal work will be sent to more expensive (but perhaps more expert) outside counsel and how much legal work will be done in-house. The company also must decide how many resources to devote to in-house legal departments. Better pay will attract better in-house lawyers, which will reduce the need to use outside counsel.

There are some significant advantages to developing a large in-house legal department. These lawyers will be particularly familiar with the firm and its needs. In-house counsel also help the company efficiently use outside counsel, when necessary. In-house counsel is always on hand to respond quickly to crises.

One of the greatest advantages to in-house counsel is its close involvement with management and ability to engage in *preventive* legal analysis. The firm's general counsel is a member of senior management near the top of the corporate hierarchy. In this position, a general counsel can insist on early legal involvement in business actions to prevent future legal problems. In-house counsel can educate employees to avoid sources of liability. The in-house counsel of Digital Equipment Corporation, for example, devotes 50 percent of its time to preventive actions.[5]

There are some disadvantages to in-house counsel, though. Some suggest that they actually increase the total legal costs of a corporation because its desire "to provide the company with maximum legal protection" actually produces more work for outside counsel.[6] In-house counsel may also have more difficulty giving independent legal advice, divorced from business considerations.

The decision of whether to employ in-house or outside counsel is closely analogous to ordinary production decisions made by companies. Manufacturing companies typically must decide whether to buy raw material inputs for their products or to invest capital resources and make their own raw material inputs. Capital budgeting models are available to make this type of decision.

The legal services area presents unique factors that must be considered in the choice between

---

[5] Chayes & Chayes, "Corporate Counsel and the Elite Law Firm," 37 *Stanford L. Rev.* 277, 287 (1985).

[6] Samuelson, "The Changing Relationship Between Managers and their Lawyers," 33 *Business Horizons* 21, 25 (1990).

in-house and outside counsel. For example, outside counsel may better protect the attorney-client privilege between a corporation and its lawyer. The privilege exists for communications between a corporation and its in-house counsel. A court may be more likely, however, to find that a discussion with in-house counsel was a business discussion rather than a protected legal discussion.

In-house counsel may have other disadvantages in litigation. Many trials require one side to disclose trade secrets or other sensitive business information. When this material is disclosed, it is often subject to a protective order. The protective order might limit disclosure of the trade secret to the attorneys and require that the attorneys keep the information secret.

Some courts have been reluctant to permit in-house counsel to see such sensitive materials. The fear is that in-house counsel may be so closely connected with a company's management that maintaining secrecy is difficult or impossible.

Litigation Strategy

When a company is involved in litigation, as either a plaintiff or a defendant, the company may take a combative posture. The opposing litigant becomes defined as the enemy, who must be vanquished at all costs. This attitude is an inefficient one, however, and companies should consider litigation strategy as simply another business decision, to be guided by concern for the financial success of the enterprise.

This means that companies should seriously consider settling claims and take a rigorous approach to settlements. In fact, over 90 percent of lawsuits brought in the United States end in settlements. How can a company decide whether to settle a claim and for how much?

A company's litigation strategy should consider three key factors. First, the company should consider its prospects or probabilities of success in the action. Second, the company should consider the financial consequences if it does succeed or if it fails in the litigation. Third, the company should consider the costs involved in pursuing the litigation to a conclusion.

A standard way for considering these factors is through the use of a decision tree. This is a mechanism for evaluating the consequences of various choices and ascribing a present value to each of these choices.

Exhibit 20-1 presents a decision tree analysis of the following hypothetical case. ChemCorp purchases raw materials from LedCorp and turns them into final products that are sold to AmCorp. LedCorp breaches its contracts with ChemCorp by failure to provide raw materials, which costs ChemCorp $1 million in profits on its AmCorp contract. Then AmCorp considers ChemCorp an undependable supplier and exercises its right to cancel other contracts, costing ChemCorp another $4 million in profits.

ChemCorp sues LedCorp for breach of contract, and claims $5 million in damages. LedCorp's attorneys and ChemCorp's attorneys get together to discuss settlement. LedCorp's attorneys state: "We think we have a defense to the breach of contract count, and we don't have any liability for the $4 million lost profits, because this was unforeseeable and therefore cannot be recovered." The LedCorp attorneys go on to say that they will be "nice guys" and agree to settle the whole case for $1 million payment to ChemCorp. Should ChemCorp accept this settlement offer?

The offer obviously has some appeal. Accepting the settlement eliminates any risk of losing at trial and also avoids the need to spend litigation costs. Plus, ChemCorp will be covered for its immediate losses. But look at the problem more rigorously.

The ChemCorp attorneys decide that they have an 80 percent probability of winning the case at trial but only a 50 percent probability of winning the full $5 million in damages as foreseeable. In addition, a full trial of the case will cost the company $500,000. These calculations are then plugged into the decision tree found in Exhibit 20-1.

This decision tree considers the probability of each consequence. If ChemCorp wins at trial, it has a 50 percent chance of making $4.5 million ($5 million minus $500,000 in costs) and a 50 percent chance of making $500,000 ($1 million minus $500,000 in costs). The expected value of a win at trial is therefore $2.5 million (50 percent of $4.5 million plus 50 percent of $500,000).

Of course, there is a 20 percent possibility that ChemCorp will lose at trial. The consequences of this outcome are a net loss of $500,000 in litigation costs with no counterbalancing recovery. When this risk is factored in, the expected value of going to trial is $1.9 million.

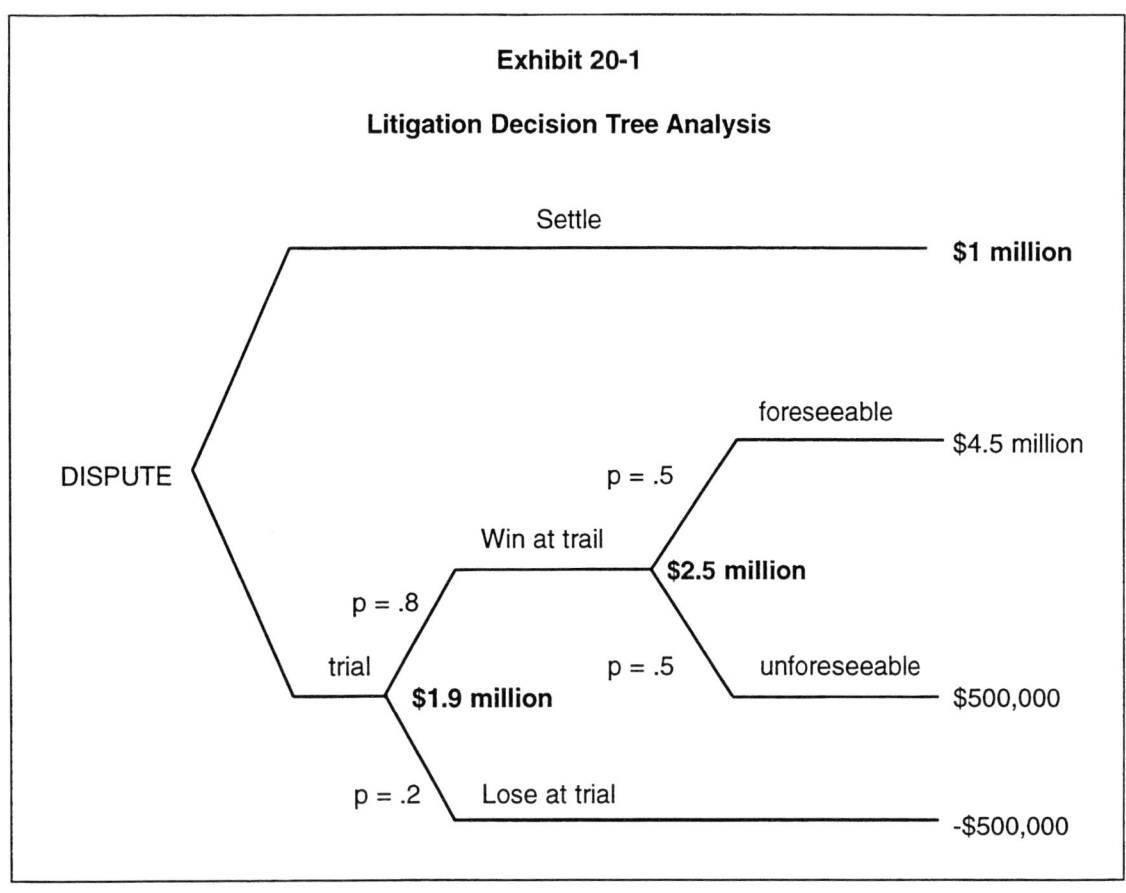

Based on this assessment, assuming that ChemCorp's probabilities are reasonably accurate, ChemCorp might decide to reject the settlement of at least $1.9 million to forego litigation.

The decision tree presents a financial analysis of litigation. But legal issues present other issues that must be factored into a decision, even if they cannot be so readily quantified.

A business might have strong reasons to settle the case. Litigation might expose trade secrets or facts that could embarrass the business and injure its position in the marketplace. Defendants often want to settle personal injury cases, because settlements are not officially reported. If a defendant tries a case and loses, that case becomes a precedent that both alerts and assists other plaintiffs in similar circumstances.

In contrast, a business might want to litigate in order to set a precedent for future circumstances. If a company faces a recurring legal problem, the company may benefit significantly from settling the problem conclusively. If the business wins, it may avoid future litigation and associated expenses. If the business loses, at least it has more certainty to plan for the future.

Alternative Dispute Resolution

The above discussion assumed that the only choice in resolving a dispute was litigating or settling. Businesses are increasingly turning to a third alternative that has become known as **alternative dispute resolution**, or ADR. ADR involves a variety of nontrial procedures, with the most common being arbitration and mediation. ADR is discussed in some detail in Chapter 3 of *West's Business Law, Seventh Edition,* and in Chapter 4 of *West's Legal Environment of Business, Third Edition.*

ADR is typically less expensive than litigation because it is less formal. In a dramatic example, Texaco and Borden had been litigating a $200 million antitrust and contract case for several years and then tried ADR. They were able to settle the case within three weeks.[7]

Arbitration is the most common form of ADR. Arbitration is also much like a trial, though somewhat less formal. The system is adversarial in nature, as both sides present witnesses and often are represented by attorneys. An arbitrator or a panel of arbitrators substitute for a judge or jury, however, and the rules of evidence are typically relaxed in arbitration.

Arbitration has advantages and disadvantages opposed to litigation. Arbitrators are not bound by legal precedents and have great discretion in structuring a remedy. This means that they have flexibility to do justice, but it also means that they may ignore the law and reach unpredictable results. Arbitration decisions generally cannot be appealed.

Arbitration does not create a binding precedent and generally permits less discovery, which may be good or bad depending upon the circumstances of the parties. Arbitration gives parties some ability to select a decision maker with business experience who understands the industry, rather than a less informed judge or jury.

One of the greatest advantages of arbitration is secrecy. In the course of a trial, documents will be publicly unearthed that may prove embarrassing or that may reveal business secrets. The law provides for protection of trade secrets, but this protection may be insufficient. In arbitration, it is much easier to preserve confidentiality. The arbitrator's code of ethics requires total confidentiality.

A party, even a plaintiff, may not simply choose arbitration, however. Most arbitration requires the consent of both parties. This consent may be expressed in advance. Thus, many business contracts provide that any disputes arising out of the contract must be arbitrated and not taken to court.

The law is very supportive of these arbitration agreements and enforces them. If there is an agreement to arbitrate and one side ignores the agreement and sues in court, the other side may halt the trial and compel arbitration. The winner in an arbitration can go to court if necessary and get a judgment compelling the loser to pay the damages found in arbitration.

---

[7] Allison, "Five Ways to Keep Disputes Out of Court," *Harvard Business Review*, January-February 1990, at 11.

Ethical Perspectives

Whistle-Blowing and the Corporate Counsel

As previously discussed, employee whistle-blowing presents several ethical dilemmas. The ethical problems of whistle-blowing are complicated when the individual is an in-house lawyer of a corporation. The ethical code of lawyers holds them to an especially high standard of loyalty to their clients, which whistle-blowing may violate.

In-house counsel typically has a broad mandate to audit the corporation and investigate potential legal problems. Thus, these lawyers are especially likely to discover unethical or illegal actions taken by the company. If the lawyer discovers such actions and tries to correct them, higher corporate officers may refuse to cease the unethical or illegal behavior. Should the lawyer then report the action to a government agency or to the press?

In addition to the duty of loyalty to the client, the lawyer's problem is further complicated by the attorney-client privilege. Attorneys are bound to preserve the confidences told them by clients. Whistle-blowing also seems to violate this duty.

There are countervailing ethical concerns as well. Suppose that a lawyer for Western Automobile Corporation discovers that the company is installing defective seat belts in order to save costs in its new convertible model. If the lawyer informs government agencies, he or she may be violating ethical duties of loyalty and the attorney-client privilege. But if the lawyer fails to disclose the defective seat belts, he or she may be contributing to the deaths of innocent persons.

Because the attorney-client privilege is a legal matter, the courts have had to deal with lawyer whistle-blowing. In one case, an in-house attorney for a corporation was told to destroy documents to protect the company in litigation. This would violate another ethical duty of lawyers, so the attorney refused, and the corporation fired the counsel. After the counsel sued the corporation, an Illinois court held that the firing was lawful.[8]

Another recent Illinois decision reached a somewhat different result. An in-house lawyer was fired after he informed the Food and Drug Administration that his employer was selling defective dialysis machines. The court held that this firing violated public policy and permitted the attorney to sue the corporation.[9] That court emphasized the societal harm that would result from a failure to blow the whistle.

In yet another case, an attorney for IBM believed that a Colorado facility was discriminating against minority employees and was fired for complaining. He released to the press confidential internal IBM documents even after IBM had obtained a court order prohibiting their disclosure. The lawyer currently faces criminal contempt of court charges for disclosing the information.

Becoming an attorney does not answer all ethical problems in favor of the client, and the in-house counsel may have an ethical responsibility to blow the whistle on especially wrongful corporate practices. The special situation of the attorney should affect the whistle-blowing decision, however. The attorney should exhaust all opportunities to correct the problem in-house. If this fails, the attorney might blow the whistle to correct the problem, but should do so in a manner that protects client confidences as much as possible.

---

[8] *Herbster v. North American Co. for Life and Health Insurance*, 501 N.E.2d 343 (Ill. App. 1986).

[9] *Balla v. Gambro, Inc.*, 560 N.E.2d 1043 Ill. App. 1990).

International Perspectives

International Practice for U.S. Attorneys

An increasingly important issue, from both legal and business perspectives, is the international legal representation of American companies. To what extent can United States lawyers practice law in foreign nations? This issue arises in many important contexts, including international finance law, international tax law, international antitrust law, international trade and contracts, and international litigation arbitration.

As U.S. companies extend their global reach, foreign representation becomes more significant. Most companies have an established relationship in the United States with a lawyer or a law firm that has served the company as a trusted counselor and advocate. The U.S. company understandably believes that its longstanding American lawyer can best represent it and is reluctant to rely upon unknown foreign attorneys, even for foreign legal problems.

Many law firms are attempting to expand overseas to provide legal services. Differences in legal systems and language complicate the ability to practice law in foreign countries, however. In addition, foreign nations may have rules restricting the practice of nonnationals as attorneys.

In Japan, an American attorney cannot become a "lawyer" (*bengoshi*) but may serve as a legal consultant. The legal consultant, though, may not give advice on Japanese law and may not litigate in the courtroom. The European Community ("EC") is relatively open to American lawyers. The EC directive on lawyers' freedom to provide services prohibits certain forms of discrimination against foreign lawyers.

Lawyers practicing in foreign nations must be careful to follow local ethical codes. For example, a number of nations prohibit attorney advertising and contingency fees, which are accepted in the United States.

Clients also must be aware of transitional differences in the attorney-client relationship. For example, a 1982 opinion of the European Court of Justice addressed the attorney-client privilege in Europe. The court held that the privilege did not apply to communications with in-house counsel and was limited with respect to foreign lawyers not licensed under the laws of the European nation.

Questions and Case Problems

1. MiraCo is negotiating a merger with Simple, Inc. The negotiations are far along and the merger agreement is nearly complete. MiraCo consults its attorney regarding whether the company should disclose the imminent merger agreement in documents sent to shareholders. The attorney advises that the company should disclose the merger under federal securities law, but the company decides not to do so. Should the lawyer disclose this violation or withdraw from representation of MiraCo?

2. The water pollution control laws require that a company report any accidental discharge of chemicals into a river. ChemCo suffers such an accidental discharge, but the company's president directs its in-house counsel not to report the discharge as required by law. In-house counsel agrees with the president that disclosure will lead to many unjustified lawsuits against the company, because the discharge was small and harmless. Should the in-house counsel go along with the admonition not to report the discharge?

3. Jill Apsit is an outside attorney representing the Growth company. At an emergency meeting of Growth, with Jill present, an engineer reports that Growth is emitting a chemical that causes cancer into the community. Jill advises that Growth take steps to halt these emissions. The Growth chief executive officer then discharges Jill, saying that she doesn't understand how business works. Jill fears that the emissions may cause multiple deaths in the community, which is wholly unaware of this risk. May Jill disclose this information to the public?

4. Four major officers of Sandro Corporation were considering conducting a management-led takeover of Sandro. The Sandro chief executive officer, Susan Becker, approached an outside attorney, John Lamar, about the takeover. He suggested that they form an acquisition company, which they did, naming it SA Acquisition. After the takeover was completed, a creditor of Sandro claimed that Susan and the other officers had engaged in fraud and acquired the company at an unfairly low price. The creditor demands that Lamar testify about his discussions with Susan. He claims that these discussions are confidential, but the creditor claims that he was representing SA and not Susan. Should Lamar be compelled to testify concerning his discussions with Susan?

5. An attorney represented a corporation in connection with a share issuance. Subsequently, individuals who purchased shares in the corporation sued the company for violation of securities laws in a shareholders' derivative action. This is where shareholders sue on behalf of the company itself to protect the company's assets. The shareholders sought to obtain the testimony of the attorney regarding the advice that he gave the corporation, but he defended with the attorney-client privilege. The shareholders claimed that they were the client and that their derivative action was on behalf of the client, so the privilege did not apply against them. How should the court rule on this matter? [*Garner v. Wilfinbarger*, 430 F.2d 1093 (5th Cir. 1970)].

6. John Thomason and Jerry Mitchell represent Hall-Kimbrell Environmental Services, Inc. They were retained by the owners, the Kimbrells, and consulted with them on EPA enforcement actions. The Kimbrells sold majority ownership to PSI, Inc. PSI investigated the EPA complaints and then locked the Kimbrells out of their offices and filed a damages action against the Kimbrells for damages in the EPA matters. The Kimbrells sought to disqualify Thomason and Mitchell from this lawsuit, claiming that they had a conflict of interest. How should the court rule? [*Professional Service Industries, Inc. v. Kimbrell*, No. 90-01326-C (D. Kan. 1991)].

Glossary

A

Actually foreseen test A principle holding accountants liable in negligence to non-client third parties that the accountants know will rely on the accountants' work.

Affirmative action A policy that gives some special preference to minority groups or women in order to overcome present effects of past discrimination.

Alternative dispute resolution The use of non-judicial procedures, such as arbitration or mediation, in order to resolve disputes, including legal disputes.

Ambiguity doctrine A principle of law that states that unclear insurance policy provisions will be construed in favor of the policy holder and against the insurance company.

Antidilution statutes State laws that restrict the use of new trademarks that may diminish the value of established trademarks.

Antidumping duties Tariffs charged importers who sell goods in the U.S. at unfairly low prices.

Appraisal The right of shareholders to reject the price offered for their shares in a merger and invoke a special proceeding to set a fair value for those shares.

Arbitration A method for resolving legal disputes through agreed-upon submission to a disinterested third party, rather than to a court.

Assumption of risk A doctrine that bars a plaintiff's recover in tort when the plaintiff has knowledge of a danger and its nature and voluntarily accepts that danger.

At-will contracts An employment agreement that permits employer or employee to cancel the agreement at any time.

Attorney-client privilege A rule of law providing that confidential communications between a client and an attorney are generally protected from disclosure at law.

Attorney-client relationship The special affiliation created when a person retains a lawyer for legal representation, creating special duties for the attorney.

Average worker test Rule permitting workers' compensation recovery for stress so severe that the ordinary employee would be harmed.

B

Bailment An agreement in which goods or personal property of one person (the bailor) are entrusted to another (the bailee), who is obligated to return the property to the bailor or dispose of it as directed.

Bank holding companies Umbrella corporations that control a number of banks in different states, but which are regulated by federal law in order to preserve competition in banking.

Bank mergers The acquisition of one bank by another, regulated by both banking and antitrust laws.

Bill of lading A document serving as evidence of the receipt of goods for shipment and as documentary evidence of title to the goods.

Branch banking The ability of a bank to establish divisions in other geographic areas, which remains limited by state laws.

Break-up fee A provision in which a company seeking a merger partner agrees to pay that company's costs in the event that the merger fails to succeed.

Bridging the gap The probability that a trademark user may expand its use of the mark into new product lines.

Burden of proof The presumption that a party must overcome in order to establish its case; the burden of proof on most issues lies with the complainant.

Business judgment rule A rule that immunizes corporate management from liability for actions taken in good faith, so long as such actions are within the power of the corporation and the authority of management.

C

Changes clause A provision in government contracts that gives the government the unilateral right to insist upon necessary changes in the original contract during the course of its performance.

Charitable immunity A doctrine that charities cannot be found liable for certain torts; now largely abandoned.

Charter The federal authorization from the Comptroller of the Currency required for entry into banking.

Chinese Wall An office procedure that isolates groups of workers in an attempt to avoid a conflict of interest.

Churning A prohibited practice in which stock brokers trade excessively in a client's account in order to accumulate greater commissions.

Collateral Property that is used as security for a loan.

Community ascertainment A requirement of communications licensing that a broadcaster research the needs of the local community.

Comparable worth compensation A policy intended to equalize the pay between jobs traditionally held by women (such as nursing) and those traditionally held by men (such as plumbing).

Comparative advertising The practice whereby the advertiser for one company compares its product with those of its competitors.

Comparative negligence A theory of tort law under which the liability for injuries resulting from negligent actions is shared by all persons who where negligent (including the injured party), on the basis of proportional negligence.

Constructive fraud Fraud that results from a party's failure to disclose material facts, notwithstanding a duty to disclose.

Contracts of adhesion An agreement in which one party has a stronger bargaining position and requires acceptance of its contract language without negotiation, such as in an insurance contract.

Control-share acquisition statutes State laws that limit the voting rights of corporate acquirers once they obtain "control share" of stock, such as 33% or 50% ownership.

Cost justification The principle that permits price discrimination among buyers if the price differential is reflective of different costs.

Cost plus incentive fee contract A cost reimbursement contract in which the contractor is provided financial incentives to cut costs and accomplish the contract more efficiently.

Cost reimbursement contract A government contract in which reimbursement is based upon the actual costs of completing the contract.

Countervailing duties Authorization of U.S. law that requires additional tariffs be paid on imports to offset effects of foreign subsidization of an industry.

Convenant A promise in a contract to undertake or not to undertake certain actions.

Coverage In insurance law, when an occurrence is within the scope of the policy, requiring the insurer to pay.

Crown jewels A corporation's most profitable asset.

D

Debarment A prohibition on contracting with the government for an extended time.

Defalcations by a corporation's employees Illegal actions by workers that steal from or defraud an employer.

Defamation A tort providing damages when a spoken or written statement causes injury to another's good name, reputation or character.

Defamatory statement A remark that injures the reputation of another person.

Defective pricing A bid by a party seeking a government contract that contains inaccurate or inflated estimates of its true costs of contracting.

Deficiency judgment A judgment against a debtor for the amount of a debt remaining unpaid after collateral has been repossessed and sold or after foreclosure proceedings.

Deposition A generic term referring to any evidence verified by oath and generally applied to the pretrial testimony of a witness taken under oath.

Diagnosis-Related Groups Organizations administering the federal health care reimbursement system that set schedules of payments for specific categories of medical procedures.

Discovery requests A pretrial procedure in which a party to litigation seeks information in the possession of the opposing party.

Disparagement Economically injurious falsehoods referring to the product or property of another.

Disparate impact discrimination A rule of civil rights law that prohibits certain employment practices or procedures that, while neutral on their face, have a significant discriminatory effect against members of a certain protected class.

Disparate treatment discrimination A rule of civil rights law that prohibits intentional employment discrimination against members of a certain protected class.

Distribution License A special permit facilitating the export of even sensitive groups to certain approved countries.

Doctrine of compelled self-publication A principle that permits a person to sue for defamation if he or she is required to repeat the defamatory statement of another.

Doctrine of increased risk A rule permitting employee recovery in workers' compensation when the job created an enhanced risk of the type of injury suffered by a worker.

Doctrine of positional risk A rule permitting employee recovery in workers' compensation when the job placed the worker in the position that caused an injury.

Draft Any instrument drawn on a drawee (such as a bank) that orders the drawee to pay a certain sum of money.

Dram shop laws Statutes that make alcohol servers liable for harm caused by patrons who become drunk.

Due-on-sale A clause in mortgages that accelerates the date of full payment whenever the mortgaged property is sold to another.

Dumping Selling goods in a foreign country at a price below that charged for the same goods in the domestic market.

Duty of fidelity An ethical and legal responsibility of loyalty in certain circumstances, such as an agent's duty to a principal.

E

80 percent rule A guideline suggesting the presence of discrimination when an employment selection procedure chooses members of one protected class at a rate less than 80% of that for choosing members of another protected class.

Employee stock option plan A corporate program that enables employees to acquire stock in the corporation.

Escape clause A provision enabling U.S. companies to obtain financial relief from imports that seriously injure domestic producers.

F

Failing company defense A legal doctrine permitting even those mergers that significantly increased market concentration when the acquired company is on the brink of failure.

Fair competition A defense to business torts that permits certain accepted market activities, such as advertising a low price.

Fairness opinion A statement by a financial adviser that makes conclusions regarding the financial fairness of an offer such as a tender offer.

Faltering company exception A circumstance in which a company need not provide 60-day advance warning for a plant closing, because the company was seeking capital to keep the plant open.

Fixed price contract A government contract in which the private contractor will receive a set payment determined in advance.

Fixed price contract with economic price adjustment A fixed price contract that allows for modification during the contract to account for increased cost or other changed circumstances.

Flip-in poison pill A corporate program that grants shareholders some special benefit (such as stock options) whenever an outsider purchases a large stake in their corporation.

Flip-over poison pill A corporate program that permits shareholders to acquire discount shares of stock in any corporation that seeks to acquire the company.

Foreclosure A procedure in which a lender takes possession of real property after the borrower has failed to make mortgage payments.

Fraudulent concealment Doctrine permitting employee to sue employer in tort if employer covers up the presence of a harm to the employee.

Free agency The ability of professional athletes to switch teams in order to obtain a better contract.

G

General duty clause A requirement of the Occupational Safety and Health Act that businesses be maintained free of known hazards that could cause serious injury to workers.

General License A permit required for the export of goods other than especially sensitive goods.

Generally Accepted Accounting Principles The conventions, rules and procedures necessary to define accepted accounting practices at a particular time.

Generally Accepted Auditing Standards A set of professional qualities and judgments for accountants set by the American Institute of Certified Public Accountants.

Generic trademark A mark that merely states what the product is (such as aspirin) and is unprotected by trademark law.

Going private merger A combination of companies that has the effect of eliminating public shareholders by purchasing their shares.

Going-private transaction A corporate restructuring action of purchasing all public shares of the company, leaving the corporation owned by a single entity or small group.

Golden parachutes Provisions that provide large severance payments to corporate officers who lose their jobs as a consequence of a takeover.

Good cause defense A response to wrongful discharge actions that permits the firing of employees who have taken certain actions deemed to justify discharge.

Good character A standard for obtaining a government communications license that considers the past behavior of the party seeking the license.

Goodbye fee A payment made by a company to an acquirer who seeks but fails to take over the company.

Greenmail A procedure in which a party purchases shares and threatens a takeover of a corporation in order to get its management to repurchase their shares at a premium price.

Guest-innkeeper relationship A special affiliation between a hotelkeeper and a guest that imposes specific duties on the hotelkeeper.

H

Hazard communication standard An OSHA rule that requires that employees be informed of certain hazardous substances in the workplace.

Hello fee A payment made to a party in order to induce them to make a takeover offer for a company.

Hostile environment harassment A prohibited practice in which continual sexual slurs or comments makes it difficult for an employee to work.

I

Implied contract of employment A legally enforceable employment agreement in addition to a written contract arising out of the conduct of the parties.

Implied warranty of suitability An unstated promise in a contract for lease of real estate to the effect that the property will suit the needs of the party leasing the property.

Implied-in-fact contract A contract formed in whole or in part from the conduct of the parties (as opposed to express language).

In the course of Rule that limits workers' compensation recovery to injuries that resulted while an employee was on the job.

Independent contractor One who works for, and receives payment from, an employer, but whose working conditions and methods are not controlled by the employer (and therefore is not an employee).

Innocent purchaser defense A rule of Superfund liability that permits certain acquirers of property to escape damages for cleanup costs on that property, if the acquirer meets certain conditions of innocence.

Insider lending A practice whereby a bank makes loans to its officers, directors or leading shareholders, which are permitted but restricted by federal law.

Intentional infliction of emotional distress A claim of action in tort when one party's outrageous action purposefully causes severe emotional distress in another.

Intentional tort exception Rule that permits employee to sue employer in court if employer intentionally causes harm to worker.

Interstate commerce Business that crosses state lines or affects enterprise in other states; defined very broadly.

Investment banker A financial professional who performs services such as valuation of stock in connection with mergers and acquisitions.

J

Joint bidding A procedure that creates an exception to antitrust laws in order to promote exports.

Junk bonds Debt securities that carry a high risk of default, such as those issued in connection with a leveraged buyout.

K-L

Lending limits A legal restriction on banking that sets a ceiling on loans to a single person or entity.

Leveraged buyout A corporate takeover financed by loans secured by the assets of the corporation to be acquired, resulting in a high level of debt financed with junk bonds.

Licensing standards Rules by which the government grants a limited authority to enter into a service, such as a radio or television station.

Limited liability company A business structure in Hungary that roughly parallels U.S. corporations.

Liquidated damages A provision in a contract that establishes an amount of damages owed in the event of a breach of the contract.

Liquidation A final government determination of tariff duties owed in international trade.

Lock-up An agreement where a corporation conditionally agrees to sell some asset to a third party at a specified and usually discounted price.

M

Malice A requirement that a public figure may not succeed in a defamation claim unless the defendant's statement was knowingly or recklessly false.

Management buyout A procedure in which the executive officers of a corporation obtain ownership of the corporation by purchasing the shares of public shareholders.

Manager's privilege A principle that allows corporate officers to interfere with the contracts of their employer, so long as the interference is in the employer's interest.

Material safety data sheets Documents that set forth the risks of hazardous chemicals found in the workplace.

Mechanics' lien security interest A doctrine that gives builders a security interest in a building until they are paid for their services in erecting or repairing the building.

Mediation A method of dispute resolution employing a neutral third party, who acts as a communicating agent between the parties in order to promote a voluntary settlement of the dispute.

Minority ownership A standard for granting communications licenses that encourages the participation of minority groups, such as African Americans or Hispanics.

Misappropriation A tort creating liability for a party that uses the likeness or other attributes of a person without permission.

Mortgage A written instrument giving a creditor (the mortgagee) an interest in the debtor's property as security for a debt.

N

Negligence A source of tort liability for failure to exercise reasonable care.

Negligence per se A doctrine that holds that a party who violates a law is therefore automatically considered negligent.

Negotiated procurement A government contracting procedure where the government negotiates contract terms with specific contractors.

Newsworthiness The right to publish private information about another due to the legitimate public interest in the information.

No-shop clause An agreement between an acquirer and the company to be acquired in which the latter's management promises not to seek out competing offers.

O

Opinion A non-verifiable statement of a subjective view, as distinguished from a fact.

Opinion shopping A practice in which a client retains a series of accountants in order to find one that produces results favorable to the client.

Ostensible agency liability A doctrine holding hospitals potentially liable for torts of non-employee doctors who use the hospitals' facilities.

P

Paramour liability A form of sexual discrimination in which a supervisor favors one employee because of their private relationship.

Parody A comment (such as a political cartoon) that makes light of a person or event and is largely protected by freedom of speech.

Participation agreement A contract in which two or more banks combine to extend credit and which has become a common source of lender liability litigation.

Peer review organization A group of physicians that review the health care decisions of other physicians to determine if they are reasonably and medically necessary.

Penalty clause A provision in a contract that appears to provide for damages in the event of breach but that is unenforceable because it is intended as a penalty and not an estimate of damages.

Per se negligence See negligence per se.

Personal animosity exception Exception to workers' compensation recovery when an injury results from personal relationship of worker and not the workplace context.

Personal injury by accident Rule of workers' compensation that limits employee recovery to harms that resulted in injury by accident (as opposed to intentional action).

Poison pill A corporate program that makes the company unattractive to a hostile acquirer, such as a shareholder rights plan.

Pollution exclusion A provision of insurance contracts that eliminates coverage for damages resulting from gradual pollution by the policyholder.

Possession liability A doctrine that provides that the possessor of property is liable for certain harms produced by the condition of the property.

Posting A requirement that certain warnings or notices be placed prominently, such as hotel disclaimers of liability for personal property.

Predatory pricing A prohibited practice of selling goods at a very low price in order to destroy the competition and monopolize a market.

Prehearing discovery An opportunity for disputants to obtain information about the other's case in advance of the hearing on their dispute.

Prepayment prohibitions A provision in a loan such as a mortgage that precludes the borrower from paying off the loan before the end of its term.

Price discrimination A practice in which the same good is sold at different prices to different customers and which is sometimes illegal under the Robinson-Patman Act.

Primary line competition Harm to competition from price discrimination, where the practice reduces competition among sellers of goods.

Privilege In tort law, a defense providing the ability to act contrary to another person's right without liability.

Privity The relationship that exists between the two or more parties to a contract.

Programming A standard for communications licensing that considers the type of shows offered by broadcasters.

Proximate cause The "substantial" or legal cause in tort law used to determine whether a defendant should bear the burden for a plaintiff's injuries.

Proxy card A card sent to shareholders in order to authorize a specific person to vote their shares at a shareholders' meeting.

Public policy A rule that prohibits firing employees for certain highly objectionable reasons, such as refusal to violate the law.

Purchase and assumption transaction A method in which the federal government seeks to salvage a failed bank by getting a solvent bank to take over its assets and liabilities.

Q

Quasi contract An obligation or agreement imposed by law in the absence of an actual agreement, in order to prevent unjust enrichment.

Qui tam actions The authority for private citizens to bring suits for fraud in government contracting and obtain part of the government's recovery.

Quid pro quo harassment A prohibited employment action in which an employee is forced to grant sexual favors in order to obtain an employment opportunity.

R

Real estate Property in the form of land and buildings fixed to the land that is immovable, as opposed to personal property that can be moved (also real property).

Reasonable expectations doctrine A legal principle that states that insurance policies cover claims that are within the reasonable expectations of the policyholder.

Redemption right The opportunity for a borrower to pay off a mortgage loan even after the lender has declared a default and begun foreclosure proceedings.

Related products rule A principle that permits a trademark holder to sue producers of similar products that use an infringing trademark.

Renewal expectancy A presumption in favor of the incumbent holder of a broadcast license in an ownership challenge in a government relicensing proceeding.

Restructuring A corporate program that usually provides shareholders with a substantial dividend that is financed by taking on additional corporate debt.

S

Scalping A prohibited practice in which brokers purchase shares and then promptly resell them to their clients at a profit.

Sealed bid procedures A government contracting procedure in which private contractors submit secret offers and the government selects a winner without negotiations.

Secondary line competition Harm to competition from price discrimination, where the practice reduces competition among purchasers of goods.

Secondary meaning The association of a trademark with a particular maker's product, required for protection of descriptive or unregistered trademarks.

Section 1981 A statutory provision prohibiting race discrimination in private contracts.

Self tender A procedure in which a company makes a tender offer to purchase its own stock.

Setoff A rule permitting banks to take money from one account of a debtor to pay off an overdue obligation in another account with the same institution.

Sex plus discrimination A rule that discriminates based on a person's sex plus another characteristic, such as prohibiting males from wearing long hair.

Shareholders rights plan A program in which shareholders of a corporation receive some valuable right (such as purchase of additional shares) that usually vests in the event of a takeover.

Shark repellants Provisions in a corporate character or bylaws that make a takeover more difficult or unattractive.

Sole source contracting A government contracting procedure when a single contractor can perform the required work.

Special duty clause The requirement that employers comply with the specific regulations promulgated by OSHA.

Stakeholders Employees, bondholders and others who have a financial interest in the continued operation of a corporation.

Standing The requirement that an individual must have a sufficient stake in a controversy (actual injury or threat of future injury) before he or she can maintain a lawsuit.

Substantial privity test A rule that holds accountants liable in negligence to certain parties, not their client, but who are in a close connection with the accountants.

Successor liability The rule that holds the surviving corporation in a merger liable for the debts of the company that was merged out of existence.

Suggestive trademarks Product marks that suggest the attributes of the product but do not directly describe them.

Superlien A provision in environment law that gives a priority security interest to ensure that resources are available to clean up hazardous wastes.

Supermajority vote A requirement that the approval of more than a majority of shareholders (e.g., 75%) is required for certain significant corporate actions.

Suspension A temporary prohibition on an individual's ability to contract with the government.

T

Tender offer A procedure for taking over a company by making a pubic offer to all shareholders to purchase their shares for a set price.

Termination for convenience The authority of the government in contracts enabling it to cancel a contract at any time, if the contract becomes unnecessary.

Trademark A word or symbol that has become sufficiently associated with a good or registered with the government such that others may not use the trademark without illegal infringement.

Transactions with affiliated banks A regulation of banking that restricts loans to associated banks.

Treasury shares Stock in a corporation that is owned by the corporation itself.

Truth-in-menu laws Statutes requiring an accurate description of the food served in restaurants.

Two-tier tender offer A tender offer that offers different prices for the shares of a target corporation, depending on the timing of acceptance of the offer.

U

Unpreventable employee misconduct defense An employer's defense to a job injury arising where the harm resulted from the fault of the employee and the employer could not reasonably have prevented this action.

V

Valid trademark A product mark that is defensible at law against infringers.

Validated License Permit required for the export of certain products that the government considers sensitive or to certain countries.

Vicarious liability A doctrine whereby one party, such as an employer, may be liable for the torts of another party, such as an employee.

W-Z

White knight An ally of management enlisted to purchase a company in order to avert a hostile takeover.

White squire An ally of management who purchases shares in a company with a promise not to tender those shares to a hostile acquirer.

Work product privilege The right of attorneys and their clients to keep documents prepared for litigation secret.

Wrongful constructive eviction claim A tenant's allegation that the landlord has rendered the lease property uninhabitable.

Wrongful discharge tort A claim of action in tort enabling an employee to sue an employer for a firing that is conducted unfairly.

Wrongful eviction A tort in which a guest can sue a hotel for improperly removing the guest from a room without justification.

Table of Cases

The principal cases are in bold type. Cases cited or discussed are in roman type.

A

A & N Cleaners and Launderers, Inc., United States v., 232
A. P. Smith Manufacturing Company v. Barlow, 13-14
Abkco Music, Inc. v. Harrisongs Music, Ltd., 271
AC Acquisition Corp. v. Anderson Clayton & Co., 144
Ackerman v. Western Electric Company, 66
Adames, United States v., 24
Algonac Manufacturing Co. v. United States, 320
Amanda Acquisition Corp. v. Universal Foods Corp., 144
American Home Products Corp., *In re,* 216
American Home Products v. Johnson & Johnson, 217
American Medical Association v. Bowen, 245
Aromin v. State Farm Fire & Casualty Company, 146-148
Arthur Young & Co., United States v., 100
Avondale Industries, Incorporated v. Travelers Indemnity Company, 149-150

B

Baker v. F & F Investment, 307
Bakers Franchise Corp. v. Federal Trade Commission, 213
Balla v. Gambro, Inc., 351
Bank of Shaw, The v. Posey, 191
Banks v. National Collegiate Athletic Association, 260-261
Barber v. Time, Inc., 311
Barrera v. State Farm Mutual Automobile Insurance Co., 155
Basic, Incorporated v. Levinson, 113-114
Bay Cities Services, Inc., 335
Bayless v. Philadelphia National League Club, 266
Beauford v. Helmsley, 120-122
Becker v. Club Las Vegas, 282-283
Berger v. State, 296
Bhattal v. Grand Hyatt-New York, 288-289
Bick v. Peat Marwick and Main, 93
Billings Clinic, The v. Peat Marwick Main & Co., 101
Bily v. Arthur Young & Company, 90-92
BMY, A Division of HARSCO Corp., 335
Bose Corp. v. Consumers Union of U.S., Inc., 202
Boykin v. Hermitage Realty, 171
Bradler v. Craig, 188
Bratt v. International Business Machines Corp., 48
Brewer v. Roosevelt Motor Lodge, 296
Brickner v. FDIC, 180
Brooke Group Ltd. v. Brown & Williamson Tobacco Corporation, 204
Brown & Williamson Tobacco Corporation v. Jacobson, 310-311

C

C&J Fertilizer, Inc. v. Allied Mutual Insurance Co., 146
Camel Manufacturing Co. v. United States, 26
Campbell v. Acuff-Rose Music, Inc., 273
Cardinal Consulting Co. v. Circo Resorts, Inc., 292
Carl M. Loeb, Rhoades & Co., 107
Carson v. Here's Johnny Portable Toilets, Inc., 219
Castleglen, Inc. v. Commonwealth Savings Association, 190
Catellus Dev. Corp. v. United States, 242
Charles of the Ritz Dist. Corp. v. FTC, 212
Charles of the Ritz Group v. Quality King Distributors, Inc., 225
Cher v. Forum International, Ltd., 274
Chiarella v. United States, 111
Chiari v. City of League City, 66-67
Circon Acme, 335
City of Lost Angeles v. Preferred Communications, Inc., 317
Cleland v. Bronson Health Care Group, Inc., 251-253

363

Clifford v. Hollander, 313
CMI South, Inc. v. Occupational Safety and Healthy Review Commission, 74-75
Coca-Cola Co. v. Gemini Rising, Inc., 200
Coca-Cola, Inc. v. Tropicana Products, Inc., 217
Coleman v. Gulf Insurance Group, 160
Community for Creative Non-Violence v. Reid, 270
Con-Tech Sales Defined Benefit Trust v. Cockerham, 228
Connecticut v. Teal, 58
Conner v. Fort Gordon Bus Co., 70
Connor v. Great Western Savings & Loan Association, 188
Coolspring Stone Supply, Inc. v. American States Life Insurance Co., 160
Cooper v. Amster, 258
Cooper v. Jevne, 173
County of Broome v. Aetna Casualty & Surety Co., 148
Crain v. Burroughs Corp., 41
Credit Alliance v. Arthur Andersen & Co., 96
Crinkley v. Holiday Inns, Inc., 283-284
Cruz v. Ortho Pharmaceutical Corp., 242
Cutler-Hammer, Inc. v. United States, 335

D

DAR Construction, Inc., United States v., 239
Datapoint Corp. v. Plaza Securities Co., 135
Daugherty v. Kessler, 170
Davidow v. Inwood North Professional Group—Phase I, 166-168
Dawn Associates v. Links, 274
DC Comics, Inc. v. Filmation Associates, 273
DeFillippo v. National Broadcasting Co., 279
DeMatteo Construction Co. v. United States, 320
Doe v. New Bedford Housing Authority, 176
Doe v. Sarasota-Bradenton Television Co., 314
Dold v. Outrigger Hotel, 290-291
Dominguez v. Brackey Enterprises, Inc., 101
Donald Schutte, 331
Drotzmann's, Inc. v. McGraw-Hill, Inc., 309
Duane Jones Co. v. Burke, 19

E

EEOC. *See* Equal Employment Opportunity Commission
Eldridge v. Downtowner Hotel, 285
Elkins, United States v., 24
Emergency Devices, Inc., *In re,* 212
Emily v. Bayne, 175
Entrepreneur, Ltd. v. Yasuna, 169
Equal Employment Opportunity Commission v. Arabian American Oil Co., 70
Equal Employment Opportunity Commission v. Carolina Freight, 59
Equal Employment Opportunity Commission v. Townley Engineering & Manufacturing Co., 71
Ernst & Ernst v. Hochfelder, 125
Eversharp, Inc., *In re,* 216

F

Falls v. Sporting News Publishing Co., 47
Fargo Women's Health Organization, Inc. v. FM Women's Help and Caring Connection, 223
Federal Communications Commission v. Midwest Video Corp., 304, 318
Federal Communications Commission v. Sanders Bros. Radio Station, 302
Federal Food Service, Inc. v. Donovan, 331-332
Federal Trade commission v. Borden, Co., 208
Fera v. Village Plaza, Inc., 170
57 E. 54 Realty Corp. v. Gay Nineties Realty Corp., 169
First Federal Savings and Loan Association v. Twin Cities Savings Bank, FSB, 4-5
First Overseas Inv. Corp. v. Cotton, 285
Fish v. Los Angeles Dodgers Baseball Club, 265
Five Platters, Inc., The v. Purdie, 274
Flanigan v. Prudential Federal Savings & Loan Ass'n, 53
Fleet Factors Corp., United States v., 242
Florida State Conference of Branches of the NAACP v. Federal Communications Commission, 299-300
Flynn v. Bass Brothers Enterprises, 113
Foley v. Interactive Data Corp., 44
Ford v. Gouin, 280
Fossett v. Davis, 170
Foxx v. Williams, 268
Fragrante v. City and County of Honolulu, 71
Francis College v. Al-Khazraji, 55
Francisco v. Hartford Gynecological Center, Inc., 249
Freeman & Mills, Incorporated v. Belcher Oil Co., 4
FTC. *See* Federal Trade Commission

G

Gargiulo v. Gargiulo, 80
Garner v. Wilfinbarger, 353
Garrett v. Coast & Southern Federal Savings and Loan Ass'n, 176
Garzilli v. Howard Johnson's Motor Lodges, Inc., 283
Gilliam v. American Broadcasting Companies, Inc., 274-276
Globe Newspaper Co. v. Superior Court, 308
Goncalves v. Regent International Hotels, Ltd., 287
Gordinier v. Aetna Casualty and Surety Co., 146
Grand Jury Investigation, *In re,* 340
Grand Metropolitan PLC v. Pillsbury Co., 144
Great American Insurance Company v. Aetna Casualty and Surety Company, 156
Greenstein, Logan & Co. v. Burgess Marketing, Inc., 93
Greenway Investments General partnership v. Signet Bank/Maryland, 185-186

H

Haagen-Dazs, Inc. v. Frusen Gladje, Ltd., 219
Hackbart v. Cincinnati Bengals, 265
Halla Nursery, Inc. v. Baumann-Firrie & Co., 93
Hancock v. American Steel & Wire Co., 198
Hansen Brothers Logging, 78
Hardy v. Procter & Gamble Mfg. Co., 222
Harmonica Man, Inc., The v. Godfrey, 202
Harris v. Forklift Systems, Inc., 60
Hartford life Ins. Co. v. Randall, 176
Hayes Int'l Corp., United States v., 238
Heen & Flint Associates v. Travelers Indem. Co., 152
Helle v. Landmark, Inc., 41
Helman v. Murry's Steaks, Inc., 341-342
Henderson v. Heyer-Schulte Corp., 247
Herbster v. North American Co. for Life and Health Insurance, 351
Hoffman v. Federal Deposit Insurance Corporation, 180-181
Hoffman v. Red Owl Stores, Inc., 7
Hoflin, United States v., 236-238
Holloman v. Life Insurance Co., 157
Home Box Office, Inc. v. Wilkinson, 317
Houchins v. KQED, 308
Hustler Magazine, Inc. v. Falwell, 317
Hutchinson v. Proxmire, 317

I

Idaho v. Bunker Hill Co., 230
In re _____ (see name of party)
Internal Revenue Service (IRS), 93
International Boxing Club, Inc. v. United States, 262
International Business Machines Corp., 325
Ives Laboratories, Inc. v. Darby Drug Co., Inc., 208

J

Jackson v. Fontenot Building, Inc., 172
Japan Line, Ltd. v. County of Los Angeles, 36
Johns Manville Products v. Contra County Superior Court, 84
Johnson & Johnson-Merck Consumer Pharmaceuticals Company v. Rhone-Poulenc Rorer Pharmaceuticals, Inc., 218
Jones v. NCAA, 260
Jordache Enterprises, Inc. v. Hogg Wyld, Ltd., 198-199

K

Kayser-Roth Corp., United States, v., 241
Kelley v. Schlumberger Technology Corp., 49, 53
King-Seeley Thermos Co. v. Aladdin Industries, Inc., 197
Kingsmen v. K-Tel International, Ltd., 280
Kirshoffner v. Quam, 265
Korr v. Thomas Emery's Sons, Inc., 281
Kraft v. Metromedia, Inc., 45
Kumpf v. Steinhaus, 53

L

L. L. Bean, Inc. v. Drake Publishers, Inc., 201-202
Landon v. Twentieth Century-Fox Film Corp., 279
Larimore v. Comptroller of the Currency, 180
Larsen v. United Federal Savings & Loan Association, 187
Las Vegas Television, Inc., 299
Latecoere International, Inc. v. U.S. Department of the Navy, 325-326
Lazar v. Thermal Equipment Corp., 87
Lee v. Beauchene, 266
Lee v. National League Baseball Club, 265
Leigh Furniture & Carpet Co. v. Isom, 195-196
Letter to Lonnie King, 304

Levy v. Bendetson, 171
Lewis v. United Airlines, 48
Life Insurance Co. v. Lopez, 157
Lincoln Grain, Inc. v. Coopers & Lybrand, 92, 104
Lindner v. Barlow, Davis & Wood, 90
Lititz Mutual Insurance Co. v. Commonwealth, 152
Lockheed Aircraft Corp. v. United States, 335
Los Angeles Memorial Coliseum v. National Football League, 262

M

Mansfield v. American Telephone & Telegraph Corporation, 45-47
Maybelline Co. v. Noxell Corp., 217
Medico-Dental Bldg. Co. v. Horton & Converse, 176
Memorex Corp., 326
Memphis Publishing Co. v. Nichols, 309
Mennen Co. v. Gillette Co., 219
Merritt v. Colonial Foods, Inc., 141
Messina V. Sheraton Corporation of America, 283
Midler v. Ford Motor Company, 221-222
Miller Brewing Co. v. G. Heileman Brewing Co., Inc., 197
Milliron v. Francke, 248
Minnesota v. Mid-Minnesota Associated Physicians, 255
Mobile Drilling Co., 321
Monroe Communications Corporation v. Federal Communications Commission, 301
Montandon v. Triangle Publications, Inc., 309
Mosley v. Perpetual Savings & Loan Association, 187
Motown Record Corporation v. Brockert, 270
Mottolo, United States v., 234

N

National Basketball Association v. Williams, 263
National Collegiate Athletic Association v. Board of Regents of the University of Oklahoma, 260
National Collegiate Athletic Association v. Tarkanian, 262
National Funeral Services, Inc. v. Rockefeller, 210-212
National Helium Corp. v. Morton, 327
National Realty and Construction Co., Inc. v. OSHRC, 74
National Refining Co. v. Benzo Gas Motor Fuel Co., 208

NCAA. *See* National Collegiate Athletic Association
New York Life Insurance Company v. Johnson, 153-155
999 v. CIT Corporation, 184
Normand v. Research Institute of America, Inc., 71
Northeastern Pharmaceutical and Chemical Co., Inc., United States v., 235
Norton v. Argonaut Insurance Company, 258
Novosel v. Nationwide Insurance Co., 42

O

O'Brien v. Pabst Sales Co., 222
O'Connor v. CertainTeed Corporation, 16-17
O'Hagan, United States v., 112
Ocean Spray Cranberries, Inc., United States v., 238
Ocean State Physicians Health Plan, Inc. v. Blue Cross & Blue Shield of Rhode Island, 258
Oki America, Inc. v. Microtech International, Inc., 3-4
Oliver Productions, Inc., *In re* Request of, 303-304
Olivia N. v. National Broadcasting Co., 276

P

Paolillo v. Dresser Industries, Inc., 65
Paramount Communications, Inc. v. QVC Network, Inc., 133
Parker v. Centre Group Limited Partnership, 266-267
Paramount Communications, Inc. v. Time, Inc., 136
Patrick v. Burget, 244
Patterson v. McLean Credit Union, 62
Pedroza v. Bryant, 258
People v. Thorpe, 296
Pfizer, Inc., *In re*, 225
Pierce v. Ortho Pharmaceutical Corp., 42-44
Pine River State Bank v. Mettille, 38
Pinter v. Dahl, 109-110
Platner v. Cash & Thomas Contractors, Inc., 70
Poling v. Wisconsin Physicians Service, 159
Poommipanit v. Sloan, 163
Porter v. Dallas Independent School District, 81
Posadas de Puerto Rico Associates v. Tourism Company of Puerto Rico, 210
Presto v. Sequoia Systems, 194
Professional Service Industries, Inc. v. Kimbrell, 353

Protex Industries, Inc., United States v., 236
Prudential Insurance Co. v. Executive Estates, Inc., 187
Purcell v. Zimbalman, 249

Q

QualMed, Inc. v. Office of Civilian Health and Medical Program of the Uniformed Services, 322-323

R

R. H. Bishop Co., 79
Raritan River Steel Co. v. Cherry, Beckaert & Holland, 98
Red Lion Broadcasting Co. v. FCC, 307
Reed v. Classified Parking System, 166
Reed v. King, 171-172
Removatron International Corporation v. Federal Trade Commission, 214-215
Reves v. Ernst & Young, 100
Revlon, Inc. v. MacAndrews & Forbes Holdings, Inc. 136
Rewe-Zentral, AG Bundesmomopol ver Waltung fur Branntwein, 36
Richards Medical Company v. United States, 27-28
Riverside Market Development Corp. v. International Building Products, 234-235
Robert Wooler Company v. The Fidelity Bank, 94-95
Robinson v. McAllen State Bank, 184
Rose v. Giammati, 264
RSO Records, Inc. v. Peri, 271
Rulon-Miller v. International Business Machines Corp., 39-40

S

Sahadi v. Continental Illinois National Bank and Trust Company of Chicago, 184
St. Louis S.F.R. Co. v. Wade, 194
Salisbury v. St. Regis-Sheraton Hotel, 287
Samjens Partners I v. Burlington Industries, Inc., 136-138
Savers Federal Savings & Loan Association v. Reetz, 164-165
Schatz v. York Steak House, 84
Scher v. Liberty Travel Service, 291
Schoenbaum v. Firstbrook, 33

Schreiber v. Burlington Northern, Inc., 125
Seattle Stevedoring Co., 87
Securities and Exchange Commission v. Ridenour, 118-119
Securities and Exchange Commission v. Texas Gulf Sulfur, 111
Security Insurance Co. v. Nasser, 81-82
Seelbach, Inc. v. Cadick, 285
Sentry Insurance v. Brown, 152
Serbin v. Ziebart Intern. Corp., 219
Severn Companies, Inc., 325
Shamrock Holding, Inc. v. Polaroid Corp., 135
Sheinkopf v. Stone, 338-339
Sheppard v. Maxwell, 314
Silberg v. California Life Insurance Co., 151
Silver Hills Country Club v. Sobieski, 106
Sipple v. Chronicle Publishing Company, 312-313
Siskind v. Newton-John, 271-272
Sletteland v. Federal Deposit Insurance Corporation, 179
Smiley v. Manchester Insurance & Indemnity Company of St. Louis, 345-346
Smith v. Van Gorkom, 129-131
Smith-Corona Group v. United States, 36
Spancrete Northeast, Inc. v. Occupational Safety and Health Review Commission, 76-78
Spargnapani v. Wright, 175
Sperka v. Little Sabine Bay, Inc., 296
Spiller v. Barclay Hotel, 282
Sportsmen's Boating Corporation v. Hensley, 196
Stephens Industries, Inc. v. Haskins & Sells, 98
Steuer v. National Medical Enterprises, 253
Sunshine State Bank v. FDIC, 191
Swerdloff v. Miami National Bank, 187
Sztorc v. Northwest Hospital, 248

T

Taggart v. Time Incorporated, 63-64
Tanglewood East Homeowners v. Charles-Thomas, Inc., 229-230
Teca-Print A.G. v. Amacoil Machinery, Inc., 36
Technical Tape Corp. v. Industrial Commission, 83
Tenants' Corp. v. Max Rothenburg & Co., 104
Tennant v. Lawton, 173
Thomas v. Bourdette, 53
Todorov v. DCH Health Care Authority, 254-255
Torncello v. United States, 327-328

Toussaint v. Blue Cross & Blue Shield of Michigan, 53
Turner Broadcasting System, Inc. v. CBS, Inc., 134
Turner Broadcasting System, Inc. v. Federal Communications Commission, 306
TW Services, Inc. v. SWT Acquisition Corp., 144

U

U-Haul, Int'l v. Jartran, Inc., 218
U.S. Health Care v. Healthsource, 255
United States v. _____ (see name of party)
United States Steel Group v. United States, 30-31
Unocal Corp. v. Mesa Petroleum Co., 132
Upjohn Co. v. United States, 339

V

Variety Children's Hospital v. Osle, 258
Vaughn v. Edel, 56-58
Verway v. Blincoe Packing Co., 45
Vidal Sassoon, Inc. v. Bristol Myers Co., 225
Video Ventures, Inc., 322
Virgil v. Sports Illustrated, Inc., 311
Virginia State Board of Pharmacy v. Virginia Citizens Consumer Council, 209

W

Wagenheim v. Alexander Grant & Co., 99
Waggoner v. STAAR Surgical Company, 343-344
Walker v. IRS, 56
Walt Disney Productions v. Air Pirates, 272
Walters v. Fullwood, 264
Ward, United States v., 228
Warner Brothers, Inc. v. Gay Toys, Inc., 208
Weinberger v. UOP, Inc., 139-140
Wetherbee v. United Insurance Co. of America, 151
Whaley Engineering Corp., 78
White, United States v., 330
Wickline v. State, 245-246
William R. Davis & Son, Co., 74
Wisconsin Ave. Associates, Inc. v. 2720 Wisconsin Ave. Co-Operative Association, 163

Y

Yale Electric Corp. v. Robertson, 200
Young v. Caribbean Associates, Inc., 285

Z

Zamora v. Columbia Broadcasting Systems, 276
Zenith Radio Corporation v. United States, 29

Index

A

Abandonment
  of leased property, 169-170
  of trademark, 200
Acceleration clause, 162, 163
Accounting law, 89-104
  actually foreseen test in, 94-95
  balancing test in, 96
  confidentiality in, 97-99
  disclaimers in, 97
  ethics in, 100-101
  international business law and, 101
  liability in, 94-98
  privity test in, 94-95
  reasonable foreseeability test in, 96
  Restatement (Second) of Torts and, 94-95
Acquired immune deficiency syndrome (AIDS)
  health care law and, 257
  insurance law and, 157-158
  real estate and, 174
  testing for, 49-50
Acquisitions, 127-144
  bank holding companies and, 183
  control-share acquisition statutes and, 138
  directors' duties in, 128-138
  international business law and, 142-143
  See also Mergers; Takeovers
Actually foreseen test, 94-95
ADA. *See* Americans with Disabilities Act (ADA)
ADEA. *See* Age Discrimination in Employment Act (ADEA)
Administrative law judge (ALJ), 212
ADR. *See* Alternative dispute resolution (ADR)
Ad valorem rate, 27
Advertising, by attorneys, 352
Advertising law, 209-226
  comparative advertising and, 215-219, 220, 224
  deceptive advertising and, 212-215
  ethics and, 223-224
  false testimonials and, 213
  First Amendment and, 202, 209-212
  government regulation of advertising and, 210-219
  honesty duty and, 6
  international, 224-225
  Lanham Act and, 216-219
  misappropriation and, 219, 221-222
  negligence in, 222-223
  private regulation of advertising and, 219
  social responsibility and, 223-224
"Advertorials," 210
Affirmative action, 61-62
  government contracts and, 324
Africa, 239
AFTRA. *See* American Federation of Television and Radio Artists (AFTRA)
Age discrimination, 62-65
Age Discrimination in Employment Act (ADEA), 62-65
Agricultural Foreign Investment Disclosure Act, 175
AICPA. *See* American Institute of Certified Public Accountants (AICPA)
AIDS. *See* Acquired immune deficiency syndrome (AIDS)
Alcohol service, 293
ALJ. *See* Administrative law judge (ALJ)
Alternative dispute resolution (ADR), 349-350
American Association of Advertising Agencies, 6
American Bar Association, 339
Americans with Disabilities Act (ADA), 49-50, 65-68
American Federation of Television and Radio Artists (AFTRA), 267-268, 269
American Institute of Certified Public Accountants (AICPA), 89-92, 94, 99
  management consulting and, 99-100
American Medical Association, 257
Ambiguity doctrine, 146
ANCOM. *See* Andean Common Market (ANCOM)
Andean Common Market (ANCOM), 34-35
Antidilution statutes, 200-202
Antidumping duties, 30
Anti-takeover statutes, 138
Antitrust laws
  bank mergers and, 183
  health care law and, 244, 253-255
  HMOs and, 255
  hospitality management law and, 294
  and legal representation of business, 351
  lender liability and, 186-187
  mergers and acquistions and, 141
  sports law and, 260, 262-264
  unfair competition and, 206
Appraisal, 141, 183
  negligent misrepresentation in, 188
Arbitration, 349, 350, 351
Arms Export Control Act, 22-26
ARPA. *See* Association of Representatives of Professional Athletes (ARPA)
Artists, 266-268, 270
  rights of, 274-276
  See also Entertainment law
Asian law, 102
Association of Representatives of Professional Athletes (ARPA), 277
Assumption of risk, 285
Attorney-client privilege, 339-340
  ethics and, 350, 351
  exceptions to, 340-342
  international business law and, 351-352
  whistle-blowing and, 350-351
Attorney-client relationship, 337-339
  settlements and, 345
Attorneys/lawyers
  business and, 337
  foreign, 351-352
  work-product privilege and, 342
At-will contract, 37-38
  public policy exception to, 41-44
Auction
  foreclosure, 164
  government contracts and, 323
  for shareholders, 136-138
Auditing, 89, 93-98
  disclaimers and, 98
  ethics in, 100-101
  social, 18
  unaudited reports and, 93-95
  See also Generally Accepted Auditing Standards (GAAS)

Australia, health care law in, 257
Austria
  advertising law in, 224
  environmental law in, 241

B

Bad faith
  in insurance law, 150-152, 155
  unfair competition and, 205
Bailment, 288
Balancing test, 96-98
Bank holding companies, 183
Bank Holding Company Act, 183, 186-187
Bank Merger Act, 183
Bank of Japan, 34
Bank of North America, 177
Banks, 177-191
  closure of, 182-183
  ethics and, 188-189
  failure of, 181-182
  international business law and, 189-190
  junk bonds and, 142
  loan termination by, 184
  mergers of, 183
  mortgages and. *See* Mortgages
  participation agreements by, 184-185
  unsafe and unsound practices of, 180-181, 182, 190
Belgium, advertising law in, 224
Berne Convention, 278
"Bespeaks caution" doctrine, 109
Bill of lading, 27
Bill of Rights, fairness and, 9
Board of directors. *See* Directors (board of)
Bona fide news event, 302-304
Books, 266, 270
"Bounty-hunter" provision, 329
Branch banking, 183, 190
Brazil, copyright law in, 279
Breach of contract, 184
  auditing and, 89
  bad faith in, 205. *See also* Bad faith
  in commercial leasing, 168-169
  defenses to, 194-195
  in employment, 37, 39-40
  fair competition and, 194-195
  "fundamental," 22
  in government contract, 327-328
  hotel reservations and, 294
  international business law and, 21, 22
  liquidated damages for, 164
  malice and, 194
  material, 168-169
  mortgages and, 164
  opportunistic, 205

  privilege of, 194
  sports law and, 264
  See also Interference with contract
Breach of duty
  of due care, 129-131, 222-223
  entertainment law and, 266-267
  insider trading and, 122, 123
  lender liability and, 184
Break-up fee, 134
Bridging the gap, 200
British law
  accounting in, 102
  advertising in, 224
  hospitality management in, 295-296
  See also United Kingdom
Broadcasting
  cross-border, 316-317
  licenses for, 298-302
  regulations for, 302-305
  spectrum of, 297-298, 307
  See also Communications law; Radio; Television
Building codes, hospitality management law and, 293
Burden of proof
  in deceptive advertising cases, 213
  in employment discrimination, 62
Business, legal representation of. *See* Legal representation
Business, international. *See* International business law
Business beneficence, 10-15
Business ethics, 1-20
  advertising law and, 223-224
  AICPA and, 99, 100-101
  AIDS and, 157-158
  attorney-client privilege and, 342
  of banks, 188-189
  business beneficence and, 10-15
  codes of, 6, 15-17. *See also* Code of ethics
  communications law and, 315-316
  comparable worth and, 68-69
  corporate counsel and, 343, 350-351
  and export of hazardous waste, 239-240
  government contracts and, 321, 332-333
  health care law and, 255
  hospitality management law and, 294-295
  insurance law and, 157-158
  law and, 2-5. *See also* Legal representation
  mergers and, 141-142
  occupational safety and, 84-85
  profit maximization and, 1-2, 5
  in real estate, 173-174
  requirements of, 6-11
  social audits and, 18
  in sports law, 276-278

  unfair competition and, 206-207
  See also Whistle-blowing
Business judgment rule, 131, 132
Buy American Act, 324, 334

C

Cable Communications Policy Act, 305-306
Cable television, 305-306
Cable Television Consumer Protection and Competition Act, 306
Canada, accounting law in, 102
Care
  duty of due, 129-131, 222-223
  reasonable, 92
  standard of, 90-92, 247
Caribbean, hospitality management in, 295
Cartagena Agreement, 35
CBCA. *See* Change in Bank Control Act (CBCA)
CCL. *See* Commodity Control List (CCL)
Cease-and-desist order, 182, 213-214
Cellular car phones, 298
CERCLA. *See* Comprehensive Environmental Response Compensation and Liability Act (CERCLA)
Change in Bank Control Act (CBCA), 178-181
Changes clause, 327
Charitable immunity, 248
China
  advertising law in, 224
  health care law in, 257
Chinese wall, 101
Churning, 117-118
Civil law
  accounting law and, 98
  communications law and, 307, 308
  reporter's privilege and, 307-308
  restaurants and, 293
  securities law and, 115
Civil Rights Act, Title VII of. *See* Title VII (of Civil Rights Act)
Clayton Act, 255
Clean Air Act, 228, 232-233, 238-239
Clean Water Act, 238. *See also* Federal Water Pollution Control Act
COBRA. *See* Comprehensive Omnibus budget Reconciliation Act (COBRA)
Code of ethics, 6, 15-17
  of American Bar Association/attorneys, 339, 342, 350
  government contracts and, 332-333
  See also Business ethics
Code, Procurement, 334
Code of Professional Responsibility, 339
Code on Takeovers and Mergers, 143

Collateral, 161-162
   takeovers and, 128
Collective bargaining, in sports, 262-263
Commercial leasing, 166-170
Commercial speech, 210-212
Commission on Freedom of the Press, 315
Commodity Control List (CCL), 23
Common areas, 285, 287
Common carriers, 297, 304-305
   multipoint distribution service and, 306
Common law
   disparagement under, 202
   employment under, 37-38, 48, 79-80
   health care under, 250, 251
   hospital liability under, 248
   hotels under, 286, 288
   lender liability and, 184, 186
   securities law and, 117
Communications Act, 305
Communications law, 297-318
   broadcasting licenses and, 298-302
   broadcasting regulations and, 302-304
   common carriers and, 297, 304-305, 306
   defamation and, 47-48
   ethics and, 315-316
   First Amendment and, 302, 304, 307-308
   international, 316-317
   media malpractice in, 314
   reporter's privilege in, 307-308
   See also Mass media
Community ascertainment, 300
Comparable worth compensation, 69
Comparative advertising, 215-219, 220
   in international law, 224
Comparative negligence, hospitality management law and, 285
Compelled self-publication (doctrine of), 48
Competition in Contracting Act, 321, 322
Comprehensive Environmental Response Compensation and Liability Act (CERCLA), 186, 227-235
Comprehensive Omnibus budget Reconciliation Act (COBRA), 251-253
Confidentiality
   in accounting law, 97
   AIDS and, 257
   attorney-client privilege and, 340-341
   health care law and, 247, 257
   reporter's privilege and, 307
Conflict of interest
   in accounting law, 100-101
   in employment, 39-40

in legal representation of corporations, 342-344
Congress, business ethics and, 2
Consideration (in contract), 7
Constitution, U.S.
   and drug testing of employees, 49
   fairness and, 9
   privacy rights and, 48
Consumer protection laws
   cable television and, 306
   hospitality management law and, 294
Contingency fees, 352
Contract liability, 187
Contracts
   accounting and, 90
   of adhesion, 145
   business ethics and, 2-3
   cost plus incentive fee, 320
   cost reimbursement, 319-320
   employment. *See* Employment
   entertainment, 266-270
   fixed price, 319
   fixed price with economic price adjustment, 319
   government, 319-336
   implied-in-fact, 320
   insurance, 145-160
   interference with, 170, 193-196
   international, 21-22. *See also* International business law, 351
   legal representation and, 351
   loan. *See* Lender liability; Mortgages
   malicious denial of, 3-4
   promise in, 7
   quasi-, 320
   sports, 264, 277-278. *See also* Entertainment law
   torts and, 3-4
   work-product privilege and, 342
   See also Breach of contract
Contributory fault, 247
Contributory negligence, in accounting law, 91-92
Control-group limitation, 339-340
Control-share acquisition statutes, 138
Conversion, hospitality management law and, 288-289
Copyrights, 266, 270-273
   "fair use" and, 272-273
   international business law and, 278-279
   licensing and, 273
   piracy and, 278-279
Corporations
   accounting for. *See* Accounting law
   attorney-client privilege and, 339-340
   business ethics and, 1-2, 5-20
   charitable contributions by, 10-15
   defalcations by employees of, 92

environmental law and. *See* Environmental law
   fraudulent disclosures by, 113-115
   legal representation of, 342-346
   manager's privilege in, 194
   mergers of, 127-144
   negligence of, 249
   securities law and. *See* Securities law
   work-product privilege and, 342
Cost justification, 205
Cost plus incentive fee contract, 320
Cost reimbursement contract, 319-320
Council of Europe, 256
Countervailing duties, 29-32
Court of International Trade, 29-32
Covenants, 168
Credit regulations, hospitality management law and, 293
Criminal False Claims Act, 330
Criminal False Statements Act. 329, 330
Criminal law
   accounting law and, 100
   attorney-client privilege and, 342
   banks and, 180
   communications law and, 307, 308, 314
   environmental law and, 235-239
   government contracts and, 329-330
   OSHA and, 79
   reporter's privilege and, 307-308
   securities law and, 114-115
   Sixth Amendment and, 9
Crown jewels, 134
Customs Service, 26-32, 207-208

D

Damages
   in advertising law, 215, 217
   in communications law, 309
   for defamation, 309, 310-311
   double or treble, 205
   in hospitality management law, 291
   in insurance law, 150
   in international business law, 21, 22
   liquidated, 164
   punitive, 44
   torts and, 44
Dango, 335
DBS spillover, 315-317
Death benefits, under workers' compensation, 83
Debarment, 330-332, 333
Deceit, attorney-client privilege and, 341
Deceptive advertising, 212-215, 223
   comparative advertising and, 217
Deceptive trade practices, 204-205
   in sports, 264
Decision tree analysis, 349
Defalcations, 90

Defamation
    communications law and, 308-311
    international business law and, 317
    truth as defense to, 309
    wrongful discharge and, 45, 47-48
Default, 164-166
Defective pricing, 328
Defense Contract Audit Agency, 328
Defense contracts. *See* Government contracts
Defense Industry Initiatives on Business Ethics and Conduct, 333
Deficiency judgment, 164-166
Depositions, 325
Diagnosis-Related Groups (DRGs), 244-245
"Dial-a-porn," 305
Directive 73/239, 159
Directors (board of)
    on banks, 180-181, 183
    duties of, 128-138
    staggered terms for, 135
    stakeholders and, 141
Directors Guild of America, 274
Disabled persons
    employment discrimination and, 65-68
    workers' compensation and, 83-84
    See also Americans with Disabilities Act (ADA)
Disclaimer
    in accounting law, 97
    in employee manual, 41
Disclosure
    accounting law and, 97, 98
    attorney-client privilege and, 342, 351
    defamation and, 48
    environmental law and, 233
    fraudulent corporate, 113-115
    medical malpractice and, 247
    real estate and, 171-173, 173-174
    securities law and, 113-115, 116
    of "soft" vs. "hard" information, 113
Discovery requests, 346
Discrimination
    in access to information, 308
    age, 62-65
    AIDS and, 174
    by banks, 188
    employment. *See* Employment discrimination
    against foreign lawyers, 352
    against homosexuals, 174
    pretext and, 56, 64
    racial. *See* Racial discrimination
    real estate and, 174
    sex, 58
Dishonesty
    attorney-client privilege and, 341

    See also Honesty duty
Disparagement, 202-203
Disparate impact, 58-59
    under ADA, 68
    affirmative action and, 62
Disparate treatment, 56-58
    under ADA, 68
Distribution License, 23
Diversity of media ownership, 299
Doctrine of. *See* specific doctrine
Document retention and destruction, 346-347, 351
"Double-leasing," 169
Double damages, 205
Draft Convention on the Hotelkeeper's Contract, 295-296
Dram shop laws, 293
DRGs. *See* Diagnosis-Related Groups (DRGs)
Drug-Free Workplace Act, 49
Drug testing, 49
Due process, 9
Due-on-sale clause, 162
Dumping
    of merchandise, 29
    of patients, 250-253
    of waste, 148
Duress, lender liability and, 184
Duties (on imports), 26-32
Duty of
    accountants, 90
    care, 251
    due care, 129-131, 222-223
    fair dealing, 141
    fairness, 139. *See also* Fairness
    honesty. *See* Honesty duty
    loyalty. *See* Loyalty duty
    rescue, 251, 285-286
    See also Fiduciary duty
Duty to
    defend, 149-150
    investigate insurance claim, 155, 157
    survey property under construction, 187

E

ECCN. *See* Export Commodity Control Number (ECCN)
EEOC. *See* Equal Employment Opportunity Commission (EEOC)
Electronic Communications Privacy Act, 50
Embargos, 24
Emotional/mental distress
    and drug testing of employees, 49
    hospitality management law and, 291, 292
    intentional infliction of, 39-40, 45-48
    media malpractice and, 313

    See also Mental anguish
Employee Polygraph Protection Act, 48-49
Employees
    accounting law and, 92
    AIDS testing of, 49-50
    drug testing of, 49
    enhanced monitoring of, 50
    government, 49
    international business law concerning, 86-87
    negligence by, 74-75
    polygraph testing of, 48-49
    privacy of, 39-40, 48-50
    rights of individual, 37-53
    See also Occupational safety
Employee stock option plan (ESOP), 134-135
Employers
    affirmative action and, 61-62
    liability of, 61, 78
    OSHA and, 78
Employment
    at-will contracts for, 37-38, 41-44
    business ethics and, 7-8, 16-17
    cable television and, 306
    Family and Medical Leave Act and, 50
    implied contract of, 38-41
    loyalty duty and, 7-8
    whistle-blowing and, 44, 51
    wrongful discharge from. *See* Wrongful discharge
    See also Occupational safety
Employment discrimination, 55-71
    affirmative action, 61-62
    based on age, 62-65
    arrest records and, 59
    cable television and, 306
    comparable worth and, 69
    disparate impact, 58-59, 62
    disparate treatment, 56-58
    FCC and, 299-300
    hospitality management law and, 294
    international business law and, 69-70
    racial, 55-59, 62
    Section 1981 and, 62
    sex discrimination in, 58
    "sex plus," 58
    sexual harassment and, 59-61, 62
    Title VII and, 55-62
Employment manuals, 38-41
Endangered Species Act, 239
Enhanced monitoring, 50
Entertainment law, 266-280
    artists' rights in, 274-276
    copyrights in. *See* Copyrights
    royalty payments in, 273
Environmental Crimes Unit, 235
Environmental law, 227-242
    business liability in, 231-233

CERCLA and, 227-235
criminal liability in, 235-239
defenses in, 230-232
ethics and, 239-240
individual liability in, 234-235
international, 241
See also Hazardous waste; Pollution
Environmental Protection Agency
 (EPA), 235, 238-239
 RCRA and, 239-240
EPA. *See* Environmental Protection
 Agency (EPA)
Equal Employment Opportunity
 Commission (EEOC), 58-59
 ADA and, 68
 age discrimination and, 63
Equal time rule, 302-304
ESOP. *See* Employee stock option plan
 (ESOP)
Ethics. *See* Business ethics
Ethics Resource Center, 333
Europe
 advertising law in, 224-225
 artists' rights in, 274
 communications law in, 316-317
 environmental law in, 241
 government contracts in, 334
 health care law in, 256
 hospitality management in, 295-296
 social audits in, 18
European Community (EC)
 accounting law in, 103
 advertising law in, 225
 banks in, 189-190
 communications law in, 316-317
 employment discrimination in, 70
 government contracts in, 334
 insider trading in, 125
 insurance law in, 158-159
 legal representation in, 352
 takeovers in, 143
European Human Rights Convention, 317
Eviction, by hotel, 290
Exclusivity clause, HMOs and, 255
Exclusivity system, 84
Expected clause, 148
Export Administration Act, 22, 23-26
Export Administration Regulations, 26
Export Commodity Control Number
 (ECCN), 24
Exports, 22-26
 hazardous waste and, 239-240

F

Failing company defense, 255
Fair competition, 194-195
Fair Credit Reporting Act, 183
Fairness
 business ethics and, 8-9
 communications law and, 304
 mergers and, 139-141
Fairness opinion, 139-141
Fair use, 272-273
False Claims Act (FCA), 329
False representation
 in accounting, 90, 92-93
 in advertising. *See* Deceptive
  advertising
 by banks, 180
 in corporate disclosures, 113, 115
 in real estate fraud, 171, 173
 See also Misrepresentation
False testimonials, 213
Family and Medical Leave Act
 (FMLA), 50
FASB. *See* Financial Accounting
 Standards Board (FASB)
FCA. *See* False Claims Act (FCA)
FCC. *See* Federal Communications
 Commission (FCC)
FDIC. *See* Federal Deposit Insurance
 Corporation (FDIC)
Federal Acquisition Streamlining Act,
 323-324
Federal Communications Commission
 (FCC), 297-306
 cable television and, 305-306. *See
  also* Television
 common carrier regulation and,
  297, 304-305
 multipoint distribution service and,
  306
Federal Deposit Insurance Corporation
 (FDIC), 177-183
Federal Insecticide, Fungicide and
 Rodenticide Act, 239
Federal Reserve Board, 177-178
Federal Trade Commission (FTC), 141,
 205, 212-216
Federal Water Pollution Control Act,
 228, 238
Fiduciary duty
 of accountant, 90
 auction and, 137-138
 entertainment law and, 266-267
 insider trading and, 122, 123-124
 lender liability and, 184
 mergers and, 137-138, 139
Fifth Amendment, 9
Financial Accounting Standards Board
 (FASB), 89, 98
Financial Institutions Reform,
 Recovery and Enforcement Act
 (FIRREA), 183
FIRREA. *See* Financial Institutions
 Reform, Recovery and
 Enforcement Act (FIRREA)
First Amendment
 advertising and, 202, 209-212
 communications law and, 302, 304,
  306-308
 disparagement and, 202
 fairness doctrine and, 304
Fixed price contract, 319
 with economic price adjustment, 319
Flip-in/flip-over poison pill, 132
FMLA. *See* Family and Medical Leave
 Act (FMLA)
Foreclosure, 164-166
Foreign capital markets, 32-33
Foreign direct investment, 33-36, 174-175
Foreign Investment in Real Property Tax
 Act, 175
"Foreign trade zones," 29
France/French law
 artists' rights in, 274
 copyright law in, 278
 health care in, 257
 hospitality management in, 295
 takeovers in, 143
Franchises, cable television and, 305
Fraud
 accounting, 96
 advertising law and, 223
 attorney-client privilege and, 342
 business ethics and, 4-5
 communications law and, 305
 contractor, 328, 329-332
 environmental law and, 233
 international business law and, 32-33
 lender liability and, 184, 185
 mail and wire, 120
 Medicare, 246
 real estate, 170-173
 securities, 32-33, 113-115. *See also*
  Securities law
 silence as, 173
 wrongful discharge and, 45
 See also Statute of Frauds
"Fraud on the market" theory, 115-116
Fraudulent concealment, workers' compensation and, 84
Fraudulent corporate disclosure, 113-115
Free agency, 262
Freedom of the press
 commission on, 315
 defamation and, 309, 311
 See also First Amendment
Freedom of speech
 commercial speech and, 210-212
 wrongful discharge and, 41
 See also First Amendment
FTC. *See* Federal Trade Commission
 (FTC)

G

GAAP. *See* Generally Accepted
 Accounting Principles (GAAP)
GAAS. *See* Generally Accepted Auditing
 Standards (GAAS)

GAO. *See* General Accounting Office (GAO)
GATT. *See* General Agreement on Tariffs and Trade (GATT)
General Accounting Office (GAO), 325, 326
General Agreement on Tariffs and Trade (GATT), 334
General duty clause, 73-75
Generalized System of Preferences (GSP), 28-29
General License, 23, 24
Generally Accepted Accounting Principles (GAAP), 89-90
   international business law and, 101-102
   SEC and, 98
Generally Accepted Auditing Standards (GAAS), 89-90, 98
General Services Board of Contract Appeals (GSBCA), 325, 326
Generic trademark, 197
"Gentlemen's agreement," 184
Germany/German law
   accounting law in, 102
   advertising law in, 225
   environmental law in, 241
   hospitality management in, 295
Globalization, 21
Going-private transaction, 113, 128
Golden parachutes, 135
Goodbye fee, 134
Good cause defense, 44-45
Good character, 299
Good faith
   in accounting, 90
   in advertising, 213
   insurance law and, 148, 157
   lender liability and, 185-186
   medical malpractice and, 247
Good samaritan statutes, 247
Government contracts, 319-336
   affirmative action and, 324
   competition for, 321-324
   Criminal False Claims Act and, 330
   Criminal False Statements Act and, 329, 330
   ethics and, 332-333
   False Claims Act and, 329
   formation of, 320-321
   fraud in, 328, 329-332
   international, 334
   scandal involving, 1
   suspension and debarment regarding, 330-332, 333
   Truth in Negotiations Act and, 328-329
   types of, 319-320
Government regulation
   of advertising, 210-219
   of banks, 177-191
   business ethics and, 3
   of cable television, 305-306
   of communications, 297-318
   environmental, 227-242
   of health care, 243-258
   of hotels, 293
   of mortgages, 162
   of restaurants, 293-294
   of securities, 115-116, 117-120
   of takeovers, 141-142
   trademark infringment and, 197-198
"Grey market," 207-208
Gross negligence
   in accounting law, 96
   in bank liability, 184
GSBCA. *See* General Services Board of Contract Appeals (GSBCA)GSP. *See* Generalized System of Preferences (GSP)
Guest-innkeeper relationship, 281-296

H

Habitability, warranty of, 168
Handicapped persons, 65. *See also* Americans with Disabilities Act (ADA)
"Hard" information, 113
Harm, avoiding, 8
Hart-Scott-Rodino Antitrust Improvements Act, 141
Hazardous waste, 227-235
   ethics and export of, 239-240
   insurance law and, 145, 149-150
   See also Environmental law; Pollution
HCQIA. *See* Health Care Quality Improvement Act (HCQIA)
Health and Human Services (HHS), Department of, 244
Health care law, 243-258
   antitrust liability and, 253-255
   ethics and, 256
   HMOs and, 255
   international, 257
   medical malpractice and, 246-249
   mergers and, 255
   patient "dumping" and, 250-253
   reimbursement controls in, 244-249
Health Care Quality Improvement Act (HCQIA), 244, 249, 255
Health maintenance organizations (HMOs), 255
Hello fee, 134
HHS. *See* Health and Human Services (HHS), Department of
HMOs. *See* Health maintenance organizations (HMOs)
Homosexuals, discrimination against, 174

"Honest error in judgment" rule, 247
Honesty duty, 6
   advertising law and, 213
   in AIDS disclosure, 174
   insider trading and, 123-124
   loyalty duty and, 7
   real estate and, 174
   See also Dishonesty
Hospitality management law, 281-296
   ethics and, 294-295
   rights of guests in, 292
   rights of innkeepers in, 292-293
Hospitals
   antitrust liability of, 253-255
   COBRA and, 251-253
   ethics and, 255
   HCQIA and, 244
   JCAH and, 246
   liability of, 248-250
   patients "dumped" at, 250-253
Hostile environment harassment, 59-61
Hostile takeover, 132. *See also* Mergers; Takeovers
Hotels, 281-293, 294-296
   bailment and, 288
   common areas of, 285, 287
   duty of rescue by, 285-286
   ethics and, 294-295
   eviction from, 290
   international business law and, 295-296
   liability limits for, 286
   reservations for, 290-292, 294-296
Hungarian law, 34
Hungarian National Bank, 34

I

IASC. *See* International Accounting Standards Committee (IASC)
ILO. *See* International Labour Organization (ILO)
Implied contract of employment, 38-41
Implied-in-fact contract, 320
Implied warranty of suitability, 166-168
Imports, 26-32
Impossibility of performance, 7
Incitement, 276
Increased risk (doctrine of), 81
Indecency, 304
   cable television and, 306
Independent contractors, doctors as, 248
Informed consent, medical malpractice and, 247
In-house counsel, 350-351
   in Europe, 352
   vs. outside counsel, 347-348
Innkeeper's lien, 293-294
Innocent purchaser defense, 230-232
Insider lending, 178
Insider trading, 110-112, 120

business ethics and, 1, 123-124
ethics and, 1, 123-124
international business law and, 125
RICO and, 122
Insider Trading and Securities Fraud Enforcement Act, 120
Insurance law, 145-160
AIDS and, 157-158
amiguity doctrine in, 146
defenses in, 152-156
duty to defend in, 149-150
ethics in, 157-158
failure of notice in, 155-156
international, 158-159
policy exclusions and, 148
reasonable expectations doctrine in, 145-148
wrongful issuance of life insurance in, 155-156
wrongful nonrenewal of policy in, 152
wrongful treatment of claimants in, 150-152
Intended clause, 148
Intentional infliction of emotional distress, 39-40, 45-48
hospitality management law and, 291
media malpractice and, 313
Intentional interference with contract, 193-194
Intentional tort exception, 84
Intentional torts, 194
hospitality management law and, 288-289
workers' compensation and, 84
See also Tort(s)
Interference with business relationship/expectancy, 193-196
lender liability and, 184
Interference with contract, 170, 193-196
intentional, 193-194
negligent, 196
International Accounting Standards Committee (IASC), 103
International business law, 21-36
accounting in, 101-102
advertising law and, 224-225
banks and, 189-190
communications and, 316-317
copyrights in, 278-279
defamation and, 317
employment discrimination in, 69-70
environmental, 241
exports in, 22-26
FCC and, 305
foreign capital markets and, 32-33
foreign direct investment and, 33-36
government contracts and, 334-335
health care and, 256

hospitality management law and, 295-296
imports in, 26-32
insider trading and, 125
insurance in, 158-159
legal representation in, 351-352
occupation safety in, 86
real estate and, 174-175
takeovers in, 142-143
trademark protection and, 207-208
See also specific countries
International Institute for the Unification of Private Law (UNIDROIT), 295
International Investment Survey Act, 175
International Labour Organization (ILO), 86
International Labour Organization Employment Policy Convention, 70
International Trade Commission (ITC), 32
Interstate commerce
anti-takeover statutes and, 138
Robinson-Patman Act and, 203
"In the course of" requirement, 82-83
Invasion of privacy, 311-312. *See also* Privacy rights
Investment bankers, 128, 139
Italy
accounting law in, 102
hospitality management law in, 295
ITC. *See* International Trade Commission (ITC)

J

Japan/Japanese law, 33-34
acquisitions in, 143
Bank of, 34
communications law in, 317
copyright law in, 278
government contracts in, 334-335
insider trading in, 125
legal representation in, 352
securities law in, 32
wrongful discharge in, 52-53
JCAH. *See* Joint Commission on Accreditation of Hospitals (JCAH)
Joint and several liability, environmental law and, 230
Joint Commission on Accreditation of Hospitals (JCAH), 246
Joint ventures, 33-34, 35, 175
Junk bonds, 1, 128
Jury trial
communications law and, 308, 314
employment discrimination and, 62

K

Kabushiki kaisha (Japanese stock company), 34

L

Landlord/tenant, 169-170
Lanham Act, 200, 203, 216-219
Late payment, 184
in commercial leases, 169
in mortgages, 163-164
Latin American law, 35-36, 279
Law
business ethics and, 2-5
importance of, to business, 337
See also Legal representation
Lawyers. *See* Attorneys/lawyers
LBO. *See* Leveraged buyout (LBO)
Leasing, 166-170
Legal malpractice, 342, 344
settlements and, 345-346
Legal representation, 337-353
attorney-client privilege and, 339-342
of corporations, 342-346
document retention and destruction and, 346-347, 35
ethics in corporate, 350-351
in-house counsel for. *See* In-house counsel
international, 351-352
litigation strategy in, 348-349
malpractice in, 342, 344, 345-346
whistle-blowing and, 343, 350-351
See also entries beginning Attorney
Lender liability, 184-191
indirect, 188
statutory sources of, 186-187
Lending limits, 178
Leveraged buyout (LBO), 128, 139-141, 142
Liability
of accountants, 90-96, 98-102
of banks, 177-191
of broker-dealers, 117-118, 125
in commercial leasing, 170
contract, 187
for cross-border broadcasting, 316-317
of employers, 61, 78
environmental, 227-242
of hotels, 286-292
joint and several, 230
of mass media, 309-317
ostensible agency, 248
of physicians. *See* Malpractice, medical
product, 84
of real estate brokers, 173
real estate finance and, 161-178
in securities law, 109-110, 113-120

seller's, 233
strict. *See* Strict liability
successor, 233
vicarious, 248, 249
Licenses
broadcasting, 298-302
copyrights and, 273
exports and, 22, 23-26
for hotels, 293
for restaurants, 293-294
Lie detector (polygraph) tests, 48-49
Life-extending technologies, 256
Likelihood of confusion, 198-200, 208
Limited liability, of hotels, 288-289
Limited liability company (LLC), 34-35
Limited partnerships, securities law and, 106
Liquidated damages, 164
Literary works, 270. *See also* Copyrights
Litigation strategy, 348-349
"Little FTC act," 204
LLC. *See* Limited liability company (LLC)
Lock-up, 134, 135
Loss-in-progress clause, 148
Loyalty duty, 7-8
insider trading and, 123
and legal representation of corporations, 342-343, 350-351
mergers and, 128-129, 142

M

Magazines, 307. *See also* Mass media
Malice, 194, 309
Malpractice
accounting, 90
legal. *See* Legal malpractice
media, 314
medical, 244, 246-249. *See also* Hospitals, liability of
Management advisory services (MAS), 99-100
Management buyout (MBO), 135, 139
Management consulting, accounting law and, 99-102
Manager's privilege, 194
MAS. *See* Management advisory services (MAS)
Mass media, 297, 302-304
ethics and, 315-316
First Amendment protection of, 307-308
liability of, 309-317
malpractice by, 314
newsgathering right of, 308-309
See also specific media; Communications law
Material breaches of contract, 168-169
Material nonconformity (in government contracts), 321

Materiality
insurance law and, 153-155
real estate fraud and, 171-173
securities law and, 113, 116
MBO. *See* Management buyout (MBO)
MDS. *See* Multipoint Distribution Service (MDS)
Mechanics' lien security interest, 187
Media malpractice, 314
Mediation, 349
Medicaid, 243, 244, 246
patient dumping and, 250
Medicare, 243, 244
COBRA and, 253
fraud, 246
hospital mergers and, 255
patient dumping and, 250
"Meeting competition" defense, 204
Mental anguish, medical malpractice and, 247
Mergers
appraisal and, 141
auction and, 136-138
of banks, 183
and business judgment rule, 131
directors' duties in, 128-138
ethics and, 141-142
FCC and, 305
FTC and, 141
of hospitals, 255
international business law and, 142-143
leveraged buyouts and, 128, 139-141, 142
management buyouts and, 135, 139
restructuring after, 134
second-step, 138-141
securities law and, 113-117, 127-144
stakeholders and, 141-142
white knight in, 128, 134
See also Takeovers
Mexican law, 35-36, 279
Migratory Bird Treaty Act, 239
Minimum capital ratios, 179, 190
Minimum compensation requirement, 268
Minority ownership (in broadcast licenses), 299
Misappropriation
advertising law and, 219, 221-222
entertainment law and, 273, 274
as invasion of privacy, 312
Misdemeanors, by banks, 180
Misrepresentation
advertising law and, 222-223. *See also* Deceptive advertising; Negligence, advertising law and
attorney-client privilege and, 341

insurance law and, 152, 153-155
negligent, 187
by restaurants, 294
See also False representation
Monitoring, 50
Mortgages, 161-166
default and foreclosure in, 164-166
lender liability and, 187-188
Movies/motion pictures, 273-274
international business law and, 278-279
piracy of, 278-279
and tort of incitement, 276
See also Entertainment law
Multipoint Distribution Service (MDS), 306
Musicians, 270, 273. *See also* Communications law
"Must carry" rules, 306

N

NAD. *See* National Advertising Division (NAD)
NAFTA. *See* North American Free Trade Agreement (NAFTA)
NARB. *See* National Advertising Review board (NARB)
NASD. *See* National Association of Securities Dealers (NASD)
National Advertising Division (NAD), 219
National Advertising Review board (NARB), 219
National Association of Intercollegiate Athletics (NAIA), 259
National Association of Securities Dealers (NASD), 117
National Basketball Association (NBA), 262, 263
National Collegiate Athletic Association (NCAA), 259-264
National Football League (NFL), 262, 264, 265
NBA. *See* National Basketball Association (NBA)
NCAA. *See* National Collegiate Athletic Association (NCAA)
Negligence
in accounting, 89-97
advertising law and, 222-223
by banks, 184, 185, 187
business ethics and, 8
under common law, 79-80
comparative, 285
contributory, 91
corporate, 249
defenses to, 285
environmental law and, 238
hospitality management law and, 285, 288-289

Index 377

of hospitals, 249, 255
in legal representation, 345-346
medical malpractice and, 247
per se, 222-223, 285
workers' compensation and, 79-80, 84
wrongful discharge and, 45, 47
Negligent interference with contract, 196
Negligent misrepresentation, 187
Negotiated procurement, 321-324
Netherlands
environmental law in, 241
takeovers in, 143
Newspapers, 307, 309. *See also* Mass media
Newsworthiness, 311-313
NFL. *See* National Football League (NFL)
North American Free Trade Agreement (NAFTA), 36
environmental law and, 241
Norway, government contracts in, 334
No-shop clause, 134

O

Obscenity, 302, 304, 305
cable television and, 306
print media and, 307
Occupational disease, 83
Occupational safety, 73-87
ethics and, 85-86
general duty clause and, 73-75
international business law and, 86-87
special duty clause and, 75-76
workers' compensation and, 79-84
Occupational Safety and Health Administration/Act (OSHA), 73-87
employer responsibility under, 78
ethics and, 85-86
inspections and citations by, 79
variance and, 76
Occupational Safety and Health Review Commission (OSHRC), 79
Office of Criminal Enforcement, 235
Office of the Inspector General (OIG), 244
Office of the United States Trade Representative (USTR), 86
OIG. *See* Office of the Inspector General (OIG)
Omnibus Trade Act, 334
Opinion, privilege for, 311
Opinion shopping, 98
Opportunistic business behavior, 205, 206-207
Oral assurances, 41
OSHRC. *See* Occupational Safety and Health Review Commission (OSHRC)

Ostensible agency liability, 248
"Outlaw" industries, 212
Overseas Private Investment Corporation, 86

P

P&A. *See* Purchase and assumption (P&A) transaction
Packard Commission, 333
Panama, health care law in, 257
Parody, privilege for, 311
Participation agreements, 184-185
Peer review organization (PRO), 244, 255
PEG television. *See* Public, Educational and Governmental (PEG) television
Penalties, OSHA and, 79
Penalty clause, 164
Performance, international business law and, 21, 22
Perjury, 342
Per se negligence, 222-223, 285
Personal animosity exception, 81-82
Personal injury
by accident, 83
workers' compensation and, 80-85
See also Occupational safety
Pesticides, 239
Photographers, 266, 308, 309
Physicians
peer review by, 244, 255
reimbursement for, 244-249
antitrust laws and, 253-255
HMOs and, 255
See also Malpractice, medical
Piracy, 278-279
Poison pill, 132-134
Pollution
business ethics and, 8, 10
insurance law and, 145, 149-150
See also Environmental law; Hazardous waste
Polygraph (lie detector) tests, 48-49
Positional risk (doctrine of), 81
Posting, 287
Predatory pricing, 203, 204, 206
Prehearing discovery, 325
Prenatal care, 255
Prepayment prohibitions, 162-163
Price discrimination, 203-205
defenses to, 204
Primary line competition, 203
Print media, 307. *See also* Communications law; Mass media
Privacy rights
cable television and, 306
communications law and, 308-309, 312-314, 315
of employee, 39-40, 48-50

First Amendment and, 307
hospitality management law and, 293
Privilege
accountant-client, 98-99
attorney-client, 339-342
to interfere with contract, 194
manager's, 194
of press, against defamation actions, 309, 311
reporter's, 307-308
work-product, 342
Privity test, 94
PRO. *See* Peer review organization (PRO)
Procurement Code, 334
Product liability, workers' compensation and, 84
Professional sports. *See* Sports law
Profit maximization, business ethics and, 1-2, 5
Programming, 300, 304
Promise-keeping, 7
insider trading and, 122
loyalty duty and, 7, 8
takeovers and, 142
hotel reservations and, 294
Promissory estoppel, 184
Protected classes, 55-59
under ADA, 65-66
affirmative action and, 62
in international business law, 69-70
sexual harassment and, 59
Proxy regulations, 115-116
Publication, 309
Public, educational, and governmental (PEG) television programming, 306
Public health and safety, hospitality management law and, 293
Public policy, 38, 41-44
Punitive damages, 44
advertising law and, 223
for defamation, 310-311
for employment discrimination, 62
lender liability and, 184
for medical malpractice, 247
Purchase and assumption (P&A) transaction, 182

Q

Quality-of-patient-care defense, 255
Quasi-contract, 320
Quid pro harassment, 59
Qui tam actions, 329
Quito Protocol, 35

R

Racial discrimination
by banks, 188
in employment, 55-59, 62
FCC and, 299-300

Racketeer Influenced and Corrupt Organizations (RICO) Act, 99, 120-123
Radio
  broadcast spectrum of, 298, 307
  FCC and, 299-302
  First Amendment protection of, 307
  international business law and, 316-317
  See also Communications law; Mass media
RCRA. *See* Resource Conservation and Recovery Act (RCRA)
Real estate
  AIDS disclosure and, 174
  broker liability, 173
  ethics in, 174
  finance for, 161-178
  foreign investment in U.S., 175
  fraud, 170-173
  international business law and, 175
  lending standards for, 184
Real Estate Investment Trusts, 161
Real Estate Settlement Procedures Act, 162
Real property, 161, 175
Reasonable access, 304
Reasonable accommodation, 66, 68
Reasonable care
  in accounting, 90
  lender liability and, 187
Reasonable expectations doctrine, 145-148
Reasonable foreseeability test, 96
"Reasonable and prudent" physician standard, 247
Recklessness, business ethics and, 8
Recycling, 241
Redemption right, 164
Rehabilitation Act, 49, 65-68
Remedies
  under ADA, 68
  in advertising law, 213-219
  in health care law, 251
  in international business law, 21, 22
Renewal expectancy, 300
Renting. *See* Commercial leasing
Reporter's privilege, 307
Republication, 309
Reserve clause, 262
Resource Conservation and Recovery Act (RCRA), 232, 238, 239-240
Respondeat superior, sex harassment and, 59, 61
Restatement (Second) of Contracts, 168
Restatement (Second) of Torts, accounting law and, 96-97
Restaurants, 293-295
Restructuring, 134
RICO. *See* Racketeer Influenced and Corrupt Organizations (RICO) Act

"Right to die," 256
Risk of loss, international business law and, 22
Robinson-Patman Act, 203-205

S

Satellites, international business law and, 315-317
Savings and loan institutions, 177
  mortgage loans by, 161, 187
  scandal regarding, 1
Scalping, 117
Sealed bid procedures, 321
Search and seizure, hotel guests and, 292
SEC. *See* Securities and Exchange Commission (SEC)
Secondary line competition, 203
Secondary meaning, 198
Second-step mergers, 138-141
Section 1981, 62
Securities Act of 1933, 32, 98, 105-108
Securities Exchange Act of 1934, 32, 98, 110-111
  broker-dealers and, 120
  Williams Act and, 116-117
Securities and Exchange Commission (SEC), 33, 98-99, 105-126
  important rules/schedules of, 118
  insider trading and, 110-112
  and legal representation of corporations, 343
  management consulting and, 99-100
  opinion shopping and, 98
  Securities Act of 1933 and, 105-106
  takeovers and, 141
Securities law, 105-126
  accounting and, 98-99
  environmental law and, 232, 233
  insider trading and. *See* Insider trading
  international, 21, 32-36, 124-125
  lender liability and, 186
  proxy regulations in, 115-116
  regulation of broker-dealers in, 117-118
  tender offers and, 116-117, 122
  tipper/tippee theory in, 111-112
  in United Kingdom, 143
  Williams Act and, 116-117
Self tender, 135
Seller's liabilities, 233
Settlements, 345-346
Sex discrimination, 58
"Sex plus" discrimination, 58
Sexual harassment, 59-61, 62
Shareholder rights plan, 132

Shareholders
  accounting law and, 96, 103
  of banks, 189, 190
  business ethics and, 1-2, 5-20
  corporate charity and, 10-15
  international business law and, 35
  and legal representation of corporations, 343
  mergers and, 127-144
  minority, 139, 141
  right of appraisal of, 141
  securities law and, 113-116. *See also* Securities law
  stakeholders vs., 142
  supermajority vote by, 135
Shark repellents, 135
Sherman Act, 253-255
  hospital mergers and, 255
  NCAA rules and, 260
"Shield laws," 307
Shipper's Export Declaration, 26
Single European Act, 316
Sixth Amendment, 9
Small Business Administration, 324
Social audits, 18
Social responsibility, 223-224
Society of Professional Journalists, 316, 342
"Soft" information, 113
Sole proprietorship, business ethics and, 1
Sole source contracting, 323
Songwriters, 271-272
South American law, 35-36, 279
South Korea
  communications law in, 316
  government contracts in, 334
Spain, advertising law in, 224
Special duty clause, 75-76
Sports law, 259-266
  athlete cases in, 265-266
  ethics and, 276-278
  spectator cases in, 264-265
  sports agents and, 264, 276-278
  torts in, 264-266
Stakeholders, 141-142
Standard of care
  in accounting, 90-91
  medical malpractice and, 247
Standing, 325
Statute of Frauds, 41
  interference with contract and, 194
Stock option plans, 135
Strict liability
  environmental law and, 230, 238
  of hospitals, 250
  of hotels, 286-287, 288, 295
"Subject matter" test, 340
Substantial privity test, 94
Successor liability, 233
Suggestive trademarks, 197
Suitability, warranty of, 166-168

Superfund, 227-235
Supermajority vote, 135
Suspension, 330-331
Sweden
    advertising law in, 224
    health care law in, 257
Switzerland
    advertising law in, 224
    communications law and, 317

T

Takeovers, 127-144
    advocates of, 142
    anti-takeover statutes and, 138
    antitrust laws and, 141
    defensive measures against, 132-136
    ESOPs and, 134-135
    ethics and, 141-142
    federal regulation of, 141-142
    friendly, 127, 136, 143
    hostile, 132, 143
    international business law and, 142-143
    "just say no" case in regard to, 135-136
    See also Mergers
Tariff Act, 29, 32, 207
Tariffs (of common carriers), 305
Tax law, 93
    and foreign investment in real estate, 175
    hospitality management law and, 294
    legal representation in, 351
Television, 266, 273
    broadcast spectrum of, 298, 307
    cable, 305-306. *See also entries beginning* Cable
    defamation and, 309-312
    FCC and, 298-304
    First Amendment protection of, 307
    international business law and, 316-317
    and tort of incitement, 276
    See also Communications law; Entertainment law; Mass media
Tender offers, 116-117, 122
    anti-takeover statutes and, 138
    ESOPs and, 134
    Hart-Scott-Rodino Antitrust Improvements Act and, 141
    "just say no" case in regard to, 135-136
    self tender and, 135
    takeovers and, 128
    two-tier, 132
    Williams Act and, 138, 141
Termination for convenience, 327
Title VII (of Civil Rights Act)
    affirmative action and, 61, 62
    arrest records and, 59
    employment discrimination and, 55-59
    international business law and, 69-70
    sexual harassment and, 59-61, 62
Tort(s)
    accounting law and, 90, 99
    business ethics and, 2-3
    contracts and, 3-4
    conversion, 288-289
    disparagement, 202
    environmental law and, 233
    hospitality management law and, 288-289
    incitement, 276
    intentional. *See* Intentional torts
    interference with business/contract, 193-196
    invasion of privacy, 48, 49, 311-313. *See also* Privacy rights
    lender liability and, 184
    sports, 264-266
    wrongful discharge. *See* Wrongful discharge
Trade, 29-32, 36, 86
    deceptive. *See* Deceptive trade practices
    legal representation and, 351
    unfair. *See* Unfair trade practices
    See also Interstate commerce
Trade Act of 1984, 334
Trademark infringement, 197-202
    entertainment law and, 273-274
    hospitality management law and, 294
    international business law and, 207-208
Trademark Law Revision Act, 216
Trade secrets, 8
Transactions
    with affiliated banks, 178
    environmental liability in business, 231-233
    environmental liability in individual, 234-235
    going-private, 113, 128
    purchase and assumption (P&A), 182
"Transport packaging," 241
Treasury shares, 134
Treble damages, 205
Truth defense, 309
Truth in Negotiations Act, 328-329
Truth-in-Lending Act, 162, 293
Truth-in-menu laws, 294
Two-tier tender offer, 132

U

Unaudited reports, 92-93
Undue reliance, 206
Unfair competition, 8, 193-208
    deceptive advertising as, 212
    disparagement in, 202-203
    entertainment law and, 273
    interference with contract/business and, 193-196
    Lanham Act and, 200, 203
    opportunistic behavior, 205, 206-207
    Robinson-Patman Act and, 203-205
    state laws on, 204-205
    trademark infringement and, 197-202
Unfair Insurance Practices Act, 152
Unfair programming, 300
Unfair Settlement Practices Act, 152
Unfair trade practices, entertainment law and, 273
UNIDROIT. *See* International Institute for the Unification of Private Law (UNIDROIT)
Uniform Commercial Code, international business law and, 22
Unions, in sports, 262-263
United Kingdom
    health care law in, 257
    hospitality management in, 295
    takeovers in, 143
    See also British law
United Nations Convention for the International Sale of Goods, 21-22
United Nations General Assembly, 316
United States Constitution. *See* Constitution, U.S.
United States Football League (USFL), 262
United States Trade Representative (USTR), 86
Universal Copyright Convention, 278
Unlawful intrusion, 313
Unocal test, 132
Unpreventable employee misconduct defense, 74-75
Unsafe and unsound practices, 180-181, 182, 190
USFL. *See* United States Football League (USFL)
USTR. *See* Office of the United States Trade Representative (USTR)
Usury laws, late payment charges and, 164

V

Validated License, 23, 24
Valid trademark, 197
Vicarious liability, 248, 249

W

Warrant, search, hospitality management law and, 292
Warrantless search, hospitality management law and, 292

Warranty(ies)
    of habitability, 168
    international business law and, 21
    of suitability, 166-168
Whistle-blowing, 44, 51
    and legal representation of corporations, 343, 350-351
White knight, 128, 134
    management buyout and, 135
White squire, 134
WHO. *See* World Health Organization (WHO)
Wildlife protection, 239
Williams Act, 116-117, 141
    anti-takeover statutes and, 138
"Wireless cable," 306
Workers' compensation, 73, 80-87
    "Acts of God" and, 82
    bad faith and, 152
    benefits under, 83-84
    docrine of increased risk and, 80
    docrine of positional risk and, 80-81
    fraudulent concealment exception to, 84
    intentional tort exception to, 84
    "in the course of" employment requirement and, 82-83
    personal animosity exception to, 81-82
    wrongful discharge and, 41
Work-product privilege, 342
Works for hire, 274
World Health Organization (WHO), 257
Wrongful construction eviction claim, 169

Wrongful discharge, 38-48
    defamation and, 45, 47-48
    good cause defense and, 44-45
    intentional infliction of emotional distress in, 39-40, 45-48
    in Japan, 52-53
    negligence and, 45, 47
    public policy exception and, 41-44
    punitive damages for, 44
Wrongful eviction (from hotel), 290
Wrongful interference. *See* entries beginning Interference
Wrongful issuance of life insurance, 156-157
Wrongful nonrenewal of policy, 152
Wrongful treatment of claimants, 150-152